second edition

Research Methods for Criminal Justice and Criminology

DEAN J. CHAMPION

Minot State University

PRENTICE HALL, Upper Saddle River, New Jersey 07458

Library of Congress Cataloging-in-Publication Data

Champion, Dean J.
   Research methods for criminal justice and criminology / Dean J. Champion.—2nd ed.
      p.   cm.
   Includes bibliographical references and index.
   ISBN 0-13-013904-1
      1. Criminology—Methodology. 2. Criminal justice, Administration of—Methodology.
   I. Title

   HV6018.C43 2000
   364′.072—dc21   99-053409

Acquisition Editor: Neil Marquardt
Assistant Editor: Marion Gottlieb
Editorial Assistant: Susan Kegler
Managing Editor: Mary Carnis
Project Manager: Linda B. Pawelchak
Prepress and Manufacturing Buyer: Ed O'Dougherty
Cover Director: Jayne Conte
Cover Design: Bruce Kenselaar
Marketing Manager: Shannon Simonsen
Proofreading: Ellen Denning

This book was set in 10.5/12 Garamond
by The Clarinda Company and was printed
and bound by RR Donnelley & Sons, Inc.
The cover was printed by Phoenix Color Corp.

Printed in the United States of America
10   9   8   7   6   5   4   3   2   1

ISBN 0-13-013904-1

Prentice-Hall International (UK) Limited, *London*
Prentice-Hall of Australia Pty. Limited, *Sydney*
Prentice-Hall Canada Inc., *Toronto*
Prentice-Hall Hispanoamericana, S.A., *Mexico*
Prentice-Hall of India Private Limited, *New Delhi*
Prentice-Hall of Japan, Inc., *Tokyo*
Pearson Education Asia Pte. Ltd., *Singapore*
Editora Prentice-Hall do Brasil, Ltda., *Rio de Janeiro*

Contents

2
Theory and Research in Criminal Justice and Criminology 35

3
Frames of Reference and Problem Formulation 71

4
Ethics in Research 99

5
Research Designs 134

6
Data Collection Strategies I:
Sampling Techniques, Purposes, and Problems 170

7
Data Collection Strategies II: Questionnaires 214

8
Data Collection Strategies III: Interviews 251

13
Hypothesis Testing and Theory Verification   457

14
Statistics in Criminal Justice and Criminology:
Some Descriptive Applications   483

15
The Normal Curve and Sampling Distributions   516

16
Inferential Statistics, Tests of Significance, and Correlation 553

appendix A
Statistical Tables 609

appendix B
Using Computers in Criminal Justice 631

appendix C
Writing Papers and Research Reports 647

appendix D
Answers to Mathematical Problems at the Ends of Chapters 668

Preface

Research Methods for Criminal Justice and Criminology (2/e) describes methods of conducting research and applying statistical techniques and tests. Within the social sciences, a broad range of research strategies, data collection techniques, and analytical tools exists to serve the needs of most professionals who conduct independent research investigations. Although certain research procedures and statistical techniques may be relevant for only certain specialized types of investigations, numerous techniques and procedures may be generalizable and applicable to most fields, including criminology and criminal justice.

■ LEVEL OF BOOK

This text has been written with the beginning student in mind. Therefore, much of the technical language and symbolic notation used to describe methodological and statistical strategies has been simplified. At the same time, consideration has been given to those who may wish to use this book as a reference or guide in their future research work. Thus, several topics have been included that are often given extended coverage in more advanced texts. A useful feature that enhances student comprehension of more difficult material is the extensive use of examples drawn from the criminological and criminal justice literature. Students should find this book user-friendly and relate easily to new concepts and principles that are introduced in the context of criminological language and examples.

ORGANIZATION

The first chapter explains the activity of doing research and includes a discussion of some of the kinds of research topics undertaken by professionals in criminology and criminal justice. An integral part of any research activity is the creation of a theoretical scheme or explanatory framework that accounts for relationships between things. The role of theory in the research process is described and discussed in Chapter 2. The research enterprise is a process that consists of several important parts. Each part is given appropriate attention. Like a chain that is no stronger than its weakest link, the research enterprise is no better than the weakest part or stage of that enterprise. And all stages or parts of this process are equally important for influencing the quality of the final research product.

When investigators start their research, they begin with an idea of what they want to study and how they will study it. Those who study juvenile delinquency, for instance, approach this topic using one explanation or another—perhaps the idea that delinquency is largely the result of family instability, or that it is largely the result of the significant influence of one's delinquent peers, or that it is largely the result of cultural deprivation. These are ways of looking at and accounting for the phenomenon to be studied. They are also frames of reference. Researchers also make up a research plan to carry out their study. The plan may start with a research proposal, including specific objectives or goals sought by the researcher. Throughout the entire process, these researchers maintain a code of ethics that operates to objectify their investigations and causes them to refrain from questionable conduct that might undermine the integrity of their research. Chapters 3, 4, and 5 examine frames of reference, problem formulation, research ethics, and research designs.

Each research plan includes provisions for collecting data or information about the problem studied. Most research involves samples of persons studied under different types of research conditions. There are several different kinds of sampling plans. Each of these plans has certain weaknesses and strengths, depending on the researcher's purposes. Chapter 6 examines sampling schemes in great detail.

Several different data collection methods are described in Chapters 7, 8, and 9, including observation, questionnaire administration, interviewing, and analysis of reports and other published information available in libraries. Because much criminological research involves contacting others and soliciting information concerning their ideas and attitudes, attention is also given to the measures we use to quantify the information collected. Do our measures have validity; that is, do they actually measure what we say they measure? Are these measures reliable? Can we depend on them to give us consistent results over time? Accordingly, Chapters 10 and 11 examine methods of measurement and the evaluation of their reliability and validity.

A general objective of the research enterprise is to verify or refute the explanations we have chosen to account for criminological phenomena. We subject our theorizing to different types of testing. Theories can be tested in many ways, ranging from qualitative tests (i.e., use of observation, interviewing, and other nonmathematical data gathering) to quantitative ones (i.e., the use of correlations, sophisticated statistical models, computer simulations, and other mathematical analyses). For tests of theory that rely on quantitative analysis, many statistical techniques exist for specific research applications. These procedures assist in describing the data we have collected and making inferences about the general adequacy of our theories or explanatory schemes.

Chapter 12 describes how we code and tabulate our information, including some preliminary descriptive strategies we may use. Chapter 13 describes how we create and test hypotheses under different research conditions. Chapters 14, 15, and 16 present and describe a wide variety of statistical tests that are used by criminal justice professionals and criminologists in making decisions about their data. These decisions invariably influence their impressions about the utility of their theories.

Often, the application of statistical procedures is more of an art form rather than a mechanical, perfunctory process. Each research investigation poses particular problems for researchers that differ from other projects. Thus, it is important to retain a high degree of flexibility so that easier adaptations to unusual situations may be made whenever they are encountered. Almost every research project has a degree of serendipity, when investigators discover unexpected events that were not anticipated. Finally, every research project should be regarded as a tentative reflection of social reality. No single project, regardless of its magnitude, is the final word on any research topic. Replication of research, time and time again, is crucial as we move forward to establish greater certainty about the events we study. Therefore, researchers are at the same time both pioneers and verifiers. They pave new paths in less explored subject areas, and they add to the growing body of literature about these same subject areas through their inquiry.

■ USING THIS BOOK MOST EFFECTIVELY

Perhaps the best way to approach the material in this book is as a collection of strategies for problem solving. Each strategy that might be employed in the investigation of particular criminal justice-related or criminological problems has weaknesses and strengths, limitations and benefits. These features must be weighed carefully as they are considered for application in problem solutions. The problems are research questions, questions about criminological and criminal justice-related phenomena about which we seek information and answers.

Because the research process is multidimensional and involves numerous phases or stages, each exhibiting technical and sometimes complicated procedures, it might be helpful to regard this collection of strategies from the standpoint of building blocks. Thinking of a pyramid, base blocks form the foundation, and blocks on higher levels can be supported only by the foundation we have provided. Thus, our knowledge of research methods proceeds accordingly, as we master knowledge of basics and proceed to more technical strategies in later chapters. And, like the pyramid that, once in place, is a beautiful, complete assemblage of blocks, the research process unfolds similarly to yield a distinctive whole that can best be appreciated when viewed as an interconnected constellation of numerous components.

The general intention is to improve our understanding of the events that occur around us. Perhaps our investigations will lead to certain practical policy decisions. However, our investigations may be unrelated to public policy or to anything of practical value other than a simple understanding and appreciation for why certain events occur. My position is that we should seek a healthy balance between our practical, substantive concerns and our theoretical ones. While some research may have direct relevance for a particular intervention program to be used for parolees in halfway houses to assist in their community reintegration, other research may not be adapted easily to any helping program. This state of affairs is perhaps as it should be, especially in view of the great diversity of interests among criminologists and criminal justice professionals, the problems they select for study, and the ways they choose to investigate these problems.

■ SPECIAL FEATURES AND ANCILLARIES

The book has several special features:

- Complex statistical formulae have been minimized, with careful, step-by-step instructions about how to complete calculations.
- All statistical and methodological procedures are fully explained, and their interpretation is simplified with examples from the criminological literature.
- Current illustrations have been extracted from the literature of criminology and criminal justice. Topics for illustrations were deliberately chosen because of their variety and because of their topical importance in view of their frequency of treatment in the professional literature. All statistical procedures covered in this book were found among these articles, and the ideas from these articles were the basis for each example provided.
- Questions are provided at chapter ends for review, together with a list of key terms. All of the key terms are included in a glossary at the end of the text.
- Chapters containing statistical tests have problems to solve at the conclusion of the chapter. Answers to all computational problems are provided in

an appendix so that students may check the accuracy of their computations.

■ Interpretive tables are inclued in an appendix, including a table of squares and square roots and a table of random numbers. All interpretive tables for statistical procedures include headnotes or footnotes describing how they are to be used; thus, it is unnecessary to go back in the book to where these procedures were originally discussed in order to see how observed statistical values should be interpreted.

■ Instructional aids include an instructor's manual and a computerized test bank of 1,000 questions and problems that are available for examination preparation. Versions of the computerized test bank are available on computer diskette and hard copy.

■ ACKNOWLEDGMENTS

Many persons play important parts in the production of a textbook. I would like to acknowledge the generous support and assistance of my editor, Neil Marquardt, who provided encouragement and helpful criticisms at key points throughout the project development. A special thanks is extended to Linda Pawelchak, who facilitated and supervised the production of the book through copy editing to page proofs. Finally, a textbook reflects the constructive criticisms of other professionals who review book chapters and help to clarify subject matter discussed. I gratefully acknowledge the helpful input of George Knox, Chicago State University; David Neubauer, University of New Orleans; James S. E. Opolot, Texas Southern University; Dave Parry, Endicott College; Sudipto Roy, Indiana State University; Jeanne B. Stinchcomb, Florida International University; and Ronald E. Vogel, California State University, Long Beach. And last but not least, I wish to thank the many contributors who sent me biographical information and photos for inclusion at critical points throughout the book. I think that a book's value is enhanced by true-to-life experiences of real researchers who are currently working in the field and can share their experiences with students. I found these contributions to be most interesting and hope students will find them likewise.

Dean J. Champion
Minot, North Dakota

About the Author

Dean J. Champion is professor and chair, Department of Criminal Justice, Minot State University, North Dakota. Dr. Champion has taught at the University of Tennessee-Knoxville and California State University-Long Beach. He earned his Ph.D. from Purdue University and B.S. and M.A. degrees from Brigham Young University. He also completed several years of law school at the Nashville School of Law.

Dr. Champion has written more than 25 texts and/or edited works and maintains memberships in 11 professional organizations. He is a lifetime member of the American Society of Criminology, Academy of Criminal Justice Sciences, and the American Sociological Association. He is former editor of the ACJS/Anderson Series on *Issues in Crime and Justice* (1993-1996) and the *Journal of Crime and Justice* (1995-1998). He is a contributing author for the *Encarta Encyclopedia 2000* for Microsoft. He was the Visiting Scholar for the National Center for Juvenile Justice in 1992 and is first vice president of the Midwestern Criminal Justice Association.

His published books for Prentice Hall include *Basic Statistics for Social Research* (1970, 1981); *Research Methods for Criminal Justice and Criminology*

(1993, 2000); *The Juvenile Justice System: Delinquency, Processing, and the Law* (1992, 1998, forthcoming); *Corrections in the United States: A Contemporary Perspective* (1990, 1998, forthcoming); *Probation, Parole, and Community Corrections* (1990, 1996, 1999); *Policing in the Community* (with George Rush, 1996); and *The Administration of Justice Systems* (forthcoming). Other works include *The Sociology of Organizations* (McGraw-Hill, 1975); *Research Methods in Social Relations* (John Wiley & Sons, 1976); *Sociology* (Holt, Rinehart and Winston, 1984); *The U.S. Sentencing Guidelines* (Praeger Publishers, 1989); *Juvenile Transfer Hearings* (with G. Larry Mays; Praeger Publishers, 1991); *Measuring Offender Risk* (Greenwood Press, 1994); *The Roxbury Dictionary of Criminal Justice: Key Terms and Leading Supreme Court Cases* (Roxbury Press, 1997); and *Criminal Justice in the United States 2/e* (Wadsworth, 1998).

Dr. Champion's primary research interests relate to attorney use in juvenile justice proceedings and plea bargaining.

chapter 1

The Research Enterprise in Criminal Justice and Criminology

■ INTRODUCTION

Here are some potential research questions for criminologists:

- ■ Are teen courts effective at reducing juvenile delinquency?
- ■ Should probation and parole officers carry firearms during their contacts with probationer/parolee-clients in dangerous neighborhoods?
- ■ What are the factors contributing to police cynicism, and does such cynicism influence police response to community-oriented policing programs?
- ■ Do persons who plead guilty to crimes through plea bargaining receive greater leniency in sentencing compared with those who are convicted of the same crimes through jury trials?
- ■ Do Asian, black, white, and Hispanic youth gangs exhibit different levels of violence?

Each of these questions and thousands of others are often asked in criminological and criminal justice research. Annually, thousands of articles are published, papers presented, and reports prepared to provide tentative answers to such questions. These are research questions, or questions that must be investigated more thoroughly before final and conclusive answers can be provided. This chapter is about the research enterprise or process. It presents and defines various essential components of this process.

What do professionals do when they conduct research? While this entire book answers this question, this chapter presents an overview of the research process. Additionally, several important functions performed by the research enterprise are described. An integral feature of the research enterprise is statistical analysis and description. We will examine how statistics and research are closely intertwined. Finally, in order to do research and pursue the research enterprise fully, several assumptions must be made about the targets of our investigations. These will be identified and described.

■ OVERVIEW OF THE RESEARCH PROCESS AND STATISTICAL ANALYSIS

The Research Enterprise

The **research process** or research enterprise consists of all activities that pertain to problem formulation and definition. **Research** consists of all investigations, studies, or systematic efforts designed to increase our knowledge about events and their occurrence. Research includes developing a theoretical explanation for why problems exist, collecting information that will verify or refute the explanation of problems, and then analyzing, presenting, and interpreting this information. Finally, tentative conclusions must be drawn that will either support or refute the theoretical explanation provided. More simply, you become interested in certain events and ask why those events occur. You speculate about the causes of these events. A reasonable explanation for the event occurs to you, but you are uncertain about it. You collect evidence that will help you to test your explanation of the event and whether the explanation is plausible. You examine your evidence and evaluate whether the explanation of the event is acceptable or feasible. The strength of the evidence you have gathered may require that you collect additional evidence and retest the explanation elsewhere, in new social settings. You repeat this process until you achieve an acceptable level of certainty about why the event has occurred.

Stages of the Research Enterprise: An Overview

Conceptualization of Problem for Study. Conceptualizing a **research problem** means to identify a general topic for study, to specify a particular dimension of the topic for more intensive examination, and then to pose several pointed questions that will guide the investigator's inquiry. Research problems are events in need of explanations. The questions posed at the beginning of this chapter are examples of research problems. Other types of research problems include the following questions:

1. Is intensive supervised probation more effective at reducing client recidivism when compared with standard probation?
2. Is it feasible to allow death row inmates to mingle in the general prison population, as opposed to isolating them in maximum-security death rows?
3. Are furloughs for prison inmates helpful in fostering their community reintegration and rehabilitation?
4. Do juvenile status offenders generally escalate to more serious delinquent offending over time?
5. What factors contribute to correctional officer turnover in jail and in prison settings?

Each of the questions above directs our attention toward a researchable problem. From the above questions, we know that our investigations will target probationer recidivism; or death row inmate adaptability to mingling in the general prison population; or the use of furloughs for rehabilitative and reintegrative purposes; or a study of career escalation from juvenile status to delinquent offending; or the factors causing correctional officers to quit their jobs.

Different experiences of researchers cause them to explore certain topics. Often, investigators have worked in law enforcement or corrections or with juveniles. Or perhaps these researchers have read interesting articles about the subjects they plan to study. Most of us who do research are going to investigate topics of interest to us. For instance, Sam Torres, a professor at California State University at Long Beach, has investigated different ways that probation officers can supervise substance-abusing probationer-clients. Torres had previously been employed as a U.S. Probation Officer for the Central District of California. Torres continues to teach courses in probation and parole, and his research in these areas is a strong reflection of his own background and personal interests and experiences.

Sometimes our employment may create conditions for studying the settings where we work. For instance, James Marquart, a professor at Sam Houston State University, was able to work as a prison correctional officer in the Texas Department of Criminal Justice. Subsequently, Marquart documented his personal experiences in several well-known articles about correctional officer–inmate interactions (Marquart, 1986).

Development of Alternative Explanations of Problem. When we identify a problem for investigation, we usually have a pretty good idea of which explanation we are going to use for why the problem exists. Our research will test whether our explanation is good or bad, productive or unproductive. For instance, we may think that one-parent families may have a greater incidence of delinquency than two-parent families. Our thoughts may be that one-parent families are less stable than two-parent families, and that youths in one-parent family situations may be more inclined to commit delinquent acts. However, we may find that there are *more* delinquents in two-parent families than in one-parent ones, at least among the families we study. This finding suggests that our idea about one-parent families and delinquency is questionable.

It is conventional for researchers to suggest several plausible explanations for why particular events (e.g., delinquency, correctional officer turnover) occur. This activity shows that we have done some critical thinking about the problem we are investigating. We have explored various alternative **explanations** for why the problem exists, and we have chosen a particular explanation that fits the particular rationale we have created. Therefore, if we should happen to find that our explanation is *not* particularly satisfactory, we can then refer readers to other explanations we have suggested for further research.

For instance, we might investigate sentencing disparity among judges. Sentencing disparity occurs whenever judges impose quite different sentence lengths, or more or less severe sentences, on several different offenders who have committed the *same* offense. A judge may impose a ten-year sentence for one burglar, while the same judge may impose a sentence of probation for another burglar. Why does one burglar get ten years while another burglar gets probation? This is sentencing disparity and it needs to be explained.

Researchers account for sentencing disparity according to several different explanations. One explanation may be that one's race or ethnicity leads to different sentences. Another explanation is that gender differences explain disparities in sentencing. Maybe one's age or socioeconomic status contributes to such disparities. Also, whether a defendant is represented by privately acquired counsel or a public defender may explain sentencing disparities. If it is believed that racial or ethnic differences among defendants lead to different sentencing outcomes, racial/ethnic factors are investigated. Subsequently, the researcher may be unable to show that sentencing disparities vary according to race or ethnicity. However, the investigation discloses that sentencing disparities vary according to the type of legal representation. Those defendants represented by public defenders may tend to receive harsher sentences compared with those defendants represented by private counsels. While the researcher is disappointed that he or she didn't find sentencing disparities according to race or ethnicity, the public defender–private counsel finding suggests that further research should be conducted in other jurisdictions using this alternative explanation.

Data Collection and Analysis.   Once a problem for study has been identified, investigators must decide how best to collect information or **data** that will help them answer their research questions. Suppose we wish to know whether death row inmates can be blended into the general inmate populations without incident. Answering this question requires that we find a prison where authorities are willing to release death row inmates into the general inmate population. Further, we must be in a position to observe whether incidents between inmates occur during this blending process. This involves a process known as **data collection.** Suppose we study the integration of death row inmates with the general inmate population for a year. Suppose that death row inmates behave in an orderly fashion, and that no serious incidents among inmates occur. At the end of a year, we report our findings that show that at least for this particular prison, death row inmates assimilate well into the general inmate population. Our data are our observations of inmate conduct and inmate incidents.

In another study we may focus on furloughs (i.e., short, unescorted leaves) of inmates from prisons. Usually, inmates who are within a year or so of being paroled will be permitted furloughs or some type of work or study release into their communities. These inmates are trusted by prison authorities, and the inmates must return within a fixed time period following their furloughs or work/study release. The purpose of such programs is to assist these inmates in making the transition from highly regimented prison life to their communities, where there are few restrictions on their behaviors. Therefore, we study a sample of inmates who are granted furloughs over a period of time, such as a year. We may even extend our observation period for an additional year, observing these inmates who are subsequently paroled into their communities. We might collect information from prison authorities, community law enforcement agencies, and parole officers to determine whether these furloughees have successfully reintegrated into their communities. Refraining from further criminal activity is a good indicator of the success of the furlough program. If we find that 70 percent or more of the furloughees have remained crime-free while on their furloughs and during the year following their release into their communities, this is strong evidence of the successfulness of the furlough program and its reintegrative and rehabilitative value.

Interpretation and Conclusions.   Almost every empirical investigation in which data are collected and analyzed contains a section in which an **interpretation** is made of the research findings. Interpretations of findings are both objective and subjective. Reporting actual factual information and details is an objective disclosure of what the researcher has found. Suppose the investigator who studied the influence of furlough programs on inmate reintegration into the community found that 63 percent of all furloughees engaged in no program violations while inmates, and that they remained crime-free once released into their communities. This means that 37 percent of the furloughees either had program violations or did not remain crime-free while in their communities, or both.

The *fact* of a 63 percent success rate is impressive. Nearly two-thirds of these offenders were successful. But some investigators consider the 37 percent recidivism or failure rate among furloughees as unimpressive. Thus, researchers who report this information may wish to explain why this failure rate occurred and how it can be decreased in the future with different furlough programming. Investigators are at liberty to speculate and to argue different positions about their findings. These discussions of findings and the different kinds of interpretations made are often interesting and insightful. Accompanying these discussions are tentative conclusions about what has been found.

Final Report.   The final report is a brief summarization of the study highlights and major findings. The investigator often recapitulates the study objectives, how the study was conducted, and what were the final results and their significance.

Beyond the Final Report.   The final report may contain several theoretical and substantive implications for further research. **Theoretical implications** of the research have to do with how the research illustrates and/or tests existing theory about the subject matter. **Substantive implications** relate to the practical applications of the research for practitioners.

For instance, Robert J. Beck (1997) investigated teen courts or peer courts used in different jurisdictions to hear and decide minor juvenile cases. Peer courts consist of juries of one's peers or school mates who hear cases against the accused juvenile, decide guilt or innocence, and recommend punishments. Beck believed that peer courts would be powerful sanctioning bodies against first-offender juveniles, who would learn and know that a jury of their peers disapproved of their offending. Thus, there was a good chance that teen courts would exert a deterrent effect on future delinquent behavior. This was the substantive or applied research component of Beck's study. The theoretical component involved a test of ecological development theory. This theory suggests that youths who undergo a severe, traumatic, or stressful transition in their lives (e.g., becoming "offenders") actually undergo a change of role. In this transitional mode, many juvenile offenders are highly susceptible to change toward law-abiding behavior, especially when punishment is imposed by one's peers. In the actual study, Beck found modest support for teen courts as sanctioning mechanisms and delinquency deterrence. His findings relative to the ecological development theory were inconclusive. In a final section entitled "Implications of the Research," Beck encouraged further investigation to determine which of several teen court program components were most effective and predictive of nonrecidivism. Those interested in pursuing this research further will find this section of particular interest.

Mark Jones's Study of Boot Camp Graduates.   Mark Jones, a professor at East Carolina University, investigated whether boot camps are instrumental in fostering greater compliance with juvenile probation program requirements (Jones, 1996). Jones was interested in youthful offenders and the factors influencing their recidivism rates while on probation. He focused upon the boot camp as a promising intervention for youthful offenders in need of discipline and self-control. Boot camps are short-term (six-month) interventions involving military drill and ceremony, physical training, physical discipline, hard physical labor, and education. Boot camps are aimed at youthful offenders. Specifically, Jones wanted to know whether juveniles who were exposed to boot camp training would have better success rates in their subsequent probation programs compared with juvenile probationers who did not have boot camp training.

Jones began his study by reviewing the literature about boot camps. He discussed various studies of boot camps, the types of youthful clientele involved in boot camp training, and the different success rates as measured by various types of recidivism. Jones raised two pointed questions: (1) How do boot camp graduates perform compared with other juvenile offenders, when both types of offenders are placed in the same aftercare programs for approximately the same time periods? and (2) What variables correlate with success or failure among boot camp graduates and their non–boot camp counterparts in those aftercare programs?

Jones studied 307 juvenile delinquents in the Harris County, Texas, Court Regimented Intensive Probation Program (CRIPP). Fifty-six of these delinquents were placed in the Harris County boot camp program. The remainder of the juveniles were placed in CRIPP. When the boot camp clients graduated, they were placed in CRIPP as well and their progress was charted and compared with the non–boot camp CRIPP clients. Jones's expectation was that the boot camp participants and graduates would have significantly lower recidivism rates at the end of the CRIPP compared with those juveniles not exposed to the boot camp program.

Jones's results were disappointing. First, Jones reported that only 59 percent of the original boot camp participants actually graduated from the boot camp. Of those that graduated, there was a recidivism rate of 59 percent when these graduates were compared with the other delinquents in CRIPP. The recidivism rate for non–boot camp participants was also high, about 60 percent. Therefore, the boot camp program did not have the desired effect of substantially reducing recidivism among the targeted juveniles.

Jones explored alternative explanations for what he found. First, the sample size of boot camp participants in his study, 56 individuals, was not particularly large. Further, when he separated the boot camp graduates from nongraduates, the sample dropped to 33 participants. We can only speculate what Jones would have found if a larger sample of juveniles had been used. What if he had observed the influence of the boot camp on 500 juveniles instead of 33? We won't know the answer to this question unless or until another study is conducted of boot camp effectiveness on juvenile delinquent recidivism. The next study may or may not be conducted by Jones.

When Jones wrote the "Implications" section of his article, he said that while boot camps are not necessarily effective as deterrents to further juvenile recidivism, they are considered a significant punishment. Thus, boot camps may be perceived by the general public as a suitable punishment for youthful offenders, despite the lack of promise shown for deterring delinquency, at least in the sample Jones studied. Finally, Jones noted that boot camps in other jurisdictions may be more effective as deterrents to delinquency. Some boot camps are operated for longer periods than the Harris County program. Perhaps the length of program is a crucial factor in promoting change among youthful offenders. Such speculation is both normal and essential in any research report. Some readers may be stimulated by the "what if's" of such speculation and conduct investigations of their own to answer specific **research questions.**

What if Jones had found that his boot camp **respondents** had a recidivism rate of only 10 percent? This would have meant a success rate of 90 percent. What could Jones have concluded with that finding? Relatively little. First, we must return to the matter of the sample size Jones used. Thirty-three juveniles participating in a boot camp program is considered a small sample. Further studies are needed, with both larger and more diverse samples in other jurisdictions, before we can make sweeping conclusions about boot camps generally. In the present case, Jones would have been limited to stating that at least in his study, boot camp participants seemed responsive to the boot camp intervention or that the boot camp seemed to decrease recidivism among juvenile probationers.

Depending upon the subject matter of one's study and the extensiveness of it, the research enterprise is a more or less elaborate plan we use for answering questions of interest to us. This plan will vary in complexity and sophistication. For instance, if Jones had studied 20 boot camps in various states over a two-year interval, his sample size would be much larger than 33. His findings would have more general appeal, since greater numbers of boot camp participants would be involved. However, we should not be swayed by large numbers alone. It is entirely possible that a more large-scale study of boot camp effectiveness on juvenile recidivism rates would yield findings similar to those in Jones's original study.

In Jones's study, he studied these juveniles directly and tracked them over time. In other research, investigators may mail questionnaires to study participants with requests to answer questions and mail questionnaires back to the researchers. These **mailed questionnaires** enable researchers to accumulate a large amount of information about persons rather quickly. For some types of research, we may need to participate in the activities of those we observe. Some research may involve an **interview,** where respondents are contacted directly by researchers and asked questions through a **face-to-face questionnaire administration.** Some problems studied by researchers may not be easily investigated by mailing questionnaires or conducting interviews. If we want to know whether the **crime rate** is increasing faster than the rate of normal population growth in the United States, then an analysis of public documents compiled by the FBI, U.S. Department of Justice, and U.S. Bureau of the Census may be necessary. In such investigations, it is unlikely that others will have to be contacted directly for information about these research questions.

Some investigators spend several decades compiling information about problems they have selected for study in **longitudinal research.** For instance, Wolfgang (Wolfgang, Figlio, and Sellin, 1972) studied a large Philadelphia **birth cohort,** nearly 10,000 boys born in Philadelphia in 1945, and tracked them through official records until 1963. Among other things, Wolfgang wanted to describe the characteristics and behavioral patterns of chronic recidivists, or persistent juvenile offenders. In 1975, he conducted a further analysis of a sample of these persons at age 30 to see how many committed crimes as adults and became career criminals (Wolfgang, 1983). For comparative purposes, Wolfgang selected a much larger birth cohort of more than 28,000 boys and girls born in 1958 and tracked them through official records for a similar 18-year period.

Wolfgang's research, regarded as classics by many criminologists, revealed that (1) a small core of offenders, approximately 6 or 7 percent, accounted for over 60 percent of all crimes committed by the 1945 cohort, and (2) the 1958 cohort had a violent offense rate almost three times as large as the 1945 cohort. Wolfgang speculated that successive generations of juveniles were committing increasingly violent offenses compared with earlier generations. Despite the magnitude of Wolfgang's analysis and the large samples studied, these investigators never regarded Wolfgang's findings as conclusive about chronic offender behavior patterns and characteristics. Nevertheless, it is noteworthy that Wolfgang spent over 30 years patiently investigating this phenomenon. This type of study, longitudinal research, is very laborious, because it spans a fairly lengthy time period and involves tracking the same sample at different time intervals.

Beginning students should recognize that, generally, the pace of research is slow. Some topics, such as job burnout among probation and parole officers, are not investigated frequently, while other topics, such as the causes of delinquency, are investigated often. Therefore, research information in different topic areas accumulates at an uneven rate.

Pure and Applied Research

Research may also be pure, applied, or both. **Pure research** is often more difficult for students to understand and appreciate, because it may have intuitive relevance only for those investigators who do such research. It doesn't excite everyone to know that reported crime in the United States increased at a higher rate during the 1990s compared with general population growth. But for radical, critical, or Marxist criminologists, crime rate fluctuations may enable them to draw parallels between crime and changing political, economic, and social conditions. It doesn't always matter that the terms used to describe crime in relation to politics, social, and economic conditions are diffuse or intangible. Consider the following:

> Capitalist interests have perpetuated an exploitative system wherein the rich dominate the poor. Laws are the manipulative tools of the capitalist class, and state repression of working class interests is evident in the differential punishments society imposes for street crimes compared with anti-trust or white-collar crime.

It would be difficult to know where to begin in order to test these statements. Who composes the capitalist class or the working class? What are capitalist interests? The intent here is not to malign pure research or radical criminology, but rather, to illustrate its diffuseness compared with applied research. Pure research is undertaken often simply for the sake of knowing. "Knowledge for the sake of knowledge" underscores what motivates many pure researchers. When you ask such persons what can be done of a practical nature with the research they have conducted, they may or may not be able to tell you. Questions about the practical aspects of what they do are often considered irrelevant.

Applied or **basic research** is research undertaken mostly for practical reasons. Mark Jones's study of boot camp effectiveness had an applied aspect. One practical outcome was knowing whether boot camps were effective as interventions in reducing juvenile recidivism and improving program success among juvenile probationers. If Jones's results had been more impressive, then perhaps public policy could be affected in terms of allocations of funds to various jurisdictions to reduce delinquency and probationer recidivism. If the cost of boot camp operation and delinquency deterrence were effective, then boot camps would be used on a large-scale basis in many jurisdictions as a means of preventing future criminality.

President Bill Clinton's Crime Bill of 1994 was a large step toward beefing up law enforcement in many communities, putting 100,000 additional police officers on the streets to prevent crime. Other monies were allocated under the Crime Bill of 1994 for various programs. In the late 1990s, evaluation research was forthcoming about the impact of the 1994 Crime Bill and whether it exerted its intended effects of lowering crime. Presently, the findings are inconclusive regarding the Crime Bill's effectiveness. Some lawmakers are skeptical about whether more police officers will cause crime reductions. But the Crime Bill also authorized money for further research about crime and its causes. Therefore, more research is being conducted and intervention programs are been evaluated to determine which solutions to crime seem to work best.

Pure and applied research can also be distinguished by the influence of such research on various community programs and public policies. Investigations of probation officer job burnout and dissatisfaction may change how administrators in probation agencies supervise their officers and assign them duties. Studies of peer group influence on juvenile delinquency may help to establish intervention programs where delinquent peers are used to "undo" delinquent behaviors through self-study and individual counseling (Empey and Erickson, 1972).

Research is not always exclusively pure or applied. It may be both simultaneously. Studies of judicial discretion in sentencing offenders may show sentencing disparities that are explained by race, ethnicity, gender, or socioeconomic status. Radical or critical criminologists may investigate sentencing patterns in different jurisdictions and find these disparities. Their work may show support for the influence of social class on the criminal justice system (a pure research objective), but it may also lead to sentencing reforms to remedy sentencing disparities because of race, gender, or social class, such as a shift from indeterminate to presumptive sentencing (an applied research objective).

■ STATISTICAL ANALYSIS

One of the last courses taken by many students in criminal justice and criminology is statistics. For many students, statistics is like a red flag, a frightening and seemingly difficult hurdle to overcome. Doesn't it involve lots of numbers and complex formulas, and don't you have to be a mathematical whiz kid to complete such a course satisfactorily? Isn't it painful? Don't most students who take such courses fail or do poorly? The subject of statistics should not be threatening or painful. While it may not be the most exciting topic studied in a criminal justice program, it is no more painful, threatening, or difficult than specific courses in methods of research.

Statistics has several meanings. First, it is a field of study. Second, it often refers to numerical evidence that has been compiled, such as the *Vital Statistics* compiled by the U.S. Bureau of the Census. Those who respond to questions asked by census-takers or who complete and return U.S. Bureau of the Census questionnaires become a part of the vital statistics of the U.S. population for particular years. The birthrate, death rate, murder rate, the Philadelphia Phillies' batting averages, the average height of Mrs. Brown's third grade class in Bangor, Maine, the average number of dropouts at the University of Tennessee, and the average yards gained per game by the Green Bay Packers are all statistics. Thus, statistics may refer to hundreds of descriptive indicators of things.

Third, statistics can mean a collection of tests and techniques used to describe and make decisions and inferences about collected research data. Statistics may enable researchers to determine the degree of association between things, such as the relation between the length of time parolees have spent in prison and the length of time on parole before some of them commit new crimes. Other statistical techniques help to determine many factors simultaneously or the causal influence of multiple factors on a single event. How do age, gender, socioeconomic status, race, history of drug use, employment status, and family stability relate with one another, and what is their collective impact on recidivism? Some of these statistical procedures help to determine whether differences exist among groups on some measured characteristic. For instance, John Whitehead of East Tennessee State University used statistical tests to determine whether males differed significantly from females in their job burnout and dissatisfaction scores.

Several chapters of this book are devoted to statistical techniques that are useful for those in criminology and criminal justice programs. Statistical analysis is an integral feature of many research projects, although some types of research do not use statistics. In these projects, investigators obtain information about things by observing others. Their observations may be presented in lengthy written accounts, and inferences about social patterns may be drawn from these observations.

Using or not using statistical procedures separates **quantitative research** from **qualitative research.** Those involved in quantitative research are considered "data crunchers" or "number crunchers." They are sometimes criticized by others for their strong, quantitative rigor. However, quantitative criminologists may believe that there is too much subjectivity in qualitative research, and that numerical quantities and sophisticated applications of statistics can improve the quality and objectivity of **data analysis** and interpretation. Both perspectives have much to offer. In a sense, each makes important contributions not provided by the other. Thus, claims that quantitative analyses of data are better or more important than qualitative analyses of data are unjustified.

One important theme throughout all studies of statistics is learning to determine when, where, and why statistical procedures should be applied in research. Statistics enters the research process largely in the data analysis and interpretation phase. Various statistical tests and descriptive procedures are helpful to researchers as they present their work to others and evaluate the significance of their findings. No statistical procedures presented in this book involve calculations beyond simple addition, subtraction, multiplication, division, and square root skills. Since pocket calculators are inexpensive and available in all colleges and universities, even computing square roots has been reduced to mere button-pushing. Even so, a table of squares and square roots for numbers 1 to 1,000 is provided in an appendix for easy reference.

■ SOME BASIC ASSUMPTIONS ABOUT CRIMINAL JUSTICE AND CRIMINOLOGY

All scientific inquiry is based upon several important assumptions. These assumptions relate to **prediction,** to the predictability and regularity of any relation between two or more variables. A high degree of predictability and regularity among variables exists in the field of chemistry, for instance. Particular combinations of certain chemicals have regular, recurring, and predictable outcomes or reactions that can be forecast accurately in advance of their combination. Such predictability and regularity are more apparent among variables associated with the hard sciences (such as, chemistry, biology, physics, and engineering), where the controlled variables are tangible. In these situations, these variables' interrelations with other variables, as well as environmental factors, are heavily controlled. Interactions of measured amounts of different chemicals under certain temperatures for designated time periods reflect the high degree of variable control achieved by chemistry, for example. But people are not chemicals and cannot be studied under such controlled conditions.

For example, in criminology and criminal justice, many of the variables we study, such as attitudes, ideas, and opinions, are intangible. Therefore, the presence or absence of these social and psychological variables must be inferred largely from other, indirect, indicators. Attitudinal phenomena are not immediately apparent through observation, although the influence of attitudes or an assessment of their existence can be made by constructing various attitudinal scaling devices.

The greater measurement difficulties associated with certain variables do not automatically exclude them from scientific investigation, however. It means that social scientists must make extraordinary efforts to establish these more elusive phenomena as behavioral predictors. While chemists can measure quantities of chemicals and observe their effects on other chemicals, criminologists must devise indirect indicators of attitudinal variables in order to assess their effects on behaviors. Attitudes cannot be seen, but their presence may be inferred from how persons behave or respond to questions about their feelings and thoughts. Thus, attitudinal measures require a high degree of empirical proof of their accuracy and consistency. This is a major reason why we spend so much time studying the validity (accuracy) and reliability (consistency) of our attitudinal measures.

Research in criminal justice and criminology is **scientific** and attempts to explain and predict relations between variables. What is the influence of diet on criminality? Do convicted black offenders receive harsher sentences compared with convicted white offenders? What barriers slow the influx of women into correctional officer and probation/parole officer work roles? How do our perceptions of powerlessness influence our adaptability to our jobs? What factors reduce stress and burnout? Is there a rise in female delinquency, and if so, why? Are successive generations of delinquents more violent than previous generations of delinquents? Can criminals be rehabilitated? If so, what intervention strategies seem to work best for purposes of rehabilitation? Considerable research is required in order to answer these questions. Before undertaking any investigation of relations among variables, several assumptions are made by criminologists and criminal justice professionals. These assumptions are not unique to criminology or criminal justice. Rather, they extend to all types of **scientific inquiry.** In the present instance, these assumptions have been adapted to fit criminology and criminal justice applications.

1. A pattern exists among certain variables of interest to criminologists. This assumption is generally accepted by those conducting criminological research. If we do not believe that there is a pattern associated with certain variable interrelationships, then prediction, forecasting, and regularity cannot be assumed. This means that relations between sentence length and socioeconomic status, between probation officer turnover and burnout and stress, between police cynicism and effectiveness of community-oriented policing, between family stability and delinquency, and between police use of force and public perceptions of police effectiveness are random. Few of us believe that these and similar variable interrelations are purely random.

2. Patterns of variable interrelationships can be described and used as the bases for hypothesis tests. This assumption stems from the first. It coincides with the empirical nature of criminological phenomena. It means that we can use the identifiable patterns of interrelationships between variables for the purpose of testing our theories about these variables.

3. A **causal relation** exists between certain criminological variables. While we are interested in establishing **causality** or cause-effect relations among the variables we study, it is also true that causal relations between phenomena are difficult to establish. Nevertheless, a major aim of criminologists is to determine which variables cause other variables to occur and to describe these causal relationships. For example, if we believe that judges discriminate in the sentences they impose on convicted offenders according to their race or ethnicity, and if minority offenders draw longer and harsher sentences compared with nonminority offenders where both have been convicted of essentially the same crimes, then these sentencing disparities can be minimized or eliminated entirely by restricting judicial sentencing discretion. Restricting judicial sentencing discretion may

Box 1.1

Robert Agnew
Emory University

Statistics: B.A. (social psychology),
Rutgers College; Ph.D. (sociology),
University of North Carolina
at Chapel Hill.

Interests: My main interest while in school was social psychology. In particular, I wanted to explore the ways in which the social environment—family, school, friends, community—affected the values, attitudes, and behaviors of individuals. I did not intend to become a criminologist at that time, and I never had a formal course in criminology. I did not become interested in criminology until my last year of graduate school, when I was looking for a dissertation topic. I came across a survey that has excellent measures of the individual's social environment and of the individual's delinquent behavior. I thought that it would be interesting to examine the impact of the social environment on delinquency.

I began to read the literature on the causes of delinquency, and I became especially interested in strain and anomie theories. The dominant versions of strain theory at that time said that individuals engage in delinquency because they want to achieve monetary success or middle-class status, but they are prevented from doing so through legal channels (for example, getting a good education and then getting a good job). In particular, most persons in the United States are encouraged to place a strong emphasis on monetary success by family, friends, school officials, the mass media, and others. But lower-class people often are prevented from achieving monetary success through legal channels. Their parents do not provide adequate preparation for school; they attend inferior schools, or their parents do not have the funds to send them to college or set them up in business. As a consequence, they want money but cannot get it legally. They become frustrated or strained and they *may* turn to crime as a result. For example, they may attempt to get the money they want through theft, prostitution, or selling drugs.

While strain theory made a lot of sense to me, I felt that the theory was incomplete. In particular, I felt that there were many sources of frustration or strain—not just the failure to achieve monetary success. When I looked at my own life and the lives of those around me, it was easy to list numerous sources of frustration and anger (such as harassment by peers, conflict with parents or romantic partners, poor grades in school, poor working conditions). Likewise, the social psychology literature—especially the literature on stress and justice—suggested that there were many sources of strain. Further, I felt that strain theory had not fully explained why some people react to strain with crime and others do not.

My dissertation tried to build on existing strain theories by describing additional sources of strain besides the failure to achieve monetary success. I continued to work on strain theory after I left graduate school and got a job at Emory University. My work culminated in a 1992 article about general strain theory (GST) of crime and delinquency. GST draws on previous versions of strain theory, the social psychology literature, and my own experiences and ideas.

GST tries to describe the major sources of strain and the factors that influence whether one reacts to strain with crime. Three major sources of strain include (1) preventing or threatening one from achieving positively valued goals (for example, monetary success or autonomy from adults); (2) removing or threatening to remove positively valued stimuli one possesses (for example, your romantic partner threatens to break up with you); and (3) presenting or threatening one with negatively valued stimuli (for example, insulting or physically assaulting you). People who experience strain may turn to crime for several reasons: crime may allow them to achieve their goals, protect or retrieve positively valued stimuli, or terminate or escape from negative stimuli (for example, run away from home, hit the person who is harassing you). Crime may also be used to seek revenge against those who have wronged you or to deal with the strain you are experiencing (for example, take drugs to forget about your problems). A number of factors influence whether you will respond to strain with crime, including such things as your coping skills and resources, social support, level of social control, and association with delinquent peers.

I think GST is important because it significantly expands the scope of strain theory, and in doing so, it has helped to generate new interest in strain theories of crime. The research on the causes of crime is now dominated by control and social learning theories. But GST supplements these theories in an important way. Rather than arguing that people engage in crime because they are free to do so or because they learn to engage in crime, GST basically argues that they engage in crime because they are treated badly, they get mad or angry, and crime is one way to deal with their anger. I and several other researchers have attempted to test GST using data from surveys of adolescents. Also, certain observational studies have examined the theory.

Advice to Students: If you are planning on doing research on strain theory or on the causes of crime more generally, you first need to familiarize yourself with the work that has been done in the area. A review of the literature will be helpful. But do not be afraid to critique or go beyond what has already been done. Ask yourself whether a particular theory or argument makes sense to you—does it jibe with your experiences, with your observations of others, or with what you have studied in other courses? If not, you may want to suggest an extension or revision in the theory. Likewise, ask yourself whether the empirical tests of the theory make sense—are adequate samples employed, are all major concepts measured, or are good measures employed? It is not as difficult as you might think to make an original contribution to the literature.

be accomplished by modifying existing sentencing structures to a guidelines-based scheme, where judges must impose sentences within certain ranges for different crimes. While other variables may be manipulated to invoke the desired response or outcome, such as greater fairness in sentencing, the fact is that we can sometimes effect changes in one variable by manipulating other variables that are causally related to it.

4. Relevant variables for criminal justice professionals and criminologists are empirical and amenable to measurement. **Empirical** means being amenable to our senses. This means that we can identify variables, their interrelations with other variables, and that we can measure their existence. If we study the influence of peer groups on delinquency, for example, this means that we must devise a measure of peer group influence. Definitions of delinquency are reasonably standardized, although there are some jurisdictional variations regarding whether certain behaviors should be classified as delinquency. Despite this variability, delinquency is easily conceptualized (e.g., delinquent or nondelinquent), although peer group influence is less easy to quantify.

5. Inconsistencies exist among studies of the same phenomena, and these inconsistencies are not necessarily indicative of no association between various phenomena. Smith and Jones might find, for instance, that criminal behavior tends to decline with increasing age. However, Anderson and Freedman may find that the incidence of crime among the elderly is increasing annually. What should we conclude about the relation between age and criminal behavior? Apparent contradictory findings should not discourage us from pursuing our research interests enthusiastically. After all, there are different jurisdictions involved, different samples of criminals investigated, different types of crime examined, and a myriad of other factors that can explain away these inconsistencies. Thus, research is cumulative, and, through replication and repetition, our knowledge about variable interrelations is greatly enhanced. Eventually, we discover general patterns of relations between variables, although these patterns may exhibit occasional inconsistencies. Again, we must not be too hasty and conclude that because inconsistencies in findings exist, there must not be any continuity in the interrelationships of the variables investigated.

These are only a few of many **assumptions** made about our fields of inquiry. Criminology and criminal justice offer a wealth of interesting information for research. Investigators are limited only by their imaginations of what can be studied and how. Subsequently, we will examine more closely the notions of theory, frames of reference, variables, and hypotheses, and how each of these relates to the research process.

■ WHY DO RESEARCH?

Some of the major reasons for conducting criminological research include (1) acquiring knowledge for the sake of knowledge; (2) determining answers to practical questions; (3) adding to the growing body of knowledge in the profession; and (4) acquiring useful knowledge and skills to transmit this information to others and to direct their investigations.

1. Some people are interested in simply knowing about things. The "knowledge for the sake of knowledge" position has been related to pure research. The practical implications of pure research are often not apparent. In fact, the practical ends served by such theorizing are simply ignored. Thus, the objective in pure research is to study the complexities of explanations, not to solve current social problems.

2. Some practitioners seek answers to practical questions. Regardless of their rightness or wrongness, decisions are made about public policy or program components. For example, research investigations of judicial sentencing patterns in certain jurisdictions have disclosed evidence of sentencing disparities. While these disparities may not be overt, it is strongly implied by researchers that subtle, yet significant, disparities exist. Thus, state legislatures may seek to correct these disparities by modifying their state sentencing systems. This is not intended to mean that all judges are biased or that they deliberately sentence offenders of different genders or races to different incarcerative terms, despite their offense similarities. Rather, legislatures may wish to take preventive action to eliminate possible allegations or the appearance of judicial favoritism or wrongdoing.

3. Most investigators wish to add to the growing body of knowledge in each criminological or criminal justice topic area. Whether we are interested in the relation between age and crime or offense escalation among juveniles arrested for status offenses, our knowledge of these and other topics is enhanced through the objective research that is conducted. Any profession is noted for a body of grounded literature pertaining to specific subject areas. Systematically undertaken research can do much to enhance the sophistication of this body of literature so that others may benefit from it.

4. A fourth reason relates to understanding the work reported by other investigators and how such work relates to our professional interests. Students entering criminology or criminal justice will carve out an interest area or area of specialization. They will read research reported in various professional journals and trade publications, and it is in their best interests to acquire extensive knowledge of the work of others. If they should eventually teach subjects reflecting their areas of specialization, their previously acquired information will be an invaluable resource from which to draw examples and illustrations. They will be more capable of directing the research of students who seek to conduct their own investigations of topics of interest to them.

■ THE EMERGENCE OF SCIENCE AND CRIMINAL JUSTICE

Criminology and criminal justice are social sciences. Criminology is the study of crime, the science of crime and criminal behavior, the forms of criminal behavior, the causes of crime, the definition of criminality, and the societal reaction to crime. It is an empirical social-behavioral science which investigates crime and criminals. Criminal justice is an interdisciplinary social science that studies the nature and operations of organizations providing justice services to society. As academic disciplines, they are considered products of sociology, a key social science. Sociology is a relatively young discipline, and the first national sociology organization, the American Sociological Association, was founded in the 1890s. Prior to such formal organization, independent researchers, both sociologists and criminologists, worked to explain various forms of criminality and deviance. August Comte (France), Herbert Spencer (England), Cesare Lombroso (Italy), Cesare Beccaria (Italy), Emile Durkheim (France), and many of their contemporaries were prolific writers and analysts during the 1800s. Much of their writing formed the foundations of social science and criminology as we know these fields today.

Criminal justice was spawned by criminologists and sociologists in the 1960s. The Law Enforcement Assistance Administration (LEAA) was created by the President's Crime Commission in 1968. The LEAA was designed to provide resources, leadership, and coordination to state and local law enforcement agencies to prevent and/or reduce adult crime and juvenile delinquency. Millions of dollars were allocated to researchers and police departments over the next decade for various purposes. Departments of criminal justice were established in hundreds of colleges and universities during this same period. In 1998 there were over 30 departments of criminal justice offering Ph.D. degrees, and over 150 departments offering master's degrees. The major national organization for criminal justice, the Academy of Criminal Justice Sciences (ACJS), was founded in 1963. The American Society of Criminology (ASC), the primary national organization for criminologists, was founded in 1948. Most persons interested in crime and delinquency belong to both organizations, where the membership lists of the ASC and ACJS correlate at about 75 percent or higher.

Members of both the ASC and ACJS consider themselves to be scientists. Science is a way of knowing about things, and it imposes strict guidelines for its users to follow. A key feature of science is that it studies empirical phenomena which are amenable to our senses. Science as a method of knowing about things embraces four fundamental elements:

1. Science is **empirical.** As criminologists, we study what is amenable to our senses or whatever is tangible. If we study attitudes or psychological factors that are not directly observable, these phenomena are rendered observable through the construction of various indirect measures. Questionnaires and observation are indirect ways of investigating phenomena that are not directly observable, such as peer group influence, burnout, stress, or police cynicism. Observable phenomena, such as criminal activity, delinquency, race/ethnicity, age, gender, and socioeconomic status, easily fall within the scope of criminologists and criminal justicians.

2. Science is cumulative. This means that the information about any given phenomenon we study accumulates over time. The research conducted by different investigators is cumulative in that it builds until there are obvious trends and characteristics that can be described. Journal articles contain research about a wide variety of topics. Reviews of the literature are indicative of the cumulative nature of criminology and criminal justice as scientific disciplines.

3. Science is ethically neutral. Whenever criminological investigations are undertaken, researchers are obligated to be neutral in their inquiry. They may observe findings that are inconsistent with what they expect to find. Using science as a way of knowing, they must set aside their values and personal beliefs, to the extent that they can, and objectively assess whatever is yielded from their scientific inquiry.

4. Science is theoretical. There is a pervasive theoretical basis to all social scientific research. Theory explains and predicts relations between different phenomena studied. Theory ties together different ideas and enables investigators to generalize their findings to larger populations and settings.

The Probability Nature of Science

The general public has a limited understanding of what science is. Scientific facts are presented daily about diverse subjects. Scientific factual information is often accepted as true in an absolute sense, without question. Scientists themselves in every field, however, admonish everyone to consider their information as tentative, subject to further evidence and confirmation. As we will soon see, *tentativeness* is a key word in any type of scientific investigation or inquiry.

In the 1960s the Surgeon General of the United States produced a document indicating that cigarette smoking was hazardous to one's health. A link between various forms of cancer and cigarette smoking was implied. An analysis of hundreds of studies of smoking and health was conducted. An impressive panel of statisticians and health experts reviewed past research and re-analyzed investigations. The Surgeon General's report was based on the tentative conclusions from these reports. The tobacco companies and most smokers took issue with the Surgeon General and countered with their own evidence showing cigarette smoking to be safe and not a cause of cancer.

Seven years would pass before cigarette companies would be forced to place warnings on cigarette products and packages. The first warning read, "Cigarette smoking *may be* hazardous to your health" [italics mine]. Several years later, other warnings would include the word *is*. "Cigarette smoking *is* hazardous to your health" [italics mine]. Of course, in the 1990s, tobacco companies have settled multibillion dollar lawsuits with most states and private citizens, where tobacco has been causally linked with cancer and millions of deaths have resulted because of cigarette smoking. All public buildings in the United States are now smoke-free, and increasing numbers of private establishments are prohibiting smoking because of the high risk of cancer from second-hand smoke. Who would have predicted this outcome?

The point is that scientists originally studied cigarette smoking and its association with cancer. Early research was tentative. Later research was tentative. At least 70 years of research eventually led to a general policy change regarding tobacco consumption and the enactment of laws and legislation prohibiting smoking in public buildings and conveyances, such as buses, airplanes, and trains. In retrospect, we can say that the process of changing public attitudes about smoking was clearly sluggish. Like a movie in slow-motion, we can review the pace of change in smoking policy over time. More than a few citizens today say, Why did it take so long? Why didn't lawmakers and the public accept the scientific findings that were presented as facts and make policy changes in the 1960s? Wouldn't these changes have saved hundreds of thousands of lives? Unfortunately, we do not have the benefit of knowing the future. We can only look back at historical events that have already transpired. Armed with this information, it is easy for us to say what should have been done earlier.

If it took so long for policy changes to occur with such heavily researched subjects as cigarette smoking and cancer, we can certainly understand why less heavily researched subjects, such as juvenile delinquency intervention programs, community policing programs, diversion programs, intensive supervised probation programs, electronic monitoring and home confinement programs, and victim-offender reconciliation programs are not easily sold to the public and adopted on large-scale bases. It takes considerable time and experimentation before we accept a particular explanation for, or solution to, a problem.

When any scientific project is undertaken and scientific findings are presented, these findings are *always* presented in a tentative context. Scientists do not say with certainty, We have proved this or that. Rather, scientists say, We have provided support for this or that idea or solution. This tentativeness and caution is very much justified. This is because all scientific inquiry is couched in the context of probability.

Every study of any phenomenon where science is used is considered a single incident or test or experiment. It takes numerous studies by many investigators to establish the sort of consistency we require to believe that a cause-effect relation exists between variables. The tobacco-cancer relation is a lesson for all of us. What about Mark Jones's study of boot camps and their effectiveness at reducing juvenile probationer recidivism? Jones's study was only one study. If we examine the literature and count the number of articles about boot camps generally, in 1999 there were only 125 studies of boot camps reported by the popular abstracting service *Criminal Justice Abstracts*. Only 29 of these articles/reports pertained to juveniles and were only generally related to the study conducted by Mark Jones, in which boot camps were viewed as a means of reducing recidivism among juvenile probationers. How many more studies do you think should be conducted before we can reach the level of certainty about the relationship between boot camps and juvenile probationer recidivism that we have with the relationship between tobacco and cancer? How long do you think it would take for these studies to be conducted, summarized, and reported?

Science also uses **probability theory** when evaluating research findings. We have alluded to the application of statistical tests when analyzing research data. Whenever scientific findings are reported, there is usually a probability accompanying these reports of findings. For instance, a probability might be stated as "Smith and Anderson found that an association exists between job stress and probation officer turnover in an Illinois probation agency. This association was

Box 1.2

Bruce Arrigo
California School of Professional Psychology, Institute of Psychology, Law and Public Policy

Statistics: B.A. (politics and philosophy), St. Joseph's University; M.A. (psychology), Duquesne University; Ph.D. (administration of justice), Pennsylvania State University.

Interests: Throughout my academic training, I relied substantially on theory as a vehicle to make sense of pressing social problems. My present research interests include the intersections of critical criminology with models of social justice; criminal and civil aspects of mental health law and policy; and the application of postmodern theory (including chaos theory, topology, and psychoanalytic semiotics) to application topics in crime, law, justice, and community.

My research interests emerged in response to my practice work prior to pursuing a career in academe. I was a community organizer and social activist for the homeless, the mentally ill, the working poor, the frail elderly, the chemically addicted, abuse survivors, and the decarcerated. I became very frustrated with how the criminal justice, the juvenile justice, the mental health, and the social welfare systems, knowingly or not, fostered a climate in which troubled and vulnerable constituencies were unnecessarily marginalized, victimized, criminalized, or otherwise oppressed.

My research has been significant particularly in the context of exploring and developing new theoretical vista in the interdisciplinary and integrated study of law, crime, and deviance. This is particularly the case in the areas of postmodern thought, semiotics, chaos theory, and psychoanalysis. Moreover, my research has been important for better understanding some of the psychological dimensions of crime and justice, especially in relation to selected controversies in mental health law.

I find that my research is thoroughly satisfying when I discover something new about how peace and justice can be meaningfully assured notwithstanding the profound problems of violence and crime in our society and around the world. Thus, I am most gratified when prospects for deepening or restoring our humanity as a people and as a culture is advanced, in part, through my contributions as a researcher and scholar.

significant at the .05 level of significance." Virtually *every* scientific finding has a probability attached. The .05 level of significance in the hypothetical Smith and Anderson study means that 5 percent of the time, the association between job stress and probation officer turnover may *not* be significant. The association might be due to a chance fluctuation between the two variables. The fact is that scientific findings include probability as part of their very natures, and they are not absolute certainties. It is *not* an absolute certainty that job stress and probation officer turnover are always related in every probation agency in the United States. The reported scientific finding pertained only to the Illinois agency and to the sample of probation officers studied. Other contrary findings *may* occur if we were to study probation officer labor turnover and job stress in several other jurisdictions, but the probability of this is low.

Returning to our original elements of scientific inquiry, science is empirical. Science is theoretical. Science is ethically neutral. And to the extent that research must be replicated and repeated numerous times before we can achieve certainty about events and associations between variables, science is also cumulative. Previous knowledge or information about variables and subjects is cumulative and builds upon itself. A virtual mountain of evidence, or scientific findings, is necessary to establish causality between variables. This is the probability nature of science.

Objectivity in Scientific Research

Let me tell you what I believe, what I *strongly* believe, about plea bargaining. I believe that plea bargaining gets criminals greater sentencing leniency than if they were to go to trial and get convicted and sentenced for the same crime. I really believe this. For example, I believe that if you are a criminal, Joe Jones, charged with armed robbery and the police have a great deal of evidence against you, you should have your lawyer, Mike Smith, work with the prosecutor, Phil Anderson, to cut a deal or plea bargain. You should enter a guilty plea to the armed robbery charge and accept whatever Phil suggests as a punishment. I believe that if Joe is stubborn and insists on his legal right to a trial by jury, he will be found guilty and the judge will sock it to him and impose a very hefty prison term. Suppose Phil says, "Listen Mike, we have a clear-cut case against your client, Joe. He was caught in the act of robbing a bank. We've got bank videotapes showing Joe holding a weapon, taking the money, menacing customers. If Joe will plead guilty to armed robbery, I'll recommend a sentence of 5 years. If Joe fights this in court, he'll be convicted and the judge will probably slap him with 20 years in prison, minimum, maybe even 40 years! Take it or leave it." Mike discusses the plea with Joe, and while Joe doesn't want to go to prison, he would rather do 5 years than 20 to 40 years. Joe accepts the plea bargain, the judge approves, and Joe gets 5 years. This is what I believe. A criminal defendant will do much better and receive greater leniency through plea bargaining compared with going to trial and taking his or her chances with the judge.

Now, suppose I study thousands of cases in North Dakota and Minnesota and find that there are only *slight* differences in the severity of sentences when criminals plead guilty as compared with when they go to trial. This evidence I have found is definitely contrary to what I would expect to find and what I personally believe to be true. I have a dilemma of sorts. I have just written a nice introduction to a research article where I have argued persuasively that plea bargaining results in greater leniency for criminals compared with punishments resulting from jury trial convictions. I have quoted from various articles that support what I believe to be true. But now my research findings say otherwise. How should I resolve my dilemma?

As a scientist, no matter what I believe otherwise, I must report what I have found. In this instance, at least, I found that there is no difference in sentencing between those who plead guilty through plea bargaining and those who are found guilty and are sentenced as the result of jury trials. This is the objectivity required of me as a social scientist when I conduct research. I conduct my research, not especially to advance my own agenda about what I believe to be true, but rather, to investigate and report my findings.

The more sensitive the topic, the more important it is to be objective about what one finds. Suppose you are a death penalty opponent. You conduct death penalty opinion research. You collect survey information from thousands of citizens and ask them whether they are for or against the death penalty. Seventy-five percent of them report that they are in favor of the death penalty. This disappoints you because you are against the death penalty. But you are also a social scientist. You must report what you have found.

Some researchers who are death penalty opponents have focused upon those few persons who have actually attended executions of criminals. These researchers think perhaps that if one sees an execution, one will be less likely in the future to be in favor of capital punishment. After all, the shock of seeing a criminal executed is traumatic for many persons. Suppose the researcher asks 500 persons who have witnessed executions whether they are for or against capital punishment. Perhaps 60 percent of these persons say that they oppose capital punishment. The researcher likes this finding because it agrees with his personal views.

But scientific inquiry isn't about what we like and dislike or our views about events that we may oppose or favor. Science demands that we use objectivity at every stage of our investigation. Thus, even our finding that 60 percent of our sample of persons who have witnessed executions oppose capital punishment does not preclude additional study where it may be found that a majority of persons who witness executions also approve of capital punishment. Again, further study is needed before we can make conclusions about events with certainty. We must maintain a posture of scientific neutrality, at least in our data collection, analysis, interpretation, results, and implications of the research we conduct. We can only insinuate our personal opinions and thoughts and conjecture as prose at appropriate points at the end of our research report.

Returning to my beliefs about plea bargaining and sentencing, I can present my findings and then speculate at length in the "Implications" or "Discussion" section of my research report. I might point out that North Dakota and Minnesota may not be typical of other states. I might say that the sample of cases I chose to analyze may not be typical of the average case in other criminal jurisdictions. I might conjecture at length and speculate about a dozen problems with my study that may have led to my findings. All of this soothes my feelings about why I didn't find what I expected to find. But I did my duty as a scientist and reported the findings as they occurred, despite the fact that they didn't agree with my personal feelings. This is as it should be.

■ FUNCTIONS OF RESEARCH AND STATISTICS

Research methods and statistics as applied to criminal justice and criminology fulfill several important functions. These functions are (1) exploratory, (2) descriptive, (3) experimental, and (4) decision making.

Exploratory Functions

In some areas of criminology and criminal justice, little is known about observed events. Why do serial murderers kill? Why do spouses abuse each other and their children? What types of policing are best for particular neighborhoods or communities? What influence does the gender of criminal defendants have on juries composed of the opposite gender? Are older judges more lenient in sentencing older offenders compared with younger judges? While some research exists to provide partial answers to these and other questions, few complete answers are presently available. More adequate research will be needed.

For instance, a correctional innovation introduced on a limited scale in recent years is electronic monitoring (Ball and Lilly, 1985). Many legal, moral, and ethical questions have arisen about the use of electronic monitoring and its subsequent application for managing larger offender populations. While preliminary reports have been completed about the cost of using these systems in various jurisdictions, there are still unanswered questions about the technological implications of electronic monitoring and the logistical problems to be solved if such equipment is to be used on a large scale. Therefore, exploratory studies are being undertaken to answer some of these questions.

Exploratory research identifies factors that seem to have more relevance than others for explaining things. Exploratory studies narrow our investigations to explanations of events that are more promising than others. For instance, electronic monitoring has raised constitutional questions, such as the right to privacy. The U.S. Supreme Court has not ruled on the constitutionality of electronic monitoring in supervised release programs, and few, if any, jurisdictions have statutes that prohibit its use. But an exploratory study might disclose little about the constitutionality of electronic monitoring, and, therefore, we might be better off studying the cost and logistical implementation of such monitoring in communities.

Descriptive Functions

It is important to note that descriptive research has a more focused quality compared with its exploratory counterpart. A descriptive study of marijuana growers was conducted by Sandra Hafley and Richard Tewksbury (1996). Hafley and Tewksbury wanted to describe the community culture within which marijuana growing thrives. They selected a Kentucky county known for its illegal marijuana production, and on the basis of interviews with several community residents, they were able to characterize the culture of marijuana growing and distribution in great detail. Using the pseudonym, "Bluegrass County," Hafley and Tewksbury learned about different roles performed by largely male members of the community. Some of the roles performed were communal grower, hustler, pragmatist, young punk, and entrepreneur. Women in Bluegrass County were also described as performing several support roles, including decent women, strumptets, and women-in-between.

Penetrating the marijuana culture of any Kentucky county is difficult. However, one of the researchers was, in fact, a life-long resident of rural Kentucky. Personal contacts and kinship network introductions were crucial in gaining access to the closed marijuana culture. Assurances of anonymity were mandatory before citizens agreed to share information with these researchers. Once trust had been established, Hafley and Tewksbury gathered extensive information about the Kentucky marijuana business. Communal growers, for instance, were those who believed that growing marijuana made a social statement to those opposed to marijuana use. Hustlers were those who have both used and sold marijuana. Pragmatists were those who grew marijuana because of economic hardship. They knew it was wrong, but they needed the money. Young punks were marijuana grower "wanna-bes."

Women's roles included strumpets—women of loose morals who provided sexual companionship and support for male marijuana growers. Decent women were highly respected and never placed in jeopardy by their men. These women are married or related to male marijuana growers and are indirectly supportive of their husbands' activities, even though the activities are illegal. Women-in-between is a new category composed of women who are neither decent nor strumpets. They are relatively new to the community and sometimes replace males who have been arrested for such activities as transporting marijuana or selling it to others. They are in transitional roles, where community residents have yet to categorize them one way or another for acceptance purposes.

Hafley and Tewksbury enriched their research with actual remarks from those interviewed. One entrepreneur said, "You don't know what it's like to work in that factory. I been shut up in that place for ten years, day after day. I ain't making no money. Hell, when I retire, I won't draw nothin'. I spend my life in that box and will be ready to die when I leave it. Why shouldn't I grow a [marijuana] crop? So what if the law don't like it? A crop or two and I'll be set. At least I'll have something to put by" (Hafley and Tewksbury, 1996:82). These remarks were made by a community member who was disgusted with his factory job and wanted to earn more money by entering the marijuana-growing business. These and other remarks are very helpful in providing explanations for why community residents might engage in deviant or criminal behavior. **Descriptive research** sets the stage for more controlled experimentation later, where certain factors may be manipulated and controlled observations may be made.

Experimental Functions

The experimental function of research pertains to the amount of control researchers exercise over the variables (factors) or subjects (persons) they study. **Experimental research** is designed to see which factors make a difference in modifying a particular outcome. A standard type of experimental research is called the **before-after method** or **before-after design.** Ordinarily, the experimental subjects (persons who are being studied by the researcher) are examined in one time period, administered a stimulus (an experimental factor or variable), and then examined again in a second time period. Comparing the subjects' Time 1 and Time 2 scores supposedly discloses the impact of the experimental factor on their behavior.

An example of an experimental study is the study of pregnant, substance-abusing probationers conducted by Vicki Markey, Sunny Areissohn, and Margaret Mudd (1997). Markey and her associates were interested in the growing problem of pregnant, drug-abusing offenders and the subsequent births of infants with defects and deformities attributable to the mother's drug use. The San Diego County Probation Department began a program in 1992 designed to decrease or eliminate birth defects among newborn infants by controlling the social environments of pregnant female probationers. The program was known as WATCh, or Women And Their Children. In 1992, for instance, there were 607,000 births in California, with 69,000 (11 percent) born to mothers who used alcohol and/or drugs prior to their deliveries. About 4,000 infants are born each year in San Diego County with alcohol and/or drugs in their systems. Costs to taxpayers for each of these infants are as much as $400,000, including medical, foster care, and special education costs.

Markey, Areissohn, and Mudd observed that prior to the implementation of the WATCh program, pregnant probationers were supervised by probation officers without any specialized training. Caseloads of officers ranged from 200 to 2,000 probationers. Many pregnant offenders continued to use alcohol and drugs, although they were expected to participate in a community recovery program. The primary focus was upon the comfort of the pregnant offender rather than on the health and welfare of the developing fetus.

When the WATCh program was commenced, probation officer caseloads were drastically reduced to 35 per officer. The WATCh model provided for no tolerance for illicit alcohol consumption or drug use. Specialized probation officers were used to test pregnant women frequently for alcohol or drug use, and to ensure their immediate treatment and custody in the event that they tested positive for alcohol and/or drugs. All probation officers supervising pregnant probationers underwent special training and were made aware of several helpful emergency prenatal community-based organizations. At least two urine tests were administered per week. Judicial support was obtained for the no tolerance policy. Under the WATCh program through 1994, there were 90 births among 84 probationer-mothers. Only 7 infants (8 percent) tested positive for alcohol or drugs, while 83 (92 percent) were alcohol/drug free. It was estimated that the program resulted in savings of $33.2 million.

Markey, Areissohn, and Mudd concluded that their experiment was significant and showed low program costs of only $2,500 per probationer per year. Subsequently the WATCh program was applied to pregnant teenagers who were in trouble with the law. By the end of January 1995, 124 adult women and 15 teenagers have delivered alcohol- and drug-free babies while in the WATCh program. This result was a 92 percent success rate for the WATCh program.

The experiment these researchers conducted was a comparison between standard probation officer-client supervision and the more intensive supervision according to WATCh program guidelines. A much larger percentage of babies with alcohol and/or drugs in their systems were associated with women under standard probation supervision compared with those delivering babies under the WATCh program. These researchers rightly concluded that "while the demonstration sample is too small to make sweeping statements, the outcomes are supportive of an optimistic view. Intensive probation does work to . . . bring about the birth of healthy, drug- and alcohol-free babies" (Markey, Areissohn, and Mudd, 1997:23).

One convenient way of distinguishing between these different studies and the functions they serve is to envision a continuum of uncertainty and certainty such as the one shown below.

Uncertainty ———————————————————— Certainty

Exploratory ————→ Descriptive ————→ Experimental

As we move from the extreme left (uncertainty), our studies change in quality from exploratory, to descriptive, to experimental. Thus, experimental studies are those characterized by a high degree of certainty. What this means is that our knowledge of which factors are important has increased to the point that we can conduct specific tests and exert some degree of control over various factors. However, it is unlikely that any study ever reaches the absolute right-side extreme of total certainty. Some studies are closer to the certainty end of the continuum than others. Those closer to the uncertainty end of the continuum are more likely to be exploratory or descriptive studies rather than experimental ones.

Decision-Making Functions

The major functions of statistics in research are to help us describe the phenomena we study, make decisions about our observations, and identify relationships between two or more variables. For instance, suppose we are interested in the frequency of inmate lawsuits filed against prison officials and correctional personnel. We study two prisons, noting that prison A has an inmate grievance counsel, where a board composed of inmates hears complaints and allegations against prison officials lodged by other inmates. In prison B, there is no inmate board. Assuming the two prisons are of equal size, suppose the rate of lawsuits filed in prison A is 3 per 100 inmates, but in prison B the rate is 7 per 100 inmates.

Statistics can give us an objective appraisal of the significance of difference between these rates, although by inspection, we can see that the two rates are numerically different. That they differ is important, but for statistical purposes, we want to determine if these differences are "significant," where statistical significance is evaluated according to certain "chance" expectations about whatever we observe.

■ EVALUATION RESEARCH

Evaluation research consists of any study designed to assess the outcome of a particular program, intervention, or experiment, and whether the program or intervention goals have been achieved. Program evaluation is the process of assessing any law enforcement, corrections intervention, or other program for the purpose of determining its effectiveness in achieving manifest goals. Program evaluation investigates the nature of organizational intervention strategies, counseling, interpersonal interactions, staff quality, expertise, education, and the success or failure experiences of clients served by any program. Several examples below illustrate what is meant by program evaluation. (Much of the material in the following section has been adapted from Champion, 1996:559–565.)

Example 1. Corrections officials might say that one reason criminals get into trouble initially is because they lack social skills and abilities enabling them to have normal human relationships. Whether we agree or disagree with this statement is irrelevant. The fact is, some researchers believe this. In fact, some researchers engage in experiments to determine whether *changing* one's level of social skill development and interpersonal abilities will modify their behaviors to the extent that they will be less likely to engage in criminal behavior in the future. Sue McCulloch (1993) studied the impact of a *Social Skills and Human Relationships Training Program* for sex offenders in Queensland, Australia. A *Self-Evaluation Scale* and a *Social Reinforcement Survey Schedule* were administered to six sex offenders who participated in the project. A personal history interview was conducted with each.

The program consisted of several small-group sessions with a counselor and interventionist. Subject matter of the program consisted of short-term courses on interpersonal behaviors and educational information. Measures were taken for all six offenders at the beginning of the program as well as at the end of the program, and the scores on these different instruments were compared. Results showed marked improvement in the level of offender social skills and human relations development, as well as more favorable self-images and self-evaluations. Some questions arose concerning the applicability of this experience to subsequent reintegration of these offenders into their communities and whether they would refrain from future sex offending. While this was a small sample, McCulloch (1993) was impressed with the intervention strategy enough to recommend it for more general application to Australia's sex offender population. *The program evaluation consisted of comparing scores before and after the intervention (coursework and small-group sessions) had occurred. Score differences in favorable directions indicated program promise for reducing recidivism among sex offenders.*

Example 2. Some juvenile corrections officials may think that youths with severe psychological dysfunction and behavioral problems and aggressiveness are more violence-prone and tend to become violent offenders. If this aggressiveness can be curbed, and if these behavior problems and severe psychological impairments can be remedied some way, then it follows that perhaps their propensity toward violent conduct can be controlled or decreased. Again, whatever we believe is irrelevant. In the present case, a study was conducted by Hagan and King (1992), using 55 youths classified as suffering from severe psychological dysfunction, having various behavioral problems and extraordinary aggressiveness. These youths had been incarcerated in the Intensive Treatment Unit of Ethan Allen School, a state juvenile correctional facility in Wales, Wisconsin.

The intervention program utilized a positively based behavior modification strategy that included family and group therapy and instruction in independent living skills. A two-year follow-up was used to determine whether any change in these youths' behaviors had occurred. Hagan and King found that one-third of the youths received future state correctional placement (failed), a third had no further convictions (a high success level), and a third had further convictions but their offending was nonviolent, less severe, and they were not incarcerated in state facilities (moderately successful). *The program evaluation consisted of contrasting the behaviors of these youths during the two-year follow-up period and determining whether there were any behavioral changes as indicated by rearrests or reincarcerations.* Hagan and King (1992) believed that their findings showed that two thirds of the youths either engaged in no further violent offending or engaged in less violent conduct, supported the *therapeutic efficacy* of the Intensive Treatment Unit experiment.

Example 3. Investigators interested in electronic monitoring and home confinement as sound reintegrative strategies designed to deter criminal conduct may believe that clients who experience home confinement will be less likely to reoffend. Again, whether we agree with this point of view or argument is irrelevant. Maxfield and Baumer (1992) studied the effectiveness of electronically monitored home detention in Indianapolis, Indiana, for 224 defendants during 1988–1989. One of their aims was to determine whether this electronic monitoring with home confinement acted as a sufficient deterrent to further criminal conduct. These 224 defendants were carefully screened, were low-risk, relatively stable property offenders. Most offenders completed the program without incurring any program infractions or new arrests. Maxfield and Baumer believed that successful completion of monitored detention was more likely if these persons had (1) suitable living arrangements, where parents or a spouse lived and (2) a criminal record consisting of only minor offenses. *The program evaluation consisted of monitoring the behaviors of these 224 clients during the period of monitored detention and determining the incidence of new offending. An absence of new offending is indicative of program successfulness in this instance.* These researchers were careful to indicate that program effectiveness in their study depended heavily upon careful defendant screening, organization, and effective management of the monitoring, as well as close coordination between judges, prosecutors, and probation personnel.

Example 4. Some researchers think that if juveniles are subjected to positive peer experiences while incarcerated in state industrial schools, they will have a greater chance at reintegrating into mainstream society when paroled. Whether we believe this view is irrelevant. The Minnesota Corrections Department (1972) conducted a study of 242 boys who were transferred from the Minnesota State Training School for Boys in 1969 and placed in a *Positive Peer Culture*, a guided-group interaction program. The program attempts to reverse the effects of the delinquent subculture by substituting positive sets of values and goals through peer pressure and staff guidance. The method is the basic treatment modality for the institution and consists of group meetings, 90 minutes in length five nights per week. During these meetings, group leaders serve to redirect, guide, and bring into focus problem areas that might be contributing to a juvenile's difficulties, and then the leaders allow the group to work on the problem.

During 1969, 219 boys were paroled. A follow-up disclosed that 51 percent (111 boys) had their parole programs revoked because of one or more program violations. But the 49 percent success rate was regarded as successful by these researchers. Although no official standards presently exist to define good or bad recidivism rates, informal standards suggest that recidivism of 30 percent or higher among any given sample is considered high recidivism. However, recidivism rates of two-thirds or 65 percent or higher are commonly observed for both juvenile and adult parolees in the following 12 months or more after their initial release. Thus, the 49 percent "success rate" was considered good by investigators, because it is substantially lower than the usual 65 percent. *The program evaluation consisted of comparing the recidivism rates of these juvenile parolees with the standards observed in other comparable jurisdictions. Since all youths in the Minnesota facility received the Positive Peer Culture program, no control groups were available with which to compare these parolees. In the present case, the researchers compared their parolee successes with a comparable program in California, the James Marshall Treatment Program, a 90-day intervention program, and their results were similar.*

The American Probation and Parole Association (APPA) has been involved in a longitudinal investigation and survey to determine various alternative outcome measures for assessing intermediate punishment program effectiveness. The APPA Board of Directors consists of probation and parole administrators, probation and parole line staff, and representatives from various affiliate organizations (e.g., American Correctional Association, American Jail Association) throughout the United States and Canada. The APPA distributed a survey instrument to all APPA board members and prefaced their questionnaire with the following:

> *Assume that your department is going to be evaluated by an outside evaluator. The results of the evaluation will determine the level of funding for the next fiscal year. What outcome measure(s) would you want the evaluator to use in "measuring" the success of your program(s)? What outcome measure(s) would you not want the evaluator to use in the evaluation?*

The survey yielded a response from 30 different board members. This was a response rate of 31 percent, since survey instruments were originally sent to over 90 persons. Table 1.1 shows the relative rankings and ratings of the top 23 criteria cited by these board members as *alternative outcome measures they would like to see used.*

An inspection of Table 1.1 shows that the *amount of restitution collected* tops the list of criteria preferred by these board members. Logically, this would be a direct empirical, tangible indicator of agency effectiveness. As we have seen in previous chapters, community-based programs are increasingly incorporating elements that heighten offender accountability. Making restitution to victims or to the community is an increasingly common program element. Employment is also a key agency goal of many community-based agencies. Thus, many board members selected *number of offenders employed* as another preferred indicator of agency effectiveness. Other criteria in the top five included *technical violations, alcohol/drug test results*, and *new arrests.* Possibly because agencies have more effective monitoring mechanisms in place and improved supervision styles, it is less likely for program clients to engage in technical program violations, fail in alcohol/drug test results, and be rearrested for new offenses. When asked which measures were *not* preferred for program evaluation, the responding board members cited 12 program components. These are shown in Table 1.2.

Table 1.2 shows that board members at least would downplay recidivism rates, revocation rates, technical violations, and new arrests as outcome measures of program effectiveness. Boone (1994:20) said that "there was considerable confusion among the 30 respondents as to exactly what outcome measures should or should not be used to evaluate their respective programs." Interestingly, the top four outcome measures cited by board members in Table 1.2 are either direct or indirect *recidivism* measures. Ideally, more effective programs have lower recidivism rates than less effective programs. *All* agencies want to exhibit low rates of recidivism among their clientele. Any agency disclosing a recidivism rate

TABLE 1.1 Alternative Outcome Measures from APPA Board
          of Directors Survey: Top 23

Measure	Number of Board Members Selecting Measure
Amount of *restitution* collected	10
Number of offenders *employed*	10
Technical violations	9
Alcohol/drug test results	9
New *arrests*	8
Fines/fees collected	7
Number *completed supervision*	6
Hours *community service*	6
Number sessions of *treatment*	5
Number/ratio *revocations*	5
Percent *financial obligations* collected	5
Employment stability/days employed	5
New arrests: crime type/seriousness	4
Meeting *needs of offenders*	4
Family stability	4
Education attainment	4
Costs/benefits/services/savings	4
Days *alcohol/drug free*	4
Number of *treatment referrals*	3
Time between *technical violations*	3
Marital stability	3
Wages/taxes paid	3
Compliance with *court orders*	3

Source: Harry N. Boone, Jr. (1994). "Recommended Outcome Measures for Program
Evaluation: APPA's Board of Directors Survey Results." *APPA Perspectives,* **18**:19.

of 10 percent or less would most certainly be considered for federal or private
funding, since the program would be demonstrably successful. But such low recidivism rates are hard to obtain in most agencies. Again, an informal standard of
30 percent has existed for several decades. This 30 percent standard suggests
that programs with recidivism rates *30 percent or less* are successful programs,
while those with rates *more than 30 percent* are not successful. Some observers
use the word *failure* to describe such programs.

In many respects, it is unfair to label any particular program as a "failure" or
a "success" on the basis of demonstrated client recidivism rates (Matthews,
Boone, and Fogg, 1994). Every agency deals with a different breed of offender—
sex offenders, property offenders, chronic delinquents, persistent property offenders, shoplifters, robbers, and thieves. For instance, Wilson and Vito (1990) describe samples of persistent felony offenders they investigated in Kentucky.
Designing intervention programs that will decrease the chronicity of such offenders is probably an impossible task, since these offenders *persist* in their of-

TABLE 1.2 Outcome Measures Not Preferred for Measuring Program Success

Measure	Number of Board Members Selecting
Recidivism	8
Revocation rates	6
Technical violations	5
New arrests	4
Single measure	2
Public/media perception	2
New convictions	2
Number of positive drug tests	2
Cost of services/efficiency	2
Number of contacts	2
Number of clients	2
Client evaluation	2

Source: Harry N. Boone, Jr. (1994). "Recommended Outcome Measures for Program Evaluation: APPA's Board of Directors Survey Results." *APPA Perspectives,* **18**:20.

fending, no matter what types of intervention strategies are applied. Also, *different time lengths are used to gauge recidivism.* Some standards stipulate a year following one's program commencement, while other standards are two or three years. Some standards are even shorter, as short as three or six months. With such different time dimensions over which to determine the recidivism of clientele, a meaningful discussion of recidivism in any general sense is of little or no consequence when assessing the merits and weaknesses of particular programs.

■ KEY TERMS

Applied research
Assumptions
Attitudes
Basic research
Before-after method or
  before-after design
Birth cohort
Causality
Causal relation
Crime rate
Data
Data analysis
Data collection
Descriptive research
Empirical

Evaluation research
Experimental research
Explanations
Exploratory research
Face-to-face questionnaire
  administration
Interpretation
Interview
Longitudinal research
Mailed questionnaires
Prediction
Probability theory
Pure research
Qualitative research
Quantitative research

Research   Science
Research problem   Scientific inquiry
Research process   Statistics
Research questions   Substantive implications
Respondent   Theoretical implications

■ QUESTIONS FOR REVIEW

1. What is the distinction between pure and applied research? Must any research be either pure or applied? Why or why not?

2. What is a research question? Formulate five research questions apart from those presented in the text and list them. You may turn to the research literature in professional journals for your answers.

3. What is the research process? What are some functions of the research process?

4. What is meant by evaluation research? What is an example of it?

5. What are several meanings associated with statistics? How are statistics and research methods interrelated?

6. Distinguish between criminology and criminal justice. What was the influence of the LEAA on the development of criminal justice?

7. What are three general functions performed by research and statistics? Describe each of these functions. How does our degree of certainty about subject matter relate to these functions?

8. What are four assumptions about the nature of data studied in criminology and criminal justice?

9. What are four crucial elements of science found in criminology and criminal justice?

10. Why is it important to be objective in our scientific inquiry?

chapter **2**

Theory and Research in Criminal Justice and Criminology

INTRODUCTION

This chapter is about theory and how it relates to the research process. Theory is defined, and several important functions of theory are described. There are different types of theory that criminologists and others can use when conducting their investigations. Some of the more important types of theory will be illustrated.

All theories are composed of several variables. These represent the phenomena to be explained as well as various phenomena used to explain them. Variables are conceptualized in alternative ways. Because the particular methods of data collection and statistical procedures we will eventually choose to use are largely dependent upon the nature of the variables we are investigating, it will be important to illustrate different ways variables can be conceived. Variables are an integral part of theories and perform several important functions. These functions will be identified and described.

Social scientists, criminologists, and criminal justice professionals seek to establish causal relations between variables, although it has been noted that causality is difficult to establish when the variables investigated are somewhat elusive empirically. Theories tie variables together in logical ways, and research permits investigators to explore the validity of these relationships. Thus, there is a complementarity between research and theory, where each assists the other. Like the horse and carriage, theory and research, for all practical purposes, are quite compatible. Each may be defined and described independently, but both depend upon each other for their maximum utility. Investigators almost always use theory to guide their research activity, and their research activity leads to either refutation or confirmation of their theories. The value of both theory and research will also be explored.

THEORY DEFINED

Some writers regard **theory** as a collection of concepts. Others say theory is an interconnected set of hypotheses. Other writers say theory is a set of **concepts** plus the interrelationships that are assumed to exist among those concepts (Selltiz, Cook, and Wrightsman, 1976:16). Another way of viewing theory is as a system of explanation. Some professionals regard theory as a conceptual scheme, a **frame of reference,** or a set of **propositions** and **conclusions.** If we consult a dictionary, one of the worst places to look for a clear definition of theory, theory is a mental viewing, a contemplation, conjecture, a systematic statement of principles, or a formulation of apparent relationships or underlying principles of certain observed phenomena which has been verified to some degree (Guralnik, 1972:1475).

All of these definitions of theory are true. Yet, no single definition above pulls together all of theory's essential elements. Perhaps one of the clearer and more comprehensive definitions of theory may be gleaned from a synthesis of two definitions provided by Robert Merton (1957:96–99) and the late theorist, Arnold Rose (1965:9–12). According to these social scientists, theory is an integrated body of assumptions, propositions, and **definitions** that are related in such a way so as to explain and predict relationships between two or more variables.

Assumptions, Propositions, and Definitions. First, let's distinguish between assumptions and propositions. Assumptions are similar to **empirical generalizations** or observable regularities in human behavior (Merton, 1957: 95–96). For our purposes, assumptions are statements that have a high degree of certainty. These are statements that require little, if any, confirmation in the real world. Examples of assumptions might be, "All societies have laws," or "The greater the deviant conduct, the greater the group pressure on the deviant to conform to group norms." Other assumption statements might be, "Prison inmates devise hierarchies of authority highly dependent upon one's physical strength and abilities," or "Most types of delinquency are group-shared phenomena," or "Most delinquents commit delinquent acts in the company of other delinquents." While some of us may take issue with these statements, there is little need to verify each of them. Social scientists and criminologists have found extensive support for each. We take these statements for granted.

In contrast, propositions are also statements about the real world, but they lack the high degree of certainty associated with assumptions. Examples of propositions might be, "Burnout among probation officers may be mitigated or lessened through job enlargement and giving officers greater input in organizational decision making," or "Two-officer patrol units are less susceptible to misconduct and corruption than one-officer patrol units." Another proposition might be, "Reducing prison overcrowding will result in a proportionate decrease in inmate discontent and prison condition-related court litigation." Each researcher has more or less strongly held beliefs about the truth or certainty of these statements. Sometimes, the same statement may be labeled as a "proposition" by one researcher and an "assumption" by another researcher. Depending upon one's experience with the subject matter being investigated, varying degrees of certainty are associated with different statements made about the real world.

Theories consist of both assumptions and propositions. At any given point, researchers will construct theories that contain assumptions and propositions, although over time, these various statements change in the degree of certainty we associate with them. Accruing research in a given subject area will eventually transform propositional statements into assumptions. Many of our assumptions have evolved from the propositional statements of earlier times. As more research is conducted and information is compiled, we gradually improve our understanding of why certain events occur. We become more certain about things.

Other components of theories are definitions. Definitions of terms we use or definitions of the factors we consider significant in influencing various events assist us in constructing a logical explanatory framework or theory. A common problem is that often, the same terms are assigned different definitions by different investigators. If we use the term *peer influence* in a statement about delinquents and their delinquent conduct, how should peer influence be defined?

Ronald L. Akers
University of Florida

Statistics: B.S. (secondary education), Indiana State University; M.A. (sociology), Kent State University; Ph.D. (sociology), University of Kentucky.

Box 2.1

Interests: I have conducted research in many areas of criminal and delinquent behavior, law, social control, and the criminal justice system. These include studies on self-reported delinquency; group conflict in the formation of laws; political power and the administrative component of organizations; adolescent and adult substance use and abuse, cross-national comparisons of prison organization and inmate systems; juvenile detention, diversion, and shelters; intermediate criminal sanctions; the exclusionary rule; fear of crime, rape; and the effects of natural disaster on law and social control. Most of this research has been cross-sectional and longitudinal studies on the causes of crime and delinquency, but it has also included applied research on the functioning and effectiveness of programs and policies. Over the years, research on adolescent drug, alcohol, and tobacco use and abuse to test theories of crime and deviance has commanded the largest share of programs and policies.

Theory has been central to my research in many ways, analyzing, criticizing, or testing the major theories of crime, deviance, law, and criminal justice. I have written more than a few books, including *Criminological Theories* (1997); *Law and Control in Society* (1975); and *Deviant Behavior* (1985). But I think it is fair to say that the contributions that are considered the most important have come in formulating, developing, and testing the *social learning theory* of crime and deviance. This theory was first proposed with Robert Burgess as an integration of Sutherland's differential association theory and behavioral learning theory. I was introduced to differential association theory as an undergraduate, but I became most interested in it during my graduate studies in sociology in which I chose criminology as my major specialty. My interest in reformulating social theory started in the first year after graduate school through conversations and collaboration with Burgess, who had been trained in behavioral learning theory and research. I have continued working on the theory until the present time. It is proposed as a general theory that is applicable to all types of criminal and deviant behavior. My current research involves testing the extent to which the social learning variables mediate the effects on delinquent behavior of age, gender, family structure, race, class, and other social structural variables.

It was also during the early years after completing my graduate studies that I became very interested in drugs and alcohol in society. I was teaching a class in social problems and deviant behavior in the mid-1960s when alcohol use was increasing, and consumption of marijuana and other drugs began to be apparent on college and university campuses (and shortly thereafter in the high schools). The signs were that drug and alcohol abuse threatened to become a more serious problem in society than it had ever been at the same time that crime rates were increasing. Therefore, I felt it was important for the students in the course to learn as much as they could about drugs, alcohol, and society. While preparing course materials on these topics, it became obvious that we had much to learn about the distribution and causes of drug behavior, and that we particularly had little knowledge of youthful drug use. I began immediately to apply social learning theory in an effort to explain drug use and addiction, but it was not until a decade later that I was in a position to conduct a large-scale study of teenage drinking and drug use. The findings from this study have been published in many articles and chapters on topics ranging from tests of competing theories to the link between adolescent drug use and delinquency. However, the one that is most often cited in the literature is the test of social learning theory applied to adolescent drinking and marijuana use that was published in 1979.

Advice to Students: I would advise students interested in doing research in any of the areas mentioned here to first understand that the most effective research is that guided by theory and the most valuable theory is that which is tested by and responsive to empirical research. Even so-called applied research is best when it is informed by theory and the findings from such research have implications for theory. It is only through such research that we can determine the empirical validity and the practical usefulness of theory.

Second, learn and apply the best and most appropriate methods for the theory or issue at hand. Let the problem addressed or questions asked guide the selection of data collection and analysis technique rather than seeking problems to fit a particular technique.

Third, do not become convinced that all of the important or innovative research and theory have been done. In the latter part of the twentieth century, great strides have been made in the quality and sophistication of research methods, in the understanding of causes of crime, and in understanding what programs and policies are and are not likely to be effective in controlling it. But we have a long way to go. In spite of some increases in teenage substance abuse in the 1990s, the overall level of drug, alcohol, and tobacco use and the general level of crime are significantly lower now than in the 1970s. Will that remain true in the next decade? You are in the position at the end of this century that I and others were in at its midpoint. You are able to learn from and build on what has been done before, with the chance to go beyond and improve on it.

How should stress be defined if we are investigating the relation between stress and probation officer power within a probation agency? How should power be defined? As we will see later, there is a conceptual "Tower of Babel" phenomenon in most sciences, as different investigators assign different meanings to the same terms. Differences in definitions assigned common terms sometimes explain inconsistencies in research findings.

When different definitions are given to a common term, it is likely that researchers will arrive at different conclusions about variable interrelationships in independent investigations. For instance, Researcher Smith might study Probation Agency A. If Smith defines stress as physical fatigue and exhaustion, this may characterize how probation officers in Probation Agency A feel while performing their jobs. However, if Researcher Jones studies Probation Agency B and defines stress as an increasing inability to perform a variety of tasks involving conflicting expectations and the psychological frustration resulting from such role performances, it is likely that Jones will find that the probation officers studied in Agency B may not exhibit "stress" in the same way as officers exhibit it in Agency A. This is one of the many explanations we give for contrary or inconsistent findings when the same variables are researched by different investigators. Researchers Smith and Jones are using the same terms, but their different definitions of those terms yield different kinds of associations with other important variables.

In criminology and criminal justice, theory is utilized frequently to account for most phenomena. In most criminology and criminal justice books, for example, theories of deviant conduct and crime are presented that link these phenomena with glandular malfunctions, early childhood socialization, unusual chromosomatic patterns such as the XYY Syndrome, body types, peer group associations and influences, criminal and delinquent subcultures, feeblemindedness and/or mental impairment, differential association, broken homes, cultural deprivation, anomie, social bonding, opportunity, hedonism, class conflict, unequal access to success goals, labeling, learning, cognitive developmentalism, behaviorism, gender, race, age, ethnicity, and social power differentials. For each of these linkages, such as the link between crime and labeling, for instance, an explanatory scheme is advanced that accounts for how labeling is related to criminal behavior.

Labeling theory, for example, explains deviant and criminal conduct by focusing upon social definitions of acts of crime and deviance rather than on the acts themselves. Some of the assumptions underlying labeling theory are that (1) no act is inherently criminal, that (2) persons become criminals through social definition of their conduct, that (3) all persons at one time or another conform to or deviate from the law, that (4) "getting caught" begins the labeling process, that (5) persons defined as criminal will, in turn, cultivate criminal self-definitions, and that (6) they will eventually seek out and associate with others who are similarly defined and develop a criminal subculture (VanderZanden, 1984:206; Bernstein, Kelly, and Doyle, 1977; Lemert, 1951).

The impact of social influence is strong in labeling theory. Accepting the definitions of others and acquiring self-definitions of criminality seems to lead to further criminal behavior. While the empirical evidence to support labeling theory as a good explanation for criminal conduct is inconsistent and sketchy, it is nevertheless an explanation accepted by more than a few criminologists. Some professionals might regard labeling theory as grounded conjecture, where occasional instances of support for the labeling perspective have been observed.

Another theory of criminality is the XYY Syndrome. Sociobiologists and geneticists have studied the chromosomatic patterns of many criminals in an attempt to link these patterns with different types of criminal conduct. X and Y are sex chromosomes persons inherit from their parents. Male infants are typified with an XY chromosomatic pattern, while females are typified by an XX pattern. Y chromosomes are considered aggressive, while X chromosomes are considered passive.

Spectacular news events such as mass or serial murders stimulate interest in criminological theories. When Richard Speck murdered eight student nurses in Chicago during the 1960s, he was eventually studied by sociobiologists. They found that Speck had an unusual XYY chromosomatic pattern, with an extra Y chromosome. This aggressive chromosome provided at least one instance of support for the idea that crime and chromosomatic patterns are related. In Speck's case, his mass murders of nurses were thought attributable, in part, to his highly aggressive genetic structure. However, subsequent tests of chromosomatic patterns among incarcerated criminals, even violent offenders, have failed to disclose any systematic relation between chromosomes and particular criminal behaviors (Mednick and Volavka, 1980; Shah and Roth, 1974). In fact, Shah and Roth (1974) found that only 5 percent of a large sample of criminals had the XYY pattern. Although this percentage is slightly higher than that estimated for the general U.S. population, it is not significant as a consistent predictor of criminal behavior.

In both the labeling and XYY Syndrome theories, various phenomena, social definitions and self-definitions of certain behaviors and chromosomatic patterns, are highlighted and featured as primary causes of other phenomena, criminal behaviors. Those who use these explanations for criminal conduct write elaborate arguments to provide logical and plausible support for their beliefs. Eventually, research is conducted that provides some degree of support for these assertions and explanations. If researchers look hard enough, they can find support for their theorizing somewhere. Richard Speck's case was considered proof of the plausibility of the XYY Syndrome, although this proof was insufficient to justify incarcerating all persons with an XYY chromosomatic pattern because of some suspected propensity to commit mass murder. These examples illustrate two important functions of theory: explanation and prediction.

Explanation and Prediction

Explanations of events are often given higher priority compared with predictions of events. There is not much difference between explanation and speculation. Brainstorming and thinking up ideas about which factors seem to create probation officer burnout, delinquency, or rising crime rates usually involves much speculation, often mislabeled as theorizing. When criminologists say, "My theory about why this or that occurs is . . . ," what they usually mean is that their *belief* is that a particular factor seems responsible for causing some event. They *speculate* about what causes an event to occur. Seldom do they sit down and patiently and painstakingly develop a systematic explanatory scheme linking certain events with their believed "causes" of those events. True theorists among criminologists and criminal justice professionals are comparatively few in number.

Theories can be rank-ordered according to their ability to predict events or occurrences. Theories with the greatest predictive utility are used most often, whereas those lacking predictive utility or promise are discarded and forgotten. Anyone can explain anything, but that doesn't mean that the explanations advanced are good ones. Often, the critical test is whether theories can predict events adequately or accurately.

For instance, judges and parole boards are in the business of predicting a convicted offender's behavior. Judges must make decisions about whether to place convicted offenders on probation or to incarcerate them for specific time periods. Parole boards must decide whether certain prisoners should be released from prison short of serving their full sentences. Different sentencing and early-release criteria are applied by judges and parole boards in their decision-making activity. In most instances, their decisions are influenced, in part, by references to rational, nonrational, and/or irrational criteria, such as race, ethnicity, age, gender, socioeconomic status, prior record, alcohol or drug dependency, presence or absence of a family support system, nature of the conviction offense, compliance or noncompliance with prison rules and regulations, acceptance of responsibility for their criminal actions, and the prestige of their defense attorneys. These decisions may also be guided by abstract references to vague theories, partial theories, or syntheses of several contrasting theories of crime and criminal conduct.

Decisions made by judges and parole boards are flawed in various ways. Many offenders placed on probation or granted parole eventually recidivate and commit new crimes. The criminal justice system considers these cases failures. These failures are empirical evidence of poor judicial and parole board judgment to forecast the future behaviors of probationers and parolees.

Consistent with the idea that theories may be evaluated as either good or bad on the basis of their degree of predictive utility, sometimes theories may be considered more or less important according to the types of policy decisions that are influenced by them. In the early 1900s, for example, when the scientific community of criminologists believed heredity to be an important factor in causing criminality, prisoners in various states such as Oklahoma and Virginia were sterilized so that they would be incapable of fathering children. At the time, sterilization seemed to be a sound and logical step society could take to prevent the birth of future criminals. During the rehabilitation era of 1940 to 1970, for another example, many prisons offered educational and vocational-technical training, as well as counseling programs for inmates. These programs were believed to be remedies for various inmate deficiencies, since many prisoners lacked formal education, vocational skills, and a basic understanding of the etiology of their criminal conduct. However, both sterilization (subsequently declared unconstitutional in *Skinner v. Oklahoma*, 1942) and many rehabilitative programs for inmates have failed to decrease or reduce criminality. In recent years, while most prisons have continued to offer a broad range of inmate programs, the emphasis in corrections has shifted from rehabilitation to crime control. This is evidenced by the great increase in probation and parole programs in recent years that stress close or intensive offender monitoring or greater probation/parole officer–offender/client contact.

Further, increasing numbers of prisons are merely incarcerating offenders rather than attempting to rehabilitate them. This fact has caused more than a few critics of prisons to accuse corrections administrators of "warehousing violence." The public expects to be protected from criminals, at least for the period of their sentence durations. Whether rehabilitation in prisons occurs is unimportant to many citizens. They simply want offenders punished and out of public view for as long as possible. Thus, the "warehousing violence" charge against correction administrators is probably accurate.

■ TYPES OF THEORY

Although there are many kinds of theorizing, this discussion will focus upon four types: (1) deductive theory, (2) inductive theory, (3) grounded theory, and (4) axiomatic theory.

Deductive Theory

Deductive theory is more common in social science today than inductive theory. It is based on deductive reasoning from the work of the ancient Greek philosopher Aristotle (384–322 B.C.). Logical statements are deduced or derived from other statements. Typically, assumptions are made and conclusions are drawn that appear to be logically connected with these assumptions. A common example is "All men are mortal. Aristotle is a man. Therefore, Aristotle is mortal." Symbolically, "All A's are B's; C is a B, therefore, C is also an A."

In research, any event that needs to be explained provides a foundation for deductive theory building. Some examples of problems or unanswered questions or occurrences that may need to be explained are

1. sentencing disparities among judges
2. juvenile delinquency
3. child sexual abuse or spousal abuse
4. crime among the elderly
5. the prisonization process
6. probation/parole officer burnout and stress
7. prosecutorial discretion
8. social class variations in crime rates

Researchers will choose problems of interest to them, and then they will devise an explanation for their problems. They will include in their explanation certain assumptions, propositions, and definitions of terms. The interrelatedness of these linkages among assumptions and propositions is a logical formulation. From this logical formulation, deductions may be made. These deductions are always considered to be tentative deductions. They must be tested by gathering data.

Through data gathering and analysis, researchers learn whether their deductions are valid. If the data suggest that these deductions should be questioned, further testing is done in other settings. Even if findings support certain deductions, further tests are ordinarily conducted, since these investigators want to be certain of their conclusions.

One example of deductive theorizing is Richard Johnson's (1986) study of family structure and delinquency. Johnson reexamined the "broken home–delinquency" relation by using self-reports from 700 high school sophomores. Because of space limitations in professional journals, researchers are not always able to elaborate their theories for readers. Rather, they provide a sketchy view of their assumptions and propositions and how they are interconnected. Johnson's reported research is no exception. Johnson acknowledges initially that broken homes have, for many years, been thought to be a major factor in the cause of juvenile delinquency (p. 65). Also, he acknowledges that there is general, although inconsistent, support for this view in the professional literature.

A careful reading of his introduction and the discussion of what he found when the responses of 700 youths were examined permits us to identify several of his theoretical premises. For instance, Johnson observes that the process whereby delinquency and broken homes become related begins with a family breakup. The family breakup reduces the quality of parent-child relationships, possibly through the physical and/or psychological separation inherent in the breakup. The breakup, like ripples in a pond, influences different dimensions of a youth's life. Problems of familial breakups may lead to school difficulties, where the child has difficulty concentrating on schoolwork. Furthermore, Johnson notes that often official agencies respond to children from broken homes in different ways compared with their responses to children from intact homes. Johnson's crucial question is, "Is there in fact an association between family structure and delinquency?" (p. 66). His data disclosed support, although moderate, for the claim that family structure is related to delinquency. Considerable statistical evidence is presented to support his tentative conclusions. Although Johnson prepared a more elaborate version of these events and the interrelatedness of his basic assumptions and propositions, the skeletal aspects of his theorizing are there.

Several traumatic events in a child's life trigger assorted problems of adjustment to other life events. We glean from his analysis that there are psychological rewards that youths obtain from intact familial experiences, and that physical separation minimizes or frustrates the youth's fulfillment of these rewarding experiences. School difficulties, one possible product of such frustration at home, generate further adjustment problems for affected youths. One product of such frustration is the commission of delinquent acts. Johnson doesn't claim that all youths from broken homes will become delinquent. Rather, he indicates that disruptive homes contribute with other factors in youths' lives to elicit delinquent behaviors. His discussion of these other factors (e.g., gender, age, and race of juveniles, mother-stepfather/father-stepmother situations, and official reports from police versus self-reports from delinquents themselves) are excellent suggestions for follow-up research projects to be pursued by other interested investigators.

Johnson's study is largely deductive, where various assumptions and propositional statements have been made about the association between familial stability and propensity of juveniles toward delinquent conduct. A more comprehensive or sophisticated analysis of the problem would encompass an explanation or delineation of the nature of psychological rewards stemming from intact families, the reasons for mother-stepfather/father-stepmother differences in the incidence of delinquent behaviors among their respective children, and a detailed outline of why various "agents of society" would be inclined to respond differently toward children from intact homes compared with children from family breakups. Specific agencies of society could be identified, and a rationale could be given in each instance for why these agencies would respond in peculiar or unique ways to youths from broken homes. All of this would be encompassed within a more comprehensive and sophisticated theoretical framework. Space limitations for journal articles, however, do not permit more extensive discussions of theory.

Johnson started by making a theoretical sketch of the relation between broken homes and delinquent behavior, and he found a setting where his theorizing could be tested. His data analysis led him to some of the conclusions noted previously. He logically deduced an explanation for delinquent behavior and sought empirical confirmation or refutation of his explanation. All of this was accomplished through deduction.

Inductive Theory

Induction or **inductive logic** is a process whereby a specific event is examined and described, and where generalizations are made to a larger class of similar events. Suppose we wanted to devise an explanation for why offenders become recidivists and commit new crimes. Through induction, we could examine a sample of known recidivists from Connecticut prisons, or inmates who have a history of prior convictions. As the result of our observations and analyses of the Connecticut inmate sample, we might conclude that our recidivists are younger, black males who have alcohol or drug dependencies, who are in the lower socioeconomic strata, who were unemployed or underemployed when originally arrested and convicted, and who have less than a high school education. From these observations, we might make several generalizations about the broader class of recidivists nationally.

Or perhaps we are interested in learning about those persons most likely to "fail" while on parole or in probation programs. Again, judges and parole boards wish to know which criteria seem most relevant in forecasting the successfulness of prospective probationers and/or parolees. Observing samples of New York probationers and parolees who have been incarcerated or reincarcerated for violating one or more program conditions will enable us to delineate some of their social, demographic, and psychological characteristics and backgrounds. From our descriptions of New York probationers and parolees who have "failed" while on probation or parole, we might generalize to the broader class of probationers and parolees on a nationwide basis.

Now, let's back up for a moment and see what has been done in each of the instances. In both cases, samples have been obtained and described. Then these descriptions have been generalized to the broader class of persons represented by the samples. Are these generalizations we have made in each instance good generalizations? Should we therefore deny parole or probation to *all* young, black male offenders with alcohol or drug dependencies, who were unemployed or underemployed when they were initially arrested and convicted, and who lack a high school education? This general policy would prompt much controversy, to say the least.

In both instances, we have examined the "events" (i.e., the samples of Connecticut inmates and New York probationers and parolees who have failed) and described various characteristics of these events. Then, we have attempted to generalize to the broader class of similar events. Clearly, our research goals include both explanation and prediction. We will tentatively explain recidivism and probation/parole program failures by using the characteristics of samples of recidivistic inmates and probation program failures as predictors. But now we must see whether these predictors or characteristics will permit us to forecast recidivism and program failures in advance of their potential recidivism and program failure.

Using deduction, we abstract by generalizing. Using **inductive theory,** we generalize by abstracting. Although both deduction and induction help us achieve common research objectives, including data gathering and theory verification, they lead us to these objectives through different paths. In a deductive context, we state what we believe is a rational theory to explain some event such as delinquency. Then we obtain samples of delinquent and nondelinquent youths to test the adequacy of our theory. Using induction, however, we may examine a few delinquents and nondelinquents, describe their similarities and differences, and attempt to generalize the characteristics uniquely possessed by these delinquents to a larger class of delinquents nationally. But again, we must follow up our induction with an empirical test situation and determine whether the characteristics we have identified on a smaller scale help us to predict delinquent behavior on a larger scale.

The distinction between deduction and induction can also be made according to whether we construct a logical explanatory and predictive scheme and observe facts consistent with that scheme, or whether we observe certain facts and generalize from the facts observed. It has been noted that "there are those who feel that the entire research process is initiated with theories. Deduction occurs when we . . . gather facts to confirm or disprove hypothesized relationships between variables [derived from theory]. Whether there were facts that precipitated the [theory] does not really matter. What matters is that research is essentially a hypothesis-testing venture in which the hypotheses rest on logically (if not factually) deduced relational statements" (Black and Champion, 1976:65). Thus, deduction and induction are simply alternative ways for constructing theory.

Grounded Theory

Barney Glaser and Anselm Strauss (1967) have described another type of theorizing known as grounded theory. **Grounded theory** is the view that investigators enter research settings without preconceived theories and hypotheses about what they will find. Essentially, investigators will immerse themselves into the research setting and describe what they have found. On the basis of observations, interviews, and other data-gathering methods, investigators will generate explanations about various phenomena that are developed directly from what they see and understand. Thus, their theories about events are grounded in the empirical reality of their study settings. As researchers continue to discover more facts about the settings they observe, their theorizing will be modified and undergo a metamorphosis of sorts, as new information suggests changes in their theoretical explanations.

Grounded theory is distinguished from deductive theory, where a theoretical explanation of an event is developed in advance of the actual study. Subsequently, the deductive theory is tested by examining a research setting and discovering whether what one has hypothesized is true or untrue. Grounded theory is, therefore, probably closer to induction than deduction theory. But the appeal of grounded theory is that any theoretical explanation devised is rooted in observed behaviors and social exchanges. Glaser and Strauss believe that grounded theorizing is more realistic than other types of theorizing, and that more valid hypotheses will emerge from empirical data.

Karen Rosen (1992) used grounded theory in her study of how young women cope with dating violence. She selected a sample of ten women from a college campus. These women had previously been identified as victims of dating violence. Rosen conducted in-depth interviews with these women to determine which interpersonal, intrapersonal, and contextual factors seemed relevant in enabling these women to cope with their victimization. Major constructs that were disclosed through interviews included women's vulnerabilities, couple imbalances, seductive processes, and disentanglement processes. Rosen found that vulnerable young women who formed fused, imbalanced relationships with vulnerable men tended to use system-maintaining coping strategies to deal with the violence and were subject to powerful seductive processes until they began to disentangle themselves from their relationships. Rosen eventually generated a contextual stress and coping theoretical framework which had been grounded with in-depth interviews and observations.

Another study using grounded theory was conducted by Tony Ward et al. (1995). Ward and his associates studied 26 incarcerated child molesters, who were interviewed and asked to describe their most recent or typical offense. Their descriptions of events, including the contributing factors, cognitive and behavioral components, led Ward et al. to develop a theoretical model of an offense chain, incorporating the possible interactions among various stages and factors. Subsequently, Ward et al. applied the developed model to an independent sample of 12 other child molesters to see whether the model had predictive value.

An additional study by Pettus (1986) used grounded theory to investigate jury decision making. Pettus rejected existing theories about jury decision making. Rather, she conducted in-depth interviews with former jurors and inquired about which factors were most influential on jury verdicts. Jurors were also asked about which stages in a trial were the moment of their personal decision regarding conviction or acquittal. What contributions to the total decision-making process do jurors report coming from the deliberations? Pettus was able to generate several models of jury decision making as well as a general theory of jury deliberating behavior.

In each of the three previously cited studies, investigators evolved theoretical schemes to account for what they observed. Their explanations of events were grounded in empirical facts disclosed through interviews and observation. Each of the investigators would presumably use their developed models in other settings to test their validity and predictive utility. Consistent with grounded theory, as these researchers would conduct further investigations, new and different factual information might mean that they would refine or refocus their initial theories, shaping them in accordance with additional empirical evidence gathered from new subjects.

Some investigators have been critical of grounded theory. They maintain that grounded theory is self-serving and might lead to researcher bias. The argument is that theories derived from empirical observations of research settings will be couched in the interpretations of events by investigators. These interpretations of observed events are perhaps flawed because of a researcher's own input into what is observed and what it means. Furthermore, subsequent observations of similar settings with new research subjects will no doubt be influenced by a researcher's previous interpretations of similar events. This argument is weak, however, since grounded theory "in action" is a self-correcting enterprise. It's very nature is one of continual refinement and development, as new factual information is disclosed about new research settings. It is difficult to imagine how one's own feelings, sentiments, and biases would significantly intrude, where the discovery of new information would be the actual basis for changes in theoretical models or frameworks. Nevertheless, grounded theory has had a modest following among criminologists and criminal justicians, and it continues to be used with some successfulness.

Axiomatic Theory

Unlike grounded theory, which is somewhat similar to inductive theory, axiomatic theory is closely associated with deductive theory. **Axiomatic theory** uses **axioms,** or truisms, as building blocks from which testable hypotheses can be derived and tested. Axioms are the equivalent of statements about reality which are accepted as true. Sufficient numbers of these assertions that are believed to be true will enable theorists and researchers to derive tentative statements, hypotheses, that can be tested through subsequent social research.

Norman Denzin (1989:60–61) says that the ordering of propositions into a theoretical scheme is conventionally seen as the logical outcome of concept formulation, construction of definitions, and the collection of data. Denzin notes that in axiomatic theorizing, certain propositions are treated as axioms; further, lower-level predictions or theorems are derived. From this strategic blend of axioms and theorems, hypotheses are logically deduced and subjected to empirical test.

For example, the French sociologist, Emile Durkheim, wrote about suicide and the reasons why it is committed. Durkheim analyzed vast data sets in France in the late 1800s relating to suicides investigated by police. He was able to develop various propositions and axioms from which statements about the causes of suicide could be deduced. The following statements are some of the types of axioms Durkheim may have used in his theory of suicide:

1. Persons are gregarious and desire close social bonds with others.
2. Close social bonds provide persons with security and comfort.
3. Disruptions in one's life that alter social bonds are traumatic and generate social and psychological stress.
4. Persons with greater attachments and bonds to others are less stressed compared with persons who have few or no attachments or bonds to others.
5. Suicide is more prevalent among persons who suffer greater stress compared with those who suffer no or little stress.

Are these true or accepted statements? Should we be expected to agree or disagree with them generally? Let's engage in a little "If-then" reasoning. This is the type of reasoning that says, *If* statement A is true, and *if* statement B is true, and *if* statement C is true, *then* we can generate one or more other statements that should logically follow. Let's assume for the sake of illustrating axiomatic theory that the previous statements are true. Furthermore, let's assume that Durkheim developed these statements and accepted them as true.

Durkheim devised additional, more specific, statements, possibly theorems, that were used to enhance other more general statements. For instance, Durkheim observed that some religions, such as Protestantism, emphasized individual means of achieving a spiritual salvation. Thus, Protestants might be more inclined to rely on their own individual efforts and work as a means of becoming "saved" than persons of other religious faiths where individuality was not considered a prominent factor. Catholicism and Judaism were examined by Durkheim. Based on his understanding of the different basic belief systems in each religious faith, he speculated that compared with Protestantism, persons with Catholic beliefs would be more inclined to be less individualistic in their thoughts about their own salvation. Persons of the Jewish faith might be even more disinclined toward individuality in their worship and salvation. Thus, Durkheim argued, we might find the closest social bonds among those of the Jewish faith, followed by Catholics, followed by Protestants. Protestants, according to Durkheim, would emphasize individuality and thus play down the significance of social bonds. Using the axioms and theorems about persons developed previously, persons with greater social bonds would be less inclined to suicide, while those persons with fewer social bonds would be more inclined to suicide. This thinking led Durkheim to examine suicide rates among Catholics, Protestants, and Jews and compare them. He found that Jews had the lowest suicide rates, while Protestants had the highest suicide rates. In this respect, his theorizing about suicide and its relation to social bonds was supported by the evidence he disclosed about religious affiliation and suicide rates.

Durkheim didn't end his research with these religious comparisons. He also investigated other scenarios where social bonds varied. He noted that older persons tend to have fewer social bonds compared with younger persons. He reasoned that older persons would have fewer close ties with others because of the increased likelihood of natural death. Those with the greatest likelihood of having the lowest social bonds were older men. Through his analysis of French suicide records, he discovered that suicide rates were highest among elderly men.

Durkheim's research about suicide rates and social bonds directly illustrates how we can use axioms and theorems to derive testable hypotheses. In Durkheim's case, he had access to national data about suicides and the circumstances under which they occurred. It was relatively easy for him to see whether suicide rates varied according to various specific social or individual variables such as religion or age. Thus, axiomatic theory might be used to construct various criminological theories about events. However, a search of the *Criminal Justice Abstracts* in 1999 showed that only a handful of abstracted articles alluded to axiomatic theory. This is one indicator of its popularity and use.

■ VARIABLES AND THEORY

Variables refer to any phenomena that can assume more than one value. Again, there are varying definitions of variables. Two alternative definitions are that variables are "categories that may be divided into two or more subcategories" (Fitzgerald and Cox, 1987:311) and "concepts that have been operationalized or 'concepts that can vary' or take on different values of a quantitative nature" (Hagan, 1989:15). Both of these alternative definitions of variables are true. However, the first definition cited is preferred because it avoids usage of terms such as "operationalization" and "concepts." In the context of this book, these terms have particular meanings.

What are "phenomena that can assume more than one value"? First, any attitudinal phenomenon we can name (e.g., prejudice, achievement motivation, burnout, work satisfaction, alienation, positive feelings toward police officers) are variables. We can have much burnout, low work satisfaction, strong positive feelings toward police officers, a high degree of alienation, and low achievement motivation. Precisely what are meant by "high," "low," "strong," and "high degree" depend upon how we measure these phenomena. Other phenomena that can assume more than one value are

gender
social class
race
ethnicity
political affiliation
religious affiliation
urban-rural background
age

income

types of crime

crime rates, delinquency

city size and population

judicial, prosecutorial, and parole board discretion

police-community relations

employment discrimination

Sometimes, the use of the term "value" is misleading. For example, gender assumes more than one "value." The values are subclasses on the gender variable, called **variable subclasses,** including "male" and "female." Different values on the "type of crime" variable might be "violent offenses" and "property offenses." Different values on the political or religious affiliation variables might be "Democrat," "Republican," "American Independent," "Catholic," "Protestant," and "Jewish." These are more like designations than values in a numerical sense. It is helpful to think of these variables simply as consisting of different subclasses. And we decide which subclasses will be used in our research for any variable.

Any research problem we choose to investigate is also a variable. We use other variables to explain the variable we are investigating. We illustrate the interconnectedness of these variables (the variable to be explained and the explanatory variables) in our theory. Thus, our definition of theory makes more sense now as "an integrated body of assumptions, propositions, and definitions that explain and predict the relationship between two or more variables." One of these variables is the problem we wish to explain, while one or more "other" variables are used to explain or account for the existence of the problem (i.e., the variable to be explained). In Emile Durkheim's suicide research used in the previous example, suicide was the problem Durkheim wanted to explain. Social bonds was used as the explanatory variable. Durkheim found different situations in which the nature of social bonds varied. When variation in the degree of social bonds could be observed, Durkheim reasoned, then variation would also be observed in suicide rates. This reasoning led him to theorize about different religious faiths and persons of different ages, and whether suicide rates fluctuated in predictable ways according to one's religious faith or age.

Variables, essential to all theories, perform different functions. In order to best portray these functions, some distinctions between variables can be made. These include considerations of variables as (1) independent, (2) dependent, (3) discrete, and (4) continuous.

Independent Variables

Independence and dependence mean that some variables cause changes in other variables, while some variables are influenced by other variables. **Independent variables** are those that elicit changes in other variables. **Dependent variables** are those whose values are affected by independent variables. Two illustrations assist us in understanding the differences between independent and dependent variables and their interrelations.

Gunderson (1987) investigated the relation between the types of uniforms worn by police and their degree of credibility in the eyes of the public they serve. Three types of police uniforms (e.g., blazers and slacks, Eisenhower jackets and slacks, and standard paramilitary uniforms) were chosen for investigation by Gunderson. These different types of uniforms were "subclasses" on the variable "type of uniform." Gunderson wanted to know whether wearing one type of uniform or another had any significant influence on officer self-perceptions of professionalism and whether the public would perceive officers wearing certain kinds of uniforms as more or less professional.

It is quite clear here that "self-perceptions of professionalism" and "public perceptions of police professionalism" were the designated variables thought by Gunderson to be influenced by the independent variable "type of uniform." His findings supported the idea that officers who wore blazer uniforms not only had higher self-perceptions of professionalism, but they were also regarded by the public as more professional compared with officers wearing other uniform styles. Although this research was not conclusive, it illustrates what an independent variable is and how it functions in relation to other variables.

The Gunderson study was fairly matter-of-fact, and it was reasonably easy to measure "type of uniform" and "self-perceptions of professionalism." Often, however, certain variables may be more elusive, and their relationships with other variables must be inferred largely from independent, abstract criteria. For instance, Anson (1983) investigated the relation between inmate ethnicity and suicide rates among prisoners in state and federal prisons. Anson noticed that different state and federal prisons exhibited different rates of inmate suicide. Attempting to explain this problem, called "prison suicide rates," Anson conjectured that the proportionate ethnicity of particular inmate populations might have something to do with the prison suicide rates. He devised a theoretical scheme wherein "ethnicity of prison population" was designated as the independent variable. Subclasses on this variable were varying proportions of ethnic inmates in the prisons he examined. His ethnic/racial categories included blacks, whites, Orientals, Hispanics, and Indians.

Anson observed that those prisons with higher inmate suicide rates also had larger proportions of white inmates. In fact, he eventually concluded from his research that the following ethnic groups may be ordered from the highest to the lowest on self-inflicted injuries: Indians, blacks, Orientals, Hispanics, and whites. Therefore, "proportion of inmate ethnicity/race" was considered to be the independent variable and a prime factor in prompting self-inflicted injuries among inmates, including suicides. Again, although Anson's findings are not conclusive and do not necessarily typify inmate suicides in all U.S. prisons or jails, the example serves to illustrate the "function" of an independent variable in relation to one or more other variables, in this case, inmate suicides.

Dependent Variables

Dependent variables are those phenomena that derive their values largely from the influences or actions of other variables. In the Gunderson and Anson studies mentioned previously, "self-perceptions of professionalism," "perceptions by the public of police officer professionalism," and "inmate suicides" were dependent variables. Virtually any "problem" we choose to investigate becomes a dependent variable.

In criminology and criminal justice, dependent variables are easy to identify. Often, they are "standardized" as dependent variables. That is, their use as either independent or dependent variables is fairly consistent from study to study. A nonsensical but informative illustration is the gender-delinquency relation. Which variable, gender or delinquency, would be the more likely choice as the independent variable in relation to the other? Obviously, differences in gender are far more likely to produce changes in delinquent behavior than differences in delinquent behavior producing changes in gender. Dependent variables from various components of the criminal justice system might be

probation officer burnout and stress

crime rates

prisonization

prosecutorial, judicial, and parole board discretion

police officer discretion to use deadly force in apprehending fleeing offenders

police professionalism

police misconduct

inmate suicides

inmate rioting frequency

inmate rehabilitation

parolee and probationer success in conditional intermediate punishment programs

turnover among correctional personnel

The list is endless. These are common dependent variables, since we so often wish to explain their occurrence or development. However, we should not always assume that these and other variables are "fixed" as permanent dependent variables. Sometimes, we formulate complex combinations of variables in our research plans. In the examples presented thus far, we have looked at "two-variable" relations, in which one variable was related or interconnected with one other variable. What if we wanted to relate more than two variables? Adding a third variable to our analysis of some research problem might be illustrated as follows.

Suppose we wish to study the relations among type of correctional officer supervision, correctional officer stress, and correctional officer turnover. We may read research reports indicating that if correctional officer supervisors were to involve their correctional officer subordinates in decision-making power more often, they might reduce the amount of burnout or stress experienced by correctional officers. Also, burnout reductions may incline correctional officers to consider remaining for longer employment periods with their prisons or jails. We have just linked three variables together. We will need to explain how each re-

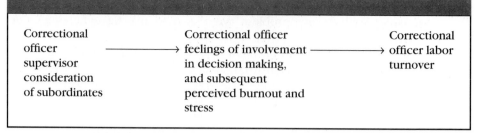

FIGURE 2.1 Hypothesized relation between correctional officer supervisor consideration of subordinates, correctional officer self-perceptions of involvement in decision making, and correctional officer labor turnover.

lates to the other, but this will be done in our theoretical scheme. The three-variable linkage we have formulated might look something like Figure 2.1.

Notice in the diagram that correctional officer self-perceptions of involvement in decision making and subsequent perceived burnout and stress are considered influenced by behaviors of correctional officer supervisors, namely, their consideration of subordinates in decision-making matters. Notice also that these correctional officer feelings of burnout and stress are linked in an implied causal fashion with labor turnover. Therefore, if you're the boss and don't give your workers power in decisions affecting their work, they will stress out, burn out, and possibly quit their jobs.

In the case in Figure 2.1, correctional officer burnout and stress is functioning in a dual capacity—it is a dependent variable in relation to correctional officer supervisor consideration of subordinates, and it is an independent variable in relation to correctional officer labor turnover. Labor turnover, is, of course, the major dependent variable in this example. Usually, when researchers formulate theories to explain things, they specify which variables will be considered relevant and how they will be used—as independent, as dependent, or as both independent and dependent under certain circumstances. It is important to maintain a high degree of flexibility when considering how variables function in theoretical schemes. Under most circumstances, many variable treatment and definition options are available to the investigator.

Discrete Variables

Discrete variables are phenomena that have a limited number of exclusive subclasses. Gender is a discrete variable, for all practical purposes. You are either "male" or "female." You cannot be in the two subclasses simultaneously. Type of crime is also a discrete variable. Divisions or subclasses on this variable include violent and property crime, misdemeanor and felony, or some other discrete designation. There are exceptions, of course. In biology, varying the amount of estrogen, androgen, or testosterone in the bodies of males and females may make them more or less male or female. In fact, biologists may be able to make a convincing case for "degrees of maleness or femaleness." Also, criminals may commit several types of crime during a crime spree. They may steal a car, burglarize a dwelling, rob a bank, kill a teller, and kidnap the bank president. Later, they may assault a police officer, resist arrest, and commit perjury on the witness stand at their trial. For convenience, however, criminologists will likely place them in one criminal category or another, depending upon the type of research conducted. They will either be classed as "violent offenders" (most likely), or possibly "property offenders" (least likely).

Continuous Variables

Continuous variables are phenomena that can be infinitely divided into a variety of subclasses. All attitudinal variables are continuous variables. Income is a continuous variable. The crime rate is a continuous variable. Each of these phenomena may assume an infinite or nearly infinite number of values. As a practical matter, however, and largely for the convenience of the researcher and reader, virtually every continuous variable is reduced more or less arbitrarily to a limited number of discrete categories. For instance, we could report incomes of 50,000 city residents to the penny. Frank Smith earns $30,267.83 per year, and Jane Jones earns $16,271.26 per year. But more often than not, income is reported in a series of discrete categories, such as "High Income," "Moderately High Income," "Moderately Low Income," and "Low Income." Dollar amounts can be assigned each of these categories, so that we will know where to place Frank Smith and Jane Jones. Zero dollars to $5,000 will define the "Low Income" category, while $5,001–$10,000 will define the "Moderately Low Income" category. The "High Income" category may be $30,000 or over, depending on the community we study and how we have chosen to define our categories.

Again, the subjective element is present here. We usually decide how many categories or subclasses will constitute given variables, and we usually make up our own definitions or criteria for those categories or variable subclasses. These decisions we make are often arbitrary. We will see that certain guidelines, conventions, or standards may be invoked for the construction of variable subclasses.

■ CAUSAL RELATIONS BETWEEN VARIABLES

One long-range aim of theoretical schemes is to identify causal relationships between two or more variables. Logically, if we know what variable or variables cause another variable to occur or change in value, we might be able to exert some control and produce expected and desirable outcomes. When elementary school teachers hear about some of their former third- or fourth-graders who are now teenagers and have committed serious offenses, they might say, "I just knew so-and-so was going to turn out that way—you just 'know' about certain children like that! Something could have been done earlier to prevent that!" What the teachers are alluding to may be an intervention program of some sort that may have "caused" the child to grow up differently and not become delinquent. While it is often difficult for teachers to define the specific nature and properties of an

effective intervention program that might deter children from becoming delinquents, it is significant that they believe that "something" could and should have
been done (as an intervention) for certain "problem children," whomever they
are, and that "something" could have "caused" a different outcome.

Some of the research described in this chapter has causal overtones. Johnson's (1986) study of delinquency and intactness of families emphasized family
stability as a contributing factor. Why? Gunderson's (1987) study of police officer uniforms and self-perceptions of professionalism also implied causality between self-perceptions and type of uniform worn. Does wearing a particular
type of uniform "cause" police officers to adopt more favorable self-perceptions
of professionalism? Can we directly improve the perceptions of community residents of the professionalism of their police officers by changing officer attire?
How does the type of uniform worn by police officers influence community perceptions of officer professionalism? And why? Can we decrease suicide rates in
prisons by adjusting the racial and ethnic compositions of inmate populations in
various ways? What proportion of whites and blacks is considered ideal for preventing or at least minimizing suicides? And why is this proportionate distribution relevant?

Most of the research in the professional literature avoids using "cause–
effect" phraseology. Rather, more conservative tones are ordinarily adopted. Statements such as, "There is an apparent association between X and Y," or "There
may be a connection between X and Y," or "Evidence suggests that X may contribute to Y" are typical of the conclusions drawn by most researchers. And this
is precisely how it ought to be. We may be in the business of attempting to establish cause–effect relationships between variables, but we also understand that
it is a very difficult business.

John Stuart Mill (1806–1873), the English philosopher and political econo-
mist, recognized certain problems of establishing cause–effect relationships between variables. He formulated three different methods whereby cause–effect
relationships could be implied. These included the **method of agreement,** the
method of difference, and the **method of concomitant variation.** Mill said
that the method of agreement states that if the circumstances leading up to a
given event have in all cases one factor in common, then this factor may be the
cause sought. The method of difference was that if two sets of circumstances differ in only one factor, and the one containing the factor leads to the event and
the other does not, we may consider the factor as the cause of the event. The
method of concomitant variation is that if variation in the intensity of a given
factor is followed by a parallel variation in the effect, then this factor is the cause
(Mill, 1930:32–33).

Mill illustrated these principles, in part, with an analogy to rats. Suppose we
have two batches of rats, under identical circumstances, that are fed identical
diets, except that one batch of rats also receives a certain drug. The fact that all
rats in the batch with the included drug die immediately might be grounds to
conclude that the drug killed the rats. Mill contended that while this might be
so, it did not prove absolutely that the drug killed the rats. He reasoned that the
result may be due to chance, or that the rats probably would have died anyway
from natural causes. The difficulty, noted by Mill, is connected with the expres-

Box
2.2

James R. Acker
University of Albany

Statistics: J.D., Duke Law School; Ph.D.
(criminal justice), University of Albany.

Interests: Immediately following my graduation from Duke Law School, I had the good fortune of being taken under wing by a brilliant, indefatigable, and scrupulously principled lawyer whose practice focused heavily on criminal defense work. Under his tutelage, I witnessed abstract legal doctrine that was the stuff of book-learning in law school alternatively corrupted and vindicated, and vulgarized and animated, in the day-to-day operation of criminal justice and the judicial system. Practicing law, as I did for four years, was a continuing education. It was an experience that provoked anger and bitter frustration when, with a cynical wink and a nod, the law was subverted through manipulation and outright dissimilation by the very officials sworn to uphold it. Yet, it was enormously satisfying when the law worked to advance constitutional values, to maintain a proper balance between people prone to abuse their authority and those most vulnerable to abuses, and to help correct injustices.

I retreated from the rough and tumble world of law practice, secure that advocates like my law partner would effectively serve that calling, and returned to the relatively calm and detached arena of academia. I sensed that I would be more comfortable and more effective in an educational environment trying to sort out the mystifying disjunctures I had observed between the written law and the law in practice. My dissertation in criminal justice at the University of Albany examined how the law, as formulated through U.S. Supreme Court opinions, assembles and makes use of research evidence about the world in which its principles are expected to operate.

Capital punishment law soon became one of my central interests. In no other context is the law's role as an instrument of social control and its function as a guardian of individual rights in such dramatic tension. Death-penalty cases are so rich with controversial issues that they are a veritable microcosm for studying the fundamentals of criminal justice. For example, what factors account for or explain a murderer's shocking criminal behavior? What process must be observed in the investigation and proof of criminal wrongdoing before punishment as awesome as death is implemented? What qualities of the offense and what characteristics of the offender should dictate punishment decisions? What penological interests, if any, are served by capital punishment that are not as effectively served by alternative, less severe sanctions? To what extent does the Constitution, or do other principles of law and ethics, constrain legislative and judicial authority to impose capital sentences? What normative and empirical assumptions influence death-penalty policies, and to what extent are those premises supported logically or in fact?

In trying to help answer questions such as these, it is important not to confound science and ideology, or confuse impartial analysis and personal sentiment. Although it is as whimsical as it would be lamentable to insist that an individual must renounce whatever passion or personal attachment is felt about an issue before being qualified to study it, a researcher must unflinchingly observe disinterested *procedures* of inquiry if the work product is to be defined other than as partisan scholarship. Especially productive researchers tend to be methodological and substantive bridge-builders. For example, they can successfully integrate law and social science, meld theory and practice, and apply sophisticated statistical techniques to data without ignoring their inner eyes and ears. The issues they investigate are not neatly unidimensional, and neither their disciplinary knowledge nor their analytical techniques can afford to be so limited.

Advice to Students: Experience is an indispensable teacher. I would not trade my years spent practicing law for double the opportunity to study books or the chance to observe and talk with others about their own experiences with law. Still, only a fool declines to explore beyond his or her own experiences. A good mentor can enrich a learning opportunity immeasurably. A student's corresponding debt is repaid in part by venturing beyond the safe confines of the mentoring relationship, accepting new challenges, and in some way imparting to others what has been gained in the process. Good scholarship—be it legal, social scientific, or interdisciplinary—can make important theoretical and principled contributions to knowledge and ways of thinking, and also can affect people's lives and help shape social policies. I know of few enterprises that are as potentially rewarding and fulfilling as the research, teaching, and public service components of academia.

sion "identical circumstances." No two circumstances are ever exactly identical. At the very best they must differ either in time or in place and will in fact differ in a practically infinite number of other respects as well (Mill, 1930:32–33).

Gunderson's (1987) study of the type of police uniform and self-perception and public perceptions of officer professionalism highlights some of the cause–effect difficulties noted by Mill. Were public perceptions of the types of uniforms worn by police officers influenced by contemporary fashion trends? Did residents of different races or ethnicities regard different uniform styles differently? Perhaps some of the officers wearing particular types of uniforms were disliked by specific community residents interviewed. Perhaps those officers who had low self-perceptions of professionalism had deep-seated personality problems or underconfidence. Perhaps these problems would not be mitigated significantly by changing uniforms. Maybe height, weight, or gender of officers wearing particular uniforms functioned in various ways to alter resident perceptions of their professionalism. Perhaps a self-selection process had occurred, in which certain officers chose to wear particular types of uniforms and "felt better" and "more professional" as a result. Again, the list of possible explanations for differential reactions to uniform type is endless.

Establishing cause-effect relations between variables also causes us to regard certain antecedent variables (i.e., variables or conditions that precede any observed associations between other variable interrelationships) as either necessary, sufficient, contributory, or contingent. **Necessary conditions** are those that must occur if the phenomena of which they are a "cause" are to occur. **Sufficient conditions** are those that are always followed by the phenomena of which they are "causes." **Contributory conditions** influence the occurrence and degree of change in other phenomena. Contributory conditions are not necessarily followed by the caused event. Rather, contributory conditions or variables, acting with other conditions or variables, operate to change dependent variables. **Contingent conditions** are those acting as "intervening links" in the presence of an observed relation between two other variables (Selltiz et al., 1959:81).

Much of the research conducted today in criminology and criminal justice identifies contributory conditions, or those variables that precede other variables. Few researchers make cause-effect statements. In fact, current statistical procedures, such as path analysis, show predictable "contributions" of certain independent and intervening variables upon dependent variables. These procedures include intercorrelations among variables, although path analysis is also designed to disclose cause-effect path relationships. Ultimately, we attempt to identify the direct and indirect influences of certain variables upon others. If cause-effect relations between variables are later established, this is a fringe benefit of our work.

It is possible to generate various combinations of variable functions by using necessary, sufficient, contributory, and contingent variable criteria. For instance, a variable might be a necessary (and obviously a contributory) condition, but it may be insufficient to bring about a given phenomenon. Or a variable may be a contributory condition but not necessary for a given phenomenon to occur. Variables can function as sufficient, but not necessary, and so on. The point is that almost every variable can be treated in several different ways simultaneously in relation to other variables in the analysis and determination of a causal relation. The theoretical scheme we devise to account for given phenomena in criminology and criminal justice provides the necessary structure for showing the precise relation or contribution of each variable in relation to other variables used in our hypotheses.

Hyman (1955) and Hirschi and Selvin (1967) recommend the inclusion of intervening variables in any causal analysis of variable interrelationships. They say that holding a match to a pile of leaves is a cause of their bursting into flames, although we cannot describe fully the intervening chemical reactions. It makes a difference whether the leaves are wet or dry (Black and Champion, 1976:41-42; Hirschi and Selvin, 1967:123-130). On the subject of explaining and predicting the incidence of delinquency, for instance, Hirschi and Selvin note that they have detected at least six "false criteria of causality" in their investigations of delinquency literature. These are to

1. *Falsely assume that to be causal, relations between variables must be perfect.* Relations between social and psychological variables are seldom perfect.

For example, possessing greater verbal skills and higher education may enable many police officers to relate more effectively with community residents. However, not every police officer possessing greater verbal skills and higher education always relates well with the public. Some less-educated officers do well in their community relations. Nevertheless, better verbal skills and higher education seem helpful in fostering better police-community relations. Therefore, police officer recruits may be selected, in part, because of their better verbal skills and higher degrees of education. The relation between police-community relations and verbal skills and educational attainment is not perfect, but there does appear to be a general relationship.

2. *Falsely assume that causal relations are equivalent to characteristics.* Variations that occur infrequently in variables are not necessarily characteristic variations. Many psychological variables are beyond our immediate grasp. If we hire correctional officers who seem to be confident and secure and capable of handling stress, the instruments we use as indicators of these traits are imperfect. Thus, when some officers "crack" under the pressure of a prison riot, for example, these exceptions do not typify all correctional officer reactions to stress-producing situations. Rather, they indicate the presence of individual factors that were previously unknown or beyond the scope of our existing measures of one's confidence and ability to handle stress.

3. *Falsely assume that variables whose relations are restricted to a specific social context can be used to comprehend relations between similar variables in other contexts.* We may find, for example, that probation officers who take a course on report writing may do quite well in writing presentence investigation reports for convicted offenders and have higher self-esteem. However, it cannot be assumed that police officers who take the same report writing course will necessarily do a better job of writing accident or arrest reports in their own work or have higher self-esteem.

4. *Falsely assume that an* **intervening variable** *may eliminate the original causal relation observed between two variables.* Variables that add to our overall comprehension of an original relation between variables do not necessarily diminish the importance of the original relation we observed between those variables. For example, we may observe a low recidivism rate among probationers who are selected for an intensive supervision program. Probation officers may have supervised their clients very closely, having as many as five face-to-face visits per week with numerous alcohol and drug checks. We may conclude that the intensity of supervision is causing the low recidivism rate among probationers, because the probationers have little opportunity to violate program rules or commit crimes. It may be, however, that the intensive supervision program is selectively applicable only for first-time offenders convicted of property crimes, such as theft and burglary. Perhaps these are offenders who would not re-offend or recidivate anyway. Perhaps these are also persons who do not use alcohol or drugs. If the intensive supervision probation program were applied to drug offenders, those convicted of driving while intoxicated, those convicted of violent crimes, or chronic recidivists with extensive prior records, it may be that the intensity of supervision may not appear to cause low recidivism among these types of clients. This wouldn't necessarily mean that intensive supervision does not induce conformity with program requirements. We would be wrong to reject intensive supervision as a potential cause of low recidivism rates because it doesn't work as well with some types of clients as with others.

5. *Falsely assume that measurable variables are not causes.* Some researchers believe that the real causes of criminological phenomena lie beyond our immediate grasp and outside of the realm of our methodological sophistication. Most variables can be measured. Not all measures we devise for these variables are necessarily good measures, but this doesn't prevent us from exploring cause–effect relationships between variables. If the true causes of criminological phenomena were indeed beyond our methodological grasp, then applications of science in criminology and criminal justice would be worthless. Current evidence suggests that these fields are expanding and growing in theoretical and methodological sophistication, and these fields are not "throwing in the scientific towel" as far as scientific investigations are concerned.

6. *Falsely assume that relationships between variables are dependent upon other variables and that the independent variable is not a cause of the dependent one.* Some researchers mistakenly believe that single independent variables are incapable of inducing specific outcomes or changes in dependent variables, and that relationships between all variables are necessarily complex ones. No doubt this line of thought has contributed to the greater use of complex methodologies and statistical procedures, where less complex strategies might be equally adequate for explaining and predicting things (Hirschi and Selvin, 1967:123–130). Obviously, criminological phenomena are complex. Single-factor explanations of events may be incomplete, but a certain amount of predictive power can be attributed to each independent variable.

One additional topic in our discussion of causal relations between variables is **spuriousness.** Often, we cite agreement or concomitant variation among variables as evidence of a causal relation between them. For instance, we may study the supervisory practices of parole officers and their influence on the recidivism/nonrecidivism of parolee-clients. Obtaining records from 100 parolee-recidivists and 100 parolee-nonrecidivists for instance, may yield results such as those shown in Table 2.1

We may tentatively conclude from these data that 75 percent of the parolees who receive close supervision from their parole officers are nonrecidivists, whereas 75 percent of the parolees who receive general supervision from their parole officers are recidivists. One implication is that if parolees receive general supervision, this contributes to recidivism. It makes a case for encouraging parole officers to supervise their parolee-clients closely. An appropriate rationale for this case can be created easily, including continuous monitoring of client behavior, less opportunity for parole program rule violations, and greater support from parole officers as supervisors. However, what if we were to take

TABLE 2.1 Relation Between Type of Supervision by Parole Officer and Recidivism/Nonrecidivism of 200 Parolees

		Parole Officer Supervision		
		Close	General	Totals
	Nonrecidivists	75	25	100
Parolee Recidivism	Recidivists	25	75	100
	Totals	100	100	200

into account a third variable, such as when parolee-clients are on electronic monitoring and must wear an electronic wristlet or anklet during their parole program? We would have to see whether this modifies our original data pattern. Table 2.2 shows our data recast, where electronic monitoring has been taken into account, and where recidivism/nonrecidivism of parolees is observed in relation to close or general supervision by parole officers.

In Table 2.2, all of the parolee-recidivists are found in the category where electronic monitoring is not used, regardless of whether the parolee is supervised closely or generally. Furthermore, all of the nonrecidivist parolees are found in the category where electronic monitoring is used. This "washes away" or overrides the original relation we presumed existed between parolee recidivism/nonrecidivism and close or general parole officer supervision. This brief exercise illustrates the potential impact of a third variable on an original two-variable relation. This is spuriousness. Spuriousness is an apparent relation between two variables that is subsequently explained by the presence of a third, unknown, variable. The potential for spuriousness in any variable interrelationship is an additional important reason for us to exercise caution when interpreting our research findings and drawing conclusions about observed relationships.

Testing for spuriousness is not difficult. Much depends upon our actual knowledge of the research problem, and whether possible alternative explana-

TABLE 2.2 Relation Between Close and General Parole Officer Supervision of Parolee-Clients and Recidivism/ Nonrecidivism of 200 Parolees, Controlling for Electronic Monitoring and No Electronic Monitoring

Type of Parole Officer Supervision	Electronically Monitored		Not Electronically Monitored		Totals
	Close	General	Close	General	
Recidivist	0	0	25	75	100
Nonrecidivist	75	25	0	0	100
Totals	75	25	75	25	100

tions for variable interrelationships exist. Additional time and patience are required, as the researcher puts each of these alternative explanations of the originally observed outcome to rest through empirical tests and tabular arrangements such as those illustrated in Tables 2.1 and 2.2. If an originally observed relation between variables is later determined to be spurious, then much has been accomplished. Researchers can then focus their attention on those variables that created the spuriousness.

■ THE COMPLEMENTARITY OF THEORY AND RESEARCH

There is an inevitable interplay between theory and research. More often than not, theory is a guide for subsequent research activity. Theory focuses our research in particular directions, and it directs us to examine certain variables and disregard the influence of other variables. Thus, theory is like blinders on horses: With blinders horses see directly ahead and are less disturbed or distracted by events not directly in their field of vision. Theory is also value-laden, because it is formulated in the context of our beliefs about what causes certain events. If we believe that criminal behavior is a function of glandular malfunction, we will be unlikely to focus our attention on delinquent subcultures or the socialization process of differential association. Instead, we will look at potential relations between different types of crime and glandular irregularities or problems among criminals. However, if we adopt labeling theory as our favored explanation for criminal behavior, we will be concerned with public reactions to and definitions of crime and the criminal's response to such reactions. We will not conduct biochemical analyses of criminals to determine the possible presence of glandular irregularities.

Research enables us to test our theories empirically. We can evaluate whether our theories adequately account for events we attempt to explain. Our predictions of events can be supported or refuted, depending upon what we observe from the collected data. We may discover things about our data and the events we attempt to explain that were formerly unknown, or if they were known, were considered unimportant or inconsequential at the time. Upon further analysis, however, it seems that certain variables have taken on greater importance to us. This is sometimes called serendipity—when we find out important things about the people we study that we weren't looking for initially. On these occasions, we might reformulate our theoretical schemes and include these formerly unknown or known but considered "unimportant" variables. Thus, research we conduct may suggest theories, the application of different strategies to collect and analyze data, or the modification of existing theories according to newly discovered criteria.

Hypotheses and Theory: A Preliminary View

Research is the means whereby theories are tested. We must collect and examine relevant data in order to show whether any theory is supported or refuted. Conventionally, investigators will focus upon a research problem, select or

Box 2.3

Stacy L. Henley
University of West Florida

Statistics: A.A. (criminal justice),
Okaloosa-Walton Community College;
B.S. (criminal justice), University
of West Florida.

Interests: Law enforcement, homicide investigation, forensic investigations, psychological profiling of killers, and investigative processes.

I am a criminal justice major at the University of West Florida, graduating *summa cum laude.* My plans are to continue with a master's degree in criminal justice. Most recently I was president of the Alpha Phi Sigma chapter of the Criminal Justice Honor Society, as well as a member of the Southern Criminal Justice Association. In addition to being on the President's and Dean's lists at the University of West Florida, I was also a member of the Phi Theta Kappa Honor Society while at Okaloosa-Walton Community College. I am currently working as an intern with the Pensacola Police Department Investigations Division. I have worked with this department for three years, both as an auxiliary officer and as an intern. My main interest in criminal justice is homicide investigations.

I became interested in criminal justice as a teenager, and I always had the desire to become a law enforcement officer. My interest was not in patrol work or administration, but in solving homicides. My extensive reading includes nonfiction crime books, articles, and research involving forensic investigations, the psychological profiling of killers, and the investigative process. I want to become one of the best homicide investigators in the field. I have put that dream on hold for at least eight years since graduating from high school. When I enrolled in criminal justice courses, I was fortunate to receive excellent advice from various professionals, including Dr. Ginger Haddad, an excellent instructor as well as an experienced defense attorney.

After completing my A.A. degree, I transferred to the University of West Florida and was inspired by Dr. Cheryl Swanson, a dynamic teacher and criminal justice professional. Dr. Swanson was critical in guiding me in the right direction for my course of study, reflecting my interests relating to homicide investigations and forensics. At the same time, I obtained a position with the Pensacola Police Department as an auxiliary officer. The experience and training in that position were invaluable, and I learned much about the laws of the state, proper police procedure, police codes, and the details of patrol work. I wanted to go further and to become more deeply involved in criminal investigations, especially of homicides.

During one semester, the police department offered me the opportunity of going undercover in order to detect sales of illegal drugs, such as crack cocaine and heroin. I assisted in other aspects of investigations, including interrogations; surveillance; and drug, burglary, and prostitution ring investigations. Included in this training were wiring vehicles for both audio and visual recordings in order to gather incriminating evidence against suspects. I assisted in interviewing witnesses of homicides and learned valuable techniques of interrogation. This work was very exciting and helped me to learn how to do so much more in the field of law enforcement. My work also included a brief involvement with the Medical Examiner's Office, where I attended and assisted in performing autopsies. One learns first-hand what defense wounds are, the significance of blood spatter, what the human body can endure in the most unlikely of death situations, what human beings are capable of doing to other human beings, and so much more. Working in the field and having the opportunity to volunteer with different agencies gave me the certainty of my career choice.

My plans are to seek employment with the Florida Department of Law Enforcement or Federal Bureau of Investigation and to apply the skills I have acquired through both education and experience in the area of murder investigations. I plan to work in the field for several years before taking my education and experience back to the classroom and teaching at the university level.

Advice to Students: My advice to students coming into criminal justice and criminology would be to always talk with persons who are already in the profession that interests you most. If you can, for two reasons, secure a position in a voluntary capacity in a field of study that interests you most. First, you want to ensure that this is what you want to do with your education. Second, you want to have the opportunity to experience what your future job will be like and what it will demand of you. You will learn much as a volunteer, getting first-hand experience and becoming useful to the agency where you may eventually apply for professional work.

As a student, be sure to always apply yourself to the fullest extent of your capacity. Do not settle for just "getting by." It is your future that you are developing while in school, and you must make the most out of these educational experiences as you acquire skills and knowledge. You should get involved as much as possible in professional societies offered by your school and department. You should plan on attending and participating in regional and national professional conferences. You can present papers and convert these into publishable articles. Don't be afraid of approaching your faculty with a request for becoming involved in their research projects. Furthermore, always conduct yourself in a professional manner. Eventually you will realize your goals and be proud of your own accomplishments.

devise a theoretical scheme to explain the problem, and then generate specific hypotheses to test. These hypotheses are directly deduced from theories. In Durkheim's study of suicide, he theorized that social bonds among groups were crucial in accounting for or explaining suicide. He hypothesized about different scenarios where variations in social bonds would occur. Durkheim didn't know what he would eventually find, nor did he know whether his findings would support or refute his theory of suicide and social bonds. Therefore, he hypothesized about different situations. Based on French suicide records and descriptive information of suicide victims, some of Durkheim's hypotheses included the following:

1. Protestants will have higher suicide rates compared with Catholics.
2. Catholics will have higher suicide rates compared with Jews.
3. Elderly persons will have higher suicide rates compared with younger persons.
4. Men will have higher suicide rates compared with women.
5. Single persons will have higher suicide rates compared with married persons.
6. Married persons with no children will have higher suicide rates compared with married persons with children.

All of these statements are **hypotheses** that can be tested. Durkheim had access to this French data; his father was a French government official with political connections. Durkheim analyzed suicide data for a period of years and found that each and every one of his hypothesis statements was supported. He based his tentative conclusions on empirical data.

In another example, Wang (1996) was interested in Asian gang affiliations, and whether Asian gang affiliation patterns were different from other types of gang affiliation patterns, including those of white, black, or Hispanic gangs. Wang noted that some gang investigators who had studied Asian gangs had found essentially no differences between these and other types of racial/ethnic gangs according to how they are formed and perpetuated. Yet Wang also described the research of others who believed that Asian gangs are influenced by their traditional belief systems and unique culture, as well as by ethnocentric identity crises. Wang decided to use the social developmental model, a blend of social control theory and social learning theory. These theories stress factors such as attachment, commitment, involvement, belief, peer influence, and the impact of school and neighborhood environments. He applied the statistical method of multiple regression analysis to isolate variables relevant to gang affiliation patterns. Wang collected data from 358 Asian-American high school students from 20 cities in five regions of the country. Wang believed that on the basis of the theory he used, he would *not* find significant differences separating Asian gang affiliation patterns from other racial or ethnic gang affiliation patterns previously described by other researchers. Thus, he set forth a hypothesis where he predicted no differences among gang affiliation patterns according to race/ethnicity. His results supported his hypothesis. The support of this hypothesis was also support for the social developmental theory he tested.

Generally, criminologists and criminal justicians proceed in this fashion. They identify a problem for study. They devise a theoretical explanation for the problem. They fashion various hypotheses from their theory to test. They collect data relevant to their hypothesis tests and generate findings that either support or refute these hypotheses. Supporting or refuting hypotheses derived from theory is the equivalent of supporting or refuting the theory itself. However, a single study, such as Wang's gang affiliation investigation, does not by itself prove or disprove a theory. Many subsequent studies must be conducted before we can cautiously conclude a theory has been proved or disproved. In the meantime, we use careful language to guard against rushing to judgment about a given theory. Thus, we "find support for a theory," or we "fail to find support for a theory," or "tentative support for theory X has been found," or "on the basis of these findings, we cannot support theory X."

■ THE VALUE OF THEORY

Often, distinctions among social scientific fields have been made according to their theoretical sophistication. Some evidence exists that criminal justice has not advanced theoretically to the same degree as criminology (Willis, 1983; Morn, 1980; Conley, 1979). Despite this evidence or its validity, there is a strong trend within criminal justice departments in the United States to improve the current state of theory throughout the discipline (Henderson and Boostrom, 1989).

Theoretical sophistication has also been equated with the degree of professionalization in any academic discipline (Dingwall and Lewis, 1983). One reason for the perceived absence of theory in criminal justice has been its historical emphasis on process and application within the criminal justice system. In contrast, criminology has historically emphasized crime causation (Henderson and Boostrom, 1989:37). Whatever the merits of these arguments, the fact is that theory is receiving greater attention from both criminologists and criminal justice professionals. Theory is increasingly perceived as the integrating medium through which the administration of justice, the criminal justice system, and explanations of crime can be productively blended.

Intermediate punishment programs such as intensive supervised probation, furloughs, work/study release, and home incarceration/electronic monitoring must increasingly respond to questions about those inmates and criminal candidates most likely to benefit from these supervisory services. In turn, these services may be treated by criminologists as intervening factors in theoretical schemes, in which these factors may change criminal behaviors and reduce recidivism in different ways. Theory not only functions to explain and predict events, but it also acts as a general policy guide for how offenders are or should be processed throughout the criminal justice system. The observed factual information—crime rates, recidivism rates, crime escalation, effects of decriminalization, plea bargaining, shock probation, short- or long-term incarceration—all conspire to tell us something about the validity of theories we have formulated.

Atheoretical Evaluations

Not every study is based upon or grounded in a theory. Conventionally, criminologists and criminal justicians perhaps prefer that criminological investigations are theoretically based in some way, because theory enables researchers to generalize their findings to wider varieties of settings. However, some research is undertaken simply to answer direct questions unrelated to theory of any kind. In these cases, the investigators who conduct such research have inquiring minds and simply want to know. These are known as **atheoretical evaluations.**

For instance, Mangus Seng (1996) studied campus thefts at the main and downtown campuses of Loyola University in Chicago. Seng himself described studies of theft as generally not being especially newsworthy or popular. But Seng set forth to describe campus thefts, at least on these two campuses. He didn't know much, if anything, about it, since campus theft studies were practically nonexistent. He simply wanted to study campus theft to "increase our knowledge of college-campus theft . . . and to relate . . . findings to [theft] prevention strategies" (Seng, 1996:34). After much description, data analysis, and comparisons, Seng concluded that at least for the two campuses he studied, no differences in theft patterns existed. There were no differences in items stolen, type of victim, or gender of victim. However, Seng found that thefts were more likely to occur in libraries or in faculty offices on both campuses. He speculated about different crime prevention measures that might reduce thefts on campuses generally, and what faculty and students could do to reduce thefts from libraries and campus offices.

Because Seng didn't know much about campus thefts and because little or no research literature existed on the subject, this piece of research might be defined as exploratory and descriptive. Seng never attempted to advance a particular theory of campus theft. Thus, his research was atheoretical.

There is more than a little atheoretical research conducted and reported in conventional journal outlets. The fact that theory is not used does not mean that the research itself is somehow unscientific. Seng was very conscientious in using sound scientific principles while conducting his investigation. A great deal of evaluation research discussed in Chapter 1 is atheoretical. In evaluation research, investigators want to know whether programs work, what their level of effectiveness is, and what can be done to make programs work better.

THE VALUE OF RESEARCH

Research supports or refutes our theories. Generally, research advances our knowledge, raising our level of certainty about why events that are of interest to us occur in the ways that they do. Much of the research used in previous examples throughout this chapter will benefit greatly from additional study. We may eventually be able to describe fully the process whereby police officers acquire professional attitudes about themselves and how the types of uniforms they wear influences this process. We might eventually learn the true relation between delinquency and homes that are or are not intact. Furthermore, some day we may be able to predict with amazing accuracy those settings in which inmate suicides will be highest, and we may be able to structure or juggle inmate environments in ways that curb inmate suicidal propensities.

Research is not limited exclusively to testing theories, however. As we have seen, some research is evaluative, wherein we seek to discover the efficacy of a particular intervention strategy or the influence of certain factors on others. Of course, we can carry our research findings into the classroom to enhance our lectures on specific subjects. Student interest in course content is frequently stimulated by presenting some of the findings from new research on selected subjects. Research uncovers topic areas that need further study. Research suggests ideas that might be useful in modifying older theories or developing new ones.

■ KEY TERMS

Assumptions	Independent variables
Atheoretical evaluations	Induction
Axiomatic theory	Inductive logic
Axioms	Inductive theory
Concepts	Intervening variable
Conclusions	Labeling theory
Contingent conditions	Method of agreement
Continuous variable	Method of concomitant variation
Contributory conditions	Method of difference
Deductive theory	Necessary conditions
Definitions	Propositions
Dependent variables	Spuriousness
Discrete variable	Sufficient conditions
Empirical generalizations	Theory
Frame of reference	Variables
Grounded theory	Variable subclasses
Hypotheses	

■ QUESTIONS FOR REVIEW

1. What is meant by theory? What are two important functions of theory? Give an example from the criminology or criminal justice literature to highlight each of these important functions.

2. What is meant by atheoretical evaluations? What is grounded theory?

3. What are variables? How are variables utilized in research? Show at least four functions performed by variables. Give an example of each from your own experience.

4. What conditions must prevail in order for causality among variables to be established? Do these conditions mean a cause–effect relation between variables exists if we adhere to them? Why or why not?

5. What are three methods proposed by John Stuart Mill whereby we can demonstrate causality?

6. Differentiate between assumptions, propositions, and definitions.

7. Which is more important for theories: explanation or prediction? Give a brief rationale for your choice.

8. What is the importance of convention relative to variables and how they are used or conceptualized in the research literature? Give an example.

9. Distinguish between independent and dependent variables. Select an article of your choice from the criminal justice or criminological literature, and isolate those variables designated as independent and dependent. How can variables perform both independent and dependent functions simultaneously? Explain and give an example.

10. What are five false assumptions about causality highlighted by Hirschi and Selvin (1967)?

11. What is spuriousness? Why is it an important consideration when attempting to establish a causal relation between two or more variables? Give an example of spuriousness apart from the example provided by the text.

12. Discuss the interplay between research and theory and how each complements the other.

chapter 3

Frames of Reference and Problem Formulation

■ INTRODUCTION

This chapter is about frames of reference or ways of looking at problems that are of interest to criminologists and those who study the criminal justice system. The first part of the chapter examines different kinds of frames of reference that guide researchers in their various projects and investigations. Several topics for investigation by criminal justice experts and criminologists are listed and described.

Since many persons entering these areas as professionals may be overwhelmed by the wide array of interest areas to pursue, some attention will be devoted to examining the decision-making process of determining what should be studied. Whenever investigators are deciding what to study, they must consider their own limitations as well as their strengths. How accessible are the elements or persons they plan to study? What can be ideally assumed about their research objectives and how to attain them? What are the realistic considerations they must take into account that will alter whatever it is they are attempting to do?

Almost every research project begins with an idea about some phenomenon to study. However, certain topics are more easily accessible than others to researchers. Investigators interested in studying inmates of jails or prisons must not only obtain permission from jail or prison authorities to study inmates, but they must also get the permission of inmates. In these heavily controlled settings, obtaining permission from correctional authorities and/or inmates to study them may be difficult or impossible. Thus, we examine some of the ideal and real considerations researchers must pursue whenever they decide to study specific groups or organizations.

The last part of this chapter examines the steps for conducting research. An examination of numerous research articles from different journals will show that while individual article formats vary, there is a consistency about how articles are crafted and arranged structurally. Thus, articles that present analyzed data usually have an introduction, a statement of a research problem, an explanation of the setting and sample to be studied, the presentation and analysis of data, and the conclusions and implications for future research. Some articles are expositional pieces, in which the authors describe a particular viewpoint or explore the different sides of a controversial issue. Perhaps a particular criminological theory is described, and the potential applications of the theory are suggested. Even in these articles, readers will detect a structure similar to formats in which analysis of data has been conducted. In these expositional articles, there is usually an introduction, a statement of the issue or theory to be described and discussed, a presentation of different viewpoints and contrasting perspectives, a more or less extensive discussion of the viewpoint, and conclusions. The steps in the research process will be described.

■ WHAT ARE FRAMES OF REFERENCE?

A *frame of reference* is the way researchers or investigators view the problem selected for study. It is the approach chosen for problem-solving situations. Several examples from criminology literature will be helpful here. Suppose we were interested in studying the influence of various deterrents to criminal behavior. How might we approach this subject and investigate it?

One view (frame of reference) toward crime deterrence is that tougher sentencing policies will deter criminals from committing crimes. If criminals know that there is a good chance that they will be caught and sentenced to substantial time behind bars, then they may be less inclined to engage in new criminal conduct. Wicharaya (1995) decided to study whether sentencing reform laws would cause crime deterrence over time. Using aggregate data from the 1970s and 1980s, the National Prisoner Statistics, the **Uniform Crime Reports (UCR),** and the *Sourcebook of Criminal Justice Statistics,* Wicharaya used complex statistical procedures, time-series and pooled time-series analyses, to determine whether legislative control over sentencing discretion through sentencing reform increased the certainty of punishment and led to crime deterrence. Wicharaya found that although the rate of incarceration declined, the new sentencing policies had no deterrent impact on violent crime rates.

A different frame of reference toward crime deterrence was adopted by Rouse (1985). Rouse investigated whether changes in police personnel, policing styles, and patrols had an impact on reducing crime. He studied different jurisdictions throughout the United States and found that police presence and varying patrol styles had little perceptible effect on crime reduction.

A leading explanation for crime deterrence is based on the utilitarian rational choice model of Ehrlich (1975) and Becker (1968) (Sampson, 1986:274). These researchers have asserted that much crime is committed because the utility of the criminal behavior or the expected benefits accruing as the result of that activity outweigh the benefits that might otherwise accrue to criminals from other, possibly legal, activities (Sampson, 1986:274). Thus, if the expected benefits derived from crime are frustrated or hindered by police or community residents, the likelihood of criminal behavior as utilitarian activity decreases.

Each of these frames of reference functions like blinders on a horse. Carriage horses wearing blinders are prevented from seeing directly to either the left or right, and thus they are inclined to move in the direction intended by the carriage driver. Frames of reference function similarly. While the researcher knows or is aware of other possible explanations for or approaches to the problem under investigation, selecting one frame of reference over others directs the researcher's attention in one direction only; and other possible explanatory factors are given lower priority.

Let's look at another example of a frame of reference. Suppose we wished to examine the phenomenon of police response to spousal abuse. When spouses physically abuse one another, police response in different jurisdictions varies. In a majority of spouse abuse situations, police response is situational, and considerable discretion is given to police officers about making an arrest. In other police departments, mandatory arrest policies are in effect, whereby police officers must arrest one or both spouses whenever they investigate reports of spousal abuse. The fact that police officers react in different ways when investigating spousal abuse has been studied by several researchers.

One explanation for differential police response to spousal abuse is whether the abuse occurs in a rural area or in an urban area. Neil Websdale and Byron Johnson (1997) speculated that rural police officers respond more slowly to reported domestic violence. One reason for this difference is that rural battered women are less likely than urban battered women to report their abuse to police. Further, when investigations of rural spousal abuse occur, it seems that rural women are less likely to come forward and testify against their spouses. Websdale and Johnson interviewed 100 battered women in spouse abuse shelters in Kentucky. These researchers also rode with police to investigate spousal abuse incidents and observed the police action taken. Websdale and Johnson found support for the idea that rural police officers took longer to serve emergency protective orders, and in some cases, these officers did not serve them at all. Their frame of reference focused upon the rural and urban contexts of spousal abuse. Using this frame of reference, these investigators were able to observe and isolate apparent differences between rural and urban police officers according to how these officers responded to domestic altercations. Further, battered women from rural and urban backgrounds seemed to respond differently when reporting or not reporting spousal abuse.

Another frame of reference toward domestic violence is the leniency thesis (Fyfe, Klinger, and Flavin, 1997). According to the leniency thesis, police officers are more lenient toward men who abuse their spouses compared with men who abuse women with whom they are intimate but not married. These researchers studied 392 felony assaults in Chester, Pennsylvania. They separated felony assaults according to whether the couples were married or unmarried. Consistent with the leniency thesis, their frame of reference, police officers made arrests in only 13 percent of the cases involving married spouses, whereas arrests were made in 28 percent of the cases involving unmarried couples. Frames of reference do not prove that any particular explanation is true, or the best explanation, but they do direct our attention to certain variables that explain behaviors like police response to spousal abuse.

Other frames of reference toward spousal abuse exist. For instance, Burgess and Draper (1989) report that spousal abuse is attributed to ecological instability, underemployment, financial pressures (which no doubt stem, in large part, from underemployment), anxiety, and alcohol abuse. Ecological instability as a frame of reference to account for a high incidence of spousal abuse might refer to relocating frequently to new geographical areas (perhaps in search of employment or better promotional opportunities). Such moves might involve a loss of immediate kin support or signify changes in the marital balance of power. Financial pressures, underemployment, and alcoholism might suggest a high degree of marital tension over how money is spent or allocated, disputes over who should make such decisions on the basis of each spouse's relative contribution to family income, and a loss of inhibitions resulting from alcohol intake. Other explanations for spousal abuse suggest that abusers were abused as children by their own parents (Johnston, 1988; Seltzer and Kalmuss, 1988). Further, there is a "universal risk" theory, a frame of reference that considers all women at risk and subject to wife battering largely as the result of liberal and radical feminist movements within a predominantly patriarchal society (Schwartz, 1988).

Choosing a Frame of Reference

One's choice of frame of reference is based on several factors. First, when a review of recent literature is conducted, investigators learn which frames of reference seem most popular. Although the popularity of certain frames of reference compared with others may be indicative of their success in explaining some phenomena, they may not be the best frames of reference to use. However, new investigators are drawn toward more popular frames of reference as a conservative move, particularly if they are new to the discipline and are hesitant to risk selecting less popular frames of reference for their investigations. Another reason why certain frames of reference are chosen over others is that perhaps the researcher is simply more familiar with a particular frame of reference and believes it is the best one to use. Other researchers may select particular frames of reference that reflect their earlier coursework and experience.

Values and Frames of Reference

Values and frames of reference are closely connected. **Values** are standards of acceptability we acquire from our peers or from society in general. These values cause us to prioritize, or to allocate greater importance to some things and less importance to others. Thus, each of us learns to value things differently, and these differences explain, in part, the diversity of approaches to various subjects or the different frames of reference chosen to account for or explain events.

Great subjectivity is reflected in our values. It follows, therefore, that the research we conduct is subjective. Most often we choose the topics we will investigate. We study certain problems and issues because of our interest in them. We also select particular frames of reference over others, often because we find them more interesting or important. Our choice of methodology and how we collect data and analyze it also reveals our priorities and interests, although we may be unaware of alternative research strategies. All of these choices are value-laden choices.

Apart from the requirements of degree programs and the personal preferences of the professors who guide us in our graduate research, the decisions we make often reflect our own value system. That our decisions are closely linked with our values is not necessarily bad. But we need to recognize the influence of values in our research choices at the outset, lest we label someone else's research choices and approaches as poor or irrelevant. The state of the art today in criminology and criminal justice is such that no single frame of reference in any topic area is considered the best one. Differences of opinion abound as to how events ought to be explained. And you will always have a chance to link your frame of reference to the event you want to explain through theory.

A frame of reference points us in a given direction as we attempt to unravel the complexities of criminological problems. The frame of reference is crucial at the outset, since it is the foundation of our explanation for why certain problems exist or events occur. The way we decide to view the problem under investigation is also the way we have chosen to explain it. The next step in the research process is to enunciate, articulate, or spell out in plain language how your explanation of the event relates to the problem in some logical fashion.

Thus, frames of reference and theory are, for better or worse, inevitably related. Our theory consists of numerous statements reflecting linkages between variables. If we are studying crime deterrence, for example, and we decide to use a demographic approach, our theory becomes the explanatory and predictive tool we will use to show how it came to be so that crime deterrence and demographics are related. If we choose to view crime deterrence largely as a function of police aggressiveness or family instability, we must demonstrate the possible causal relation between crime deterrence and police aggressiveness or between crime deterrence and family instability in our theory or theoretical scheme. If we study spousal abuse and wish to explain it or account for it by using underemployment or alcoholism as predictor variables, then our theoretical scheme should lay out our reasoning for why spousal abuse and underemployment or spousal abuse and alcoholism are related.

Some researchers specialize in theory construction, and they heavily stress the importance of different theoretical components such as axioms, propositions, assumptions, and postulates. In a logical fashion, they weave an explanatory and predictive web that yields certain "tentative" conclusions (hypotheses) that may be tested empirically. For instance, it is insufficient to say simply that because someone is unemployed or underemployed, he will feel bad and beat his wife. It is insufficient also to say simply that if one consumes enough alcohol, he will become drunk and physically abuse his spouse. We want to know why these events are related or interconnected. Why should underemployment or unemployment contribute to or cause spousal abuse? Why should family instability raise crime rates? Why should excessive alcohol consumption precipitate family violence?

As we attempt to explain the "whys" involved, we must continue searching for answers until we have exhausted an explanation or have given a reasonably full account of how the events are related. What is reasonable? Again, value judgments enter the picture, and we must rely on our own standards and assessments about what constitutes an adequate amount of completeness. No one agrees on how "complete" our theoretical explanations ought to be. In fact, theory is perhaps the weakest link in the chain of events we regard as the research process because it is difficult to develop, construct, or create theory.

At least the frame of reference we adopt in relation to any given problem or event focuses our attention on a limited number of explanatory options. But remember that whenever we choose one frame of reference over others, we are barring ourselves from considering these other options. Our choices may not be

Robert M. Bohm
University of Central Florida

Statistics: B.A. (psychology), University of Missouri at Columbia; M.A. (secondary education), University of Missouri at Kansas City; Ph.D. (criminology), Florida State University.

Interests: My present research interests are diverse, but they include various aspects of capital punishment, especially death-penalty opinion, crime and delinquency causation and prevention, and criminal justice generally. I have taught at Jacksonville State University and the University of North Carolina at Charlotte. I served as president of the Academy of Criminal Justice Sciences in 1992–1993.

After graduating in 1972 with a degree in psychology, I returned to my hometown of Kansas City, Missouri, and went to work in the retail business. I managed an automobile radio and stereo store owned by one of my father's friends. I hated that job and quit after just seven months. I opened a pinball arcade called the 39th Street Phantasmagoria and Pinball Emporium. I owned and operated the arcade for almost two years, but for reasons beyond my control, I had to shut it down. I needed a job badly, and so I took a civil service examination. I was invited to interview for a correctional officer job at the Jackson County, Missouri, Jail. I was offered the job and took it, not knowing then that it would eventually lead to a career in academic criminal justice.

I worked as a correctional officer for about seven months. Then the jail received a federal grant to create and implement a county work release program—one of the first of its kind. The program administrators needed someone with a psychology background to create an educational and motivational program for prework release inmates. My new title was Instructor/Counselor in the Model Inmate Employment Program. I held this position for two years. During that time the federal government, through the Law Enforcement Assistance Administration (LEAA), instituted a program that encouraged in-service criminal justice personnel, like myself, to pursue advanced educational degrees. I took advantage of the program and earned my M.A. and Ph.D. degrees.

I seem to have always had an interest in human behavior, but I did not become interested in criminal behavior per se until I went to work at the jail. My work with the inmates at the jail made me curious about why they did the things for which they were incarcerated. My graduate education exposed me to theories that purportedly answered that question. However, few of the theories made much sense to me in light of what I knew from my correctional experience. And so I began a search for more satisfying theories of criminal and delinquent behavior and, perhaps even more important, for ways of preventing those behaviors from occurring. That question has been a principal focus of my research ever since.

In 1985 I read in the newspaper that pro–death penalty opinion in the United States had reached the highest level ever recorded: 75 percent of Americans favored the death penalty for persons convicted of first-degree murder. What struck me as interesting was that so large a percentage of Americans could agree about anything, let alone the death penalty. That chance event instigated my effort to understand why people supported (and opposed) capital punishment. From that beginning, my interest in capital punishment has expanded to include other aspects of the penalty and its administration.

My research into other issues of criminal justice, such as the mythology of crime and criminal justice, stems from my teaching the subject since 1979 and my prior correctional experience. I have found that what many people think they know about criminal justice is either wrong or terribly misunderstood. Over the years, I have made an effort to rectify the situation.

It is hard to estimate what contribution, if any, my research has made to criminology and criminal justice. I would like to believe that it has made a difference, but I do not know. I do know that criminology and criminal justice are fascinating subjects, and I will never be able to research all of the questions I would like to answer myself. However, I am grateful that people are willing to pay me to try.

Advice to Students: My advice to students who are contemplating a career doing criminal justice or criminological research is to be inquisitive, skeptical, a little cynical, and open to serendipity. It is also useful to be motivated by an idealistic goal. One of mine is to improve the quality of everyone's life.

the best ones, and our results may be inconclusive as good explanations for and predictors of the problems we investigate. This is one reason why so much replication and reinvestigation occurs in any kind of social research. And perhaps this is as it should be, considering how science operates and affects what we do. We acquire knowledge and certainty about things slowly, and we continually subject our views and explanations for events to experimentation and empirical testing. Gradually, some explanations emerge as better predictors than other explanations. Over time, we develop a stronger sense of what fits and what doesn't fit, of what seems to work and what doesn't seem to work.

■ DECIDING WHAT TO STUDY: TOPICS OF INVESTIGATION FOR CRIMINAL JUSTICE AND CRIMINOLOGY

Choosing a topic for investigation in criminology and criminal justice is often associated with one's interests and previous experience. Persons who have been law enforcement officers or correctional officers or probation/parole workers may seek out topics that pertain to these areas. It is not unusual to find that researchers who study police officers have previously been police officers themselves. Many investigators find it comfortable to study topics in areas in which they have some familiarity. Some former corrections officers may study prison settings and prisoners, or they may study the lives of corrections officers.

For some researchers, their research topics may be chosen for them. If you are in a graduate department or working toward a graduate degree, or if you are working as a graduate research assistant on a grant supervised by one of your professors, deciding what topics to study may not be one of your options. In short, you may already be locked into a particular topic and expected to investigate a particular aspect of it. However, in most graduate departments, there is considerable latitude extended to researchers concerning what they study and how they study it.

It is unnecessary to list each and every interest area in criminology and criminal justice in which research may be conducted. At professional meetings, such as the annual meeting of the American Society of Criminology, criminologists convene and present papers or give reports about research they have conducted. These papers reflect the diverse interests among these professionals. An examination of the program for the annual meeting of the Academy of Criminal Justice Sciences, which was held in Orlando, Florida, in March 1999, disclosed that more than 400 panels, workshops, and roundtable discussions were offered, with an average of three or four papers per session. These panels included topics such as the impact of AIDS on law enforcement, psychosocial aspects of criminal behavior, police officer safety, a historical perspective of women in criminology, crime control trends, the sexual integration of prison and jail guard forces, community corrections models, victimization, crime prevention strategies, police education, electronic monitoring and house arrest, sentencing policies, elderly abuse, prisoner rights, juvenile gang patterns and trends, and corrections institutional management.

The subject matter of criminal justice and criminology is boundless. While there are some standard topic areas related to different components of the criminal justice system (e.g., law enforcement, courts, corrections), an infinite number of subtopics may be investigated. In the area of prosecution and the courts, for example, plea bargaining has been a popular topic for investigation. What factors influence prosecutorial discretion? How do race, ethnicity, gender, and socioeconomic status influence the plea bargaining decision and the contents of a plea bargain agreement? What are the implications of different types of sentencing schemes for various types of offenders? Are defendants more likely to receive greater leniency from judges at the time of sentencing if they pleaded guilty through plea bargaining or if the guilty verdict was rendered against them by a jury through a jury trial?

Regarding jury trials, many researchers have investigated the jury deliberation process. What are the dynamics of jury deliberations? Does the racial and/or gender composition of juries make a difference and influence these deliberations depending upon the race or gender of the defendants? Can jury verdicts be predicted with any degree of accuracy? Are smaller juries more likely to reach consensus compared with larger juries? Is there an optimum jury size? What can prosecutors and defense attorneys do to influence juries? These are just a few of the many questions researchers raise when investigating juries, jury deliberations, and other jury-related factors.

When investigating police officers, some researchers focus upon factors that influence the exercise of police discretion in effecting arrests of suspects. Does a more-educated police officer relate to the community better than a less-educated officer? What types of training should police officers receive in order to prepare them for the realities of police work? Is there a distinctive police personality? How much stress do police officers experience while on the job? What coping mechanisms are put into play as a means of handling such job stress? How do stress and burnout affect job performance? Are one- or two-officer patrol units more effective in combating crime? Again, a virtually limitless range of topics within the component of law enforcement may be selected for scientific study.

Before we make a final decision about what to study, however, we should assess our abilities, our personal strengths and weaknesses, and our interests. Sometimes, inexperienced researchers will identify grandiose research problems that are well beyond their means, both personally and financially. The topics selected may be noteworthy, but often, the study objectives are unobtainable, simply because they are beyond the investigator's financial means. We might wish to conduct a study of a large sample of all officers of the Los Angeles Police Department. But we quickly find that the cost of such a study would be prohibitive. This is one reason why professors, researchers, and others apply for grants from public and private funding agencies. Perhaps we want to study a sample of district attorneys in various cities in several states, but we don't at first consider the travel time involved, the appointments we would have to make, and other logistical factors that would make it possible for our study to materialize.

If we plan to study others in public organizations or agencies, one of the first things we do is assess our connections. Do we know anyone who can help us get our foot in the door? Are we personally employed at an agency that would allow us to study it? In short, we identify whom we know relative to the problem we intend to study, or we assess the connections of others who may be in a position to help us in our research endeavors. If our choice is to do library research and rely exclusively on the contents of documents and other library materials for information, it is unnecessary to obtain permission from anyone or go through the often difficult and tedious process of gaining access to organizations and agencies. But even if "quiet" research is done in a library setting, practical concerns must still be addressed beyond our immediate research interests. We must pay attention to some of the dilemmas that often arise between what ideally should be done and what, in reality, can be done. This is the ideal-real scenario that is common to all researchers in all subject areas.

■ REVIEWING THE LITERATURE

Getting started in any research project requires that investigators become very familiar with existing literature about the problem to be studied. It is conventional in all social and criminological research to conduct a **literature review.** What is known about the problem to be studied? What have other researchers written about it? What other research has been done and what has been found?

One important purpose for a literature review is to determine whether your ideas are current and relevant. Some novice researchers think that they have a highly interesting research problem or a novel way of studying it. But when they seek out articles and information about the research problem, they discover that many other researchers have investigated the topic in the past and no longer consider it important. Further, the "novel" approach used to study the research problem may turn out to be an old approach no longer used by contemporary investigators. Thus, the literature review is a learning experience in several respects. We learn about what information exists about the problem we are studying. We glean ideas about studying the problem from what other researchers have done. We become aware of possible controversies and issues surrounding the problem.

The most logical place to begin a literature review is the library. A college or university library will contain much information about any research topic. Libraries maintain more or less extensive collections of journals and periodicals. Journals publish research findings by criminologists and others. Articles cover an array of subjects and may be essays or analyses of data. If you are studying correctional officer labor turnover and why it occurs, there are specialized journals that cater to studies about institutional corrections and corrections officers. *The Prison Journal* publishes such articles. If you are studying probation officer burnout and stress, the Administrative Office of the U.S. Courts publishes *Federal Probation*, a journal that includes numerous articles about probation work. Libraries have sourcebooks that list all journals and periodicals. It is fairly easy to scan this list and determine which journals might contain information you are seeking.

There are also technical reports and books about the subjects you study. Suppose you are interested in international terrorism. Library personnel are available to assist you in locating technical reports and books on terrorism sources. And once you have located certain areas in which these sources about terrorism are found, you will see other books about terrorism on the same library shelf. Whether you examine books or articles or both, you will glean much informative material from your examination of the literature. What you learn from published reports and research will often cause you to rethink your original research problem or modify your frame of reference.

Sources for Literature Reviews

Besides the library, there are other sources for conducting literature reviews. For example, since 1968 Willow Tree Press in Monsey, New York, has published a quarterly periodical of abstracts from articles and books. Called *Criminal Justice Abstracts*, this publication has been used by thousands of researchers who investigate criminological problems. Abstracts are abbreviated summaries of research articles or book contents. An abstract of a research article might include the focus of the study, the sample selected and methods used for data analysis, a synopsis of findings, and some statement about the significance of the article. Abstracts are usually one or two paragraphs long. These abstracts are very informative for researchers.

Since the early 1990s, Willow Tree Press has made these abstracts available on CD-ROM, including annual updates of abstract information, such as 1968–1998, 1968–1999, and so on. Each year a new CD is issued. These CDs contain more than 100,000 abstracts of articles and books. With the proper CD-ROM and a computer, researchers can conduct data searches using key words. If a researcher wanted information about probation officers and firearms, deadly force, police cynicism, correctional officer professionalism, judicial sentencing disparity, or virtually any other valid criminal justice topic, simply entering key words and pressing a computer button will yield several hundred abstracts on a particular subject. These abstracts can be downloaded onto a computer diskette and translated into some software format, such as MS Word for Windows or WordPerfect. From there, a document can be printed that contains all of the downloaded abstracts. These abstracts can be scanned to determine what is known about a given subject. Interestingly, when you scan 25 or more abstracts on a given subject, you begin to acquire a sense of what is known about the subject and how investigators have studied it. Since abstracts report research findings, you can easily spot contradictory articles.

Contrary findings in any given subject area are common and should not be interpreted as indicating that the field is in disarray or that researchers haven't developed any consistent information about a topic. For instance, suppose we are studying judicial sentencing disparity. Disparities in sentencing occur when convicted offenders with similar criminal histories and conviction offenses are given widely different sentences. Disparities are attributable to any of several factors, including race/ethnicity, socioeconomic status, use of private counsel or public defender, gender, or age. An examination of abstracts of articles studying sentencing disparities may disclose seemingly inconsistent findings. One abstract, a hypothetical article by Smith and Jones, may show that a study of 35 judges in Pennsylvania revealed that in 550 sentences imposed for offenders convicted of the same felonies, 56 percent of the white convicted offenders were placed on probation, whereas 38 percent of the nonwhite convicted offenders received probation. However, in another hypothetical study, Peters and Johnson found that of 728 same-felony sentences in Georgia, 64 percent of the white convicted offenders received probation, while 65 percent of the nonwhite convicted offenders received probation. Thus, it would seem that sentencing disparity was found in the Smith and Jones study but not in the Peters and Johnson study.

If we were to look more closely at these studies, however, we may find that actual sentence lengths were quite different, depending upon whether the offenders were white or nonwhite. We might find that for *both* the Smith and Jones and the Peters and Johnson studies, white offenders spent an average of four years in prison, while the nonwhite offenders spent an average of six years in prison. While these figures do not prove that judges or parole boards discriminate against nonwhite offenders, the differences in time served raise serious questions about the equity of the sentences imposed.

In order for us to make a serious case showing sentencing disparities, we must examine the findings of many studies. Surveying the abstracts on sentencing disparities will give us a very good idea about how much disparity exists and which variables seem to explain sentencing disparities in different jurisdictions.

There are many other sources for literature reviews. Besides the *Criminal Justice Abstracts* on CD, the *National Criminal Justice Reference Service Document Data Base* is also available annually on CD. This database is funded by the U.S. Department of Justice National Institute of Justice. This database contains more than 140,000 abstracts of articles, books, and government publications. One significant difference between this resource and *Criminal Justice Abstracts* is that it contains a much larger variety of government document abstracts. There is also some duplication, as both sources abstract many of the same articles and books. The *National Criminal Justice Reference Service Document Data Base* CD is used in the same way as the *Criminal Justice Abstracts* CD, using word searches on a computer program. Abstracts on selected subjects can be downloaded to a computer diskette and subsequently formatted and printed. Various other abstracting services relevant for specific fields, such as sociology and psychology, are available. Many of these sources are found in university libraries. Table 3.1 shows various journals and abstract databases that might be used to locate relevant articles and other types of publications.

Depending upon the magnitude of the research project, whether it is a class or term paper or the beginning of a full-fledged research study, the literature review should be a fairly thorough coverage of existing literature on the subject. Literature reviews are not meant to be exhaustive. That is, you don't have to summarize the 650 articles that may be available. Many of the sources you cite will be somewhat repetitive. Thus, if 40 articles report similar findings regarding a given subject, it is only necessary to reference 10 to 12 articles and briefly summarize what they have concluded. If there are different findings reported in other articles, you can easily document these differences in findings. Often, these study differences heighten reader interest. Why are there discrepancies in the research literature? What factors might account for these discrepancies? A part of your job might be to offer one or more explanations for these contrary study findings. Indeed, your major or only task might be to explain them.

Literature reviews vary in their complexity and extensiveness, depending upon the particular paper or research project. Term papers written to satisfy the requirements of an undergraduate course may contain 15 to 20 references. If the research is a master's thesis or doctoral dissertation, the writer may include 100 or more references in the literature review. Appendix B of this book contains a detailed discussion about writing papers and research reports. Different types of reports and papers are described and distinguished. Generally, the literature review is geared to acquaint readers with what is known about the subject studied.

A warning is in order for students and others who turn to textbooks for literature review summaries. While it is true that most textbooks summarize some of the literature in selected areas, it is also true that textbooks are limited. Textbooks must cover a lot of material; this means that articles are often discussed as "one-liners," where the author merely asserts a specific study finding. For example, such a summary might say, "Rogers found that correctional officers who worked on death row at Suburban Penitentiary had significantly greater stress

TABLE 3.1 Journals and Abstract Compilations

Journals

American Jails

American Journal of Criminal Justice

American Journal of Police

American Journal of Sociology

American Sociological Review

APPA Perspectives

Corrections Compendium

Corrections Today

Crime and Delinquency

Criminal Behavior and Mental Health

Criminal Justice and Behavior

Criminal Justice Ethics

Criminal Justice Policy Review

Criminal Justice Review

Criminology

FBI Law Enforcement Bulletin

Federal Probation

Journal of Child Sexual Abuse

Journal of Contemporary Criminal Justice

Journal of Contemporary Law

Journal of Crime and Justice

Journal of Criminal Justice

Journal of Criminal Law and Criminology

Journal of Legal Studies

Journal of Offender Counseling, Services and Rehabilitation

Journal of Offender Rehabilitation

Journal of Quantitative Criminology

Journal of Research in Crime and Delinquency

Judicature

Justice Professional

Justice Quarterly

Law and Society Review

Police Chief

Police Studies

Prison Journal

Social Problems

Abstracts

Abstracts on Police Science

Criminal Justice Abstracts

Criminal Justice Periodical Index

Criminology and Penology Abstracts

National Criminal Justice Reference Service Document Data Base

Police Science Abstracts

Psychological Abstracts

Social Science Index

Sociological Abstracts

and burnout levels compared with correctional officers who worked in the general inmate population," or "Smith showed that a sample of police officers in Detroit, Michigan, admitted to accepting illegal gratuities from businesses while on foot patrols." These observations are interesting and probably help to illustrate certain topics in textbooks. But they are of little value in literature reviews. Further, by the time a textbook is published, the printed material is already dated by one or more years. This is because it takes about a year to publish a textbook once the final manuscript has been submitted to the publisher. Thus, textbooks generally are not good resources to consult for generating up-to-date or timely literature reviews. Textbooks *do* provide interesting ideas for potential research topics, however. And examining the bibliographies of textbooks can identify classic works on a wide variety of topics.

■ "HANDS-ON" RESEARCH AND INVESTIGATIONS FROM A DISTANCE

"Hands-On" Research

Anyone doing research has several choices. By far the most difficult choice is to actually collect original data and conduct "hands-on" research. "Hands-on" research means that a target population must be identified, such as all police officers or probation officers in a community, county, or state. Then, a sample of these persons will need to be contacted in some way. Commonly used methods for contacts include personal visits and interviews, telephone calls, or mailed questionnaires. Prior to making these contacts, questions that reflect the investigator's research goals and objectives will have to be formulated. Much preliminary work is involved before the research project is launched.

Data collection may not be easy. Persons may refuse to be interviewed. Some persons are simply inaccessible. Organizations may have policies that bar researchers from contacting their employees. Even if data are eventually collected, analyses of data will have to be made. A knowledge of statistics and analysis techniques is required. Once data have been tabulated and interpreted, a summary of major findings and implications of the research will have to be prepared. Thus, considerable work goes into carrying out an actual research project involving direct contact with samples of the persons to be studied.

Investigations from a Distance

An easier choice is an investigation from a distance. This means that a researcher can study data already collected by others. It is possible for a researcher to spend his or her professional lifetime examining data collected and reported by others. One of the largest data sources is state and federal governments, which publish statistical and descriptive information about every criminal justice topic. An annual compilation of general criminal justice statistical information is the *Sourcebook of Criminal Justice Statistics.* Not only is a hard copy of this sourcebook published annually, but it is also available on CD. Thus, for $15, any person may obtain a CD version of the *Sourcebook* covering recent years.

A growing number of agencies are producing data sets available in a variety of formats. One of the most popular formats is a computer diskette. The National Center for Juvenile Justice (NCJJ), headquartered in Pittsburgh, Pennsylvania, distributes free diskettes of juvenile justice data to professionals at annual conferences of the Academy of Criminal Justice Sciences and the American Society of Criminology. Interested persons can write the NCJJ for these diskettes as well. Other diskettes, for various years, are produced by the

National Judicial Reporting Program. With their home computers, investigators can analyze these large data sets rather easily, as well as perform simple cross-tabulation functions. The National Institute of Justice annually publishes lists of existing data sets, and this information is available to interested consumers for a nominal charge.

The *Uniform Crime Reports* and *National Crime Victimization Survey*

Another data source is the *Uniform Crime Reports (UCR)*, compiled by the Federal Bureau of Investigation. This publication includes statistics about the number and kinds of crimes annually reported in the United States by more than 15,000 law enforcement agencies. The *UCR* is the major sourcebook of crime statistics in the United States. The *UCR* is compiled by gathering information on twenty-nine types of crime from participating law enforcement agencies. Crime information is requested from all rural and urban law enforcement agencies. However, not all agencies report their crime information on a regular basis to the FBI. Others don't report at all, while still others report their information inconsistently (e.g., New Mexico authorities and California authorities may report the same offense in a different way to the FBI).

The FBI has established a crime classification index. Index offenses include eight serious types of crime used by the FBI to measure crime trends. Information is also compiled about 21 less serious offenses ranging from forgery and counterfeiting to curfew violations and runaways. Index offense information is presented in the *UCR* for each state, city, county, and township that has submitted crime information during the most recent year. The eight index offenses and their definitions according to the Uniform Crime Reporting Program are shown as follows:

1. Murder and Nonnegligent Manslaughter: the willful (nonnegligent) killing of one human being by another.
2. Forcible Rape: the carnal knowledge of a female forcibly and against her will; assaults or attempts to commit rape by force or threat of force are also included.
3. Robbery: the taking or attempt to take anything of value from the care, custody, or control of a person or persons by force or threat of force or violence and/or by putting the victim in fear.
4. Aggravated Assault: an unlawful attack by one person upon another for the purpose of inflicting severe or aggravated bodily injury.
5. Burglary: the unlawful entry of a structure to commit a felony or theft.
6. Larceny-Theft: the unlawful taking, carrying, leading, or riding away of property from the possession or constructive possession of another; includes shoplifting, pocket-picking, purse-snatching, thefts from motor vehicles, and thefts of motor vehicle parts or accessories.
7. Motor Vehicle Theft: theft or attempted theft of a motor vehicle including automobiles, trucks, buses, motorcycles, motorscooters, and snowmobiles.

8. Arson: any willful or malicious burning or attempt to burn, with or without intent to defraud, a dwelling house, public building, motor vehicle or aircraft, and the personal property of another.

The **National Crime Victimization Survey (NCVS)** is another source of information. The *NCVS* is a compendium of crimes reported by crime victims from an annual survey. The *NCVS* was implemented in 1972 and originally known as the *National Crime Survey*. In 1991, the name was changed to the *NCVS*. It consists of an annual national survey of 50,000 households involving more than 100,000 persons. These households are subdivided into subsets of 10,000 households each, and each subset is interviewed each month. Every six months one subset of 10,000 households is dropped from the survey and replaced by a fresh subset of 10,000 households. This feature ensures household diversity and incorporates transitional elements that keep the *NCVS* up to date. The reported material is usually referred to as victimization data. The *NCVS* distinguishes between victimizations and incidents. A victimization is the basic measure of the occurrence of a crime and is a specific criminal act that affects a single victim. An incident is a specific criminal act involving one or more victims.

Criticisms of the UCR and NCVS.   Even though the *UCR* publishes the most current crime figures from reporting law enforcement agencies, it is inaccurate in several respects. First, when criminals have been questioned about other crimes they have committed, the results show discrepancies between *UCR* figures and the "self-report" information. In short, criminals escape detection or capture for many crimes they commit. Thus, it is generally accepted that there is more crime committed each year than official estimates such as the *UCR* disclose. Second, not all law enforcement agencies report crimes in a uniform manner. Many jurisdictions define the same crimes differently. Errors also occur in tabulating arrest statistics by clerks in local police departments (e.g., a clerk may classify a robbery as a burglary). Thus, the *UCR* may be more a reflection of police arrest practices rather than a true measure of the amount of crime that really occurs. Third, in some jurisdictions, police crackdowns will lead to numerous arrests, but there will be few convictions. The implication is that arrest statistics are more a measure of police activity than criminal activity. Fourth, not all law enforcement agencies report their crime figures on a consistent basis. Sloppy record keeping and lax record-keeping policies contribute to faulty reporting. Also, many crimes are never reported to the police. Fifth, when a crime is reported and a report is submitted to the *UCR*, only the most serious offense is often reported. For example, a burglary suspect is arrested at a crime scene in possession of burglary tools—a law violation—stolen goods—another law violation—and a concealed weapon—another law violation. However, law enforcement officials may report a single crime, burglary. This practice (i.e., reporting the most serious offense when more than two offenses have been committed by a single suspect), together with the fact that many crimes remain undetected or are not reported, causes some experts to charge that the *UCR* underestimates the actual amount of crime committed in the United States. The result of comparing *NCVS* (victimization) information with *UCR* (officially reported) data is that the amount of crime reported by the *NCVS* is two to three times greater than the amount of crime reported by the *UCR*.

There are also several criticisms of the *NCVS*. Some crime victims cannot remember when or where the offense occurred. Other victims are reluctant to report a rape, particularly if the rapist is known, perhaps a family member or close friend. Nonreporting is also related to victim fear, feelings of helplessness or apathy, the perceived powerlessness of police, and fear of the authorities themselves. The poor are especially reluctant to report crime because they fear reprisals from the criminals who are often known to them. Additionally, both the *UCR* and *NCVS* overemphasize street crimes and deemphasize corporate crimes.

■ STEPS TO CONDUCT RESEARCH IN CRIMINAL JUSTICE

Many different kinds of research may be conducted, but all usually follow certain basic steps. There is no perfect research format, although most researchers follow a general organizational plan when conducting their investigations. Such a plan includes (1) problem formulation, (2) research design, (3) data collection methods, (4) analysis of data, (5) presentation of findings, and (6) conclusions.

Problem Formulation

Problem formulation refers to focusing upon a subject for study and defining one or more specific research questions to be answered. Suppose we were interested in juveniles and the extent to which they are represented by attorneys in juvenile court. Given the greater rights extended to juvenile offenders during the last few decades and the increasing criminalization of the juvenile court itself, we might suspect that juveniles have greater cause to use attorney services. Further, we might want to know whether the use of attorneys by juveniles results in greater leniency from juvenile court judges compared with adjudications of juveniles who are not represented by counsel. Finally, we might want to know if attorney use varies according to juvenile offense seriousness, or whether there is greater attorney use by juveniles regardless of the nature of their offense.

This particular research problem is unique, since relatively little is known about attorney involvement in juvenile matters. Also, we have little direct evidence about the impact of attorneys on juvenile court outcomes and leniency. The problem we have selected is noteworthy, in part, because of increasing juvenile violence in recent years. Media attention has focused upon juvenile courts in different states and how especially violent juveniles have been disposed by these courts.

Another problem we might select for study might focus on the factors affecting police officer decisions to engage in a "code of silence," that is, the decision not to report the misconduct of other officers. What factors cause police officers to look the other way when their fellow officers violate the civil rights of persons when making arrests or obtaining evidence?

A third problem we could select for study might involve probationers and their reaction to electronic monitoring. Is electronic monitoring an effective offender management method? Does electronic monitoring reduce the likelihood of offender recidivism?

In each of the previous problems, we will need to collect information from either juvenile courts, police officers, or probationers. We will need to identify potential sources of pertinent information and attempt to collect data that will enable us to answer our research questions.

Research Design

Each of the problems formulated previously requires that we formulate a research plan. This plan is referred to as a **research design.** Research designs are blueprints for research activity. Common research designs include exploratory, descriptive, or experimental research objectives. Do we merely wish to collect information about our research problem and describe what we have found? Do we want to conduct an experiment to determine the effect of one variable upon another variable? The research design, therefore, is our plan of attack. It sets forth the steps we will follow to answer our research questions.

Data Collection Methods

Depending upon the goals of our research, we will use one or more types of **data collection methods.** For the juvenile court study of attorney use, we might obtain information from the National Center for Juvenile Justice. This organization maintains computerized records of juvenile arrest and adjudication activity in every state. These records are kept for many years, starting when each state began automated compilations of juvenile justice information. We may wish to study juveniles in all states, or we may focus our attention on only a few states. We will probably want to narrow our time frame to a block of years, such as 1990 to 1996. This will help us to observe trends in attorney use by juveniles over time. We can also select certain variables for study, such as type of offense, type of attorney (e.g., private counsel or public defender), gender, age, prior adjudications, dispositions, and ethnicity/race.

For the study of police misconduct and the code of silence, no computerized records are likely to be available. We will probably have to interview police officers. We might want to select a large police department for our study site. Since it will be difficult to get reliable information from most police officers about their perceptions of misconduct by other officers, it may be necessary to work with some of our police officer friends, if we have any. Some of our work associates may know officers in various police departments. Working through these connections, we can establish a rapport with a few police officers. With assurances of anonymity, we might be able to obtain much valuable information about the nature and frequency of police officer misconduct.

For the study of probationers and how electronic monitoring might operate to decrease their recidivism, we might wish to contact probation officers. These probation officers can arrange visits and/or interviews with various probationer-clients who are on electronic monitoring. Perhaps the probation office maintains records of recidivism activity for offenders involved in their electronic monitoring program. However, we might wish to interview or send questionnaires to a sample of probationers for additional information. Personal interviews or questionnaires may sensitize us to how electronic monitoring influences probationer behaviors and how these probationers react to this offender management method.

Each research problem suggests one or more data collection methods. More than one data collection method might be used for the same study. Thus, data collection methods are usually selected depending upon the type of research problem we have formulated and the nature of the data required to provide answers to our research questions.

Analysis of Data

Data analysis involves tabulating our information and arranging it into a form that can be interpreted. If we interview probationer-clients, we will need to translate our interview information into useable data. If some probationer-clients have negative reactions to electronic monitoring, we might wish to quote some of their answers to our questions as a way of highlighting these negative reactions. We might also codify the different answers they give to certain questions. Codification means creating categories into which different responses can be placed. Codifying data greatly simplifies our ability to make sense out of whatever we have found.

Tables and charts can also be used in our study of juvenile justice and attorney involvement in juvenile cases. We can chart the percentage of attorney use in juvenile cases over time. We can distinguish between public and private counsel as well. This information can be cross-tabulated with the types of dispositions juveniles receive. Dispositions are tantamount to adult criminal sentences, including probation or jail/prison time. Tabular information can disclose whether leniency toward juvenile offenders varies according to the type of counsel used. We can also examine attorney use trends over time to determine whether the extent of attorney use has actually increased.

Presentation of Findings

Presenting our findings will include the use of tables, figures, and other forms of graphic presentation, including pie charts and bar graphs. These visual effects are supplemented with a more or less extensive discussion of the study highlights. If we have found considerable evidence of a code of silence among police officers, for instance, we can describe it. We can also enrich our discussion with quotations from officers who explain why such behavior is condoned.

In our study of probationers and electronic monitoring, we can describe how electronic monitoring is used and whether it is effective, at least for the sample of probationers we have examined. For the juvenile justice study of attorney involvement in juvenile cases, we can describe attorney use trends for various jurisdictions. We can describe which offenses seem more closely associated with attorney use. We can illustrate differential adjudication and disposition decisions, and this information can be compared with attorney involvement or noninvolvement.

The presentation of findings should be a concise portrayal of what the researcher has found. It should be directly relevant to one's original research questions. Readers should be able to examine the presentation of findings and acquire an understanding of what has been found and how it is interpreted. Tentative answers to one's research questions are provided in this section of one's research report.

Conclusions

The final section of any research report consists of major conclusions based upon the findings and tabulated results. Most researchers adopt a conservative stance when presenting their conclusions. Thus, they regard their conclusions as tentative, subject to further research on the subject. In the spirit of the cumulative nature of scientific inquiry, investigators will consider their own work as merely one additional bit of information that contributes to the growing knowledge of a particular subject. The study conclusions themselves summarize the major highlights.

More often than not, investigators will include in their discussion of conclusions suggestions for future research. These suggestions are often the result of unanticipated problems or emerging new questions found in the course of conducting one's study. No investigator can anticipate every conceivable contingency when a research project is implemented. In almost every investigation, researchers realize that they have omitted certain critical questions from their interview schedules or questionnaires. Perhaps an interviewee says something that leads to a new line of inquiry. It is very difficult to reformulate one's questionnaire or interview schedule in the middle of the study. Researchers may wish that they had included a particular question or added another variable to their questionnaire. These afterthoughts prompt researchers to alert other investigators about how a similar study might be improved in the future. These suggestions for future research are also a valuable source of ideas for novice researchers. Many graduate students have obtained ideas for their master's thesis or doctoral dissertations from "suggestions for future research" sections in research articles.

Finally, the conclusions section might contain various implications of a substantive or theoretical nature. Substantive implications refer to how the information yielded by the study might be used in some practical way to solve contemporary problems. For instance, perhaps probation departments can modify the use of electronic monitoring and supplement it with house arrest and intensive face-to-face visits by probation officers as a means of reducing client recidivism.

Theoretical implications pertain to the use of study findings for purposes of bolstering a particular theory or approach in studying criminological problems. Perhaps the study of police officers and the code of silence might enhance the understanding of the sociological phenomena of primary groups and group solidarity. Theoretical implications are not tied directly to practical applications. Rather, theoretical implications relate to reinforcing existing theoretical schemes or explanations of social events. Can these findings be generalized to a theory of decision making in police organizations? Ultimately, theorizing about decision making or primary groups or group solidarity will be grounded in actual research settings. One or more solutions to practical problems in different organizations might be suggested from theories generated from and modified by criminological research.

ISSUES IN FORMULATING RESEARCH PROBLEMS

It is difficult to refrain from structuring ideal research scenarios for yourself as you prepare to examine one topic or another. One major reason is that most of your academic work in preparation for research, including your statistics and methods courses, has presented you with the ideal way of proceeding under maximally ideal conditions. Many of the articles you have read describing the research of others may have given you the impression that everything proceeded smoothly, without complications of any kind. Few research reports contain detailed descriptions of data gathering, of the actual interviews conducted, of the reactions of others to being observed by researchers and the researchers' assistants. We seldom hear about having doors slammed in the researchers' faces, of investigators being told off by various irate respondents who have been sent questionnaires by anonymous persons and agencies for the past ten years or longer.

This doesn't mean that making ideal plans for investigating certain research problems is necessarily bad or should be discouraged. What it does mean, however, is that often our ideal plans about how to proceed may be fraught with problems, hurdles, and all manner of obstacles from the outset. And that even if everything were seemingly to go as smoothly and perfectly as we initially planned, other obstacles of a theoretical or philosophical nature might intervene and adversely affect the interpretations we have made of our findings. It is good to devise our research plans in ways that adhere to the ideal formulations and conceptions we have learned. But at the same time, we must recognize that in all likelihood, those ideal scenarios we have structured will not be realized fully, and that we will to some extent fall short of them. This is the "gap" between the ideal and real worlds. But the standards to guide us are still in place at all stages of the research enterprise.

The reality is that some departure from these standards is inevitable, and it is the price paid for engaging in research of any kind. Therefore, we must prepare ourselves for these "less than perfect" experiences and for what we will say about our work when it is completed. The researcher decides almost everything about the implementation of a research project and oversees it through its completion. But dealing with people poses various risks and certain problems that widen the ideal–real gap. Even in those research situations, in libraries, where secondary sources are exclusively relied upon for research information, certain problems exist that require us to adjust our original objectives and procedures at various research stages.

It is important that some consideration be given to both ideal and real situations that may be confronted as the investigation progresses. Several pitfalls

George W. Knox
National Gang Crime Research Center,
Chicago State University

Statistics: B.A., University of Minnesota;
M.A., University of Texas at Arlington;
Ph.D., University of Chicago.

Interests: Groups and organizations have always fascinated me. My first gang publication came in 1975 as a result of my master's thesis, surveying delinquents in the Dallas Juvenile Detention Center. My interest in gangs expanded when I got to Chicago for my Ph.D. program. Mentored by Morris Janowitz, taking independent study courses on gangs with Irving Spergel and on neo-Nazi groups with James Coleman, I developed a million intellectual questions about gangs, many of which remain unanswered today.

Upon getting my Ph.D., I did not want to teach. I wanted to do research full time. The American Sociological Association at the time was certifying persons like me as "applied criminologists" (law and social control). It required five years of full-time field experience and publications. I was one of the first six ever to get that now nonexistent designation.

In 1988 I did someone a favor by taking over courses for an ill professor at Chicago State University, and I have found myself teaching there ever since. In 1990, I founded the National Gang Crime Research Center, and in the next year established the *Journal of Gang Research*, a professional quarterly which is in its seventh-volume year. The center carries out large-scale gang research using various methodologies. It disseminates information on gang problems, and provides gang-research training. Obviously, I try to conduct research that is scholarly and penetrates new frontiers, but which is also useful to the practitioner.

may or may not occur in the research we conduct. We cannot forecast their occurrence, but it might be wise to store up various alternate strategies or "Plan B's" in such cases. When things don't go the way we want, when we rely on someone to provide us with certain important information and that person lets us down and fails to provide it, when the findings (for some reason), turn out precisely opposite the way we originally predicted, when we are promised access to an organization and that access is later denied—these are some of the real experiences that frustrate our investigative efforts and contribute to the ideal–real gap. The following list is by no means exhaustive, but it does provide an indication of the sorts of things to be aware of, to possibly anticipate, as the research investigation proceeds.

1. A common pitfall is not containing your research objectives within manageable limits. When a topic is selected, a frequent tendency is to be too ambitious and to extend the problem boundaries beyond your personal means. Researchers must carve out investigations that can be completed within reasonable time frames. For example, it would be foolish, most likely impossible, for graduate students to design a longitudinal study over a ten-year period (e.g., observing a cohort of youths from age 11 until they reach age 21 for purposes of determining factors that may influence some of them to adopt delinquent behaviors), since the graduate schools of their universities limit the time students have to complete their degree work. In many cases, students must finish their research work (e.g., their dissertations and theses) within a six-year or nine-year period after they have completed their coursework. These are maximums, and few students ever stay that long in any given graduate department. Thus, much of the research conducted by graduate students is of short duration. Also, it is common to define a topic in such a diffuse way that there are many loose ends. The researcher may never be able to connect these loose ends within a reasonable time frame.

2. If permission is required to study certain **elements** (persons in this case), it may not be granted. Some investigators may wish to study a sample of juveniles at a secure detention facility, or inmates in a prison or jail. They may do all of their preliminary work, prepare their research design, write their study objectives, define the population to be studied, and construct measuring instruments and questionnaires. Then, when they approach the target institution with their study proposal, permission to interview, observe, or in other ways examine the detained delinquent youths is denied by institution authorities. Even when permission to study a particular setting is granted in advance, that permission may be withdrawn later with little or no notice.

3. When samples of persons are designated for study, some of those persons selected may refuse to participate. If you mail questionnaires to respondents, they may trash them. If you visit people with the idea of interviewing them, they may refuse to be interviewed. This is **nonresponse.** No matter how well you plan ahead and identify persons for investigation, little, if anything, can be done to force them to comply with your requests. Even when your research doesn't involve people directly and your research efforts are exclusively library related, the materials you examine may not always be directly relevant for your specific research interests. Whenever data have been collected by others, their personal objectives may not directly coincide with yours. Therefore, if you design a research project involving the **analysis of secondary sources** in the library, that material may not exist, or it may not exist in the form that would best fit your own objectives. Thus, researchers often adjust their original investigative sights to fit the data available.

4. The instruments designated for studying various samples may be deemed unsuitable, because they may elicit actions on the part of participants that may be detrimental to the goals of the organization. If the proposed research is threatening in any way to the participants or those in charge of specific settings, they may refuse cooperation. Asking prisoners whether their grievance procedures are adequate, for instance, may evoke negative, and unwarranted, responses. It may even provoke lawsuits filed by inmates against corrections officials, if the inmates believe they should be entitled to a grievance procedure they don't already have. Questionnaires are not only a source of information for the investigator, but they can also educate respondents about things that are not always favorable for the organization. For instance, considering the previous example, asking penitentiary inmates whether they have inmate grievance committees or various privileges may precipitate minor rioting if they have no such committees or lack certain privileges. Thus, seemingly innocent-appearing questionnaires can be a key source of future respondent discontent.

5. The measures selected for use in the research project may lack **validity** and **reliability.** This means that even if everything else is going well for the researcher, there is always a problem relating to the adequacy of measures measuring what they are supposed to measure, and also the extent to which these measures are consistent. Measuring social phenomena accurately is a complex task. At the outset, it is important to recognize that our measures of social and psychological variables are flawed in various respects. Besides these instrument flaws, some persons who know they are being studied may act in ways that are different from the way they might behave if they were not being observed. Such behavior is known as **reactivity,** and it can adversely affect one's findings.

6. The problem selected for investigation may have been heavily researched in the past. Regardless of how fresh one's approach to a field of study is, the researchable problem and a solution may have already been implemented and found to be unproductive. This means that recent familiarity with the topic area may not disclose earlier approaches that were not considered noteworthy. The researcher needs to experiment with different research methods, and also with different frames of reference, before actually implementing a research project. It is confusing, and especially frustrating, for a researcher to investigate a problem in a certain way that may have been researched earlier using the same approach, the same explanation, and the same investigatory techniques.

7. The data collection methods selected for use may not be the best for the problem under investigation. Sometimes, researchers will select problems for investigation that lend themselves to specific kinds of data collection techniques. Some techniques may be more appropriate for certain kinds of research than others. Again considering the previous example of inmates, it would be unreasonable to expect researchers to investigate inmate grievance procedures in prisons through the use of surveys (e.g., questionnaire administration). The superficial nature of responses to questionnaires would not provide researchers with a complete picture of the grievance process used by inmates. There might be some hesitancy on the part of correctional officials to disclose their own procedures for processing grievances, and inmates may not be entirely truthful about the administrative and internal grievance mechanisms that are currently in place for the resolution of interpersonal or legal problems, especially when they are required to respond in writing. If correctional officers or administrators see the written responses of prisoners, some inmates may be subject to reprisals later or have their privileges withdrawn. Personal interviews and observations of the grievance process in action would be better depictions of what is going on and why.

8. Depending upon the data collection method used, respondents may say things that they believe the researchers want to hear but are not necessarily true. Investigators have termed these kinds of responses **social desirability,** the propensity of respondents to place themselves in a favorable light when being interviewed or questioned. Black interviewers, for instance, may not obtain truthful answers from white respondents if the subject area has racial overtones. Topics such as race prejudice or the death penalty are touchy subjects for many persons, and often there is an element of cat-and-mouse interplay between an interviewer and an interviewee. Once interviewees sense that the interviewer has a particular attitudinal disposition or mind-set, they may say and do things that they believe the interviewer wants to hear or see. Regardless of whether they are untruthful, their statements of opinion and belief are nevertheless distorted to conform to an acceptable social image.

9. The samples selected may not be representative of the population from which they have been drawn or of the population-at-large. If investigators study police officers in Omaha, Nebraska, for example, how do we know that Omaha police officers are typical of police officers in other jurisdictions, such as Los Angeles, Chicago, or New York? We don't know how typical they are. Thus, some caution should be exercised in generalizing our findings to settings beyond those immediately studied. There is little researchers can do to influence the representativeness of the samples they obtain for research investigation. There are absolutely no guarantees that certain samples are better than others.

10. If subject participation is coerced, responses may not be an accurate portrayal of the subject's real world. Studies of detained juveniles, jail or prison inmates, or probationers and parolees are basically studies involving a degree of coercion. If permission is granted to study persons with any of these or similar characteristics, such research may be tainted by respondent retaliation because of the coercive nature of their involvement. These are captive audiences. Inmates of prisons and jails may deliberately lie to researchers. Detained juveniles may overdramatize their involvement in delinquent activities and admit to juvenile acts they never committed or contemplated committing. Probationers and parolees studied by investigators may feel compelled to participate in research projects because of their belief that failure to comply might dispose their probation/parole officers to file negative reports about them. Again, the coercive nature of their involvement raises the serious question of the meaningfulness of their responses. It is not so much that they will say what they think we want to hear, but rather, they may say what they want us to hear. We have no direct ways of controlling for the influence of coercion on participant responses. We can recognize some of the elements of coercion in the research we conduct and act accordingly and cautiously when interpreting our data.

As noted previously, this is not a comprehensive listing of all of the ideal-real problems that can influence the research enterprise. However, the listing does bring to our attention the idea that many factors can operate in a variety of ways to complicate or frustrate our research efforts and shake the investigation's ideal foundations. Throughout the book, you will detect a strong element of conservatism. This is not political conservatism, but rather a conservatism that urges us to be cautious when collecting data, analyzing it, and drawing conclusions about it. There are simply too many weak points in the research process where things can go wrong. Murphy's Law may apply here: If something can go wrong, it probably will go wrong. Although investigators should be prepared to accept some failure in their work, they should also recognize that research has many rewarding features.

■ KEY TERMS

Analysis of secondary sources
Data collection methods
Elements
Literature review
National Crime Victimization Survey (NCVS)
Nonresponse
Problem formulation

Reactivity
Reliability
Research design
Social desirability
Uniform Crime Reports (UCR)
Validity
Values

■ QUESTIONS FOR REVIEW

1. What is social desirability? How can it distort responses to survey instruments or questionnaires? Is reactivity the same as social desirability? Why or why not? Explain.

2. What is a frame of reference? Do all criminal justice professionals and criminologists use the same frames of reference in approaching a common research problem such as juvenile delinquency? Why or why not?

3. How do values influence our decision making at different stages of the research process? Can you think of any stages of the research process at which our values have little or no impact? If so, what are these stages and why would our values be of little consequence?

4. How do you believe nonresponse might cause our samples to be unrepresentative of the populations from which they are drawn?

5. What are some elements of coercion in data collection? How might coercing respondents cause distortions to occur in our collected data? Think of

two situations (apart from those mentioned in this chapter) in which coercion might be found in the research process.

6. Why is our instrumentation important in testing our theoretical schemes?

7. How do frames of reference influence our theoretical schemes? What is the relation between explanations for research questions (or problems) and our theoretical schemes?

8. Why is it important for researchers to consider both ideal and real aspects of the research process?

9. Who chooses our research problems? What factors can you think of that influence our choice of research topic? In each case, explain how the factor mentioned influences our research choices.

10. Do certain research questions lend themselves to one specific data collection technique and not to any others? If so, what are they?

11. Suppose you decide to study a group of juveniles in detention in a small community. Before you conduct your study, what are some considerations you should make?

12. Who selects frames of reference for our research investigations? What criteria do we often use for selecting certain topics for study and specific frames of reference?

chapter 4

Ethics in Research

■ *Suppose you are against the death penalty. You think the death penalty is morally wrong and you are adamantly opposed to any view that is supportive of it. Suppose you are in a position to do research at a major university. You decide to conduct a survey of attitudes of a random number of persons from the community about whether they are for or against the death penalty. You construct a questionnaire, including items that disclose whether persons are for or against the death penalty under any circumstances. You provide various criminal scenarios (e.g., murder, rape, aggravated assault, hate crimes, drug trafficking, burglary) and ask whether the death penalty is acceptable under any of these circumstances. When you tabulate your results, you learn that about 70 percent of all respondents are in favor of the death penalty for persons convicted of murder. However, about 90 percent of all respondents do not favor the use of the death penalty for the other crimes you have listed. You write a research report saying that "my research found that 90 percent of all persons surveyed are against the death penalty under any circumstances." Other researchers read your study survey and quote you in their own work. You acquire a good reputation over time as a death penalty researcher.*

■ *Suppose you are a researcher in a criminology department at a medium-size university in the Midwest. You are seeking a promotion in rank from assistant professor to associate professor, and you also want tenure. You have been advised by administrators that you must "publish significant research" in refereed journals in order to get your promotion and tenure. You decide to write a fictitious article, describing a study in which questionnaires were distributed to inmates in a prison in a nearby state. You devise an elaborate data analysis scheme, complete with a large inmate sample and interesting research questions. You create fake tables and inmate responses. The study findings are very significant, since you are making them up as you go along. You craft a well-written article based upon this fictitious data and submit it to a prestigious journal. The journal decides that your article is interesting, and with minor editing your article is subsequently published. You show a copy of it to your university superiors and eventually you are promoted with tenure.*

■ *Suppose you are a student in an undergraduate research methods class. The professor has assigned the class a research project involving all students in collecting and analyzing data from various community residents. Suppose the professor gives each student 20 questionnaires with questions about religious affiliation; church attendance; and religious commitment, belief, or religiosity. You are instructed to visit 20 households in the community and ask the heads of these households to complete one of the questionnaires. The professor gives you the names and addresses of the 20 households you must contact. All other students have been given 20 different household contacts as well. You are given two weeks to perform this task. However, it is spring semester and the campus has lots of parties and interesting activities going on. You decide to put off distributing these questionnaires and making house visits and have some fun. When the two weeks are almost over, you realize that you haven't distributed a single questionnaire. You live in a men's dormitory, and you decide to go up and down the hall, knocking on doors. Your friends are asked to fill out these questionnaires for you, as though they were the heads of the households you were supposed to contact. You convince several of your friends to complete these questionnaires, and you fill out a few of them yourself. The following week, you turn in these questionnaires as though they were from the 20 households you were supposed to visit. The professor collects this information and combines it with the other questionnaires. Later, the professor tabulates the different responses to questions and asks the students to break up into groups of five each and prepare a written summary of the study findings as a part of their course grade. You help four other students in the class prepare the report. You get a "B" in the class.*

■ *Suppose you are conducting interviews with various prison inmates in a state prison over a two-week period. Your research is about inmate interactions and you wish to describe day-to-day activities of inmates and what is important to them. You promise each inmate that you will keep whatever they say confidential. As you talk with more inmates each day, some inmates ask you questions about what their inmate friends said. At first you tell them that you have to respect the confidentiality of others you have interviewed. But some inmates get downright nasty and say that they aren't going to talk with you anymore unless you tell them what they want to know. You want information from them, and so you disclose what other inmates said earlier. Some of this information concerns drug trafficking in the prison and is considered sensitive by virtually every inmate. It is a violation of the inmate code to talk about it. After you leave the prison and publish your findings about prisoner interaction patterns and behaviors, referring to the prisoners anonymously, you learn that three inmates at that prison have been mysteriously killed by other inmates. You wonder why that happened, but since you never mentioned any inmate names in your published research, you don't give the inmate murders much thought. You get ready for your next research project, a study of probationers and parolees.*

■ INTRODUCTION

Each of the presented scenarios involves some type of deception. In the first scenario, an investigator presents misleading findings about the death penalty. Instead of reporting that 70 percent of the respondents supported capital punishment for murderers, the researcher deceives readers by reporting that 90 percent of the respondents were opposed to capital punishment under any circumstances. This finding is not true. It is a deliberate attempt to slant the research findings in such a way as to be consistent with the views of the researcher.

The second scenario involves a professor who completely fabricates a research project from beginning to end. The entire project never occurred and the findings are completely fictitious. The professor wants to get promoted and does whatever it takes, including contriving a false study, to get a publication and eventual promotion.

The third scenario involves an undergraduate student who is basically lazy and doesn't want to go to the trouble of completing a class assignment. Instead, he uses his friends to make up answers to questions intended for the heads of households in his community. The questionnaires are meaningless, containing responses from other college students who have no idea how these heads of households would have responded had they been contacted.

The fourth scenario involves a professor who is conducting a study of inmates in a prison. She has promised each inmate that his responses will be confidential. However, pressures from other inmates cause her to violate her earlier promises of confidentiality. Some inmates die as a result of her carelessness and deceit.

In all of these scenarios, **unethical conduct** occurred. Deception of varying degrees of severity was practiced. All of this deception occurred in the context of criminological and social research. This chapter examines the application of ethics to the research process. First, the term *ethics* is defined. Ethical practices in research are distinguished from ethical dilemmas in criminal justice organizations. Ethics and social responsibility in criminological research are discussed.

Several types of ethical problems in the research process are highlighted, including producing fraudulent research; engaging in research that might harm human subjects; deceiving respondents in various ways; accessing and studying confidential records and information; studying sex offenders; and gaining access to subordinates, potentates, and juveniles. The Nuremberg Code is presented and discussed. The ethical codes of conduct of different professional associations are described, including the evolution of ethical research standards and university guidelines for projects that involve human subjects.

The last section of this chapter examines selected ethical issues including sponsored research and investigator interests; informed consent and the use of personal information about victims, arrestees, defendants, and prisoners; fraudulent research; objectivity and research; ethics and public policy; and ethics and evaluation research. The chapter concludes with a consideration of legal remedies for ethical violations.

ETHICS DEFINED

Ethics are the standards of professional groups or organizations, the normative behaviors of right and wrong. Ethics involve the prescription of a moral **code of conduct** that is normatively binding on the members of a professional group or organization. Implicit in accepting membership in an organization is the agreement to abide by the ethical standards of the organization. Violating one or more ethical standards is not necessarily illegal, although other members of the organization would define unethical conduct as immoral and improper. Various sanctions, including exclusion from the group or organization, are applied whenever ethical standards or the code of conduct is violated in any way. For instance, the Academy of Criminal Justice Sciences states that "violations of the Code of Ethics may lead to sanctions associated with membership in the Academy of Criminal Justice Sciences, including restrictions on or termination of that membership" (*ACJS Today*, 1998:14).

ETHICAL PRACTICES IN CRIMINAL JUSTICE ORGANIZATIONS DISTINGUISHED FROM ETHICAL DILEMMAS IN RESEARCH

The focus of this chapter is on the various ethical practices of researchers who identify potential research topics and conduct investigations. The scenarios at the opening of this chapter involved different types of unethical behavior committed by persons conducting research. Existing ethical standards apply to research conducted by members of different professional organizations, such as the Academy of Criminal Justice Sciences and the American Society of Criminology. Fairly clear guidelines of acceptable and unacceptable behaviors exist for all investigators to follow.

Ethics and ethical issues involved in the research process are substantively different from the ethics and ethical issues of law enforcement organizations, the courts, and corrections. In law enforcement organizations, for example, there are codes of professional responsibility. If some police officers engage in misconduct, such as roughing up suspects during routine arrests, these incidents should be reported. When such incidents are observed by other officers and not reported, this is a violation of one of their ethical standards. Officers should testify truthfully on the witness stand in any criminal case. When one or more officers lie on the witness stand, they not only commit perjury, but they also violate one of their ethical codes of conduct (Frank et al., 1995; Prenzler, 1994).

Defense attorneys as well as prosecutors are expected to abide by American Bar Association (ABA) codes of professional responsibility. Defense attorneys are obligated to uphold the confidentiality between themselves and their clients. Any conflicts of interest involving any attorney or court officers are prohibited by certain ABA codes of conduct. If a defense attorney discusses a case with others and discloses confidential information about his or her client, this is considered unethical and a violation of ABA standards (Elliston and van Schaick, 1984). If a prosecutor has reason to believe that a defendant is innocent and has exculpatory information but decides not to disclose it and persists in the criminal prosecution, this behavior is considered unethical and inconsistent with ABA standards. If the prosecutor asks a prospective prosecution witness to give misleading testimony against a criminal defendant, testimony that will tend to incriminate the defendant, this practice may not be illegal but it is considered immoral and inconsistent with the canons of professional responsibility outlined by the ABA (Anderson and Winfree, 1987; Brannigan, Levy, and Wilkins, 1985). If a judge in a criminal case has a relative (e.g., uncle, brother, son, cousin) on the jury and does not disclose this relationship to all parties, this conduct is considered improper. Judges are expected either to dismiss these jurors or recuse themselves from the case. If they don't, then they are violating the ethics of their profession. They may also be violating the law.

In corrections settings, if prison administrators hire their relatives or close friends to perform correctional officer functions or lower-level administrative tasks, such nepotism, though not necessarily illegal, is probably unethical and/or immoral. If jail or prison correctional officers ask certain prisoners to "snitch" on other prisoners concerning institutional rule violations, or if these

Box 4.1

Celesta Albonetti
University of Iowa

Statistics: Ph.D.(sociology), University of Wisconsin at Madison

Interests: Sociology of law, organizational theory, criminology.

During my graduate work at University of Indiana at Bloomington, I became interested in studying discretionary decision making in the courts. I worked on a grant to study bail, guilty pleas, and sentencing decisions in the federal courts, with John Hagan and Ilene Nagel as principal investigators. I worked on the sentencing section of the grant and especially with sentences involving white-collar offenders. Our findings were published in the *American Sociological Review* in 1982. Looking back, reading works by John Hagan, Abraham Blumberg, Herbert Packer, Austin Turk, and W. Boyd Littrell ignited my interest in conducting research and understanding how discretion in the adjudication process affects outcomes during the pretrial and sentencing stages.

My interest in doing research intensified at the University of Wisconsin at Madison, where I took courses in sociology of law in both the sociology department and the law school. The research assistantships during my graduate training gave me ample opportunity to apply to my study of the courts the statistical techniques that I was learning in my courses. The social significance of the decisions made in the adjudication system in terms of depriving persons of their liberty, and the realization that these decisions were played out so frequently in informal negotiations added to my desire to conduct research on discretionary decision making in federal and state courts.

My research has attempted to identify the effects of defendant characteristics, legally relevant case information, and process variables on prosecutorial and judicial discretion. Two studies of prosecutorial discretion uncovered the strong effects of the defendant-victim relationship, gender, and a prior record of felony convictions on prosecutors' decisions to pursue prosecutions at the initial screening stages and later at the postindictment stages of adjudication. These studies revealed that prosecutors systematically consider case information that is unrelated to the strength of evidence.

My research on pretrial release outcomes in the federal system found that the defendant's race, stratification resources (education and income), and community ties affected the severity of the bail outcome. Black defendants received less advantage from their education, income, and ties to the community at the bail hearing than did white defendants. My recent studies of sentencing under the Federal Sentencing Guidelines indicate that judicial departures from the guidelines strongly reduce sentencing severity for white-collar offenders. In addition, the research reveals that blacks and Hispanics receive substantially less sentence reductions from guidelines departures compared with whites. Taken together, my work has sought to contribute to the fields of criminology and sociology of law by empirically testing theories that suggest that disadvantaged groups in society are also disadvantaged throughout the criminalization process.

officers smuggle contraband to certain prisoners and overlook rule violations, such conduct is often a violation of their code of professional responsibility as outlined by the American Correctional Association (American Correctional Association, 1993).

Whether we are discussing law enforcement, the courts and court officers, or corrections, we are dealing with professional codes of conduct and responsibility that govern the behaviors of persons performing different organizational roles. The performance of each role in these different types of organizations will involve either ethical or unethical conduct. These forms of ethical or unethical conduct are not relevant for this chapter. The only forms of such conduct examined here are behaviors that relate to the research process.

■ ETHICS AND SOCIAL RESPONSIBILITY

All ethical matters pertaining to the research process involve **social responsibility.** Each of us assumes that if we engage in research, we will be socially responsible and not do anything that departs markedly from the boundaries of professional propriety. We expect that others who do research will behave similarly. The product of one's research is eventually going to be consumed by others. When we read the research of others, we have a legitimate expectation that the investigators followed certain rules throughout the entire research process. Thus, we can rely on the evidence they have presented as genuine.

Does the End Justify the Means?   Those of us who conduct research of any kind, however, eventually realize that different persons have different interpretations of what it means to be socially responsible. Social responsibility is a relative term. Some researchers will condone minor or drastic departures from codes of accepted conduct, while other researchers will be intolerant of any departure from accepted standards of behavior. For example, an investigator mailed a survey questionnaire to several thousand persons in different states. The cover letter said that "all responses are confidential and anonymous." A self-addressed, stamped envelope was conveniently enclosed in order to encourage those contacted to respond. But the investigator was interested in knowing the identities of the respondents. In a seemingly unobtrusive way, the investigator used invisible ink to mark the insides of return envelopes. Thus, when each questionnaire was returned, a chemical was used to reveal the numerical code on the inside of the envelope, and each respondent's identification code was written on their questionnaire by the researcher. This deception seemed innocent enough. The investigator considered the written assurance of anonymity a necessary white lie, since the only purpose was to identify respondents and utilize public information available from city directories. Later, such information could be correlated with respondents' answers on the questionnaires. However, several other researchers learned about this deception and were openly critical of it on moral grounds. Was the investigator who engaged in this deception immoral or unethical? Were any respondents harmed by this deception? It is unlikely that any respondent was ever harmed. But this ignores the fact that a lie was told in order to induce research subjects to return their questionnaires.

Does a Large Response Overwhelm Minor Departures from Scientific Procedure? In another research project, an investigator collected 400 ten-page attitudinal questionnaires from students in a large introductory criminology class. The researcher discovered that among the questionnaires, several revealed missing information. For instance, some of the pages on some of the questionnaires were simply blank, as though the pages had been skipped. In truth, some of the student respondents were in a hurry to answer the questions and therefore careless, simply turning two or three pages at once, not recognizing that they had skipped pages. Approximately 15 questionnaires had missing information. Instead of throwing out these questionnaires, the researcher merely filled in the blank spaces with fictitious choices. Later these questionnaires and responses were combined with the other 385 questionnaires and research results were yielded. Even though less than 4 percent of all questionnaires contained small portions of fictitious information, the study was eventually published in a popular criminological journal. No mention was made of the incident involving the missing data or the manufacture of fictitious information. The investigator later admitted, "Well, I didn't think it'd hurt anyone. What I did made no difference to the final result anyway!"

What if the researcher had reported the information just from the 385 valid questionnaires? Suppose that this valid information was very similar to that filled in by the researcher on the incomplete questionnaires. Suppose the researcher was right, and that the inclusion of these false responses made no difference to the final result anyway. Was this an unethical act? Yes. Was this a violation of any particular code of professional responsibility or conduct? Yes. Did it hurt anyone? Probably not. But whether anyone is injured by these particular actions of researchers misses the point of the results of these unethical behaviors. The point is that proper procedures were violated and conventional research rules were not followed. The reported research evidence was unreliable to the extent that these violations occurred.

It is apparent that whenever unethical research conduct occurs, it is seldom evident and detected. Often this misconduct occurs behind closed doors, and the researcher is the only one who knows whether proper research procedures were followed. Unless the researcher tells others about not following proper procedures or admits to the misconduct, there is little that can be done by any professional organization to correct the problem.

Several reasons exist for the difficulty in detecting unethical research practices. The major reason is that it is customary to present findings in an anonymous context. A study of plea bargaining might occur in "a large southern state" or "in a large, urban western county." Prisoners may be studied at "a large state prison in the Midwest." Thus, some unscrupulous researchers are protected from discovery by the very guarantees of anonymity that are extended to most research subjects. If lawyers in "a large Midwestern state" are interviewed, how do we know *which* lawyers in *which* state? We don't know. If we don't know, we cannot verify or authenticate any of the reported information.

Another reason why it is difficult to detect unethical research practices is that much of the time, data analysis, interpretation, and dissemination is directly within the absolute control of the individual investigator. If the investigator chooses to be deceptive or dishonest, who is going to know about it?

Sometimes, the findings reported by unethical researchers are so outrageous and inconsistent with the research reported by others that we are alerted to possible research dishonesty. But here again, we are prevented from verifying or authenticating the research since we don't know who was contacted and interviewed. Furthermore, contradictory and inconsistent findings are endemic to criminological and social research of any kind. No subject is free from inconsistencies. We have no way of knowing whether an anomalous finding is the product of deception and dishonesty or an actual research inconsistency in comparison with other studies.

No one knows how much dishonesty occurs. By far the majority of researchers engage in reputable projects, which are often sponsored by legitimate organizations, such as the National Institute of Justice or the Office of Juvenile Justice and Delinquency Prevention Programs. But such sponsorship does not immunize any researcher from misrepresenting or "massaging" data in ways that slant research findings one way or another. Much research is also unsponsored. This fact does not mean that unsponsored research is inherently inferior to sponsored research. Most persons who conduct independent investigations of criminological phenomena do so in scrupulously ethical ways. Ultimately we must have faith in other investigators who report their findings to us in diverse outlets.

ETHICS AND CRIMINOLOGICAL RESEARCH

Criminological research and studies of the criminal justice system are ideal breeding grounds for a variety of ethical issues. Criminal behavior is interesting to study. However, investigations of criminal behaviors and criminals are often intrusive. Whether juveniles or adults are studied, the matter of confidentiality arises. It is imperative in many investigations that criminologists and criminal justicians have access to information that only criminals can provide. If criminals are interviewed, observed, or surveyed, they may disclose potentially damaging information about themselves or others. Researcher integrity protects a respondent's anonymity and the information shared with investigators.

A few examples are in order to illustrate some of the ethical problems that are created in the process of studying criminals and delinquents. Suppose you are conducting interviews with various probationers and parolees. As a researcher you want to know how these probationers and parolees are responding to their probation and parole programs. You ask these offenders about themselves, about their use of drugs and alcohol, and their general conformity to program rules. In the course of your interviews, you might ask these clients whether they have committed new crimes. Thus, through self-reports, these clients disclose considerable information about themselves. Some of this information might get them into trouble if it came to the attention of their probation or parole officers. Suppose a probation officer asks you how your study is progressing. In your conversation with the probation officer, you might say that some of the clients are having trouble complying with program rules. The probation officer may push you to reveal if any program violations have occurred that have previously been undetected. Under this pressure, you might reveal what you have been told by others. This information could have serious implications for certain probationers.

In a study of delinquent youths in Provo, Utah, during the early 1960s, for instance, the Ford Foundation funded research about the subculture of delinquency. Researchers worked with the juvenile court in Provo to obtain more than 200 juvenile participants in a delinquency prevention experiment over a three-year period. In small groups, delinquents were encouraged to share their delinquent experiences with other group members, and then they were to introspect and determine why they had committed these delinquent acts. Open conversation among these youths was encouraged by researchers who promised total anonymity and confidentiality, regardless of whatever was said or disclosed in these group sessions. All group sessions were tape-recorded.

One goal of the group therapy was to enable these youths to understand the etiology of their delinquent conduct and form close social bonds with other delinquents. As they came to understand why they had committed their delinquent acts, they could actually unlearn their delinquency in the same group milieu in which they originally acquired their delinquent attitudes and behaviors. This method of creating substantial attitudinal change was premised in part on the confidentiality of the situation. However, researchers were pressured by police and the courts to reveal whatever these boys had said in the context of their closed-group discussions. Researchers learned much from the boys about unsolved community crimes and who had committed them. Some of the perpetrators were participants in these groups. But despite the pressure to disclose information, the investigators respected the boys' confidentiality and refrained from reporting them to police. It would have been highly unethical of these researchers to violate the confidences of these boys, and such behavior probably would have defeated an otherwise successful delinquency intervention program.

The fact is that criminologists are thrust into many situations in which they are obligated to respect the confidentiality of others they examine. For example, if they wish to study the cultural context of marijuana production in the hills of Kentucky, or if they want to examine the attitudes and opinions of prisoners at Leavenworth, or if they want to study a delinquent gang and understand gang operations, they must be prepared to honor their code of ethics and respect the confidentiality of their respondents, especially if they have guaranteed it. Information yielded by respondents in different situations can be quite damaging to them if made available to the wrong persons, agencies, or organizations. Thus, it is imperative that persons used as respondents in research and experimentation should be made fully aware of the implications of their involvement. Their informed consent to participate as subjects in research is an essential respondent right.

■ TYPES OF ETHICAL PROBLEMS IN RESEARCH

Several types of ethical problems in research have been described. These include (1) plagiarism; (2) fraudulent research and statistical manipulation; (3) research potentially harmful to human subjects; (4) deception or lying to respondents; (5) accessing confidential records and information; (6) studying sex offenders, including examinations of their sexual histories and conducting stimulus-response experiments on them; and (7) granting permission to study subordinates, potentates, and juveniles.

Plagiarism

Plagiarism means to use someone else's published work and represent it as your own. It is a type of fraud in which the ideas and/or work of others is used without acknowledgment. If you borrow a term paper from another student, put your name on it, and submit it to a professor as something you have written, this is plagiarism. If you quote from one or more sources and do not cite these sources, this is plagiarism. In the early 1990s at California State University at Long Beach, for instance, some graduate students in the Department of Criminal Justice obtained an "A" grade on a term paper written by a California Highway Patrol officer. All of the corrected term papers for a given class were placed in a tray outside the professor's office so that students could claim them. A graduate student picked up the patrol officer's paper surreptitiously. Other students tore off the cover sheet containing the name of the patrol officer and put their own names on the paper. The same paper was recycled at least half a dozen times in subsequent criminal justice courses before this plagiarism was discovered. The highway patrol officer had been unwittingly exploited by other students. Once the plagiarism was detected, the students received failing grades in the courses where the patrol officer's paper had been "recycled" by them.

Double-Duty Papers.   Another form of fraud is to use the same paper you have written in more than one course. More than a few students write a term paper for one course, and then they decide to replace the cover sheet with a new course title and submit the same paper again. Thus, the student obtains course credit by using the same paper again and again. Some professors may accept papers prepared originally for other courses, but most professors would consider this practice unethical.

Plagiarism by Professors.   Students aren't the only ones who commit plagiarism. Various investigators have used the work of others without proper citation or referencing. Sometimes the author of an article submitted to a professional journal will replicate lengthy passages from articles written by others. This is also plagiarism. If detected, the plagiarist may be barred from publishing in the journal to which the article was submitted. Professional organizations may also sanction the plagiarist in different ways, such as withdrawing his or her membership and other privileges. If the plagiarist is a faculty member at a university, the university may consider such plagiarism as grounds for dismissal or reduction in academic rank.

Mail-Order Papers.   In an increasing technological age of computers and information access, numerous paper services exist on the Internet and elsewhere, offering papers for a fee on a variety of subjects for different college courses. Anyone can order one or more papers from these sources. The papers are represented as original and properly referenced. The usual marketing strategy is to offer papers on different topics, noting the number of references used. Some students order these papers and submit them in their courses. It is increasingly difficult to detect this type of plagiarism when it occurs, but it is clearly unethical.

Dual-Submissions of Articles to Different Journals and Other Outlets.
Another unethical practice committed by article writers is simultaneously submitting the same article to two or more journals. The article review process is time-consuming. Sometimes it takes up to six months or more for an article to be reviewed. With increasing pressure on professors to publish, time is precious. Some professors do not want to wait for these reviews. Further, the rejection rates for certain high-quality journals are high. As many as 95 percent of all journal articles submitted to *Criminology* and *Justice Quarterly* are rejected annually. The *Journal of Crime and Justice* has a rejection rate of 75 to 80 percent. With these high rejection rates, more than a few professors might be inclined to submit their research articles to more than one journal at a time. The major problem is that two (or more) journals may decide to publish the same article at the same time. Sometimes these decisions are made without proper notification of the author. When the article eventually appears in two or more journals, readers consider the author to be unethical. Thus, most journals today have a **dual-submission policy,** advising authors that it is against journal policy to review any submitted article that is presently under review by another journal.

When I was editor of the ACJS/Anderson Monograph Series on *Issues in Crime and Justice* (1993–1996), I had the occasion to work with the co-editors of a collection of original essays. These co-editors had spent a great deal of time screening numerous articles and essays for inclusion in their work. Eventually, they had narrowed their selection of articles to 12. As the project moved toward completion, I received a telephone call from one of the co-editors. He was very upset. It seems that one of the original articles accepted for their edited work had just appeared in a major journal. I inspected the journal article as well as the article submitted for publication in the Monograph Series. Sure enough, both articles were identical. The titles were different, but the articles were the same. Both the co-editors of the book and I wrote the authors of the article and chided them for this dual submission. They had warranted that their work was original and unpublished elsewhere. But the journal publication told a different story. It is clear what they had done. And these were professionals at a prestigious university. They had been unethical in their dealings with me and the co-editors of the work, and I told them so. Luckily, we had caught this duplicity in time to remove the article from the edited work. It was never published in the Monograph Series.

Fraudulent Research and Statistical Manipulation

Fraudulent research occurs when the study or significant parts of it are fabricated or falsified. An investigator might invent a population and sample to study. Fake data are invented and analyzed. Perhaps no real analysis ever occurs. The researcher simply invents tables and inserts fictitious data in them. Statistical tests are applied to these fictitious data, and meaningless results are yielded. Bogus conclusions and implications for future research are discussed. The "significance" of the research is described. The fake research is published in different outlets, such as journals and periodicals. Other professionals may reproduce these fake studies in books of readings, not realizing that the material is falsified.

The "publish-or-perish" pressure generated by virtually every university causes some professors to resort to falsifying studies or study findings. If professors don't publish, or if they don't publish significant results, they may not be promoted or granted tenure at their collegiate institutions. They may even be terminated for failing to publish. When one's livelihood is seriously threatened under these "publish-or-perish" conditions, the production of fraudulent research may result.

Or in another case, an investigator may actually carry out a legitimate research project. He or she may collect data from real human subjects and may actually tabulate and analyze the data. However, the actual results yielded by the study may not be significant or worthwhile to anyone. Editors of most journals are reluctant to publish studies in which nothing significant was found. They therefore become silent co-conspirators with universities and colleges by rejecting articles lacking significance or originality and increasing "publish-or-perish" pressures. (In past years, some short-lived journals made fun of the more prestigious journals, including *The Journal of Irreproducible Results* and *The Journal of Insignificant Findings*.)

When insignificant or nonsignificant data exist, an investigator may change the distribution of responses in tables and graphs so that statistical significance increases or occurs. As a major consequence, the investigator can write up the study, showing that the findings are significant in different respects. The fact that the study findings are now "significant" enhances the chances of the article being accepted for publication in some journal or periodical. And the chances of promotion and tenure for the professor are also greatly improved.

Research Potentially Harmful to Human Subjects

Some research may be harmful to **human subjects.** The research may be either biologically or physically harmful or psychologically harmful. During World War I, the U.S. military experimented with various types of noxious gases to determine their debilitating effects. Inmates from prisons were typically used as human guinea pigs in these experiments. At that time, prisoners had few rights and could not effectively challenge the legality of their forced participation in these experiments. Some inmate deaths occurred, and more than a few inmates suffered chronic or serious side-effects from exposure to these gases and other substances.

Well into the 1940s, many male inmates of prisons in Oklahoma and Virginia were routinely sterilized or castrated. It was believed at the time that criminal behaviors were genetically transmitted. Thus, if criminals were castrated or sterilized, then they could not pass on hereditary criminal characteristics to a new generation. Mass sterilization and castration of male prisoners were considered valuable means of future crime prevention. Prevailing criminological beliefs suggested that these practices were fully warranted as aggressive measures to prevent future criminality. Today these practices are considered unlawful and no longer used. However, from time to time, a judge will offer sex offenders, both male and female, the option of sterilization as an alternative to hard prison time. Such judicial actions have been declared unconstitutional.

The Tuskegee Syphilis Study.   One of the most notorious medical experiments of the twentieth century occurred from 1932 to 1970. It has become known as the **Tuskegee Syphilis Study,** carried out at the Tuskegee Institute under the auspices of the U.S. Public Health Service. At the time, little was known about syphilis, a sexually transmitted disease. It was known that if left untreated, syphilis would cause degeneration of the bones, heart, and nerve tissue. Death usually resulted. Penicillin was available as a known treatment for syphilis at the time, although investigators were uncertain about how penicillin worked. They succeeded in soliciting nearly 1,000 black male laborers as volunteers. All of these volunteers had syphilis. Researchers treated one-half of all subjects with penicillin, while about 400 of these laborers were not given anything to treat their syphilis. At least 425 of these blacks subsequently died from syphilis. While experts concede that the study yielded much information about how penicillin acts on spirochetes, the parasitic bacteria that cause syphilis, the study itself was a most inhumane biomedical experiment (Brandt, 1978).

The Tearoom Trade.   Some potentially harmful research is unobtrusive, in that the researcher observes others without their knowledge. In the late 1960s, Laud Humphreys investigated male homosexual behavior. He secreted himself in certain locations in public restrooms, known as "tearooms," and observed numerous homosexual encounters. On some occasions, he represented himself to homosexuals as a voyeur or "watch queen," who wanted to watch others perform sex acts. Later, he followed these persons and wrote down their automobile license plate numbers. Using his connections with the police department, he learned where these persons lived and later visited them, pretending to be a mental health professional.

Humphreys discovered much about persons who carry on homosexual liaisons with others in public restrooms. His investigation revealed much about the sociodemographic characteristics of homosexuals. Humphreys defended his research by claiming that no one was ever harmed by his unobtrusive observations of their behaviors. He never disclosed the names of any of the homosexuals to the media, and he scrupulously maintained their anonymity. However, his research was widely criticized as unethical, inasmuch as he failed to disclose to those he observed that he was a social scientist who was studying homosexuals. He never gave these persons the option of refusing to participate in his research. Humphreys (1970) contended that he was under no obligation to disclose his research intentions to those he observed. In fact, he said, these persons were more than willing conspirators in his observation of them as a voyeur. Admittedly, it is unlikely that Humphreys would have obtained such extensive information about homosexual behavior patterns if he had advised all of those he observed of his true research intentions. But did this fact necessarily justify his actions and deceit? Did the ends justify the means used to gather important information?

Obedience Research. In the 1970s Stanley Milgram, a professor at Yale University, conducted several experiments involving obedience to authority. Milgram was interested in explaining why so many Germans and others routinely carried out orders from superiors in World War II and executed millions of Jews in death camps.

At Yale University, Milgram (1974) constructed a small laboratory where he could conduct **obedience research** experiments. He hired a middle-aged man to act as his "stooge" and pretend to react in certain ways in response to how other persons treated him. The experiment involved 40 student volunteers, who would sit at an electrical panel and administer a series of progressively more severe electric shocks to the stooge, who was sitting in a chair and hidden from view on the other side of the electrical panel. The experimenter explained to his volunteers that the study involved a word-association learning test. An electrical shock would be administered to the stooge each time he gave an incorrect answer. Each time an electrical shock was administered, the intensity of the next electrical shock would be increased by 15 volts. The shock range was from 15 to 450 volts. The electrical panel showed various levels of volts, with printed words showing "Slight Shock" to "Severe Shock." In reality, the electrical panel was fake, and there were no shocks administered to the stooge. However, each volunteer believed that he was administering increasingly severe electrical shocks to the stooge, referred to as the "learner." Each time the learner gave an incorrect answer, an electric shock would be administered by the volunteer at the direction of the experimenter. A red light on the instrument panel would blink as the "shock" was administered to the stooge. The experiment was structured so that the learner would give a sufficient number of "incorrect" responses so that excessive shock voltages would have to be administered.

Milgram wanted to see how far these volunteers would go when ordered to administer progressively more severe electrical shocks. As each volunteer sat at the instrument panel and apparently administered increasingly severe electrical shocks to the stooge, the stooge would cry out or hit the wall with his fists, as though he were responding to the painfulness of the shocks. Although the volunteers were reassured that the shocks, regardless of their severity, would not cause any permanent tissue damage or scarring, the situation created severe emotional conflicts for many of the volunteers.

Milgram found that five volunteers refused to administer any shocks beyond the 300-volt range. However, he found that 26 out of the 40 volunteers administered the most intense 450-volt shock when ordered to do so. Milgram concluded that his study supported the idea that even when senseless orders were given to inflict pain on anonymous test subjects, many persons would obey these orders without hesitation and administered seemingly severe shocks. Thus, the study helped researchers to understand the motivations and responses of subordinates in death camps in Nazi Germany during World War II.

More than a few critics contended that Milgram's research was unethical in several respects. Deceit was practiced when the experimental subjects were not advised that they would not actually be harming anyone. Of course, had they been advised of this fact, it would have defeated the whole purpose of Milgram's experiment. Some deception, therefore, was essential if the experiment was to be considered valid. Other critics took issue with the whole idea of subjecting persons to an emotionally exhausting experience in which they thought that they were causing injury to a test subject. Was such an experiment ethical? Could Milgram have studied his theory of obedience in ways that would not have been controversial? Probably not.

Zimbardo's Simulated Prison Study.   Philip Zimbardo, a professor at Stanford University, conducted an experiment that was perhaps even more controversial than Milgram's study. Zimbardo (1972) solicited and paid student volunteers to act as either prison guards or prisoners. A "prison" was constructed in several rooms in the basement of a building on the Stanford University campus. Some students were designated as "guards," while others were designated as "prisoners." The experiment was designed to last two weeks. Prisoners were issued inmate jumpsuits or smocks and shower caps, while guards were issued guard uniforms, nightsticks, and other guard-related equipment. Prisoners were fed regularly, and they had bathroom facilities and cots. Zimbardo wanted to study the interaction patterns of prison guards and inmates through this simulation.

After the student volunteers were chosen, they began to play out their roles. Guards became increasingly abusive, both physically and verbally. Prisoners were dehumanized and began to act both passive and hostile toward their keepers. The experiment was short-lived, however, when the emotional strain became too much for some of the prisoners. After only six days, Zimbardo terminated the experiment because of certain adverse effects observed among the various student participants.

Zimbardo, who also played the role of warden, was criticized for this research, since the emotional states of experimental subjects were altered in different ways. Zimbardo defended his research, observing that the students had knowingly volunteered for the experiment and were, in fact, being paid well for their participation. He contended that it was never his intention that anyone would be physically injured or psychologically abused as the result of the experiment. However, evidence to the contrary suggested that several students emerged from the experiment with serious emotional scars.

It is clear that social research of any kind may generate harmful effects upon human subjects. We cannot possibly know all of the potential adverse consequences of conducting experiments involving human subjects, regardless of how innocent our research objectives and procedures may appear. Certainly Zimbardo, Milgram, and Humphreys never expected that others would cast aspersions on their research and label them as unethical.

Deception: Lying to Respondents

Deception is used in social research projects as a means of obtaining unbiased research results. In several studies, human subjects are advised that their responses are anonymous, when in fact the researcher knows exactly who they are. This type of deception is justified by these researchers as a way of preserving the objectivity of respondent's reactions (Vohryzek-Bolden, 1997).

Deception is also used whenever investigators infiltrate social groups that they wish to examine. For example, if someone wishes to study juvenile gangs, they might hire certain juveniles to join these gangs and report gang activities and behaviors to them. On other occasions, social scientists might pose as bikers and join biker's groups such as the Hell's Angels for a period of time. The intent of these researchers is to describe the behavior patterns of close-knit gangs of either juveniles or adults. Access to these gangs would ordinarily be restricted, and conventional requests to study these gangs by social scientists would also be rejected.

At the University of California at Riverside, a married couple joined a "swinger's" club, where persons would routinely swap spouses for sexual intercourse. The couple joining the swinger's club was actually a pair of sociologists who wanted to study the behavior of swingers and describe the culture of swinging. They participated in the swinger's club for a year, including the physical intimacy of sexual intercourse with other couples. At no time did they advise the club that they were researchers collecting data. Eventually, they left the club and wrote a book about their swinger experiences, detailing the culture of swinging and swinger norms and behaviors.

Is any of this deception justified? If we were to be totally truthful with the groups we wanted to study, would we be permitted to study them? If these groups knew who we really were and were aware of our true research purposes, would *they* deceive *us* by behaving differently? Under what circumstances, if any, is deception warranted for certain research purposes? While deception is generally disapproved of by professional codes of ethics, the fact is that deception is practiced by at least some researchers every year. No precise figures are available to indicate the extent of deception in the research process, although it is probably relatively infrequent.

Accessing Confidential Records and Information

An incredible amount of information is available about people through the Internet and various official sources. Public statistics are published on a regular basis by different governmental agencies and organizations. Nevertheless, much information is privileged and confidential.

Box 4.2

Mark Blumberg
Central Missouri State University

Statistics: B.A. (sociology), University of Kansas; M.A. (criminal justice), State University of New York; M.A. (sociology), University of Kansas; Ph.D. (criminal justice), State University of New York.

Interests: The impact of HIV/AIDS on criminal justice policy; myths regarding crime, drugs, and the justice system; police use of deadly force.

I became interested in these issues because of the misinformation that often appeared in the mass media. For example, there was a great deal of public hysteria regarding HIV/AIDS in the early days of the epidemic. Much of this was fueled by misleading and alarmist information that was being presented on television. This motivated me to examine such issues as whether prisons and jails really were breeding grounds for the transmission of the AIDS virus, whether correctional officers were at risk of infection as a result of their occupational duties, and whether a sizeable number of female sex-workers were transmitting HIV to their male clients. My research indicated that none of these scenarios were in fact true.

I was able to write numerous journal articles and book chapters that examined various aspects of criminal justice and correctional policy that were impacted by the AIDS virus. Eventually, I was able to turn much of this material into an edited book published by Prentice-Hall, entitled *AIDS: The Impact on the Criminal Justice System.* There is nothing more satisfying than to receive a call from a person working in an agency and be told that my work has been helpful in clearing up various misconceptions and developing sound policies for their agency.

Advice to Students: I would advise students not to accept the conventional wisdom presented by the media. Students should do a thorough review of the literature and not limit their search to criminal justice publications. In my own work, I consulted journals and periodicals in the fields of medicine, law, psychology, sociology, and public health.

Governmental Safeguards to Ensure Confidentiality. In 1973, the federal government established confidentiality provisions to shield persons from the prying eyes of researchers. Under the Omnibus Crime Control and Safe Streets Act, the government proclaimed that no officer or employee should disclose to anyone any research or statistical information of a personal nature, including any research sponsored and funded by the federal government. The intent of this provision was to protect research subjects from having personal details of their lives disclosed to others, apart from those actually conducting the research. Thus, it would be both illegal and unethical to disclose specific information about research participants when they could be easily identified by name. Such a provision, however, would not preclude any legitimate governmental agency, such as the Internal Revenue Service, a U.S. district court, or U.S. probation office, from securing personal information about any person targeted for investigation.

It would, therefore, be unethical for a researcher to disclose personal information about research subjects involved in a study sponsored by the National Institute of Justice or the Office of Juvenile Justice and Delinquency Prevention. In almost every case in which researchers obtain sensitive information for their research, they refer anonymously to the research subjects studied. It is not their intent to name individuals or their characteristics.

Creating Anonymity and Disclosing Confidential State Data.   Some confidential information may be provided when personal identification characteristics have been obliterated. In 1994, a woman was completing her master's degree at a North Dakota university. She telephoned officials at two juvenile detention facilities in Mandan and Minot. The Mandan facility was a secure juvenile institution containing about 150 juveniles, while the Dakota Boy's Ranch in Minot contained about 75 boys. The graduate student was interested in examining only "closed files," files of boys who were no longer in confinement. Authorities permitted the researcher to inspect 250 records of juveniles, where the names of juveniles had been omitted. Thus, even though this information was originally confidential and privileged, it was released to the woman with the provision that the identities of all boys would not be known. Subsequently the student wrote a master's thesis detailing the use of risk or dangerousness scores of youths and the varying lengths of their placement in these secure facilities. It was unnecessary to know the names of these boys to realize her specific study objectives. No ethical codes were violated.

On Ethics and Dating.   In another case involving juvenile records, a graduate student at California State University at Long Beach was dating a woman who oversaw juvenile records for the city of Long Beach. The graduate student was also a Long Beach police officer. He was interested in collecting data for a master's thesis and wondered if his female companion could assist him in inspecting juvenile files. The woman agreed to let him inspect these files, which had been maintained in a secure area of a city building since the early 1960s. Ordinarily, these files are closely guarded, and few persons are granted access to inspect them. She even let him photocopy numerous files and prepare them for research analysis. He was also allowed to carry these files from the building and study them for several weeks. This was a very questionable action on the woman's part. No doubt the fact that she and the police officer were dating was the sole reason she allowed him to inspect and use otherwise confidential juvenile information.

Because of a shift change in his work schedule, the police officer had to postpone his graduate work for a few months. In the interim, he ceased dating the woman and returned the juvenile files. About three months later, when his shift schedule was changed again, he decided to pursue an inspection of some of these juvenile files that he had earlier examined. When he went to the city building and department where these records were maintained, a different woman was on duty. She advised him that his previous acquaintance had been transferred to another department. When the officer asked to inspect the juvenile records, this woman said that under no circumstances, other than with a court order, could he examine these sensitive records. Furthermore, she said, she was going to report the other woman, his acquaintance for permitting him to illegally inspect these records on an earlier occasion. According to the police officer, he finally persuaded the new woman to agree to forget about the incident. He did not study these juvenile files for his master's thesis research.

Sex Offenders: Sexual Histories and Stimulus-Response Experiments

Studies of sex offenders and the methods used to treat them have raised several ethical issues. Public sentiment against sex offenders was heightened when a New Jersey sex offender stalked, sexually assaulted, and murdered a young child. New Jersey passed Megan's Law, a significant piece of legislation requiring that all sex offenders register in the communities where they reside; notify community leaders of their residency; and suffer lengthy civil commitments if they are regarded as serious, dangerous, and mentally ill (Brooks, 1996). Considerable attention has also been directed toward the treatment of sex offenders and preventing them from committing new sex crimes.

In the 1970s researchers conducted experiments with sex offenders using aversion therapy. Sex offenders would be exposed to various visual sexual stimuli (e.g., graphic sexual photos and scenes), and then they would receive electrical shocks or chemical injections that would tend to make them ill or nauseous. These and other similar treatments were largely unregulated and unstandardized. The result was that some sex offenders were permanently injured or suffered psychological traumas well beyond the scope of the intended treatment and the goal of sex crime prevention (Wardlaw, 1979).

In the 1990s experiments with sex offenders continued, with greater regulation and control. For male sex offenders, one method of charting their reaction to sexual stimuli was phallometry, or penile plethysmorgraphy, which measured erectile function of their penises resulting from exposure to visually stimulating sex scenes. Such methods have been deemed well suited to challenge sex offender denials that they are stimulated by sexual deviance of any kind. Investigators have used phallometry and other methods to assess a sex offender's treatment needs and to predict future deviant sexual behavior (Launay, 1994).

Despite the effectiveness of these and other treatment methods, several investigators have raised ethical questions about the assessment and treatment procedures used and the amenability of patients to counseling. Relatively little has been done to provide aftercare for sex offenders in communities. Further, professional guidelines have been espoused by some of those who treat sex offenders. These guidelines include the development and design of more standardized stimulus material to discourage patient faking; providing more reliable data; and carrying out validation studies with forensic and nonforensic populations, which would include detailed analyses of subjects' sexual histories, motivations, and fantasies (Launay, 1994).

Granting Permission to Study Subordinates, Potentates, and Juveniles

Often, researchers contact heads of organizations and agencies for the purpose of studying their employees or obtaining different kinds of information about them. Investigators who study inmates in prison settings, for example, will contact prison administrators to obtain their permission to study prisoners. Prison wardens and others in authority want to know how much time it will take and what type of inmate involvement will be required. Do researchers wish to interview certain inmates? Do researchers want to distribute self-administered questionnaires to inmates? Do researchers want to study prisoners on death row or those maintained in maximum-security areas? Who is sponsoring the research?

Granting Permission to Study Subordinates. If investigators wish to study probation officers, they may contact probation agencies and discuss their contemplated research plans with agency heads. Sometimes agency heads or administrators will consent to have the researcher study their agency personnel. Investigators may be at liberty to use every potential resource and contact in the organization to their research advantage. If a researcher has a friend who is politically connected with others in agencies or organizations where certain information is desired, then this friend can make appropriate introductions. This doesn't mean that permission will automatically be granted to study persons in these settings, but at least the researcher has an opportunity to make a pitch for why the study should be conducted.

Investigating Potentates. Some investigators want to study the characteristics of law enforcement administrators, chiefs, commissioners, and other functionaries. These persons are often insulated from the public. They are **potentates** or very powerful people. Gaining access to these people is difficult. It is helpful if the researcher is connected with an established agency, university, or research institution. Using agency, university, or research institution letterheads and auspices, researchers can often get their foot in the door of offices that would otherwise be closed to them. Before any researcher decides to study special samples of potentates, it is a good idea to determine whether or not they can be accessed by conventional research methods.

Studying Juveniles and Their Records. Juveniles pose particularly difficult problems. Numerous protections and safeguards are in place to shield juveniles from research investigations. If a researcher were to show up at an elementary school and ask the principal to distribute a questionnaire to all fifth-grade students concerning their possible delinquent conduct, there is no doubt that the researcher would be turned away and flatly refused admission. If investigators wished to inspect juvenile court records and study delinquency trends, they would quickly find that these records are safeguarded from the general public, including social scientists.

Most juvenile courts have retained their status as civil bodies. When juveniles are declared delinquent by juvenile court judges, they are not convicted of crimes. Rather, they are adjudicated delinquent in a civil proceeding, and at a later date when they become adults, their records will likely be sealed or expunged. Many authorities believe that youths who get into trouble should not have their juvenile records count against them as adults. Thus, in a majority of states, the records of juvenile offenders are either expunged or sealed when the juveniles reach adulthood. This means that only a limited number of agencies or officials can gain access to these records at some later date. These records are not available for public inspection.

Increasing numbers of states, however, are changing their policies concerning the privacy of and restricted access to these juvenile records. In some states these juvenile records are maintained for many years beyond one's age of majority or adulthood. Removing the cloak of anonymity from juveniles and their records is a relatively new strategy used to combat delinquency and crime. Traditional methods for dealing with delinquency have been ineffective, and many juveniles express contempt toward juvenile courts because of their known leniency. The new "get-tough" movement toward crime has extended to juveniles so that accountability for their actions has been heightened. Making juveniles who commit crimes increasingly visible to the public is one way of making them take a new look at the law and their own responsibilities. Despite the get-tough movement and its effects, it is still difficult to obtain juvenile records or study juveniles in most jurisdictions.

■ THE NUREMBERG CODE

During World War II, Nazi Germany engaged in mass genocide against Jews and others. The German dictator Adolf Hitler believed in the purity of Aryan and Nordic ethnicities, meaning certain white Germanic peoples, and thought that Germany should be ethnically cleansed of all non-Aryan persons. Numerous death camps were established in several European countries controlled by German troops, and routine executions and exterminations occurred over a period of years. During World War II it is estimated that more than 6 million Jews were put to death in these camps.

At the same time that Jews were being executed, more than a few Nazi physicians were conducting inhumane experiments on people calculated to change "less desirable" biological characteristics and features of prisoners to "more desirable" features. For example, consistent with the blond, blue-eyed Nordic ideal envisioned by Hitler and his close associates, German physicians injected blue dye into the eyes of brown-eyed patients/prisoners in the fruitless effort to change their eye color. The testicles and ovaries of thousands of Jews were removed surgically, without anesthetic. Some of these experiments were designed to discover how much pain human beings could endure before dying. Other experiments were conducted in which men, women, and children were made to stand nude in rivers during the cold winter months. These experiments were calculated to test how long it would take for persons to freeze to death under varying conditions of exposure to the elements.

These atrocious experiments, and many others, were subsequently revealed and described at the Nuremberg, Germany, trials of war criminals following World War II. Many surviving victims testified against those who tortured them in the name of medical science. When the trials of war criminals were concluded, several countries including the United States adopted what became popularly known as the **Nuremberg Code,** a set of principles specifying conditions under which human subjects could be used in social and medical experiments. The critical provisions of the Nuremberg Code that have become widely adopted by virtually every research institute are that (1) any experimental subject must participate in any research project on a voluntary basis and give their **informed consent,** and (2) any potential research participant must be advised of any known or anticipated harmful effects arising from the contemplated experiment before the research is undertaken.

Despite these standards and potential safeguards, some agencies and individuals have conducted unethical and illegal experiments. During the Vietnam war in the early 1970s, for example, several experiments were conducted by various military investigators. These experiments involved knowingly exposing selected samples of American soldiers to different chemical agents. For example, Agent Orange, the code name for a highly toxic herbicide, was used extensively in the jungles of Vietnam to remove vegetation where enemy troops could hide. Numerous soldiers were exposed to Agent Orange and contracted serious illnesses, and more than a few died. Other experiments were conducted with LSD and other drugs to determine their behavior-altering effects on soldiers. In the early 1990s, American soldiers were once again exposed to toxic chemicals in Operation Desert Storm, a military action against Iraq.

■ PROFESSIONAL ASSOCIATIONS AND THE DEVELOPMENT OF ETHICAL STANDARDS FOR RESEARCH

Most national, social, and criminological professional organizations in the United States have evolved codes of ethical standards for researchers to follow. Because of the diverse views and opinions of persons in these different organizations, consensus has been difficult to achieve and some codes of professional responsibility and conduct are in different stages of revision. Some of these organizations moved to adopt codes of ethics in the 1990s. In 1996, the American Society of Criminology established a committee charged with the responsibility of drafting a code of ethics acceptable to its membership. In 1998, an Ethics Committee was formed by the Academy of Criminal Justice Sciences (ACJS) at its annual meeting in Albuquerque, New Mexico. Both of these organizations tended to emulate the code of ethics established years earlier by the American Sociological Association.

A good example of a **code of ethics** is the one evolved by the ACJS. Ethics committee members originally crafted a detailed document, outlining a code of ethics and other standards. In December 1998, the seventh draft of this code of ethics was published in the *ACJS Today*, a bimonthly newsletter sent to the membership. The draft was published in order to permit all members to examine it and vote on whether it should be adopted as ACJS policy at its annual meeting in Orlando, Florida, in 1999. It is beyond the scope of this book to reprint the entire text of this document. Rather, a 22-point section will be reprinted that pertains to "Objectivity and Integrity in the Conduct of Criminal Justice Research." The relevant text follows:

III. Ethical Standards.

Objectivity and Integrity in the Conduct of Criminal Justice Research.

1. Members of the Academy should adhere to the highest possible technical standards in their research.

2. Since individual members of the Academy vary in their research modes, skills, and experience, they should acknowledge the limitations that may affect the validity of their findings.

3. In presenting their work, members of the Academy are obliged to fully report their findings. They should not misrepresent the findings of their research or omit significant data. Details of their theories, methods, and research designs that might bear upon interpretations of research findings should be reported.

4. Members of the Academy should fully report all sources of financial support and other sponsorship of their research.

5. Members of the Academy should not make any commitments to respondents, individuals, groups, or organizations unless there is full intention and ability to honor them.

6. Consistent with the spirit of full disclosure of method and analysis, members of the Academy, after they have completed their own analyses, should cooperate in efforts to make raw data and pertinent documentation available to other social scientists, at reasonable costs, except in cases where confidentiality, the client's rights to proprietary information and privacy, or the claims of a field worker to the privacy of personal notes necessarily would be violated.

7. Members of the Academy should provide adequate information, documentation, and citations concerning scales and other measures used in their research.

8. Members of the Academy should not accept grants, contracts, or research assignments that appear likely to violate the principles enunciated in this Code, and should disassociate themselves from research when they discover a violation and are unable to correct it.

9. When financial support for a project has been accepted, members of the Academy should make every effort to complete the proposed work on schedule.

10. When a member of the Academy is involved in a project with others, including students, there should be mutually accepted explicit agreements at the outset with respect to division of work, compensation, access to data, rights of authorship, and other rights and responsibilities. These agreements should not be exploitative or arrived at through any form of coercion or intimidation. Such agreements may need to be modified as the project evolves and such modifications should be clearly stated among all participants.

11. Members of the Academy have the right to disseminate research findings, except those likely to cause harm to clients, collaborators, and participants; those which violate formal or implied promises of confidentiality; or those which are proprietary under a formal or informal agreement.

Disclosure and Respect of the Rights of Research Populations by Members of the Academy

12. Members of the Academy should not misuse their positions as professionals for fraudulent purposes or as a pretext for gathering intelligence for any individual, group, organization, or government.

13. Human subjects have the right of full disclosure as early as it is appropriate to the research process, and they have the right to an opportunity to have their questions answered about the purpose and usage of the research.

14. Subjects of research are entitled to rights of personal confidentiality unless they are waived.

15. Information about subjects obtained from records that are open to public scrutiny cannot be protected by guarantees of privacy or confidentiality.

16. The process of conducting criminal justice research should not expose respondents to more than minimal risk of personal harm, and members of the Academy should make every effort to ensure the safety and security of respondents and project staff.

17. Members of the Academy should take culturally appropriate steps to secure informed consent and to avoid invasions of privacy. In addition, special actions will be necessary where the individuals studied are illiterate, under correctional supervision, minors, have low social status, are under judicial supervision, have diminished capacity, are unfamiliar with social research, or otherwise occupy a position of unequal power with the researcher.

18. Members of the Academy should seek to anticipate potential threats to confidentiality. Techniques such as the removal of direct identifiers, the use of randomized responses, and other statistical solutions to problems of privacy should be used where appropriate. Care should be taken to ensure secure storage, maintenance, and/or destruction of sensitive records.

19. Confidential information provided by research participants should be treated as such by members of the Academy, even when this information enjoys no legal protection or privilege and legal force is applied. The

obligation to respect confidentiality also applies to members of research organizations (interviewers, coders, clerical staff, etc.) who have access to the information. It is the responsibility of administrators and chief investigators to instruct staff members on this point and to make every effort to insure that access to confidential information is restricted.

20. While generally adhering to the norm of acknowledging the contributions of all collaborators, members of the Academy should be sensitive to harm that may arise from disclosure and respect a collaborator's need for anonymity.

21. All research should meet the human subjects requirements imposed by educational institutions and funding sources. Study design and information gathering techniques should conform to regulations protecting the rights of human subjects, regardless of funding.

22. Members of the Academy should comply with appropriate federal and institutional requirements pertaining to the conduct of their research. These requirements might include, but are not necessarily limited to, obtaining proper review and approval for research that involves human subjects and accommodating recommendations made by responsible committees concerning research subjects, materials, and procedures (*ACJS Today*, 1998:15–16).

Notice in the code of ethics that certain elements of the Nuremberg Code have been incorporated into items 13, 14, and 16. Reassurances of respondent anonymity are also pervasive throughout the document. Most of the other provisions of this code of ethics address matters relating to researcher conduct. Essentially, investigators are admonished by this code to be honest, objective, and sensitive to proper research procedure that characterizes the discipline.

■ UNIVERSITY GUIDELINES FOR RESEARCH PROJECTS: THE USE OF HUMAN SUBJECTS

Colleges and universities are known for conducting extensive research on virtually every academic subject. Botany and other sciences, such as chemistry and physics, seldom rely on the participation of human subjects for experiments. However, the social sciences, including sociology, psychology, anthropology, criminology, and criminal justice, conduct numerous studies and experiments in which human subjects are involved.

Most of the time, social scientific research consists of soliciting information from human subjects in different contexts. Probation or parole officers are interviewed or surveyed in order to determine their work interests and motivation. Inmates of prisons and jails may be studied for various reasons. Corrections officers and administrators might be studied. Judicial decision making or plea bargaining between defense counsels and prosecutors might be investigated. Patterns of behavior might be described. The decision-making process in law enforcement might be portrayed.

University professors and both undergraduate and graduate students carry out ongoing research to answer various questions relating to their discipline.

Most of the time, conventional data collection techniques are used, including questionnaires or surveys, interviews, and/or observation. Seldom are research subjects exposed to chemical substances or drugs, or to other physical stimuli that might expose these subjects to some type of biological harm or injury.

Despite the fact that much criminological research seems harmless to humans in terms of the potential for adverse physical or biological effects, it is possible for them to suffer certain psychological effects. In fact, exposure to certain types of questions, either in interviews or on questionnaires, is an educational experience in a sense. Interviewers and investigators may actually trigger certain thoughts and ideas among their respondents. Some respondents may feel that "Whatever these interviewers are asking me must be important. Perhaps I ought to be concerned about it." Furthermore, merely asking respondents questions in their work settings or habitats may set off chain reactions that substantially change these work settings or habitats.

For instance, as a graduate student, I studied a sample of bank employees near my university. This was an integral part of my doctoral dissertation and research. I thought my questions were harmless. Among other things, I wanted to know about employee job satisfaction and work motivation. When I gave questionnaires to these bank employees and interviewed them, I sensed that they were very uncomfortable with the questions I asked. Later I confided my feelings about their reactions to a bank officer who had earlier granted me permission to study these employees. She nodded knowingly and said, "You don't know this, but we had a large amount of money missing a few months ago. We decided that all of our employees must submit to a lie detector test or lose their jobs. We had to find out who embezzled the money. Needless to say, the morale of these employees went through the floor. They have been unhappy campers ever since!" Suddenly I understood the significance of their reactions to me. I was the "enemy" in a sense, since my study coincided with the embezzlement. How were they to know I was acting independently of the bank and doing research for my own self-interest?

Later, as a professor at a large university, I had the occasion to prepare a simple questionnaire and send it home with students in my research methods class. The questionnaire was a survey of parents' opinions about different topics. None of the questions contained anything offensive, at least in my view. About a week later, I was called into the office of my department head. He handed me a large envelope containing one of my questionnaires. It had been torn into many pieces. He advised me that one of the parents had visited him earlier that day and told him that he didn't want "any damn professor" at the university giving his daughter some "sex" questionnaire. He didn't want that "filth" in his home. I was flabbergasted. The only reference to sex in my questionnaire was an item indicating whether the respondent was male or female. The other questions were items about the United States space program and how space on the moon might be utilized if somehow we were eventually able to cultivate it. Other items were of a sociodemographic nature, such as urban-rural background, age, years of education, religious and political affiliation, and other factors. I showed another copy of my questionnaire to the department head and he immediately recognized the overreaction of the parent.

Subsequently I was approached by the woman student whose father had torn up my questionnaire. She apologized for his behavior and explained that a few weeks earlier, a psychology graduate student had given her psychology class a questionnaire inquiring about the sexual habits and behavior patterns of college students. Her father happened to see the questionnaire as she was completing it at home. Some of the items asked about sexually explicit details of one's behaviors. Her father threw a fit and spent several hours cursing the university and its professors. He hadn't even read my questionnaire, assuming that if another professor at that "damned university" sent a questionnaire home with his daughter, it must be like the first one. Thus, because of the thoughtlessness of one graduate student, the reputation of the university was irreparably damaged for at least one parent.

Today most universities and colleges have policies and provisions relating to research conducted under their sponsorship. Any research project conducted by any university employee must first be reviewed by a **human subjects committee** or **institutional review board.** This committee ascertains whether there are any aspects of the research that might potentially be harmful to human subjects. The committee determines which safeguards, if any, have been implemented to ensure that human subjects are protected. Such screening of research projects is imperative especially if any drugs or experimental substances are used or if human subjects might be exposed to biological or physical harm.

When human subjects are going to be interviewed, exposed to questionnaires, or observed, the research instrumentation and methodology are scrupulously examined to determine if there are any potentially offensive or psychologically harmful effects. Provisions are made for human subjects to be made fully aware of the research goals or purposes. Human subjects must be in a position to give their informed consent, and they may decline to participate.

These and other safeguards are incorporated into human subjects committee policies. One purpose is to protect the university from subsequent lawsuits if any physical or psychological harm to any human subject occurs. Another purpose is to ensure that all researchers conform to the codes of ethics of their professions. The point is that everything that can be done is done to protect human subjects in every way. At least that is how any university-sponsored research should ideally proceed. But, there are few sanctioning mechanisms in place in most schools to prevent professors from conducting various types of social research on their own. Anyone can create a questionnaire, photocopy it, and mail it to numerous respondents. It is quite difficult to police such independent research efforts. Despite university and professional ethical standards, there are always some persons who depart from them from time to time.

ETHICAL ISSUES

Ethical issues in research studies include (1) whether the research is sponsored by an outside agency or the individual investigator, (2) the rights of human subjects, and (3) informed consent and how personal information about subjects is used.

Sponsored Research and Investigator Interests: Choice or Chance?

Money is available from external sources to fund research projects. A substantial number of consumers who accept external research funds are university faculty. Most universities and colleges have **seed money** available, or small monetary sums to assist individual faculty in modest research projects. Usually seed money is furnished to professors in order to help defray their paper and postage costs as they prepare questionnaires and distribute them to a chosen set of respondents. If a professor wants to study the local police department or survey its officers, for instance, there will be some expense incurred as the research progresses. Duplication and mailing of questionnaires may be expensive. If the investigator wishes to use interviewers to gather some of the data, then these interviewers will have to be paid. Students are sometimes used as part-time interviewers. Small amounts of $1,500 to $2,000 may be available for faculty to use for these limited research purposes to help defray investigation costs.

The National Institute of Justice and Office of Juvenile Justice and Delinquency Prevention are two agencies that fund criminal justice and criminological research. These organizations issue requests for research proposals, or RFPs, on an annual basis. They provide guidelines for the preparation and submission of proposals, where prospective investigators describe their research ideas and how they intend to implement them. Committees within these different agencies review submitted proposals and select those for funding that appear to fit agency guidelines and needs.

One example of requests for proposals is seen in the National Institute of Justice Solicitation for Fiscal Year 1997. A 12-page booklet was mailed to thousands of persons throughout the United States in June 1997. It was entitled *Policing Research and Evaluation: Fiscal Year 1997*. The booklet contained hundreds of suggestions and requests for research proposals on a variety of topics. The NIJ solicitation contained the following:

> In this solicitation, NIJ seeks local evaluations that will contribute to our understanding of police agencies' efforts to move toward community-oriented policing. NIJ is particularly interested in learning of efforts to implement community-oriented policing across a variety of community settings including cities, rural communities, small towns, and sheriff's departments. In addition to understanding the process of implementing community-oriented policing, NIJ seeks evaluations that advance our understanding of the consequences of specific community-oriented policing strategies, practices, and styles, including: recruitment and training strategies; use of performance and reward structures; the realignment or redefining of supervisory roles; and strategies that promote collaboration or resource-sharing with other public and private agencies and institutions . . . NIJ anticipates supporting up to 7 awards of varying sizes totaling up to $1.5 million. (National Institute of Justice, 1997:2–3)

In the same publication, the NIJ stated that it

is interested in the application of problem-solving strategies across a range of topics, including firearms violence, especially among youth; illegal gun markets; gangs and gang violence; the changing nature of drug markets; family and intimate violence; prostitution, panhandling, and other illegal street solicitations; and other predatory crimes, such as auto theft, auto robbery, and ATM-related robbery . . . grants will be made for up to 24 months. Multisite research is encouraged. NIJ anticipates supporting up to 12 awards totaling up to $2 million under this section of the solicitation. (National Institute of Justice, 1997:3–4)

For NIJ purposes, small grants range from $1,000 to $50,000. Large grants are in excess of $50,000.

This is **sponsored research.** Applicants for this and other grant money must tailor their research proposal to fit the interests of the funding agency, such as NIJ. Thus, if a professor applies for NIJ funding, the proposal must be directly relevant for a specific NIJ interest, even though the NIJ says, "While NIJ encourages potential applicants to identify the specific area under which their research application should be considered, promising research applications that *do not fit precisely within a given section of this research agenda* or that may cross over areas may still be considered" (National Institute of Justice, 1997:2, italics added).

Being the Director or Being Directed?   There is a clear difference between doing one's own research and doing research for others. In the former case, a research project is envisioned, planned, and implemented. The research goals and aims are outlined by the investigator. The investigator determines how data will be collected and how they will be presented and interpreted. The summary and implications of the study will be totally within the control of the researcher. However, in the latter case, when the researcher receives grant money from an external agency such as the NIJ, the interests of the agency are of primary importance. In the case of the NIJ, this organization chooses the research topic, not the researcher. The research objectives for any specific project within NIJ guidelines are also chosen by the NIJ.

For many researchers, the difference between choosing specific research topics and engaging in studies involving predetermined research topics is irrelevant. Rather, the most important consideration is receiving funding. This is because universities and colleges evaluate professors in part on their ability to secure external research funds. Promotions and tenure are granted in part on the basis of one's success in securing research grants from virtually any source.

Some researchers consider doing work under the sponsorship of a federal agency or a private corporation as a form of intellectual prostitution. Investigators are paid for performing a service, not necessarily of their own choosing. This ethical issue generally arises as the result of doing sponsored research. Using the previous NIJ example, it is clear from the solicitation that the NIJ favors and supports community-oriented policing. One method of implementing community-oriented policing is to involve different community elements (e.g., neighborhoods and neighborhood leaders, different ethnic groups and races, business persons, labor organizations). Any integrative theme that explores ways to facilitate acceptance of community-oriented policing is encouraged as a research objective. Similarly, the focus of the NIJ on firearms violence, illegal gun markets, and gangs and gang violence mildly suggests that research on gun control, a policy opposed by organizations such as the National Rifle Association, will be favored.

When an investigator accepts federal money from the NIJ for a specific research purpose, this does not mean that the researcher will deliberately slant findings from the study to fit the goals of the agency agenda. Rather, the entire research project is couched in a particular context that may or may not be consonant with the researcher's own interests and agenda. Presumably, researchers who apply for external funds from any agency or organization have some interest in the topics proposed for study. Thus, in practice, the issue of the ethics of doing sponsored research may be a relatively unimportant one.

Rights of Human Subjects

The rights of human subjects involved in any criminological investigation are addressed in the codes of ethics of relevant national organizations, such as the American Society of Criminology and the Academy of Criminal Justice Sciences. Regional organizations, such as the Midwestern Criminal Justice Association, Southern Criminal Justice Association, and Western Society of Criminology, have evolved or are developing their own codes of ethics to apply to their respective memberships.

Any federally sponsored research today automatically includes regulations promulgated by the Department of Health and Human Services and the National Research Act of 1974. Some of the regulations pertain to the informed consent of research subjects who are or may become involved in any study supported by federal funds. One consequence of the National Research Act was the establishment of institutional review boards on university campuses. Institutional review boards are internal committees that screen research proposals when federal funds are solicited. The screenings are designed to protect the rights of human subjects who may become involved in the proposed research. These screenings are especially important for biomedical experiments and studies, in which the potential for physical harm is heightened. For social science proposals, the potential for human subject harm is minimized. Nevertheless, these screening committees scrutinize all research proposals to determine if all ethical standards are properly observed. Institutional review boards may also screen projects for which federal funds are not sought. These boards may evolve their own standards apart from those mandated under the National Research Act.

Informed Consent and the Use of Personal Information: Respecting Confidentiality

Informing research subjects about their participation in research may mean communicating with specific types of respondents involved in the criminal justice system in different ways. These types of respondents include (1) victims, (2) arrestees and defendants, (3) prisoners, and (4) persons involved in illegal behaviors.

Victims.   Some criminal justice researchers are interested in crime victims and how they respond or react to being victimized. Perhaps a researcher wants to study police investigation and police report writing in which one or more victims are involved. It has been found that in at least some jurisdictions, police officers do not always file reports from victims who have been robbed or assaulted even though they are supposed to do so (Barker and Carter, 1990). One of the most frequent reasons given for not filing reports is avoiding the extensive paperwork involved in writing up a street crime incident, which some police officers tend to trivialize. The incidents are certainly not trivial to the victims, however, especially when personal injuries have been inflicted by the perpetrators. Thus, interviews with various crime victims may disclose certain police officer improprieties. Researchers may learn the names of police officers who investigated the complaints of several victims. Seeking out these officers or examining their paperwork, or lack of it, may create further problems for crime victims. Officers involved in these incidents may retaliate in different ways. They may harass some of these crime victims. Therefore, attention must be given to preserving victim anonymity in such investigations. Their confidentiality must be respected (Esbensen, 1991).

Frequently victims testify at parole hearings or provide written reports about how they have been affected by a perpetrator's crime. These reports are victim-impact statements, and they are often appended to presentence investigation reports prepared by probation officers. Some convicted offenders are very vindictive toward those testifying or giving negative information against them. In the state of Washington, for instance, a female rape victim testified against the rapist who was sentenced to 10 years in prison. When the rapist was released, he tracked the woman down to her home in Oregon and killed her. He had obtained information about her relocation through documents filed by the probation officer who had prepared the rapist's presentence investigation report. While this information was not generated by a research investigation, it was collected in a way that did not protect the woman's anonymity and whereabouts from public scrutiny, including a request for information from the rapist himself.

Over time, a victim's bill of rights has been established to protect crime victims from further victimization. In the late 1970s, the New York State Compensation Board established a bill of rights for victims of serious crimes. Among other provisions, the victim's bill of rights includes the protection of victims from criminal violence. Furthermore, victims must be kept informed by law enforcement agencies of the status of the defendant(s) in custody and if and when the defendant(s) are released. They should be notified of a plea bargain arrangement or any other discretionary disposition of their case. They should also know the release date of the incarcerated defendants.

Any studies of crime victims should include provisions for their informed consent and protection. The information they provide investigators should be treated as confidential. Any victim surveys should be sensitive to the ethics of survey research (Garofalo, 1977).

Arrestees and Defendants.   Arrested persons and criminal defendants are sometimes selected for research investigations. Since these persons have not yet been convicted of a crime, information they might disclose to interviewers could be regarded as potentially incriminating. Sometimes arrestees are eventually released without formal charges being filed against them. Many persons arrested for spousal assault fit this scenario (Williams and Hawkins, 1992). Researchers might contact potential subjects when their names have been reported in local newspapers as alleged spouse abusers. Follow-up interviews with these persons might be conducted in an effort to determine the factors that contribute to spousal violence.

Prisoners. Inmates in jails and prisons are literally captive audiences. Historically, prisoners have been subjected largely to biomedical experimentation, involving tests of prescription drugs and other substances (Schroeder, 1983). Involuntary treatment of mentally ill prisoners with antipsychotic drugs and other types of social or medical intervention has sometimes resulted in inmate deaths or serious personality and physical disorders (Burlington, 1991; Schroeder, 1983; Todd, 1975). Inmates are often in the position of failing to comprehend the full nature and scope of their involvement in social or medical experiments (Schroeder, 1983). There is the very serious question of whether mentally ill inmates can give their informed consent for full research participation in such experiments (Burlington, 1991). Indeed, the very nature of prisons may be so inherently coercive that it would be virtually impossible for any inmate to give an informed consent to being a subject in research (Smodish, 1974).

For criminologists and others who conduct social research, investigating inmate populations is largely a matter of distributing self-administered questionnaires and/or direct interviewing. But researching inmate populations is not as simple as it seems. For instance, some researchers have conducted extensive interviews with death row inmates and their families (Goldhammer, 1994). Other research has involved the families of death row inmate victims (Dicks, 1991; Smykla, 1987). Interviewing any death row inmate is an emotional experience. Interviewers know or have good reason to suspect that the persons they interview will eventually be executed for their crimes. It is difficult to retain objectivity under such circumstances.

Some studies of death row inmates and the conditions under which they are supervised and maintained are designed to advance political agendas. For instance, Amnesty International is an organization that opposes the death penalty for any reason and under any circumstance. Amnesty International has conducted studies of death row inmates in several prisons, including Oklahoma State Penitentiary (Amnesty International, 1994). Predictably, Amnesty International proclaimed the Oklahoma maximum-security unit, where death-row inmates are housed, as a good example of what is meant by cruel and unusual punishment. Amnesty International noted the physical conditions, such as windowless cells, inadequate exercise yards, the length of confinement (23½ hours per day), isolation, and the lack of education or other ameliorative programs.

Inmates are now afforded certain rights by prison administrators. Thus, they may refuse to become involved as research participants. Most prisons have informed consent provisions to guard against involuntary participation in social research projects. The concern for inmate rights is almost universal, with provisions to protect inmates implemented in Australia, England, and Japan (Bowery, 1997; Dixon, 1997; Yokoyama, 1994).

People Involved in Illegal Behavior and Self-Reports. Harold Grasmick, Robert Bursik, and John Cochran (1991) studied 330 adult respondents who disclosed religious and tax-related information about themselves. These researchers wanted to know what factors might be influential for deterring persons from cheating on their income taxes. Respondents disclosed in **self-reports** certain factual information about their religious commitment. Also, they furnished information about the likelihood that they might violate the law and not pay their full taxes. It was found that persons who were deeply religious were more inclined to pay their full share of taxes in order to avoid potential social embarrassment and shame. While this study is interesting, it depicts a situation in which the respondents were asked to admit to illegal behavior, that is, whether or not they paid their taxes in full. As information about these respondents was collected, the investigators were in the position of identifying tax cheaters.

Kevin Minor (1988) studied 45 delinquent youths who had been adjudicated by the juvenile court and placed on probation. Minor was able to obtain self-reports from these youths about their illegal activities. He was particularly interested in the effectiveness of an intervention program for reducing their illegal activity. The intervention program involved job preparation workshops, outdoor adventure experiences, and family relationship counseling. While Minor's findings were inconclusive, the fact is that Minor obtained a substantial amount of incriminating information from these delinquents about illegal acts they had committed.

Were Grasmick, Bursik, and Cochran under any special duty to report their tax cheaters to the Internal Revenue Service? Should Kevin Minor have reported to police the fact that certain delinquent youths had admitted to various illegal acts? In these instances, the illegal behaviors were not reported to the IRS or any law enforcement agency. The information solicited by these researchers was generated in a research context, regardless of the illegality of it.

Sometimes investigators discover information about research participants that may not be illegal but is otherwise potentially dangerous to others. For instance, an investigation conducted by Ralf Jurgens and Norbert Gilmore of prison inmates in a Canadian federal correctional institution led to the identification of several HIV-infected prisoners (Jurgens and Gilmore, 1994). In the context of examining the state of correctional health care, were these researchers under any obligation to report that certain prisoners had the HIV virus? In another similar study of HIV among prison inmates, Hammett and Dubler (1990) found that when HIV-infected inmates were identified in different U.S. prisons, they were administratively segregated from the rest of the inmate population and treated differently. Thus, their confidentiality was not respected and they considered themselves discriminated against because of their illness. The fact that certain inmates were discriminated against because they were HIV-infected raises a serious ethical question. For some investigators, the ethical question is difficult to answer. The rights and interests of HIV-infected inmates must be recognized. However, the direct, hazardous risk of HIV to uninfected inmates must be considered as well. Thus, the dilemma exists over whose rights are more important. Prison institutions have already resolved this matter by segregating infected inmates from uninfected ones. But investigators should recognize that depending upon the details of their investigations in such settings, ethical considerations will emerge that are not easily resolvable.

■ KEY TERMS

Code of conduct
Code of ethics
Deception
Dual-submission policy
Ethics
Human subjects
Human subjects committee
Informed consent
Institutional review board
Nuremberg Code

Obedience research
Plagiarism
Potentates
Seed money
Self-reports
Social responsibility
Sponsored research
Tuskegee Syphilis Study
Unethical conduct

■ QUESTIONS FOR REVIEW

1. What is meant by ethics? What are the purposes of codes of ethics for professional organizations?

2. How can we distinguish between ethics in the research process and ethics involved in the performance of law enforcement or corrections work?

3. Why is it difficult to detect fraudulent research when it occurs?

4. What is plagiarism? What are some forms of plagiarism?

5. Why is the dual-submission policy of professional journals important?

6. What was the significance of Stanley Milgram's obedience research?

7. What ethical problems were obvious in the study of the "tearoom trade" by Laud Humphreys?

8. What is the Nuremberg Code and why was it established? Is it applicable today? What elements of the Nuremberg Code have been preserved in contemporary codes of ethics?

9. How is deception harmful to human subjects? What are several forms of deception?

10. Whenever juveniles are studied, what safeguards are taken to preserve their confidentiality? Why are these safeguards in place?

11. What is an institutional review board? What are its functions?

12. What ethical problems are associated with sponsored research?

13. What is meant by informed consent? Under what conditions should informed consent be extended to research participants?

chapter 5

Research Designs

INTRODUCTION

The research interests of criminologists and criminal justice professionals are limited only by their imaginations. Any social setting is a potential target for scientific examination, whether it is a prison or probation agency or something else. Despite the diversity of subject matter that criminologists and others might study, all types of social scientific research are characterized by a limited number of types of research plans or research designs. Research designs are detailed plans that specify how data should be collected and analyzed.

This chapter describes various types of research designs, including explorative, descriptive, and experimental plans. The goals and functions of these research designs will be discussed. Given space limitations, it is not the intention of this chapter to cover all possible designs that may be applied in criminological research. Rather, several plans have been selected for discussion—those that appear to have the greatest amount of utility in terms of their frequency of usage throughout the research literature.

QUALITATIVE AND QUANTITATIVE RESEARCH

There are many different kinds of research conducted by criminologists and criminal justicians. Often, two broad categories are used to distinguish between different types of research. These categories are qualitative and quantitative. Qualitative research is the application of observational techniques and/or the analysis of documents as the primary means of learning about persons or groups and their characteristics. Sometimes qualitative research is called fieldwork, referring to the immersion of researchers into the lives and worlds of those being studied. Investigators may observe persons or groups from afar, or they may join groups and describe their experiences and interactions with group members. Qualitative research is intended to enrich our descriptions of social settings and persons participating in them. Such research offers a level of detail that is generally missing from a self-administered questionnaire or interview situation.

One example of qualitative research is the work of Richard A. Wright and Colette Soma (1996). These investigators were interested in describing the most-cited scholars in criminology, based on a citation analysis of several popular criminology textbooks. They examined all criminology texts published from 1989 to 1993. They carefully compiled a listing of the citations of works by various authors. These findings were compared with other studies of citations from earlier years. Thus, they were able to describe important trends in citation patterns in criminology textbooks spanning a 30-year period. Eventually they were able to identify a list of seven elite scholars, whose work has had an enduring impact on the course of criminology in the United States.

As another example, Mary Ann Farkas (1997) conducted a qualitative study of the normative code among correctional officers. She conducted in-depth interviews with 79 correctional officers from "Prison Town Prison" and "Urban Prison," both penitentiaries in a midwestern state. Her interviews yielded much rich information about how correctional officers perceived their work surroundings and the rules by which they lived in relation to dangerous inmates. Her important work tested various theories about social solidarity and behavioral regulation, as different officers described the processual aspects of their jobs. Farkas supplemented her own writing with direct quotes from correctional officer interviews. This type of detail is very difficult to quantify. Rather, we glean much from these quotes and officer observations that would be glaringly lacking in any type of statistically oriented quantitative study. As Farkas said, "This qualitative study [explores] the normative code of correctional officers . . . Examining this code will provide greater insight into the functions which it serves and its impact on behavior and interactions among organizational members" (Farkas, 1997:26).

Quantitative research is the application of statistical procedures and techniques to data collected through surveys, including interviews and questionnaire administration. Quantitative researchers are known as numbers-crunchers, since a wide variety of sophisticated statistical techniques exists to describe what they have found. By far the lion's share of articles in contemporary journals are quantitative. Elaborate tables, charts, and graphs are constructed to portray numerical data. An advanced knowledge of statistics is often required to understand what researchers have done and to interpret their findings. Quantitative research is most often associated with different types of experimentation.

An example of quantitative research is a study by Gennaro F. Vito and Thomas J. Keil (1998). These investigators studied the death penalty and surveyed public opinions about it. They found several factors that seemed to influence support for capital punishment, including the nature of the homicide (the degree of premeditation); the personal characteristics of the offender; and the circumstances surrounding the offense. They utilized several sophisticated statistical techniques and portrayed their data in several elaborate tables. Statistical tests were used to assess the statistical significance of what they found. They relied heavily on these statistical results to support the findings generated.

More than a few studies combine aspects of both qualitative and quantitative research. For instance, Alexander Weiss and Steven Chermak (1998) investigated the news value of African-American victims and the media's presentation of homicides. They collected all articles covering homicides in Indianapolis, Indiana, during 1995. They examined each of these articles and determined the number of victims, and gender and racial/ethnic information. These investigators created various categories of media coverage based on their impressions of the articles they read. This was a heavily qualitative dimension. They also counted words in each article, as well as the numbers of articles published about each murder incident. Subsequently, they applied several statistical techniques to this information in an effort to discover any correlations or statistical observations that might be significant and interesting.

RESEARCH OBJECTIVES AND DESIGNS

The goals of researchers may be conventionally grouped according to (1) exploration, (2) description, and (3) experimentation. No single research design is universally applicable for all investigators at any particular time. Each type of research design functions to allow researchers to conduct their social inquiries in different ways and at different levels of sophistication. Selecting the appropriate research design, therefore, is dependent, in part, upon the kinds of questions researchers wish to answer. Often, several research design objectives may be combined in the same research project to shed light on specific social questions. However, most research projects will likely emphasize one design over the others. Decisions about selecting the best designs must be made by considering the weaknesses and strengths of each design relative to the others. There is no prohibition that would prevent researchers from customizing their investigations with elements of several different kinds of research designs.

Exploration and Exploratory Objectives

Research designs may have predominantly exploratory objectives. An **exploratory design** is characterized by several features. First, it is assumed that investigators have little or no knowledge about the research problem under study. A general unfamiliarity with a particular group of people does not provide investigators with much opportunity to focus upon specific aspects of the social situation. One of the chief merits of exploratory research is that potentially significant factors may be discovered and may be subsequently assessed and described in greater detail with a more sophisticated type of research design.

For instance, if researchers wanted to study social interaction patterns among inmates in prison systems but knew little or nothing about the structure and functioning of penal institutions, an exploratory research project would be in order. Such was the case in the early 1930s, when Joseph Fishman described inmate subculture and sexual aggression. Little was known about prisoners and prison life, and even less was known about their sexual aggressiveness and patterns of sexual assault. Fishman was a federal prison inspector who became interested in depicting various dimensions of prisoners' lives. In 1934 Fishman's *Sex in Prison* was published. Although this classic work described the prevalence and nature of inmate homosexuality behind prison walls, it also acquainted the outside world with several new concepts and inmate jargon that suggested to other researchers a new and rich source in need of greater social description. Fishman used the term *subculture* to describe unique social arrangements among the separate, smaller social system of prisoners behind prison walls, but within the greater societal culture.

Fishman's work stimulated other investigators to describe similar prison environments and inmate culture. Donald Clemmer wrote *The Prison Community* in 1940, which described inmate subculture in Menard Penitentiary in Illinois. Clemmer was a correctional officer who spent nearly three years observing inmate life and interviewing various prisoners. Especially noteworthy was his description of how new inmates were introduced to prison life. He described new inmates using inmate jargon. Thus, new inmates or "fish" would undergo a certain amount of "prisonization" (a term equivalent with the sociological concept of socialization, or learning through contact with others), where older inmates would take them aside and tell them about the do's and don't's of prison life at Menard. Prisonization was the descriptive term that portrayed the learning of inmate customs and about who in prison controlled the flow of scarce prisoner goods and contraband as well as certain inmate privileges.

The works of Fishman and Clemmer stimulated other social scientists to provide more detailed descriptions of prison life in later years. For example, one of the most precedent-setting classic studies of prison life is *The Society of Captives* (1958) by Gresham Sykes. Sykes acknowledged the influence of both Fishman and Clemmer on his own research and writing when depicting inmate culture at the New Jersey State Maximum Security Prison at Trenton. His analysis of prisoner culture introduced us to terms such as "rat" (an inmate who informs or squeals on other inmates), "merchant" (an inmate who barters scare goods in exchange for favors), and "real man" (an inmate who is loyal and generous, but tough in his relations with other inmates). Sykes extended his analysis of prisoners to include a description of the inmate code and pecking order.

The distinguishing feature of exploratory studies is that relatively little is known about the target of one's research. Thus, investigators who wanted to study delinquent gangs in the 1940s and 1950s had to become acquainted with gang norms and patterns of formation and persistence before they could conduct more sophisticated descriptive investigations. Today, many metropolitan police departments have special gang divisions and specialty teams of officers, whose exclusive function it is to monitor gang movements and activities in their jurisdictions. For uninitiated observers several decades ago, the significance of different types and colors of wearing apparel among juvenile gang members would be largely unknown. Currently, much descriptive information is available about gang members, their colors and signs, and the meaning of certain types of graffiti in their "turfs" or neighborhood territories. Thus, in many schools throughout the United States today, both teachers and students who are not gang members refrain from wearing certain colored clothing for fear of being victimized by juvenile gangs. It has been found, for instance, that random, drive-by shootings of innocent bystanders are perpetrated by juvenile gang members, in part, based upon the "wrong" colors worn by pedestrians.

Exploratory studies, therefore, serve primarily to acquaint researchers with the characteristics of research targets that should be described or examined more extensively. Another example of early exploratory research would be the initial investigations conducted by researchers into the drug culture of the 1920s and 1930s. At one time in our history, marijuana was believed to cause irreversible insanity and to cause persons to murder others. Gradually, we have learned much about marijuana and other drugs, and under certain medical conditions, different types of illicit drugs have potential therapeutic value, such as marijuana which is helpful for the disorder of glaucoma. Thus, over a 60-year period, we have gradually moved our level of inquiry about the social, biological, and psychological influence of different drugs from exploration to description, and from description to experimentation.

Description and Descriptive Objectives

Description is the most common design objective in criminology and criminal justice. Before we can discover patterns for various phenomena, such as sentencing disparities, prison violence and rioting, civil disorder, probation and parole officer burnout and stress, law enforcement officer misconduct, the use of excessive force by police, or any other event we wish to explain, we must first acquire large amounts of descriptive information about these phenomena.

A **descriptive design** means depicting the characteristics of whatever we observe. We select settings for investigation, we target particular features of those settings for special attention, and we describe in various ways whatever we find. Different data collection strategies can be used for this purpose. All of the information derived from various data collection strategies provides rich descriptions that often have explanatory value for researchers. It should be noted, however, that description, true scientific description, is considerably more structured than casual description of social settings. Researchers know in advance what they wish to describe, and their accumulated data reflect a focus upon specific social and psychological dimensions of persons and their environments.

The works of Fishman and Clemmer described previously have inspired more than a few researchers to investigate new inmate populations and describe existing inmate codes. The work of Paula and William Faulkner (1997) is an indepth description of the inmate code of conduct at a maximum-security state penitentiary in the Midwest. When the Faulkners conducted their study, there were 550 inmates housed in the facility. They obtained a random sample of 67 inmates, with subsequent participation by 33 inmates. The Faulkners wished to describe the existing inmate code, as well as status relations among inmates. Extended interviews with inmates yielded much descriptive information. The inmates said that primary inmate code characteristics were (1) loyalty ("don't be a snitch"), (2) "doing your own time," (3) "standing up" for one's self, and (4) "smartness." The type of conviction offense had a significant impact on one's status among other inmates. The Faulkners concluded that the inmate code in the prison they studied was virtually identical to the inmate codes described by previous researchers, including Fishman and Clemmer. Thus, it is significant that inmate culture of the 1990s is not particularly different from inmate culture of the 1940s. The Faulkners also discussed certain historical changes in the structure and organization of penitentiaries in their analysis and the relevance of their findings for sociological theory and prison policy.

Contrasted with exploratory studies, descriptive designs are more specific in that they direct our attention to particular aspects or dimensions of the research target. The heuristic value of descriptive studies must be considered a major contribution as well. Descriptive studies may reveal potential relationships between variables, thus setting the stage for more elaborate investigations later. In the research by Long, Shouksmith, Voges, and Roache (1986), several important relationships among different variables were disclosed. Subsequently, revised training programs for prison officers can be examined to see experimentally whether debilitating job stress is decreased substantially. Reorganized shift work and job hours for employees can be studied to see if stress emanating from family conflicts is reduced to a significant degree. The point of a descriptive design is that it enables us to move forward to the most valuable type of investigation—experimentation. This is the type of investigation where it is possible to establish cause-effect relationships between variables.

Experimentation and Experimental Objectives

Designs with the objective of experimentation implicitly include the control of variables. Researchers experiment by observing the effects of one or more variables on others, under controlled conditions. The use of the term **control** in criminological investigations has several connotations. First, control means to hold constant one or more factors while others are free to vary. For instance, if the variable, gender, were believed to be a crucial factor in an experimental situation, then gender is controlled by observing the differential reactions of males and females in relation to some specific stimulus or an experimental variable. An experimental variable might be a sound, an electrical shock administered to the skin, a dosage of some drug, a changed social situation (such as replacing a lenient supervisor with one who is strict), or any other external condition to which the sample of males and females is exposed. If we control for the variable age, for example, then this variable is said to be held constant. In other words, how do all individuals between the ages sixteen and nineteen behave compared with individuals in the age category twenty to twenty-three when exposed to a common stimulus?

An illustration of how variables are controlled is shown below and is based on a research idea by Kowalski, Shields, and Wilson (1985). These researchers conducted a descriptive study of female murderers in Alabama during the years 1929 to 1971. Among other things, they wanted to know about the contributory effects of alcohol and other possibly precipitating events, as well as whether there has been increased use of firearms among female offenders. Among the descriptive information they compiled were questions about race, age, the nature of the victim-offender relationship, and the type of weapon used. Table 5.1 shows a hypothetical distribution of race and the method whereby victims were murdered.

TABLE 5.1 Hypothetical Relation Between Race and Method Used by Female Offenders to Commit Homicide

	Race of Offender	
Method of Murder	Black $N_1 = 125$	White $N_2 = 140$
Shooting	36%	64%
Stabbing	55%	10%
Beating	3%	18%
Other	6%	8%
Totals	100%	100%

In Table 5.1, the variable race has been controlled and divided into two categories, "Black" and "White." An inspection of this cross-tabulation (i.e., the method of murder has been cross-tabulated with the race of offenders) shows that the majority of black murderesses stabbed their victims, while a majority of white murderesses used a firearm. A substantial number of white offenders murdered their victims by beatings, while beatings accounted for very few murders by black offenders. Had we wished to "experiment" with the variable race, and determine its relation with the method whereby these murders had been committed, then Table 5.1 would have given us the relevant information we would need.

More elaborate tables can be constructed, and several variables may be controlled simultaneously. Suppose we wished to determine whether one's race has any bearing on the original charges filed and the final charges associated with the murder conviction. Some hypothetical information is shown in Table 5.2.

In Table 5.2, it would appear that 60 percent of the black offenders were charged with first-degree murder initially and that that charge was the subsequent conviction offense. This figure is contrasted with only 20 percent of the white offenders who were originally charged with first-degree murder and eventually convicted of it. It would also appear that a substantial portion of white offenders had the charges against them reduced to less serious charges compared with black offenders. For instance, about 7 percent of the black offenders had their second-degree murder charges reduced to manslaughter, whereas 60 percent of the white offenders had their second-degree murder charges reduced to manslaughter. Although these findings are hypothetical, they demonstrate certain possibilities that tentative conclusions about variable interrelationships may be drawn from cross-tabulations such as these.

Another meaning of the word *control* is a reference to groups or individuals who are not exposed to experimental variables, whatever they might be. For

TABLE 5.2 Hypothetical Cross-tabulation of Original Charges Filed and Eventual Conviction Offense, by Race

Final Charge	Original Charge					
	First-Degree Murder		Second-Degree Murder		Manslaughter	
	(Race)					
	Black *N = 50*	*White* *N = 55*	*Black* *N = 20*	*White* *N= 60*	*Black* *N = 55*	*White* *N = 25*
First-degree murder	60%	20%	23%	10%	5%	0%
Second-degree murder	30%	50%	70%	30%	35%	15%
Manslaughter	10%	30%	7%	60%	60%	85%
Totals	100%	100%	100%	100%	100%	100%

instance, if we were to administer a particular drug to persons in one group and withhold the drug from persons in another group, the group receiving the drug would be called the **experimental group,** whereas the group not receiving the drug would be called the **control group.** Ordinarily, the reactions of the experimental group and the control group are observed and compared. Differences between the two groups are attributed largely to the effects of the **experimental stimulus,** or in this case, the drug.

In such experimental situations, it is assumed that the two (or more) groups are equated in some way. Persons or groups are matched in some respect, or persons are used as their own "controls" in a before-after experiment. That is, persons are measured according to some characteristic in one time period, and then the same persons are measured again according to that same characteristic in a later time period. In the interim, researchers introduce some experimental variable that is predictably designed to change behaviors. In the general case, it would be predicted that the dependent variable measured in the first time period would change between the first and second time periods. The experimental variable, an independent variable, would be regarded as responsible for any score changes observed between the two time periods, since its introduction was the only new event to influence dependent variable values. Experimental studies may be more or less elaborate or sophisticated in terms of the number of variables used and controlled.

■ SOME CONVENTIONAL RESEARCH DESIGNS

In this section we examine several conventional research designs used by criminologists and others to answer various kinds of questions. Perhaps the two most popular research designs chosen by investigators are surveys and case studies. A third, more complex design is the classic experimental design.

Surveys

Survey research is defined simply as gathering information about a large number of people by interviewing a few of them (Backstrom and Hursh, 1963:3). Hyman (1955) differentiates between exploratory and descriptive surveys, and although no formal definition of **survey design** is apparent in his classic work, the meaning of survey research implicit in his writing is very similar to that described by Backstrom and Hursh. Generally, survey designs are specifications of procedures for gathering information about a large number of people by collecting information from a smaller proportion of them.

Survey researchers apply at least three standards in their research work that center around the quality of data collected. First, the quality of surveys depends, in part, on (1) the number of people obtained for the study, (2) the typicalness of persons sampled in relation to the populations from which they are drawn, and (3) the reliability of data collected from them.

An example of survey research is the work of Finn-Aage Esbensen and Thomas Winfree (1998). These researchers were interested in studying the de-

Obie Clayton
Morehouse College

Statistics: B.A. (religion and sociology), Millsaps College; M.S., Ph.D. (sociology), Emory University.

Interests: I have taught at Millsaps College, Atlanta University, University of Massachusetts at Boston, and the University of Nebraska at Omaha. My research and teaching interests are primarily in the areas of crime and delinquency and stratification and social inequality. I just completed a longitudinal study of homicide in Nebraska. This study was funded by the state of Nebraska.

My current funded research is in the area of urban inequality, and I am part of a research team which is studying this problem in four major U.S. cities: Atlanta, Boston, Detroit, and Los Angeles. This study is funded by the Ford and Russell Sage foundations.

Other research projects in which I have been involved include (1) a study of the impact of immigration on the Atlanta work force, (2) jobs and job training for African-Americans, and (3) the impact of mass transit in Atlanta. In addition to these activities, I sit on the Board of Trustees of the Metropolitan Atlanta Crime Commission and the Atlanta Center on Health and Aging.

I became interested in the field of criminology and criminal justice as a graduate student at Emory University. Working under the direction of Dr. John Doby, a social psychologist, we conducted a study of criminal behavior in Georgia. This research was picked up by the Georgia Department of Corrections and resulted in my dissertation. Though my research interests are varied, I still find the academic study of crime and criminality central to my research agenda. Specifically, my studies of domestic violence are longitudinal in design, and I hope to have had some impact in assisting police departments in both Omaha and Atlanta in acknowledging and designing programs to treat domestic violence.

Advice to Students: I would advise any student thinking about a career in the criminal justice area to get solid training in both research methods and statistics. These tools will be of great importance regardless of the area of specialization chosen. Criminal justice is a dynamic field, full of challenges and opportunities.

mographic composition of gangs and the level of delinquent activity of gang members compared with nongang members. Supported by a grant from the National Institute of Justice, Esbensen and Winfree worked with officials in charge of the Gang Resistance Education and Training (G.R.E.A.T.) Program, a school-based gang prevention program. These researchers were able to use records furnished by the Bureau of Alcohol, Tobacco, and Firearms to identify several prospective sites for their survey. Site selection was limited to agencies with two or more trained officers who could teach G.R.E.A.T., and locations with considerable geographic and demographic diversity. Eventually, 11 sites were selected.

Esbensen and Winfree distributed questionnaires to eighth-grade students in these 11 site areas, yielding a final sample of 5,935 students, representing 315 classrooms in 42 different schools. Questionnaires given to students contained demographic, attitudinal, and behavioral measures. Self-reported delinquency and gang affiliation questions were included, and gang membership was measured through self-identification. Responses from self-identified gang members were compared with nongang members on several salient dimensions. The results of their survey were illuminating. These researchers found that white involvement in gang activities was more extensive than previously reported by other studies. Furthermore, 38 percent of self-identified gang members were female, a much larger percentage than other studies have disclosed. Since this was a survey, Esbensen and Winfree did not interview or observe any self-identified gang members. It is unknown whether additional information from these other methods would enhance their study in any way, although we suspect that it would. But sufficient survey information was generated by these investigators to challenge prevalent notions about gender and race/ethnicity and the extent to which each characterizes gang members.

Another example of a survey design is the ***National Youth Survey (NYS),*** an ongoing longitudinal (over time) study of delinquent behavior and alcohol and drug use among the American youth population. The NYS uses a fairly typical sample of youth ranging in age from 11 to 17. Self-report questionnaires are administered, where youths disclose whether they have committed any status or criminal offenses and whether they have been apprehended for any of these offenses. The NYS utilizes this sample of youth over successive time periods as a panel. A panel is some designated sample that is studied repeatedly over time, and comparisons are made between "panels" or the responses given by these youths within each time frame. Krisberg et al. (1987) used the NYS to investigate the differential rates of incarceration of minority youth. Key research findings were that minority youth were being incarcerated at a rate three to four times that of white youths, and that over time, minority youth incarcerations are increasing proportionately. Self-reports of delinquent conduct among both whites and minorities disclosed similar patterns, and therefore one's minority status is seen as a primary predictor of subsequent incarceration or involvement with police compared with being white.

Both of these studies involve somewhat superficial examinations of data. However, this is not an unfavorable observation. By their very nature, survey designs are superficial. In each case, limited numbers of social and personal characteristics are solicited from respondents. These characteristics are tabulated and analyzed statistically. They yield broad conclusions about large aggregates of persons. No attempt is made to conduct in-depth investigations of family systems, personality systems, or any other intimate details of the participants' lives. Details such as these are disclosed by means of an alternative design known as the case study. Case studies will be examined in the next section.

Advantages and Disadvantages of Surveys.   The major advantages of survey designs are the following:

1. Surveys can provide information about a large number of persons at relatively low cost.
2. Generalizability to larger populations of elements is enhanced because of the larger numbers of persons who are included in survey designs.
3. Surveys are flexible enough to permit the use of a variety of data collection techniques.
4. Surveys sensitize researchers to potential problems that were originally unanticipated or unknown.
5. Surveys are useful tools that enable investigators to verify theories.

Some of the disadvantages of survey designs are the following:

1. Surveys are superficial reflections of population sentiments.
2. Surveys, particularly political surveys, are unstable reflections of population characteristics.
3. Researchers have little or no control over individual responses in surveys.
4. Statements about populations from which samples are drawn are tentative.

Case Studies

Although some investigators might claim that a **case study** is not a design in a technical sense, a **case study design** is one of the most popular types of research designs used by criminologists and other social scientists today. Case studies are relatively thorough examinations of specific social settings or particular aspects of social settings, including detailed psychological and behavioral descriptions of persons in those settings. Words such as "intense" and "in-depth" characterize the type of information yielded by case studies, whereas survey designs yield data of a superficial and broad nature, as we have seen. An example of a case study is the work of Charles (1989).

Charles investigated the social and psychological impact and effects of electronic monitoring on six juvenile delinquents. Charles conducted in-depth interviews with probation officers, the parents/guardians of the juveniles, the juveniles themselves, and probation department administrators. His close contact with juveniles themselves disclosed details about wearing electronic wristlets associated with electronic monitoring programs that he otherwise wouldn't have known had he not conducted the case study. For example, the activity of "hanging out" frequently led to delinquent acts, since youths who "hung out" were bored, with little or nothing to do. Charles found that youths could avoid trouble in their schools by using their wristlets as a "crutch" to withstand peer pressure and refuse invitations to "mess around," "hang out," and commit delinquent acts (Charles, 1989:168). The wristlet worn by these participating youths also reminded others of their probationary status. Thus, Charles was able to penetrate the social worlds and minds of these boys to a limited degree and to understand their motives and rationales for different behaviors.

One interesting characteristic of case studies is that much rich information about social settings is disclosed. Another example of such research is an ambitious case study undertaken by Frazier and Bishop (1990). In 1987, these researchers sent observers and interviewers to Florida's 67 county jails to investigate booking and inmate processing. They were particularly interested in the extent to which Florida jails were in compliance with a general mandate to remove juvenile offenders from adult jails and lock-ups. Jail personnel were interviewed, and the ways and places in which juveniles were processed and detained were observed. Approximately 13 percent of all juvenile jail admissions were considered out of compliance with the Juvenile Justice and Delinquency Prevention mandate.

Through conversations with jail officials and other personnel, Frazier and Bishop found that both law enforcement officers and jail officials held basic misconceptions about detaining juvenile status offenders. Although holding juvenile offenders in adult jails is a violation of Florida law, 237 cases in 1985 and 219 cases in 1986 were reported where juvenile status offenders were held for various periods in these county jails. Some officials believed that juvenile offenders could be held in adult jails, as long as sight and sound separation was provided, or as long as they were placed in general holding areas and not in individual cells. Interviews and casual conversations also disclosed that many jail officials were resistant to unwanted reform and had complacent attitudes about jailing juvenile offenders of any kind.

A good point made here is that this quality of information could not have been obtained through more superficial survey instruments. It took an intense investigation and description of these settings, together with detailed interviews with jail officials and examinations of jail records, before such information emerged. After all, not many jail officials are going to admit to violating any Florida statute on an anonymous questionnaire mailed or distributed to them. Further, they are probably not going to say that they have complacent attitudes about whether juveniles are jailed in their facilities with adults or that they are stubborn or resistant to juvenile jailing reforms. Case studies, therefore, provide us with an in-depth grasp of social environments. However, because they consume so much time and energy of researchers, they are not conducted on the same broad magnitudes as surveys. This is one reason why both types of designs have offsetting weaknesses and strengths.

Some Advantages and Disadvantages of Case Studies. Some of the more important advantages of case studies for criminologists are the following:

1. Case studies are flexible in that they enable researchers to use multiple data-gathering techniques, such as interviewing, observation, questionnaires, and examinations of records and statistical data.

2. Case studies may be conducted in almost any type of social environment.

3. Case studies are specific instances of tests of theories. If researchers have adequately prepared a theoretical framework within which to cast the research activity, then case studies provide them with an opportunity to test theories. Thus, case studies may be viewed as a test of a more general theory to the same degree that survey designs are able to achieve this objective. Surveys make possible certain generalizations to the extent that the elements surveyed are representative of the population from which they are drawn.

4. The flexibility of case studies may be extended to virtually any dimension of the topic(s) studied.

5. Case studies may be inexpensive, depending upon the extent of inquiry involved and the type of data collection techniques used. A researcher's costs may be kept to a minimum if data can be collected firsthand. It is not unusual to find researchers conducting case studies of social settings of which they are a part.

Disadvantages of Case Studies.   Some disadvantages of case studies are the following:

The primary disadvantage of case studies is that they have limited generalizability. Although they are geared to provide detailed information about social units, they are often criticized for being quite limited in scope and insufficient for meaningful generalizations to larger social aggregates. Representativeness, however, is a primary question in the assessment of the quality of survey information as well. On a theoretical level, it may be argued that findings from case studies lend support to or provide refutation of theories. Researchers do not regard case study findings as conclusive proof of anything. Neither do survey researchers. Only through the accumulation of information from many case studies and many surveys investigating similar phenomena can we begin to generate statements about the social world that have little or no exception.

Figures 5.1 and 5.2 illustrate more clearly how each type of research design treats the social aggregates studied and their generalizability to larger populations. Figure 5.1 shows that a survey derives elements from the total population, which is generally known. Characteristics of a sample of elements are generalized tentatively to the entire population of elements. Figure 5.2 depicts case studies in relation to some unknown population. The typicality or representativeness of the case under investigation is unknown and is all but impossible to assess. However, because social situations are usually involved, certain theoretical propositions and hypotheses can be put to the test, again on a tentative basis.

Comparison of Surveys and Case Studies

It is clear that both types of research designs discussed previously may be used for hypothesis testing. In fact, in some instances, both types of study designs may be used to test the same hypotheses. Case studies appear to have greater utility for hypothesis tests about certain structural and procedural characteristics

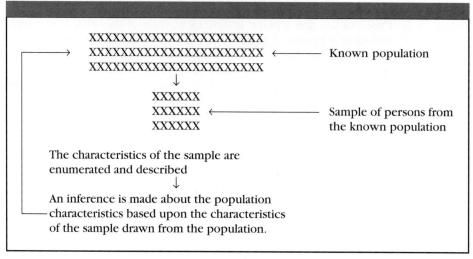

FIGURE 5.1 An illustration of the generalizability of samples studied with survey designs.

FIGURE 5.2 An illustration of the generalizability of samples studied with case study designs.

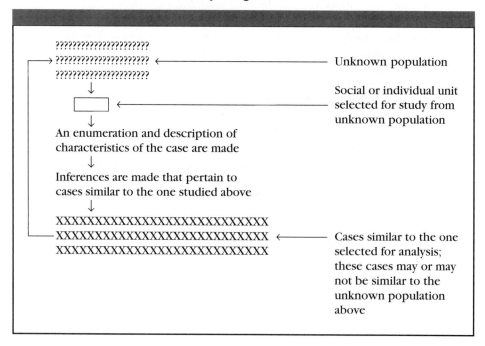

(e.g., mobility patterns, status relations, interpersonal characteristics) of specific social units (e.g., organizations, small groups, cliques, communities). In addition to their descriptive value, surveys are of great utility for testing hypotheses about large social aggregates (e.g., female criminals between the ages of 20 and 25, the background differences among convicted felons, sentencing disparities among judges that pertain to racial or ethnic factors, or describing the social and demographic characteristics of juvenile delinquents).

Classical Experimental Design

Experimental research designs generally are those that seek to control conditions within which persons are observed and analyzed. The natures and types of experimental designs range from simple to complex and are quite varied. Any conventional or **classical experimental design** contains three important elements: (1) experimental and control groups, (2) equivalent groups, and (3) pretests and posttests.

Experimental and Control Groups. In any discussion of experimental designs, two types of groups must be distinguished: (1) experimental groups and (2) control groups. Conventionally, **experimental groups** consist of persons who are exposed to experimental variables or treatment variables. **Experimental variables** or **treatment variables** might be a new type of group or individual counseling method; a different method of supervision; increased pay or job benefits; larger or smaller client caseloads for probation or parole officers; longer or shorter working hours for correctional officers; or the creation of inmate grievance councils in prisons. We might want to know if a new type of group or individual therapy is effective in treating sex offenders. Or we might want to know if changing the method of supervision, the pay, or the job benefits has any effect on the morale of police officers in a police department. Or we might want to know if changes in working hours change the job satisfaction levels of corrections officers. Or we might want to know if decreasing client caseloads for probation officers makes the officers more effective in their supervision of offenders. Or we might want to know if creating inmate grievance councils in prisons decreases inmate violence. All of these variables that we intend to manipulate or change are possible experimental variables.

Control groups consist of those persons *not* exposed to experimental or treatment variables. A comparison of the attitudes and behaviors of the experimental and the control group should tell us whether the experimental or treatment variable had any effect on those attitudes or behaviors. Effects of treatment or experimental variables are detected whenever there is a change in behaviors or attitudes of the experimental group but the attitudes or behaviors of the control group remain unchanged.

Equivalent Groups and Establishing Equivalence. The classic experiment assumes that the two groups to be compared, the experimental and control group, should be *equivalent*. This means that the two groups should share many of the same characteristics. If we compared two groups, one consisting entirely of females and one consisting entirely of males, we would not consider these groups equivalent. Likewise, a group of 80-year-olds would not equate favorably with a group of 16-year-olds. Generally, any two-group comparison should be conducted where it can reasonably be assumed that for all practical purposes, the two groups are very similar in their shared characteristics. Therefore, researchers attempt to equate control and experimental groups on as many salient characteristics as possible (e.g., gender, age, rural or urban background, socioeconomic status, prior criminal record, years of experience, years of education, and certain personality factors). Then, when theorized changes occur within the experimental group but not within the control group, investigators may tentatively infer a cause-effect relation between the experimental variable and the changed behavior, whatever it might be. The behavioral changes, therefore, are more likely attributable to the experimental variable than to obvious differences in the sociodemographic composition of the experimental and control groups.

In order to achieve equivalence between two or more groups designated for experimentation, social scientists select one of the following four methods: (1) individual matching, (2) persons used as their own experimental controls, (3) group or frequency distribution control matching, or (4) random assignment.

Individual Matching. **Individual matching** or simply **matching** is the most difficult method of equating two or more groups. If researchers wanted to match 25 persons in an experimental group with 25 other persons according to several important characteristics, it is often necessary that a large population base must exist in order to find sufficient numbers of persons who will match up with those in the experimental group. Usually, experimenters will want to match persons according to their gender, age, years of education, socioeconomic status, occupation, race or ethnicity, and perhaps, some additional personality factors. The addition of each new matching characteristic greatly limits the available pool of persons from which matching individuals may be drawn. And assuming "matches" can be made, there are no guarantees that those who are found to match others will participate in one's research as a part of the control group. Even if persons participate later who have been matched with others on certain characteristics, there is a definite likelihood that the two groups will remain unmatched on numerous other important characteristics. Thus, if differences are later observed between the two groups on some dependent variable, then it will be unknown whether the experimental variable caused changes in variable values or if unknown differences between the two groups were responsible for these discrepancies. Figure 5.3 illustrates individual matching.

Using Persons as Their Own Experimental Controls. One way of overcoming the matching problem and equating persons more directly is to use **persons as their own controls** in an experimental situation. Therefore, a target sample of persons is identified, measures on some dependent variable are taken, the group is exposed to some experimental variable, and then measures

EXPERIMENTAL GROUP		CONTROL GROUP
Individual:	MATCHED WITH:	Individual:
1	⟨-------------------⟩	7
2	⟨-------------------⟩	8
3	⟨-------------------⟩	9
4	⟨-------------------⟩	10
5	⟨-------------------⟩	11
6	⟨-------------------⟩	12

FIGURE 5.3 A hypothetical illustration of individual matching.

are again taken on the dependent variable. Score changes observed under this circumstance cannot be attributed to differences between individuals, since the same persons who were tested in the first time period were also tested in the second time period. An example of persons used as their own controls is illustrated in Figure 5.4

In Figure 5.4, the same persons are measured on some dependent variable in two or more time periods. Perhaps a new program is being implemented in a parole agency to bolster morale and work attitudes, or to improve interpersonal relations. The new program is the experimental variable. Perhaps the researcher has a *quality of life* scale that measures contentment with the working environment and one's work associates. Scale scores in time 2 and are compared with these same scale scores in time 1, and differences observed are attributed more to the new program than to "individual differences" between the two groups in the two time periods, since it is the same group of people in both time periods.

Group or Frequency Distribution Control Matching. **Group distribution matching** or **frequency distribution control matching** means to

FIGURE 5.4 A hypothetical illustration of persons used as their own controls in a before-after experiment.

TIME 1	EXPERIMENTAL VARIABLE INTRODUCED	TIME 2
Individual:	E	Individual:
1	⟨---------- ↓ ----------⟩	1
2	⟨---------- ↓ ----------⟩	2
3	⟨---------- ↓ ----------⟩	3
4	⟨---------- ↓ ----------⟩	4

EXPERIMENTAL GROUP $N = 100$	CHARACTERISTICS USED FOR MATCHING PURPOSES	CONTROL GROUP $N = 100$
34.1 ⟨ --------------- 1.	Average age --------------------⟩	34.2
14.9 ⟨ --------------- 2.	Average years of education ---------⟩	15.3
35/65 ⟨ --------------- 3.	Male-female composition ----------⟩	33/67
83.9% ⟨ --------------- 4.	Percentage favorable -------------⟩ toward issue X	81.8%
etc. ⟨ ----------------------- etc. ----------------------⟩		etc.

FIGURE 5.5 A hypothetical example of group matching or frequency distribution control matching.

equate two groups on the basis of their aggregate similarities. Suppose we identified two groups of 250 prison inmates each distributed as follows according to following characteristics:

Characteristic	Group 1	Group 2
Average age	34.2	33.9
Gender	40% female	42% female
Prior record	3.2 felonies	3.3 felonies
Prior delinquency	39% prior delinquency	40% prior delinquency
Race	40% black, 60% white	38% black, 62% white
Urban background	72%	75%
Average level of custody	94% medium-security	95% medium-security

On the basis of group or aggregate characteristics, these two groups have much in common. They are on the average approximately 34 years old; are 40 percent female; have 3+ felonies for prior records; are 40 percent black; 72 percent are from urban backgrounds; and 94 percent are in medium-security custody. These two groups may have other characteristics in common. They may have similar attitudes about prison life; similar write-ups or incidents of misconduct; similar good-time credit earned; and similar sentence lengths to serve. We justify their equivalence on the basis of how many characteristics they share. The more characteristics the two groups share, the more they are equivalent for experimental purposes. Figure 5.5 shows these two groups and their characteristics.

Random Assignment. The fourth method for equating groups is to select them from an overall sample by means of **random assignment.** Thus, we might draw a sample from some population, such as a sample of students from a large

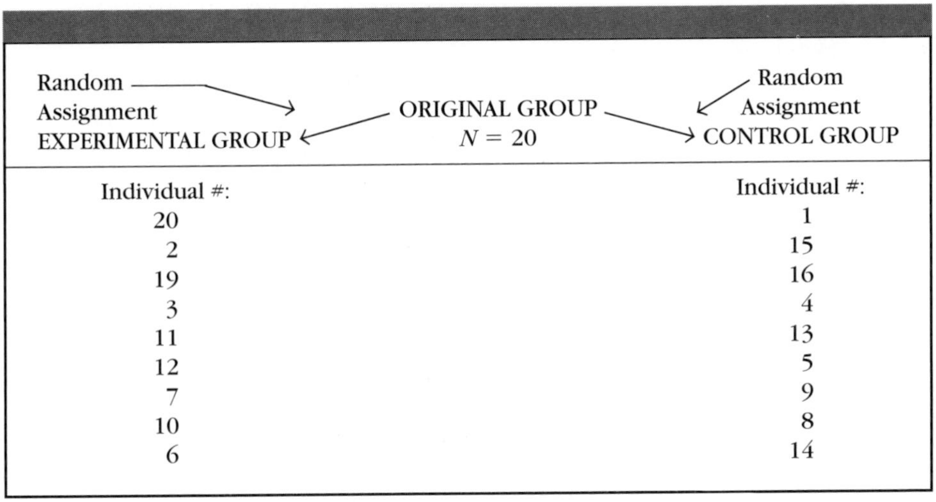

```
Random ────────────                                    Random
Assignment          ────→ ── ORIGINAL GROUP ──    ←── Assignment
EXPERIMENTAL GROUP ←──         N = 20            ──→ CONTROL GROUP
```

Individual #:		Individual #:
20		1
2		15
19		16
3		4
11		13
12		5
7		9
10		8
6		14

FIGURE 5.6 A hypothetical illustration of random assignment.

introductory criminal justice course. Suppose we drew a sample of 20 students from a large class. Using random assignment, we would place 10 students in the experimental group and 10 students in the control group. Figure 5.6 shows how random assignment would divide these persons. In Figure 5.6, 20 students have been numbered from 1 to 20. Using a random procedure, each of the 20 students is placed in either the experimental group or the control group.

Pretests and Posttests.   The third integral feature of **experimental designs** is the inclusion of pretests and posttests. What is the general condition of the experimental and control groups before any experimentation has been conducted? What is the general condition of the experimental and control groups after experimentation has occurred?

Assuming that we have two equivalent groups for purposes of carrying out an experiment, we need to know whether the two groups we are comparing manifest any substantial differences in their attitudes and behaviors before the experiment occurs. Thus, we observe and measure certain important characteristics of both the experimental and control groups before the experimental variable is introduced. This activity is known as a **pretest.** Thus, we pretest the experimental and control groups and record their present behaviors and attitudes.

Following the administration of an experimental or treatment variable, we will conduct a **posttest.** This means that we will measure our experimental and control group members according to their behaviors and attitudes following the experiment. Ideally, we expect that a comparison of pretest and posttest results for the control group will show that for all practical purposes, the control group has not changed in any way. Since the control group was not exposed to the experimental variable, it was not expected to change. However, when the experimental group pretest and posttest results are compared, we anticipate that the experimental group changed in some way. After all, the experimental variable was supposed to cause one or more changes in the behaviors or attitudes of the experimental group.

Suppose we have two groups of 25 parole officers in two different parole agencies, Agency A and Agency B. We determine that the two groups are generally equivalent for experimental purposes. The parole officers in both agencies have average caseloads of 75 client/parolees each. Designating Agency A parole officers as the experimental group and Agency B parole officers as the control group, we obtain measures of their morale and job interest in a pretest. Later, we reduce the caseloads of parole officers in Agency A to 25 client/parolees each, while we leave alone the caseloads of those parole officers in Agency B. We think that reducing one's client/parolee caseload will improve morale and raise job interest because of the more personalized attention officers can direct to fewer numbers of clients. After an interval of three months, we subject both groups of parole officers to a posttest, again assessing their work morale and job interest. We find that morale and job interest has increased appreciably for the parole officers in Agency A, while the morale and job interest levels of parole officers in Agency B remained the same over time. This finding supports our idea that lowering caseloads of parole officers will heighten their morale and job interest. We might also conjecture that the client/parolees themselves will benefit as well from the improved morale and job interest of their parole officers.

In the above example, we carried out a classical experiment. We had an experimental group and a control group. We had equivalent groups. And we had a pretest and a posttest. When an experimental variable was introduced, we determined that it had a predictable effect on the behaviors or attitudes of the parole officers in the experimental group. Our evidence showed this. Further, our evidence showed that no change occurred in the parole officer sample where the experimental variable did not occur. With these concepts in mind, we can now look at a typical experimental scenario where an experimental and a control group are used. Figure 5.7 shows a hypothetical experimental situation involving one experimental group and one control group.

The classical experimental design is easily illustrated by an example provided by Goode and Hatt (1952:76–78): " . . . in its simple statement, it can be formulated in this fashion: If there are two or more cases, and in one of them observation Z can be made, while in the other it cannot; and if factor C occurs when observation Z is made, and does not occur when observation Z is not made; then it can be asserted that there is a causal relationship between C and Z." Figure 5.8 illustrates the classical experimental design defined by Goode and Hatt.

Another illustration is helpful here. Suppose we were to observe two random samples of parolees over a two-year time period. Both samples of parolees have similar prior records, and all parolees were earlier convicted of robbery. Further, suppose that previous information about these parolees indicates that one sample has a history of alcohol or drug abuse, while the other sample of parolees does not show any alcohol or drug use or dependencies. From the literature we know that if recidivism is going to occur, it usually occurs within a two-year time interval from the time inmates are paroled from prison. If we ob-

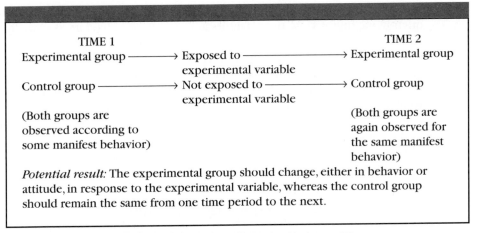

FIGURE 5.7 A hypothetical illustration of an experiment with an experimental group and a control group.

serve these two samples of parolees over the next two years, we might find that no parolees within the group with no alcohol or drug abuse history have recidivated, whereas all parolees in the group with a history of alcohol or /drug abuse have recidivated and have been returned to prison. This hypothetical example would suggest that a history of alcohol or drug dependency or abuse would be a strong predictor of subsequent recidivism among parolees. Unfortunately, our findings about parolees and other groups throughout the criminal justice system are not that clear-cut. We might find higher rates of recidivism within one group compared with another, or we might find higher levels of work satisfaction among one group of parole officers compared with another. Seldom, if ever, do we find "all" or "none" differences that might be suggested under a pure or perfect classic experimental design format.

The idea of "all" or "none" is important, however. Thus, if the presence of certain factors triggers certain events or behaviors, even a greater frequency of those events, and the absence of those same factors does not elicit the same

FIGURE 5.8 The classical experimental design.

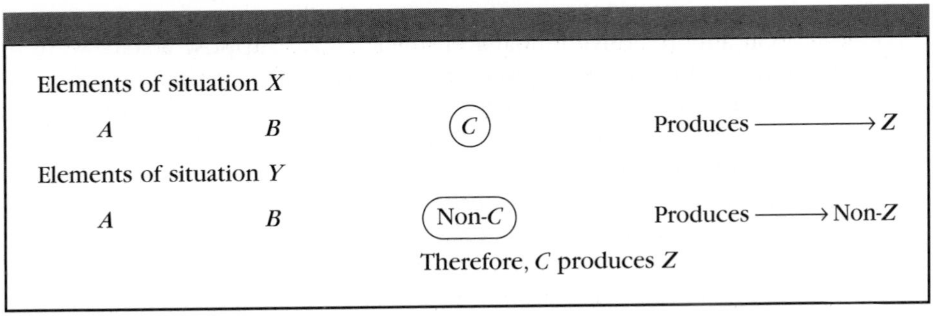

Elements of situation X

    A B C Produces ────────→ Z

Elements of situation Y

    A B Non-C Produces ────────→ Non-Z

           Therefore, C produces Z

events or behaviors, or if the same events or behaviors are not elicited as frequently, we might view these factors and events or behaviors as causally related.

Criticisms of the Classical Experimental Design. Goode and Hatt (1952:78–81) caution, however, that when it comes to "proof" of the effectiveness or impact of an experiment, the classical experimental design has certain weaknesses. Some of these weaknesses are that (1) researchers are unable to control all relevant variables in the research project, (2) there is a lack of clarity in the causal relation between the two variables, (3) there are unpredictable effects produced by the factor of time, and (4) there may be an oversimplification of cause-effect relations between the different variables.

Modifications of the Classical Experimental Design

The classical experimental design has manifested itself in different forms in the criminological literature. Variations of this design include (1) the after-only design, and (2) the before-after design.

The After-Only Design. The **after-only design** seeks to compare an experimental group with a control group after an experimental variable has been introduced to one group but not the other. Sometimes, the terms *experimental group* and *control group* are loosely defined. In some instances, these terms may refer to similar neighborhoods or similar cities. For instance, police departments throughout the United States have experimented with various police patrol methods either to prevent crime or decrease it. An example is the Tampa (Florida) Police Department.

Believing that a "back-to-the-people" program might be helpful in reducing Tampa crime, the Tampa Police Department inaugurated sector patrolling, where police officers would be assigned particular city sectors. Offices were established in each sector and manned 18 hours a day. Police officers were assigned to patrol specific neighborhoods and became familiar with residents and merchants. Supposedly, reported crime in those areas of the city receiving sector patrolling, compared with other city areas, decreased "significantly" during the first six months of the program and greater police-citizen cooperation occurred (Smith and Taylor, 1985). In this case, the "experimental group" was composed of those city sectors receiving sector patrolling, while the "control group" consisted of those city areas not receiving sector patrolling.

On a more conventional and smaller scale, suppose a state were to change the type of administrative leadership in several of its probation offices in various cities. State officials might believe that different, more authoritative leadership would improve officer accountability and responsibility. Assuming we had measures of officer accountability and responsibility, those offices undergoing this administrative change (the experimental group, in this case) could be contrasted with those offices with no administrative changes (the control group, in this case). Subsequently, the two sets of offices would be compared in an after-only contrast, and any differences in officer accountability and responsibility would be noted. Theoretically, those offices that underwent administrative changes would subsequently have greater officer accountability, as indicated by the appropriate instruments.

Criticisms of the After-Only Design. Unfortunately, the after-only design fails to identify the respective conditions of the experimental and control groups before changes have occurred. Thus, it is difficult to make conclusive statements about any observed differences between the experimental and control groups that might be more attributable to general differences within the groups themselves rather than to the experimental variable. One weakness of the after-only design is that unless some method has been used to establish the equivalency of the experimental and control groups, it is impossible to assess the impact of the experimental variable with certainty.

The Before-After Design. An improvement over the after-only design, the **before-after design** consists of obtaining measures on some dependent variable for two groups that are presumed equivalent for experimental purposes, introducing an experimental variable to one group and withholding it from the other, and comparing the two groups after the experiment has been completed. An example of the before-after experiment, again using police patrol styles as the theme, is the work of Kelling et al. (1974).

Kelling et al. (1974) conducted what became known as the classic Kansas City Preventive Patrol Experiments between June 1972 and September 1973. Funded by a grant from the Police Foundation, the Kansas City Police Department varied the numbers of routine preventive patrols within fifteen of Kansas City's police beats. The beats were divided into three groups of five each. In the "control" beat grouping, patrols were continued according to previously "normal" patterns. In the two "experimental" beat groupings, routine patrols were both increased and eliminated. In one experimental beat grouping, known as the "proactive" beats, the "normal" one-car patrols were increased to three-car patrols. In the other experimental beat grouping, the "reactive" beats, all one-car patrols were removed, and police officers serviced those areas strictly on the basis of calls from residents who reported crimes as they occurred.

It was expected, and predicted, that crime would increase in the reactive beats, decrease in the proactive beats, and remain about the same in the "control" beats. The experiment failed to produce these results. Crime remained about the same or occurred with about the same frequency in all beats, regardless of the patrol style used. These results generated much controversy, since police agency funding is based, in part, upon the argument that more police presence tends to deter crime. Clearly, this was not the case, at least in those experimental and control beats studied. In fact, since crime did not increase in those areas where police patrols were withdrawn, some citizens questioned the value of police patrols in any city sector. In all fairness to the Kansas City Police Department, some experts surmised that criminals "thought" that police patrols were continuing as usual. After all, how were criminals supposed to know that the city was experimenting with varying police patrol styles? Thus, a "phantom effect" was described to account for the lack of increased crime in those areas not patrolled by police.

Criticisms of the Before-After Experimental Design. The principal advantage of the before-after experimental design is the ability of the researcher to evaluate experimental and control group subjects both before and after experimentation, and to isolate and eliminate (or take into account or take into consideration) extraneous factors that might otherwise obscure the true effect(s) of the experimental variable. In the Kansas City study, for instance, crime rates in various beats were known before the experiment was conducted. Thus, comparisons were easily made among beats after the experiment ended to determine the experimental effects on crime rates of varying the intensity of police patrols. Again, reference may be made to Figure 5.7 where the before-after experimental design is illustrated.

True Experiments and Quasi-Experiments

Depending upon the method researchers use to establish equivalence between experimental and control groups, they may conduct either true experiments or quasi-experiments. True experiments involve comparisons of two groups in which random assignment has been used to establish their equivalence. The classical experimental design described earlier is an example of a **true experiment.**

Frequently, researchers conduct experiments where random assignment has not been used to establish equivalent experimental and control groups. Under these circumstances, such experiments are known as **quasi-experiments.** Quasi-experiments utilize matching, frequency distribution control matching, or persons used as their own control in before-after experiments.

A good example of a quasi-experimental research investigation is a study by Suman Kakar (1998). Kakar studied families who had children involved in delinquent gangs or children at risk of becoming gang members. She compared these families with a sample of other families where the children were not at risk or involved in any gang activity. According to Kakar,

> The sample consisted of 114 families. Half of these families, the experimental group, had children identified either as gang members or at risk of being gang members. These families participated in the Gang Reduction and Sports Program (GRASP), where the child is officially identified as a gang member or is officially identified as at risk of being a gang member . . . The other half of the families, the control group, were participating in the Police Athletic League (PAL), located in Miami, Florida, . . . The only condition for enrollment in the [PAL] program is that the child is not officially identified as delinquent or as a gang member.

Kakar's research goals were to contrast these families according to their different levels of satisfaction and subjective well-being and to investigate the effect of the number of children in gangs on parental well-being. She matched the two sets of families according to (1) the responding parent's age, (2) the number of children in the family, (3) the ages of the children, (4) the child's grade in school, (5) the family's socioeconomic status measured by annual income,

(6) family structure, (7) church attendance and (8) the gender of the child in the program. Her findings showed that parents with children in gangs report significantly lower scores on subjective well-being than parents without children in gangs. Also, having more than one child from the same family involved in gangs lowered parental subjective well-being.

Another quasi-experimental type of study was conducted by Kevin Knight and Matthew Hiller (1997). These researchers studied 492 probationer/clients who became involved in a Texas substance abuse program during a one-year period from 1993 to 1994. Knight and Hiller determined that of the original 492 participants, 100 were expelled because of program violations and other reasons, and 41 clients were transferred out the program elsewhere. The 351 graduates were compared with the 141 expelled/transferred clients according to their recidivism. The graduates were considered as the experimental group, while the expelled/transferred clients were considered the control group. Subsequent comparison for recidivism revealed that the expelled/transferred clients had re-arrest/recidivism rates twice as high as the graduate (experimental) group.

In Knight and Hiller's study, the expelled/transferred clients became the control group, inasmuch as they no longer were participating in the experiment designed to bring about change among drug users. The substance abuse program was the experimental variable. As a result of this experimental variable, according to Knight and Hiller, graduates should recidivate at a lower rate compared with those who were not exposed to the drug abuse program. The findings were supportive of this position. But Knight and Hiller rightly noted in a conclusion that "this study did not include random assignment, and causal attribution cannot be determined" (1997:67). In "research-ese," this means that the study was not absolute proof of a cause-effect relation between the drug abuse program and lower recidivism rates. But they also said that the study demonstrated that "probationers who receive treatment for their substance abuse problems are less likely to recidivate than are those who do not receive treatment [at least as shown in this study]" (1997:67).

Other types of research involving quasi-experimental designs might include comparisons of different inmate populations and inmate subcultures, where several salient inmate characteristics have been controlled; comparisons of different samples of correctional officers according to officer-inmate ratios; or comparisons of different groups of citizens according to their attitudes toward capital punishment or plea bargaining.

Criticisms of Quasi-Experimental Designs.   The major advantage of quasi-experimental research is that so many natural situations exist for such experimentation. There are first offenders and offenders with prior records. There are black and white or male and female corrections officers. There are drug abusers and people who do not use drugs. These are alcoholics and nondrinkers. There are program participants and people not in programs. There are parolees in halfway houses and parolees not in halfway houses. There are plea bargained cases and cases concluded by trials. The list of such different segments of society is endless. From a purely functional point of view, it is the easiest of experimental research strategies to use without a great deal of design complexity. Quasi-experimental research is simple, and natural situations where it can be applied are abundant.

A disadvantage is that quasi-experimental research lacks the equivalence between experimental and control groups that random assignment would provide. Therefore, conclusions drawn from such research are more tentative. But scientific research in general is tentative anyway. We are trained not to draw absolute conclusions on the basis of a single study, regardless of its magnitude or complexity. Research about different topics accumulates gradually, and over time we develop sound explanations for why certain events occur. Quasi-experimental research is a sound tool for contributing a growing amount of evidence for explanations of criminological problems.

Time-Series and Multiple Time-Series Designs

Time-Series Designs. More than a few experiments occur over long periods of time, such as 10, 15, or 20 years. Investigators may examine phenomena such as the murder rate over time. For instance, we might chart the murder rate for the United States, beginning in 1960, and track the murder rate through 1990. At certain points in this yearly murder rate tracking, we might note significant U.S. Supreme Court decisions about how murderers are punished, such as the use of capital punishment or its nonuse.

It has been argued, for example, that the application of the death penalty is not a significant deterrent for prospective murderers. Other investigators say that the death penalty *is* a deterrent to murder. In 1972 the U.S. Supreme Court ruled against the death penalty according to how it was being applied in a racially discriminatory manner in Georgia in the case of *Furman v. Georgia* (1972). Georgia and other states using the death penalty temporarily suspended its application. This suspension lasted four years, until the U.S. Supreme Court ruled again in *Gregg v. Georgia* (1976) that the application of the death penalty in Georgia was no longer discriminatory and therefore constitutional. Thus, researchers were presented with an ideal situation for examining murder rates in the United States under conditions where the death penalty was allowed or disallowed.

Contrary to the beliefs of persons supporting the death penalty, the murder rate in the United States did not escalate appreciably when the death penalty was suspended for four years. Neither did the murder rate decline when the death penalty was reinstated in 1976.

The significance of this example is that it illustrates a **time-series design.** Time-series designs include numerous observations of a variable (e.g., the murder rate) over time. During these observations, another variable, an intervening variable, occurs (e.g., suspension of the death penalty). Observations of the original variable (murder rate) continue to be made. Eventually, investigators can draw tentative conclusions about the impact of the intervening or treatment variable (suspension of the death penalty) on the original variable (murder rate).

Symbolically, the time-series design involves numerous observations (O) with an experimental variable (E) introduced at some point among these observations. Changes likely attributable to the experimental variable can then be charted (e.g., the preexperimental variable period and the postexperimental variable period). A conventional time-series design, also known as an interrupted time-series design because of the introduction of the experimental variable, E, is

Time 1	Time 2	Time 3	Time 4	Time 5	E	Time 6	Time 7	Time 8	Time 9	Time 10
O	O	O	O	O	↓	O	O	O	O	O

Another example is an examination of attorney involvement in juvenile court cases over time. In the 1950s and 1960s, attorney involvement in juvenile court cases was minimal. However, the U.S. Supreme Court ruled in several cases that led to greater constitutional rights and protections for juveniles from 1966 to 1976. Since greater constitutional rights for juveniles might also mean greater responsibility and accountability on their part, it has been suspected by many researchers that the juvenile court has become increasingly criminalized. Thus, greater attorney involvement in juvenile cases will probably occur, largely as the result of a greater need for attorneys in defense of juveniles.

The National Center for Juvenile Justice in Pittsburgh, Pennsylvania, compiles information about juvenile court cases in most states. This information has been collected for many years. If we were to examine juvenile cases across many years in different states, we could see whether attorney involvement in juvenile cases increased or remained the same. Several studies of attorney involvement in juvenile court cases have indicated greater attorney involvement over the years. In states such as California, attorney involvement has increased over the years from 40 percent of the cases in 1960 to over 90 percent in 1994.

The experimental or treatment variable in this case might be a U.S. Supreme Court decision about particular juvenile rights. We might also use an event such as the "get-tough" movement toward crime and delinquency, which seems to have gained considerable momentum since the mid-1980s. The get-tough movement promotes tougher sanctions or penalties, sentences, or dispositions for both adult and juvenile offenders. Tracking attorney involvement during the 1980s during a time when the get-tough movement evolved, we might see a dramatic upsurge of attorney involvement in juvenile cases seemingly coinciding with the get-tough movement.

Another application of the time-series design might be a study of the impact of divestiture of certain juvenile court cases in a certain jurisdiction. For example, in the 1980s the juvenile court in Yakima, Washington, divested itself of jurisdiction over status offenders (e.g., runaways, truants, and curfew violators). This meant that juvenile court judges would no longer hear cases involving juvenile status offenders. Rather, the juvenile court would concentrate solely on more serious delinquent offenders (e.g., those commiting theft, robbery, rape, and murder). It was predicted that divestiture would be followed by a reduction in the sheer numbers of cases to be processed by the juvenile court. Using the number of juvenile court cases processed by the Yakima juvenile courts on a

Box 5.2

Jeffrey A. Butts
Program on Law & Behavior,
Urban Institute, Washington, DC

Statistics: B.S. (sociology), University of Oregon; M.S.W. (social work), University of Oregon; Ph.D. (social work and sociology), University of Michigan.

Interests: Criminal justice issues; juvenile justice programs and policy, especially concerning juvenile courts and juvenile corrections programs for young offenders.

I am a senior researcher with one of the most recognized organizations in the field of social policy research. More than 300 people work at the Urban Institute in Washington, DC, and I am one of 25 persons at the Institute who focus exclusively on criminal justice issues. My work at the Institute spans the fields of policy analysis and program evaluation. For example, in 1998 I began a three-year evaluation project for the U.S. Department of Justice's Juvenile Justice Office that measured the impact of teen courts on young, relatively nonserious juvenile offenders. My colleagues and I collected data on teen court operations in several cities and compared individual youth outcomes in teen court cases with similar cases handled in traditional juvenile court. The findings of the study were designed to aid federal, state, and local decision makers that were considering expanding the use of teen courts.

In a project that was funded by the Department of Justice in 1999, in response to a direct request from the U.S. Congress, my colleagues and I studied trends in the demand for juvenile detention and corrections space nationwide. The purpose of the study was to examine the methods that state governments use to plan for future juvenile corrections capacity and to develop new techniques of estimating future demand that were more sensitive to policy and programmatic factors.

Before joining the Institute in 1997, I worked for six years at the National Center for Juvenile Justice in Pittsburgh, Pennsylvania. My primary responsibility at the center was to manage the National Juvenile Court Data Archive, maintained for the U.S. Department of Justice. The archive is basically a warehouse of automated case records including more than half of the juvenile court cases handled nationwide. In addition to producing national reports for the Department of Justice, my colleagues and I analyzed these data for other studies as well. For instance, I relied on the archive's data files for a federally funded study of processing delays in the juvenile justice system that resulted in several published articles.

Like many criminal justice researchers, my background is rather mixed and reflects my interest in the application of research findings as well as the research itself. I earned an undergraduate degree in sociology in 1981 at the University of Oregon. My first job was with the Lane County Juvenile Department in Eugene, where I provided counseling and drug education workshops to youth charged with alcohol and drug offenses. I also earned a master's degree in social work and worked for two years as a caseworker in the state agency responsible for abused and neglected children. Then I went to the University of Michigan where I received my Ph.D. in social work and sociology in 1992. My studies at the University of Michigan concentrated on organizational theory and youth policy research.

I began to train seriously for a career in research while at the University of Michigan. I took every opportunity while in graduate school to work on short-term research and consulting projects. I would argue that these temporary research positions were at least as important as my classwork in preparing me for work as a researcher. They allowed me to work in more than a dozen states, meeting frequently with state and local officials to design and manage studies of juvenile detention centers, training schools, and community programs. I was often responsible for analyzing data, authoring reports, and presenting the findings, often in meetings with executive and legislative staff but occasionally in legislative hearings.

One of my central goals as a researcher is to make research findings more accessible to nontechnical audiences. Unlike most of the problems studied by those in the physical sciences, the areas investigated by criminal justice researchers are subject to political manipulation and ideological disputes. It is one of the jobs of a researcher, I would argue, to bridge the communication gap between the legislator and the scientist, or between the truck driver and the professor. If researchers fail to take the time to translate the results of their own work to nonresearchers, others will do the translation for them. This has often led to confusing or even harmful use of research findings.

Advice to Students: I encourage students interested in criminal justice research to use their time in school to learn the tools of the trade. First, make sure that your degree program includes one or two good writing courses. If your school or university does not offer one, go elsewhere. Bad writing is an unforgivable sin for a researcher. Second, take every statistics course that you can feasibly take. Every student hates that part of graduate school, but this is the only time in your career when you will have the opportunity, and probably the energy, to train those mental muscles.

Finally, choose one thing and learn everything you can about it. That one thing might be prison privatization, electronic monitoring technologies, or recidivism measures. Whatever you choose, you need to have one area about which you know more than almost anybody. Joining a new professional field is like trying to force your way to a buffet table already jammed by hungry eaters. Don't expect them to step aside for you; you have to elbow your way to get where the goodies are. The way to do that is to offer an expertise that only you can provide. Once you are reasonably established, then you can let your interests take you into other areas.

monthly basis, a time-series design would track these cases over several years. Following divestiture of jurisdiction over juvenile status offenders, it was found that actual numbers of juvenile court cases *increased* appreciably. This didn't make any sense to investigators. However, researchers learned later that the divestiture action was not received well by Yakima police officers, who perceived divestiture as a challenge to their decision-making authority when confronting juveniles on city streets. In fact, Yakima police were "redefining" juvenile status offenses as delinquent acts and arresting more youths in the postdivestiture period than in the predivestiture period. Many of the arrested youths in the post-divestiture period would have received only verbal warnings in the predivestiture period. A time-series design was useful in detecting this unusual police activity and response to divestiture.

Multiple Time-Series Designs. **Multiple time-series designs** are similar to conventional time-series designs, with the exception that an additional comparison group or population is examined. For instance, in our previous discussion of time-series design used to track murder rates in the United States and the application of the death penalty, the entire U.S. murder rate was examined. But suppose we wanted to compare the murder rates of two states over time, where one state used the death penalty and the other state did not use it. For example, Texas uses the death penalty for capital offenses. In recent decades, Texas suspended its application of the death penalty only as the result of *Furman v. Georgia* (1972). Texas reinstated the death penalty in 1976 when *Gregg v. Georgia* (1976) was decided. Suppose we were to track the murder rate in Texas over time, encompassing the 1972 to 1976 period when the death penalty was temporarily suspended. Further, suppose that we were to track the murder rate of another state where the death penalty is not used, such as Michigan. We might suspect that suspending the death penalty in Texas might cause changes in the Texas murder rate, whereas for the same period of time, the Michigan murder rate might not fluctuate. This multiple time-series design might be illustrated as follows across the years 1968 to 1979:

Murder Rate by Year

	1968	1969	1970	1971	1972	E	1973	1974	1975	1976	E	1977	1978	1979
						↓					↓			
Texas	O	O	O	O	O	E	O	O	O	O	E	O	O	O
Michigan	O	O	O	O	O	E	O	O	O	O	E	O	O	O

The above example actually shows two *E*'s, the first being the *Furman v. Georgia* (1972) decision. The second *E* is the *Gregg v. Georgia* (1976) decision. We might expect that the murder rate in Texas would increase following the 1972 decision, since capital punishment was suspended for murder. However, when capital punishment is reintroduced in 1977 following the *Gregg v. Georgia* (1976) decision, we might expect the murder rate in Texas to decline. But in Michigan, we would expect little or no change in the murder rate across these same years, since Michigan has no death penalty and made no changes relative to it. All of these expectations are premised on the idea that the death penalty per se is a profound deterrent to murder. Indeed, if we saw the murder rate significantly rise in Texas for the years 1973–1976, and then if the murder rate were to decline substantially in 1977, 1978, and 1979, we might conclude that the death penalty deters persons from committing murder.

Criticisms of Time-Series and Multiple Time-Series Designs. A compelling strength of a time-series research design is that changes in our observation of a single variable over time may be indicative of the influence or impact of a treatment or experimental variable. If appreciable changes occur in the variable under observation, and if these changes occur contemporaneously with the new event or the intervening treatment, or experimental variable, then a potential cause-effect relation may be established. For instance, if several new juvenile rights are conveyed by the U.S. Supreme Court in 1966 and we are tracking the percentage of attorney use in juvenile cases, we might infer that these changes of rights cause increased attorney involvement in juvenile court cases if we observe something like the following:

Percent of Attorney Involvement in Juvenile Court Cases

E

1960	61	62	63	64	65	66		67	68	69	70	71	72	73	74	75	76
40%	40%	40%	40%	40%	40%	40%		55%	60%	70%	80%	81%	82%	85%	85%	86%	90%

where E = more rights for juveniles because of U.S. Supreme Court decisions

Our analysis of this trend in attorney use by juveniles in juvenile court cases would certainly arouse our suspicions that U.S. Supreme Court decisions conveying more rights to juveniles seemed to prompt greater attorney involvement in juvenile cases.

One drawback of time-series designs is that we don't know for sure if a variable such as the murder rate for any given state would have changed anyway or remained the same, regardless of events or U.S. Supreme Court decisions. For instance, attorney use may have escalated in juvenile court cases because of new state legislature provisions mandating attorneys for juveniles in all serious cases. The fact that juveniles have more rights in the post-1966 period than they did in the pre-1966 period may be irrelevant.

Even where multiple time-series designs are used, there are problems regarding whether the two samples or populations being compared are equivalent. Murder rate comparisons between Texas and Michigan may be influenced by factors other than whether these states use or don't use the death penalty. The U.S. economy fluctuates. Persons may engage in more violent crime when unemployment is high. The death penalty may be an irrelevant consideration. Thus, the presence and potential influence of one or more factors unknown to us may actually cause changes or not cause changes in the variables we examine. This is one important reason why researchers conduct investigations of the same events and variables again and again. After considerable investigation, we are able to discern patterns in our findings that give us more confidence in our explanations of events.

Cost-Benefit Analyses

Another type of research design is **cost-benefit analysis.** The focus of cost-benefit analysis is upon the useful and practical results of an intervention or experimental variable and the cost of these results compared with alternative interventions.

Electronic Monitoring versus Conventional Probation Supervision. Suppose we are interested in determining the cost of electronic monitoring as one supervisory option for offenders who have been placed on probation. Perhaps we are unsure about the value of electronic monitoring compared with various forms of intensive supervised probation that we currently use to monitor offenders. We want to know whether electronic monitoring will have any discernable effect on reducing client recidivism compared with conventional monitoring methods. The start-up costs of electronic monitoring are approximately $50,000, which includes 50 electronic wristlets that can be worn by offender/clients. Included also in this expense is the apparatus and equipment located in our central probation office.

Over the next year we place 100 clients on electronic monitoring at different times and for varying durations, such as three months, six months, or nine months. Next, we determine the rate of recidivism among those who have been electronically monitored compared with 100 probationers who have been supervised by more conventional methods (e.g., intermittent contact with probation officers on a face-to-face basis in the community). We determine that the recidivism rate is about 28 percent for those who have been electronically monitored compared with a 65 percent recidivism rate among conventionally monitored probationers. Further, we calculate that apart from the initial start-up costs of electronic monitoring, it costs about $4 per day to monitor each probationer compared with $10 per day to monitor them with conventional monitoring methods. A comparison of the costs of supervising offenders, either by electronic monitoring or conventional probation officer supervision, together with a comparison of the recidivism rates of the two sets of probationers, reveals that electronic monitoring is less costly and reduces recidivism of probationer/clients substantially. In this example, the costs and benefits of electronic monitoring can be directly calculated and compared with conventional probation supervision practices.

Studying At-Risk Youths and Delinquents. Cost-benefit analyses are not always that easy to make. Suppose we are interested in comparing different types of delinquency interventions to see whether one intervention program is better than another at preventing delinquency. One program, Program A, is geared to identify "at-risk" youths in elementary schools who have not yet committed any delinquent acts. "At-risk" youths are identified on the basis of their family instability, lower socioeconomic status, school adjustment problems, and other factors. We have fairly reliable information that suggests these characteristics seem to be associated with older delinquent youths who have had troubled pasts. Perhaps if we can work more closely with at-risk youths, we might be able to interrupt the chain of events that leads them to commit delinquent acts as they grow older. Program A requires hiring several special school counselors and social workers, as well as some clinical psychologists. These persons can work as a team to target at-risk youths and expose them to the delinquency prevention components of Program A.

Program B is designed to work with youths in these same schools who have already committed delinquent acts. Program B includes bringing eight or ten delinquent youths together on a regular basis for introspective group counseling and therapy. A part of this therapy includes periodic visits to a local prison, where several inmates can speak directly to these youths and warn them of the potential dangers of delinquency that might lead to incarceration. Thus, there is an attempt in Program B to shock youths or scare them away from further delinquent offending.

Both Program A and Program B involve hiring specialists and psychological therapists who can work with youths of different ages. Both programs are calculated to prevent delinquency. A cost-benefit analysis of the two programs can be made. We must prepare for a long-term examination of participating youths over a period of years.

After six years, we are able to compare participating youths in both Program A and Program B according to whether they have committed delinquent acts. Perhaps 15 percent of the at-risk youths in Program A have engaged in some form of delinquent behavior during the six-year period of our research. Also, we have found that about 20 percent of all delinquent youths in Program B have committed new delinquent acts. However, we note that following this six-year time interval, *other* youths in these schools who were not involved in either Program A or Program B have committed one or more delinquent acts. These are youths previously unidentified as being at risk or delinquent. These other youths make up about 2 percent of all students in these schools.

Our cost-benefit analysis is somewhat inconclusive. We know what it costs to hire the specialists, psychologists, and social workers for both programs. But it is difficult to gauge which of the two programs is the better one for preventing future delinquency. Program A seems to have the better record for curbing delinquency among those previously defined as at-risk. But Program B has fairly good results as well, inasmuch as only 20 percent of the delinquent youths committed future delinquent acts.

Ultimately it may come down to deciding which of the two programs is easier to operate. External factors may persuade us to go with one program instead of the other. Perhaps some of the parents in Program A are offended that we have identified their children as being at-risk. Perhaps they feel that we have singled out their children and are discriminating against them, despite our good intentions to help them. We may find that it is easier to deal with those youths who have already demonstrated their capacity for delinquent conduct. We may also find that the school board is concerned about the different programs and which ones are the least intrusive. Our cost-benefit analysis of these programs may be influenced by many factors.

The Detroit, Michigan, Ministation Program. A third example may involve an experiment with police department ministations in communities used as a means of preventing crime in neighborhoods. Ministations are small substations staffed by one or two police officers. These are often located in high-crime neighborhoods and offer neighborhood residents an additional means of connecting with police officers apart from foot and cruiser patrolling. The Detroit Police Department experimented with ministations during the late 1980s. It was believed that the ministations would reduce crime in those neighborhoods where they were placed. After several years, crime rates were compared for the preministation years and the postministation years. The difference in crime rates for the two periods was negligible, signifying that ministations did not appear to significantly decrease crime in those neighborhoods where they were located. But officials were quick to point out that the ministation program *did* heighten community acceptance of police officers and that the ministation program was a good public relations strategy. In those neighborhoods with ministations, citizens felt safer and had more positive attitudes toward the police. During times when police departments of various cities have serious public relations problems because of the misconduct of some of their officers, any strategy that improves police-community relations, such as the ministation program in Detroit, is viewed as a desirable strategy. It is impossible to calculate the value of improved public relations between police and their communities.

Criticisms of Cost-Benefit Analysis.   When investigators seek to determine the effectiveness of an intervention, program, therapy, drug, or other experimental variable, they may have a vested interest in the outcome. If their research is sponsored by a private organization, their vested interest in the outcome may be heightened. Also, cost-benefit analyses are often subjective. Researchers are trained to be objective, although some investigators may be tempted to focus only on the most positive aspects of study outcomes.

Depending upon the variables examined, cost-benefit analysis may be a simple and direct way of determining which of several interventions is best at bringing about desired results at the least cost. However, demonstrating the effectiveness of an intervention may take considerable time. Longitudinal studies, or studies that span one or more years, may be inconclusive, when study findings are diffuse. It may be difficult to distinguish between several competing strategies because of mixed results. Increasingly, the National Institute of Justice and other funding organizations are obligating research grantees to limit the time frames of their investigations, so that research results are reported more quickly. The shorter-term nature of research projects might reflect the greater impatience of organizations and agencies for study results that can be used to support changing policies and procedures.

■ KEY TERMS

After-only design	Control group
Before-after design	Cost-benefit analysis
Case study	Descriptive design
Case study design	Equivalent groups
Classical experimental design	Experimental designs
Control	Experimental group

Experimental stimulus
Experimental variables
Exploratory design
Frequency distribution control
  matching
Group distribution matching
Individual matching
Interrupted time-series design
Matching
Multiple time-series designs
National Youth Survey (NYS)

Persons as their own controls
Posttest
Pretest
Quasi-experiments
Random assignment
Survey design
Survey research
Time-series design
Treatment variables
True experiment

■ QUESTIONS FOR REVIEW

1. What is meant by a research design? Identify two major types of research designs and discuss briefly their major objectives and limitations.

2. What are three major research objectives? Give some examples of each objective different from those in the chapter and that are drawn from your own perusal of criminal justice literature.

3. How does the amount of information we have about a given sample to be studied influence our study design choices? Explain.

4. Define what is meant by "control." Illustrate how different variables might be manipulated or controlled by the investigator.

5. What is cross-tabulation? Give a hypothetical example of variable control in a cross-tabulation using at least three variables of your choice.

6. Differentiate between experimental groups and control groups. In what sense might the term *group* be used when the research target might be more broadly conceived? Hint: Review the Kansas City Preventive Patrol Experiment.

7. What are four methods whereby groups are equated for experimental purposes? Describe each and discuss their respective limitations.

8. What is a survey? In what sense is a survey considered superficial? Discuss.

9. What is a case study? What are some drawbacks of case studies? In what respects can case studies be more informative than surveys?

10. Describe the classic experimental design by using hypothetical variables of your choice from the research literature.

11. What is meant by time-series designs? What are some criticisms of time-series designs?

12. What are after-only experimental designs? How are these designs variations of the classical experimental design?

13. How does a before-after experimental design improve upon after-only designs? Discuss briefly.

14. What is meant by cost-benefit analysis? What are some criticisms of it?

chapter 6

Data Collection Strategies I
Sampling Techniques, Purposes, and Problems

■ INTRODUCTION

*A major component of most research projects is **sampling.** Essentially, sampling involves targeting populations and selecting some of them for subsequent investigation. For instance, researchers may wish to study correctional officers from jails and prisons in order to compare their degrees of professionalism. Or researchers may want to know opinions of professionals in community-based probation agencies about agency volunteers and how the effectiveness of these volunteers is determined. Other investigators may want to see whether shock probationers make better adjustments in their communities compared with those offenders who do not participate in shock probation. Some researchers may want to profile the characteristics of convicted female murderers currently serving time in penitentiaries.*

Each of these topics raises several common questions. These are (1) Where will data be obtained? and (2) How will it be obtained? Many researchers know in advance where data can be found. Also, they have a general idea about how they will get the data needed to answer their research questions. Perhaps they have important contacts within various institutions and agencies. Some researchers may be employees of organizations they wish to study. Using one's organizational contacts or the contacts of others is a good means of initially getting one's foot in the door to conduct research.

A third question is suggested by each of these topics: What sampling process will be used to obtain persons from the larger category of those we wish to study? Because there are so many different topics, so many target audiences available for study, and so many different conditions that might exist whenever studies are conducted, no single sampling method has universal application. Over the years, many sampling techniques have evolved. Each technique has different strengths and weaknesses, depending upon the unique circumstances of its application.

The organization of this chapter is as follows: Several conventional terms of sampling methods are identified and described. Sampling fulfills several important functions. These functions are outlined. Questions about why we sample are answered. All of the major sampling plans discussed here have been grouped into probability sampling plans and nonprobability sampling plans. Respectively, these plans either permit or do not permit generalizations to populations we have selected for study. Several types of probability and nonprobability sampling plans have been devised to meet investigator needs under different kinds of research conditions. Each of these types of sampling plans is illustrated, and the weaknesses and strengths of each is discussed. Suggested applications are made for each type of plan in relation to problems that may be investigated in criminal justice or criminology.

Finally, several important sampling issues are examined. Investigators may want to know whether their samples are representative or typical of the general class of persons they are studying. What factors intervene to affect the representativeness of samples adversely or favorably? What should researchers do if some persons they want to study refuse to participate or fail to return their mailed questionnaires? What should be the appropriate sample size?

Some samples are difficult to access, since permission may be required to study them. Prisoners and juveniles are examples of persons requiring the consent of others before they may be studied. Some persons may not require the permission of others before they can be studied, but they may be nearly inaccessible. Judges and prosecutors are often insulated from researchers by a protective group of assistants and a loyal secretarial pool. Thus, the broad class of potentates will be examined as a sampling problem and consideration. These and other issues will be presented and discussed.

■ WHAT IS SAMPLING?

Statisticians refer to the units they study as elements. *Elements* refer either to things or people. Thus, we may study light bulbs, shoes, telephones, or people, and, in the general case, our references to them will be as elements. In the social sciences, "a study of 100 elements" means that researchers are studying 100 persons. Usually, these persons have characteristics of interest to the researcher. These characteristics may be male juvenile delinquents, female murderers, probation officers, defense attorneys, juvenile court judges, intake officers, jail or prison inmates, correctional officers, wardens or superintendents, or volunteers in a community-based correctional agency. They constitute the **sampling frame.** Because of our research interests, we seek information about these persons. Sampling means to take a proportion of persons from the whole class of persons about which we seek information.

Populations and Parameters

A **population** comprises the entire class or aggregate of elements about which one seeks information. For example, we may seek information about the inmates in the Kentucky State Penitentiary. We may want to study Illinois probation officers. Or we may seek information about juvenile delinquents in Las Vegas, Nevada. Therefore, the three populations about which we seek information are all inmates at the Kentucky State Penitentiary, all probation officers in the state of Illinois, and all juvenile delinquents in Las Vegas, Nevada. In each of these cases, the characteristics of these populations of elements are designated as **parameters.** Thus, the average age of all Kentucky State Penitentiary inmates is a parameter. The average caseload of all Illinois probation officers is a parameter. And the average height of juvenile delinquents in Las Vegas, Nevada, is also a parameter or population characteristic. We want to know about these and other characteristics or parameters of these populations.

But because of the sheer magnitude of these populations, it is frequently difficult for researchers to study all of the population elements. We can appreciate this difficulty more easily by imagining what our task would involve if we wanted to study all probation officers or juvenile delinquents or inmates in the entire United States! Imagine the time, money, and personpower it would require to complete this task. However, our task of studying these populations is greatly simplified if we are less ambitious and choose to study only samples of elements taken from these populations.

Samples and Statistics

Samples are proportions or smaller collections of elements taken from the larger population of them. Using the population examples above, samples of them would be (1) a sample of all Kentucky State Penitentiary inmates, (2) a sample of all Illinois probation officers, and (3) a sample of all Las Vegas, Nevada, juvenile delinquents. If the Kentucky State Penitentiary inmate population consists of 1,200 inmates, we might study 200 of these inmates as our **sample** of elements. The characteristics of our inmate sample would be designated as statistics. Statistics are characteristics of samples of elements taken from a population of them. Some sample statistics might be the average age of a sample of Las Vegas, Nevada, juvenile delinquents or the average caseload of a sample of Illinois probation officers. Table 6.1 illustrates the population-sample relation.

Generalizability and Representativeness

A persistent concern of researchers who study samples of elements rather than entire populations of them is whether their samples are representative of those populations. Can investigators make generalizations about populations of elements by only studying samples of them? How do we know if our samples are representative of the populations from which they were taken? As long as we study samples of elements rather than entire populations, we may never know if our samples are representative of those populations.

Generally, **sample representativeness** is assumed or implied, depending upon how the sample is selected and depending upon its size in relation to the population. If we must choose between two samples of different sizes that have both been selected using the same sampling procedure, the larger sample would be assumed to be more representative of the population than the smaller sam-

TABLE 6.1 The Distinction Between a Population and a Sample

Population (100%)	Sample (20%)
1. All Kentucky State Penitentiary inmates	1. Some Kentucky State Penitentiary inmates
2. All Illinois probation officers	2. Some Illinois probation officers
3. All Las Vegas, Nevada, juvenile delinquents	3. Some Las Vegas, Nevada, juvenile delinquents
Some Characteristics of Elements	
1. The average age of all inmates in the Kentucky State Penitentiary	1. The average age of the sample of inmates in the Kentucky State Penitentiary
2. The average caseload of all Illinois probation officers	2. The average caseload of the sample of Illinois probation officers
3. The male/female proportion of all Las Vegas, Nevada, juvenile delinquents	3. The male/female proportion of the sample of Las Vegas, Nevada, juvenile delinquents

ple. If different sampling procedures were used, however, we could not make this statement about the two samples, regardless of their respective sizes. Thus, the **sample size** alone does not make the sample representative of its population. For instance, we may want to generalize about all incarcerated adult offenders in the United States. But if we select a sample of 20,000 offenders from only half of all U.S. maximum-security penitentiaries, we would have no inmate representation from jails (facilities that house short-term or less serious offenders) or other, less secure, incarcerative facilities. Although quite large, our sample of prison inmates would be unrepresentative or atypical of all inmates, since only the most serious and long-term offenders would be included in our sample, and all short-termers in jails or less serious offenders housed in medium- or minimum-security facilities would be excluded. (See Table 6.1.)

In another research situation, investigators may have responses from 350 out of 375 inmates of a particular prison. If the investigators want to generalize only to the inmates of that prison, then the sample size of 350 is considered quite large for generalization purposes. Over 90 percent of all inmates have been obtained as elements. However, what if the researcher wants to use the sample of 350 inmates and generalize to all inmates of all U.S. prisons? Because of the dramatic shift from the population of a single prison to the population of all U.S. prisons, the sample of 350 inmates diminishes in significance when we attempt to generalize from it to all U.S. prison inmates. Therefore, answers to questions about the representativeness and generalizability of one's sample on the basis of its size are relative. Much depends on what the researcher wants to do with the results and how large the sample is in relation to the population from which it was drawn.

■ THE DECISION TO SAMPLE

When the research design has been formulated, specifications have usually been made about what elements to include. An analysis of much of the current literature in criminal justice and criminology shows that the bulk of it describes data collected from samples. The decision to sample is made on the basis of at least three criteria: (1) the size of the target population, (2) the cost of obtaining the elements, and (3) the convenience and accessibility of the elements.

Size of the Target Population

How large is the target population? If researchers want to study the effectiveness of defense counsels in criminal cases, for instance, their target population might be all licensed criminal lawyers in the United States or all criminal defense counsel who are members of the American Bar Association. Perhaps the investigator wishes to study how AIDS inmates are segregated and treated in prisons and jails. Maybe the project is focused on the amount of knowledge correctional officers have about their legal liabilities in their interactions with inmates. These are fairly large populations, and it would be a demanding task to study all of these elements, even if they could be identified and contacted. Bureaus of social research, survey research centers, and most other large-scale public or private research organizations have the resources to conduct research projects on a grandiose scale. Nevertheless, even these large bureaus with extensive resources limit the scope of their inquiry to samples of elements rather than entire populations. However, most independent researchers must engage in small-scale studies with limited funds, unless one's project is funded by the Department of Justice, the Bureau of Justice Statistics, or some other public or private funding agency.

Cost of Obtaining Elements

How much money is available for the study? The cheapest ways of collecting data include observing others or going to libraries and analyzing information from surveys and reports. The *Uniform Crime Reports, National Crime Victimization Survey,* or the *Sourcebook of Criminal Justice Statistics* contain much information about crime and criminals. Another excellent source of data relevant to crime and the criminal justice system is the National Archive of Criminal Justice Data, which is sponsored by the Bureau of Justice Statistics, U.S. Department of Justice and operated by the Inter-University Consortium for Political and Social Research, headquartered in Ann Arbor, Michigan. Working through universities and colleges, professors, students, and others may access all types of information, including data sets; surveys; statistical compilations about runaways, truants, and prison and jail inmates; judicial decision guidelines; career offender characteristics; national crime figures; and correctional facility censuses. Nominal fees are charged for such services, which have been converted into computer-readable formats.

Convenience and Accessibility of the Elements

Consideration must be given to the convenience and accessibility of the elements to be studied. Students are frequent research targets, simply because researchers are often professors who teach large university classes. It is easy to distribute questionnaires to large numbers of students and ask them their opinions about diverse issues.

However, if someone wishes to interview HIV-positive inmates in prisons and discover how they are treated, permission must first be obtained from the wardens or superintendents of those facilities. The consent of HIV-infected inmates is then required. Wardens and superintendents of prisons may not grant researchers permission to carry out their study. Even if they did, there are no guarantees that HIV-infected inmates would consent to being studied. The best research plans may be devised, but they may never be implemented, simply because of the inaccessibility of the target population.

Briefly summarizing, decisions to sample are based, in part, on the size of the population, the anticipated cost of the study in relation to the budget of the researcher, and the convenience and accessibility associated with obtaining the elements. Other factors are involved in this decision as well. Some of these factors will discussed in a latter portion of the chapter.

■ SOME FUNCTIONS OF SAMPLING

The functions of sampling include (1) economizing resources, (2) manageability, (3) meeting assumptions of statistical tests, and (4) meeting the requirements of experiments.

Economizing Resources

Sampling saves researchers time, money, and personpower. Fewer elements are selected, and less expense is incurred as the result of sending fewer questionnaires to respondents or interviewing fewer of them. In addition, fewer assistants are necessary to help perform these chores.

Manageability

Sampling helps to make data tabulation and analysis more manageable. It is easier to tabulate information from smaller numbers of elements. Also, many statistics programs for personal computers have data limitations, where the number of variables is restricted and smaller sample sizes are recommended. But small numbers of variables and sample sizes are not necessarily small. A computer program may prescribe that it be used only for data sets with 40 or fewer variables and sample sizes of 1,200 or fewer. This size data set will cover 99 percent of all research projects conducted by criminologists and criminal justice professionals. Much of the time, samples analyzed in the current literature (e.g., articles, reports) contain fewer than 500 elements.

Meeting Assumptions of Statistical Tests

Certain assumptions associated with statistical test applications must be satisfied. **Probability sampling** is a requirement of all statistical procedures involved in statistical inference and decision making. Other assumptions must be satisfied as well, besides the probability sampling requirement. The importance of meeting the assumptions is that meaningful and valid interpretations of test results can be made only if these assumptions are fulfilled.

Also, each statistical test and measure of association has a "recommended sample size range" where optimum sample sizes are specified. Some procedures are designed for small samples, where "small" means 12 persons or less. Other procedures prescribe a range from 25 to 250 persons for optimum application. Applying these tests outside of these sample ranges can be done, but the reliability and dependability of these tests is adversely affected. We cannot be sure of what the numerical test results mean under these less-than-optimum conditions.

Meeting the Requirements of Experiments

Certain types of research experimentation require that samples be of specified sizes. In some experimental situations, several samples of elements must be obtained. A requirement of an experiment might be that the samples should be of equal size and that they share other characteristics or similarities. For instance, these sample similarities may be equivalent proportions of males and females, equivalent proportions of different criminal offense categories, or equivalent proportions of years on the job, depending upon the target population being investigated. Specialized statistical procedures have been devised to analyze these unusual experimental situations as well.

PROBABILITY SAMPLING PLANS

Probability sampling plans are those that specify the probability or likelihood of inclusion of each element drawn from a designated population. Technically, the following facts need to be known by the researcher in advance of selecting the sample:

1. The size of the target population or universe from which the sample will be obtained must be known. (The term *universe* is used interchangeably with population, since it refers to all persons about which one seeks information.)
2. The desired sample size must be specified.
3. Each element in the population or universe of elements must have an equal and an independent chance of being drawn and included in the sample.

Symbolically, when comparisons of population and sample sizes are made, N is the actual population size, while n is the desired sample size. Under many conditions, these ideal criteria can be invoked. If we are seeking information about all inmates in a particular state penitentiary, a complete listing of inmates is available for our use in identifying all population elements. Another example is provided in a study by Larzelere and Patterson (1990). These researchers investigated the influence of parental management as a primary antecedent of delinquency. They believed that parental management skills would override factors such as socioeconomic status (SES), divorce, and exposure to criminal elements as contributors to juvenile delinquency.

In order to test certain hypotheses, these researchers identified in advance a target population of youths from the Oregon Youth Study (OYS). Among other things, the OYS identified those schools in the Eugene-Springfield area that had the highest per capita juvenile arrest rates. They drew their sample of youths from "all fourth-grade boys in these schools" (1990:308). Since there were existing records of these youths in the Eugene-Springfield area, it was relatively easy for them to draw the desired number of elements from these records. Similarly, membership lists of various organizations, such as the American Correctional Association, the American Probation and Parole Association, the American Jail Association, or the American Bar Association, will help us to identify various aggregates or potential target populations and enumerate them.

Some populations of elements are more elusive and cannot be enumerated easily, if at all. Studies of the parental characteristics of abused children are difficult to conduct, since child abuse is infrequently reported. Even if it is reported, many cases are not handled by courts but rather by referrals to social welfare agencies. Prostitution and illegal gambling are other phenomena that are difficult to study, since the incidence or extent of these activities is largely hidden or unknown. Even if we know about the target population and where it can be located, there may be serious logistical problems encountered when attempting to sample from it. Knowing about the population of all jail inmates in the United States is theoretically possible, but our attempt to enumerate them would be frustrated by the fact that this population changes daily through admissions and releases.

A practical approach is best for dealing with large populations of elements. We will scale down our target population to a more manageable level. If we wish to study inmates, correctional officers, or juvenile delinquents, we can limit the scope of our investigation to a particular jurisdiction, such as a state, county, city, or suburb. Even if these smaller populations of elements do not include everyone, we can nevertheless conduct meaningful research and suggest to others that our findings are potentially generalizable to other settings. Researchers will often make qualifying remarks or statements in their work that highlight deficiencies in the target population or problems that occurred in the selection of sample elements.

Natural conditions may exist that limit the population's magnitude. For example, Meadows and Trostle (1988) studied police misconduct in the Los Angeles (California) Police Department for the years 1974–1986. They wanted to describe the nature of the misconduct alleged as well as the legal outcome. The city attorney's office permitted them to examine 79 closed cases during that time interval. From their research report, it is unknown whether these 79 cases represented a small or large proportion of the total number of police misconduct cases handled by the city attorney's office between 1974 and 1986. Under these circumstances, the researchers had no alternative but to label their sample "nonprobability," since it was not possible to enumerate all cases from which their sample of 79 was obtained.

In another study, Walters (1988) wanted to examine correctional officers' perceptions of powerlessness in their work. Powerlessness was defined as the probability that individuals could not determine the occurrences or outcomes they seek. Walters wanted to know if powerlessness was perceived by correctional officers, and whether powerlessness was the result of specific environmental factors and self-concepts. Walters identified a large prison in the "Intermountain West." The facility housed 750 inmates and employed 193 correctional officers. Walters sent questionnaires to all 193 officers, but only 126 completed questionnaires were returned, meaning a 65 percent response rate. In this study, no attempt was made to enumerate all of the officers. Rather, the entire population of 193 was targeted, although only two-thirds responded. Two-thirds of the population of officers is a rather large proportion under these circumstances. Despite this large proportion of responses, the sample cannot be considered as a probability sample. The reasons for officer nonresponse are unknown, but Walters's results may have been quite different had some or all of these nonrespondents actually responded and returned their completed questionnaires.

Some studies are conducted where it is impossible to identify the target population. In these cases, researchers must settle for a microcosm of the population, and there may even be additional limitations. For instance, Charisse Coston and Lee Ross (1996) studied a sample of female prostitutes and streetwalkers who had been arrested for soliciting in a large city in the East. These investigators wanted to know about the nature and extent of victimization occurring among these women who were considered high risks as crime victims. Coston and Ross identified 77 women who had been arrested and attempted to interview all of them. Eighteen women refused to be interviewed, leaving Coston and Ross with only 59 women. Thus, 30-minute interviews were conducted with 59 women out of their original sample of 77 prostitutes. Compared with the study by Walters where the entire population of prison correctional officers was known, Coston and Ross were dealing with only a small number of prostitutes in a single city. Their sample was not random, and Coston and Ross could not say with certainty what population these prostitutes were from. But these limitations did not detract from the fact that Coston and Ross were able to generate much informative data about prostitute victimization.

Finally, a study by Jacqueline Helfgott (1997) of ex-offender needs versus community opportunity was conducted in Seattle, Washington. Helfgott wanted to know about ex-offender needs in Seattle, what employment and service opportunities existed for them, and what could be done locally to maximize their opportunities. Ex-offender needs included food, clothing, housing, transportation, mental health counseling, medical and dental care, legal assistance, employment, and social relationships. Her research targeted 326 community transition agencies, 500 employers, 500 property managers, 22 educational institutions, and 1,440 community residents drawn from a Seattle telephone directory.

All of these agencies and persons were drawn at random from various directories and listings. Helfgott didn't obtain the cooperation of everyone she contacted. Her sample results were as follows: 56 out of 326 community transition agencies (17 percent); 156 out of 500 employers (31.2 percent); 196 out of 500 property managers (39.2 percent); 22 out of 22 educational institutions (100 percent); and 306 out of 1,440 community residents (21.2 percent). She also obtained the cooperation and involvement of 20 out of 40 ex-offenders, a 50 percent response. Thus, in just about every category she targeted, Helfgott only obtained a portion of those she sought to include. While her subsequent investigation of the participants yielded much valuable information about how the community could assist ex-offenders in meeting their diverse needs, it was virtually impossible for Helfgott to say with certainty that her findings typified any particular population. This says much about the difficulty of acquiring a probability sampling plan despite our best efforts to do so.

Randomness

The crucial features of probability sampling plans have to do with the **equality of draw** and **independence of draw** found in our selection of elements for inclusion in our samples. Actually, equality and independence are essential defining characteristics of randomness, which is the process of selecting elements such that each element has an equal and independent chance of being included. **Randomness** is the primary control governing all **probability sampling plans.** Equality of draw refers to giving all population elements an equal chance of being

Box 6.1

Mark Jones
East Carolina University

Statistics: B.S. (education), University of Georgia; M.S. (criminal justice), Georgia State University; Ph.D. (criminal justice), Sam Houston State University.

Interests: Community corrections, criminal justice ethics, organized crime, and criminal justice history.

My research interests mirror my teaching interests, and not by coincidence. One enjoyable aspect of conducting research is sharing it with the students in my courses. I have written and published in each of my teaching areas. There is a symbiotic relationship between research and teaching: one assists the other. My attraction to teaching in these areas stimulates my desire to conduct research.

I have never had a job assignment that I enjoy as much as writing and conducting research. I do not view publication as daunting or burdensome. One of the attractive aspects of conducting original research is purely egocentric: Face it: It is a bit of an ego trip to see your name in print. My attraction to research also stems from the desire to learn something new, something that I have discovered on my own, and something that, in a sense, no one else besides me knows at that time.

There is another reason I conduct research: It is fun and I enjoy it. But viewing the finished product is not the only satisfaction I derive. When you are engaged in something you enjoy, you do not just enjoy the end result. If a baseball player wants to be a great hitter, the constant, solitary repetition of batting practice must be just as enjoyable as hitting a grand slam in front of 50,000 people. If a researcher wants to enjoy the satisfaction of a finished product, he or she must enjoy the repetitive process of constant editing and reediting that is necessary to attain the finished product.

I hope that my research will positively affect the administration of justice. I hope that the people who read my research will somehow derive some benefit from it. I like to think that policymakers, academicians, and students will look beyond quick fixes, feel-good solutions, and panaceas. I often remind students that criminal justice is in dire need of creative solutions about how to administer justice and deal with crime. Our graduates who enter the criminal justice field need to be taught how to devise creative solutions to the problem of crime, rather than being stuck in the myopia and **paradigm** analysis that grips our field. Research stimulates this kind of badly needed creativity and critical thinking.

Advice to Students: Good writing, and especially good organizational skills acquired through writing, greatly benefits any criminal justice practitioner. Any student who aspires to work in criminal justice can benefit from practice at organizing and writing reports or investigations. One way to develop effective writing skills is by conducting research. Conducting research also helps us to stay current in the dynamic entity of criminal justice study. Heraclitus said that one cannot step into the same river twice. Criminal justice practitioners must be sensitive to changes in their field, and so must criminal justice professors. To some extent, while we can stay current in our field by reading the writings of others, it is very advantageous to use one's own firsthand research experience to stay current.

For students who are considering conducting research, I would suggest that you try it—you might like it. Do not be afraid or intimidated. Each time in my life that I have been given a writing or research assignment, from grade school to the present day, it seems that the most difficult part is writing the first sentence. I am probably not alone here; many of my students have the same problem. There is only one solution, however: Just do it. Keep in mind that there is no such thing as perfect research, especially in a social science like criminal justice where a perfect laboratory setting is unattainable.

If you do not aspire to make research a career, you owe it to your agency and your profession, whether it is law enforcement, corrections, or any other criminal justice system component, to be an informed consumer. To use a colloquial analogy, a person should not have to be a professional auto mechanic when purchasing a new car. But a basic knowledge of automobiles is a great asset when looking for a car. In the same way, people who possess degrees in criminal justice should be able to recognize good criminal justice research and aid their profession with that recognition.

included in the sample. Independence means that the draw or selection of one element will not affect the chances of the remaining elements being drawn later.

Equality of Draw.   Equality of draw is simply illustrated by the following hypothetical example. Suppose we were studying defense attorneys in Detroit, Michigan. Our records might show that there are 2,000 defense attorneys in Detroit. We will use a sampling method that will give each of these 2,000 attorneys 1/2,000th of a chance of being included in our sample n. If our population $N = 50,000$, then everyone should have 1/50,000th of a chance of being included. If our population N were 100, then everyone would have 1/100th of a chance of being included. This is what is meant by giving everyone in the population an equal chance of being included.

Independence of the Draw.   Independence of draw means that the draw of any particular element will not influence the chances of other population elements being included in the sample. An example known as the **fishbowl draw** will be used to illustrate what is meant by independence. First, all elements in the population are enumerated from 1 to N. Second, their numbers are placed on identical slips of paper. Next, these slips are placed in a fishbowl. Next, someone who is blindfolded reaches into the bowl and selects slips of paper, one at a time. Then the numbers are recorded, and those persons matching the numbers become a part of our sample.

Suppose our target population consists of 100 elements. We number each person from 1 to 100, write these numbers on slips of paper, and place them all in a fishbowl. After mixing the slips of paper in the bowl, we reach in, blindfolded, and select the first slip of paper. Our first selection is a random one, since all element numbers were in the bowl and each had 1/100th chance of being included on the first draw. However, we have withdrawn one slip of paper. That leaves 99 pieces of paper in the bowl. The next time we dip into the bowl to retrieve a slip of paper, the remaining elements will have 1/99th chance of being included in our sample. Thus, by continuously drawing slips of paper from the bowl we will slightly increase the chances of the remaining elements being included (e.g., 1/98th, 1/97th, 1/96th, and so on). These are not independent draws, since the chances of the remaining elements being included in our sample are increased each time a slip of paper is removed from the bowl. Therefore, we will not have a **random sample** using this method.

What if we replace the slips of paper once we have drawn them? This way, there would always be 100 slips of paper in the bowl, and each person would have a 1/100th chance of being drawn each time. Actually, this is an appropriate strategy for insuring both independence and equality of draw, and it has been given a name by statisticians: **sampling with replacement.** The earlier method of withholding slips of paper from the bowl after they have been drawn, once we have selected and recorded them, is called **sampling without replacement.** In the social sciences, all probability sampling plans as well as all of the statistical tests used that require probability samples as one of their requisite assumptions assume that sampling with replacement has been used.

However, when sampling with replacement is used, some of us are going to worry about drawing slips of paper from the bowl that have been drawn before. Under these circumstances, the best procedure is to continue drawing slips of paper from the bowl, with replacement, until n desired elements are obtained. Simply skip or ignore those numbers that have already been drawn, replace them in the fishbowl, and continue to draw slips until you have selected n different numbers. Better procedures are available for selecting random samples of elements other than the fishbowl draw. We can obtain randomness by using either a table of **random numbers** or a computer-determined draw.

Simple Random Sampling and Random Numbers Tables

A **table of random numbers** is almost exactly the way it sounds. It is a table of digits randomly derived, where no digit occurs in any particular sequence and no digit occurs any more frequently than any other digit. Table A.2 in Appendix A, pages 620–623, is a table of random numbers. Examine Table A.2 and observe that digits have been bunched up into groups of five rows and five columns, with spaces above and below, as well as on either side of these bunches. There is no significance attached to these particular groupings. The blank spaces between the bunches of digits are simply for reading ease. Imagine what this table would look like if all of these bunches of digits were pushed together toward the centers of the pages. Following is a segment reproduced from the first page of Table A.2, specifically the two bunches of digit groupings in the upper left-hand corner on page 620.

10097	32533
37542	04805
08422	68953
99019	02529
12807	99970

We use this table as follows. First, we identify our target population. Suppose it is an inmate population at the Colorado State Penitentiary. Suppose the population of inmates is $N = 850$. Suppose we wish to draw a sample n of 50 from this population of 850. We will first assign these inmates numbers from 001 to 850, and then we will select 50 different random numbers from Table A.2. We begin this task by counting the number of digits in our population N, that is, three digits: 8, 5, and 0. We will move through this table in a systematic fashion, examining groupings of three digits each. Let's decide to start our selection of sample elements with the first three digits shown in the upper left-hand corner of page 620. These are the digit groupings reproduced earlier for your convenience. Let's record the first three digits, 1, 0, and 0. For our purposes, this is inmate 100. Moving directly downward in the table, we pick up the next three digits immediately below 100, or 375. This is inmate 375. Continuing to move downward toward the bottom of the table, we select 084 or inmate 84, then 990, the 990th inmate, and 128, the 128th inmate. Did you just sense something wrong? Yes. The "990th inmate" doesn't exist, since our population size extends only to 850 inmates. Therefore, we skip or ignore all inmate numbers that don't fit the limits of our population.

When we reach the bottom of page 620, our last three-digit grouping is 690 or inmate 690. Where do we go from here? We go back to the top of the page, almost where we started initially. But now, we will move over to the right precisely one digit, and then pick up the next three-digit sequence. In this case, it will be 009, or the 9th inmate. The next, moving downward directly, is 754, or inmate 754, then 842 or the 842nd inmate, then 901 (skip it), then 280 or the 280th inmate, and so on, until we reach the bottom of the page again. We repeat this process by moving to the top of the page, moving over precisely one digit, selecting the next three-digit sequence, which is 097 (inmate 97), and move downward again, making our selections. The next time we go back to the top of the page, we will move over to the right again one digit, and pick up the next three digits. In this case, we will pick up 973. The next three-digit groupings below this one in the previous example are 420, 226, 190, and 079 respectively. The spacing between groups of digits means nothing, and it is intended only for ease of readability. We continue our selection process until we have identified 50 different random numbers for our desired sample size. By definition, this is a random sample of 50 elements from our population of 850.

Researchers often have access to computer systems with programs capable of generating n random numbers from a population of N elements through a **computer-determined draw.** This is a computer-determined random sample.

In fact, this is precisely how Table A.2 was generated by the Rand Corporation—by computer. Thus, the computer-determined draw and a draw of elements from a table of random numbers are synonymous.

Simple random samples are samples of size n taken from a population size of N. An example of simple random sampling is provided in a study by Crouch and Marquart (1990). These researchers were interested in the effects of prison reforms introduced by the Texas Department of Corrections (TDC) during a period of massive court-ordered reforms during the years 1978–1981. They wanted to know whether significant changes occurred in prison conditions, violence levels, and perceptions of safety among prisoners before, during, and after court-decreed reform implementation. Using TDC-assigned six-digit numbers that identified each inmate, Crouch and Marquart obtained simple random samples of inmates from different prison units, eventually drawing 614 numbers or about 5 percent of the inmate population. However, 123 inmates were not available when these researchers collected their data. Some were ill, others were on furloughs, and others were in solitary confinement. Thirty of the available inmates refused to participate. Therefore, what started out as an ideally selected random sample of TDC prison inmates eventually dwindled to 461 inmates.

What should we call this sample of a simple random sample? First, the sample is no longer a random sample. Of the 614 inmates originally selected as the simple random sample, 153 inmates were either unavailable or refused to participate (1990:107). This nonresponse represents nearly 25 percent of the original sample of 614 inmates. Who knows what effect this substantial number of inmates would have made had their responses been included in the data analysis?

What happened to Crouch and Marquart is what happens in almost every study researchers conduct. These investigators obtained only a portion of the original number of elements selected. This is where our ideal–real gap between following the rules of sample selection to the letter and our final sample obtained is most apparent. In defense of their sample of a random sample, Crouch and Marquart said, "These refusals showed no pattern that would bias the sample" (1990:107). Unless we know what the responses of refusals would have been to our questions, we really have no way of assessing their impact on the final study outcome. The refusals refused to participate for various reasons. This certainly makes them different compared with those who did participate. For all we know, they may have been the hardcore leadership of the Mexican Mafia or Aryan Brotherhood, and their responses to questions about prison violence and inmate safety would have been most enlightening. When confronted with substantial nonresponse or refusals, therefore, it is probably best simply to acknowledge it and not comment about its significance, nonsignificance, or biasing effects. Nonresponse is merely one of several research shortcomings.

Advantages and Disadvantages of Simple Random Sampling Plans. Simple random sampling plans have the following advantages:

1. All elements in the population are selected randomly, each having an equal and an independent chance of being included. Theoretically, at least, the sample obtained will have a good chance of being representative of the population.

2. This plan is used in conjunction with all other probability sampling plans. It serves as the foundation upon which all types of random samples are based.

3. It is easiest to apply of all probability sampling plans.

4. The true composition of the population does not need to be known in advance. Simple random samples theoretically reflect all important segments of the target population to one degree or another.

5. The amount of **sampling error** can be computed easily. While a more extensive discussion of sampling error will be presented later in this chapter, sampling error is the degree of departure of various sample statistics from their respective population parameters. Ordinarily, larger samples have less sampling error than smaller samples.

The disadvantages of simple random sampling plans include the following:

1. These random sampling plans may not exploit fully the knowledge researchers may have of the target population studied. Sometimes, researchers may know more about certain characteristics of the population that would enable them to draw more representative samples using some alternative probability sampling plan, such as a stratified random sample. Simple random sampling ignores these valuable characteristics. For instance, in sampling from a prison inmate population using simple random sampling, suppose there are 20 inmates out of 800 who have AIDS. Unless something is done to provide for the inclusion of AIDS inmates, it is likely that because of their few numbers, they will not be included in the subsequent sample. Again, a stratified random sample would overcome this limitation.

2. Compared with stratified random samples of the same size, there is usually more sampling error in simple random samples. This is because stratified random samples use more information about the population to enhance representativeness, whereas such information is not ordinarily considered under the simple random sampling format.

Stratified Random Sampling

Stratified random sampling plans take into account one or more population characteristics. **Stratification** means to control for one or more variables and insure their subsequent inclusion in a sample. If we study probation officers and determine from the population of them that 30 percent are nonwhite and 70 percent are white, we can "stratify" on race/ethnicity and insure that both whites and nonwhites will be included. Further, suppose that 10 percent of the population consists of females. We can stratify on gender as well, and we can insure that some of the female probation officers will be included in our sample. Thus, **stratifying** means to take one or more variables into account in our sample selections and insure their inclusion. Two types of stratified random sampling plans are presented here: (1) disproportionate stratified random sampling, and (2) proportionate stratified random sampling.

Disproportionate Stratified Random Sampling. When investigators possess some knowledge concerning the target population, such as its offense characteristics, or race, or gender characteristics, or some other variable, they may select their samples in such a way so that one or more of these characteristics are represented. These types of sampling plans are improvements over simple random sampling, since it is entirely possible when selecting a simple random sample that some of these relevant characteristics will not be included. In order to use **disproportionate stratified random sampling,** researchers divide their population into categories based on those variables considered important. Then they select their sample from each of these subcategories.

For example, McShane (1987) studied prison inmates in the Texas Department of Corrections (TDC). She wanted to know whether inmates who are illegal aliens, alien inmates, receive differential punishment and more severe punishment compared with nonalien inmates. At the time of her study, McShane found that the TDC had 27 prison units housing 36,653 inmates. About 1,500 of these were alien inmates. Because she wanted a substantial number of alien inmates to compare with nonalien inmates, it would be unlikely using a simple random sampling plan that she would randomly include many alien inmates. She decided to divide the entire inmate population into subpopulations of alien and nonalien. Next, she drew two separate simple random samples, called **subsamples**—one from the alien inmate population and one from the nonalien inmate population.

Her alien inmate subsample consisted of 590 prisoners, while her nonalien subsample consisted of 603 prisoners. These different subsamples, roughly equivalent in size, were subsequently examined. If McShane had combined these subsamples into one large sample, her overall sample, randomly selected, would be disproportionate in relation to the general inmate population on the alien/nonalien variable. About 1.6 percent of the TDC inmate population consisted of alien inmates. However, her sample was made up of about 50 percent alien inmates. Therefore, these inmates were disproportionately represented or overrepresented in her sample. Accordingly, nonalien inmates were underrepresented in the sample, since they made up nearly 99 percent of the TDC inmate population.

While McShane made direct comparisons of the two subsamples of inmates according to various factors such as sentence lengths, good-time credit, and status level, she had other investigative options. She could have combined the two subsamples into one large sample of 1,193 (590 + 603 = 1,193) and made other analyses of her data. She would have referred to the combined subsamples as a "disproportionate stratified random sample, stratified according to alien/nonalien inmate status." Using some general figures that roughly parallel those reported by McShane, Table 6.2 illustrates disproportionate stratified random sampling for the TDC inmate population.

Advantages and Disadvantages of Disproportionate Stratified Random Sampling. The major advantage of disproportionate stratified random sampling is that it enables researchers to guarantee that specific characteristics or

TABLE 6.2 Disproportionate Stratified Random Sampling Illustrated for 36,000 Texas Department of Corrections Inmates, Controlling for Alien/Nonalien Status

Population (Stratified by Alien/Nonalien Status)		Sampling Method	Sample
Alien Inmates	2,000 (1.6%)	Simple Random ⟶	600 (50%)
Nonalien Inmates	34,000 (98.4%)	Simple Random ⟶	600 (50%)
Totals	36,000 (100.0%)		1,200 (100%)

important variables that exist in the population will also be represented in their samples. The disadvantages are the following:

1. This sampling method does not give each of the subpopulations (total alien and total nonalien inmates in the TDC population in the above case) weight in the sample in accordance with their proportionate weight in the population. In this respect, the resulting sample is less representative of the population. However, an overriding consideration is the guaranteed inclusion of small numbers of elements that possess desired traits or characteristics, so that meaningful comparisons may be made between subsamples.

2. This method requires some in-depth knowledge about the **target population** in advance. This information is not always available, depending upon the target population investigated. In McShane's case, TDC files helped her to determine those belonging in one subpopulation or another so that she could draw simple random samples from them.

3. Whenever samples are stratified on any variable, there is the possibility that classification errors may arise. In studies of the influence of socioeconomic status (SES) on delinquency, for instance, one's SES and the type of delinquency may be defined according to several broad categorizations. Subpopulations of persons on the SES variable will be identified, as well as subpopulations of juveniles on the delinquency variable. Some of these elements may be improperly assigned to certain categories. A nonviolent property juvenile offender might be misclassified as a violent offender, or persons classified as upper-class may really be middle-class. Using simple random sampling, however, will minimize errors that may result from misclassifications of elements.

Proportionate Stratified Random Sampling. The major difference between disproportionate and **proportionate stratified random sampling** plans is that in proportionate plans, stratified characteristics exist in samples in the same proportionate distribution as they exist in the population. In McShane's study of TDC inmates, for example, it would have been easy to sample these inmates proportionately instead of disproportionately. She would have proceeded to identify the two **subpopulations** the same as before, but in the present instance, her interest would be in carrying over the proportionate distribution of

TABLE 6.3 Proportionate Stratified Random Sampling Illustrated for 36,000 Texas Department of Corrections Inmates, Controlling for Alien/Nonalien Status

Population (Stratified) by Alien/Nonalien Status)		Sampling Method	Sample
Alien Inmates	2,000	Simple Random ⟶	19 (1.6%)
Nonalien Inmates	34,000	Simple Random ⟶	1,181 (98.4%)
Totals	36,000 (100%)		1,200 (100%)

alien/nonalien status into her resulting sample. For example, if she knew that 1.6 percent of the 36,000 TDC inmate population were aliens and 98.4 percent were nonaliens, then her sample would be made up of 1.6 percent aliens and 98.4 percent nonaliens. For comparative purposes, let's assume she wanted a large sample of 1,200.

Wishing to preserve the proportionate distribution of alien/nonalien status, she would insure that 1.6 percent of 1,200 ($.016 \times 1,200 = 18.2$) or 19 (rounding off to the next whole number) aliens would be included, and 1,181 nonaliens would be included. This would make her resulting sample a "proportionate stratified random sample, controlling for alien/nonalien status." Table 6.3 illustrates this procedure. In each case, McShane would simply calculate how much of her sample should consist of persons exhibiting certain characteristics. Since alien inmates made up 1.6 percent of the population, then her sample of 1,200 should have this proportion included, or $.016 \times 1,200 = 19$. Nineteen of these 1,200 sample elements should be alien inmates, provided that she wanted to have a proportionate stratified random sample, stratified according to alien/nonalien inmate status.

Advantages and Disadvantages of Proportionate Stratified Random Sampling. The advantages of this sampling method include the following:

1. Proportionately stratifying a sample on one or more important characteristics enhances the representativeness of the sample in relation to the population.

2. The resulting sample is superior to a simple random sample of the same size as the basis for estimates about population parameters or characteristics.

3. The amount of sampling error in proportionate stratified random samples is generally less compared with that found in simple random samples of the same size. This is because there are more similarities between the sample and the population.

The disadvantages of this sampling method include the following:

1. The researcher needs to know something in advance about the composition of the population in order to insure proportionality on one or more

characteristics. Like disproportionate stratified random sampling, this information is not always readily available.

2. Compared with simple random sampling, this method is more time-consuming, since subpopulations of elements with certain characteristics must be identified first before random samples can be taken from them.

3. Similar to disproportionate stratified random sampling, stratifying always creates the possibility that misclassifications may occur regarding population element placements in one sample or another. Simple random sampling overcomes misclassification problems.

Area, Cluster, or Multistage Sampling

If we consider that simple, disproportionate, and proportionate stratified random sampling are three different types of probability sampling plans, then **area sampling,** also known as **cluster sampling** or **multistage sampling,** is a fourth type. Area (sometimes areal) sampling is used primarily for the purpose of surveying public opinion about issues within a vast geographical territory, such as a country, state, or city.

Area sampling has its origin in agriculture. Farming experiments were often conducted to determine the effects of various types of fertilizers and soil nutrients as well as various planting methods on crop yield. A map of some specified acreage would be identified, and vertical and horizontal grids would be drawn for the entire area, creating numerous smaller squares or land plots. These squares would be enumerated, and a simple random sample of squares would be obtained by using the table of random numbers. Once the sample of land squares was obtained, the researcher could combine them into one large sample of land squares, calculate crop yield for the aggregate of squares, and compare the yield with the yield of some other aggregate of squares taken from land treated by different nutrients or fertilizers.

Social science applications of this method have been closely connected with public opinion polling and survey designs in field research. Thus, geographical divisions and horizontal and vertical grid lines are designated on a map of some previously identified territory, community, or neighborhood. Squares of smaller portions of territory are formed by the intersecting grid lines. These squares are numbered, and a simple random sample of squares is obtained. These individually selected squares are again crisscrossed with horizontal and vertical grid lines, the resulting squares are numbered, and a simple random sample of territorial squares is again taken from each of the previously drawn squares. This process involves different sampling stages, hence the term, multistage sampling. This probability sampling method is illustrated in Figure 6.1.

Suppose the geographical territory was a part of the United States as pictured in Figure 6.1. Note that vertical and horizontal grids have been drawn and squares numbered. A simple random sample of these squares is obtained using the table of random numbers that we have already discussed. These squares constituting our initial sample are known as first-stage units. We will subdivide each of these first-stage units or territorial squares as shown, using similar horizontal and vertical grid lines. We will number these resulting second-stage squares and

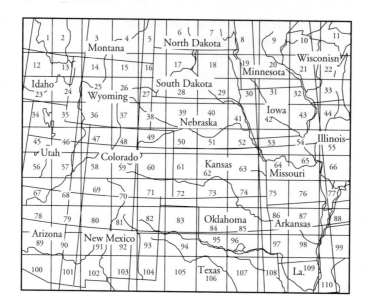

A hypothetical unit taken randomly from Figure 6.1.

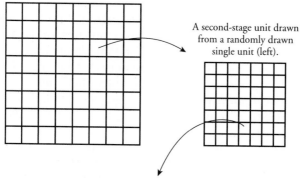

A second-stage unit drawn from a randomly drawn single unit (left).

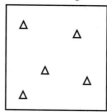

A third-stage unit drawn randomly from N second-stage units.[a]

[a] Δ = a farm home or other dwelling unit within a third-stage unit.

FIGURE 6.1 Illustration of area sampling.

take simple random samples of them. We continue this procedure, possibly through a second-stage to third-stage units as shown. We then combine all of the third-stage units into one large sample. This becomes our probability sample for a large geographical territory. From here, we identify persons who dwell within the territories of the squares we selected.

Perhaps one of our third-stage units is a six-square-mile area in Kansas. Five farms are located within this area as is shown in Figure 6.1. We might send an interviewer to the area to interview the heads of all families living in this "cluster" of farms, hence, the name *cluster* sampling. This saves a lot of interviewer travel time, since interviewers only have to go to a few localities and interview all or most of those who live there.

Numerically, we might begin area sampling by selecting 10 squares from the original grid. Once these 10 squares (first-stage units) have been identified, each is vertically and horizontally crisscrossed again to yield numerous squares that are numbered. Suppose we take 10 squares at random from each of the first 10. This will give us 100 squares (second-stage units). We can grid these squares with vertical and horizontal lines, thus creating numerous other squares. Of course, these squares are becoming smaller and smaller geographical areas. Taking 10 squares from each of these 100 squares will give us 1,000 squares (third-stage units as shown in Figure 6.1). Then, clusters of elements living in those third-stage units are interviewed or surveyed.

If it occurs that one of these squares is a city block of large apartment buildings in Los Angeles, it might be cost-prohibitive to canvass all persons living in that block of apartments. Perhaps we will interview every tenth family throughout all of these apartment buildings in the block. Actually, this is using systematic sampling (discussed later as a nonprobability sampling plan) with a probability sampling plan, but it does save us some time, particularly if we are conducting interviews.

While area or cluster or multistage sampling is primarily conducted by demographers and pollsters, criminologists and others might be interested in soliciting opinions about different controversial issues, such as abortion or the constitutionality of the death penalty. On the basis of survey data, researchers may eventually influence public policy relating to these issues.

An example of the use of cluster sampling to obtain a cross-section of police officers is a study by William McCamey and Gayle Carper (1998). McCamey and Carper were interested in learning about the level of social skills police officers acquired as the result of attending mandatory training classes in a Midwestern state. A cluster sampling technique was used to select several subpopulations of 200 police officers from various locations throughout the state where these mandatory training classes were being conducted. This sampling technique yielded a probability sample and permitted McCamey and Carper to use certain statistical techniques in their analysis, where probability sampling was assumed. These investigators learned much about what police officers learned from their mandatory training, and although further research was recommended, McCamey and Carper found supporting evidence for the popularity of community-based policing and the importance of police social skills.

Advantages and Disadvantages of Area Sampling. Area sampling includes the following advantages:

1. It is much easier to apply compared with simple random sampling, whenever large populations are studied or when large geographical areas must be canvassed. It is easier in the sense that researchers do not have to have predetermined lists of elements who inhabit the areas selected. Random geographical areas are included, and these are believed to be representative of the general population.

2. Compared with other sampling methods, especially where a large geographical territory is involved, area sampling is less expensive. Interviewers may concentrate their efforts in specific regions, and consequently they save time and money by not having to travel great distances to interview different people living at random points in a geographical area.

3. Not everyone may respond when contacted by the researcher. Since clusters of elements are sampled, however, individual refusals are less harmful to the sample's representativeness compared with a simple random sample of elements from the entire territory.

4. If field research crews or work units are dispersed throughout a state or territory, cluster sampling saves them time and money by focusing their efforts in selected areas. This advantage is especially relevant for large research corporations rather than for individual investigators.

5. This sampling method offers flexibility, since a combination of sampling strategies might be employed to sample elements from densely populated areas.

The disadvantages of area sampling include the following:

1. There is no way to ensure that each sampling unit included (second- or third-stage units) will be of equal size. The researcher has little control over the size of each cluster sampled. This may introduce some bias in the final sample obtained.

2. Area samples have a greater amount of sampling error compared with simple random samples of the same size.

3. It is difficult to ensure that all elements surveyed in all clusters are independent of one another. For instance, someone interviewed in one cluster area may be visiting relatives. That person may travel to another area and be interviewed by other researchers involved in the same research project. Thus, the same person's opinion would be counted at least twice. The chances of this event occurring are remote, however.

■ NONPROBABILITY SAMPLING PLANS

Many types of research designs do not require that random samples be obtained. Rather, investigators may only be interested in obtaining sufficient numbers of elements to satisfy limited research objectives. Perhaps the investigator is testing certain research instruments or the readability of questionnaires. Only a sufficient number of "warm bodies" would be required to assist the researcher in pretesting these instruments. In such cases, it is often unimportant if these persons have characteristics that are similar to those in the intended target population.

Some types of research are such that it is impossible to enumerate population elements in advance to draw random samples from them. For instance, if we were interested in describing the behaviors of looters who steal from others in the aftermath of natural disasters, such as earthquakes or floods, these types of events cannot be forecast with any accuracy. Also, some types of behaviors we might want to examine pertain to satanic cults and nefarious rituals carried out in secret, away from the prying eyes of others. If researchers should gain access to such groups, the formality of obtaining random samples of elements would have to be abandoned.

The main distinction between probability and **nonprobability sampling plans** is that probability samples use randomness as the primary control feature and nonprobability sampling plans do not. Randomness permits inferences to be made about population characteristics based on observed sample characteristics. Random samples of elements are commonly considered generalizable to larger populations from which they are drawn, within a probability context. In the case of nonprobability samples, we cannot make inferential statements of any value about population parameters. We don't know what populations our nonprobability samples represent or typify. But this limitation does not mean that such samples are without merit. On the contrary, much of what we do in criminal justice and criminology is based on descriptions of nonprobability samples.

Another compelling argument suggesting that nonprobability samples have heuristic value is that often researchers begin their investigations ideally seeking random samples to study. As so often happens, however, these researchers frequently fail to obtain all the persons they originally included in their sampling plan. Relatively few research projects report that all of those originally selected for inclusion in the sample are subsequently included and studied.

MacKenzie and Shaw (1990) were fortunate in this respect in their investigation of inmate adjustment to shock incarceration. Shock incarceration involved placing convicted offenders in a jail for a period of up to six months. These persons were then brought back into court, and, provided that they behaved well while in jail, were paroled under intensive supervision. The shock of confinement does much to induce conformity to societal rules and parole program conditions. MacKenzie and Shaw studied inmates who participated in a Louisiana Department of Public Safety program known as IMPACT, or the Intensive Motivational Program of Alternative Correctional Treatment. They wanted to know whether the shock incarceration program was more effective at changing offender attitudes and behaviors than plain "flat time" or incarceration as the standard penalties. They asked all 90 offenders who were entering the IMPACT program during a specified time interval if they would like to participate in their research. All offenders agreed to participate. This 100 percent response is rare in any social scientific project.

Nonprobability samples are categorically easier to obtain compared with probability samples. In this section, seven nonprobability sampling plans are presented. These include (1) accidental sampling, (2) systematic sampling, (3) purposive or judgmental sampling, (4) quota sampling, (5) snowball sampling, (6) dense sampling, and (7) saturation sampling.

Accidental Sampling

Accidental sampling, sometimes known as **convenience sampling,** is exactly what it sounds like. Researchers make virtually no effort to identify target populations in advance and ensure all elements an equal and an independent chance of being included. Rather, they attempt to obtain as many persons as they believe will make it possible for them to test their theories and the hypotheses derived from them. The roving reporter interviewing passersby on the street is obtaining an accidental sample of respondents. Persons who call others at random by telephone and solicit their opinions about different controversial issues are obtaining accidental samples. The professor who distributes questionnaires to large sections of criminal justice or criminology courses and surveys students has acquired an accidental sample.

An example of obtaining an accidental sample is a study of the effect of victim-offender relationship on the sentence lengths of violent offenders by Leonore Simon (1996). Simon wanted to know if the sentence lengths of offenders differed according to whether they were strangers or acquaintances in relation to those they victimized. Previous research shows that stranger-offenders are usually sentenced to longer prison terms compared with non-stranger-offenders, where they knew their victims. Simon went to a penitentiary in Arizona and with prison permission, she approached 341 inmates for possible interviews. These were all of the inmates identified by prison records as having been convicted of assault, homicide, kidnapping, sexual assault, and robbery. Subsequently, 273 consented to be interviewed, a response rate of 80 percent. Although Simon had narrowed her search of offenders only to those who had committed violent crimes, her sample was still an accidental one. She had no way of knowing which of the inmates she contacted would ultimately volunteer to be interviewed. Interestingly about half of those she interviewed knew their victims, while the others did not. Simon had no way of knowing that her accidental sample would divide on this dimension so evenly. Simon found that at least for the sample of inmates she studied, sentence lengths were unaffected by whether the offenders knew or did not know their victims.

Advantages and Disadvantages of Accidental Sampling. The primary advantages of accidental sampling are convenience and economy. The disadvantages include limited generalizability, considerable bias, and no evidence of a probability sample. Regarding bias, researchers often select elements because of their particular location in relation to the researcher. In Alexis Durham's study, for example, the elements were students in large classrooms. Durham distributed questionnaires to several classrooms of criminology students. He didn't go to classes consisting of engineering students, education students, or history students. If researchers study their own organizations, they do not know whether their organizations are typical or atypical of other organizations like theirs. The major drawback of accidental sampling is that researchers have little or no idea about what population the sample is supposed to represent. This fact explains the limited generalizability, the bias, and the nonprobability nature of such samples.

Systematic Sampling

Systematic sampling is a popular technique for selecting elements from alphabetized listings or other compilations of elements. Basically, it involves selecting every nth person from a list, whether the list is a telephone directory, inmate listing, or the membership list of a national or local professional association. In some instances, lists may not be involved. If investigators wish to canvass a particular geographical territory, such as a city block or small community, they can anticipate in advance how many persons or households exist. Then, they can select every nth household in the neighborhood or community for inclusion in their systematic sample.

This technique has some probability sampling aspects, although it is questioned as a probability sampling plan. When investigators determine the size of the target population, they calculate how many persons they want to include in their sample. Then they divide the population by their desired sample size and derive their value of n. For instance, if a listing of persons contained 5,000 names, and if researchers desired a sample size of 200 elements, they would need to select every nth person, where $n = N/n$ or $5,000/200 = 25$. Thus, every 25th person on the list or every 25th household in the neighborhood or community would be contacted. Automatically excluded from the sample are the persons between each 25th person. For some researchers, at least, these exclusions are troublesome. This is because one's placement on a list determines whether he or she will be included in the sample.

An illustration of the application of systematic sampling is found in the work of Kenney (1986). Kenney wanted to investigate the influence and effectiveness of various citizen groups that are created to combat street crime. In this particular study, Kenney focused upon the group known as Guardian Angels. The Guardian Angels formed in 1979 and originally patrolled subways in New York City in an effort to minimize muggings and other subway crimes. One aspect of his investigation involved direct interviews with subway passengers about their perceptions of the effectiveness of the Guardian Angels. Therefore, a systematic sampling of subway passengers was obtained, consisting of passengers who were contacted while exiting subways as well as those waiting on subway platforms. Kenney notes that "individual passengers were then chosen in a systematic manner until the assigned number of interviews was completed" (Kenney, 1986:484). About 79 percent of all passengers contacted by Kenney and his assistants responded to face-to-face interviews. We are not informed by Kenney's report as to the magnitude of n in "every nth person being selected," although Kenney's resulting sample was substantial, consisting of 2,693 passengers.

Advantages and Disadvantages of Systematic Sampling. The primary advantages of systematic sampling include the following:

1. This method is easy to use, especially contrasted with having to use a table of random numbers in the identification of elements.
2. Because it is a nonprobability sampling form, mistakes in drawing certain elements are relatively unimportant. Mistakes might occur if one miscounts on the listing of elements and draws the 51st person instead of the 50th person, for example. But this mistake is trivial.
3. If checks are employed to verify the accuracy of sample selection, systematic sampling makes it easier to spot mistakes that might have been made in counting. However, questions about the accuracy of systematic sampling are relatively unimportant, again because of the nonprobability nature of the method.
4. Systematic sampling is a fast method for obtaining a sample. If researchers are in a hurry to make their sample selections, systematic sampling would be much faster than any of the probability sampling methods discussed earlier.

The major disadvantages of systematic sampling include the following:

1. Systematic sampling will systematically exclude persons from being included in the selected sample. Thus, it is sometimes questioned as a probability sampling method. Representativeness and generalizability are affected adversely as a result.
2. If the listing of elements is alphabetically arranged, some degree of ethnic bias will enter the picture. Sampling error will be increased accordingly, as some groups with minority or ethnic surnames, Oriental or otherwise, are selected less frequently compared with selections of names beginning with "Mc," "Smith," "Jones," "Anderson," or "Johnson." This bias will affect the generalizability of findings accordingly.
3. If the listing of elements is arranged according to some other characteristic, such as "severity of offense," "educational level attained," "age," or some other similarly ordered characteristic, some bias will be introduced. Those characteristics most frequently listed will be overrepresented, while less frequently listed characteristics will be underrepresented.

Purposive or Judgmental Sampling

Purposive sampling or **judgmental sampling** involves handpicking elements from some target population. The researcher's intent is to ensure that certain elements will be included in the resulting sample. Because some or most elements will be included in the sample deliberately and others will be excluded deliberately, purposive sampling is a nonprobability sampling form. Why would researchers want to sample in this fashion? One explanation is that the investigators might have extensive familiarity with the population to the extent that they know those elements who would be most representative of it. Because of their knowledge about the population, the researchers may, in fact, be able to obtain a sample that would be better (i.e., more representative) than any probability sampling plan would yield.

Purposive or judgmental sampling has been used in the social sciences, particularly where studies of small communities are involved. Someone who is well known in the community and is familiar with most residents is asked to handpick representative numbers of elements who typify the range of community sentiment on some issue. Thus, if a researcher wanted to know community sentiment about abortion, or civil rights issues, or capital punishment, the handpicked sample, the "judgmental" sample, would be a good indication about what the community at large thought about the issue.

Because the application of judgmental sampling has been sparse in the criminal justice literature, a hypothetical illustration will be used, based upon an actual study conducted by Charles (1989). Charles studied the effectiveness of electronic monitoring of the whereabouts of selected juveniles. Because of the initial costs of establishing electronic monitoring programs, not all jurisdictions have them. Those jurisdictions that use this equipment usually operate it with relatively few offenders. Charles studied juveniles who were adjudicated delinquent and sentenced to the Indiana Boys School in Fort Wayne (Allen County), Indiana.

In Charles's study, youths who wanted to participate in the electronic monitoring program and not enter the Indiana Boys School could volunteer. Probation officers would select those youths deemed to be the most acceptable electronic monitoring candidates. Hypothetically, suppose Charles wanted to evaluate the effectiveness as it might influence the recidivism of boys who represented several offending categories. He might select some boys who were violent offenders, some who were property offenders, and perhaps some who were juvenile status offenders but had violated court orders. Working with probation officers who knew all the boys and were familiar with their backgrounds, Charles could handpick those youths believed to be "typical" of different offender categories. This would enable him to obtain a reasonably representative sample for study, although it would not be a random one.

Advantages and Disadvantages of Purposive Sampling. The major advantage of judgmental samples is that certain elements will definitely be included in the resulting sample. If researchers know a great deal about the population of elements they are studying in advance, this handpicked sample could be a better representation of the population as a whole than any group picked with a probability sampling method. Additional advantages are that this method is less cumbersome compared with probability sampling plans. The elements selected are likely to be more accessible to the researcher and to relate more directly to the study objectives. On the negative side, no amount of judging can forecast accurately that the sample will be a truly representative one. Unknown biases may enter into the selection process and make the sample quite atypical. There are generalization problems, as well, since these samples do not conform to the requirements of probability sampling. Tests of statistical significance and inference would be inappropriate here, and their use undermined by the nonprobability nature of sample selection.

Finally, an extensive amount of information about the population is required in advance of such element selections. This is seldom the case when researchers approach the target population for the first time. Thus, judgmental or purposive sampling plans are only infrequently applied in criminology or criminal justice research projects, although some investigators regard their representativeness as superior to all probability sampling plans.

Four other nonprobability sampling plans are discussed next. These include quota sampling, snowball sampling, dense sampling, and saturation sampling.

Quota Sampling

Compared with snowball sampling, dense sampling, and saturation sampling, quota sampling is the most popular, largely on the basis of its more frequent use in criminology and criminal justice research. **Quota sampling** is obtaining a desired number of elements from the population by selecting those that are most accessible and have certain characteristics of interest to the researcher. The selection of elements is comparable to proportionate stratified random sampling, without randomness as the primary control. The characteristics sought in the elements might be age, gender, race, ethnicity, type of offense, profession, or any other factor that might be measured. Investigators want to obtain persons that possess certain characteristics that typify some population, and they want to obtain similar proportions of these characteristics in their samples. Thus, if a population is known to consist of 80 percent whites and 20 percent blacks, efforts will be made to secure a sample consisting of 80 percent white and 20 percent black participants. Quota sampling has been called "the poor man's proportionate stratified sample."

A hypothetical illustration is provided by reference to a study of staff perceptions of volunteers in a correctional program conducted by Lucas (1987). In Lucas's original study, he wanted to sample probation and parole officers in Missouri and obtain perceptions from them about the quality of performance of volunteers in a state-sponsored Volunteers in Corrections (VIC) program. Lucas determined that there were 300 officers working in 28 districts in 5 state regions. In the actual study, Lucas limited his investigation to 7 of the 28 districts. But suppose Lucas had wanted to obtain a quota sample of probation and parole officers statewide? Further suppose that he determined that of the 300 probation and parole officers, 60 percent (180) were male, while 40 percent (120) were female. Also, suppose he learned that 10 percent (30) of these officers were black (15 males and 15 females), while 90 percent (270) were white (165 males and 105 females).

Let's assume that Lucas wants to obtain a third of these officers (100) from the state for study. But he wants to use a quota sample, controlling for gender and race. Therefore, he would need to obtain 60 males and 40 females. Also, 10 percent of his sample of 100, or 10 elements, would need to be black. Since half of the blacks are female, he would want to include five black female and five black male probation and parole officers. Of the 270 whites, 165 (61 percent) are males, while 105 (39 percent) are females. Therefore, of the remaining 90 elements he wants in his sample, 61 percent need to be males and 39 percent need to be females. This breaks down to a 54–36 split. Thus, he would select 54 white male officers and 36 white female officers for his remaining 90 elements. Combining these subsamples of male and female blacks and whites will give him a quota sample, controlling for race and gender. Concerning his choices of elements, they do not have to be randomly selected. He would commence his search in any of the 28 districts and obtain sufficient numbers of respondents that fit these desired characteristics. Remember that Lucas hasn't done any of these things. We are merely using his research topic to illustrate hypothetically how quota sampling might be applied in that real situation.

Advantages and Disadvantages of Quota Sampling. The advantages of quota sampling are best appreciated when contrasting this sampling method with probability sampling plans. Quota sampling is considerably less costly than the probability sampling method. Furthermore, if quick, crude results are desired that will satisfy certain short-range research objectives, quota sampling is useful. Finally, use of quota sampling ensures the inclusion of certain types of elements, whereas simple random sampling might not. The major disadvantages of quota sampling are that while the most accessible elements are included that fit the desired characteristics of the researcher, these elements may not be typical of the rest of the population. There is limited generalizability, since this sampling method is a nonprobability one. Some bias may enter his selection procedure as the result of misclassifying elements. Of course, this may happen in any stratified sampling plan when we control for the inclusion of specific variables. Finally, although certain variables can be controlled for and their inclusion assured by quota sampling, other relevant variables perhaps unknown to the investigator might be better to use and have greater theoretical significance compared with the **control variables** the researcher has chosen.

Snowball Sampling and the Use of Informants

For special sampling situations, Coleman, Katz, and Menzel (1957) have suggested **snowball sampling** as a type of relational analysis. These researchers were interested in studying the diffusion of medical information among physicians. Snowball sampling, named as such because of the "snowball effect" achieved by the method itself, relies on the use of initial element contacts to furnish researchers with additional element contacts, and so on, until some constellation or social network is outlined. These researchers asked several physicians to name those other physicians with whom they shared information about new pharmaceuticals or drugs. Those physicians named were contacted by researchers and asked the same question: "With whom do you share information about new drugs or pharmaceuticals?" These physician-respondents would supply additional names of other physicians, who would be contacted and asked the same question, until eventually Coleman and his associates observed various group patterns.

Another application of snowball sampling in criminal justice is to use **key informants.** If investigators wish to study the drug subculture in a given community and how drugs are distributed, they might begin by using an **informant.** An informant is someone who knows others who are involved in various types of activities. Police officers use informants to gather incriminating information about criminals. In much the same way, researchers can use informants, such as known drug users, to find out about the drug community.

Informants can introduce researchers to other drug users and dealers. It is imperative that a degree of trust is established between the researchers and those they wish to study, especially if the activity is illegal. One introduction leads to other introductions, and eventually researchers are able to describe drug distribution patterns.

It may be recalled from an earlier chapter that Sandra Hafley and Richard Tewksbury (1996) studied the marijuana-growing business of "Bluegrass County" Kentucky. They relied heavily on informants to introduce them to community residents who were involved in growing and distributing marijuana illegally. These researchers used a form of snowball sampling in their data-gathering process.

The use of informants is not limited to criminals and descriptions of illegal activities. Perhaps investigators are interested in studying police officer or correctional officer culture. Accessing police or correctional officers may be difficult, since few officers wish to disclose the nature of their work to others. However, if researchers know one or more police officers or corrections officers, their work is made easier to the extent that these officers can arrange introductions with other officers. Once a relationship has been established between researchers and the officers involved, other introductions can be arranged. In time, researchers can describe police and correctional officer interaction patterns and such phenomena as the police personality or correctional officer–inmate relations.

Advantages and Disadvantages of Snowball Sampling.   Some possible applications of snowball sampling in criminology and criminal justice might be discovering inmate communication and goods distribution networks in prisons and jails. Snowball sampling could be used to discover drug-distribution patterns in cities or the recreational patterns of and interpersonal relationships among undercover law enforcement officers who work irregular hours and shifts. The major advantage of this technique is that it permits researchers to chart social relationships that are difficult to detect using conventional sampling strategies. But statistical procedures might have limited application in these situations, since randomness is not assured. Further, if the population is large, the number of social networks detected might become unwieldy.

Dense and Saturation Sampling

Both **dense sampling** and **saturation sampling** are intended to overcome the deficiencies of a lack of randomness and small sample size that may hinder generalizability. Coleman (1959) suggested these sampling methods might be applied to the study of large-scale organizations. However, his work has been extended by others to applications in a variety of fields.

The theory behind dense and saturation sampling is fairly simple. If your sample size is substantial enough in relation to the population from which it was drawn, it won't make much difference whether randomness was used in the draw of sample elements. Coleman said that "dense sampling is sampling densely" and elaborated further. He indicated that dense samples would involve the use of at least 50 percent of all population elements. Thus, if the population consisted of 500 juvenile delinquents, the dense sample would be any 250 delinquents or about 50 percent of them. The overwhelming numbers of such a sample, even obtained accidentally, would be sufficient to warrant some amount of generalizing to and inferences about populations.

Saturation sampling, according to Coleman (1959), is almost like not sampling at all, since almost everyone in the population is subsequently included in the sample. When criminal justice professionals and criminologists send out questionnaires to all target population elements or seek to interview most if not all of them, saturation sampling is likely the method employed. Crank et al. (1986) used saturation sampling in their study of police chief cynicism among all Illinois police chiefs. They sent questionnaires to all 771 police chiefs in all jurisdictions, although the return rate was about 67 percent (519 chiefs responded). This large return was boosted, in part, by several follow-up letters to those chiefs who did not initially respond. According to Coleman's guidelines, Crank et al. would have a sample somewhere between a dense sample and a saturation sample. Nevertheless, the sheer numbers of police chiefs involved in their research seem convincingly representative of most police chiefs in Illinois. Of course, about a third of these chiefs did not respond, and again, we have no way of evaluating the influence of their impact on the final results had their responses been included and reported.

Advantages and Disadvantages of Dense and Saturation Sampling.   Virtually any occasion when researchers seek to include all respondents suggests that a saturation sample has been obtained. A study of spousal abuse conducted by Bersani, Chen, and Denton (1988) is an example of saturation sampling applied to records and files. Among other things, these researchers wanted to know about the effectiveness of certain treatment programs offered to those convicted of spousal abuse. Through previous agreements with judges in six municipal courts "in a city with well over 200,000 population," these researchers obtained a handpicked sample of convicted spousal abusers between October 1983 and May 1985. A therapeutic program called Time Out was being offered to spousal abusers in an effort to help them change their behaviors and choose nonviolent solutions to resolve marital conflict. Judges agreed to refer only those convicted offenders who had not been charged with domestic violence in the four years prior to their present convictions until the desired sample size had been obtained. Eventually, a sample of 120 males was obtained through this purposive sampling method. This sample represented almost all offenders processed during the targeted 1983 to 1985 dates.

If the target population is fairly small, and if the instrumentation selected is not time-consuming, dense and saturation sampling plans might be useful, since they do not require time-consuming randomness procedures. With dense and saturation sampling, the results of any research are almost certainly applicable to the general population, since so much of it is included in the samples obtained. The size of the target population is relative. Generally, any population of 1,000 or more would be considered a large population. If interviewing were proposed for such an investigation, the costs of interviewing using a dense or saturation sampling format would be prohibitive. Distributions of questionnaires to these elements for data-collection purposes would be another matter altogether. In cases where survey instruments are used, such as questionnaires, dense or saturation samples would be extremely valuable in terms of their generalizability. Nevertheless, the technical requirements of probability sampling plans would not be fulfilled, and therefore, statistical applications would have to be viewed with caution.

■ TYPES OF SAMPLING SITUATIONS

The types of sample situations presented here include studies of a single sample of elements (sometimes called **one-shot case studies**), studies of two samples, and studies of k samples.* A further distinction is whether the two- or k-sample situations involve independent or related samples. These terms will be defined below.

Single-Sample Situations

The most common research scenarios are studies of a **single sample** at one point in time. A professor may administer a questionnaire to several classes of criminology students and combine these questionnaires to form a large sample. An investigator may study decision making of the Utah Parole Board. Another may describe jail inmate characteristics in a particular county jail. Another researcher may study a sample of New York City delinquents. All of these studies have in common the fact that a particular population has been targeted and a sample has been drawn from it. It makes no difference whether these elements have been randomly selected or chosen as the result of saturation or dense sampling. A single sample is described, interviewed, questioned, and/or observed. Statistical tests applied to such sample situations are referred to simply as "single-sample tests of significance."

It is a common misconception that a single sample of elements must be taken from a specific location. For instance, a study of Ohio forensics experts taken from numerous Ohio counties is simply a single sample of Ohio forensic experts. It is not a study of numerous samples of forensic experts taken from assorted Ohio counties. An investigation of Tennessee circuit court judges will

---

*k technically means "two or more." Applied to samples, k would mean "two or more samples." However, statistical tests of significance of difference are conventionally categorized as "two-sample" and "k-sample" tests, where k is understood to apply to situations involving more than two samples.

likely involve responses from judges in many county jurisdictions throughout the state. The resulting sample will be referred to simply as "a single sample of Tennessee circuit court judges."

Two- and *k*-Sample Situations

Researchers may wish to investigate two or more samples for comparative purposes. For example, Fagan, Forst, and Vivona (1987) studied two samples of chronically violent juvenile delinquents in order to determine whether racial factors were important in affecting their likelihood of being adjudicated in juvenile court or being transferred to criminal court jurisdiction for adult processing. Are more minority youths transferred to criminal courts compared with white youths charged with similar offenses? Since transfer implies that these youths are either too dangerous for juvenile court sanctions or beyond rehabilitation, a comparison of two samples of chronically violent juvenile offenders was made. These investigators drew two samples of delinquents from juvenile court records and court petitions. Controlling for previous offense behaviors and juvenile records, these researchers examined two large samples of youths. One sample of youths had been adjudicated and sanctioned by juvenile courts. The other sample consisted of those youths who were designated for transfer to criminal courts. The study disclosed minimal differences in treatment between the two samples of juveniles examined.

Statistical tests have been formulated to fit **two- and *k*-sample situations.** Two-sample tests of significance of difference determine whether two samples of elements differ significantly on some characteristic or exhibit only nonsignificant differences.

The *k*-sample situations are simply extensions of the two-sample case. For example, Fagan, Forst, and Vivona (1987) could have studied the influence of race among three samples of juvenile probationers, juvenile parolees, and juvenile detainees. Additional samples of juveniles could be obtained by considering whether the detention facilities were publicly or privately operated. Another example might involve an investigation of three samples of inmates under minimum-, medium-, or maximum-security confinement conditions. Additionally, an investigator might describe five different types of administrative styles in five different police departments. Samples of police officers from each of these departments could be collected and studied according to whether they differ on self-perceptions of professionalism. Thus, this would be a *k*-sample situation or a five-sample study of police officers.

Independent Samples

For the two- and *k*-sample cases or situations, specific statistical tests have been devised for application according to whether the samples are independent or related. **Independent samples** are those that contain elements that are **mutually exclusive** of one another. The study by Fagan, Forst, and Vivona (1987) described previously involved two independent samples of juvenile delinquents. The hypothetical five-sample study of police officers would be a five-independent-sample situation or a *k*-independent sample case. Elements in one sample are mutually exclusive of those in the other sample or samples. In these situations, the samples were drawn separately, each from a particular population of elements. Independent samples may be established by other means, however.

Suppose a researcher has obtained a large sample of 400 prison inmates. If the researcher desired, the entire sample of 400 inmates could be described, and hypotheses relevant to that sample could be tested. Single-sample statistical tests would be applied for more extensive data analyses. But the original sample of 400 could also be broken down or stratified according to type of conviction offense. This would be equivalent to treating various subsamples of elements as separate samples under either proportionate or disproportionate stratified random sampling methods discussed earlier in this chapter. Perhaps the researcher wanted to divide inmates according to whether they were violent or property offenders. A division of inmates according to this **dichotomy,** violent and property offenders, might yield 200 violent offenders and 200 property offenders. This would be a two-independent-sample scenario. This scenario has been created artificially by dividing the original sample according to criteria deemed important by the investigator.

It is apparent that similar breakdowns could be completed according to age, race, ethnicity, security level, years of confinement, inmate-gang membership, or any other relevant variable. If these 400 inmates belonged to five different gangs and the researcher separated them according to their particular gang affiliation, the result would be a five-independent-sample case. Membership in one gang would rule out membership in the other gangs. The different gang subdivisions would be mutually exclusive of one another. Therefore, it is not necessary to visit five different prison sites to obtain five different samples of offenders. All of this can be accomplished by drawing one large sample of inmates initially and subdividing them later on selected variables.

Related Samples

Two or more related samples involve two- or k-sample cases, where the samples are not mutually exclusive of one another. **Related samples** are useful whenever researchers conduct experiments and wish to know whether the experimental variable induces changes on some behavioral or attitudinal **dimension.** If the samples are related, they are treated as though they are equivalent. Thus, any differences observed between the related samples on some measured characteristic are believed attributable to the experimental variable rather than to other extraneous factors, such as individual differences among sample elements. There are three ways of obtaining related samples. These include (1) using persons as their own controls in before-after experiments, (2) matching elements among samples, and (3) group or frequency distribution control matching.

■ SOME SELECTED SAMPLING PROBLEMS

In this concluding section, we will examine several important sampling issues that often arise in the course of one's research. No hard-and-fast rules exist to function as standards against which our own research efforts can be assessed.

The fact that gaps frequently exist between what ideally ought to be done to obtain samples and what actually occurs generates several questions that have no universal answers. We might rely to some extent on conventions followed by one discipline or another. In criminology and criminal justice, there are conventional guidelines that we may use for decision making, but individual research circumstances and limitations frequently require departures from these guidelines. Issues selected for discussion include (1) determining the sample size, (2) the problem of nonresponse, (3) evaluating the representativeness of samples, (4) the relation of sampling techniques and statistical analyses, (5) the ideal–real gap in sampling procedures, and (6) the inaccessibility of potentates and special populations.

Determining Sample Size

How large should our samples be in relation to the populations from which they are drawn? For purposes of generalization and statistical inference, a conventional rule of thumb is that the sample size, n, should be 1/10th of the population size, N, or $n/N = 1/10$th. This is called the **sampling fraction.** Applying this rule of thumb, if the population size is 500, the sample size should be 50. If the population size is 20 million, the sample size should be 2 million. However, this particular rule of thumb leads to unwieldy sample sizes whenever larger populations of elements are involved. Few researchers have the resources to obtain samples of 2 million elements. Do we necessarily need 2 million elements to make inferences about 20 million elements? No. Fortunately, the 1/10th rule of thumb becomes less important and may even be ignored whenever one's target population reaches or exceeds 2,500 elements. While this "2,500" figure is somewhat arbitrary, note that the 1/10th rule would yield a sample size of 250 in this instance. Larger populations would yield sample sizes larger than 250.

There are several logical reasons for limiting our sample sizes and violating the 1/10th rule of thumb by drawing samples that account for less than 10 percent of their respective population sizes. First, we can manage smaller samples more easily than larger ones. Sample sizes of 150 to 250 are more manageable than sample sizes of 1,000 or more. Second, samples that are extremely large are not proportionately more informative than smaller samples. A "diminishing returns" effect occurs as we increase our sample sizes substantially. In short, we do not double the accuracy of our sample statistics as estimates of population parameters if, for example, we were to double our sample sizes from 250 to 500. As more persons are added to our samples, many of these additional elements have characteristics similar to those elements we have already obtained. Thus, our larger samples are more costly than smaller samples, but they are not substantially more accurate for making inferences about population values as a whole. Provided a probability sampling plan is used for one's sample selection, larger samples are generally more accurate for estimating population parameters than smaller samples. The point is that this improvement in accuracy is only minimal in relation to the greater cost of obtaining additional elements.

A third reason relates to the statistical procedures we may use for data analyses. Most statistical procedures are designed to be applied to sample sizes of 250 or less. Most tests of statistical significance are most effective when they are applied to sample sizes within designated ranges, sometimes called reasonable operating ranges. For instance, some statistical tests discussed elsewhere require that one's sample size consists of fewer than 25 elements (e.g., Fisher's Exact Test) (Champion, 1981; Siegel, 1956). Some tests have even smaller sample size requirements, limiting procedures to situations where *12 or fewer elements are examined* (e.g., the randomization test for two independent samples, the randomization test for matched pairs) (Champion, 1981; Siegel, 1956). Other procedures require sample size ranges of from 25 to 250 (e.g., the chi square test) (Champion, 1981). When statistical tests are applied to samples beyond these reasonable operating ranges, the statistical results are distorted. The nature of this distortion is that our numerical results are grossly inflated. Thus, researchers may erroneously interpret certain statistical findings as significant when, in fact, one's very large sample size has caused unusually large and distorted statistical results.

Certain statistical procedures have been proposed as objective means for determining one's sample size, given the size of the target population and other factors. However, all of these procedures are artificial contrivances and have inherent weaknesses. None of these procedures is qualitatively better than the 1/10th rule of thumb discussed above. For discussions of these exotic procedures, the reader is referred elsewhere (Blalock, 1972). Even if ideal sample sizes for research purposes could be forecast with great accuracy, almost all investigators have seen their ideal sampling plans dashed because of nonresponse.

Nonresponse and What to Do About It

Nonresponse is the proportion of the originally selected sample not included in the final sample studied by the investigator. If researchers have used a table of random numbers to identify 100 sample elements from their target population of 1,000 elements, nonresponse occurs when one or more of these sample elements is not included in the final sample studied. For example, if questionnaires are mailed to 5,000 persons and 2,000 of them do not return their completed questionnaires, this is a nonresponse of 2,000/5,000 or 40 percent. Nonresponse is not limited to questionnaire administration. Interviewers may attempt to interview certain subjects, only to be refused. Often those selected for interviews may not be at home or keep their appointments with interviewers. Some persons, by virtue of their status, are simply inaccessible (see the subsequent discussion of potentates).

Almost all studies that describe and analyze samples drawn from larger populations have some degree of nonresponse. The amount of nonresponse varies among studies and no standards exist that define normal nonresponse rates. Different textbooks report "average" nonresponse rates from 20 percent to 70 percent, although these estimates are largely impressionistic. An analysis of social science literature suggests that "average response" rates to mailed questionnaires are about 30 percent. On the average, the response to direct interviews is much higher, since this data collection method involves face-to-face contact between the interviewer and interviewee.

Professors and other researchers who administer questionnaires to students in large classrooms frequently report response rates of 100 percent. High response rates in these "captive audience" situations are commonplace, since classrooms are implicitly coercive settings. Sometimes teachers will require student compliance in completing administered questionnaires as one of several course requirements, or additional points will be awarded to those students who respond. Thus, many students participate to avoid being penalized.

The major problem with nonresponse is that it affects adversely the typicality or representativeness of one's sample in relation to the population from which it was drawn. If ideal criteria are applied in one's initial sample selection, nonresponse detracts from these ideal sampling objectives. There is little we can do about it. We can encourage those who did not respond originally to reconsider. This is often done through follow-up letters to nonrespondents, if mailed questionnaires are used. These follow-ups require that we somehow keep track of and identify those who do and do not respond. But anonymity cannot be assured under this circumstance. And we often offer anonymity to potential respondents as a means of encouraging them to return completed questionnaires that contain personal and/or confidential data. But even follow-up letters usually result in small increases in the final response rate. Among other strategies that have been used to prompt larger response rates are (1) using hand-stamped postage (compared with metered postage) on return envelopes to "personalize" them, (2) using **altruistic appeals** with cover letters that appeal to the potential respondent's altruistic spirit, (3) using **egoistic appeals** with letters offering goods or money for responding, (4) using prizes that are awarded based on lottery selections from among those who respond, (5) using special delivery follow-up letters to nonrespondents, (6) using direct telephone calls to all nonrespondents, and (7) using home visits to nonrespondents.

Sometimes for experimental purposes, researchers will deliberately **oversample** in order to obtain a desirable sample size. For example, if investigators want to obtain 200 elements in their final sample, and if they are using mailed questionnaires, they may send questionnaires to 600 elements, anticipating that their nonresponse will be about 65 percent. Unfortunately, the original 600 elements selected may have comprised an ideal random sample drawn from a table of random numbers. Excluding 400 of these elements (through nonresponse) from the resulting data analysis means that the sample is not a random one, despite the fact that the final sample consists of 200 elements, a desirable sample size. Therefore, oversampling is recommended only when investigators require minimum sample sizes for anticipated experimental research and the research designs they have formulated or for the application of particular statistical procedures.

Is the Sample Representative? Uncertainty About Representativeness

How do we know if a sample is representative of the population from which it was drawn? Never. Assessing sample representativeness accurately requires considerable knowledge about the population and its characteristics. If such knowledge about the population were possessed, it is unlikely that we would need to draw samples from it. Of course, we may select sample elements according to their known distribution in the population. We may know the different types of offenders in a state prison or local jail. Or we may know the gender and educational distribution of law enforcement officers in a large city. Or we may know some of the superficial characteristics of state correctional officers from personnel files or state records. These information sources may enable us to judge whether our samples exhibit certain population characteristics. Thus, we may say that our samples appear typical according to gender distribution, age distribution, educational level, type of offense, length of confinement, prior record, and any other recorded population information.

But thousands of other variables, attitudinal and otherwise, characterize the populations we study. Controlling our sample selections according to those criteria we know about will make those samples representative of their parent populations only for those criteria. Remaining uncontrolled are thousands of other individual, social, and psychological **attributes** and characteristics that may render our samples atypical or unrepresentative. We cannot possibly know when our samples are truly representative or unrepresentative of their parent populations in all respects, however. Thus, there is almost always considerable uncertainty about the representativeness of our samples. Investigators do not quit doing research because they are uncertain about the representativeness of their samples, however. There is much to be learned from the samples they obtain, regardless of their representativeness or lack of it. After all, the samples do come from target populations of elements. Some information is better than no information.

Sampling and Statistical Analysis

Ordinarily, investigators know in advance of conducting their **statistical analysis** which statistical techniques they intend to apply. Their familiarity with these statistical techniques will often indicate the sample sizes required for those intended statistical applications. Furthermore, any inferential tasks to be performed require the use of a probability sampling plan when a sample is selected. Randomness is an assumption underlying all statistical inference and decision making. Therefore, if we wish to generalize about population parameters on the basis of certain sample statistics or characteristics, our sample must be a random one. However, whenever the samples we obtain are less than random, as is the case when there is substantial nonresponse, the typicality and representativeness of our samples are ruined, and any generalizations and inferences about population parameters made from observed sample characteristics are similarly affected.

The **purist** view is that in order to apply statistical tests meaningfully, all assumptions and requirements underlying those tests must be met fully. Failing to meet one or more assumptions underlying certain statistical tests will automatically void the test results. However, if the purist view were adopted by all criminologists and criminal justice professionals, most research work that involves the application of statistical procedures would come to a grinding halt. This is

Box 6.2

Dilip Das
Plattsburgh State University of New York

Statistics: M.A. (English literature), University of Delhi; M.S. (criminal justice), Michigan State University; Ph.D. (criminal justice), Sam Houston State University; honorary IPS (Indian Public Service), National Police Academy, India.

Interests: My present research interest is the study of police. I am interested in leaning about current, innovative, and result-oriented research as well as operational and managerial practices from all over the world, in exchanges that take place between police practitioners and researchers, in the state of public safety and the resultant quality of life issues on global dimensions, and in practices that build partnerships between police policymakers, practitioners, researchers, and citizens around the world. I explore who the police are, what they do, and how they maintain order, administer laws, and serve their communities in different societies, including the regions beyond the frontiers of the developed nations.

I became an Assistant Superintendent of Police in 1965, after a national competitive examination to obtain a position in the Indian Police Service, an elite service, originally established by the British for the colonies throughout the empire. As I worked as a police officer, I became aware of the paradoxes of the profession. Policing was an occupational avenue that was capable of letting me do a lot of good in the community, but also a lot of harm. After 15 years of active service, I decided to study policing in the United States as a graduate student in order to understand its enormous complexities, challenges, and potentials.

Having started as a police practitioner, and later becoming a criminal justice academic, I have been trying to bring researchers and practitioners closer, to encourage cross-cultural and international dialogues among the police agencies all over the world, and to facilitate communication between police and other disciplines. With this objective in view, I started an organization, the International Police Executive Symposia (IPES), which, among other things, brings police practitioners and researchers together for a four-day symposia. Papers presented at the symposium are published as a book. The symposia are hosted by an institution of higher education or government.

Thus far, symposia have been hosted by the Canton Police of Geneva, Switzerland (Police Challenges and Strategies, 1994); the International Institute of the Sociology of Law in Onati, Spain (Challenges of Policing Democracies, 1995); Kanagawa University in Yokohama, Japan (Organized Crime, 1996); the Federal Police in Vienna, Austria (International Police Cooperation, 1997); and the Dutch Police and Europol in The Hague, Netherlands (Crime Prevention, 1998). Subsequent symposia will be hosted by Andhra Pradesh Police in Hyderabad, India (Policing of Public

Order, 1999); the Traffic Institute at Northwestern University in Evanston, Illinois (Traffic Services in the Twenty-First Century, 2000); the Military Police of Sao Paulo, Brazil (Police and Human Rights, 2001); and Plattsburgh State University of New York (Law Enforcement, Crime, and Society, 2002). The IPES has launched the journal *Police Practice and Research: An International Journal,* a quarterly that seeks to promote the aims and objectives of the IPES.

Advice to Students: Research, like swimming or playing baseball, must be learned by actually doing it. My police research in various parts of the world has enabled me to get insights into unique cultures, values, and customs in different parts of the world. This has been a fascinating experience.

because most research conducted in these fields and all other social sciences fails to satisfy completely all statistical test assumptions. But violating one or more statistical test assumptions is more the norm rather than the exception. The purist view is not particularly popular among social scientists. Ultimately, researchers apply various statistical tests, despite certain assumption violations, and report their findings with conventional cautions. Every piece of research examined should be given the appropriate degree of credibility commensurate with the study's shortcomings.

Ideal and Real Sampling Considerations

The quest to obtain samples that meet ideal criteria is a noble one. But it is unrealistic to expect that all of our sampling plans will fall into place as anticipated. Whether we use the 1/10th rule of thumb or some exotic procedure for determining the desired sample size, Murphy's Law is likely to affect our work. Murphy's Law says that "whatever can go wrong will go wrong." Nonresponse is one of these problems. Additionally, we will see that many other events and factors may contaminate our research efforts. Our choice of sampling plan is only one of the many links in the chain of events we know as the research enterprise. We must be prepared to deal with whatever elements we eventually obtain, regardless of our original ideal considerations. Eventually we do the best we can with what we have, and we encourage others who read our work to assess its importance in view of existing research limitations.

Potentates: Juveniles, Prisoners, and Permission to Sample Special Populations of Subjects

Potentates are those from whom researchers require special permission to conduct studies. Criminologists and others who study the criminal justice system often find that gaining access to specific populations targeted for study is difficult. It is not particularly easy for researchers to obtain samples of prison or jail inmates, or to gather large samples of delinquent offenders in various detention facilities. Studying probation officers, criminal court judges, law enforcement officers, federal judges, correctional officers, and district attorneys are not easy tasks. These persons are usually insulated from the general public by secretarial hierarchies, locked gates, and a general aversion to being studied by anyone.

Studies of juvenile delinquents are sometimes difficult to conduct because of the confidential nature of record keeping relating to them. Not all juvenile courtrooms are open to the public, and court dispositions and adjudications relating to juvenile offenders are considered restricted material. Even if investigators wish to examine juveniles in school settings and obtain self-report information about delinquent conduct, permission must first be obtained from principals and teachers. There is often resistance to such investigations for a variety of reasons. School board and parental opposition to having their children involved in any type of research asking them to disclose personal details of their lives are barriers to certain kinds of research. Questionnaires are sometimes perceived as threatening or informative for others. Checklists of infractions and law violations may be interpreted by some juveniles as expected behaviors. In a sense, questions dealing with prohibited behaviors may prompt some youths to engage in those behaviors or at least be more susceptible to involvement in delinquent conduct.

Studying lawyers and district attorneys may be difficult, since their time is often limited by large numbers of clients and high caseloads. The sponsorship of research by a major college or university might help researchers gain access to some of these persons. Snowball sampling might be used as a means of obtaining introductions to different attorneys, especially if some of their attorney friends have referred interviewers to them.

Sometimes there are organizational constraints that restrict access to particular populations. If an investigator wished to study FBI agents, for example, local FBI offices do not disclose information to the public about their present roster of agents, where they live, or how they may be contacted. FBI agents usually have unlisted telephone numbers, live quietly and anonymously in neighborhoods for many years, and are advised by their superiors to refrain from divulging any information about their jobs. If you happen upon FBI agents at social gatherings, chances are that these agents will reply "government service" when you ask them about their occupation or profession. This high level of secrecy about one's affairs is primarily a function of the organization itself, in much the same way that the Central Intelligence Agency would control the behaviors of its operatives.

In sum, any research plan must realistically evaluate the accessibility of target populations. It is one thing to write a research plan. It is another thing to implement it. When researchers apply for research funds from public agencies or private foundations, it is conventional for them to include supporting documentation and letters from those they intend to contact. This information lets the funding agency know that the researchers have anticipated certain data-collection problems and have engaged in preliminary efforts to ensure that the data can be obtained if the study is funded.

KEY TERMS

Accidental sampling
Altruistic appeals
Area sampling
Attributes
Cluster sampling
Computer-determined draw
Control variables
Convenience sampling
Dense sampling
Dichotomy
Dimension
Disproportionate stratified
  random sampling
Egoistic appeals
Equality of draw
Fishbowl draw
Independence of draw
Independent samples
Informant
Judgmental sampling
Key informant
Multistage sampling
Mutually exclusive
n
N
Nonprobability samples
Nonprobability sampling plans
One-shot case study
Oversample
Paradigm
Parameter
Population
Probability sampling
Probability sampling plan

Proportionate stratified random
  sampling
Purist
Purposive sampling
Quota sampling
Randomness
Random numbers
Random sample
Related samples
Representativeness
Sample
Sample representativeness
Sample size
Sampling
Sampling error
Sampling fraction
Sampling frame
Sampling without replacement
Sampling with replacement
Saturation sampling
Simple random samples
Single samples
Snowball sampling
Statistical analysis
Stratification
Stratified random sampling plans
Stratifying
Subpopulation
Subsamples
Systematic sampling
Table of random numbers
Target population
Two- and *k*-sample situations

QUESTIONS FOR REVIEW

1. Differentiate between probability and nonprobability sampling plans. Review briefly their general functions and limitations.

2. What are some major considerations in deciding to sample? Discuss these considerations briefly.

3. Discuss some of the problems researchers might have when studying potentates.

4. Sometimes systematic sampling is considered a probability sampling plan. What is the basis for this thinking? What can be said of systematic samples that might disqualify them as probability sampling plans?

5. What are some general rules that apply to determining one's sample size? Are extremely large samples necessarily better than smaller sample sizes? What factors should be considered when determining one's sample size?

6. What are some of the primary advantages of judgmental or purposive sampling plans? In what sense might some researchers consider them to be superior to probability sampling plans?

7. What is the primary control factor in probability sampling plans? Why is it important? How can this factor be achieved when samples are selected from target populations?

8. Distinguish between independence of draw and equality of draw relating to sample elements.

9. Differentiate between independent and related samples. What are at least three ways that related samples may be obtained?

10. What is meant by sample representativeness? Can we ever guarantee that a sample of elements will be representative of the population from which it is drawn? Why or why not?

11. What is an accidental sample? Under what circumstances might accidental samples be the only samples available for study?

12. Define and differentiate between population parameters and sample statistics.

13. What is nonresponse in sampling and how can it be affected?

14. Why is there often a gap between ideal sampling plans and real samples of elements obtained by the researcher?

15. What is the influence of statistical tests and techniques on sampling decisions?

16. When would area or cluster sampling be appropriate to apply? Identify at least three different situations where such a technique would be useful.

chapter 7

Data Collection Strategies II
Questionnaires

INTRODUCTION

*The most popular data-gathering tool used in criminological research today is the questionnaire. **Questionnaires** are self-administered inventories that seek descriptive information about people and their opinions about things. From our earliest years in school, we are accustomed to completing questionnaires. Schools solicit information from us about our personal backgrounds and our previous educational experience, including high schools and elementary schools attended, where we live, the occupations or professions of our parents, and our immediate and long-range interests, including our declared academic majors and professional ambitions. Perhaps you have been in a class when your instructor has distributed questionnaires in connection with a research project being conducted, or maybe the instructor has distributed questionnaires to you and your classmates on behalf of someone else conducting research.*

This chapter describes questionnaires and their functions and distinguishes between different kinds of questionnaires used for data-gathering purposes. Questionnaires are relatively easy to construct, although there are several important guidelines to follow when developing questions as well as alternative responses for them. Thus, attention is given to questionnaire construction and format as well as to some of the guidelines associated with the proper administration of questionnaires to others. Some of the problems associated with the construction and administration of questionnaires are discussed. The weaknesses and strengths of questionnaires as data-gathering tools are also examined.

QUESTIONNAIRES IN CRIMINAL JUSTICE RESEARCH

Each of the data-gathering tools discussed should not be viewed in isolation. That is, we must consider questionnaires as one of several data-gathering strategies we might employ to gather information about people and their characteristics. It is not unusual for researchers to use several types of data-gathering tools in the same research project. For example, if we were to study law enforcement officers in a particular city, we might obtain information from them through questionnaires. Further, we might observe several officers as they conduct their patrol activities. Also, we might interview them at different times to determine why particular actions were undertaken. We might even supplement all of this information with reports about the police department generally, its organization and operation, and its change over time. Whenever two or more data-gathering tools or strategies are used by researchers for investigating the same social aggregate (e.g., a police department, community corrections agency, probation office, jail inmates, or juvenile delinquents), this practice is known as **triangulation.** Therefore, we would practice triangulation if we used both questionnaires and interviews, and possibly observation, in our investigations of law enforcement officers and their patrol activities. The majority of criminal justice professionals and criminologists probably use two or more data-gathering techniques in their investigations of social phenomena. Different kinds of information are yielded about the people we study, depending upon the data-gathering procedures we use.

In order to describe fully the research contributions and limitations of these different data-gathering tools, specific chapters highlight each technique and illustrate its application. It will become more apparent that certain deficiencies inherent in one type of data-gathering tool will likely be compensated for or overcome by simultaneously using alternative data-gathering tools.

Throughout the criminal justice system, there are numerous aggregates about which we seek information. We have mentioned law enforcement officers as one important aggregate. Others include prosecutors, judges, court officials, defense attorneys, correctional officers, community corrections workers, ancillary personnel, and, of course, clients. Clients may be defendants, convicted misdemeanants or felons, probationers, jail or prison inmates, or parolees. These clients may further be distinguished according to whether they are divertees, halfway house members, work or study releasees, furloughees, shock probationers, or those participating in home confinement or electronic monitoring programs.

The literature in criminal justice and criminology is abundant with studies in which questionnaires have been used as the principal data-gathering tool. For instance, one of the more ambitious (because of the large number of persons sampled) research projects was a national study undertaken by the Research Triangle Institute for the National Institute on Alcohol Abuse and Alcoholism (Rachal et al., 1975). A two-staged stratified cluster sample of 15,000 students, grades 7–12, was obtained from the 48 contiguous states. Each student was asked to complete an anonymous, self-administered questionnaire, which included items on drinking behavior, the contexts and consequences of drinking, deviant behavior, and selected demographic, attitudinal, and personality characteristics. A **response rate** of 72.2 percent was obtained. This information was subsequently coded and became an interesting data set available for analysis by interested researchers.

In 1989, a study utilizing this data was completed and published by Thompson (1989). Thompson was interested in learning whether gender- or ethnicity-related drinking patterns among teenagers could be identified. He was also interested in whether socioeconomic status differences exerted any noticeable impact on drinking behaviors and if different types of socialization experiences seem to modify drinking habits between various age groupings. In this case, a ready-made data set was available to Thompson, based upon the numerous questionnaires completed by randomly selected samples of students in 1974.

While using existing information from previously administered questionnaires is a definite advantage for many researchers, other investigators find it necessary to devise their own instruments and tailor them to fit particular target audiences. For example, Colley, Culbertson, and Latessa (1986) analyzed the roles of probation officers, including the diverse and often contradictory demands probation agencies make of those performing such roles. These researchers wanted to compare current probation officer educational and training programs with the actual tasks performed by such officers while performing their duties. One commonly used method to evaluate personpower needs in organizations is job analysis, which includes task analyses, job inventories, and descriptions of job elements and critical incidents.

Gregg Barak
Eastern Michigan University

Statistics: B.S., M.A., Ph.D. (criminology),
University of California at Berkeley.

Interests: Presently my research interests revolve around issues of crime and crime control in the context of both criminal and social justice, including but not limited to the following subjects: integrating criminological bodies of knowledge; exploring the relationships of crime and crime control from a global perspective; examining the intersections of class, race, gender, and crime; and developing a framework for analyzing the interdisciplinary nature of violent behavior.

I came of age at Berkeley in the years from 1967 to 1973, during the turbulent days of the Oakland Induction Center, People's Park, the movement for Black Studies and Women's Studies, the invasion of Cambodia, and the struggle to defend the Berkeley School of Criminology. Although others may have spent more time there, I am unique in having completed my undergraduate and graduate degrees at the University of California. This intellectual experience, grounded as it was in the relationship between theory and practice, remains at the core of my scholarly research to this day. For example, it underpinned my newsmaking praxis as a criminologist beginning in the early 1980s and culminating more recently with the publication of two edited anthologies of original essays: *Media, Process, and the Social Construction of Crime: Studies in Newsmaking Criminology* (1994), and *Representing O.J.: Murder, Criminal Justice, and Mass Culture* (1996).

Initially, my research interests were sparked by the rising social consciousness of the 1960s and the desire for the creation of the Great Society, devoid as much as possible of racism, sexism, and classism. Concerned with the denial of civil rights to all people, with the various assaults against ordinary persons by the prevailing institutions, and with the associated crimes against humanity that were being exposed during this period, my approach to research and scholarship took me beyond the legalistic confines of criminology and criminal justice. Influenced by the revisionist history of the late 1960s and the movement to demystify "law and order" in particular, I wrote my dissertation and first book, *In Defense of Whom? A Critique of Criminal Justice Reform* (1980), on the emergence and development of the public defender system at the turn of the twentieth century.

To this day, I have always been engaged with the "big picture" or with the macrorelations of crime and social justice. Over the years, I have researched and written on a variety of topics such as state criminality, domestic violence, homelessness, and the media as each of these have related to changes in both the political economy and in the social constructions of crime and punishment.

I have a saying when it comes to my scholarship and research: I am like the Platte River, a mile wide and an inch deep. In other words, I research and write a little about a lot, rather than a lot about little. Related to the self-conscious notion that I prefer breadth to depth of knowledge, and that if I have an area of expertise or specialty, it is in the area of generalism rather than particularism, then I like to think of my contributions to criminology and criminal justice as having expanded the terrains of investigating crime and crime control. I also like to believe that my rather unconventional ideas and concepts about crime, criminals, criminology, and criminal justice have inspired others to reevaluate and to critically examine in non-traditional ways the various fields of inquiry and application of crime and social control. Finally, it is my hope that in some small way my work has, is, or will have contributed to an altering of the creative landscapes of thinking about criminality and criminology as these are related to how we habitually theorize about crime, criminals, and justice. In my efforts to facilitate what I believe is a paradigmatic shift to integration in all of its forms and guises, I refer to my edited collection of essays, *Varieties of Criminology: Readings from a Dynamic Discipline* (1994), where I brought together, under one cover for the first time, modernists and post-modernists, and where the discussion of incorporating the strands of mainstream and critical criminology was just beginning to emerge.

Advice to Students: As for the sage advice that I can pass along to those who might follow in my footsteps, I would simply say that fundamentally one must keep an open mind and one must be willing to incorporate a full array of research techniques and methodologies: qualitative and quantitative, ethnographic and interpretive, historical and empirical. To do less is to engage in a theory and practice which, at best, covers only a portion of the whole story of crime and justice. In this regard, I would also recommend that researchers of tomorrow take an interdisciplinary approach to our subject matter, especially since there are virtually no areas in the arts, sciences, and humanities that do not influence our understanding of crime and justice.

Colley, Culbertson, and Latessa found little, if any, evidence of the use of job analysis for assessing probation officer work roles in the criminal justice literature. Thus, these investigators sought to devise instrumentation that would be capable of identifying tasks making up the probation function and that would determine those skills most necessary to perform the real tasks associated with probation work (1986:68). More simply, they wanted to identify the most essential elements that would fit into a competency-based probation officer training program. Presumably, such a competency-based program could be implemented in various jurisdictions to improve overall probation officer work performance and to maximize the services and benefits they might render to their probationer/clients.

These investigators compiled an extensive list of tasks derived from the literature about probation officer training needs, training methods, and preexisting probation officer job descriptions. They also conducted face-to-face interviews with a sample of probation officers from both rural and urban counties to determine directly their individual responsibilities and job assignments. This permitted them to make comparisons between verbal responses given by these officers and the list of tasks they had earlier compiled.

Eventually, these researchers devised a three-part questionnaire. These parts assessed the frequency with which different listed tasks were performed, the relative importance of each task to the probation officer role and function, and a general information section, including questions about age, gender, race, job experience, education, and size of caseload. These investigators subsequently administered the final version of their questionnaire to 240 Illinois probation officers of adult clients or about one half of the Illinois probation officer force.

Thus, two extremes are portrayed here. In the first instance above, Thompson (1989) utilized information from questionnaires originally administered in 1974. No new questionnaire construction was necessary, since existing questions and scales yielded a data set containing much valuable information. In the second instance, Colley, Culbertson, and Latessa (1986) constructed their questionnaires completely from scratch. Also, they analyzed some of the data they eventually collected, although both studies involved quite different statistical analyses and methodological objectives.

Frequently, researchers construct questionnaires which consist, in part, of original question items and, in part, of preexisting scales that purportedly measure certain phenomena. This practice is perhaps the most common, since there are many existing scales that measure important social and attitudinal variables that are theoretically intertwined with criminal justice and criminological questions. Using existing scales exposes these instruments to further empirical testing, experimentation, and verification, while those using such scales benefit because they do not have to create their own measures. However, regardless of the popularity of certain existing scales, not everyone finds them suitable for their individual research applications. One or more questionnaire items may not fit the intended audience. Therefore, some customizing is necessary to produce questionnaires that are directly relevant for certain samples of elements.

■ FUNCTIONS OF QUESTIONNAIRES

The two basic functions of questionnaires are description and measurement.

Description

The information acquired through questionnaire administration may provide a **description** of individual and/or group characteristics that gives information on gender, age, years of education, occupation, income, political and religious affiliation, civic group or fraternal order membership, urban or rural background, and job status.

Describing elements serves several useful purposes. For instance, a knowledge of the age distribution of a sample of law enforcement officers may provide researchers with plausible explanations for certain group phenomena that occur on the job, including clique formations, liberal or conservative positions on social issues, intraofficer esprit de corps, and the type and amount of possible officer misconduct. Are younger officers more inclined to use excessive force when taking suspects into custody? The educational characteristics of particular employees may help to account for different assessments of job content, supervision, job satisfaction, and work quality. Are more-educated police officers more effective at resolving domestic disputes or quelling civil disorders? What factors seem most important for improving police-community relations? Accurate descriptions of elements in any social setting can benefit researchers in many ways. Insight, explanation, and prediction are but a few of the many contributions questionnaires make to social inquiry.

Measurement

A primary function of almost every questionnaire is the **measurement** of individual and/or group variables, particularly attitudinal phenomena. Questionnaires may contain single items or multiple items (i.e., questions about issues or simple statements) used in combination that are designed to measure various attitudinal phenomena, such as group cohesiveness, peer-group influence, burnout and stress, alienation, professionalism, job security, role clarity, anxiety, or sexual permissiveness. The list of attitudinal dimensions that may potentially be tapped by questionnaires is endless. Annually, improvements are made on existing questionnaire measures, and new questionnaire instruments are continually being constructed as well.

■ TYPES OF QUESTIONNAIRES

Questionnaires are often classified according to whether they include fixed-response or open-ended items. Sometimes, questionnaires contain both fixed-response and open-ended items.

Fixed-Response Questionnaires

Fixed-response questionnaires consist of items (questions or statements) that have a finite list of alternative responses. Respondents are asked to select from among a number of fixed choices and check the responses that best fit them. Informational items with fixed choices include the following:

1. My age is: *(Check one)*

    _____ below 18
    _____ 18–21
    _____ 22–25
    _____ 26–29
    _____ 30 or over

2. My political affiliation is: *(Check one)*

_____ Republican
_____ Democrat
_____ American Independent

3. The amount of formal education I have completed is: *(Check one)*

_____ Less than eighth grade
_____ Completed elementary school, some high school
_____ High school graduate, no college
_____ High school graduate, some college, did not graduate
_____ College graduate, no advanced graduate work
_____ College graduate, some graduate work completed
_____ Completed a graduate degree (master's, doctorate, etc.)

Besides informational items that may also include questions about race, ethnicity, income, occupation/profession, or rural-urban background, several items may be combined to form a scale. Below are three partial sets of items that form scales that purportedly measure group cohesiveness, desire for changing work tasks, and work alienation.

Partial Set of Items No. 1:

Group Cohesiveness Scale [Partial List of Items]

Below are various statements about your work group. Check the response that best fits you. (Responses include "Strongly agree," "Agree," "Undecided, probably agree," "Undecided, probably disagree," "Disagree," and "Strongly disagree.")

1. Do you feel that other members of your work group give your opinion ample consideration whenever issues concerning job matters are discussed?
(Check one)

_____ My opinion is considered very important by other group members
_____ Group members are fairly interested in my opinion
_____ Group members are somewhat disinterested in my opinion
_____ Group members ignore my opinion when job matters are discussed

2. To what extent do you and/or other members of your work group refer to your group as "we" or "us"?

_____ To a great extent (very frequently)

_____ To some extent (fairly frequently)

_____ To a small extent (fairly infrequently)

_____ To no extent at all (seldom, if ever)

3. How would you characterize the way the members of your work group get along?

_____ We get along better than most groups

_____ We get along about the same as other groups

_____ We get along less than other groups

_____ We seldom, if ever, get along well

4. To what extent do you feel other members of your work group would come to your aid if you were in trouble involving your work tasks?

_____ My work group members would come to my aid without question

_____ My work group members would be fairly indifferent about my problems

_____ I feel that I am on my own and cannot depend upon other work group members for assistance if I get into trouble on my job

Partial Set of Items No. 2:

Desire for Changing Work Tasks [Partial List of Items]

Each statement below [not reprinted here] is followed by the responses: "Strongly agree," "Agree," "Undecided, probably agree," "Undecided, probably disagree," "Disagree," and "Strongly disagree." Please check the response for each item that best fits you.

1. On my job it is important to me that I do new things frequently.
2. Changing my job to meet changing technology in the work place would be very disturbing to me.
3. I like a job where I can perform the same tasks routinely every day.
4. Assembly-line type work appeals to me.
5. I dislike frequent disruptions of my work routine.
6. I like my present job and would feel bad about having to perform some other different tasks.

7. Doing a variety of things on the job each day helps make me feel that time goes by more quickly.
8. I would tend to feel comfortable performing most any job at my place of work, should higher-ups decide to switch me around from one job to another frequently.

Partial Set of Items No. 3:

Work Alienation [Partial List of Items]

Each of the statements below [not reprinted here] is followed by the responses: "Strongly agree," "Agree," "Undecided, probably agree," "Undecided, probably disagree," "Disagree," and "Strongly disagree." Select the response for each item that best fits you.

1. On my job it is possible to make errors without too much disruption.
2. The way I do my work is important to my fellow employees.
3. Many times they think getting the job done is more important than the people who do the job.
4. If I ever stay home from work, this department would be in a real bind.
5. A person who likes to do work that requires thinking would like to perform my job.
6. Things are really regimented around here.
7. When I come to work each day, I look forward to a new and challenging experience.
8. Sometimes I wonder just how important I really am around here.
9. I think my job is too mechanical and repetitive.

These different kinds of fixed-response items contain certain implicit assumptions about the target audience. First, an assumption is made that the target sample has meaningful knowledge about the subject matter of the questionnaire. Second, it is assumed that the researcher knows enough about the sample under investigation to be able to anticipate the kinds of responses that would likely be expected and given. A third assumption is that most, if not all, relevant questions have been asked that relate to the basic research questions, depending upon the manifest goals of the researcher. A fourth assumption is that the responses people give are truthful reflections about them and how they feel. This latter assumption focuses upon the accuracy of questionnaires and whether they provide reliable information about the target sample.

Fixed-response items may be constructed to fit an infinite number of response patterns. In the previous examples, a format was used employing "Strongly agree" and "Strongly disagree" options. Other possible formats may include arrays of options, indicating a range of choice from "Favorable-Unfavorable," "Most intense-Least intense," "Strong-Weak," "All-None," "Everybody-Nobody," and "Positive-Negative." Your choices of response options are limited only by your own imagination. There are no "standard" or "conventional" response options that are universally used or accepted by all researchers.

Open-Ended Questionnaires

Open-ended questionnaires consist of questions that require short or lengthy written replies by respondents. Some examples of open-ended items follow:

1. What is the title of your present position with this probation agency?

   _____

2. What are your primary responsibilities or duties? Please specify: _____

   _____

   _____

3. What are the chances for your advancement to a higher position in this agency in the future? Please explain:

   _____

   _____

   _____

4. What are your recommendations for an "ideal" work setting?

   _____

   _____

   _____

5. Do you feel that the present method of evaluating work quality is fair?

   Yes _____ No _____ Uncertain _____ *(Check one)*

6. Why do you feel this is so? Please explain: _____

   _____

   _____

In these instances, rather than anticipating particular responses from the target sample through fixed-choice items, investigators instead simply provide several pages of open-ended items that request respondents to indicate their opinions and elaborate about them in some detail. Primarily exploratory and descriptive research designs might be more likely to include open-ended items if questionnaires are used for survey and investigative purposes.

Combinations of Fixed-Response and Open-Ended Items

Many questionnaires consist of questions that are either **fixed-response items** or **open-ended items.** If there is the likelihood that not all alternative categories for particular questions can be anticipated in advance, an "other" category is often included along with the other fixed choices. For instance, if we were to distribute questionnaires to a sample of residents in ethnically heterogeneous communities, such as Los Angeles, New York, Miami, or Chicago, and if we were to include an item about one's religious affiliation, it would be awkward to attempt a complete listing of all possible religious affiliations for these respondents. In Los Angeles, for example, there are large numbers of Cambodians, Laotians, Vietnamese, Chinese, Japanese, Indians, and numerous persons from the Middle East. Therefore, an item might be constructed as follows:

> My religious affiliation is: *(Check one or designate your faith in the space provided below)*
> _____ Catholic
> _____ Protestant
> _____ Jewish
> _____ Other. If "none," write "none." Please specify _____

There may or may not be sufficient numbers of "other" responses to justify creating additional categories when we commence our data analysis. Perhaps 85 percent of our sample of city residents are primarily Catholic, Protestant, and Jewish, but 10 percent are Buddhist (a major religion in India, Southeast Asia, and China) and 4 percent are Shintoist (the major religion in Japan). One percent might consist of 30 other religious faiths, with two or three respondents associated with each. Assuming that religious affiliation is an important variable in our theory, we would probably want to use five religious categories where sizable numbers of respondents of those faiths may be found. For this particular part of our data analysis, we might omit those in the "other" category, since statistical manipulations of such small numbers of respondents would be meaningless.

Comparison of Fixed-Response and Open-Ended Items

It is apparent that certain variables are more easily and directly taken into account by using fixed-response items. For example, gender, years of education, race, and political affiliation are almost always confined to a limited number of fixed-answer alternatives. For some variables, such as religious affiliation, "other" categories may be created and used together with a fixed-response format.

Most attitudinal measures in questionnaires are in fixed-response formats. These fixed-response formats enable researchers to score responses easily, sum individual item values, and determine overall raw scores for particular variables. Comparisons may be made directly between people or groups who possess certain raw scores or who fall within certain score ranges.

Survey research and the use of questionnaires are virtually inseparable, since it is almost always the researcher's intention to canvass large numbers of respondents who may be dispersed over large geographical areas. Questionnaires, particularly mailed questionnaires, enable researchers to acquire large amounts of data from large numbers of persons at minimal cost. Depending upon what is known about the intended targets of questionnaires, these instruments will vary in their sophistication and format. Before we examine the task of constructing questionnaires, it is helpful to highlight some of the major weaknesses and strengths of fixed-response and open-ended questionnaire formats for particular research purposes.

Advantages and Disadvantages of Fixed-Response Items. Among the major advantages of fixed-response questionnaires are the following:

1. Fixed-response items are easy to score and code. (Coding is a procedure whereby researchers assign numbers to particular types of responses—e.g., Democrat = 1, Republican = 2, American Independent = 3, and so on—in order to distinguish responses from one another in subsequent data analyses.) Researchers can more easily transfer the data from questionnaires containing fixed-response items to computers where data may be stored for subsequent statistical treatment and analysis.

2. No writing is required of respondents. Respondents merely check the responses that best typify them. In cases where respondents cannot adequately express themselves in writing, the fixed-response item is definitely an advantage.

3. Fixed-response items facilitate completion of questionnaires. Lengthy questionnaires with fixed-response items are completed more rapidly compared with those containing large numbers of open-ended items.

4. If questionnaires are mailed to designated respondents, there is greater likelihood that respondents will complete and return questionnaires more frequently if little or no writing is involved in their completion.

Some of the disadvantages of fixed-response questionnaire items include the following:

1. Researchers may not be able to anticipate or think of all relevant response alternatives. Fixed-response items, as noted previously, require some familiarity with the population under investigation. If respondents are forced to make choices between several alternatives that do not fit them, researchers may obtain erroneous or misleading information.

2. Fixed-response items, especially those used in attitudinal scales (i.e., with "Strongly agree" and "Strongly disagree" response patterns), may lead respondents to lapse into a **response set** or **set response.** A response set is a particular response pattern that has nothing to do with question or statement content, but rather, is used almost exclusively by respondents to complete the questionnaire rapidly or "to get it over with quick." Some respondents have been known to check the first responses for all statements or question items, regardless of whether such responses are true of them. For example, someone might check the "Strongly agree" response to the statement, "I like my job." Later, in the same set of items, they will also check "Strongly agree" in response to the statement, "I hate my job." It is apparent that they don't read the statements or questions asked. They are either bored with the questionnaire or consider the researcher's intrusion into their time as offensive. Thus, sometimes researchers build in **lie factors** or

lie scales that seek to detect set responses whenever it is suspected they are being given. Lie factors are nothing more than including several statements that are directly contradictory. Either agreements with both statements or disagreements with them mean inconsistency, a contradiction in response, and a possible set response.

Advantages and Disadvantages of Open-Ended Items. Some of the major advantages of open-ended questionnaires are as follows:

1. Open-ended items are particularly useful when researchers have little or no information available about the samples studied. Respondents are least restricted in terms of their possible answer choices with open-ended items. They can provide flexible responses to specific questions.
2. In certain instances, open-ended items are helpful to researchers because they provide insights into the respondent's thoughts and behaviors. There is always the possibility that researchers can anticipate many responses that respondents might give, but often the flexibility of open-ended items will elicit unanticipated and insightful replies from respondents. These responses will enhance the investigator's understanding of what is going on and why.

Some of the disadvantages of open-ended questionnaires include the following:

1. For open-ended items, written answers from respondents may be so diverse that researchers may find them difficult to code or classify into convenient categories. Also, different respondents may appear to provide similar responses to the same item on a questionnaire, when in fact, the meaning and importance each respondent attaches to the particular reply may be considerably different. Thus, although several respondents might be placed in common categories for purposes of classifying them on some measured characteristic, the results of such classifications may be erroneous or misleading.
2. A **bias** exists in open-ended questionnaires that stems from several sources. Some persons who cannot express themselves adequately on paper (and also orally) will be combined unfairly with more fluent persons. Therefore, an educational bias exists, particularly if the target population from which the sample is drawn is quite heterogeneous in this respect. By the same token, questionnaires in the general case (i.e., those containing both open-ended and fixed-response items) are subject to a similar type of educational bias. Not every respondent is equally adept in the art of self-expression.

    The socioeconomic factor may yield misleading results and incorrect interpretations of findings as well. Persons of different socioeconomic backgrounds or professions and occupations may not view issues the same way, nor will they necessarily use the same vocabulary to describe their feelings or attitudes. The wording of questionnaires at the outset has certain built-in biases that must be considered in assessing the quality and meaning of information obtained.

3. A third disadvantage of open-ended items is that they are time-consuming to complete. If researchers mail questionnaires to respondents, response rates will likely be lower where open-ended items are used compared with those situations where exclusively fixed-response items are used. Many persons feel that they do not have the time or interest to sit down and write out lengthy replies to questions. Face-to-face interviews appear to be more successful with better response compared with open-ended questionnaires that are self-administered.

4. Applicable to both open-ended questionnaires and fixed-response questionnaires is the possibility that significant portions of heterogeneous urban populations may not understand English. Large numbers of immigrants from Asian, Middle Eastern, and European countries in the last several decades have created ethnic enclaves in many cities throughout the United States. Thus, when heads of households are surveyed by using mailed questionnaires, it is very possible that some language other than English may be native to these heads of households. If English cannot be read or understood, certain respondents may simply discard the questionnaires they receive. Further, a significant minority of the citizenry is illiterate, despite the fact that their native language is English.

■ QUESTIONNAIRE ADMINISTRATION

Basically, there are two methods for administering questionnaires to target samples of elements: the mailed questionnaire and face-to-face questionnaire administration.

Mailed Questionnaires

Survey researchers utilize the mailed questionnaire extensively in canvassing large numbers of subjects located over broad geographical territories. This method consists simply of mailing questionnaires of variable lengths to previously designated subjects. Instructions for completing the questionnaire and returning it are usually enclosed and a stamped, return envelope is provided. Researchers want to maximize the rate of return whenever questionnaires are mailed. They may enclose cover letters designed to familiarize respondents with their study and the reasons it is being conducted.

After questionnaires have been mailed initially, a waiting period of about two weeks passes, while researchers collect questionnaires from early respondents. If some attempt has been made to identify respondents within the questionnaires themselves, then researchers can determine from master lists of respondents which ones have returned their questionnaires and which ones have not returned them. Those who haven't, as yet, returned their questionnaires may be sent follow-up letters with additional questionnaires included. A statement might be included, such as, "We recently sent you a questionnaire concerning . . . . (some topic) . . . and we have not, as yet, heard from you. Your responses are important to us. Because of the possibility that you may not have received the questionnaire we recently sent you, we are sending you another for your convenience, together with a stamped, preaddressed envelope so that you may complete and return the questionnaire easily. We hope to hear from you soon. Thank you in advance for your important participation in our research project."

Response to mailed questionnaires varies among survey research projects. No one knows what a normal response rate is for any target respondent audience. Estimates of what is "normal" range from 30 percent to 75 percent. In the social sciences, return rates to mailed questionnaires are usually expected to be about a third. Thus, if we were to mail 1,000 questionnaires to a random sample of city residents, we might expect about 330 to be returned. Naturally, if we receive larger numbers of completed questionnaires, this will enhance the representativeness of our respondents relative to the overall questionnaire mailing, which is usually based on some type of random sampling plan. Subsequently, we will examine the issue of nonresponse, or those instances where persons receive our questionnaires but for various reasons elect not to return them. The rate of return for any mailed questionnaire depends on many factors.

Face-to-Face Questionnaire Administration

Another common method of distributing questionnaires is **face-to-face questionnaire administration.** Researchers may distribute questionnaires directly to target audiences. Many students have been a part of a target audience in the classroom, where investigators might pass out questionnaires to them during class time. Students are frequent target audiences of researchers because they are easily accessible and investigators can obtain direct responses to their questionnaires from large numbers of students in a matter of minutes.

Unfortunately, frequently selecting students in the classroom for questionnaire administration has led some professionals to allege that, over the years, we have learned a great deal about students and their attitudes about things, but that students are atypical of the population at large in several respects. Their general educational level is somewhat higher than the average community resident. Further, many students in colleges and universities may be from elsewhere geographically. Thus, if students at some university are used for a professor's attitudinal research, and if that research is connected with one or more community issues, student responses may be interesting but irrelevant in relation to those issues.

Besides administering questionnaires to students in classrooms, investigators can visit work settings and distribute questionnaires directly to employees. Prisons may permit researchers to canvass prisoners about various matters through self-administered questionnaires distributed to various inmates by correctional officers. One advantage of such direct distributions of these questionnaires is that students or employees or prisoners may ask researchers for clarification about any statement or question which may be ambiguous or confusing to readers. Another advantage is that a large proportion of those who receive questionnaires will likely complete and return them. Thus, a high return rate is virtually guaranteed. Such guarantees cannot be made regarding mailed questionnaires.

Comparison of Mailed Questionnaires with Face-to-Face Questionnaire Administration

It should be apparent that the major benefit of mailed questionnaires is economy. Mailed questionnaires are an inexpensive means of obtaining information about particular target samples. One of the drawbacks to mailed questionnaires is that you never are sure who completes and returns the questionnaires you have distributed. If researchers send questionnaires to organizational leaders in community corrections agencies, a secretary or volunteer worker in the agency may actually complete the questionnaire and return it. However, it is assumed by the researcher that directors or agency heads were the ones who responded to the questions. Another drawback is that researchers have no way of assuring that people will return the questionnaires they have been sent. Thus, in most research projects involving mailed questionnaires, nonresponse is significant and limits the generalizability of subsequent research findings.

Another drawback of mailed questionnaires is that respondents may misinterpret certain statements or misread questions and provide answers that are unrelated to the intended statement meanings. Without the presence of the researcher as a resource, respondents must determine for themselves what the statements mean or how questions should be interpreted. Some inaccurate information is therefore expected among the returned questionnaires.

On the favorable side, mailed questionnaires allow respondents the option of completing the instrument in the privacy of their own homes or work settings, with a high degree of privacy and anonymity. If sensitive issues are being probed, or if personal behaviors or attitudes are being solicited, such as indicating one's participation in illicit drug use or sexual experiences, heightening respondent anonymity will improve the odds of greater return rates. Respondents might be more inclined to return questionnaires that contain sensitive materials if they believe their responses will be treated confidentially and anonymously. In such situations, however, follow-up letters that contain extra questionnaires might serve notice to potential respondents that the researchers know who they are and that they did not respond initially. Relatively little research has been conducted about the distinction between those topics considered sensitive and those labeled as innocuous. What is considered as sensitive by one person may not be considered as sensitive by another.

The major advantages of face-to-face questionnaire administration are that (1) researchers know who completes the questionnaires, (2) a high rate of questionnaire completion and return is expected, and (3) investigators are present to clarify any statements or questions that might otherwise be misinterpreted by respondents. A disadvantage is that researchers must actually be present during the questionnaire administration, which might involve the cost of extensive travel to diverse locations.

■ QUESTIONNAIRE CONSTRUCTION

For most persons, a questionnaire is likely to be viewed as a simple device that anyone can create or throw together, given the time and interest. For serious scientists who do social research, however, questionnaires and their construction is serious business and considered a complex task. In many instances, before the final form of a questionnaire is determined for general distribution to some target sample, researchers will probably revise it several times. These revisions include modifications of question or statement wording and questionnaire content and length. Most researchers would probably agree that constructing an appropriate questionnaire for any target audience is a tedious and arduous task. However, despite their best efforts, researchers have never devised the perfect questionnaire. Every questionnaire suffers at least a few imperfections that neither the researchers nor their assistants detected during its preparation.

This section examines some of the major factors that researchers must take into account when constructing questionnaires for selected target samples. Let's begin by considering some of the questions that arise in the initial stages of questionnaire preparation:

1. What is the definition of the population about which we seek information?
2. What is the socioeconomic and/or educational level of people who will receive and complete our questionnaires?
3. What kinds of facts do we want to know about them?
4. How accessible are these people for research purposes?
5. How will we administer the questionnaire?
6. What kinds of response patterns will we use in our questionnaire construction?
7. How long should we make the questionnaire?
8. How much control will we be able to exert over ensuring their responses to our questionnaire?

Ideally, every element in the population to be studied should be identified and given an opportunity to be included in the research project. The socioeconomic level or educational background (if known) of the intended target population will enable the researcher to design questions or formulate statements at a particular level of readability commensurate with that of the respondents. If there is a strong likelihood that the population contains a substantial number of persons who might have difficulty with the English language for one reason or another, then interviewing might be a better strategy, although it will be considerably more expensive in time and money.

The kinds of things we want to learn about the sample will directly determine the content of our questionnaires. Some of the standard social and demographic items are age, gender, occupation/profession, years/amount of education, and race/ethnicity. Other items are included as needed. For example, if we are studying probation officer burnout, we would want to include a scale that measures burnout. If we wish to assess job performance and cross-tabulate it with other variables, including burnout, we would need to include various measures that would enable us to evaluate one's job performance or effectiveness. We can use existing measures devised by other researchers or we can create our own measures.

Questionnaire length is a controversial matter and has never been resolved. Some investigators have argued that in the case of mailed questionnaires, short questionnaires are preferable to long ones. The idea is that people will be more inclined to spend their time completing and returning short questionnaires rather than long ones. Unfortunately, no one knows what the guidelines are for determining whether any given questionnaire is long or short. For instance, **postcard questionnaires** have been used in the past for soliciting public opinion about a few issues. Two or three statements can be printed on a self-addressed, stamped postcard that can easily be mailed back to researchers. These are considered short questionnaires.

I worked part-time at Knoxville College in Tennessee for several years. One semester, all faculty were required to complete a 110-page questionnaire, printed on both sides of each page. The questionnaire solicited information about teaching duties, college functions, and numerous other items. It was administered as a part of a general accreditation program for the college. One hundred percent compliance was obtained from all faculty, since completing and turning in questionnaires to the payroll office was the only way faculty could receive their paychecks. This type of questionnaire would be considered very long. But most questionnaires are somewhere in between postcard length and 110 pages.

Questionnaire length is a matter of personal preference and standards. One consideration that provides a good standard for limiting questionnaire length is how long it will take to complete. Extremely lengthy questionnaires can cause some respondents to become test-weary. Tired respondents may become somewhat careless in the responses they give, and they may drift into response sets.

Questionnaire length is also influenced by organizational time constraints. If you approach a police department and attempt to get departmental approval to administer questionnaires to all officers commencing various shifts, you will not be particularly persuasive if you tell the watch commander that the questionnaire will take about an hour to complete. You would be better off limiting questionnaire administration to 15 minutes or less. And even this short time interval may be considered lengthy by the target agency or department. Questionnaires sent to persons in their own homes and on their own time may be lengthier and take longer to complete. But again, you must balance questionnaire length against factors that would enhance the likelihood of increasing the rate of returns.

The length of the questionnaire is generally a function of the amount and type of information sought. If we assume that investigators are operating within a theoretical context and that the variables being studied are limited, then the length of the questionnaire will be determined by the inclusion of those scales necessary to measure the limited number of variables examined. Researchers should not "throw in" extraneous scales or include variables that are detached from or irrelevant for their theoretical schemes. But sometimes, novice researchers will add other variables simply because they are interesting. A good rule of thumb is to include only those relevant variables that enable you to carry out your research objectives fully. Leave out additional variables that might be more suitable for a subsequent investigation.

Selecting and Ordering the Questionnaire Items

Because the primary functions of questionnaires are description and measurement, researchers have a variety of options for selecting items for inclusion. Several classic sources exist that either tell researchers where to find existing measuring instruments in questionnaire form or provide them with compilations of measures themselves (e.g., Miller, 1977; Bonjean, Hill, and McLemore, 1967). Investigators will often want to combine several relevant existing measures with items of their own or even newly devised scales. However, many existing scales, such as those found in Bonjean, Hill, and McLemore (1967) or Miller (1991) are probably dated culturally or contain questions using phraseologies that might have different meanings in the 2000s when compared with their meanings in the 1960s or 1970s. Sometimes, the researcher may be able to adapt older existing scales to fit present problems by changing the wording of various statements. Basically, the originally devised scales are used, but they have been given an updated treatment by investigators who have modified certain statements to fit the present research problem.

Whenever any scale is used in research, whether it is a previously constructed scale or a newly devised one, researchers should perform various tests to determine whether the items are clearly worded and internally consistent with one another. Such tests are known as pretests, and they involve administering early versions of questionnaires to audiences similar to those targeted for one's research. For example, if researchers wanted to administer questionnaires to a sample of Indiana prison correctional officers, they might want to pretest their questionnaires by giving them to samples of jail correctional officers or to others who perform similar work. Jail correctional officers in the researcher's local community might be more accessible for study than prison correctional officers, where access to the prison environment is extremely limited. Sometimes, these pretests are designated as **pilot studies,** because they involve trial runs of questionnaires before audiences similar to those where the final form of the questionnaire is to be administered. Thus, pilot studies are small-scale implementations of the actual studies researchers are prepared to conduct. They enable investigators to detect faults associated with their research instruments and obtain ideas about how best to carry out the final project.

For example, these pretests are helpful in that they help researchers to detect spelling errors, awkward wordings of questions or statements, or possibly irrelevant items that do not apply to correctional officer duties or functions. Also, investigators may subject their scales to preliminary tests to determine whether they seem to provide accurate indications of the degree to which certain characteristics are possessed by respondents.

Including items whose primary function is description is a fairly easy task for seasoned researchers. But precautions need to be taken, particularly with reference to the question wording. For instance, if investigators wanted to estimate the amount of marijuana consumption among an aggregate of college students, they might draw a probability sample and ask them the following question:

How often do you smoke marijuana per month?

or

How many "joints" do you smoke per week?

Each of these questions is presumptuous in that it assumes that these students smoke marijuana, when in fact, none of them may do so. Such questions are labeled "husband-beating-wife" questions, and are similar to the question, When was the last time you beat your wife? The ridiculousness of this question is apparent. First, it assumes that respondents are married (which may not be true). Second, it assumes that all respondents are male (which may not be true). Third, it assumes that all respondents beat their wives (which may not be true). It is imperative that researchers refrain from assuming too much about the target population.

Provided that investigators have established or legitimized their research purpose with the target audience (particularly where information is requested concerning possible law violations by respondents), a safer and more reasonable approach to the marijuana question would be the following:

Have you ever smoked marijuana?

If the respondent's reply is yes, then the researcher can use the follow-up question,

Do you smoke marijuana currently?

Again, if the respondent's answer is yes, then the "frequency" question may be asked safely:

How often per week (or month) do you smoke marijuana?

These are **contingency questions,** since the answer to the first question (Have you ever smoked marijuana?) determines whether the respondent will answer additional questions about marijuana smoking. If the respondent answers no to the Have you ever smoked marijuana question, then he or she can skip the next question(s) relating to the frequency of marijuana use. Other types of contingency questions might be

Have you ever been assaulted?

Have you ever had any property stolen from your house or car?

Depending upon respondent answers to either of these questions, they may be directed to other questions about the nature of the assault against them or what types of property were stolen from them.

Caution should also be exercised when interpreting answers persons give to questions or statements. For instance, several interpretations may be made about the extent of one's professionalism as a police officer, depending upon the answer given to the following question:

How many journals, periodicals, or other police officer–oriented materials do you subscribe to on an annual basis?

_____ None

_____ One or two

_____ Three or four

_____ Five or six

_____ Seven or more

If some police officers do not subscribe to any journals or police-oriented periodicals, does this mean that they do not have professionalism or are not professional? Are officers who subscribe to "seven or more" periodicals more professional than those who subscribe to only "three or four" periodicals? We have no way of controlling for the *types* of periodicals referred to in the previous item. Are these equipment magazines that advertise police officer weapons and accessories? Are these journals from a police officer's association, such as *Police Chief*, which contain research articles about police work? Are these magazines about hand-to-hand combat or developing better public relations skills? We have no way of equating numbers of magazine subscriptions with degree of police officer professionalism.

We can ask police officers how professional they believe they are, relative to their work. Or we can ask certain officers to evaluate the professionalism of other officers. All of these questions are contingent upon what we mean by the term *professionalism*. But questionnaires are designed to function as indicators of the extent to which these various phenomena are possessed by our respondents. By probing and seeking answers to questions that relate logically to professionalism, such as membership in professional organizations, taking courses that improve one's performance on the job, or enrolling in workshops that are geared to enhance one's professional skills, we can acquire a fairly good understanding or impression of someone's degree of professionalism. However, we don't know whether these officers will necessarily do better jobs at enforcing the law or refraining from using excessive force. Indicators of one's attitudes only suggest a possible propensity to behave in given ways. Often, there are discrepancies between what our indicators reveal on questionnaires and the ways people actually behave in the real world.

Ordering the Questionnaire Items.   Constructing questionnaires is not particularly difficult. Constructing *good* questionnaires is absorbing and requires much thoughtfulness on the part of researchers. A major problem for many researchers is how to begin their questionnaires. Much of the time, questionnaires are started by some type of identification, such as one's name, address, telephone number, or other personal information. While these items seem innocent enough, they may be viewed as intrusive by some respondents.

Better questionnaires begin with interesting questions that attract one's attention. For example, if we were studying the opinions of prison inmates and inmate rights, we might plan to distribute questionnaires to a sample of prison inmates. We might begin our questionnaire as follows:

In recent years, more attention has been focused upon the rights of inmates. Please indicate your agreement or disagreement with the following statements.

1. The constitutional rights of inmates should not be ignored.

Check one:

_____ Strongly agree

_____ Agree

_____ Undecided, probably agree

_____ Undecided, probably disagree

_____ Disagree

_____ Strongly disagree

Most if not all prison inmates are going to check the "Strongly agree" option, since they have a strong vested interest in this question. It attracts their attention. In some way, inmates may feel that by responding to these items, they may influence public policy about inmate rights. At least they have a chance to express their opinion to outsiders, such as criminological researchers. Other similar statements will follow. Eventually, researchers can insert more intrusive questions about the type of conviction offense, age, socioeconomic status, gender, and other personal information about the respondent.

■ RESPONSE AND NONRESPONSE: SOME CONSIDERATIONS

Survey researchers who utilize questionnaires in their investigations are concerned about maximizing the number of respondents who are contacted initially. Also, they are concerned about the potential effects of nonresponse, if any, particularly in mailed-questionnaire situations. Some of the more important factors that affect the rate of response to questionnaires follow. Many of the facts identified are particularly relevant for mailed questionnaires, although most pertain to all types of questionnaire administration.

Questionnaire Length

Much attention has been given to questionnaire length. As we have seen, there are no consistent standards that distinguish short questionnaires from long ones. The common belief held by many researchers is that shorter questionnaires tend to be returned more often than longer ones. However, at least one study has investigated the influence of "apparent" questionnaire length upon response rate.

Researchers sent 3,000 questionnaires to random samples of residents in three Tennessee cities: Knoxville, Chattanooga, and Memphis (Champion and Sear, 1969). The questionnaires pertained to NASA spending and were directed to household heads. All 3,000 questionnaires were the same regarding content. That is, all questionnaires were exactly the same in wording. However, the researchers spaced the question items differently so that three different questionnaire lengths were produced. These questionnaire paper-lengths were three, six, and nine pages, respectively. Basically, the same questions were cramped into three pages, spread out over six pages, and even more spread out over nine pages. Thus, respondents received questionnaires where some only appeared to be longer or shorter than others. Interestingly, the nine-page questionnaires were returned more often than either six-page or three-page questionnaires. This finding suggests that at least for questionnaires within these page ranges, "apparently" longer questionnaires do not necessarily lead to lower return rates among respondents.

Other investigators might consider any questionnaire under ten pages to be short, whereas other researchers would invoke different standards of questionnaire length. We might generally assume, however, that keeping a questionnaire as short as possible, while including only the relevant scales and question items designed to accomplish one's research objectives, will elicit the highest return rates under most conditions.

Questionnaire Content and Wording: Possible Sources of Bias

Questionnaires that contain controversial material or that request respondents to reveal intimate details of their personal lives may elicit both high and low response rates, depending upon the topics investigated and the target audience. It is entirely likely that some individuals will find material on some questionnaires to be offensive and immoral, whereas others will find the same material interesting, titillating, or arousing. It would be logical to expect differential response rates from such diverse groups.

Some people may regard questionnaires as an invasion of their privacy and simply refuse to answer on such grounds. Others may see questionnaires as an opportunity to express their feelings about important issues, and therefore, the questionnaire functions for them as a means of tension release or frustration reduction, as well as a data-gathering tool for the researcher.

Hypothetically, suppose you wished to gather some public opinion information about President Bill Clinton and his 1999 impeachment trial in the U.S. Senate. You are interested in the opinions persons have about perjury and obstruction of justice generally, since these were the key charges leveled against President Clinton. You devise a questionnaire and include several items that you think are interesting. You distribute your questionnaire to numerous households in your neighborhood, advising persons that you will collect their questionnaires the following day. When you return the following day to collect the questionnaires, most persons tell you that they are not interested in your research and give you back a blank questionnaire. They are downright rude to you. The following are some of the questions you asked of these neighbors:

1. What is your name, age, and sex?
2. How many affairs have you had outside of your marriage in the last 20 years?
3. Since Republicans are sexually frustrated politicians, do you think President Clinton had a fair trial in the Senate?
4. What other kinds of sex acts are there besides plain sexual intercourse?
5. What type of perjury have you committed in a court of law?
6. Have you ever asked someone to lie for you to escape punishment?
7. Have you ever been audited by the Internal Revenue Service?
8. How much is your house worth?
9. What is your salary at work?
10. What kinds of sex acts do you think are serious enough to warrant the impeachment of a president of the United States?

Chances are that if you asked these particular questions or others like them, your neighbors will now view you as a major neighborhood snoop. These questions pry into their private sexual behaviors, finances, and other matters that might be embarrassing if disclosed. A major reason that these questions will repel most persons is that you know, and now they know you know, these things about them. Also, several of these questions make assumptions about them and their behaviors that may not be true. Items 2 and 5 presume that the respondent has had affairs outside of marriage and committed perjury in a courtroom. Item 3 is a biased statement disparaging Republicans. It may offend a respondent who is a Republican. Items 4 and 10 ask you to describe specific sex acts, a topic you may find very uncomfortable discussing, even on a questionnaire. Even if we were to somehow change the wording of these items and make them less threatening to respondents, it would be better if we provided our respondents with some type of anonymity.

Double-barreled Questions. Sometimes questions are asked that are really two questions in one or **double-barreled questions.** For instance, Are you a Republican and pro-choice? or, Did you register as a sex offender or did you use a dangerous weapon when carrying out the molestation? We need to think through these questions and determine whether they will confuse or confound our respondents. In double-barreled question scenarios, we need to break down the question into two or three items, such as What is your political affiliation? Are you pro-life, pro-choice, or do you have no opinion in this matter? Have you registered in the community as a sex offender? When you committed the offense, did you use a dangerous weapon?

The Use of Certain Key Words. What may appear to be clear to us as questions or statements may be very confusing or unintelligible to others. For police officers we might ask, Do you always do your job in a professional manner? What does that mean? What does the word "professional" mean to the officer? Does it have the same meaning for the officer that it has for us?

If we conduct a survey of halfway house parolee/clients, we may ask them if they feel if the halfway house staff are effective. What does "effective" mean? Does it have the same meaning for halfway house parolee/clients as it does for us? We may need to provide some specificity for these clients, such as, Do you think the halfway house staff does a good job at providing you with job referrals and employment opportunities?

Anonymity

Respondents may be more likely to give more truthful answers on questionnaires to the extent that their anonymity is assured. Sensitive items related to racial or religious attitudes or to sexual behavior may appear to be less threatening if the responses are anonymous. However, because of certain psychological and/or social factors presently unidentified, persons may derive some gratification (e.g., ego, sexual prowess, or deviance rewards) from disclosing sensitive information about themselves to others. No consistent pattern is evident in the literature concerning the influence of anonymity on response rates.

Regardless of whether we provide anonymity to those who respond to our questionnaires, we must consider several possible problems that anonymity creates. First, if responses to our questionnaires are anonymous, we won't be able to identify the respondents. Perhaps a meaningful interpretation of questionnaire results depends on knowing the identities of the respondents. For instance, suppose we use the city directory to obtain a list of respondents. The city directory contains much valuable information about families, such as occupation/profession of household heads, whether the family has a telephone, and the average property value of the neighborhood where the respondent lives. This information can be gleaned directly from the city directory. This means that we don't have to ask these types of potentially sensitive questions on our questionnaire. But we need to know *who* the respondents are in order to link their questionnaires to city directory information. While some researchers might consider the practice unethical, one study used invisible ink on questionnaires to identify respondents on a mailed questionnaire. Applying a special fluid to the paper of returned questionnaires enabled researchers to see the names of respondents, and, therefore, they could be linked with the city directory information. The researchers did not consider this deception as serious, since the names of respondents were used only to associate their questionnaires with sociodemographic information already in the city directory.

Second, the target sample of respondents may be so small that even though anonymity is assured, it would be easy for most anyone to identify all respondents. Suppose an investigator wanted to study a probation office. Questionnaires are administered to 30 employees in the office. Respondents are asked to indicate their job titles or positions, age, years on the job, and other salient job characteristics. With only a superficial knowledge of that work setting, researchers would know the identities of all respondents.

Third, some respondents may interpret assurances of anonymity from investigators as an indication that the questionnaire is unimportant or trivial. Respondents may assume that if researchers don't care who these respondents are, then the investigators probably don't care about what responses are given. There is no way for researchers to overcome this dilemma.

Self-Reports

Self-Report Defined.   The self-report is a data collection method involving an unofficial survey of youths or adults where the intent is to obtain information about specific types of behavior not ordinarily disclosed through traditional data collection methods, including questionnaires, interviews, polls, official agency reports, or sociodemographic summaries. The exact origin of the use of self-reports is unknown. However, sociologist Richard LaPiere used self-report information to investigate the relation between attitudes and action in the 1930s. LaPiere wanted to know whether whites who admitted prejudice toward blacks and who said they would discriminate against them would actually engage in discrimination if confronted with an opportunity to do so. LaPiere sent black couples to restaurants and hotels owned and operated by whites, following self-disclosures from these same whites who said that they would discriminate against blacks and not serve or accommodate them. Subsequently most blacks were served or accommodated at these restaurants and hotels without incident, causing LaPiere to conclude that the attitude-action relation on this issue was at best tenuous. LaPiere's research was significant in part because it called into question the use of expressed attitudes as predictors of subsequent behaviors consistent with those attitudes.

Subsequent use of the self-report method targeted juvenile delinquents. In 1943, Austin L. Porterfield investigated hidden delinquency, or delinquency neither detected by nor reported to police. He surveyed several hundred college students, asking them to disclose whether they had ever engaged in delinquent acts. While all of the students reported that they had previously engaged in delinquent acts, most also reported that they had not been caught by police or brought to the attention of the juvenile court.

In 1958, James Short and Ivan Nye became the first investigators to conduct the first self-report study of a delinquent population. They obtained self-report information from hundreds of delinquents in several Washington state training schools. They compared this information with self-report data from hundreds of students in three Washington state communities and three Midwestern towns. Their findings revealed that delinquency was widespread and not specific to any social class. Further, both the seriousness and frequency of juvenile offending were key determinants of juvenile court treatment of youthful offenders and public policy relating to delinquents.

Some of the popular self-report surveys conducted annually are the *National Youth Survey* and the *Monitoring the Future Survey*. These large-scale surveys of high school students focus upon particular behaviors. In addition, the Institute for Social Research at the University of Michigan annually solicits information from a national sample of 3,000 high school students. These informative

Diana K. Harris
University of Tennessee

Statistics: M.A. (sociology), University of
Tennessee.

Interests: I was not aware of the theft that occurred in nursing homes until
both of my parents moved to a nursing home. It wasn't long until the few things
that they had with them, such as jewelry and clothing, as well as a small amount of
money, began to disappear. Even the food that I brought them vanished. I searched
the gerontological literature to find what research had been done on this subject.
I was amazed when I discovered that there was none.

After doing two small survey studies on theft in nursing homes within Tennessee with my colleague Michael Benson, we then applied for and received a
grant to do a national study. We collected survey data from nursing home employees, family members of patients, and administrators from 47 nursing homes in ten
states. We supplemented the data with site visits to six homes where we interviewed patients, employees, and administrators.

Our findings indicated that 25 percent of the employees reported seeing or sus-
pecting their co-workers of stealing from nursing home patients. About one-fifth of
family members suspected that their relatives' possessions had been stolen by nursing home employees, and a small minority of employees self-reported that they had
stolen from their patients and done this more than once. Most of the employees
felt that if they were caught stealing (40 percent of our sample believed that this
was unlikely), the worst thing that could happen to them is that they would be
fired and not reported to police.

Our analysis provided support to the idea that nursing home theft is extensive.
The combination of motivation, opportunity, and lack of deterrence creates favorable conditions for the victimization of patients in nursing homes.

reports are frequently cited in the research literature, which attests to the integrity, reliability, and validity of this information among noted juvenile justice
professionals.

These national surveys involve administering confidential questionnaires
and checklists to high school students. Students are asked to indicate which behaviors they have engaged in during the past six months or the previous year.
Assuming that their responses are truthful, researchers believe that the results
are a more accurate reflection of delinquent behaviors than are official sources,
such as the *Uniform Crime Reports*.

High school students or others may be asked to complete a confidential questionnaire where lists of offenses are provided. Ordinarily, simple checklists are given to students, and they are asked to identify those behaviors they have done, and not necessarily those for which they have been apprehended. Considered unofficial sources of information about delinquency and delinquency patterns, these self-disclosures are considered by many professionals to be more accurate than official sources. An example of such a checklist is shown in Figure 7.1.

Delbert Elliott has described aggregate data derived from self-reports and the first eight waves of questionnaires in the *National Youth Survey*, a prospective longitudinal study involving a national probability sample of 1,725 youths. The utility of self-reporting was amply illustrated. These self-reports disclosed, for instance, that the prevalence of serious violent offending among juveniles is substantially higher than otherwise reported by different official sources; that the onset of serious violent offending occurs at earlier ages; that evidence of career escalation (e.g., progressing from less serious to more serious offending) is stronger than previously believed; that serious violent offending represents only a small proportion of all juvenile offending annually; and that a small subset of serious violent offenders accounts for a majority of all serious violent offending (Elliott, 1994).

Self-reports enable researchers to determine whether there are changing offending patterns among juveniles over time. Substantial information exists that characterizes violent juvenile offenders and catalogs the many potential causal factors that are associated with violence. Self-report data suggests that a sizeable gap exists between official reports of juvenile offenses and self-reported information. Generally, self-report disclosures reveal more delinquency than are reported by either the *Uniform Crime Reports* or *National Crime Victimization*

FIGURE 7.1 A hypothetical checklist for self-report disclosures of delinquent or criminal conduct among high school students. (*Source:* Compiled by author.)

How often during the past six months have you committed the following offenses? (*Check whichever best applies to you.*)

Offense	Frequency				
	0 times	*1 time*	*2 times*	*3 times*	*4 or more times*
Sniffed glue	_____	_____	_____	_____	_____
Shoplifted	_____	_____	_____	_____	_____
Stole a car	_____	_____	_____	_____	_____
Used marijuana	_____	_____	_____	_____	_____
Used crack	_____	_____	_____	_____	_____

Survey (Elliott, Dunford, and Huizinga, 1987). Self-reports of delinquency are commonly referred to as "hidden delinquency," because much of this delinquency is undetected through official data collection methods.

The relation between one's early childhood and the onset of status offending or delinquency has been heavily investigated. Typically, parent-child association and attachment are linked with delinquent conduct. Samples of delinquents and nondelinquents are asked to provide self-reports of their early upbringing, including their perceived closeness with parents and the disciplinary methods used to punish misconduct. Different themes are researched. For instance, the etiology of delinquency as related to different family processes according to race/ethnicity has been studied (Smith and Krohn, 1991). Does a sample of inner-city high-risk youths reflect important differences in family processes according to race/ethnicity?

Researchers who want to determine the extent to which convicted felons experienced abusive childhoods use the self-report method as a means of testing theories about childhood socialization. For example, a sample of 301 convicted male felons in a New York prison were interviewed (Weeks and Widom, 1998). On the basis of their self-reports, it was determined that two-thirds of these felons reported some form of childhood victimization and abuse. Violent offenders reported a greater incidence of childhood violence compared with property offenders, while sex offenders reported a greater incidence of childhood sexual abuse than other types of offenders. Thus, self-reports enabled these researchers to test their theory about the relation between adult criminality and childhood victimization.

Information about runaways is almost exclusively gleaned from self-report studies (Whitbeck, Hoyt, and Ackley, 1997). For example, it has been found that runaways, compared with other types of juvenile status offenders, have greater levels of family violence, rejection, and sexual abuse. Not unexpected, runaways were from families where there was less parental monitoring of juvenile behavior, and less parental warmth and support.

Not all of this research is dependent upon recollections of one's childhood and familial past. For instance, 39 community-based organizations in Miami, Florida, have provided risk-focused delinquency prevention services for over 900 families (Kakar, 1998). These organizations provided families with parenting skills and counseled both adults and juveniles about how to cope with day-to-day family problems and stresses. Self-reports from family members indicated that the program was effective and accomplishing its goal of delinquency prevention.

Self-report surveys are believed to be more accurate and informative compared with official sources of crime and delinquency information. Before self-report surveys of such information are presented, it is helpful to become familiar with some of the more popular crime and delinquency information sources and their strengths and weaknesses.

Research Applications.   The research applications of self-reports are both extensive and diverse. An inspection of research articles compiled by the *Criminal Justice Abstracts* between the years 1968 and 1998 revealed that 202 articles utilized self-reports for different purposes. Two-thirds of the articles involved studies of juveniles, while article subject matter was dominated by the themes of alcohol/drug use, sex offenses, spousal abuse, status offending and delinquency, and early childhood sexual, psychological, or physical abuse.

Generally, self-report studies accomplish two important research objectives: (1) describing and understanding behavior, and (2) predicting behavior. Self-report information provides considerable enriching details about persons under a variety of circumstances. Self-reports furnish important descriptive information about what people think and do. Such descriptions include how persons were treated as children and the events that were most significant to them as they grew to adulthood. The more that is learned about the significant occurrences in one's life, the better the predictive schemes to explain present and to forecast future behaviors. Self-reports, therefore, are an important source of information for descriptive and theoretical purposes. From a theoretical standpoint, self-reports represent one important means of theory verification.

School Violence. School violence is an increasingly important topic of discussion among parents, school officials, and juvenile justice professionals (Rosenblatt and Furlong, 1997). Although the media suggests that school violence is pervasive, the sensationalism attached to school shootings does not necessarily mean that school violence is increasing. For instance, a study of 3,364 high school seniors drawn from 113 public and 19 private schools across the United States revealed that between 1982 and 1988, school victimizations occurred at relatively low rates (Hanke, 1996). Boys were victimized more frequently than girls, and nonwhites were victimized more frequently than whites. Most victimizations were single occurrences, with dangerous weapons used in only limited instances. Verbal threats not involving injury or weapons were most commonly observed. These victimizations were noted through the use of self-reports, where juveniles were asked whether they had been victimized at school. Other researchers have reported more serious and frequent violence, especially in schools with larger proportions of at-risk youth (Levine, 1996).

Drug Use Among Juveniles and Delinquency. A frequently cited relation is between alcohol or drug abuse and delinquency. In Hillsborough County, Florida, the Juvenile Assessment Center was established as an intervention project to help at-risk youths and their families (Dembo, Pacheco, and Schmeidler, 1997). Self-reports of 114 project participants led researchers to conclude that a significant association exists between self-reported drug use and involvement in delinquent behavior. Sometimes, however, self-reports from youths about crimes or status offenses they have committed may be exaggerated. One survey of high school students reported that over half of all students smoked cigarettes, and that they had smoked cigarettes on the day they were surveyed by researchers. But saliva specimens collected from all of these students on the same day disclosed that less than 10 percent of them had nicotine in their systems. If students are untruthful on a questionnaire regarding their smoking behavior, what else will they lie about?

Verification of self-report information can be made by means other than collecting saliva specimens. Police or juvenile records may be checked against what offenses are reported, but only if we know the identities of our juvenile respondents. But most self-report surveys are conducted where anonymity is assured. Thus, it is often difficult if not impossible to verify one's responses against official records.

Sometimes investigators may use known-group validation, where self-report questionnaires are administered to a group of known delinquents. These persons can furnish researchers with anonymous information, but that information can be checked against preexisting records for authentication. In known-group validation situations, it is not necessary to know the names of specific juveniles. Rather, it is important to know about the aggregate offending characteristics of the group in order to match them with aggregate self-report information.

Investigations of Criminals. A significant amount of self-report research involves adult offenders. Recidivists and career criminals have been studied extensively in order to determine which factors seem to explain their repetitive criminal behavior. When probationers or parolees fail in their respective programs, researchers want to know which factors account for their failure to complete the program successfully. Other research using self-reports from adults focuses upon family violence and spousal abuse.

Self-Reports of Batterers and Spousal Abusers. A study of spousal violence where one of the spouses is a police officer yielded interesting information based upon self-reports (Neidig, Russell, and Seng, 1992). Self-report data were obtained from 385 male police officers, 40 female police officers, and 115 female spouses in a Southwestern city. Approximately 40 percent of the officers reported some form of marital conflict involving physical aggression. Greater marital violence was associated with the number of hours worked per week, the shift and current assignment, and the amount of leave taken. Researchers believe that based upon this self-report information, it might be possible to identify those police groups that may be at relatively higher risk for marital aggression and that such aggression might be regulated or decreased.

Self-Reports of Convicted Sex Offenders. The use of self-reports is believed helpful at highlighting the background or personal factors and attitudes of sex offenders that help to explain their crimes (Kaplan, 1990). Sex offenders have provided investigators with considerable background detail leading up to their crimes. Situational factors, such as the isolation and helplessness of victims, the physical characteristics of victims that trigger sexual urges, and the fantasies that are played out through the sexual acts themselves enable researchers to develop explanatory schemes that suggest particular therapies and individual or group counseling. Thus, through self-reports, new treatment methods are suggested as well as potential interventions.

Self-reports of crime and delinquency are a valuable source of information to researchers. Research projects with exploratory, descriptive, and/or experimental study objectives benefit from the use of self-report data. Descriptions of different types of delinquents and the development of useful intervention strategies for delinquency prevention have been assisted greatly by the use of self-reports. The broad application of self-reports in virtually every facet of criminology and criminal justice suggests the long-term application of this data collection method.

How Do You Know that Respondents Tell the Truth? The Lie Factor

Much has been written about deception practiced by researchers when contacting and studying respondents. However, respondents may also be deceptive according to how they respond to questions. Some respondents may simply lie to investigators and give false information about themselves. We don't know all of the reasons why people lie to researchers. We suspect, for instance, that some juveniles lie in order to make themselves seem tough or adultlike. Maybe some adults lie for similar reasons. Maybe they think that if they admit to criminal or embarrassing activities, this information will be made available to others and they might get into trouble or suffer social ostracism.

Whenever investigators administer questionnaires to respondents, sometimes they include a few questions that will sensitize them as to whether respondents are lying. Essentially, researchers build into their questionnaires a lie factor, consisting of several general statements with almost universal answers. Some of these items are

1. Sometimes I have thoughts that would be embarrassing if known to others.
2. Sometimes I feel anxious about a trivial incident.
3. I never lie for any reason.
4. Sometimes I feel insecure or underconfident.
5. I have never said anything that embarrasses others.
6. I have never had bad or unpleasant dreams.
7. I never worry about anything.

These and similar items are sometimes included together with other statements that describe one's self and personal characteristics. Respondents are asked to indicate whether these statements are true or false. Researchers assume that *every* one of these statements is true of most people. However, some persons deny that these statements characterize them. If a respondent gives a "false" response to most of these items, then their responses to other items on a questionnaire are suspect. Most everyone has worried about something at one time or another. Most everyone has felt anxious about a trivial incident or had an unpleasant dream. However, some persons want to convey a particular image to investigators. Maybe they think that "normal" people don't worry about things and are totally self-assured and confident. Maybe they think that it is "abnormal" to dream about unpleasant things or say something that embarrasses others. Therefore, they lie in order to appear normal. However, by lying, they appear abnormal. Thus, a lie factor is established and undermines the credibility of their responses to other items. Researchers are inclined to discard their questionnaires as useless if their lie factor is significantly high.

The Minnesota Multiphasic Personality Inventory (MMPI) is a personality assessment inventory. It consists of over 550 true-false statements and measures a multitude of personality characteristics. Some of the previous items are found on the MMPI. It also has a built-in lie factor. When persons take the MMPI, they get a lie factor score in addition to an assessment of several salient personality characteristics. The MMPI is administered for many reasons, some of which pertain to applications for employment with different agencies. Some professions, such as probation or parole officer work, are stressful. Some persons may be unsuited for such work according to their personality characteristics. Perhaps it has been found that persons with certain personality traits do not deal well with stress. Prospective job applicants may or may not be selected, depending upon how they respond on the MMPI and the personality profile they exhibit.

The Long Beach (California) Police Department (LBPD) is one police organization that uses the MMPI as a part of its officer selection process. Once, an undergraduate student told me that he wanted to become an officer with the LBPD. He said that he had heard about the "personality test," and he wondered if I had a copy of it that he could study. I told him that I did not have a copy of it, that the test was not available for general distribution, and that the MMPI was an assessment device and not something to prepare for, such as a math or verbal aptitude test. "Well then," he asked me, "is there a way I can respond that will make me look good to them [the LBPD selection committee]?" I said, "Tell the truth. Give truthful responses." Later he reported that he took the test and was not selected for the police officer position. I asked him about the responses he gave on the personality test. "Well," he said, "I answered the questions according to what I thought I ought to say." I told him to go back at the next available opportunity and retake the test. This story has a happy ending. The student retook the psychological examination and was eventually selected as a new LBPD police officer recruit. I like to think that my advice to answer the questions honestly was the clue to his success.

Many researchers in criminal justice and criminology simply construct questionnaires and assume that their respondents will be truthful. Or these investigators may use questionnaires and scales previously used by others. Lie factors in these questionnaires are relatively rare and are most frequently associated with psychological inventories and educational testing. Nevertheless, lie factor items are certainly an option if researchers wish to use them.

Cultural Values and Questionnaire Wording

When questionnaires are administered to anyone, consideration should be given to the cultural values and differences of the target audience and how questionnaire items are worded. Non-English speaking persons will be unable to read questionnaire items. For example, there are large Hispanic populations in California, Arizona, and Texas. Sometimes researchers in these states construct bilingual questionnaires, anticipating that a significant portion of their respondents will prefer Spanish over English.

Comparative research or investigations of other cultures may require that we formulate questions that are culture-specific. If we are studying the Russian Mafia and its role in organized crime in the United States, there are expressions and colloquialisms that are unfamiliar to Russians or are not directly translatable into Russian. Therefore, we must consider alternative phrases or other ways of asking about organized crime in the United States involving Russian immigrants.

Despite the best efforts of states to educate their citizens, the fact is that there is still a fair amount of illiteracy throughout the U.S. population. Some persons cannot read, while others read poorly. A **self-administered questionnaire** in the hands of an illiterate or semiliterate respondent is meaningless. Sometimes researchers may actually need to read questionnaires to respondents in a structured interview format face-to-face. However, if large numbers of questionnaires are mailed to anonymous respondents, this option is not feasible.

The educational level of target audiences varies greatly. Investigators may need to adjust the wording of their questionnaires depending upon the composition of their respondents. For instance, when Sandra Hafley and Richard Tewksbury (1996) studied marijuana distribution in Bluegrass County, Kentucky, they exercised choices about how certain questions were asked. It probably would not be appropriate for them to ask local residents,

> Can you please provide us with a description of the distributional patterns of canabis and related paraphernalia in this socioeconomic milieu as well as the political and economic ramifications of such commerce for the affected populace?

Upon reading or hearing this, more than a few Kentucky mountain folk would cock their heads and give Hafley and Tewksbury funny stares. Rather, Hafley and Tewksbury probably asked questions similar to these:

> Who are the pot-growers? Where do they sell their stuff? How do people in this neck of the woods get by? Is everybody around here in on it?

However, if we were investigating professional groups, such as medical examiners, coroners, and criminalists, we might be inclined to prepare questions that use jargon appropriate for these persons in their respective fields. Also, if we were to question police officers or corrections personnel, we might construct our questions so that they tend to fit these special audiences. Researchers must use their own best judgment about framing questions for specific target audiences.

Other Factors

If questionnaires are mailed to respondents, factors such as the type of postage used (e.g., metered, hand-stamped, special delivery), type of cover letter attached (e.g., appeals to respondent egoism or altruism), rewards for responding (e.g., money, turkeys, opportunities to express opinions), and the socioeconomic status of the target sample are considered to be influential to different degrees for eliciting greater rates of response. If questionnaires are administered on a face-to-face basis, such factors as the appearance or ethnic/racial origin of the investigator or questionnaire administrator, the readability of the questionnaire, and the types of responses required must be considered important in determining response rates. When questionnaires are administered on a face-to-face basis, many problems are encountered similar to those encountered by interviewers.

What About Nonresponse?

Two of the most frustrating questions investigators must deal with are Who are the nonrespondents? and What would be the outcome of my results if the nonrespondents were somehow added or included as a part of all data analyzed? There are various ways of identifying nonrespondents, particularly in a mailed questionnaire situation. Lists of individuals are compiled to whom questionnaires are sent. Those who respond and return the questionnaire are simply checked off these lists. Those who do not return their questionnaires may be sent follow-up letters to remind them to return the questionnaires they received. Under such conditions, it is ethical to advise respondents that their identities are known in advance and that the researcher will know if they have not responded to the mailed questionnaire.

Another method is to simply code each questionnaire or the return envelope with a number that refers to specific respondents. However, respondents will notice the number. This absence of anonymity may inhibit their response, but it will also explain why they receive a follow-up letter from researchers later if they do not respond to the original questionnaire mailed. A questionable practice mentioned earlier is using some sort of invisible ink or undetectable coding procedure on the questionnaires or return envelopes to identify all respondents. Respondents are unaware that their questionnaires have been coded so that if they are returned, researchers will know who they are. Various professional associations, such as the Academy of Criminal Justice Sciences, the American Society of Criminology, and the American Sociological Association presently scrutinize these and other research practices and seek to provide safeguards that will protect the anonymity of human subjects who are contacted by social investigators.

If researchers have made no provisions for identifying nonrespondents, they have little or no hope of being able to describe the characteristics (social, psychological, socioeconomic) of nonrespondents and contrast them with the characteristics of those who have responded. Obviously, the respondents and nonrespondents differ in at least one important respect—some of them returned the questionnaires and some did not return them. Would the inclusion of information from the nonrespondents be significant enough to change or alter one's research findings to any degree? We don't know. It would be wrong to think that the inclusion of the information from nonrespondents would make no difference to one's results, but we cannot calculate the impact the unknown information might have to our final results. Considering response rates varying from 30 percent to 60 percent, these rates would be associated with nonresponse rates of from 70 percent to 40 percent. These are sizable numbers of respondents, and it may be safely speculated that had they been included in one's data analysis, the information yielded would have made some difference. However, from a philosophical viewpoint, the effect of nonrespondents on the original research outcome is almost always purely speculative.

■ KEY TERMS

Bias
Comparative research
Contingency questions
Description
Double-barreled questions
Face-to-face questionnaire
   administration
Fixed-response items
Fixed-response questionnaires
Lie factors
Lie scales
Measurement

Open-ended items, open-end items
Open-ended questionnaires,
   open-end questionnaires
Pilot studies
Postcard questionnaires
Questionnaire
Questionnaire length
Response rate
Response set
Self-administered questionnaires
Set response
Triangulation

■ QUESTIONS FOR REVIEW

1. What are questionnaires? Identify and discuss briefly their major functions.

2. Describe what is meant by triangulation. What are some primary purposes of triangulation?

3. Identify two types of questionnaire administration. Discuss briefly the weaknesses and strengths of each administration method.

4. Differentiate between fixed-response and open-ended items. What are the positive and negative features of each type of item? Discuss each.

5. What is a response set? Can researchers do anything to control for response sets and their occurrence when constructing their questionnaires? What can be done? Discuss briefly.

6. What are some primary drawbacks to using open-ended items on culturally diverse populations?

7. What are some limitations and advantages of using existing scales devised by other researchers?

8. What are mailed questionnaires? How much nonresponse is usually anticipated in mailed-questionnaire situations? What can be done to decrease nonresponse?

9. What are some important questions we must consider before constructing our questionnaires?

10. What are follow-up letters? What are their purposes? Are there any ethical considerations to be made when sending out follow-up letters? Discuss briefly any ethical considerations you might list?

chapter 8

Data Collection Strategies III
Interviews

Michael McShane, a 15-year-old boy, was attacked by 30 members of a delin-quent gang in a New York City park one hot summer evening in 1958. He was brutally killed. Subsequently, Edward R. Murrow interviewed several of the juve-nile gang members for NBC Radio:

Question: "Can you tell me what happened then?"

Answer [from 14-year-old]: "The other guys were all over him, you know, they was kickin', punchin', stompin', stabbin'. I couldn't get near him. I had a baseball bat. And then someone stabbed him with a bread knife."

Question: "Did you ever get near enough to hit him?"

Answer: Yeah, he was all messed up. The guys backed off, I got up close, but he was all messed up. I hit him a few times, you know, around the legs, with my bat. That's the least I could do, was to hit him a little. He was real messed up."

Question: "What about you? [gesturing to 11-year-old]. Are you the one who had the bread knife?"

Answer: "Yeah, I had a bread knife."

Question: "Did you stab the boy with the bread knife?"

Answer: "Yeah, I stabbed him good. I knew, you know, that would sort of be good for my 'rep (reputation). You know, like, I wanted other guys to say, 'There goes a cold killer.' That would've given me a bigger 'rep, a bigger build-up, you know."

Question: "What about you? [gesturing to 13-year-old]. What weapon did you have?"

Answer: "I had a chain and a knife. I had it [the chain] wrapped around my fist."

Question: "Did you hit him too?"

Answer: "Yeah, I hit him. I hit him good in the mouth, once in the back, I think."

Question: "What about the knife? Did you stab him with the knife also?"

Answer: "Yeah, I kinda stabbed him once, you know, in the stomach or chest . . . I don't know . . . maybe the back . . . anyway, I stabbed him with my knife."

Question: "Why did you do that?"

Answer: "I always wanted to know what it would feel like to stick a knife through human bone. You know, and, too, I wanted people to respect me for what I had done there."

■ INTRODUCTION

One of the most direct data-gathering tools is the interview. An interview is ver-bal communication for the purpose of acquiring information. Investigators target a sample of respondents and ask them questions directly. This chapter examines the interviewing process and how criminologists and others can

---

*Excerpts from Edward R. Murrow's interview with members of a New York City gang known as the Egyptian Kings and Dragons in 1958, after a boy, Michael McShane, was attacked by 30 gang members and killed.

make use of interviews to acquire data in their research. First, several types of interviews are described as well as their general functions. Like questionnaire construction, some planning is necessary to construct appropriate interviewing tools. Thus, we will look at how interviews are arranged and conducted.

Since interviews involve direct contact between researchers and respondents, any anonymity respondents might otherwise enjoy, such as that accruing from self-administered, mailed questionnaires, is eliminated. A different kind of information is obtained through interviews, and therefore, we will assess interviews in terms of the weaknesses and strengths relative to other data collection procedures. Further, the relatively close interpersonal nature of interviewing is inherently flawed by various factors. An interviewer's appearance, race or ethnicity, manner of speech, and several other factors combine to influence the types of responses interviewees provide. Thus, several key problems associated with the interview will be identified and discussed.

■ INTERVIEWS AS INSTRUMENTS IN CRIMINAL JUSTICE RESEARCH

The interview is a very time-consuming, yet valuable, data-gathering tool that can disclose much about various types of social settings and the people within them. Interviewers are at liberty to go well beyond the limited boundaries of questionnaires, even open-ended ones, and to probe respondents for additional, insightful information about themselves, their work, and those with whom they work. There are no restrictions relating to the conditions under which interviews may be conducted. If we consider each component of the criminal justice system, no single component is immune from an interviewer's questions.

For instance, we can interview police officers and their administrators to inquire about their work roles and how they are performed, about how police officers react to job stress and life-threatening situations, and about their reactions to different patrol styles and a host of other considerations. Prosecutors and judges may be interviewed to determine their prosecutorial and sentencing priorities, which types of cases they most and least prefer, and their reactions to different types of sentencing reforms. Defendants, inmates, probationers, and parolees may also be interviewed to determine their reactions to different types of prison or jail conditions, the quality of various community-based correctional programs, and their interpersonal relations with those who supervise them. Juvenile gang members may be questioned about their behavioral patterns, their reasons for fighting other gangs, and their gang formative processes. The portion of the late Edward R. Murrow's interview with gang members from the New York City gang called the Egyptian Kings and Dragons at the beginning of this chapter proved quite insightful about the motives the boys had for killing another teenager suspected of being a rival gang member. The types of respondents and the ranges of questions they might be asked are virtually unlimited.

Most criminology students are familiar with the results of several common interview applications, such as the *National Crime Victimization Survey* (in which random households are targeted and the occupants questioned about crimes they have experienced during the past year or some other time interval), the *National Youth Survey* (in which samples of high school students disclose through interviews the incidence and types of crimes they have committed but have not been apprehended for committing), and the U.S. Census, in which random samples of households throughout the United States are contacted and interviewed concerning specific demographic, social, and socioeconomic characteristics.

The characteristic features of interviews include the following:

1. Questions are asked and responses are given verbally. The verbal nature of the questions emphasizes three points about interviews that were not sufficiently stressed in our original definition. First, interviews are not simply conversational exchanges between interviewers and interviewees. They are conversations wherein the major thrust is obtaining verbal answers to questions put verbally. Second, these verbal exchanges need not be on a face-to-face basis, even though they usually are. Sometimes, interviews with others are conducted over the telephone. Finally, interviewing may be conducted with more than one interviewee, such as an interview of partners, a husband and wife, two patrol officers, or a small group of prisoners who cell together.

2. Information is recorded by investigators rather than respondents. The fact that interviewers record information provided by respondents underscores the greater accuracy of interviewing with regard to the information obtained. Interviewers may take notes, mark interview schedules or guides, or tape-record these verbal exchanges with audio or videotaping devices.

3. The relationship between interviewers and interviewees is structured. First, this relationship is transitory. It has a fixed beginning and a fixed point of termination. Second, the relation is one where the participants are usually strangers. Even if these persons are not strangers to one another, the nature of the interviewer-interviewee relation is one of scientific objectivity, where most, if not all, threats are removed that might otherwise hinder or frustrate honest responses to one's questions.

4. There is considerable flexibility in the interviewing format. Few other data collection tools offer such a large range of question-asking formats to investigators. It seems at times that the only limitation is the ingenuity of interviewers. Such an amount of structural variability allows for greater mutual understanding of both the questions by interviewers and the answers given by interviewees.

Some researchers deliberately choose interviewing, in part, because it permits them the opportunity of moving into unexpected or uncharted areas. Even the most standardized interviews do not prohibit such spontaneity of exploration both before and after the data have been compiled through the interview.

■ INTERVIEWS CONTRASTED WITH QUESTIONNAIRES

Interviews are "Up Close and Personal"; Survey Questionnaires are Not.
Compared with mailed questionnaires used in surveys, interviews are an "up close and personal" means of data collection. There is a close interaction between the interviewer and interviewee. This type of relation does not exist under most types of questionnaire administration. Thus, respondents are more inclined to have a conversation with and be interviewed by a researcher. They are also more likely to trivialize a questionnaire sent to them and throw it away.

Anonymity is Abandoned in Interviews. Interviews are conducted face-to-face, and as such, all pretense of **anonymity** is removed from the encounter. Under questionnaire administration, at least assurances of anonymity can be made to bolster both the response rate and truthfulness of responses.

Questionnaires Yield Superficial Information; Interviews Yield In-Depth Information. Questionnaires, especially those mailed to respondents and returned anonymously, are often criticized for their superficiality. Respondents respond to checklists. There is no sound method for determining who completed the returned questionnaires, unless they are administered in face-to-face situations. Researchers are usually not in a position to clarify or explain the meaning of certain questions on questionnaires. Nor can researchers see facial expressions of bewilderment or confusion or frustration. But interviews overcome the problems of superficiality and lack of clarity concerning how questions are formulated and presented. Interviews permit additional **probes** of respondents, in order to amplify or expand their answers verbally. There is little opportunity for such amplification or expansion when respondents complete any questionnaire.

Interviews Permit Probing and Follow-Up Questions; Questionnaires Do Not. Generally, interviews permit investigators to gather more in-depth information from respondents with **follow-up questions.** Interviewees can elaborate on their answers to certain questions. Sometimes they add information that was not originally contemplated by researchers. Thus, there is an element of serendipity in many interview situations.

Interviews Generate Larger Response Rates. Also, a greater rate of response is obtained through interviewing, provided research subjects allow themselves to be interviewed. Mailed questionnaires have considerable nonresponse, perhaps has much as 50 or 60 percent on the average. An estimate of the average response rate to interviews is about 80 percent.

■ TYPES OF INTERVIEWS

Interviews are either unstructured or structured.

Unstructured Interviews

Unstructured interviews are much what their name implies. Investigators might be charged with finding out about parent-child relations relative to a sample of juvenile delinquents. They might conduct informal, unstructured interviews with several delinquents to determine what they can about how these juveniles define their relations with their parents. The interviews may vary greatly in the time taken to complete them. Further, not all questions asked of one juvenile may necessarily be asked of another. Also, the order of questions is irrelevant, as long as interviewers "cover their bases" and get all relevant material they can from the youths they interview.

Another feature of unstructured interviews is that interviewers do not need special interviewing training. They may record any observations they make and their own interpretations or impressions of any answers given. The interviews are also characterized as free-flowing, with the direction and depth of interviews determined by situational factors. If certain juveniles are obviously reluctant to talk about certain background factors, interviewers can shift gears to discuss other areas of interest. Thus, unstructured interviews come closest to the spontaneity inherent in natural conversation.

There are several advantages of unstructured interviews. First, the interview itself approaches natural conversation, and subjects often feel at ease in responding to an interviewer's questions. Second, interviewers are guided in their questions by the types of responses given. Thus, there is less likelihood that interviewers will infuse their own values and biases into the interview itself. Third, unstructured interviews offer the greatest degree of flexibility and serendipity. Researchers can spend as much time as they wish **probing** certain aspects of answers persons give in order to develop certain emerging themes.

One problem with unstructured interviewing, however, is that there may be incomparability of information derived from one interview as contrasted with information derived from other interviews. Since there is no systematic control over the question-asking procedures, the reliability of data is thrown into serious question. Also, much wasted time may be spent with respondents who have little or nothing to add to the knowledge interviewers have already obtained from others. Sometimes, interviewers may engage in repetitive or unproductive conversations with respondents.

Another problem is that some respondents may choose this opportunity to use interviewers as "therapists." For instance, one interviewer who studied employees in a large probation department reported that one older probation officer, a 63-year-old, was being singled out for early retirement. The probation officer didn't want to retire early, but probation office administrators were dissatisfied with his performance, which was diminishing rapidly. The officer continually forgot to keep appointments with various probationer/clients, failed to submit presentence investigation reports with the court, and failed to comply with other rules and regulations associated with probation officer work. In short, the administration wanted to get rid of him. Since civil service regulations were in effect at the time and mandatory retirement could not be enforced until one reached 70 years of age, one's early retirement was not mandatory. Therefore, the administration sought to make his life as uncomfortable as possible, hoping that eventually, he would take the "hint" and resign of his own accord.

The interviewer who interviewed this elderly probation officer found himself in the role of therapist, since the probation officer poured out his life experiences and disclosed what had been happening to him on the job. At one point, the probation officer broke down and cried. The interviewer was in an awkward situation, since it wouldn't be appropriate to simply get up and leave. The interviewer decided to hear him out, and this "interview," a tape-recorded one, lasted nearly seven hours. The interviewer finally was able to "get away" by noting that the sun was setting, his wife had dinner waiting, and his tape recorder had run out of tape.

Another drawback of unstructured interviewing is that there are no guarantees that the interview will be fruitful or insightful. However, this limitation may be a function of the original research enterprise implemented. If researchers have such poorly conceived research problems that unstructured interviewing is chosen as a data-gathering option, then the investigators' own lack of problem conceptualization may enhance any shortcomings of unstructured interviewing. This is not meant to suggest that such unstructured interviewing is chosen only when researchers have poorly conceived research plans. Rather, it is simply more likely that unstructured interviews will be used whenever researchers are uncertain of the information desired from target audiences or if they believe that something new or insightful will be disclosed.

Closely related to this possible drawback is that considerable time must be allocated to devising categories into which one's responses from an unstructured interview can be classified. If several interviewers are involved in the data collection effort, then problems may arise relating to interviewer–interviewee reliability. Different interviewers may ask different questions, or they may code similar responses to the same questions differently. For these and other reasons, most researchers prefer more structured interviews to less structured ones, since there is greater ease in coding and systematizing the information derived. Some unstructured interviews are given some structure by using an **interview guide.** Interview guides consist of lists of predetermined questions and/or topics about which researchers seek information. Since these questions and/or topic areas are anticipated in advance, some thought may be given to the codes devised for probable replies from respondents.

Structured Interviews and the Focused Interview

Contrasted with interview guides and unstructured interviews, **structured interviews** consist of a predetermined list of fixed-response questions or items. For the most part, interviewers adhere rather closely to the predetermined question list. Structured interviews reflect a high degree of interviewer control. Such interviewer control may be exercised over the time taken to complete the interview. The interviewer controls the clarification of any confusing questions or answers received from respondents and limits the questions only to those factors relevant for the problem being investigated. In contrast, unstructured interviewing lacks such controls. Often, it is important for those interviewed to know

Box
8.1

Hugh D. Barlow
*Southern Illinois University
at Edwardsville*

Statistics: B.S. (economics and sociology), Southampton University (England); M.A. (sociology), University of Texas at Austin; Ph.D. (sociology), University of Texas at Austin.

Interests: While in graduate school at the University of Texas, I became interested in criminology, although I never took a formal course in the subject. My Ph.D. dissertation involved a formal test of a theory of crime and punishment based on ideas by Emile Durkheim (1858–1917). As often happens in research, my findings only partially supported the theory, but I was able to show how the relationship between crime rates and punishment could be derived from a more general social theory.

After graduate school, I taught sociology at the University of Illinois at Springfield, from 1971 to 1973, and then I moved to Southern Illinois University at Edwardsville, where I have been ever since. I developed new courses in criminology and began writing a textbook on the subject. The book is in its seventh edition. I have published books on delinquency and on the relation between crime theory and public policy, and I have just finished a new text on criminal justice.

I consider good textbooks an important contribution to any discipline because they provide the groundwork for future generations of scholars. They integrate accumulated knowledge and make sense of it for beginning students. However, I have also been interested in scholarly research, although other professional commitments have severely limited the time I have available for it. In the early 1980s, I became interested in how assaults turn into homicides, and I undertook an innovative research project in St. Louis that evaluated the impact of weapons in over 289 separate incidents. No study had ever combined these independent variables. I found that while weapons used and location of injuries inflicted were the strongest predictors of assault outcomes, emergency medical services also played a role in determining which assaults turned into homicides.

Another research project that I undertook in the late 1980s involved application of Geographic Information System (GIS) techniques for the mapping of crime in a public housing project. Back then, GIS was a relatively new technology for social research, but now it is widely used by police departments as well as in academic research. This research linked up with my earlier work on homicide since it, too, treated crime as an event—in this case a spatial event—that can be understood apart from the motivations or predispositions that make some people more likely to commit crime than others. From my perspective, the important question is why does crime look the way it does?

Today my research interests have turned in a qualitative direction: I have been fascinated by a scandal that occurred in a nearby community 25 years ago in which local officials skimmed thousands of dollars from federal and state grants through a collaboration involving small business owners, elected officials, petty criminals, and a variety of professional people. I wanted to know how this network of collusion emerged, grew, prospered, and eventually died. I believed that answers would have to come from "inside," that is, from persons who participated in the network. I have spent many hours interviewing key players in the network—one eventually became an FBI informant and was largely responsible for the successful prosecution of eleven individuals connected with the case. These interviews are unstructured, allowing my subjects to wander wherever they want, although I must occasionally draw them back to an issue or topic that helps me better understand what went on and why. This research is not yet completed, but I hope in the end to illuminate an area and type of criminal activity that has been largely ignored in the research literature.

Advice to Students: My advice to students interested in research is to pick a topic that excites you, learn everything you can about it—particularly existing attempts to explain it—and then see how you can build upon that knowledge in a creative way. Your creativity may come in the way you conceptualize the topic, in the way you plan to study it (your research methodology), or in what you hope to do with your findings. There is always room for more applied research, and criminal justice is a field where the application of theory and research to practical problems is very important if we hope to reduce the victimization caused by crime—and sometimes, by our attempts, to prevent it.

how much time the interview will take to complete. Interviewing is sometimes conducted on one's job. Sometimes, employers will allocate times when interviewing may be conducted. These infringements on a company's time must be carefully controlled, since researchers do not want to jeopardize their chances of studying the same setting at a later date. Telling interviewees that the interview will only take 15 minutes, and subsequently conducting an interview that takes two hours, will do nothing but antagonize respondents and make them resistant to being interviewed again. Research projects where the same samples are studied over several different time periods rely upon access to the same samples, and, therefore, good public relations skills are essential to permit study completion.

Actually, a structured interview utilizes an **interview schedule.** An interview schedule is a questionnaire consisting of a predetermined list of questions and fixed-response replies that interviewers can fill in themselves when they conduct interviews. Often, a copy of the interview schedule is given to respondents so that they may read it along with the interviewer. If respondents think of answers that are not among those provided by fixed-responses, then the interviewer can write in their verbal replies or tape-record them.

One type of structured interview is the **focused interview** (Merton, Fiske, and Kendall, 1956). Focused interviews are interviews with respondents who have shared some common experience that has, in turn, been carefully scrutinized by investigators to generate hypotheses about the effects of the experience on participants. The interview context focuses upon the actual effects of the experience as viewed by the participants. Thus, applications of focused interviews may be directed toward samples of shock probationers or those who participate in electronic monitoring or home confinement in community-based correctional programs. Focused interviews may be conducted with police officers who have received special types of training relating to resolutions of marital disputes. It is apparent that focused interviews may be used in close conjunction with experimental types of research designs, where it is important to assess the effects of experiments on subject behaviors and attitudes.

Bahn and Davis (1991) were interested in describing the social psychological effects of the status of probationers. They wanted to learn from probationers themselves whether the probation experience was helpful and if it stigmatized them in their communities. Bahn and Davis used self-administered questionnaires and focused interviews with samples of probationers to learn about their feelings and attitudes toward their probation program. They obtained a sample of 43 probationers and exposed them to three data-gathering instruments: (1) a questionnaire, consisting of 16 open-ended questions, administered in an interview format; (2) a scalogram consisting of 15 items, with 5 choices for each item, which had been devised especially for the study by these authors; and (3) the Self-Attitude Inventory (SAI), a self-concept scale. The open-ended questions that made up their focused interview are shown in Table 8.1.

Bahn and Davis were able to learn much about probationers and their feelings through the use of these questions. They found, for instance, that probationers generally received considerable assistance from their families and

TABLE 8.1 Open-ended Questions Administered to 43 Probationers by Bahn and Davis

1. Have you told your family, relatives, and friends that you are on probation? Why or why not?
2. Have any of your family, relatives, or friends been in trouble with the law?
3. Have the actions or what was said to you by your family or friends changed in any way after they found out that you were on probation?
4. Have any of your family, relatives, or friends helped you since you were on probation? In what way? Before probation?
5. Have you told your boss that you were on probation? Why or why not?
6. Do you think about the fact that you are on probation very often? Is it something that's on your mind?
7. Is there anything you especially like about your probation?
8. Is there anything you especially dislike about your probation?
9. What would you like to go on, between me and you? What would you like to talk about?
10. What do you think the purpose of probation is?
11. Has your life changed since you have been placed on probation? How?
12. Are you afraid or anxious about probation? Why?
13. Have you felt depressed since you have been on probation? Why?
14. Do you think of yourself as a criminal since you have been on probation? Why or why not?
15. Do you think your arrest was justified? Why or why not?
16. Do you think the judge should have placed you on probation for the offense? Why or why not?

Source: Questions reproduced from Bahn and Davis (1991:24).

friends, and even from some employers. Interestingly, these researchers found that the stigma of being on probation was not as stigmatizing as many people think. For example, these probationers reported that most of their friends did not avoid them. However, they were hesitant to disclose their probationary status to employers for fear of being fired. They told the investigators that their behaviors had changed to the extent that they no longer associated with other criminals and that they tended to avoid using alcohol and drugs.

As an indication of how a scenario might develop between probationers and their probation officers, we might envision the following hypothetical interview, using one of Bahn and Davis's questions:

P = Probationer

PO = Probation Officer

PO: "Are you afraid or anxious about probation?"

P: "Yes."

PO: "Why?"

P: "Well, for one thing, you know . . . you always think they're looking over your shoulder. Like, they might be looking for a reason to bust you, or to run you in for something. I don't know . . . it just makes me feel uncomfortable."

PO: "But you haven't broken the law. You've told me that probation helps you go straight. Do you feel like law enforcement officers might pick on you more than someone else, if a crime occurs and you happen to be near there?"

P: "Yeah, well, not exactly. It's just that . . . well, what if you happen to run into somebody accidentally . . . you know . . . on the street . . . you are walking along one day, and this guy comes up to you, and he says, 'Hey, Joe, long time no see.' And suppose it's a guy you knew had committed crimes. You begin thinking, are they watching me, are they testing me? You don't really know for sure, whether its a test, or whether its just an accident . . . you know, you don't really have a whole lot of privacy . . . you want to feel like you're free, being on the outside and all . . . but they still have you . . . you are still controlled by the system . . . they can still put you away if they want . . . for any reason . . ."

PO: "But you have to do something pretty serious to get your probation revoked."

P: "Well, yeah, I know . . . but I suppose . . . I guess, it's like they might think the wrong thing, seeing you with someone else whose maybe a criminal or former criminal, like maybe, you are still doing your old thing and all . . . I don't know . . . there are just those times when I feel, like, I feel the system is looking at me and thinking I going to screw up . . ."

PO: "Are you afraid about your own willpower or will to avoid things that might get you into trouble?"

P: "Well, yeah. You know, like I might want a drink, or maybe I want to get high, or do some coke. But, you know, they got these checks, where they might come around and test me . . . I never know when to expect them . . . what if you only screw up once, have one little drink, and the next minute they're there wanting to test your pee. You don't know when they are coming around, or if they're watching . . . you get to where you don't trust anybody anymore, because there's so much at stake."

PO: "And so, being free on probation maybe doesn't mean that you are as free as everyone else?"

P: "Exactly. Anybody else, you know, they can get in a car and drive to Mexico, Canada, out of state, wherever, and who cares? But me, I drive out of the county and my PO might make a federal case out of it. I'm even afraid of the mail I get . . ."

PO: "What do you mean, 'Afraid of your mail?' "

P: "Well, you know, you're always getting things in the mail even if you didn't order them . . . well, once I got this sporting goods catalog from some company back East . . . there were guns advertised in there . . . I was looking at the catalog one day when my PO paid me a visit . . . saw that magazine, about had a fit . . . wanted to know if I was going to order a gun by mail . . . I said, 'Hey, not me, I don't want no trouble . . . I just got this thing in the mail . . . I didn't even ask for it . . . you know, it's the little things that really screw you up . . . you don't have to do anything, just be there in the wrong place at the wrong time . . . I guess what really bothers me the most, why I worry, is that I never know when I am going to be in the wrong place at the wrong time. I don't even sometimes want to go out at night because of that."

Whereas this exchange between a probation officer and a probationer is hypothetical, it is apparent that much enriching detail may be furnished to the interviewer when the respondent is able to answer freely. The interviewer may probe at various points to seek clarification of particular points. We can learn from the above interview. For instance, probationers may feel certain pressures about being on probation that would be considered commonplace occurrences for most other people. Also, there is a psychological strain that persists among many probationers, no doubt owing to the possibility that they might be in the wrong place at the wrong time. Thus, there is a persistent threat to their freedom that is inherent in their probationer status. Although probation revocation today is much more involved than it once was, it nevertheless exists as an option available to probation officers and judges if probationers violate one or more of their program conditions.

There is little disputing the fact that greater precision is achieved as the investigator's knowledge of the target population increases. The more closely investigators can approach the narrow objectives of the focused interview, the greater likelihood that they will acquire more precise data. There is also a better chance that they might make full use of the advantages inherent in interviews generally.

There are three clear advantages of structured interviews. First, data from each interview may be compared and equated with data from other interviews. Second, there are fewer problems of recording and coding data. Thus, greater precision in measurement is achieved. Third, the more highly structured the interview, the less likely it is that attention will be diverted to extraneous, irrelevant, and time-consuming conversation.

On the other hand, as interviews become increasingly structured, they tend to lose the spontaneity of natural conversation. In addition, there is the danger that investigators have structured the interview in such a way that the respondent's views are minimized and the investigator's own biases about the problem are highlighted. Finally, the possibility of exploration and probing further, although not absolutely eliminated, is less likely to occur in structured interviewing compared with unstructured interviewing.

In-Depth Interviews

Similar to questionnaires, interviews may be somewhat superficial or they may be in-depth. A more superficial interview situation is exemplified by the work of Fisher et al. (1998). Fisher and her associates studied crime committed against students on university campuses. Using 12 schools as research sites, a sample of 3,472 students was obtained. Interviewers visited these students and asked them various fixed-response questions modeled after items included on the *National Crime Victimization Survey*. Each student was asked a series of victimization screen questions. If the respondent said yes to any of the screen questions, then the interviewer completed an incident report for each yes response. Fisher and the other researchers identified the time and location of incidents (on campus or off campus) as well as the nature of the incident (what actually happened, what was tried, or what was threatened). Information was collected about violence (rape, sexual assault, robbery), theft (larceny with and without contact, motor vehicle–related thefts), living-quarters crimes (burglary and living-quarters larceny), vandalism, threats, and harassment (verbal and telephone) (Fisher et al., 1998:684). Other questions about the students' lifestyles and sociodemographic information were included. This checklist type information obtained from the interviewers was then codified and statistically analyzed. No attempt was made to study these student victims in depth.

An in-depth interview seeks to discover intimate knowledge of research sites and respondents by the use of intensive and personalized questioning. In-depth interviews are most closely associated with qualitative research, where the objective is to gain greater understanding while certain social events transpire.

Investigators have made extensive use of **in-depth interviews** as a means of obtaining greater insight into various social phenomena. In 1997, for instance, Mary Ann Farkas studied the normative code among corrections officers. Farkas obtained permission to study the correctional officers at two Midwestern state

<table>
<tr><td>Box
8.2</td></tr>
</table>

Mary Ann Farkas
Marquette University

Statistics: M.A. (criminal justice),
University of Wisconsin at Milwaukee;
Ph.D. (social science: criminal justice,
sociology, and labor and industrial labor
relations), Michigan State University.

Interests: My dissertation focused on styles of correctional officers and involved
field work at two Midwestern prisons. I interviewed a sample of officers concerning their ways of handling different situations encountered on the job. My master's
thesis also consisted of field work in correctional facilities. I was interested in the
attitudes of correctional officers and their approaches to the job. Surveys and observations of officers were the research methods utilized in the study. While a graduate student at the University of Wisconsin at Milwaukee, I worked as a research assistant helping several faculty members with various research projects. This is
where I gained rudimentary knowledge and experience with statistical computer
applications and statistical analysis. At Michigan State University, I participated in
field research investigating the disproportionate representation of females and minorities in the juvenile justice system in Michigan. I traveled to juvenile courts in
several counties to interview judges, referees, probation officers, and intake workers. I also observed court and intake proceedings to gather data on decision making regarding juveniles. I feel that my graduate work was enriched immeasurably by
these wonderful opportunities to participate in field research.

I am currently co-principal investigator along with my colleague, Dr. Richard Ze-
vitz, on a grant funded by the National Institute of Justice investigating the impact
of the new Sex Offender Registration and Community Notification Law in Wisconsin. This has been a fascinating research experience. The project employed several
research techniques: interviews, surveys, and nonparticipant observations. We surveyed law enforcement personnel concerning their responsibility for registering
sex offenders and their task of notifying the community of Level II and III (higher
risk) sex offenders. We also surveyed probation and parole agents about their supervision of sex offenders in the community. We attended community notification
meetings around the state and observed the process firsthand. Finally, we interviewed a sample of Special Bulletin Notification sex offenders regarding their experiences and reactions to the law.

In the summer of 1998, I participated in a **focus group,** Sex Offender Community Registration and Notification—Problem Avoidance and Barriers to Implementation, sponsored by the National Criminal Justice Association in Washington, DC.
Scholars, legislators, and practitioners in the area of sex offender management from
around the country were invited to share their research, insights, and experiences

with sex offender laws. I had the opportunity to present the findings from our study to the group. The ensuing discussion and debate was stimulating and insightful and resulted in several recommendations for policy and practice. This focus group illustrates how research can enhance our understanding of significant issues in criminal justice.

The opportunity to interview and observe subjects in their natural environment, and hence, to more fully comprehend the impact of laws and policies has been a very satisfying aspect of my research. Field research allows me to stay current with what is happening in the criminal justice field, particularly with regard to new laws, policies, and practices. Another satisfying aspect of my research is the knowledge that I am making a contribution to criminology and criminal justice. Findings from the sex offender project are impacting laws, policies, and practices pertaining to sex offender management. My participation in the Washington, DC, focus group gave me the chance to share my findings with practitioners, legislators, and policymakers from several other states.

Advice to Students: My advice to students interested in a career in criminal justice would be to take advantage of internship and research opportunities at their universities. Internships allow students to develop a practical and realistic understanding of the criminal justice field and provide the opportunity to explore various careers. Research projects stimulate students to question the reasons for a policy or practice, consider the short- and long-term implications for the criminal justice system and society as a whole, and to look for alternative or new solutions to problems. These analytical and critical thinking skills are invaluable, and I believe essential, for any type of career in criminal justice.

prisons. Farkas could have sent these officers self-administered questionnaires in a survey. However, she believed that face-to-face interviews would provide her with greater detail, the nature of which would enrich her investigation. She focused upon the correctional officer code, an informal abstract policy of conduct among officers, where a certain type of social solidary evolved. The dangerous nature of correctional work, together with low pay and scorn from inmates, caused many correctional officers to close ranks and devise informal ways for dealing with officer-inmate problems.

One identifying characteristic of in-depth interviews is dialogue between the interviewer and interviewee. Farkas's work was replete with quotes from various officers about their on-the-job experiences. One of the female corrections officers said:

> One of the women I work with calls the inmates "her guys." She'll walk in and say, "How are my guys tonight?" I think that you have to keep a certain distance. This is not kindergarten and these are not choir boys. She thinks I am too tough with them (inmates). If they want anything, they ask her and she'll give it to them, too. (Farkas, 1997: 28)

Another officer said,

> Don't *ever* tell inmates any details of your personal life. Don't mention names of your family members. Don't get too close with inmates. Remember that you are not their buddy. You can be nice, but remember that you have a job to do. You've got to keep your distance!" (Farkas, 1997:28)

Farkas was able to identify several important informal social norms among corrections officers, including:

1. Always go to the aid of an officer in real or perceived physical danger.
2. Don't get too friendly with inmates.
3. Don't abuse your authority with inmates. Keep your cool.
4. Back up your fellow officers in decisions and actions; don't stab a co-worker in the back.
5. Cover your ass and do not admit to mistakes.
6. Carry your own weight.
7. Defer to the experience and wisdom of veteran corrections officers. (Farkas, 1997:27-31)

It is unlikely that Farkas would have been able to identify these and other officer codes of conduct from a training manual or survey questionnaire. The fact that she was able to record and reproduce dialogue between herself and those interviewed added a very interesting and insightful dimension to her study.

Similarly, Paula and William Faulkner (1997) studied a sample of prison inmates to describe the inmate status system and how it might be affected by organizational change. The Faulkners engaged various inmates in in-depth interviews and learned much about how status among inmates is assigned. One inmate disclosed,

> I remember when I was in Kansas and this guy never showered and no one ever said anything about it to him. He got a new cell mate and he came back to his cell and the new guy had cleaned his cell and he killed the guy for it. All the inmates respected him.

Another inmate revealed some insight about toughness:

> This is the way it is done. If you are a man, you must either kill or turn the tables on anyone who propositions you with threats of force. It is the *custom* among young prisoners. In doing so, it becomes known to all that you are a man regardless of your youth. (Faulkner and Faulkner, 1997:60-61)

Again, there are certain things about social situations, such as the lives of prison inmates, that you cannot know about through conventional survey research methods and self-administered questionnaires. In-depth interviews with selected inmates can reveal much about themselves and what they respect. Researchers using in-depth interviews can learn much from their respondents.

Telephone Interviews

An interview may be conducted by telephone, known as a **telephone interview.** To some extent, at least, a degree of anonymity between interviewers and interviewees is created. But because of this physical separation, interviewers may not see puzzled expressions on interviewee's faces, or they may not know the exact identity of those interviewed. Nevertheless, the telephone interview may be used as a relatively inexpensive way of obtaining information directly from respondents.

In one profitable use of telephone interviewing, this writer was hired by an attorney to conduct telephone interviews with various persons in an East Tennessee community. A local citizen had been arrested and charged with murder and conspiracy to commit murder. He had been linked with several others and was allegedly involved directly in the murder of a North Carolina man. His trial was scheduled soon in that community, but his attorney believed that the press had prejudiced prospective jurors. Thus, the attorney sought a change of venue for his client, so that the trial might be held in another community where pretrial publicity was not as significant.

This writer called approximately 300 persons in the community and asked them various questions about their knowledge of the case. Among the questions asked were whether those contacted were voting citizens, whether they could be called for jury duty, whether they had formed an opinion about the guilt or innocence of the defendant, and if so, what was that opinion? Did they know any family members of the person charged with the murder? The results showed that most citizens had followed the case closely in their local newspapers. Furthermore, most citizens contacted had formed opinions. Most believed the defendant guilty of the murder and that he should be sentenced to death. On the basis of these telephone interview results, the attorney was able to convince the presiding judge to move the case to another county where it was believed a fair trial could be conducted.

Vince Webb, Charles Katz, and Nanette Graham (1997) used telephone interviews as a way of assessing the effectiveness of the Omaha Police Department and the performance of police officer duties. Approximately 800 respondents were surveyed at random from a population of 340,000. Interviewers dialed the home telephones of their random sample and asked respondents questions about their race, marital status, number of children, perceptions of crime, income, education, age, gender, and other general sociodemographic information. They also asked these respondents whether they had ever been crime victims and to rate the differential importance of nine different crime-control and order-maintenance police duties, using a five-point rating scale. Thus, these researchers were able to correlate specific sociodemographic characteristics with perceptions of police officer performance according to several salient dimensions.

Random-Digit Dialing and Computer-Assisted Telephone Interviewing.
Utilizing new technology, researchers who conduct telephone interviews can randomize the numbers dialed. Known as the **Computer-Assisted Telephone Interviewing (CATI)** system, any designated sample size of numbers to be dialed can be produced. More conventional methods of dialing might include using current city directories or telephone directories to obtain numbers. However, city directories and telephone directories are quickly dated as persons move and change their numbers. Also, increasing numbers of citizens have unlisted numbers. **Random-digit dialing** overcomes these problems, since numbers, listed or unlisted, new or old, are dialed randomly. Once the connection is established, interviewers can seek to obtain essential information from randomly dialed respondents.

An example of using random-digit dialing for telephone interviewing is a study of citizen attitudes about female police officers conducted in Minnesota by Michael Breci (1997). Breci wanted to know how citizens in Minnesota rated the performance of female police officers compared with their male officer counterparts. Breci observed,

> Subjects for this research were drawn from a random sample of Minnesota adults who were 18 years of age or older at the time of the interview. Respondents were contacted by telephone. A computer program generated the telephone numbers for the statewide survey. A random method of selection based on age and gender was used to assure randomness of respondents within each household. . . . In order to reach hard-to-get respondents, each number was called up to four times over different days. (Breci, 1997:156)

Breci contacted 1,115 persons, with 702 (63 percent) consenting to be interviewed. Breci found that acceptance of female police officers depended on the degree of education of respondents, with less-educated respondents being more adverse toward female officers. Breci concluded that involving female police officers in more community policing programs has the potential of reducing citizen bias against female officers generally.

Techniques Used in Telephone Interviews. In many respects, the techniques used in telephone interviews are the same as those used in conventional interview situations. The questions to be asked in telephone interviews are arranged in much the same fashion as a researcher would construct a questionnaire. An interesting, attention-grabbing question or two would be used to attract the respondent's interest. If respondents are going to hang up on an interviewer, it will probably occur during the first minute or two of the interview. The longer the amount of time an interviewer can keep the respondent on the line, the greater the likelihood that the entire interview can be conducted.

Sometimes interviewers will use a **branching technique** to narrow the range of response to a sensitive question. If the victim of a sex crime is being interviewed by telephone, it might be appropriate first to ask, Have you ever been the victim of an assault? If the victim says yes, then the interviewer can ask, Were the injuries sustained primarily psychological or physical? If the victim says physical, then the interviewer can ask, Was the assault sexual or nonsexual? The intent of branching is to gradually draw out the respondent to disclose more personal aspects of the victimization or incident. Branching is preferred to a direct question such as, Have you ever been raped or sodomized?

Criticisms of Telephone Interviews. Telephone interviews are much cheaper than face-to-face interviews. Further, researchers have the opportunity to draw out respondents and probe with follow-up questions. They can also explain complex or confusing terminology to those interviewed. However, it is difficult to verify whether the researcher is interviewing the true target of the interview. If the head of household is called, a son, other relative, or a family friend may answer the telephone and respond as though he or she were the head of the household. Also, there is no way to judge the validity of one's responses according to facial expressions or other physical criteria.

Telephone interviews contain some anonymity to the extent that the researcher is unsure of who the respondent is. It is possible for some deception to occur under these circumstances. More than a few respondents may resent the intrusion of interviewers into their homes via the telephone. For those with unlisted numbers, privacy is highly valued. Thus, interviewers who use random-digit dialing and connect with someone with an unlisted number are likely to be chastised with strong language. There are no precise figures about the average response rate to telephone interviews, although success rates reported by investigators who use telephone interviews for data collection suggest response rates of 75 percent or higher. Compared with the average response rates to mailed questionnaires, telephone interviewing yields a substantially higher rate of response.

■ FUNCTIONS OF INTERVIEWING

The major functions of interviews are description and exploration.

Description

Information obtained from interviews is particularly useful for describing various dimensions of social reality. With certain exceptions, such as certain forms of observation, no other type of research data-gathering tool performs this descriptive function as well. Most people spend much of their time with others in some sort of verbal exchange or dialogue. Being able to capture the question-and-answer process as an unfolding dimension of this dialogue permits us to catch a glimpse of social life as it is lived. Compared with the relatively stale and abstract nature of statistical results, interviewing can yield a "gut-level" understanding of how people think and behave that is more reflective of social reality than summarizing certain survey questionnaire results. Edward R. Murrow's interview with delinquent gang members at the beginning of this chapter evidenced the kind of enriching detail and insight we frequently obtain from interviews that would otherwise be missed through self-administered surveys.

Can you imagine, for instance, giving these same delinquent gang members a self-administered questionnaire designed to investigate the same murder incident?

> *Please place a check in the space that best fits you.*
> What type of weapon did you use in the attack on the youth?
> On the average, how many times did you strike the boy with your weapon? *(Check one)*
> What reasons can you cite for why you attacked the boy? *(Check as many reasons that apply—list of reasons attached).*

Needless to say, much would be lost in this highly superficial and ludicrous survey that was originally captured in Murrow's probing interviews with gang members.

Exploration

Another purpose of interviewing is to provide insights into unexplored dimensions of a topic. Surveys of work done usually only scratch the surface and yield only superficial details about the phenomena we wish to explain. However, interviews invite more in-depth probing and detailed descriptions of people's feelings and attitudes. For instance, evidence in the criminal justice literature suggests that private counsel, as opposed to public defenders, tend to have greater plea bargaining successes with prosecutors. Thus, if defendants charged with various crimes attempt to plea bargain or negotiate favorable sentences in exchange for pleas of guilty, they will probably receive more lenient treatment if they are represented by private counsels than by public defenders. Some of the logical reasons for this are that in many jurisdictions, public defenders are often new attorneys with little trial experience. Furthermore, private counsel probably have developed reputations and associations with various prosecutors so that their bargaining powers are favorably enhanced. Do prosecutors view public defenders different from private counsels, and if so, how will these different views influence prosecutorial decision making and the plea bargains eventually worked out between counsel?

Among the various studies examining prosecutorial decision making relative to plea bargaining, Champion (1988) examined prosecutorial discretion and the relative influence of private counsels and public defenders on their plea bargain decisions. In the jurisdictions examined, it was found that private counsels generally were able to negotiate more favorable plea bargains for their clients compared with public defenders. Further, of those cases that eventually went to trial, private counsels had a greater success rate through client acquittals. Prosecutors in these jurisdictions were interviewed in order to see whether they view public defenders and private counsel differently. One interview proved illuminating in that it explained some of the informality associated with plea bargaining that is often hidden from public view. Behind-the-scenes plea bargaining is inherently secretive, since no one knows the final contents of a plea bargain until it is accepted by the presiding judge. Regarding his interactions with private counsel compared with public defenders, one prosecutor said:

> One problem with public defenders is that they get stuck with a lot of cases they don't want. They don't get paid much for these cases. It's in their best interests to get their clients to cop pleas [plead guilty] and get it over with. Usually, they come to me and ask me what I recommend. If I say, "I think a year in jail and two years probation sounds good," they often agree with that without making a counteroffer. But if defendants can get themselves some high-powered counsel, well . . . let's put it this way. I know most of the big criminal attorneys in this town on a first-name basis and associate with several of them regularly. They know what and how I think and I know how and what they think. They make me an offer, and you know, more often than not, they know I'll probably go for it. They're not pushovers. I don't bluff as much with them as I do with PD's [public defenders]. (Champion, 1988)

In this interview, the intent of the interviewer was to find out whether prosecutors view public defenders differently compared with privately appointed counsel. It was apparent from these few statements what this particular prosecutor thought about public defenders. However, he said something else of interest which aroused the interviewer's curiosity. He said, "I don't bluff as much with them [privately appointed counsel] as I do with PD's." The fact that he brought up "bluffing" led the interviewer to try and find out more about prosecutorial bluffing:

Interviewer: "What do you mean by 'bluffing?'"

Prosecutor: "Oh, you know. Whenever we have a weak case, perhaps a witness is unreliable, evidence is scarce, but, you know, we think we have the guy who did the crime, because of other things . . . we might push them hard, the PD's . . . to get them thinking we have more against their clients than we actually do. You'd be surprised how much of the time it works. Not all of our cases are airtight. So we do a little bluffing."

Interviewer: "You said that you don't do that as much, bluffing, with private counsels. Why not?"

Prosecutor: "Well, most of them know me and how I operate. Some of them have even been PD's. I've been at this job for nine years. Plus, they do their own research on a case, do their homework. They have a pretty good idea whether or not I've got a solid case. If they even smell a bluff, you can bet they'll call me on it. I've had 'em do it to me. But then, sometimes it backfires."

Interviewer: "What do you mean?"

Prosecutor: "Sometimes they think I'm bluffing and I'm not. They have pushed it in some cases, in really important cases, and they've gone to trial. I've got a perfect track record with them on that . . . when I really know down deep that I've got a solid case, and they're stupid enough to push it to trial, probably because they think I've got a weak case . . . I beat 'em."

Interviewer: "Why is it easier to bluff PD's?"

Prosecutor: "For one thing, none of them want to go to trial. They don't want to drag things out. Most of their clients are sleaze-bags, anyway, and they're probably guilty, know their guilty. We just let them think we're going to play hard ball with 'em, and most of the time, it works. We make an offer, they accept it. Bam! That's it!"

Interviewer: "Do you have many PD's call your bluff?"

Prosecutor: "Sometimes. We sit on the case for a few weeks, let them steam a little . . . then we drop it. So what? We didn't lose anything by trying. It works both ways, you know."

Interviewer: "What do you mean, 'It works both ways.'?"

Prosecutor: "Defense attorneys do it to us, bluff."

Interviewer: "Do you know when they're doing it?"

Prosecutor: "Some of the time. There are some attorneys in town that do a good job at it. If I've got a weak case, I'm not going to take the chance, I mean, I'm not going to lose something for nothing. We usually work something out."

Interviewer: "Plea bargain?"

Prosecutor: "Yeah. Some attorneys I know let me know up front what they have and what they think I have. They make me an offer. You know, it kind of shakes you up, they come to you and try to dictate their terms."

At this point, the interviewer learns something else about the prosecutor-defense attorney relation: exactly who initiates the plea bargain offer and terms. A follow-up to this might be the following:

Interviewer: "Is there any pattern to this? I mean, do you get many defense attorneys coming to you with offers?"

Prosecutor: "Not too often. I'd say about 20–30 percent of the time."

Interviewer: "Is there any, do you think that those situations, where offers are made by these attorneys . . . are these situations the kind where they might have strong cases . . . as opposed to you going to them with an offer?"

Prosecutor: "Definitely. If they come to me with an offer . . . now I'm not going to say this as a policy thing . . . but if they come to me with an offer, I'll seriously consider it. I want to know what . . . I mean, I don't know what they have in their favor, but they must have something, you know, for them to come to me with the offer. If it is a "no time" deal . . . they don't want their client to do time . . . maybe probation, something like that . . . I'll probably think they've got a strong defense. It makes me think twice about pushing them."

Interviewer: "Now, let me see if I understand this. Would you say that, well, if you initiate a plea bargain, you've got a weak case, but if they initiate a plea bargain, they've got a weak case?"

Prosecutor: "No. It depends on when they bring me an offer. If they hit me with a plea bargain offer early on, like within a week or so after their client's been booked . . . they might have a weak case. But then again, we don't get approached that often. Most of the time, we approach them. I'll say this, and that is, if we approach them early with a plea bargain, we probably have a weak case. Not always, you know. But the sooner we send out an offer, well, we're hoping for a quick decision."

Interviewer: "So you think it makes a difference, who makes the offer to begin with, the attorney or the prosecutor?"

Prosecutor: "Definitely. You have to know these guys to figure out whether . . . you have to figure they've either got a weak case, and they might be bluffing, but they also might have a strong case . . . I'll bet they have a strong case if they come out with an offer of probation for a cop [guilty plea] to a lesser charge."

Interviewer: "So, it's more likely that if you make a plea bargain proposal to some attorney, especially early in the case, you might not have a particularly strong case?"

Prosecutor: "Something like that. That doesn't mean that we have a weak case. It might mean that we don't have the kind of evidence we want to be sure about nailing 'em. We've got evidence, but a lot of it might be circumstantial. First, we believe their guy's guilty. We're not going to purposely set up some shmuck and bluff him into a cop. But we're not going to lay down, either, especially when we've got incriminating stuff against the guy . . . also, you've got to understand . . . the longer you wait, well, the evidence might get cold. Witnesses might forget, move away, die. Attorneys are smart, too . . . they might try to delay things . . . you know, delays almost never hurt their cases. We had one guy, a vehicular homicide case . . . a waiter at a local restaurant . . . he was crocked, driving home from work one night. Ran over two drunks fighting in the middle of the road near his apartment. Killed 'em both. They dragged that [case] out for a year and a half . . . never did come to trial . . . the girlfriend of the two guys he killed [who was watching the guys fighting when they were killed] moved out of state. We lost track of her, couldn't get her here if we wanted. Anyway, it turns out these two guys were always in and out of jail . . . long records. Trash. Whose going to get uptight about running over trash like that? We settled the damn thing by putting the guy on probation for three years . . . he plead guilty to reckless driving. Can you beat that? Anyway, there would have been a problem or two with vehicular homicide . . . for one thing, you know, he didn't leave work that night thinking, 'I'm going to go out and run over two drunks fighting in some road.' We had a real problem with intent. Also, there was contributory negligence. The street wasn't lit up, either . . . some problem with the street lights. The trial, if there had been one, would've been a mess. Turned out the kid's dad was a physician, plenty of money. Also got himself the best criminal attorney in town. We knew it'd be tough initially, but when he got that attorney . . . well, I wasn't going to push it."

This interview was one of the more interesting conducted. It is apparent that the prosecutor's answers often open up new areas previously unexplored by the interviewer. The prosecutor's comment about hiring "the best criminal attorney in town" could have led to questions about defense attorney quality and whether those who can afford the best attorneys receive more lenient treatment than indigent clients. Suffice it to say that the interview functions as an exploratory tool every bit as much as it functions as a descriptive instrument.

■ INTERVIEW CONSTRUCTION

Constructing interview items is comparable to constructing questionnaires. Investigators who plan to use interview schedules, the more highly structured interviewing formats, use standardized items. Thus, interviewers must ask fixed numbers of questions, usually with fixed responses. If items are open-ended, then interviewers must either record a respondent's replies by hand or tape-record them in some fashion. More structured interviewing instruments may be coded more easily. Also, data from several different interviews may be compared directly.

Focused interviews, those that solicit information from subjects exposed to common stimuli or events, are structured to disclose specific details about one's experiences. The more investigators know about the target audience, the greater the precision the interviews may achieve. An excellent illustration of a structured, focused interview, with open-ended options and space for interviewer notes, is the survey instrument for the *National Crime Victimization Survey (NCVS)*, a portion of which is shown in Figure 8.1.

Figure 8.1 shows a portion of the survey instrument used by the U.S. Department of Justice in its National Crime Survey. This instrument contains

NOTICE — Your report to the Census Bureau is **confidential** by law (U.S. Code 42, Sections 3789g and 3735). All identifiable information will be used only by persons engaged in and for the purposes of the survey, and may not be disclosed or released to others for any purpose.

FORM **NCS-1 and NCS-2**
(4-10-86)

U.S. DEPARTMENT OF COMMERCE
BUREAU OF THE CENSUS

ACTING AS COLLECTING AGENT FOR THE
BUREAU OF JUSTICE STATISTICS
U.S. DEPARTMENT OF JUSTICE

NATIONAL CRIME SURVEY

NCS-1 BASIC SCREEN QUESTIONNAIRE

NCS-2 CRIME INCIDENT REPORT

PGM 2

Sample	Control number			HH
	PSU	Segment	CK. Serial	No.
J ___				

N C S 1 and 2

ITEMS FILLED AT START OF INTERVIEW

1. Interviewer identification
Code | Name
`201`

2. Unit Status
`202`
1 ☐ Unit in sample the previous enumeration period – *Fill 3*
2 ☐ Unit in sample first time this period – *SKIP to 4*

3. Household Status – *Mark first box that applies*
`203`
1 ☐ Same household <u>interviewed</u> the previous enumeration
2 ☐ Replacement household since the previous enumeration
3 ☐ Noninterview the previous enumeration
4 ☐ Other – *Specify* ⌐

4. Line number of household respondent
`204` _____ Go to page 2

TRANSCRIPTION ITEMS FROM CONTROL CARD

5. Special Place type code
`205` _____

6. Tenure
`206` 1 ☐ Owned or being bought   2 ☐ Rented for cash   3 ☐ No cash rent

7. Land Use
`207` 1 ☐ Urban   2 ☐ Rural

8. Farm Sales
`208` x ☐ Item blank   1 ☐ $1,000 or more   2 ☐ Less than $1,000

9. Type of living quarters
Housing unit
`209`
1 ☐ House, apartment, flat
2 ☐ HU in nontransient hotel, motel, etc.
3 ☐ HU permanent in transient hotel, motel, etc.
4 ☐ HU in rooming house
5 ☐ Mobile home or trailer with no permanent room added
6 ☐ Mobile home or trailer with one or more permanent rooms added
7 ☐ HU not specified above – Describe ⌐

OTHER unit
8 ☐ Quarters not HU in rooming or boarding house
9 ☐ Unit not permanent in transient hotel, motel, etc.
10 ☐ Unoccupied site for mobile home, trailer, or tent
11 ☐ Student quarters in college dormitory
12 ☐ OTHER unit not specified above – Describe ⌐

Use of telephone
10a. Location of phone – *Mark first box that applies.*
`210`
1 ☐ Phone in unit . . . . ⌐
2 ☐ Phone in common area (hallway, etc.) . . . .
3 ☐ Phone in another unit (neighbor, friend, etc.) . . . . .   } *Fill 10b*
4 ☐ Work/office phone . . . .
5 ☐ No phone – *SKIP to 11a*

10b. Is phone interview acceptable?
`211` 1 ☐ Yes   2 ☐ No   3 ☐ Refused to give number

TRANS. ITEMS FROM CONTROL CARD – Cont.

11a. Number of housing units in structure
`212`
1 ☐ 1–*SKIP to 12*   4 ☐ 5   7 ☐ Mobile home or trailer–*SKIP to 12*
2 ☐ 2   5 ☐ 5–9
3 ☐ 3   6 ☐ 10 +   8 ☐ Only OTHER units

11b. Direct outside access
`213`
1 ☐ Yes   4 ☐ Don't know
2 ☐ No   x ☐ Item blank

12. Family income
`214`
1 ☐ (a) Less than $5,000   8 ☐ (h) $20,000– 24,999
2 ☐ (b) $5,000– 7,499   9 ☐ (i)   25,000– 29,999
3 ☐ (c)   7,500– 9,999   10 ☐ (j)   30,000– 34,999
4 ☐ (d)   10,000–12,499   11 ☐ (k)   35,000– 39,999
5 ☐ (e)   12,500–14,999   12 ☐ (l)   40,000– 49,999
6 ☐ (f)   15,000–17,499   13 ☐ (m)   50,000– 74,999
7 ☐ (g)   17,500–19,999   14 ☐ (n)   75,000 and over

PGM 3   ITEMS FILLED AFTER INTERVIEW

13. Proxy information – *Fill for all proxy interviews*

a. Proxy interview obtained for Line No.	b. Proxy respondent		c. Reason (Enter code)
	Name	Line No.	
`301` ___		`302` ___	`303`
`304` ___		`305` ___	`306`
`307` ___		`308` ___	`309`
`310` ___		`311` ___	`312`

Codes for item 13c
1 – 12 – 13 years old and parent refused permission for self interview
2 – Physically/mentally unable to answer   } FILL INTER-COMM
3 – TA and won't return before closeout

14. Type Z noninterview

a. Interview not obtained for Line No.	b. Reason (Enter code)	Codes for item 14b
`313` ___	`314` ___	1 – Never available . . .
`315` ___	`316` ___	2 – Refused . . . .
`317` ___	`318` ___	3 – Physically/mentally unable to answer – no proxy available } FILL INTER-COMM
`319` ___	`320` ___	4 – TA and no proxy available . . . .
		5 – Other . . . .
		6 – Office use only

▶ *Complete 17–28 for each Line No. in 14a.*

15a. Household members 12 years of age and OVER
`321` _____ Total number

15b. Household members UNDER 12 years of age
`322` _____ Total number
0 ☐ None

16. Crime Incident Reports filled
`323` _____ Total number – *Fill BOUNDING INFORMATION*
0 ☐ None

Notes

FIGURE 8.1

275

PERSONAL CHARACTERISTICS

17. NAME (of household respondent)	18. Type of interview	PGM 4	19. Line No.

17. NAME (of household respondent)

Last

First

18. Type of interview PGM 4

`401`

1 ☐ Per. – Self-respondent
2 ☐ Tel. – Self-respondent
3 ☐ Per. – Proxy ⎫ *Fill 13 on*
4 ☐ Tel. – Proxy ⎬ *cover page*
5 ☐ Noninterview – *Fill 19-28 and 14 on cover page*

19.ᵢ Line No.

`402`

Line No.

20. Relationship to reference person	21. Age last birthday	22a. Marital status THIS survey period	22b. Marital status LAST survey period	23. Sex	24. Armed forces member	25. Education –highest grade	26. Education –complete that year?	27. Race	28. Hispanic origin
`403`	`404`	`405`	`406`	`407`	`408`	`409`	`410`	`411`	`412`
1 ☐ Reference person 2 ☐ Husband 3 ☐ Wife 4 ☐ Own child 5 ☐ Parent 6 ☐ Brother/Sister 7 ☐ Other relative 8 ☐ Non-realtive	___ Age	1 ☐ Married 2 ☐ Widowed 3 ☐ Divorced 4 ☐ Separated 5 ☐ Never married	1 ☐ Married 2 ☐ Widowed 3 ☐ Divorced 4 ☐ Separated 5 ☐ Never married 6 ☐ Not inter-viewed last survey period	1 ☐ M 2 ☐ F	1 ☐ Yes 2 ☐ No	___ Grade	1 ☐ Yes 2 ☐ No	1 ☐ White 2 ☐ Black 3 ☐ Amer. Indian, Aleut, Eskimo 4 ☐ Asian, Pacific Islander 5 ☐ Other	☐ Yes ☐ No

---

PGM 5

29. Date of interview

`501` ☐☐ ☐☐ ☐☐
Month   Day   Year

30. Before we get to the crime questions, I have some questions that are helpful in studying where and why crimes occur.

How long have you lived at this address?

Enter number of months OR number of years. If more than 11 months, enter number of years and leave months blank.

`502` _____ Months (1- 11) – **SKIP** to 31

OR

`503` _____ Years (Round to nearest whole year) – *Fill Check Item A*

CHECK ITEM A How many years are entered in 30?

☐ 5 years or more – **SKIP** to Check Item B
☐ 1-5 years – **SKIP** to 32

31. How many people 12 years of age or older were living in your previous household, including you?

`504` _____ Number of people 12 +

32. Altogether, how many times have you moved in the last 5 years, that is, since_____, 19____?
(5 yrs. ago)

`505` _____ Number of times

Notes

CHECK ITEM B Is the respondent 16 years or older?

☐ Yes – Ask 33
☐ No – **SKIP** to 35a

33. Did you work at a job or businness LAST WEEK? (Do not include volunteer work or work around the house)

INTERVIEWER – *If farm or business operator in the household, ask about unpaid work.*

`506` 1 ☐ Yes – **SKIP** to 35a
2 ☐ No

34a. Did you work at a job or business DURING THE LAST 6 MONTHS?

`507` 1 ☐ Yes – Ask 34b
2 ☐ No – **SKIP** to 35a

34b. Did that job/work last 2 consecutive weeks or more?

`508` 1 ☐ Yes
2 ☐ No

35a. Does anyone in this household operate a business form this address?

`509` 1 ☐ Yes – Ask 35b
2 ☐ No – **SKIP** to 36

35a. PERSONAL – *Fill by observation*
TELEPHONE – *Ask.*

Is there a sign on the premises or some other indication to the general public that a business is operated form this address?

`510` 1 ☐ Yes
2 ☐ No

FORM NCS-1 (4-10-86)

FIGURE 8.1 *(continued)*

HOUSEHOLD SCREEN QUESTIONS

36. Now I'd like to ask some questions about crime. They refer only to the last 6 months–between_____ 1, 19____ and _____, 19____. During the last 6 months, did anyone break into or somehow illegally get into your (apartment/home), garage, or another building on your property?
☐ Yes – How many times?
☐ No _____

37. (Other than the incident(s) just mentioned) Did you find a door jimmied, a lock forced, or any other signs of an ATTEMPTED break in?
☐ Yes – How many times?
☐ No _____

38. Was anything at all stolen that is kept outside your home, or happened to be left out, such as a bicycle, a garden hose, or lawn furniture? (other than any incidents already mentioned)
☐ Yes – How many times?
☐ No _____

39. Did anyone take something belonging to you or to any member of this household, from a place where you or they were temporarily staying, such as a friend's or relatives home, a hotel or motel, or a vacation home?
☐ Yes – How many times?
☐ No

40. What was the TOTAL number of motor vehicles (cars, trucks, motorcycles, etc.) owned by you or any other member of this household during the last 6 months? Include those you no longer own.
`511`
0 ☐ None – *SKIP to 43*
1 ☐ 1
2 ☐ 2
3 ☐ 3
4 ☐ 4 or more

41. Did anyone steal, TRY to steal, or use (it/any of them) without permission?
☐ Yes – How many times?
☐ No _____

42. Did anyone steal, or TRY to steal parts attached to (it/any of them), such as a battery, hubcaps, tape-deck, etc.?
☐ Yes – How many times?
☐ No _____

INDIVIDUAL SCREEN QUESTIONS

43. The following questions refer only to things that happened to YOU during the last 6 months – between_____ 1, 19____ and _____, 19____. Did you have your pocket picked/purse snatched?
☐ Yes – How many times?
☐ No _____

44. Did anyone take something (else) directly from you by using force, such as by a stickup, mugging or threat?
☐ Yes – How many times?
☐ No _____

45. Did anyone TRY to rob you by using force or threatening to harm you? (other than any incidents already mentioned)
☐ Yes – How many times?
☐ No _____

46. Did anyone beat you up, attack you or hit you with something, such as a rock or bottle? (other than any incidents already mentioned)
☐ Yes – How many times?
☐ No _____

47. Were you knifed, shot at, or attacked with some other weapon by anyone at all? (other than any incidents already mentioned)
☐ Yes – How many times?
☐ No _____

48. Did anyone THREATEN to beat you up or THREATEN you with a knife, gun, or some other weapon, NOT including telephone threats? (other than any incidents already mentioned)
☐ Yes – How many times?
☐ No _____

49. Did anyone TRY to attack you in some other way? (other than any incidents already mentioned)
☐ Yes – How many times?
☐ No _____

50. During the last 6 months, did anyone steal things that belonged to you from inside ANY car or truck, such as packages or clothing?
☐ Yes – How many times?
☐ No _____

51. Was anything stolen from you while you were away from home, for instance at work, in a theater or restaurant, or while traveling?
☐ Yes – How many times?
☐ No _____

52. (Other than any incidents you've already mentioned) was anything (else) at all stolen from you during the last 6 months?
☐ Yes – How many times?
☐ No _____

53. Did you find any evidence that someone ATTEMPTED to steal something that belonged to you? (other than any incidents already mentioned)
☐ Yes – How many times?
☐ No _____

54. Did you call the police during the last 6 months to report something that happened to YOU which you thought was a crime? (Do not count any calls made to the police concerning the incidents you have jsut told me about.)
`512`
*
☐ No – *SKIP to 55*
☐ Yes – What happened?
_____

CHECK ITEM C Look at 54. Was HHLD member 12 + was attacked or theatened, or was something stolen or an attempt made to steal something that belonged to him/her?
☐ Yes – How many times?
☐ No

55. Did anything happen to YOU during the last 6 months which you thought was a crime, but did NOT report to the police? (other than any incidents already mentioned)
`513`
*
☐ No – *SKIP to Check Item E*
☐ Yes – What happened?
_____

CHECK ITEM D Look at 55. Was HHLD member 12 + attacked or theatened, or was something stolen or an attempt made to steal something that belonged to him/her?
☐ Yes – How many times?
☐ No

CHECK ITEM E Who besides the respondent was present when screen questions were asked? (If telephone interview, mark box 1 only.)
`514`
*
1 ☐ Telephone interview – *Go to Check Item F*
   Personal interview – *Mark all that apply.*
2 ☐ No one besides respondent present
3 ☐ Respondent's spouse
4 ☐ HHLD member(s) 12 +, not spouse
5 ☐ HHLD member(s) under 12
6 ☐ Nonhousehold member(s)
7 ☐ Someone was present – Can't say who
8 ☐ Don't know if someone else present

CHECK ITEM F If self-response interview, *SKIP to Check Item G*
Did the person for whom this interview was taken help the proxy respondent answer any screen questions?
`515`
1 ☐ Yes
2 ☐ No
3 ☐ Person for whom interview taken not present

CHECK ITEM G Do any of the screen questions contain any entries for "How many times?"
☐ Yes – Fill Crime Incidents Reports.
☐ No – Interview next HHLD member. End interview if last rependent.

FIGURE 8.1 *(continued)*

NOTICE — Your report to the Census Bureau is **confidential** by law (U.S. Code 42, Sections 3789g and 3735). All identifiable information will be used only by persons engaged in and for the purposes of the survey, and may not be disclosed or released to others for any purpose.

FORM **NCS-2**
(4-10-86)

U.S. DEPARTMENT OF COMMERCE
BUREAU OF THE CENSUS

ACTING AS COLLECTING AGENT FOR THE
BUREAU OF JUSTICE STATISTICS
U.S. DEPARTMENT OF JUSTICE

CRIME INCIDENT REPORT

NATIONAL CRIME SURVEY

Notes

N C S 2

I N C I D E N T   R E P O R T

PGM 6

1a. LINE NUMBER ⟶ | 601 | _____ Line number

1b. SCREEN QUESTION NUMBER ⟶ | 602 | _____ Screen question number

1c. INCIDENT NUMBER ⟶ | 603 | _____ Incident number

CHECK ITEM A | Has this person lived at this address for more than 6 months? (If not sure, refer to item 30, NCS-1.)

☐ Yes (Item 30 – more than 6 months) – **SKIP** to 2c
☐ No (Item 30 – 6 months or less) – Ask 2a

2a. You said that during the last 6 months –
(Refer to appropriate screen question for description of crime.)
Did (this/the first) incident happen while you were living here or before you moved to this address?

| 604 | 1 ☐ While living at this address
2 ☐ Before moving to this address

2b. In what month did (this/the first) incident happen?
(Show calendar if necessary. Encourage respondent to give exact month.)

| 605 | ☐☐ ☐☐ – **SKIP** to Check Item B
Month   Year

2c. You said that during the last 6 months –
(Refer to appropriate screen question for description of crime.)
In what month did (this/the first) incident happen?
(Show calendar if necessary. Encourage respondent to give exact month.)

| 605 | ☐☐ ☐☐
Month   Year

CHECK ITEM B | Is this incident report for a series of crimes? (Note – Series must have 3 or more similar incidents which respondent can't recall separately.)

| 606 | 1 ☐ Yes – Ask 3a (Note – Reduce entry in screen question if necessary.)
2 ☐ No – **SKIP** to 4b

3a. Altogether, how many times did this happen during the last 6 months?

| 603 | _____ Number of incidents

3b. In what month or months did these incidents take place?
If more than one quarter involved, ASK ↗
How many in (name months)?

INTERVIEWER – Enter number for each quarter as appropriate. If all are out of scope, end incident report.

Number of incidents per quarter			
Jan., Feb., or March (Qtr. 1)	Apr., May, or June (Qtr. 2)	July, Aug., or Sept. (Qtr. 3)	Oct., Nov., or Dec. (Qtr. 4)
608 ____	609 ____	610 ____	611 ____

4a. The following questions refer only to the most recent incident.
Was it daylight or dark outside when the most recent incident happened?

| 612 | 1 ☐ Light – **SKIP** to 5
2 ☐ Dark – **SKIP** to 5
3 ☐ Dawn, almost light, dusk, twilight – **SKIP** to 5
4 ☐ Don't know – **SKIP** to 6a

4b. Was it daylight or dark outside when this incident happened?

| 612 | 1 ☐ Light – Ask 5
2 ☐ Dark – Ask 5
3 ☐ Dawn, almost light, dusk, twilight – Ask 5
4 ☐ Don't know – **SKIP** to 6a

---

5. About what time did (this the most recent) incident happen?

During day

| 613 | 1 ☐ After 6 a.m. – 12 noon
2 ☐ After 12 noon – 6 p.m.
3 ☐ Don't know what time of day

At night

1 ☐ After 6 p.m. – 12 midnight
2 ☐ After 12 midnight – 6 a.m.
3 ☐ Don't know what time of night

Or

1 ☐ Don't know whether day or night

Page 11

FIGURE 8.1 *(continued)*

6a. *ASK OR VERIFY –*
Did this incident happen inside the limits of a city, town, village, etc.?

614 | 1 ☐ Outside U.S. – *SKIP to 7*
2 ☐ Yes (inside limits) – *Ask 6b*
3 ☐ No (outside limits) – *SKIP to 6c*

6b. What is the name of that city, town, village?

615 | 1 ☐ Same city/town/village as present residence – *SKIP to 7*
2 ☐ Different city/town/village from present residence – *Specify* ↗

_____

6c. *ASK OR VERIFY –*
In what State and county did it occur?

616 | ☐☐☐☐☐

State _____ County _____

6d. *ASK OR VERIFY –*
Is this the same State and county as your PRESENT RESIDENCE?

617 | 1 ☐ Yes
2 ☐ No

7. Where did this incident take place?
Mark (X) only one box.

AT OR IN RESPONDENT'S HOME OR LODGING

618 | 1 ☐ At or in own dwelling, or own attached garage *(Always mark for break-in or attempted break-in of same)* . . . .
2 ☐ At or in detached buildings on own property, such as detached garage, storage shed, etc. *(Always mark for break-in or attempted break-in of same)* . . . .
3 ☐ At or in vacation home/second home . . . .
4 ☐ At or in hotel or motel room respondent was staying in . . . .

} *SKIP to 9a*

NEAR OWN HOME

5 ☐ Own yard, sidewalk, driveway, carport *(does not include apartment yards)* . . . .
6 ☐ Apartment hall, storage area, laundry room *(does not include apartment parking lot/garage)* . . . .
7 ☐ On street immediately adjacent to own home . . . .

} *SKIP to 8b*

AT, IN, OR NEAR A FRIEND/RELATIVE/ NEIGHBOR'S HOME

8 ☐ At or in home or other building on their property . . . .
9 ☐ Yard, sidewalk, driveway, carport . . . .
10 ☐ Apartment hall, storage area, laundry room *(does not include apartment parking lot/garage)* . . . .
11 ☐ On street immediately adjacent to own home . . . .

} *SKIP to 8b*

COMMERCIAL PLACES

12 ☐ Inside restaurant, bar, nightclub . . . .
13 ☐ Inside other commercial building such as store, bank, gas station . . . .
14 ☐ Inside office, factory, warehouse . . . .

} *Ask 8a*

PARKING LOTS/GARAGES

15 ☐ Commercial parking lot/garage . . . .
16 ☐ Noncommercial parking lot/garage . . . .
17 ☐ Apartment/townhouse parking lot/garage. . . . .

} *Ask 8a*

SCHOOL

18 ☐ Inside school building . . . .
19 ☐ On school property (school parking area, play area, school bus, etc.) . . . .

} *Ask 8a*

OPEN AREAS, ON STREET OR PUBLIC TRANSPORTATION

20 ☐ In apartment yard, park, field, playground *(other than school)* . . . .
21 ☐ On the street *(other than immediately adjacent to own/friend/relative/neighbor's home)* . . . .
22 ☐ On public transportation or in station (bus, train, plane, airport, depot, etc.). . . . .

} *SKIP to 8b*

OTHER

23 ☐ Other – *Specify* ↗

_____

} *Ask 8a*

FORM NCS-2 (4-10-86)

FIGURE 8.1 *(continued)*

8a. *ASK OR VERIFY –*
Did the incident happen in an area restricted to certain people or was it open to the public at the time?

619 1 ☐ Open to the public
2 ☐ Restricted to certain people (or nobody had a right to be there)
3 ☐ Don't know
4 ☐ Other – *Specify* _____

8b. *ASK OR VERIFY –*
Did it happen outdoors, indoors, or both?

620 1 ☐ Indoors (inside a building or enclosed place)
2 ☐ Outdoors
3 ☐ Both

8c. *ASK OR VERIFY –*
How far away from the home did this happen?
PROBE –
Was it within a mile, 5 miles, 50 miles or more?
Mark (X) first box that respondent is sure of. Then SKIP to check Item C.

621 1 ☐ At, in, or near the building containing the respondent's home/next door . . . .
2 ☐ A mile or less . . . . }
3 ☐ Five miles or less . . . . } **SKIP** to
4 ☐ Fifty miles or less . . . . } Check
5 ☐ More than 50 miles . . . . } Item C
6 ☐ Don't know how far . . . . }

9a. Did the offender(s) live (here/there) or have a right to be (here/there), for instance as a guest or a repairperson?

622 1 ☐ Yes – **SKIP** to Check Item C
2 ☐ No
3 ☐ Don't know

9b. Did the offender(s) actually get in or just TRY to get in the (house/apartment building)?

623 1 ☐ Actually got in . . . . }
2 ☐ Just tried to get in . . . . } Ask 9c
3 ☐ Don't know . . . . }
4 ☐ Didn't try to get in – **SKIP** to Check Item C

9c. Was there any evidence, such as a broken lock or broken window, that the offender(s) got in by force/TRIED to get in by force)?

624 1 ☐ Yes – Ask 9d
2 ☐ No – **SKIP** to 9e

9d. What was the evidence? Anything else?
Mark (X) all that apply. Then SKIP to check Item C.

Window

625 1 ☐ Damage to window (include frame, glass broken/removed/cracked) . . . .
* 2 ☐ Screen damaged/removed) . . . .
3 ☐ Lock on window damaged/tampered with in some way . . . .
4 ☐ Other – *Specify* ↗

_____

Door

5 ☐ Damage to door (include frame, glass panels or door removed) . . . .
6 ☐ Screen damaged/removed) . . . . **SKIP** to
626 7 ☐ Lock or door handle damaged/ tampered with in some way . . . . Check
* Item C
8 ☐ Other – *Specify* ↗

_____

Other

9 ☐ Other than window or door – *Specify* ↗

_____

9e. How did the offender(s) get in TRY to get in)?
Mark (X) only one box.

623 1 ☐ Let in
2 ☐ Offender pushed his/her way in after door opened
3 ☐ Through OPEN DOOR or other opening
4 ☐ Through UNLOCKED door or window
5 ☐ Through LOCKED door or window – Had key
6 ☐ Through LOCKED door or window – Picked lock, used credit card, etc., other than key
7 ☐ Through LOCKED door or window – Don't know how
8 ☐ Don't know
9 ☐ Other – *Specify* ↗

_____

CHECK ITEM C
Was respondent or any other member of this household present when this incident occurred?
If not sure, ASK –
Were you or any other member of this household present when this incident occurred?

628 1 ☐ Yes – Fill Check Item D
2 ☐ No – **SKIP** to 27a, page 18

CHECK ITEM D
Which household members were present?
If not sure, ask.

629 1 ☐ Respondent only – Ask 10
2 ☐ Respondent and other household member(s) – Ask 10
3 ☐ Only other HH member(s), not respondent – **SKIP** to 28, page 18

FIGURE 8.1 *(continued)*

10.	ASK OR VERIFY – **Did you personally see an offender?**	630	1 ☐ Yes 2 ☐ No

11a.	**Did the offender(s) have a weapon such as a gun or knife, or something to use as a weapon, such as a bottle or wrench?**	631	1 ☐ Yes – *Ask 11b* 2 ☐ No – **SKIP** *to 12a* 3 ☐ Don't know – **SKIP** *to 12a*

11b.	**What was the weapon? Anything else?** *Mark (X) all that apply.*	632 *	1 ☐ Hand gun (pistol, revolver, etc.) 2 ☐ Other gun (rifle, shotgun, etc.) 3 ☐ Knife 4 ☐ Other sharp object (scissors, ice pick, axe, etc.) 5 ☐ Blunt object (rock, club, blackjack, etc.) 6 ☐ Other – *Specify* ⬎

12a.	**Did the offender(s) hit you, knock you down or actually attack you in any way?**	633	1 ☐ Yes – **SKIP** *to 15a* 2 ☐ No

12b.	**Did the offender(s) threaten you with harm in any way?**	634	1 ☐ Yes – **SKIP** *to 14* 2 ☐ No

13.	**What actually happened? Anything else?** *Mark (X) all that apply.* Then **SKIP** *to 19a, page 16.*	635 *	1 ☐ Something taken without permission . . . . 2 ☐ Attempted or threatened to take something . . . . . 3 ☐ Harassed, argument, abusive language . . . . 4 ☐ Forcible entry or attempted forcible entry of house/apt. . . . . 5 ☐ Forcible entry or attempted forcible entry of car. . . . . 6 ☐ Damaged or destroyed property . . . . 7 ☐ Attempted or threatened to damage or destroy property . . . . 8 ☐ Other – *Specify* ⬎	*SKIP to 19a, page 16*

14.	**How were you threatened? Any other way?** *Mark (X) all that apply.* Then **SKIP** *to 19a, page 16.*	636 * 637 *	1 ☐ Verbal threat of rape . . . . 2 ☐ Verbal threat to kill . . . . 3 ☐ Verbal threat of attack other than to kill or rape . . . . 4 ☐ Weapon present or threatened with weapon . . . . . 5 ☐ Shot at (but missed) . . . . 6 ☐ Attempted attack with knife/sharp weapon . . . . . . 7 ☐ Attempted attack with weapon other than gun/knife/sharp weapon . . . . 8 ☐ Object thrown at person . . . . 9 ☐ Followed or surrounded . . . . 10 ☐ Other – *Specify* ⬎	*SKIP to 19a, page 16*

15a.	**How did the offender(s) attack you? Any other way?** *Mark (X) all that apply.*	638 * 639 * 640 *	1 ☐ Raped 2 ☐ Tried to rape 3 ☐ Shot 4 ☐ Shot at (but missed) 5 ☐ Hit with gun held in hand 6 ☐ Stabbed/cut with knife/sharp weapon 7 ☐ Attempted attack with knife/sharp weapon 8 ☐ Hit by object (other than gun) held in hand 9 ☐ Hit by thrown object 10 ☐ Attempted attack with weapon other than gun/knife/sharp weapon 11 ☐ Hit, slapped, knocked down 12 ☐ Grabbed, held, tripped, jumped, pushed, etc. 13 ☐ Other – *Specify* ⬎

15b.	**Did the offender(s) THREATEN to hurt you before you were actually attacked?**	641	1 ☐ Yes 2 ☐ No 3 ☐ Other – *Specify* ⬎

FORM NCS-2 (4-10-86)

FIGURE 8.1 *(continued)*

16a. What were the injuries you suffered, if any?
Anything else?

Mark (X) all that apply.

642   0 ☐ None – *SKIP to 19a*
  * 1 ☐ Raped
  2 ☐ Attempted rape
  3 ☐ Knife or stab wounds
  4 ☐ Gun shot, bullet wounds
  5 ☐ Broken bones or teeth knocked out
  6 ☐ Internal injuries
  7 ☐ Knocked unconscious
  8 ☐ Bruises, black eye, cuts, scratches, swelling, chipped teeth
  9 ☐ Other – *Specify* ⤹
  _____
  _____

CHECK ITEM E   Refer to 11b.
Did the offender have a weapon other than a gun or knife? (Is box 4–6 marked?)

1 ☐ Yes – *Ask 16b*
2 ☐ No – *SKIP to 17a*

16b. Were any of the injuries caused by a weapon (other than a gun or knife)?

643   1 ☐ Yes – *Ask 16c*
  2 ☐ No – *SKIP to 17a*

16c. Which injuries?
Enter code(s) from 16a.

644
  *   ☐   ☐   ☐
  Code   Code   Code

17a. Were you injured to the extent that you received any medical care, including self treatment?

645   1 ☐ Yes – *Ask 17b*
  2 ☐ No – *SKIP to 19a*

17b. Where did you receive this care?
Anything else?

Mark (X) all that apply.

646   1 ☐ At the scene
  * 2 ☐ At home/neighbor's/friend's
  3 ☐ Health unit at work, school, first aid station at a stadium, park, etc.
  4 ☐ Doctor's office/health clinic
  5 ☐ Emergency room at hospital/emergency clinic
  6 ☐ Hospital (other than emergency room)
  7 ☐ Other – *Specify* ⤹
  _____
  _____

CHECK ITEM F   Refer to 17b.
Is "Hospital" (box 6) marked?

☐ Yes – *Ask 17c*
☐ No – *SKIP to 18a*

17c. Did you stay overnight in the hospital?

647   1 ☐ Yes – *Ask 17d*
  2 ☐ No – *SKIP to 18a*

17d. How many days did you stay (in the hospital)?

648   _____ Number of days

18a. At the time of the incident were you covered by any medical insurance, or were you eligible for benefits from any other type of health benefits program, such as Medicaid, Veterans Administration, or Public Welfare?

649   1 ☐ Yes
  2 ☐ No
  3 ☐ Don't know

18b. What was the total amount of your medical expenses resulting from the incident (INCLUDING anything paid by insurance)? Include hospital and doctor bills, medicine, therapy, braces, and any other injury-related expenses.

INTERVIEWER – *Obtain an estimate, if necessary.*

649   $ _____ . 00   Total amount
  0 ☐ No cost
  x ☐ Don't know

Notes

FIGURE 8.1 *(continued)*

several parts, including a basic screen questionnaire that collects information about respondent characteristics. On the basis of respondent replies, a Crime Incident Report is completed, which is a lengthy, 28-page questionnaire. Some sample items have been included in Figure 8.1, commencing with page 11 of the actual Crime Incident Report, and continuing through page 15, which includes item 18b. Observe that space is provided for interviewer notes and for open-ended replies by respondents. Subsequently, these data are easily coded and transmitted to computer programs for various types of analyses. These analyses yield numerous tabular data, cross-tabulating social and individual characteristics (age, race, victim-offender relationship) with different types of crime (robbery, assault, burglary, rape).

■ CONDUCTING INTERVIEWS

Since interviews mean direct contact between the interviewer and one or more respondents, there is some strategy involved. A golden rule practiced in business is that "the customer is always right." This also applies in interview situations. The interviewee is always right. Researchers must cater to the convenience of respondents. This means that investigators must schedule their interviews in ways that maximize the successfulness of the interviews and that accommodate the interviewees.

Some of the major points to consider when conducting interviews are (1) gaining access to organizations, (2) arranging interviews, (3) training and orienting interviewers, (4) deciding how to dress for interview occasions, (5) determining when to probe with follow-up questions, (6) deciding whether to videotape interviews, (7) determining whether polygraph or lie detector tests should be used in certain situations, and (8) estimating the dangerousness of interviewing.

Gaining Access to Organizations

Conducting interviews varies in formality, depending upon the nature of the research, the sophistication of the interviewers, and the scope of the research plan. If employees are to be interviewed at their work settings, permission must first be obtained from superiors to interview these subjects. If jail or prison inmates are to be interviewed, permission must be obtained from the prison warden, county sheriff, or chief jailer. Inmates themselves must consent as well. If researchers are connected with a well-known sponsoring agency, such as the Bureau of Justice Statistics, National Institutes for Mental Health, or National Opinion Research Center, they stand a much better chance of gaining access to prospective interviewees than those investigators who are conducting research independently.

Sometimes, it is desirable to preface requests to interview employees with a letter, using an official letterhead, indicating the purposes of the interviews and the research objectives. It is advantageous to point out how the research might benefit those interviewed, or the organizations who employ them. A subsequent face-to-face meeting with higher-ups can clarify any misconceptions management might have about permitting interviewers access to their employees. Even then, access to employees may be denied. Perhaps the organization can be persuaded to permit investigators to interview employees at their homes, on their own time. This tactic has the advantage of leading subjects to believe that their organizations are sponsoring or condoning the interviews, and their cooperation with interviewers is enhanced.

If interviews are to be conducted on a door-to-door basis, there is no need to obtain permission beforehand. However, interviewers must spend considerable time visiting each home and explaining their research purposes. Again, such interviewing is enhanced to the extent that researchers have the sponsorship of well-known research agencies. While it may be ideal to contact subjects in advance by telephone, many subjects to be interviewed do not have telephones or may have unlisted numbers. Thus, investigators may have to take what they can get through door-to-door contacts. The best advice to interviewers is to expect the worse, but hope for the best, interviewing conditions. Poor weather, vicious dogs, and other distractions quickly transform one's ideal plans into reality and often present far from optimum interviewing conditions.

Arranging the Interview

Where interviewees are selected in advance, especially outside of their work settings, a time must be arranged for the interview. It is important to work closely with the interviewee and schedule an interview time that best suits them. If they are on shiftwork schedules, the only convenient time for an interview may be between 2:00 to 4:00 A.M. Daytime interviewing is preferred, especially if persons to be interviewed live in high-crime or gang-dominated areas. The researcher's best strategy is to have the respondent name the time, and perhaps even the place. The respondent's home or apartment is often the best location for an interview, but the close proximity of small children and relatives may prove to be too distracting. Sometimes a small restaurant, or city park, might be a better location. But researchers must anticipate that no matter where an interview is conducted, there are extraneous factors that may interfere with a smooth interview.

Interviewing persons at their work places may not be best. Sometimes workers may suggest their organization lunch rooms for interviews. These areas have unusually high traffic, where other employees drift in and out. Again, there is too much potential for becoming distracted. Some employees may wander over to your table and look over your shoulder: "Hey, what's up? What is that? Are you being interviewed? Do you want to interview me? What are you wanting to know?" Interview areas are best where minimal distraction occurs.

In the case of interviews with jail or prison inmates, researchers literally have a captive audience. Even under these circumstances, however, inmates can refuse to be interviewed. After all, what's in it for them? Researchers need to remember that no interviewee has anything to gain when granting an interview. The interview is an imposition and generally has relevance only for the researcher. However, interviewees have the information a researcher needs, information that will describe the setting and orientations of group members. If a theory is being tested, or crime or delinquency interventions planned, interviewees are the sources for necessary data. Everything within reasonable limits should be done to cater to an interviewee's whims concerning when and where to be interviewed.

Training and Orientation for Interviewers

Depending upon the magnitude of the study, researchers themselves may conduct interviews with various respondents. If large numbers of interviews are to be conducted, then it is increasingly likely that interviewers will have to be recruited and trained for the task. For example, J. L. Miller and Glenna Simons (1997) studied prospective jurors and the impact of news reports and media coverage of spectacular events on their opinions about defendants. Miller and Simons recruited eight graduate students at Purdue University in West Lafayette, Indiana, to conduct interviews with 117 persons. The students were trained at Purdue University and coached in various ways to minimize the chances of a refusal or a break in the interview. A role-playing exercise was conducted wherein a mock interview was completed. This enabled the interviewers to practice interviewing techniques and provided them with an opportunity to ask questions (Miller and Simons, 1997:6).

When interviews are conducted in face-to-face situations, sometimes sensitive questions are asked. Interviewers should be trained in ways that enable them to be unmoved by things they might hear from respondents. The best way to end an interview is to ask a sensitive question, hear the answer, look shocked, and say, "Oh, my!" Or, the interviewer may ask about the respondent's income. If the respondent says, "$200,000 a year," the interviewer might say, "That's a *lot* of money!" This and other judgmental reactions turn off interviewees. At the very least, the interviewer will cause the interviewee to be less than candid and more guarded for the remainder of the interview. Interviewers should refrain from looking surprised or shocked at anything the interviewee might disclose. Interviewers should look interested yet somewhat detached. This mode of behavior is acquired through interviewing experience. There is no such thing as the perfect way to behave when conducting interviews.

What Makes a Good Interviewer? Personality Factors

It is impossible to set forth a set of personality characteristics to suit all interviewers. Interviewers cannot be rigidly standardized like cans of peaches on a store shelf. There is considerable variety among persons and their personalities. Some general recommendations can be made, however. First, interviewers should be friendly and cordial. They must be familiar with the subject matter of the interview. Thus, when interviewees have questions about the meaning of certain questions or statements, interviewers should be competent enough to provide answers.

The key to a good interview is developing rapport. The interviewer can influence the rapport of any social situation. If the interview is conducted at the interviewee's home, the environment may include trappings, such as awards or plaques, which can be used to start the conversation. Perhaps a comment about one's automobile or neighborhood would help to make everyone comfortable before commencing the interview.

More successful interviewers must be able to think on their feet, to make instant assessments of situations and respond accordingly. Your objective is to blend in with the immediate social surroundings and not appear to be overly conspicuous. If you're interviewing farm families in Kansas or isolated persons in places like Rafter, Tennessee, wearing a three-piece suit from Brooks Brothers is out of the question. The interviewer's attitude should reflect an interest in the interview and respect toward the interviewee. Interviewers should relax and attempt to be comfortable, regardless of the circumstances in which they find themselves.

Dressing Appropriately

It is important for interviewers to adapt to the settings they are investigating. If executives of a large organization are being interviewed, it would be advantageous for interviewers to dress rather formally, in attire similar to those being interviewed. However, if interviewers are conducting interviews in run-down neighborhoods, formal attire is inappropriate. Casual attire is less likely to arouse the suspicions of those interviewed. Detectives often wear coats and ties, and interviewees may suspect interviewers of being law enforcement personnel. This may cause prospective respondents to become uncooperative, even refusing to answer an interviewer's questions.

Since much research is conducted by investigators working independently, it is unlikely that they will have an adequately trained interviewer pool. Only major research organizations have this degree of sophistication and training capability. Assuming, then, that most interviewers will enter the field relatively untrained, their "training" will often consist of learning some general guidelines, or do's and don'ts, associated with conducting interviews.

An interviewer's primary objective is to obtain the most accurate data from respondents. It is important, therefore, to put respondents at ease during the interview. Even the most unskilled interviewers become more at ease themselves when conducting interviews, after they have participated in ten or twenty of them. The more experienced the interviewer, the easier it becomes to create good interviewer–interviewee rapport and obtain desired information. Interviewers, therefore, should not over- or underdress in relation to those interviewed. Further, interviewers should remain interested in one's answers yet relatively neutral, depending upon an interviewee's responses. For instance, if the interviewee discloses some sexual indiscretion or admits to a crime, the interviewer should refrain from smiling, laughing, frowning, or deeply inhaling suddenly. These are some of the "don'ts" of conducting interviews. It is also possible to get too close to those interviewed. The objectivity of the interview may be impaired when either the interviewer or interviewee becomes overly friendly. Offers of alcoholic beverages or soft drinks during the interview should probably be avoided.

Probing

One of the positive features of interviewing is the fact that interviewers can seek clarification or amplification whenever respondents give one-word answers or are somewhat vague. For instance, if you are interviewing probationers about the effectiveness of probation officers who supervise them, you might ask:

Q: "Is your probation officer helpful in providing you with job contacts and referrals?"

A: "Yeah, he's OK."

Q: "What does the probation officer do to help you in that regard?" (Probe)

A: "He gives me job leads, you know, names and addresses of people to see, you know, people who might hire me."

Q: "Does your probation officer provide any other type of assistance?" (Probe)

A: "Well, beyond that, I don't know. What do you mean?"

Q: "Well, does he help you fill out job applications, or does he provide you with ideas to put on a job application?" (Probe)

A: "Ohhhh, yeahhh. That, too. He's real good at helping me fill out those forms. One time, I had forgot something I done a long time ago, and it was important for some job I was applying for. He just, you know, sort of worked with me, and helped me remember that and other things. I never would have thought of some of that stuff. He's real smart like that. Yeah, come to think of it, he was really helpful. I got the job!"

This scenario reveals the value of probing questions. Rather than allow the probationer to simply brush off the interviewer with a "Yeah, he's OK" answer to whether the probation officer is effective, the subsequent probes permit additional elaboration concerning the nature of the probation officer's effectiveness, especially regarding job assistance. This may be important for depicting areas where probation offices can improve their various services. Probes also permit investigators to gain insight into the subject matter of their investigation.

Another feature of probing is to uncover areas of inquiry previously neglected by the researcher. There is an element of serendipity associated with probing, meaning that one or more issues, topics, or ideas may be elicited that were not previously thought of by the investigators when the interview was originally constructed. Researchers can't think of everything meaningful to be included in their questionnaires or interviews.

Videotaping or Tape-Recording Interviews

In some situations it may be important to videotape or tape-record interviews. This method of data collection totally eliminates the anonymity factor and jeopardizes the truthfulness or candor of respondents. However, it may be an important feature of the interview to see the interplay between interviewer and interviewee or to hear the dialogue as it transpires. Vocal inflections and the interview tempo may be important and suggest that the interview is properly or improperly conducted. Tape-recording or videotaping the interview memorializes the event as well. The option is to rely on one's memory of events and what was said. A tape recording permits a transcription to be generated. This transcription can be consulted at any time later to authenticate what was actually said.

When police interrogate suspects or interview witnesses, videotaped and tape-recorded interviews are most helpful and reliable. Suspects will have a difficult time later recanting confessions if those confessions are videotaped. Allegations of coercion or of officer failures to "Mirandize" suspects (to tell the suspects their legal rights) can be overcome with a videotaped or tape-recorded account of the interview. Videotapes or audiotapes are also effective when played back to juries in courtrooms.

The Use of Lie Detectors or Polygraph Tests

Using Lie Detector Tests. Although the results of **polygraph tests** or **lie detector tests** are inadmissible in criminal court proceedings, the results of these devices may provide exculpatory evidence for criminal suspects. Polygraphs are devices that measure several physical characteristics and sensory responses of someone responding to a focused interview, such as heart rate and perspiration. The most frequent use of polygraphs is to determine the veracity or truthfulness of someone who is either a criminal suspect or a witness to a crime, although polygraphs may also be used in civil proceedings. "Passing" a polygraph test is interpreted as possibly excluding that person from suspicion of lying. But polygraph tests are not 100 percent accurate and reliable. Some persons may be able to lie without exhibiting any physical characteristics indicating that they are lying. Sometimes, taking certain types of drugs or narcotics prior to responding to a polygraph test will drastically alter the results.

Interviewing May Be Dangerous

A rule cannot be written to cover every interview situation or contingency. Even the most seasoned interviewers encounter unusual situations for which there are no ready-made solutions. For instance, 33 women who worked in a large Indiana bank were interviewed. The interviews were conducted at the women's homes, on Saturdays and Sundays, when they would be available to answer questions. One woman in her late forties was interviewed on a Sunday afternoon. The interviewer placed a tape recorder in the middle of the floor, started it, and then sat on a sofa in the woman's living room, opposite the woman who sat in a chair. A large German Shepherd dog rested nearby.

The purpose of the interview was to solicit these women's opinions about certain work role changes that were occurring at their bank because of the introduction of new computer equipment. The researcher wanted to know how their individual work roles would be affected. As the interviewer asked the woman various questions about her job and her interpersonal relations with other co-workers, a man burst through her front porch screen door into her living room. He cursed at the woman, calling her a whore and other unflattering names. He turned to the interviewer, called him things that would make a sailor's ears burn, and began ranting and raving about the house, breaking lamps and ceramic objects. The interviewer discreetly packed up his notes and tape recorder and quickly left. The man burst from the house and jumped into his car. He followed the interviewer for miles, at high speed, throughout the city, until the interviewer finally lost him in a back alley. Later, the woman called the interviewer, apologized, and explained that the man was her ex-husband who had been in the Korean War. It seems he was suffering from shell shock and had other mental problems. She had divorced from him a few years back, but he continued to visit her occasionally. The interviewer had indeed picked the wrong day to conduct his interview.

In another case, a young male interviewer agreed to meet with and interview a woman in her trailer park at 7:00 A.M. before she went to work. When the interviewer arrived, the thirty-something woman was dressed in a see-through negligee. She insisted on having the interviewer sit with her at the small breakfast table and have coffee. During the interview, the woman frequently changed the subject of the interview, asking whether the interviewer was married, what he did apart from interviewing, and other personal questions. She also sat provocatively. This situation made the interviewer extremely uncomfortable. The woman continued, saying that she was unhappily married to a Marine recruiter. At that point, the interviewer found some excuse to terminate the interview and made a hasty exit. While this situation was potentially compromising and conceivably dangerous, the problem was averted by the interviewer's retreat. The point is that situations like this may occur. Interviewers may need to familiarize themselves with the exits to any situation, as they might do when entering a movie theater.

Hazards are also encountered by those who conduct research in high-crime areas. More than one interviewer has been mugged or assaulted in the course of conducting research. Perhaps one reason mailed questionnaires are so popular is that they avoid certain problems that may arise in face-to-face interview situations, especially in areas of high crime or under circumstances that may jeopardize the researcher's safety. For example, some interviewers who have interviewed delinquent gang members have reported receiving threats or obscene telephone calls from various gang members subsequent to those interviews. Physical damage to an interviewer's property, such as their automobile, might occur, if interviewees suspect that the information they provide might be used against them in some way.

ADVANTAGES AND DISADVANTAGES OF INTERVIEWS IN CRIMINAL JUSTICE RESEARCH

The major advantages of interviews include the following:

1. They enable investigators to obtain desired information more quickly than data-gathering methods such as mailed questionnaires.

2. They permit investigators to be sure respondents understand questions and interpret them properly.
3. They allow greater flexibility in the questioning process.
4. They permit much more control over the context within which questions are asked and answers given.
5. Information is more readily checked for its validity on the basis of nonverbal cues from respondents.

It is clear that other forms of data collection, such as observation and questionnaire administration, share certain of these advantages. However, none of these offers such a unique combination of advantages as interviews. But interviewing is not without its flaws.

Several disadvantages of interviewing follow:

1. Whenever persons are asked questions in a face-to-face situation, any anonymity of the respondent is lost. It is generally believed that anonymity heightens the objectivity of the responses given, such as is the case with self-administered questionnaires mailed to strangers. But interviews are direct. If some of the questions pertain to intimate details of a person's life, then there is the possibility that they will not disclose some of this information. Or if any information is disclosed, it may not be true. One of the more frequent contaminators that interferes with accurate information about people is called social desirability. Social desirability is giving false, but favorable, information about yourself, either to the interviewer or on paper in a self-administered questionnaire situation. For example, a respondent may be prejudiced toward some minority, but if the respondent is asked whether he is prejudiced, he might say no, simply because it is undesirable to say yes. Therefore, respondents may say what they think the interviewer wants to hear.
2. Interviewers may become tired as they conduct several interviews during the day. Their minds may wander or they might be distracted by environmental factors. Their own reliability in recording responses accurately, therefore, may not be consistent from one interview to the next.
3. If unstructured interviews are used, there is the real possibility that inter-interviewer reliability may be poor. This is because each interviewer will give different priority to or show greater interest in certain topics compared with others. This makes it difficult to compare interview results from different interviewers.
4. Interviews may take different amounts of time to complete. Each respondent may prolong the interview, by becoming enmeshed in certain questions or by unnecessary elaboration on particular topics. It takes considerable tact on the part of interviewers to terminate a respondent without appearing rude or disinterested.
5. If interviewers tape-record their interviews, transcribing these recordings takes time. If they make notes about one's responses, they may distract respondents with their note pads and pens.

KEY TERMS

Anonymity
Branching technique
Computer-Assisted Telephone
 Interviewing (CATI)
Focused interview
Focus group
Follow-up questions
In-depth interviews
Interview guide

Interview schedule
Lie detector test
Polygraph test
Probes
Probing
Random-digit dialing
Structured interview
Telephone interview
Unstructured interviews

QUESTIONS FOR REVIEW

1. What is the focused interview? Give some examples of how focused interviews might be applied.

2. Differentiate between unstructured and structured interviews. Under what circumstances would investigators want to use each type of interview? What general kinds of research plans might be associated with these two types of interviews?

3. What is social desirability, and how might it emerge to influence respondent truthfulness during an interview?

4. What are some major functions of interviews?

5. What are some major disadvantages of interviewing?

6. What kinds of things can interviewers do to make the interviewing process go more smoothly for targeted respondents?

7. What are some characteristic features of interviews?

8. Differentiate between interview schedules and interview guides. Under what kinds of circumstances might each of these instruments be used?

9. What is a telephone interview? What are some purposes and advantages of telephone interviews? Can you anticipate any problems with these interviews? List several potential problems and discuss them briefly.

10. What are some potential hazards faced by interviewers, especially those who conduct research in high-crime neighborhoods?

11. What is random-digit dialing? How is it useful and what types of problems does it overcome?

12. What are probes? What advantages are associated with probes?

13. Define and describe in-depth interviewing.

14. What are some general guidelines for dressing and preparing for interviews?

chapter 9

Data Collection Strategies IV

Observational Techniques and the Use of Secondary Sources

■ INTRODUCTION

This chapter has a dual focus: the examination of the two remaining data collection techniques used by criminologists for research purposes. These are the techniques of observation and secondary source analysis. Observation is also known as field research. Whenever researchers immerse themselves in the settings they observe, they are engaged in field research. They may either participate in the activities they are observing, or they may observe from a distance, independent of the activities they observe.

Observation rivals interviewing as the most direct access to information people possess. In the broadest sense, researchers are constantly observing human conduct. Whether investigators are distributing questionnaires in the classroom or listening to remarks made by interviewees, they watch others and their expressions. They carefully scrutinize the circumstances under which their investigations are conducted. Sometimes, these researchers learn more by watching people than by recording what they say.

This chapter examines **observation research** *as a data collection tool. For criminologists and other social scientists, observation is much more than merely sitting in some social setting watching others behave. Criminologists who use observation for data collection purposes are usually trained to look for certain kinds of things, to structure their observations of others with specific goals in mind. Therefore, scientific observation differs from casual observation in that it is focused and linked closely with one's research objectives. Like marks made by respondents on questionnaires, observers code and classify their observations in order to make sense out of whatever they have seen. Observers may be actual participants in the activities they are observing, or they may be on the periphery of interaction as outsiders looking in. Thus, a distinction is made between participant and nonparticipant observation. We define each and examine their respective weaknesses and strengths as research tools.*

Besides observing others, researchers may inspect various resource materials in libraries or elsewhere. Government publications, especially those produced by the National Institute of Justice Bureau of Justice Statistics, are quite useful to investigators as information sources. Any information compiled by others, including public or government-sponsored research publications or reports or analyses made by private organizations, is lumped under the broad designation **secondary source analysis.** *Usually, available public or private data have been collected for purposes that are not necessarily of immediate interest to the investigator. These sources may include statistical information, archival data, case histories, letters, reports, diaries, life histories, newspaper and magazine articles, and any other available, published material. Various types of secondary source materials will be described, and certain weaknesses and strengths of secondary source analysis will be discussed.*

This chapter concludes with an examination of canned data sets, which often are made available by one or more public and private organizations. These data sets may be examined in different ways by investigators, and much interesting information is often disclosed.

WHAT IS OBSERVATION?

To appreciate the distinctiveness of observation as a data-gathering tool, we must distinguish between observations of a casual nature, those that might be by-products of one's investigations, and observations that are used exclusively and fundamentally for data-gathering purposes. It has often been said that those using observation are probably "seasoned," which means that they know pretty much what to expect in advance of their observations. This comes from having been there before, regardless of the types of studies being conducted. Most serious observers have some firsthand, on-the-scenes contact with studies they are conducting.

If properly conducted, **observation** is characterized by the following:

1. Observation captures the natural social context where persons' behaviors occur.
2. Observation grasps significant events or occurrences that might influence the social interactions of participants.
3. Observation determines what makes up reality from the worldviews, the outlooks, and philosophies of those observed.
4. Observation identifies regularities and recurrences in social life by comparing and contrasting data obtained in one study with those obtained in studies of other natural settings.

These characteristics set observation apart from any casual, sporadic, and spontaneous notations made by researchers as they conduct their investigations with other types of data gathering tools. These characteristics also highlight the distinction between observational research and experimental social research. In experimental research, observations are made, but events have been deliberately manipulated to effect certain results. Observational research, in contrast, seeks to preserve the natural context within which observed behaviors occur.

MAJOR PURPOSES OF OBSERVATION

The major purposes of observation in criminological research include the following:

1. To capture human conduct as it actually happens, to permit us to view the processual features of behavior. Whenever persons are interviewed or respond to questionnaires, these are more or less static glimpses of how people think and feel about things. Most observers claim that the difference between what people say and do is great. Observation reflects a dimension of reality that is untapped by other data-gathering methods.
2. To provide more graphic descriptions of social life than can be acquired in other ways. Observation, therefore, supplements the factual information disclosed from other data-gathering methods. For example, we may

describe delinquent behavior in terms of its incidence or frequency. However, observational methods may reveal what delinquents actually do to get into trouble. How do juveniles go about vandalizing businesses and homes, taking drugs, or stealing automobiles? Observation enriches our descriptions of social life and enables us to illustrate behaviors more graphically. Triangulation involves the application of two or more data-gathering tools (e.g., combining interview data with questionnaire and observational information) when investigating a particular subject area. Observation may be combined with other data-gathering strategies to provide us with a more complete picture of the behaviors of others.

3. To learn, in an exploratory sense, those things that should receive more attention by researchers. Observational findings often suggest topics for future research that were unanticipated by investigators when their studies were commenced.

■ TYPES OF OBSERVATION

Two major types of observation are described here: participant observation and nonparticipant observation.

Participant Observation

Participant observation is the structured observation of social settings of which the observer is a part. This is a popular form of observation, since researchers may find it convenient to describe the settings wherein they work or the groups in which they have membership. One of the best illustrations of participant observation is some research by James Marquart (1986).

Marquart participated in a project designed to evaluate correctional officer training, supervision, and turnover in the Texas prison system (1986:16). While working on his doctorate in sociology in 1979, Marquart met with officials connected with the Texas Department of Corrections (TDOC) and explained his interests. The TDOC had recently been involved in highly publicized litigation involving allegations of brutality against inmates. One of Marquart's study objectives was to observe actual officer-inmate interactions to determine whether these allegations were true. Also, he wished to describe the "building tender system," or the pattern in many prisons of using more dominant/ aggressive inmates to control other inmates.

Marquart became a prison guard in Eastham Unit (a pseudonym), a maximum-security facility housing 3,200 prisoners over age 25 who had been incarcerated three or more times (1986:16). Although Marquart acknowledged some difficulty being accepted by the prisoners and other prison guards, he was eventually able to build rapport and acquire both guard and inmate trust (1986:22). An example of one of his guard experiences describes the enriching detail that can only come from participant observation. In this case, the use of force by other guards was obviously excessive, but both prisoners and guards alike seemed to accept its occurrence. One of Marquart's guard associates recalled the following:

I was sitting at the Searcher's desk and Rick (convict) and I were talking and here comes Joe (convict) from 8-block. Joe thinks he knows kung-fu, hell he got his ass beat about four months ago. He comes down the hall and he had on a tank top, his pants were tied up with a shoelace, gym shoes on, and he had all his property in a sack. As he neared us, Rick said, "Well, Joe's fixing to go crazy again today." He came up to us and Rick asked him what was going on and Joe said they (staff) were f___ing with him by not letting him have a recreation card. I told him, "Well, take your stuff and go over there to the Major's office," and there he went. Officer A went over and stood in front of Joe, so did Officer B who was beside Joe, Officer C was in back of A, and two convicts stood next to Officer A.

Inmate James, an inmate who we "tuned up" in the hospital several days before, stood about ten feet away. All of a sudden Joe took a swing at Officer A. A and B tackled Joe. I ran over there and grabbed Joe's left leg while a convict had his right leg and we began kicking his legs and genitals. Hell, I tried to break his leg. At the same time B was using his security keys, four large bronze keys, like a knife. The security keys have these points on them where they fit into the locks. Well, B was jamming these keys into Joe's head. Joe was bleeding all over the place. Then all of a sudden another brawl broke out right next to us. Inmate James threw a punch at Officer D as he came out of the Major's office to see what was going on. James saw Joe getting beat and he decided to help Joe out. I left Joe to help Officer D. By the time I got there (about two seconds), Officer D and about six convicts (building tenders) were beating the s___ out of James. Officer D was beating James with a blackjack. Man, you could hear the crunch noise every time he hit him. At the same time, a convict was hitting him in the stomach and chest and face. These other inmates were kicking him and stomping him at the same time. It was a wild melee, just like being in war.

I got in there and grabbed James by the hair and Officer D began hitting him, no love taps. He was trying to beat his brains out and yelling, "you mother___, you think you're bad, you ain't bad, you mother___, son of a b___, you hit me and I'll bust your f___' skull." I think we beat on him alone for ten minutes. I punched him in the face and head. Then Officer D yelled, "Take him (James) to the hospital." Plus we punched and stomped him at the same time. At the hospital, Officer D began punching James in the face. I held his head so D could hit him. Then D worked James over again with a blackjack. We then stripped James and threw him on a bed. D yelled at James, "I'm going to kill you by the time you get off this unit." Then D began hitting him in the shins and genitals with a night stick. Finally, we stopped and let the medics take over. James had to leave via the ambulance. Joe required some stitches and was subsequently put in solitary."

This was clearly a dimension of prison life Marquart saw that most researchers with conventional research instruments might never see. Can you imagine a formal interview in the home of one of these officers: "Do you hit inmates with your blackjack?" "Do you use excessive force on any inmate to obtain his compliance with prison rules?" How many officers are going to admit to that? Few, if any.

Marquart's participation as a prison guard made him very much aware of some of the shortcomings of participant observation. As a guard, his relationships and rapport with inmates was changed accordingly. Because of his status, he would not become privy to certain types of inmate information. Interestingly, he might have acquired some "guilty knowledge" about drug use or other rule violations, but he did not report such infractions to authorities. He believed that this "guilty knowledge" created an ethical dilemma, although he attempted to walk the fine line of civility and legality. Additionally, much of the brutality he witnessed was difficult for him to accept emotionally. Also, since others knew that he was not really a guard, his views of what occurred may have been manipulated by other guards to a degree. However, Marquart believed that he had acquired sufficient credibility and was honest enough to solicit true reactions from those with whom he worked.

Nonparticipant Observation and Unobtrusive Observation

Another type of observation is **nonparticipant observation.** Nonparticipant observation is the structured observation of others with or without their knowledge, and without actually participating in the behaviors and activities being observed. In this situation, researchers conduct observations of various social settings from the sidelines. Their observations of others may or may not be known to those being observed.

For example, Humphreys (1970) and his associates observed homosexual exchanges that occurred in the restrooms of public parks. They secreted themselves in these restrooms, where they had a vantage point to see possible homosexual interactions. They observed numerous occurrences of homosexual behavior, followed certain persons and obtained their automobile license plate numbers, and used this information to determine their identities and residences. Later, some of those who had been seen committing homosexual acts were visited by researchers on some other pretext. Humphreys claimed that although this type of observation raised certain ethical questions, it nevertheless provided him with valuable data about attitudes concerning homosexuality from those he observed.

Many nonparticipant observers believe that a natural setting yields more accurate information about social reality than what we obtain from contrived experiments in laboratory settings. Observing persons in their natural habitats is certainly not demanding on any investigator, and **field notes** may be taken to record one's observations. Field notes are simply written entries in a field diary to refresh one's memory about what has been observed. Field research, or any research conducted in the natural habitat of those observed, builds upon whatever is observed and the interpretations we make of these observations.

As we have advanced technologically, it is now possible to record what is observed through video cameras. Such observations may be done secretly, so that those observed will be unaffected by the intrusion of cameras into their social interactions. Several different law enforcement agencies, such as the FBI,

have used videotaping to record illegal activities. The effectiveness of sting operations has been enhanced through videotaping, as criminals are filmed in the act of committing various crimes. Criminologists have used videotaping for diverse purposes. For example, some criminologists have videotaped citizen reactions to vandalism. In one instance, an unattended automobile parked on the street was broken into by paid stooges of the researchers, and reactions of passersby to this breaking and entering were photographed. Several interesting observations were made about citizen apathy or noninvolvement in events that affect others. Certain theories about victimization and public response to being victimized can be recorded and tested.

◼ ADVANTAGES AND DISADVANTAGES OF OBSERVATION IN CRIMINOLOGICAL RESEARCH

Participant and nonparticipant observation are not physically demanding on investigators. Some amount of skill is required, however, in order to record accurately whatever is observed. Nonparticipant observers may choose their settings at will, as well as the times when their observations will be conducted. Thus, there is great flexibility associated with this data collection method. Observed behaviors may be either anticipated or unanticipated. Unanticipated observations may form the basis for new research into previously unexplored areas. Observing what is anticipated may enhance theory verification. Observation is also a cheap method of acquiring data. It costs little or nothing to look at others.

An investigator's choice of participant or nonparticipant observation often depends upon the nature of the research being conducted. If private clubs, gangs, prisons, or other "closed" organizations are to be studied, it is necessary to penetrate these settings either obtrusively or unobtrusively. James Marquart became a prison correctional officer temporarily in order to gather information about officer–inmate interactions. Frequently, researchers will go "underground" to infiltrate the groups or organizations they plan to study. This may be the only way such phenomena may be studied scientifically. On other occasions, researchers may have to solicit the help of others to become informants for them as group or organization members. Juvenile gangs may be studied, for instance, by enlisting the cooperation of one or more gang members to report on gang activities and member behaviors. The use of key informants is one method whereby researchers may obtain access to restricted organizations and acquire greater knowledge about them.

The researcher's gender may influence what is studied and how it is studied. For example, Jackie Wiseman (1970) was interested in studying skid row alcoholics. Wiseman had several choices. She could walk up and down skid row, make random observations, conduct random interviews with alcoholics and street people, and generally conduct conventional interviewing and nonparticipant observation. She could pretend to be an alcoholic and attempt to "blend in" with other skid row inhabitants as one of them. Or she could enlist the aid of one or more skid row people and use them as key informants. Wiseman's observations are insightful here, as she explains how she resolved this data-gathering problem:

> On Skid Row, observations were made both by myself in the company of a paid "guide," and by paid male observers. My observations were confined to those activities in which a woman can take part on the Row without causing undue comment—walking around during the day, sitting in bars, eating in cafeterias, cafes, and shopping in grocery stores.
>
> Four male observers walked the streets of Skid Row with the men at night, stood talking to them on the street, drank in taverns with them, and met them at the bars returning from jail. These observations were spread in time through one year. Findings were further supplemented by published observations of the Skid Row area by other researchers.
>
> On Skid Row, I passed as a woman friend of a presumed resident there, as a woman looking for a lost boyfriend, and as a woman who had returned to the area after some absence and was looking for a bartender friend. In Christian Missionary prayer meeting and in free soup lines, I merely joined the men and few women recipients. At the various screening sessions held at stations on the loop, [police officers] were kind enough to allow me to sit in and pass as a secretary who was taking medical notes.

In the Jail and the State Mental Hospital, no attempt to pass was made for two different reasons: in an all-male world like the jail, it would be virtually impossible; in a calmly coeducational and research-oriented environment like the State Hospital, it seemed unnecessary. The first night at the Hospital, when I was introduced to the men in one of the alcoholic wards, they gallantly included me in a late night party based on food raided from the kitchen. From then on they treated me as one of the family.

However, while there were a greater many scenes I could observe, it became apparent that as a woman, or as a researcher, access was denied to some areas of the loop. Especially acute problems were presented by the County Jail and the Christian Missionaries (in addition to skid row at night where a woman attracts attention no matter how innocuously she is dressed).

For these three areas, as well as a fourth (the courts) where time was at a premium, observers were hired. In jail, at the Christian Missionaries, and on Skid Row they were participant observers, unknown to their subjects as researchers. Recruiting observers for the jail posed several problems. Obviously, I could not ask someone to commit a crime so as to be sentenced to the County Jail. On the other hand, there was a need for someone who could participate unnoticed in prisoner activities. The decision was to recruit within the jail. Young men who were not in jail for alcoholism were selected. There were four observers in all. These men were not used simultaneously, but two were observing and recording for three weeks and then two others working for the same period of time approximately six months later—some time after the first two had been released. In this way, it was hoped that collusion between observers would be prevented. (Wiseman, 1970:276–277)

Therefore, Wiseman effectively blended several different strategies—use of key informants, participant observation, the use of volunteers, and simple non-participant observation—to obtain her data. She was able to collect considerable data from her own observations and experiences as well as from those she paid to observe others.

Some of the limitations of observation as a data-gathering tool are that (1) the desired events to be observed may not occur; (2) certain actions of those observed may be wrongly interpreted by observers, since they are not directly involved with what is going on; (3) the observed behaviors may be atypical of the normal behaviors of those observed, given the time when the observations are conducted; and (4) it is impossible to ask those observed for explanations of their conduct, without disclosing one's identity as an observer. Two additional limitations are (5) the impact of the observer on the observed; and (6) the impact of the observed on the observer.

■ IMPACT OF THE OBSERVER ON THE OBSERVED

The Hawthorne Experiments. A classic illustration of the impact of the observer upon those being observed is the small-group experiment conducted in two rooms. One room, the experimental setting, contains a small group seated around a table. A one-way mirror is on one wall in the room, and it is known by those observed that one or more observers are viewing them from an observation booth or room on the other side of the mirror. Theoretically, those being observed eventually ignore others that are watching them, and then they behave more naturally. Critics of such experimentation indicate that those observed cannot possibly ignore that they are being observed. Thus, their actions are restrained or inhibited. They cannot act normally, since they are not in a normal setting, unhindered by observations made of them by others. A major criticism of such small-group research is that it is contrived and not indicative of real-world conditions. Experimenters counter by arguing that such settings are ideal, since they are uncluttered with extraneous factors that might otherwise jeopardize the naturalness of actions or behaviors of those observed. Both views have some validity.

An early study where observation was used, and where the influence of the observer on the observed was significant and eventually apparent, was the classic **Hawthorne experiments.** These were a series of studies conducted at the Hawthorne, Illinois, plant of the Western Electric Company. This company manufactured telephone components. One experiment involved observations of workers who were wiring telephone equipment. Experimenters manipulated the number of rest pauses of these workers, the times when they took their lunch breaks, and even room temperature.

One experiment, known as the illumination experiment, involved the use of a dimmer switch in the work area. Experimenters believed that worker productivity would increase if the lighting intensity in the room was raised. An observer sat in the room and watched workers perform their jobs. As the room was made brighter by raising the lighting intensity, worker productivity climbed. Experimenters argued accordingly that if the room lighting were decreased, productivity would drop also. But when the lights were dimmed, productivity continued to increase. Eventually, the room was lighted with the equivalent of moonlight, yet worker productivity hit an all-time high. Later, workers disclosed in interviews that, while they didn't know the purpose of these experiments, they believed the company wanted them to produce as much as possible, even under conditions of moonlight. They believed that the entire company was watching them as an example. Thus, they deliberately worked hardest when conditions of work were most adverse to them. This phenomenon became known as the **Hawthorne effect,** and such an effect is still used to explain certain behaviors of those who know they are being observed by researchers.

Too Up Close and Personal. Another dimension of the impact of observers upon the observed occurs whenever observers are actual participants in the social events observed. If observers are a part of the social situation they are observing, they may be too close to the situation to retain their objectivity. Further, their own input into what is going on may actually influence the behaviors of others in ways that detract from the naturalness of these settings. Therefore, participant observers may (1) develop friendships with (or animosities against) certain group members they are observing, and these friendships (or antipathies), in turn, may prevent them from accessing information about others; or (2) observers may profess to believe various things about group ideas and goals, and these beliefs may alter the belief systems of those being observed.

In most groups, group members have closer attachments to certain persons in the group. If observers become accepted by and closer to specific group members, this association may automatically restrict them from close access to other group members. For example, John may like Allen and Fred, but John may dislike and be disliked by Gene and Gary. If the observer, Tom, becomes close to John, he may be able to learn much from John, as well as Allen and Fred. But Gene and Gary may see Tom's association with John, Allen, and Fred as choosing sides. Gene and Gary will not disclose anything to Tom, simply because of his associations with others Gene and Gary do not like. Gene and Gary may have important information about the group that Tom needs to know, but Tom will never acquire this information because of his previously developed friendships with John, Allen, and Fred. This oversimplification illustrates an important point about participant observation. That is, in the normal course of social interaction, the observer becomes co-opted into certain cliques or groups. These cliques or groups may be socially isolated from other cliques or groups in the social setting. While it is an objective of the observer to get close to those being observed, such closeness may become a social liability for interactions with others in the same group.

■ IMPACT OF THE OBSERVED ON THE OBSERVER

Observers may prompt those observed to put on an act for the benefit of the observer.   It is presumed that if persons know they are being observed, then they may behave according to whatever they think the observers expect to see. For example, if school teachers are being evaluated by their principals or supervisors, they may dress especially nice for these occasions. Further, they may prepare canned lectures or lessons that highlight their particular teaching skills. Thus, observers develop impressions of these teachers that may or may not be accurate portrayals of their average teaching conduct. There is every reason to believe that if observers make their presence known to others, the validity of whatever is observed may be seriously questioned. This is a phenomenon similar to social desirability, where those observed behave in ways they believe are anticipated or expected by observers.

Observers may cause those observed to exaggerate their natural behaviors.   Another type of influence observers exercise upon the observed is that their own presence may reinforce certain behaviors. If observers are attending a political rally or religious meeting, their own presence may in fact heighten the emotionally charged gathering. Therefore, whatever is observed may be an exaggerated form of behavior that would not occur but for the presence of the observer.

Investigators who use observation of any kind as a data-gathering tool should be sensitive to their own influence upon those who are observed. Attempts should be made to inform readers about any influence their presence as observers may have had on reported findings. As we have seen, observation can be an excellent source of enriching detail to supplement otherwise drab statistical presentations and summaries of tabulated information from questionnaires. One general vulnerability of observation is that it often lacks well-established, coherent, methodological protocol for its implementation. The benefits of its use in criminological research are realized only to the extent that its users are skilled and are aware of its potential as well as its limitations.

■ ANALYSIS OF SECONDARY SOURCES

It is possible to engage in research projects without having any direct contact with human subjects. Some investigators spend their entire professional careers studying secondary sources. Secondary sources are any information originally collected for purposes other than their present scientific one in research studies.

Major Features of Secondary Sources

Secondary source materials are characterized by the following:

1. Secondary source materials are ready-made. Any student may visit a local school or public library to discover a vast amount of ready-made data available for analyses of any kind.

2. Secondary source materials have been collected independently of an investigator's research purposes. Researchers seek out secondary sources that contain some or all of the information they might need to answer their research questions. Often, research projects are designed around available information from secondary sources. Thus, one's research is tailored to fit existing data sets. This is different from formulating a research project in advance, and not knowing whether data are available that can answer one's research questions.

3. Secondary sources are not limited in time and space. This means that investigators who use such sources did not have to be present when and where these data were gathered.

Types of Secondary Sources

Archival Records. One of the most common sources of information are historical archives. Libraries maintain vast records and archival data available to interested researchers. Governmental agencies also compile and maintain records of criminal acts and other relevant information. For example, Marc Riedel and Tammy Rinehart (1996) studied murder clearance rates for Chicago during the period 1987 to 1991. They determined that murder records and homicide reports are sent to the Illinois Department of State Police. These reports, known as Supplementary Homicide Reports (SHRs), are maintained as Victim Level Murder (VLM) files. The Illinois Department of State Police is the state repository for crime statistics. Riedel and Rinehart eventually studied 3,066 single victim murder cases reported by the Chicago Police Department.

Riedel and Rinehart searched these murder archives conducting an **archival analysis** in an effort to determine whether the murders were committed concomitant with another felony, such as a burglary, robbery, or rape. Sometimes this research is referred to as the **historical method.** Information was also obtained about whether the murders occurred as the result of brawls or arguments. These investigators cross-tabulated murders with which other felonies were committed with murders in which the circumstances were unknown. Clearance rates were compared with these variables as well. Riedel and Rinehart eventually established several interesting correlations. For instance, they found that if the conditions that govern the acquisition of information about victim race, gender, and weapon are independent of those that govern information about circumstances, then

1. Clearances will not be related to victim race, gender, and weapon, but will be related to circumstances.
2. The relation between circumstances and clearance status will remain generally unchanged when victim race, gender, and weapon used are introduced as controls.
3. The presence or absence of circumstances information will not be related to victim race, gender, and weapon. (Riedel and Rinehart, 1996:98)

Riedel and Rinehart concluded that "cases involving missing data on circumstances may represent a variety of murders characterized by a lack of clearance relevant information. However, *the limitations of the data set prevent further testing of hypotheses drawn from these interpretations*" (Riedel and Rinehart, 1996:98, italics mine).

The Riedel-Rinehart study utilizing the Chicago Police Department archival information about murders highlights an important disadvantage of using archival information generally. That is, the information has not been collected for research purposes, such as those contemplated by Riedel and Rinehart. Therefore, these investigators could only proceed so far with their analysis of the data. While they wanted to learn more about the phenomena they were studying, they were limited to existing recorded information.

Another study involving the use of historical documents was conducted by Mitchell Chamlin and Steven Brandl (1998). Chamlin and Brandl were interested in studying the historical evolution of vagrancy laws. They focused upon Milwaukee, Wisconsin, largely because of the facts that Milwaukee is an older city that has experienced rather typical changes in its ecological structure. The records collected and maintained by the city and police department are unusually detailed and complete, and longitudinal data for vagrancy arrests are not readily available for other cities (Chamlin and Brandl, 1998:29).

Chamlin and Brandl examined historical records from 1930 to 1972. They correlated vagrancy arrests with unemployment and available sociodemographic information. They were interested in testing several propositions generated by the research of William Chamblis and his associates. Chamblis has argued, for instance, that vagrancy statutes and their codification and subsequent modification reflect changes in the social and economic structure of political units.

Specifically, vagrancy laws have been used throughout history to control the criminal propensities of those who refused to accept low-wage employment.

Chamlin and Brandl examined all vagrancy arrests during the 1930 to 1972 period as recorded in the *Directory and Report of the City of Milwaukee, 1930-1973*. They consulted other concomitant records for population data, including the *Population of Milwaukee, City, County, and Minority: 1800-1990* and the U.S. census. On the basis of their analysis, they concluded several things about vagrancy statutes. They found, for instance, that where demand for labor is low, vagrancy arrests decreased. They also found that during World War II, a 68 percent reduction in arrests for vagrancy occurred in Milwaukee. Several other interesting propositions were tested using this archival data.

Personal Documents and Biographies.   Other sources for data include various historical documents, biographies, letters, and other writings. This information doesn't always have to be historical. Contemporary biographies of criminals and influential political figures can provide interesting insights into the motives that promote criminal behaviors. Social events can be explained or interpreted by paying attention to autobiographical information. For instance, Jack Henry Abbott, twice-convicted murderer and former inmate of the Marion, Illinois, federal penitentiary calls the facility "the belly of the beast" (Abbott, 1981). His autobiographical depiction of his confinement is most illuminating for researchers who wish to characterize prison settings and describe the lives of certain inmates.

One of the most acclaimed autobiographical works was by a prison inmate, Victor Hassine (1996). Hassine was imprisoned for life without parole. His day-to-day account of life behind bars, interactions with other inmates, inmate jargon, and other features of his confinement and attempts at freedom through various appeals are described in enriching detail. Another account of prison life includes the work of former inmate Jim Quillen, who spent many years at Alcatraz in San Francisco Bay (Quillen, 1991).

Some autobiographical records examine the lives of particular types of offenders, such as Donald "Pee-Wee" Gaskins, who was a serial killer (Gaskins and Earle, 1992). Gaskins killed a series of hitchhikers in California in the late 1960s and early 1970s. In his autobiography, he recounts his life and the crimes he committed. Another autobiography was written by Joseph "Joe-Dogs" Iannuzzi, who described his experiences as a former Mafia gangster, a member of the Gambino crime family, and eventually an FBI informant (Iannuzzi, 1993).

Autobiographical information and **biographical information** has also been used to characterize and describe pedophiles and their sexual behaviors. Feierman's (1990) anthology demonstrates a cross-cultural, cross-species, and cross-historical approach to adult/nonadult sexual behavior that gives new insights into the biosocial roots of pedophilia as it occurs in industrialized societies. Feierman includes several autobiographies and clinical assessments of known pedophiles as a means of depicting their actions and providing explanations for them.

Not all biographical and autobiographical research is related to criminals and their experiences. For instance, Tom Tripodi and Joseph DeSario (1993) described the efforts of American special agents working for the CIA, the Drug Enforcement Administration, the Federal Bureau of Narcotics, and the Bureau of Narcotics and Dangerous Drugs to combat organized crime and illegal drug trafficking. They described the French Connection drug ring, government corruption, the FBI under J. Edgar Hoover, and anti-Castro operations.

Gaining Access to Records: The Freedom of Information Act (FOIA). Not all public records are open to the public. When President John F. Kennedy was assassinated in 1963, for instance, records about that incident were subsequently sealed. One important reason for sealing these records was to protect the identities and respect the privacy of witnesses who gave testimony. When Martin Luther King was assassinated in 1968, the records surrounding his assassination were similarly sealed. Subsequently, the **Freedom of Information Act (FOIA)** was passed. The FOIA permits private citizens to access information about themselves, others, and certain events, including assassination data.

Among the various provisions of the act is the stipulation that agencies that collect data on individuals are required to inform the individuals that such information is being gathered, to explain the purposes for the data collection, to tell them whether disclosure of information by them is mandatory or voluntary, and to provide them with other similar protective warnings (National Association of Attorneys General Committee on the Office of Attorney General, 1976).

There are several restrictions and exemptions. For instance, investigatory records compiled during civil and criminal enforcement proceedings are exempt if their production would deprive a person of a fair trial or impartial adjudication. Some information may constitute an invasion of privacy. Other exempted material would be the disclosure of investigative techniques and procedures, disclosure of confidential sources or information (informants), or any information that might endanger law enforcement personnel (McIntyre, 1986).

Under the FOIA, information about former FBI Director J. Edgar Hoover has been disclosed to researchers. The secret files maintained by Hoover demonstrate his interest in collecting derogatory information about prominent Americans, such as Eleanor Roosevelt, John F. Kennedy, Martin Luther King, and others (Theoharis, 1991). New revelations about Hoover's investigative techniques reveal his obsession for retaining his position and discrediting his critics.

Inmates and others also have a right under the FOIA to obtain their presentence investigation reports, although some of the contents of these reports may be censored because of confidentiality provisions relating to probation personnel or informants (Shockley, 1988). Ordinarily, access by prisoners to their presentence investigation reports has been tightly restricted by federal courts and government officials.

There is practically no limit to the sorts of materials that can serve the purposes of scientific exploration. From the most private items, such as personal letters, diaries, logs, and appointment books, to the most systematically accumulated and distributed documents, such as the publications of the U.S. Census Bureau, a bewildering array of information awaits investigators.

Secondary sources may be either public or private. Public data sources are most frequently national agencies and departments that publish and distribute

Box
9.2

Eric L. Jensen
University of Idaho

Statistics: B.S. (criminology), Washington
State University; Ph.D. (sociology),
Washington State University.

Interests: Drug policy, juvenile justice, and juvenile sexual offenders.

I was lucky to be an undergraduate student at Washington State University with its strong program in criminology. This matched my interest in crime, which was shaped as a teenager growing up in a working-class neighborhood of a small port city with relatively high levels of delinquency, street crime, and hard drug abuse.

I originally became interested in illegal drugs when a rash of IV drug abuse hit our high school. I later gained my first sociological background on drugs in the social problems course taught by William Rushing. These interests led me to read books by Edwin Schur and Alfred Lindesmith. During my senior year, I did a library research project facilitated by John Lillywhite and expanded my knowledge of this topic considerably.

I returned to drug issues and delinquency in my master's thesis under the direction of Steve Burkett. The thesis was a secondary analysis of survey data collected by Dr. Burkett, and it examined the influence of informal social controls on adolescent marijuana use.

Drug policy became a major national issue with the declaration of the War on Drugs by President Reagan in 1986. I became very interested in the creation of a war on drugs policy at this particular time since the reported use of illegal drugs had been generally declining since the late 1970s and early 1980s. My training in social constructionism by Armand Mauss was central to explaining the official definition of drugs as a major social problem at this time. Using data sources such as the National Household Survey on Drug Abuse, the *New York Times Index,* and various national public opinion polls, Jurg Gerber and I pieced together an explanation for the declaration of the War on Drugs in a period when illegal drug use was declining. It was a federal election year and politicians had no safe issues to run on, and so they chose illegal drugs.

Our initial article on the social construction of the 1986 War on Drugs has been followed by articles on drug testing in the workplace, the civil forfeiture of assets in drug-related cases, the Canadian war on drugs, and an edited book on the impacts of the War on Drugs on the criminal justice system. We are now examining U.S. influences on drug policy in other nations. Our constructionist analysis of the creation of the War on Drugs has been widely cited in criminological publications, but our research has had no discernible effect on public policy.

My research on juvenile justice includes an article testing the deterrent effect of Idaho's legislative waiver statute. I have also conducted two studies for the state government. The first was a study of the visitation patterns of youth in detention in Idaho, and most recently a study of juveniles committed to state custody for sexual offenses. A needs assessment of the juvenile justice system in Idaho found that a large proportion of the youth in secure placements were adjudicated for sexual offenses. Since Ron Sipe and I had recently coauthored an article on the recidivism of juvenile sexual offenders in young adulthood, we were asked to study the reasons for this unusually high rate of juvenile sexual offender commitment. We presented a brief summary of selected findings to a major committee of the state legislature. We are hopeful that a statewide continuum of care for juvenile sexual offenders will be established as a result of this research.

Another interesting research project emerged several years ago when I worked with two regionally prominent defense attorneys and examined the relationship between the amount of funding available to counties and the likelihood that a defendant would be sentenced to death. Based on several celebrated cases, the print media, along with various defense attorneys, prosecutors, and county commissioners, were claiming that rural, poorly financed counties could not afford to seek death sentences due to the high costs of the trial and subsequent appeals. My preliminary findings confirm the hypothesis: Death sentences in Idaho are more likely to come from counties with higher economic resources and are less likely to be handed down in counties with lower economic resources. The lead attorney on this project credits this study for influencing the creation of a state-level defense unit to assist the lower resource counties in capital cases.

One of the things I most enjoy about conducting research is simply learning more about the subject being studied. For example, I learned a great deal about the administration of capital punishment and juvenile sexual offenders from the studies mentioned above. I also enjoy the challenge of designing a research project to fit the complexities of the issues that we study. Finally, I am pleased when my research is recognized by my peers and if it is used to improve public policy.

Advice to Students: My advice to students who want to pursue research in these areas is to first find a supportive professor and begin your research career as soon as possible. This can be an extensive literature review to gain a sound knowledge of the subject, or you may be able to conduct a study in your research methods course. Second, when approaching a research problem, always remember to design a manageable project. Before embarking on the master's thesis, my overambitious research goals were often something like, What is the meaning of life? We need to understand the big picture, but the practicalities of research require focusing on a few well-specified hypotheses.

information relative to their functions and goals. All types of data are compiled. Any public information source is directly accessible by researchers, and ordinarily, research costs associated with obtaining data are low. Private sources include voluntary agencies or associations, bureaus, and societies. These organizations also publish and distribute data about their functions and goals, usually as technical reports or bulletins. Such information may or may not be distributed to all libraries. Often, researchers must do some detective work to determine whether certain types of information are available and where such data may be obtained. For instance, the Internet may be used to track down certain information, sources, or addresses.

Advantages and Disadvantages of Secondary Sources

The major advantages of analyzing secondary sources include the following:

1. There is considerable savings of time and money, since ready-made data are accessible to the public and then analyzed.
2. Information compiled often pertains to large aggregates of people and their characteristics. Thus, generalizations to larger populations have greater legitimacy than those based upon relatively small samples of elements.
3. Information from secondary sources may be triangulated with information obtained through interviews, observation, and questionnaires to yield more reliable data.
4. Researchers avoid potential ethical problems and harm to human subjects by studying documents rather than people directly.

The major disadvantages of secondary source analysis include the following:

1. Data have been collected for other purposes and may be incidentally related to the researcher's goals and interests. The answers to specific questions, which researchers would prefer to ask, may not be found in available data.
2. There is no way researchers can reconstruct missing data in available secondary sources. Nonresponse in secondary source materials is a "given," and the incompleteness of information may be an important limitation that can affect data reliability.
3. Researchers must often speculate about the meaning of phraseology in various documents, and they lack the opportunity of obtaining further clarification from respondents.
4. Researchers must devise codes in order to classify the contents of documents analyzed. If their analyses are conducted over time, it is possible that missing information may exist to frustrate their coding efforts.

In sum, the use of secondary sources in criminological research is widespread. The strengths of using secondary sources far outweigh any limitations or disadvantages. Secondary source materials are often used to supplement one's research efforts where alternative data collection procedures are used. Therefore, an additional, inexpensive, mechanism exists for bolstering a study's internal and external validity. External validation is important because it pertains to a study's generalizability to other settings and elements. A close correspondence between what is generally known about a given topic as revealed by data in secondary source materials and the information disclosed by a given study attests to the study's generalizability. Internal validity reflects the study's quality and internal consistency. Thus, information derived from questionnaires may be compared with various secondary source materials as a means of verifying its accuracy and dependability.

■ CONTENT ANALYSIS

When investigators have targeted their research objectives, and if these objectives may be achieved partially or in full through the analysis of secondary sources, these researchers may engage in **content analysis.** Content analysis is the systematic qualitative and quantitative description of some form of communication. Thus, the contents of communications of different kinds are examined for the purpose of discovering patterns and meanings. Three examples of content analysis drawn from the criminological literature are illustrated below.

Holmes and Taggart (1990) wished to compare the fields of criminology and criminal justice. They were interested in determining whether the two fields have experienced similar professional growth patterns as evidenced by the quality and sophistication of the major journals within each field. One indicator of the degree of professionalism of any academic discipline is the methodological sophistication of its publications.

These researchers focused upon three major journals: *Criminology, Journal of Criminal Justice,* and the *Justice Quarterly.* The journal *Criminology* is published by the American Society of Criminology, while the *Justice Quarterly* is published by the Academy of Criminal Justice Sciences. *The Journal of Criminal Justice* is an independent publication, distributed by the University of Michigan, publishing high-quality articles of broad criminological and criminal justice interest. These three journals enjoy considerable prestige in both the criminological and criminal justice academic communities.

Holmes and Taggart conducted a content analysis of all research articles in these journals for the period 1976–1988, with the exception of the *Justice Quarterly,* which originated in 1984. The articles in this journal were analyzed for the years, 1984 to 1988. A total of 966 articles were examined. These investigators created ten topical categories, according to which all articles could be classified. Some of these categories included law enforcement and crime prevention, crime causation/social control, courts, corrections, statistics/methods, and discipline/profession. Also, seven variables were examined, including the article topic, methodological orientation, research design, data source, time orientation, and statistical techniques used. They rank-ordered the three journals according to each of these criteria and drew various conclusions about comparative journal sophistication. Regarding topics addressed, for example, Holmes and Taggart found that *Criminology* focused primarily on crime causation/social control, juvenile delinquency, and the courts, whereas the *Justice Quarterly* contained articles that emphasized the courts, corrections, law enforcement, and crime causation/social control.

Thus, there were subtle differences in those articles receiving publication priority. *Criminology* contained articles that emphasized hypothesis-testing to a greater degree than *Justice Quarterly,* and the *Justice Quarterly* seemed to promote more articles that were concerned with problem delineation. More descriptive research articles were found in the *Justice Quarterly* compared with *Criminology.* An illustration of what these investigators found is shown in Table 9.1.

An inspection of Table 9.1 enables us to determine the types of articles that are featured the most among these journals. The predominance of certain subject matter suggests editorial priorities which, in turn, are presumably influenced by the academic disciplines themselves. Thus, considerable research about the courts, corrections, and law enforcement are featured in *Justice Quarterly* articles, whereas predominant topics in *Criminology* pertain to crime causation, social control, and juvenile delinquency. Articles about juvenile delinquency are ranked tenth in the *Justice Quarterly* relative to their frequency. This is only one analysis of several that might be made from this and similar tables.

For instance, Holmes and Taggart were able to detect certain convergences over time, where articles in all of these journals tended to exhibit similar statistical, theoretical, and methodological characteristics. Articles from these different journals in earlier issues tended to be differentiated from one another more clearly. Recent journal issues were less distinct. These researchers concluded that although certain differences in journal content continue to exist, more recent journal articles exhibited growing use of correlational research designs, cross-sectional data, and multivariate research designs. Therefore, the contents of these journals, when analyzed over time, seem to reflect the relative age and development of these respective fields.

TABLE 9.1 Distribution of Topics Appearing in *Criminology (CRIM),* *Journal of Criminal Justice (JCJ),* and *Justice Quarterly (JQ)* Articles

| | Journal | | | | | |
| | CRIM | | JCJ | | JQ | |
Topic	*Rank*	*%*	*Rank*	*%*	*Rank*	*%*
Crime causation/social control	1	26.1	5.5	9.0	3	13.6
Juvenile delinquency	2	17.2	10	2.4	10	2.5
Courts	3	12.1	3	12.2	1	21.2
Other	4	9.4	8	8.3	5	10.2
Corrections	5	8.5	2	16.1	2	19.5
Law enforcement	6	8.0	1	19.0	4	11.9
Statistics/methods	7	6.2	7	8.5	8.5	4.2
Discipline/profession	8	5.3	4	9.2	7	5.1
Public opinion/relations	9	5.0	9	6.3	8.5	4.2
Policy/planning	10	2.3	5.5	9.0	6	7.6
Totals	$N = 437$		$N = 411$		$N = 118$	

Source: Malcolm D. Holmes and William A. Taggart (1990). "A Comparative Analysis of Research Methods in Criminology and Criminal Justice Journals." *Justice Quarterly* 7:421–437.

The second example, a study by Walker (1986), illustrates the potential of content analysis for discovering certain hidden messages or meanings contained in verbatim transcripts of legal proceedings. Walker conducted a sociolinguistic examination of the contextual features of court transcripts. She obtained responses from 27 judges from both trial and appellate courts. Among other things, she asked judges to report their reading habits relative to trial transcripts. She wanted to know whether these judges believed it important to include actual witness speech characteristics in these written transcripts, such as pauses during testimony ("uh's"), hesitations, poor grammar, false starts, stammers, laughing, crying, whispering, sighing, or shouting.

Apart from these judges' opinions about what should or should not be included in trial transcripts, many of the judges believed that the transcripts should be as accurate as possible. One judge said that "laughter and shouting are direct indications of [the deponent's] state of mind and may assist in proper meaning [being] given to statements—others may or may not go to state of mind or meaning—usually more to physical state" (Walker, 1986:421).

Walker discovered several curious inconsistencies among judges about their views concerning transcript completeness and accuracy. She says,

> I found it curious, for example, that a total of 84 percent of the respondents considered the parenthetical [shouting] to be acceptable (i.e., objective), despite its close semantic connection to anger. Yet I cannot imagine any judge ever tolerating, nor any court reporter ever inserting the parenthetical [angrily] in a transcript. Equally curious was the finding reported . . . that allows the inference to be made that for some judges, at least, silent pauses are considered objective facts, while "spoken" hesitations are not. Such an evaluation really stretches the definition of objectivity and leads inevitably to problems with interpretation, raising the question of who is competent to make the distinction between a fact and an interpretation. (Walker, 1986:423)

Another example is a study by Klofas and Weisheit (1987) of the historical evolution of the insanity plea in Illinois. To some extent, it involved archival analysis, since these investigators delved into historical records and court documents in order to discover patterns. It is also an example of how evidence disclosed by content analysis may be used as the basis for policy decision making by legislative bodies. Klofas and Weisheit were interested in tracing the transformation of "not guilty by reason of insanity" (NGRI) to the more current "guilty but mentally ill" (GBMI) statute, which was established in 1981 by the Illinois legislature.

These investigators examined the contents of court data from Cook County (Chicago) to determine and document the extent to which GBMI has replaced NGRI. Besides charting the frequency of use of these statutes, these researchers also noted the type of disposition (e.g., plea, bench, or jury trial). Their content analysis of case dispositions and the frequency of use of NGRI and GBMI led them to conclude that "GBMI cases are typically resolved differently from NGRI cases" (Klofas and Weisheit, 1987:43). Interestingly, they found that although the number of GBMI cases has increased over the years, a commensurate decrease in the number of NGRI cases has not been observed.

These investigators were able to show that by leaving the insanity defense virtually intact in Illinois and adding the GBMI statute, the legislature actually compounded rather than resolved the fundamental issues surrounding the insanity defense. Their research is important, in part, because it suggests misuse of the GBMI statute apart from its original application, and that GBMI "may be used to provide excuses for behavior rather than to hold offenders accountable" (Klofas and Weisheit, 1987:49). One implication is that the Illinois legislature, as well as the legislatures of other states where similar statutes have been enacted, must face an important policy decision in future years as it attempts to further clarify the insanity issue. Thus, a very important policy issue has been highlighted by using a fairly simple, inexpensive content analysis tool in analyzing insanity defense cases over a period of years.

When investigators such as Klofas and Weisheit examine documents over an extended period of time, there are natural occurrences or events that may intervene to frustrate their research efforts. For instance, a police officer in Long Beach, California, wanted to study gang formation patterns and membership over an extended period from 1960 to 1990. He had access to all juvenile files, consisting of arrest reports and considerable personal and demographic information about juvenile arrestees. He wanted to compare these files over a sample of years. A secondary objective was that he wanted to see whether juvenile crime changed during this 30-year period. He designated specific years to study, using five-year intervals. However, when he inspected available files and records, he found that the forms for logging juvenile arrests had changed several times. Information provided on certain forms in 1960, for instance, was not provided on forms in 1970, and so on. This irregularity made it difficult for him to code the information he wanted. Also, not all arresting officers were equally proficient in completing these arrest reports. He soon found that many juvenile arrest documents were poorly completed and unusable. This is one of the major hazards of using secondary source materials.

Another interesting use of content analysis was a study by J. L. Miller and Glenna Simons (1997). Miller and Simons were interested in describing pretrial media coverage and how such coverage might impact trial outcome and sentencing severity. Besides surveying a large sample of persons available for jury duty, these researchers analyzed legal case documents and news media documents. They performed a content analysis of television film clips and all of the stories appearing in two local newspapers in a designated city. They classified and categorized the ways in which defendants were portrayed by the media. Specifically, they focused upon six factors in their content analysis: (1) the characterization of the crime, (2) the characterization of the accused, (3) statements or information not allowed in court, (4) statements or testimonies that were untested or unsupported, (5) untested or unsupported credibility of individual spokespersons, and (6) opinions about the guilt of the accused.

Miller and Simons found that prospective jurors who consume media coverage of a case identify with the state against the accused. Further, prospective jurors are likely to attribute guilt, and that the narratives contained in media portrayals of crimes provide a dimension of structure. Miller and Simons offered several proposals to remedy pretrial bias among prospective jurors.

Advantages and Disadvantages of Content Analysis

Content analysis is an inexpensive way to collect data. No one needs to be interviewed. No surveys need to be prepared. Questionnaires do not have to be mailed. Permission is not required for access to documents, such as newspapers and televised media excerpts, in order to conduct content analyses of them. Lengthy periods of time can be covered by content analysis. Researchers can conduct content analysis on their own, without the assistance of others. Permission of human subjects is not required. Content analysis is perhaps the most unobtrusive data collection method that exists. Contemporary use of computers and software make it possible for researchers to scan documents and conduct word searches to facilitate their content analysis of specific materials.

However, content analyses of documents, articles, or other materials are difficult to replicate by others who are interested in studying the same events. It is also possible for two or more researchers who examine the same documents independently to arrive at totally different conclusions about the contents examined. Each researcher may devise a particular code for classifying article or document content. There is a strong subjective element present here. Codes devised for particular content may reflect researcher bias. The subject matter of content analysis is fixed. This means that whatever the form of material examined, it is in print or on videotape. It is not subject to cross-examination or probing or follow-up questions. The clarification inherent in any document is there for the researcher to interpret.

■ OFFICIAL AND CRIMINAL JUSTICE AGENCY RECORDS

For criminal justice professionals and criminologists, much use is made of publications generated by the U.S. Department of Justice Bureau of Justice Statistics. *The Uniform Crime Reports,* published annually by the Federal Bureau of Investigation, is also tapped as a primary crime information source.

Since 1977, the National Archive of Criminal Justice Data has been operating at the Interuniversity Consortium for Political and Social Research in Ann Arbor, Michigan. This archival network makes available substantial information to analysts, policymakers, and researchers in all criminal justice fields. Data from the archive are made available to over 350 colleges and universities throughout the United States without charge. Private researchers are assessed modest fees to access this information for their own investigative purposes (National Archive of Criminal Justice Data, 1990:iii).

In 1998, the *Sourcebook of Criminal Justice Statistics* was made available on CD-ROM, including editions for previous years from 1994 through 1996. The extensive compendium of statistical information has made it possible for instantaneous data retrieval.

CANNED DATA SETS

Increasing numbers of national and state data sets are being made available to researchers for different types of analyses. These are **canned data sets.** For instance, the National Judicial Reporting Program distributes data files for various states. The National Center for Juvenile Justice distributes data disks as well, including an extensive number of variables and records relating to juvenile delinquency characteristics and juvenile court data. This information can be cross- tabulated and analyzed in many different ways. Each year new sources of information are being established and distributed to researchers for nominal costs. In some instances, this information is freely dispersed.

META-ANALYSIS

Meta-analysis is the quantitative assessment of a large number of articles and research that focuses upon a particular issue or research question (Glass, 1976). This definition may sound like the definition of a literature review. However, a literature review is an examination and synthesis of information about a specific research question and what generally has been found out about it. Those conducting literature reviews summarize the studies examined and describe the similarities and differences. However, in meta-analysis, the quantitative findings of individual studies are themselves quantified and examined for patterns or trends.

A study by James Bonta, Moira Law, and Karl Hanson (1998) illustrates a typical application of meta-analysis. Bonta, Law, and Hanson wanted to know whether the predictors of recidivism for mentally disordered offenders are different from the predictors of recidivism for nondisordered offenders. Therefore, they examined 64 studies of recidivism that yielded 35 predictors of general recidivism and 27 predictors of violent recidivism. They controlled for mentally disordered and nondisordered offenders in each of the studies. Essentially, a subsequent statistical analysis yielded no differences in the predictors of recidivism for either type of offender. Actually, Jim Bonta and his associates found that the best predictors of recidivism were criminal history variables. Thus, Bonta was able to recommend that in the future, the development and application of risk assessment instruments to mentally disordered offenders should rely less on psychopathology variables and more on social psychological criminology literature.

A close colleague and friend of Jim Bonta's, Paul Gendreau, also studied factors related to recidivism and conducted an extensive meta-analysis of 131 studies published between January 1970 and June 1994 (Gendreau, Little, and Goggin, 1996). The studies yielded 1,141 correlations between criminal recidivism and various predictor variables. Gendreau, Tracy Little, and Claire Goggin found that the strongest predictors of criminal recidivism were crimogenic needs; criminal history/antisocial behavior history; social achievement; age/gender/race; and family factors. Less important predictors included intellectual functioning, variables related to personal distress, and socioeconomic status of the family of origin. Thus, the meta-analysis performed by Bonta, Little, and

Box
9.3

James Bonta
Chief, Corrections Research
Department of the Solicitor General of
Canada

Statistics: B.A. (experimental psychology),
McMaster University; M.A. (child studies),
University of Toronto; Ph.D. (clinical
psychology), University of Ottawa.

Interests: I have always been interested in behavior modification and childhood
aggressive behavior. I have done volunteer work at local mental health clinics. After
completing my bachelor's degree, I studied at the Institute of Child Study at the
University of Toronto. I worked part-time, conducting psychological assessments
for family court. In all likelihood, I would have stopped going to school after receiving my Diploma in Child Studies, were it not for my supervisor at the clinic. He
encouraged me to continue my studies.

I entered the Ph.D. clinical psychology program at the University of Ottawa. Before starting formal studies, all clinical applicants had to have some clinical experience. Therefore, I worked as a psychometrist at a training school for a year prior to
beginning the Ph.D. program. The training school dealt with delinquents under the
age of 12. It was there that I was exposed to the I-level classification system for
delinquents.

While at the University of Ottawa, I had to submit a research report to take the
place of a master's thesis (the Institute of Child Study did not require a thesis). The
study was an examination of the factors related to juvenile court disposition. Not
only did I publish the report, but because the university required an external examiner, I met Don Andrews from Carleton University. Later, Don would become an
important colleague of mine.

While at the University of Ottawa, I completed two clinical internships. My first
internship was with mentally delayed individuals, and the experience further developed my skills in the behavioral techniques of intervention. My second internship was at a forensic unit of a psychiatric hospital. The hospital staff was routinely
administering psychological tests to the offenders, and the interns were encouraged to conduct research from this database. One of the tests struck me and another intern as not making much sense. It was the Luscher Color Test, and our subsequent analysis of this test found little empirical support for its use. For me at
least, this study was a great deal of fun. We took something that many people accepted as valid, and through research, showed the opposite. In many of my studies,
there is the theme of debunking popular myths (e.g., the detrimental effects of
prison overcrowding, the ineffectiveness of offender rehabilitation).

Interestingly, my career in corrections was not cemented by my studies at the
University of Ottawa. There were no courses in corrections/forensic psychology.
My doctoral dissertation dealt with teaching sign language to autistic children.

Part way through the program, I needed a part-time job to supplement my income (I was married and had a child). Don Andrews suggested that I speak with Paul Gendreau, who was responsible for hiring correctional psychologists in the region. Paul gave me a part-time job at the Ottawa-Carleton Detention Centre, a maximum-security remand centre for adults and young offenders. I stayed there for 14 years and established the only full-time psychology department in a jail setting in Canada.

During my years at the Detention Centre I was given considerable freedom to do research. The early studies dealt with the effects of incarceration. However, in the 1980s I became interested in offender classification. I started administering the Level of Service Inventory-Revised (LSI-R) to inmates and evaluating the predictive validity of this offender risk-needs classification instrument. This specific line of research continued for ten years and offender risk-needs assessment remains a major interest of mine.

In 1990, I joined the Solicitor General of Canada. My research covers a range of topics from offender assessment to dangerous offenders to restorative justice. I have also held various academic appointments, and at present I am an adjunct research professor at Carleton University.

Reflecting on my route to correctional research, I think that there were few notable influences. First, I have always respected the value of empirical evidence. When I worked at the Detention Centre, I quickly learned that the clinical techniques and assessment procedures that I was taught were not working with the offenders. My research on offender assessment showed that traditional clinical measures were largely irrelevant for use with offenders. In collaboration with Don Andrews, Paul Gendreau, and others, we became convinced that offender assessment and rehabilitation could be improved if our theories of criminal behavior would pay greater attention to psychological principles. These ideas culminated in a book that I co-authored with Don Andrews, *The Psychology of Criminal Conduct.*

Second, I always felt that research should lead to practical applications. It was not enough to show significant effects at a .05 probability level. My early exposure to behavior modification perhaps underscored the value of interventions that showed significant changes in behavior. The risk-assessment research also impacted on the way that some correctional systems dealt with offenders. The third factor that influenced my career was luck. I was lucky to have met two of the most influential correctional researchers in Canada: Don Andrews and Paul Gendreau. Their support and advice had tremendous influence on my own work.

What do I hope to accomplish through my research? I hope that the way our society deals with lawbreakers will become more effective, more reasonable, and more humane. There are many things that we do with offenders that are empirically indefensible. We need good research to develop effective policy. When I see some correctional systems adopting new risk-needs approaches to offender assessment, such as the LSI-R, and introducing offender rehabilitation programs based on the empirical literature, I think that we are making small but important improvements.

Advice to Students: For the student interested in a research career, I would say the following: Do not worry if you are a late-starter in the field. What you really need is an appreciation of research to improve our understanding of criminal behavior. Do not accept blindly what your professors tell you. Some can be pretty persuasive at pushing all of the right emotional buttons. Always ask: What is the evidence? For you to have this critical eye on the evidence, you have to know research methodology and statistical analysis. Although the methods and results sections of a journal article are the most boring parts for many students, they are probably the most important. Finally, get your hands dirty! Go out and collect some data with real offenders. Once you have experience with offenders, you will see the tremendous variation in these people and the opportunities for research.

Goggin resulted in identifying key predictors of recidivism and eliminating less important predictors. A literature review would only have been a superficial examination of these articles without any conclusive quantitative results.

A meta-analysis of 80 studies was conducted by D. A. Andrews (1990) to assess the effectiveness of delivery of appropriate correctional services in higher-risk cases in juvenile and adult correctional treatment. In Andrews's research, 154 coefficients were analyzed from the different studies, targeting specific criminogenic needs, and the use of styles and modes of treatment (e.g., cognitive and behavioral) that were matched with client need and learning styles.

Advantages and Disadvantages of Meta-Analysis

Meta-analysis is not new. It has the advantage of statistically synthesizing a large number of research articles and separating better predictor variables from poor ones. Meta-analysis has been used extensively in psychological studies, but its use in criminal justice and criminology is increasing. A survey of *CJ Abstracts* reveals that meta-analysis has been used in more than 60 articles from 1990 to 1998.

Meta-analysis works best where considerable data are available on particular research subjects. The examples of meta-analysis applications cited above pertained to recidivism. Much work has been done over the years to explain why recidivism occurs. Thus, when researchers have large numbers of studies to examine, perhaps as many as 50 or more, meta-analysis is an effective method for assessing this research and isolating the best predictors of recidivism or whatever phenomena are of interest to researchers. But not every research question is investigated aggressively. Some topics, such as the use of K-9s (police dogs) in law enforcement, are less intensively investigated. As a result, where few studies exist, meta-analysis would not be appropriate. Thus, it is highly dependent upon popular research questions rather than less popular or infrequently studied events.

Meta-analysis involves the application of sophisticated statistical techniques. Those who use meta-analysis must be familiar with a wide variety of statistical applications. This is because they must be familiar with the different statistical procedures used in each of the studies they examine, and they must also have the capability of translating statistical findings in the various studies into a common statistical format for use in their own meta-analysis of predictor variables. More than a few investigators may not understand the complexities or significance of meta-analyses reported in the research literature.

Additionally, there is little uniformity among studies investigating a common research question. Both qualitative and quantitative investigations are conducted. Different samples of persons are studied. Many extraneous factors are uncontrolled. Researchers may not report their numerical results. Thus, important information may be missing from certain articles subjected to meta-analysis. Despite these limitations, meta-analysis is considered a highly effective means of quantitatively synthesizing large amounts of research data where available.

■ KEY TERMS

Archival analysis	Historical method
Autobiographical information	Meta-analysis
Biographical information	Nonparticipant observation
Canned data sets	Observation
Content analysis	Observational research
Field notes	Participant observation
Freedom of Information Act (FOIA)	Secondary source analysis
Hawthorne effect	Unobtrusive measures
Hawthorne experiments	

■ QUESTIONS FOR REVIEW

1. What is meant by secondary source analysis? What are some examples of public secondary sources?

2. What is nonparticipant observation? What are some limitations of nonparticipant observation regarding the reliability of whatever is observed and its meaning? Explain.

3. What is participant observation? How can researchers who engage in participant observation "get too close" to their subjects being observed? What can be done to avoid this problem?

4. Who is a key informant? What are some purposes of key informants? What are some problems that can be anticipated from using key informants in research?

5. What is content analysis? How can content analysis be used to affect policy decision making? Give two examples.

6. What are some major problems associated with content analysis?

7. If you plan to use content analysis over a lengthy period, such as five or ten years, what types of problems might occur to interfere with your coding of data? Explain.

8. In what sense is observation a source of enriching detail to supplement questionnaire information?

9. How does observation conducted by criminologists differ from everyday, random observations by others?

10. In what ways are participant and nonparticipant observation structured? Explain.

11. What are some hazards of doing participant observation with criminals and street people?

12. What are the major limitations and strengths of secondary source analysis?

13. What is meta-analysis? What conditions maximize the usefulness of meta-analysis?

chapter 10

Measurement of Variables in Criminal Justice and Criminology

INTRODUCTION

One of the most important links in the research chain involves measuring variables. How do we know when probation officer stress levels and burnout are high or low? How do we know if prospective parolees will be dangerous to the community? How do we know how much peer group pressure is exerted upon juveniles to prompt them to commit delinquent acts? How do we know if sentencing disparities exist among judges and whether sentences imposed are harsh or lenient? How do we know whether crime is increasing or decreasing? These are measurement questions. Quite often, tests of our theories about behaviors and events depend upon our ability to measure crucial variables.

This chapter defines measurement and highlights its importance in the research process. Chapter objectives include (1) illustrating the relation of measurement to theory and the research process generally; (2) describing different levels of measurement and their relation to the data collection process; (3) highlighting some of the more important scaling procedures used for measuring criminological phenomena, including attitudes; and (4) illustrating several theoretical and substantive measurement issues in criminal justice research.

MEASUREMENT OF VARIABLES IN CRIMINOLOGY AND CRIMINAL JUSTICE

Variables are quantities that assume more than one value, and they may be discrete, continuous, dependent, or independent. All attitudinal phenomena are variables. Race, ethnicity, gender, political affiliation, religious affiliation, income, age, education, occupation/profession, and nationality are variables in the sense that they may assume different values. The persons we study have these and many other characteristics. Our attempts to describe persons and differentiate between them according to these and other characteristics involve measurement.

Some of the earlier definitions indicated that it is "the correlation with numbers of entities that are not numbers" (Cohen and Nagel, 1934), or "the assignment of numerals to objects, events, or persons, according to rules" (Stevens, 1951). A subsequent definition referred to measurement as "the procedures by which empirical observations are made in order to represent symbolically the phenomena and the conceptualizations that are to be explained" (DiRenzo, 1966).

Bailey (1987:60) has added to these previous definitions by saying that measurement is "the process of determining the value or level, either qualitative or quantitative, of a particular attribute for a particular unit of analysis." Bailey distinguishes between qualitative and quantitative measures by whether labels or names are applied to variables or whether numbers are applied to them. If labels or names are applied, such as eye or hair color, religion, political affiliation, or gender, he would describe these variables as qualitative. Descriptions of prison inmates, including "real man" or "punk," would also be qualitative. Age, income, years of education, and all attitudinal phenomena could be expressed in quantitative terms, and numerical values would be applied to them.

For our purposes, measurement is the assignment of numbers to social and psychological properties of individuals and groups according to rules, and correlating these numbers with these properties symbolically. Another way of viewing measurement is the process of using numerical expressions to differentiate between people and groups according to various properties they possess. These properties are largely behavioral and attitudinal characteristics that are amenable to measurement.

The primary functions of measurement are to

1. Describe social and psychological phenomena empirically
2. Render data amenable to some kind of statistical manipulation or treatment
3. Assist in hypothesis testing and theory verification
4. Enable researchers to differentiate between people according to various properties they possess

Conceptualizations of Social and Psychological Phenomena

Exploratory and descriptive studies of criminological phenomena depict both social settings and characteristics of persons in those settings. For example, jail overcrowding is sometimes used to explain the incidence of inmate suicides or unrest. Overcrowding is conceptualized in different ways, such as the amount of cell square footage available to inmates, the number of beds per cell, the number of inmates confined per cell, and the actual capacity of the jail facility in relation to its rated capacity. Different quantitative expressions of this phenomenon can be correlated with suicide rates, inmate anxiety, and the incidence of rioting. Describing the characteristics of burnout can help us acquire a better understanding of the effectiveness or ineffectiveness of police officers or others exposed to hazardous or life-threatening situations.

Rendering Data Amenable to Statistical Treatment

Another function of measurement is to bring various phenomena into a form that enables researchers to manipulate it statistically. In order to make sense out of data collected from different sources and respondents, it is often helpful to transform the data into numerical quantities. Once data have been cast into some kind of numerical form, we can apply various statistical tools and analyze the data more effectively.

Suppose researchers inspect recidivism rates of probationers (i.e., their arrests or convictions for new crimes while on probation) in a given state. They note that in some cities, the recidivism rate among probationers is higher than in other cities. Believing that these different rates of recidivism among probationers might be attributable, in part, to differences in the ways these probationers are managed or supervised, these researchers place themselves in several probation offices for two weeks and observe what is going on around them. They observe interactions of probation officers and their clients, supervisory practices, and the general office setting. They probably take notes about what they observe. Further, they might ask questions of officers about different ways their jobs are performed or how they feel about their work. At the end of their observation, interviewing, and questionnaire administration, they will have compiled a good bit of information about the persons in the probation office. What can they do with this data they have collected? In order to make sense out of their observations of probation officer behaviors, they may find it helpful to classify their observations into different categories.

Perhaps one result of their investigation is the finding that in those cities with higher probationer recidivism rates, the caseloads of probation officers generally seem much higher compared with caseloads of officers in cities with lower probationer recidivism rates. Probation officer caseloads are easily quantified. We can count the numbers of probationers each officer is assigned. What about less obvious dimensions of the probation officer–probationer relation? What if there are certain probation offices with lower client caseloads but higher probationer recidivism?

Observations made by these researchers may lead them to conclude that in these particular offices, probation officers do not seem especially interested in probationer problems. Probation officers in these departments may relate to probationers in an impersonal fashion, whereas in other comparable departments, probation officers may seem to take more of a personal interest in their clients. If we are going to make sense out of these observations, we are going to have to translate "appears more impersonal or distant" or "seems to take more personal interest in probationers" into numerical quantities. We are going to have to measure these probation officer-client interactions in some way. Once we have measured these types of interactions, we can compare them with different office policies about how offenders ought to be supervised, or caseloads of officers, or size of office, or any other relevant variable. After these variables have been quantified in some way, it will then be possible to apply various statistical procedures to these data in order to enhance our understanding of what is going on and why.

Assisting in Hypothesis Testing and Theory Verification

Hypotheses Defined.   An important function of measurement is to permit us to verify theories and test hypotheses derived from them. Conventionally, investigators proceed in their scientific inquiry by theorizing about events. Why does recidivism occur? What causes labor turnover in probation agencies? What causes burnout among correctional officers? How does jury nullification occur? Why do we have sentencing disparities? Why do persons support the death penalty? Researchers conjecture about why these events occur. Different explanations are considered. These explanations are translated into hypotheses, where a stated relation between an event and an explanation of it is made. Hypothesis statements may be, The greater the alcohol use, the greater the recidivism among probationers. Or, Whites receive shorter sentences compared with blacks where both are convicted of the same offense. Or, The stress of correctional work increases job burnout for corrections officers. Or, Punishment-centered citizens favor the death penalty, while rehabilitation-centered citizens are opposed to the death penalty. Or, White jurors will tend to acquit white defendants, despite

Zelma Weston Henriques
John Jay College of Criminal Justice, CUNY

Statistics: B.A. (sociology), Morgan State University; M.Sc. (social work), Columbia University; M.Ed. (applied human development and counseling psychology), Columbia University; Ed.D. (applied human development and counseling psychology).

Interests: Women and crime; imprisoned mothers and their children; race, class, and gender issues; cross-national studies of crime.

Currently I am a professor in the Department of Law and Police Science at John Jay College of Criminal Justice, the City University of New York. I was employed by the Women's Prison Association of New York as the director of a special project titled "Children of Offenders." As director of this special project, I was responsible for designing and developing research in order to document the plight of children of female offenders. This experience heightened my interest in the subject of women and crime, imprisonment, and the impact of maternal imprisonment on the lives of children. I pursued these topics as areas of interest. Later, upon returning to complete my doctorate at Columbia University, I chose to do a study of imprisoned mothers and their children.

My research represents a significant contribution to the field of criminology and criminal justice. In fact, I am referred to as a pioneer by researchers in the field, who have studied the topic of imprisoned mothers and their children.

The aspects of research that I find most gratifying are my direct interactions with the populations with whom I have worked over the many years. Such interactions have provided me with the opportunity to understand the dilemmas of race, class, and gender in the American society, and in the criminal justice system.

Advice to Students: My advice to those interested in doing research in this area would be to seek an internship experience in this field. It is also important to keep abreast of all the emerging research on the subject. In addition, one should always be cognizant of the humanity of all people, even those accused of crime.

extensive inculpatory evidence. Or, Probation officers who have to travel great distances to meet with their probationer clients will be more likely to leave their probation agencies. These are examples of different kinds of hypotheses, and they are not necessarily good ones.

Hypotheses are tentative statements, usually derived from theories, that may be refuted. Hypotheses are alternatively defined as statements of theory in testable form. Hypotheses may be assertions of a relationship between two or more variables. Hypotheses may contain a single variable. One research objective is to test various hypotheses. Initially, researchers believe their hypotheses are true. However, they must test these hypotheses in some way in order to support or refute them. The logic is that if one or more hypotheses are supported by data collected by the investigator, then the theory from which those hypotheses was derived is also supported.

Perhaps investigators learn from their investigations of various probation offices that each is somewhat autonomous from the others, and that chief probation officers administer office procedures and policies according to their personal discretion. Researchers may suspect that the probation officer–client relation is influenced greatly by office policy. Perhaps certain offices are more rule-oriented and bureaucratic than other offices. Perhaps caseload assignments are quite different from one office to the next. These investigators may conjecture about the degree of formality in probation office operations and the relation of formality–informality to probation officer–client interactions. Certain organizational theories may be used to explain probation officer behaviors and conduct. Measurement of the degree of formality–informality as well as the nature of probation officer–client interactions will permit researchers to test hypotheses about these variable interrelationships. Tests of hypotheses derived from theory are also tests of the theories from which those hypotheses were derived.

The nature of caseload assignments may have some explanatory value and account, in part, for probation officer–probationer interactions. In some offices, caseloads are determined by dividing the total number of probationers by the number of officers. This method gives each probation officer a caseload equivalent to other officers. But in another probation office, caseloads may be more specialized. Some probation officers may be assigned principally those probationers who have serious drug or alcohol dependencies. Other probation officers may be assigned violent offenders to supervise, including convicted rapists and robbers. Specialized caseload assignments such as these are often determined on the basis of a probation officer's skills and interests. Thus, it may be that where caseloads are specialized and tailored to fit particular officer interests, the probation officer–client relationship may be more personalized. The officer takes greater interest in those clients supervised and relates better to their individual problems and needs. In more generalized caseload assignment situations, probation officers may have such diverse clientele that they cannot conceivably relate to all probationer problems and needs. These officers may feel frustrated and overworked. In order to insulate themselves from the complexities of these diverse relations, they may bureaucratize their behaviors and relate to their clients impersonally, on a "strictly business" basis.

Measurement permits us to evaluate these settings and the personnel within them. We can characterize office settings and caseload assignment policies according to various criteria and correlate these factors with other variables. In the general case, if a hypothesis is about the relation between two variables, X and Y, and is of the form,

As X increases, Y increases,

then one should conceptualize variables *X* and *Y* in such a way so that this hypothesis can be tested. If variable *X* is *office formality* and variable *Y* is *probationer recidivism rates,* a hypothesis might be as follows:

> *As the formality of probation office policy increases, recidivism rates among probationers will increase.*

Both formality of probation office policy and recidivism rates of probationers will have to be measured. By the same token, if variable *X* is the nature of caseload assignments and variable *Y* is probationer recidivism rates, we might develop the following hypothesis:

> *Recidivism rates among probationers will be lower where specialized caseload assignments are made for probation officers compared with offices that use generalized caseload assignments.*

For both of these hypotheses, we can measure probationer recidivism by the proportion of those probationers who are arrested for new crimes. If there are 100 probationers and 20 are arrested for new crimes, then the recidivism rate based on this measure is $20/100 = .20$. If there are 300 probationers and 90 of them are arrested for new crimes, then the recidivism rate would be $90/300 = .30$, a higher rate of recidivism. We might develop the following tables:

	Office Procedures	
	Formal	Informal
Recidivism Rate of Probationers	.40	.30

OR

	Nature of Caseload Assignment	
	Specialized	Generalized
Recidivism Rate of Probationers	.15	.30

In each of these tables, we have created categories for office formality-informality and for the nature of caseload assignments. In each table, we have supplied hypothetical recidivism rates for aggregates of probationers. From the ways these data are arranged, it would seem that probation office formality is associated with higher probationer recidivism rates of probationers, while informality is associated with lower probationer recidivism rates. Also, those offices making specialized caseload assignments seem to have less probationer recidivism associated with them compared with those offices making generalized caseload assignments. These tables are relatively simple, but they illustrate how we might translate office characteristics into categorical expressions and contrast them with offender recidivism rates. Measurement would help us test our hypotheses about the influence of office environments on client recidivism.

Differentiating Between People According to Properties They Possess

A primary function of measurement is to make distinctions between people according to certain properties they possess. Suppose we are looking at five large tables in a room. Each table is slightly different from the rest and of a different color. We might wish to know which table is longest, which is heaviest, which is widest, and which is tallest. One solution to our problem is to grasp a ruler and take measures of length, width, and height, and then compare the five tables. We can bring in scales and weigh each table as well. These two measuring instruments, the ruler and the scales, help us answer our questions about the different properties of length, width, height, and weight shared by these five tables.

However, what if we are looking at several people and wish to know whether they differ regarding their age, educational attainment, job satisfaction levels, morale, stress and burnout, job proficiency, and attitudes toward supervision. The ages and levels of educational attainment for these persons are not difficult to determine. We may have access to employee information that tells us their ages and amounts of formal education. Or these persons may tell us their ages and amounts of education when asked. The remaining variables of job satisfaction, morale, stress and burnout, job proficiency, and attitudes toward superision are more difficult to conceptualize. True, each of these persons may tell us how they feel about their work, whether they feel stressed or burned out, whether they have high or low morale, whether they are proficient at their work, and whether they approve of how they are supervised. What if they all say they like their jobs and have high morale? What if they all deny that they are stressed or burned out? What if they all say they are proficient in the performance of their work tasks? What if they all like their supervisor and approve of the way they are supervised? Are we to assume that all of these persons surveyed are equal on each of these variables? While all of these persons may be equivalent to one another on each of these properties, social scientists generally assume that for any group, there will be differences among individual members pertaining to their behavioral and attitudinal characteristics. These differences may be either great or small, depending upon the variables or characteristics examined.

Thus, depending upon how we choose to conceptualize job satisfaction, some of these persons will have higher levels of it compared with other persons. Variation in the level of morale will also be observed among these individuals. They will differ in their job performance, with some persons performing better or worse than others. We may even find that although all appear to like their supervisors and how they are supervised, some of these persons may not like these supervisors as strongly as the other persons. Typically, we will create measuring instruments for these different variables. These measures will likely consist of questions or statements, and these persons will differ in their agreements or disagreements with these statements. We will make inferences from their responses about whether they possess these characteristics or properties to high or low degrees. This is a basic task of measurement that will permit us to classify people differently and make distinctions between them on various dimensions.

▪ HYPOTHESES: OPERATIONALIZING VARIABLES

Nominal a.ıd Operational Definitions

The process whereby variables are brought into the empirical world where they can be manipulated or controlled is **operationalization.** An **operational definition** is the result of operationalization. Operational definitions of variables may be understood by comparing them with nominal definitions.

The explication of theories is heavily dependent upon extensive use of **nominal definitions.** Nominal definitions are those we might find in a dictionary. All attitudinal terms are defined by other terms that are considered synonymous with them. This establishes a circularity or merry-go-round of terms that is confusing, since these terms are seldom defined in a uniform fashion. No consistent meaning is assigned to many of these terms, so that one, and only one, meaning of a term can be measured by independent investigators. An attitudinal example is *anxiety.* Using the latest version of *Webster's New World Dictionary, anxiety* is defined as the state of being uneasy, apprehensive, or worried about what may happen; misgiving; a thought or thing that causes this; an eager and often slightly worried desire. If we look up the word *misgiving,* we find that it means a disturbed feeling of fear, doubt, apprehension. When we look up the word *apprehension,* we find that it means foreboding, fear, dread. And when we look up the word *fear,* we find that it means to be uneasy, anxious, or doubtful, to expect with misgiving. And when we look up the word *uneasy,* we find that it means disturbed by anxiety or apprehension. In other words, according to this dictionary, *anxiety is defined as anxiety.* Such circularities in nominal definitions of things are commonplace. Nominal definitions assist us by linking different ideas in a logical fashion. For instance,

> *Bureaucratic settings are characterized by adherence to rules and impersonality. The greater the bureaucratic operations, the greater the impersonalization. Probationers often require personalized treatment in order to complete their probation sentences satisfactorily. Personalized treatment is less likely to occur in a highly bureaucratized probation office. The greater the bureaucracy of a probation office, the less individualized and personalized the treatment received by probationers from their probation officers. The less personalized the treatment received by probationers, the more likely they will re-offend or recidivate.*

All of this theorizing is done using nominal definitions of terms. Seemingly, we know or understand what *impersonal relations* implies and what *individual-*

ized treatment is. We can understand how probation office policies may inadvertently contribute to greater rates of probationer recidivism. But all of this theorizing is articulated through the use of nominal definitions of terms.

Theories are constructed mostly of nominal definitions and logical abstract linkages between different concepts. Logical interrelationships between variables are outlined, largely through the use of nominal terms and how they are intrinsically associated with other nominal terms. However, in order to test our theories, we must bring our terms into the empirical realm. The term *empirical* means "amenable to our senses" in some respect. If we can see something, smell it, taste it, touch it, or hear it, it is said to be in the empirical realm. Translating terms into empirical reality most often involves the measurement process, or the assignment of numbers to different amounts of personal and/or social properties. Transforming nominal definitions into an empirical form or rendering them measurable quantities is operationalizing them. Thus, operational definitions are quantifications of nominal definitions. Kerlinger (1965:34) defines an operational definition as "one that assigns meaning to a . . . variable by specifying the activities or "operations" necessary to measure the . . . variable."

For example, if we wanted to devise an operational definition of anxiety, we would come up with something like "anxiety is what an anxiety test measures." The anxiety test we might devise consists of agreement or disagreement with several statements that appear logically related to our nominal definition of anxiety. Certain responses are designated as anxious responses, whereas other responses would be nonanxious responses. For instance, Janet Taylor (1953) investigated anxiety and formulated an operational definition of it. Prior to creating this definition, however, she examined numerous psychoneurotic patients at a large state mental hospital. She reasoned that one of the best places to find anxious people would be a mental hospital. The patients she investigated had previously been diagnosed by psychiatrists as either psychotic or neurotic and suffering from considerable anxiety. Taylor observed these patients, their behaviors, and ailments. On the basis of her observations of large numbers of anxious persons and their behaviors, she created a manifest anxiety scale consisting of 50 statements with true or false responses. A few of the 50 items Taylor used to measure anxiety follow. "Anxious" responses are indicated in parentheses following each item:

1. I am often sick to my stomach. (True)

2. I am about as nervous as other people. (False)

3. I blush as often as others. (False)

4. I have diarrhea once a month or more. (True)

5. When embarrassed, I often break out in a sweat, which is very annoying. (True)

6. Often my bowels don't move for several days at a time. (True)

7. At times I lose sleep over worry. (True)

8. I often dream about things I don't like to tell other people. (True)

9. My feelings are hurt easier than most other people. (True)

The rationale underlying this scale and others like it is that the greater the number of anxious responses, the greater the degree of anxiety. Taylor's anxiety scale ranged from 0 (low or no anxiety) to 50 (high anxiety). This score range was achieved by assigning one point (1) for each "anxious" response, and assigning no points (0) to a nonanxious response. When administered to samples of persons in different social contexts, most of their anxiety scores generally range from 14 or 15 to 35 or 40. Few persons ever have scores below 10 or above 40. Notice that the previous nine items are related to different attitudes and behaviors. Psychological, social, and biological dimensions of anxiety are tapped by this measure. Irregular bowel or bladder functioning, loss of sleep, excessive worry, and greater sensitivity about one's thoughts and dreams seem to be closely correlated with anxiety. These characteristics are called concomitants of anxiety, primarily because they have been found to be closely correlated with it.

Taylor used psychoneurotic patients at a mental hospital exclusively for the purpose of identifying characteristics of anxiety and to devise her scale items. Later, she administered the scale to persons outside of the hospital setting, in work environments and elsewhere. She found that anxiety could be used as an indicator of personal and social reactions to changes in one's work environment or family stability. The same principles that pertained to the development of Taylor's anxiety scale are also generalizable or applicable to constructing scales of burnout, stress, the nature of the probation officer–probationer relationship, or any other attitudinal variable of interest to criminal justice professionals and criminologists.

The nominal definition–operational definition distinction is also exemplified by the use of concepts and constructs.

Concepts

Concepts are terms that have direct empirical referents. When we say *book, desk,* or *blackboard,* we can point to specific objects that these terms represent. Thus, any book may be a direct **empirical referent** of the term *book.* We would say that the term *book* is a concept because it has a tangible object as its direct empirical referent.

Constructs

Constructs are terms we use that *do not have* direct empirical referents. *All* attitudes are constructs, since we must rely on *indirect evidence* of their existence. When we say the word *anxiety,* we cannot point to some specific referent of it. However, we *can* point to an anxiety scale as a referent for the term. The scale itself contains specific items that depict behaviors that are concomitants of the term. Occasionally, the term *epistemic correlate* has been used to characterize the components of operational definitions. Thus, it is likely that underlying many attitudinal phenomena are numerous epistemic correlates. As an example, Taylor's manifest anxiety scale described earlier consisted of 50 **epistemic correlates** of anxiety.

The work of criminal justice professionals and criminologists involves the widespread investigation of constructs. Some variables, such as recidivism rate, age, gender, fractured family, or race/ethnicity, are more directly defined and amenable to measurement than other variables, such as anxiety, psychotic-aggressive personality, stress and burnout, political conservatism, offender dangerousness, reactive depression, extroversion, and acceptance of responsibility. These are just a few of the many constructs that have been gleaned from recent issues of *Criminal Justice Abstracts,* and they reflect the diversity of subject matter studied by social scientists.

While most of the instruments that are devised to conceptualize these and other variables are of the paper-pencil variety and are often administered in a questionnaire format, some attitudinal variables may be measured through other creative means. For example, Thompson, Dabbs, and Frady (1990) studied 17 adult male first-offenders who were exposed to a 90-day shock incarceration program. The program was modeled after a military boot camp, and offenders were examined over time regarding their stress levels and self-concepts pertaining to social status. These researchers found, for instance, that these offenders' stress levels were lowest and their perceptions of social status were highest at the time of their admission to the boot camp. However, stress for most program participants heightened during the first four weeks, and their social status perceptions decreased during the same period. Eventually, their stress levels dropped and social status perceptions increased.

These researchers were able to chart these changes by testing saliva samples and varying levels of testosterone concentrations. Levels of testosterone appeared to decrease in response to increased stress and loss of social status, coincidentally during the first four weeks of boot camp. Eventually, testosterone levels for most participants increased, varying positively with decreased stress and higher perceptions of social status. Although this particular means of tracking stress is not unique, it is imaginative and suggests alternative ways of evaluating attitudinal dimensions. Furthermore, precise levels of testosterone can be measured or gauged.

In sum, we construct our theoretical schemes and use nominal definitions liberally as a way of logically relating attitudes and behaviors and developing explanations for events. When hypotheses are derived for empirical test, we must devise operational definitions for the terms used in our hypotheses. Operational definitions of terms are created by using epistemic correlates or observable characteristics that can be empirically determined. While some of our terms may be concepts, inasmuch as they have direct empirical referents, other terms we use must be conceptualized as constructs. Constructs involve the use of indirect indicators of phenomena of interest to us. Operationalization is the process of developing operational definitions from nominal ones. Operationalization is also described as establishing constructs for some of the less empirical terms used in our theories.

Some variables are more a part of our empirical world (concepts) than other variables (constructs). Concepts and more elusive variables (constructs) are brought into the empirical world through quantification, where numbers are ultimately assigned. The fact that some of these variables are less tangible than others (e.g., attitudes, the psyche, stress) means that the numbers assigned to such intangible phenomena will vary in their meaning. Four different meanings have been assigned to numbers that represent social and psychological phenomena. These meanings are described as levels of measurement and are crucial to our data presentation, analysis, and interpretation.

LEVELS OF MEASUREMENT

Four levels of measurement have been distinguished. These are the nominal, ordinal, interval, and ratio levels. Some investigators use other labels to describe these levels of measurement, such as classifiables or countables, rankables, and measurables (Peatman, 1963). In a sense, numbers pretty much mean the same thing from one application to the next. For instance, higher level mathematics uses numbers in a consistent way, regardless of their application. In another sense, numbers mean different things, depending upon what they are used to represent. When numbers are assigned to social and psychological variables, they take on different meanings, depending upon how the variable has been measured. If we assign a "1" to a male and a "2" to a female, for example, the "1's" and "2's" will have a different meaning compared with the "1's" and "2's" we use in our description of ages. We will not be able to average the "1's" and "2's" assigned to gender categories, for example, since these numbers are simply used to distinguish males and females in our sample from one another (e.g., classifiables). Numbers assigned to different socioeconomic statuses or basketball ratings can be ranked (rankables). And numbers assigned various ages can be summed and averaged (measurables). Thus, numbers are interpreted differently depending upon whatever they stand for in criminological research.

This section presents several popular levels of measurement. This arrangement of levels moves from low to high, beginning with the nominal level and ending with the ratio level. The importance of distinguishing between different levels of measurement is that researchers have a greater range of data analysis and statistical test options where higher measurement levels can be assumed to underlie the data they have obtained. The fewest statistical and analytical options are associated with the nominal level of measurement, whereas the greatest number of options would be associated with the ratio level of measurement.

Nominal Level of Measurement

The lowest form of measurement is the **nominal level of measurement.** This level involves the classification or categorization of variables into nominal subclasses. Gender, for instance, has two nominal subclasses: male and female. Political affiliation has several nominal subclasses, including Democrat, Republican, American Independent, Communist. Delinquency may be treated as a nominal-level variable, where different types of delinquent conduct can be distinguished. Felony and misdemeanor are two nominal subclasses on the type of crime variable. Different types of deviant behavior also may be placed into nominal subclasses. Each of these variables is a **categorical variable.** When numbers are assigned to these nominal subclasses, the numbers mean nothing more than to differentiate one subclass from another. Thus, nominal-level measurement is highly qualitative and serves to distinguish between people according to discrete attributes.

Ordinal Level of Measurement

A higher level of measurement compared with the nominal level, the **ordinal level of measurement** not only allows researchers to distinguish between persons according to certain attributes, but the numbers assigned certain attributes are considered either higher or lower compared with one another. Socioeconomic status is generally measured according to the ordinal level of measurement. Supreme Court Justices may be ranked higher than university professors or district attorneys or correctional officers. The numbers assigned these various professions or occupations permit researchers to say that a "1" is higher or lower than a "2," which may be higher or lower than a "3," and so on. Other variables that might be measured according to an ordinal scale might be police professionalism, correctional officer work satisfaction, prisonization, ego strength, and a force continuum. Most attitudinal variables are considered measurable according to ordinal scales.

Assignment of numbers to data measured according to an ordinal scale permits researchers to make "greater than" or "less than" distinctions between different scores. However, we cannot know or determine actual distances between scores on a scale. Consider the intensity continuum of police professionalism on the following scale:

Nonprofessional   Professional

—— / — / ————— / – / ————————————— / —
15   25   26 30   31

Points or units to the far left are toward the "nonprofessional" end of the continuum, whereas points or units toward the far right are toward the "professional" end of the continuum. Therefore, some police officers are more professional than others. Some officers are less professional than others. However, we cannot say *how much more professional* or *less professional* these officers are from each other. Observe that these points are not equidistant from one another. The scores of 15 and 25 are close together, while the scores of 25 and 26 are far apart. There is a great distance between 30 and 31. Yet there is only a small distance between 26 and 30. This is the nature of ordinal scales. Ordinarily, we can say that one score is higher or lower in relation to other scores, but we are not permitted to say "how much higher" or "how much lower" these scores are from other scores. The magnitude of differences between scores on an ordinal scale has little meaning other than to locate scores relative to others along a continuum. There is no standard distance between units along the horizontal axis of an ordinal continuum.

This particular feature of ordinal scales limits the statistical and data analysis options available to researchers. Some statistical procedures require that we can specify the magnitude of score differences for certain arithmetic operations, such as averaging, square root functions, summing, multiplying, and dividing. Thus, averaging numbers derived from ordinal scales is not a legitimate arithmetic function. There are several reasons for these conventional misapplications of statistical procedures, and they will be discussed subsequently. However, there are conventional applications of certain statistical measures to ordinal data even though a higher level of data is required.

Interval Level of Measurement

Data measured according to the **interval level of measurement** are also assigned numbers. These numbers permit nominal differentiations between values. Further, these numbers permit determinations of "greater than" or "less than." Additionally, these numbers have equal spacing along an intensity continuum, and researchers may say that there are specified distances between units. In the study by Thompson, Dabbs, and Frady (1990), for example, levels of testosterone in saliva specimens provided by several boot camp shock probationers would be measurable according to an interval scale. Thus, if we had several boot camp participants' testosterone levels indicated by scores on a testosterone scale, we might see something like this:

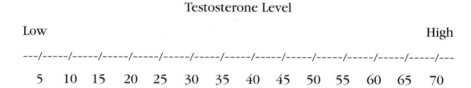

Testosterone Level

Low   High

---/-----/-----/-----/-----/-----/-----/-----/-----/-----/-----/-----/-----/-----/---
    5   10   15   20   25   30   35   40   45   50   55   60   65   70

This hypothetical testosterone level continuum is gradated according to five-point intervals. These intervals are considered equal distances from each other. The distance between 5 and 10, for example, would be identical to the distance between 50 and 55. The distance between 10 and 30 would be equal to the distance between 50 and 70. This equal spacing of interval scales is desirable, because it permits us to use statistical procedures and other data analysis techniques that involve arithmetic operations such as averaging and square rooting. Comparing our hypothetical police professionalism scale with this hypothetical testosterone level scale, we would not be able to determine meaningful average police professionalism scores, whereas we would be able to compute meaningful average testosterone level values.

Ratio Level of Measurement

The **ratio level of measurement** is identical to the interval level of measurement with one exception. The ratio level of measurement assumes an absolute zero on some ratio continuum. Income is a ratio-level variable, since income may be measured according to a scale having an absolute zero. Persons can have no money. Where an absolute zero is assumed, values may be proportionately related to other values. Therefore, $50 is to $100 as $10,000 is to $20,000. Interval scales lack an absolute zero, and therefore, ratio statements are not permissible with such scales.

However, no procedure discussed in this book and in most other texts in statistics and methodology requires levels of measurement beyond the interval level. For instance, although income is actually measurable according to a ratio scale, it is treated as though it were an interval measure. Since income has ratio-level properties, it also embraces properties of all other lower levels of measurement, including the interval level, the ordinal level, and the nominal level.

In later chapters, statistical measures and techniques are presented according to different levels of measurement. Therefore, it is important to know how variables are measured initially before we decide which statistical procedures to apply. If a statistical procedure happened to require that our data should be measured according to an interval scale, we would not be in a good position to apply this measure if our underlying levels of measurement were either ordinal or nominal at best. Consider the following summary of permissible actions we may take, as shown in Table 10.1, depending upon the level of measurement we may assume with the data collected.

Table 10.1 says that analytical tools and statistical procedures may be used according to whether certain levels of measurement have been achieved. The characteristics of all lower levels of measurement are embodied within higher levels of measurement. Therefore, the interval level of measurement may also be treated as an ordinal scale, and it may be divided nominally. However, if we elect to divide interval scales according to some lower-level-of-measurement standard, we lose a certain amount of information. In the case of reducing an interval scale to a nominal one, we lose the equal spacing between units as well as the "greater than" or "less than" qualities it possesses. This is throwing away valuable data. Researchers may be faulted for "underutilizing" analytical techniques if they have the data to warrant applications of procedures suitable for higher measurement levels. A case of underutilization would be to take various age scores for some sample of elements and divide them into two categories, "old" and "young." By dichotomizing such values, we destroy the interval features of the scores. The statistical measures we might apply to such dichotomies may not be as sophisticated as those measures that require the interval level of measurement for their application.

Alternatively, some researchers attempt to do too much with the data they have collected. If they apply a statistical technique or analytical procedures to data measured according to an ordinal scale, when those procedures require at least an interval scale, then they are violating one assumption underlying those techniques or procedures. In the social sciences, this is a common occurrence

TABLE 10.1 Levels of Measurement and Statistical Applications

If the measurement level required by our statistical tests is	Then, we may apply:
1. Nominal	1. Nominal-level procedures
2. Ordinal	2. Nominal- and ordinal-level procedures
3. Interval	3. Nominal-, ordinal-, and interval-level procedures
4. Ratio	4. Nominal-, ordinal-, interval-, and ratio-level procedures

and has come to be regarded as conventional. The frequent application of averages or means to data measured according to ordinal scales, such as attitudinal scores, is typical of such a violation. If we observe police professionalism scores of 10, 20, 25, 30, and 15, for example, their sum is 100. The average score would be 100 divided by the number of scores. Since there are five scores, the average score would be computed as follows: 100/5 = 20. The average professionalism score is 20. What does the score of 20 mean? Not much. Again, the reason is that in order for averages to be computed, scale scores must be equal distances from one another along a continuum. We saw previously that the hypothetical police professionalism continuum does *not* have equal spacing along the intensity continuum. Nevertheless, attitudinal scores are frequently averaged by researchers. Therefore, two major pitfalls to be avoided by researchers are the following:

1. Underutilizing information collected by using lower-level-of-measurement tests and procedures with higher-level-of-measurement data
2. Overanalyzing data by applying tests requiring higher levels of measurement to data measured according to lower levels of measurement

■ TYPES OF SCALING PROCEDURES FOR MEASURING VARIABLES

The measurement of social and psychological variables may be accomplished by applying several popular methods devised by researchers. These include (1) Likert scaling or the method of summated ratings and (2) Thurstone scaling or the method of equal-appearing intervals.

Likert-Type Scales

Rensis Likert (1932) was instrumental in devising the **method of summated ratings** as a means of distinguishing between persons according to differing degrees of ordinal-level characteristics. Subsequently labeled a **Likert scale,** this procedure is probably the most popular attitudinal scaling method used in criminology and other social sciences today.

Likert scales are easy to identify in the research literature. We may identify them according to the response patterns that accompany attitudinal items in questionnaires geared to measure ordinal-level attitudinal phenomena. Respondents are provided a list of statements with which they agree or disagree to varying degrees of intensity. For example, the following items are typical Likert-style items:

SA = Strongly agree
A = Agree
U,A = Undecided, probably agree
U,D = Undecided, probably disagree
D = Disagree
SD = Strongly disagree

Check (Or Select) The Response That Best Fits You.

1. Firearms ownership in the United States should be limited to law enforcement officers and military personnel.
   (SA) (A) (U,A) (U,D) (D) (SD)
2. The right to bear arms is fundamental for all U.S. citizens.
   (SA) (A) (U,A) (U,D) (D) (SD)
3. When guns are outlawed, only outlaws will have guns.
   (SA) (A) (U,A) (U,D) (D) (SD)
4. There is a high relation between access to firearms and violent crime.
   (SA) (A) (U,A) (U,D) (D) (SD)
5. Firearms don't kill people; other people kill people.
   (SA) (A) (U,A) (U,D) (D) (SD)
6. Children should receive firearms instruction when they are very young.
   (SA) (A) (U,A) (U,D) (D) (SD)

These items obviously have something to do with firearms ownership and use in the United States. The categories, "Strongly agree," "Agree," "Undecided, probably agree," "Undecided, probably disagree," "Disagree," and "Strongly disagree" constitute a gradated pattern indicative of **weighting.** Respondents choose the response that best fits them. These responses are weighted numerically. Depending upon the choices one makes, the **item weights** of selected responses are summed to yield a raw score; hence, the term, summated ratings.

An assumption made by researchers is that those persons who favor or disfavor gun control to varying degrees will select more or less intense responses for each question. Those strongly in favor of gun control and limiting firearms possession only to law enforcement officers and military personnel would tend to agree with items 1 and 4, and they would tend to disagree with the other items. Those favoring gun ownership and private use of firearms would tend to agree with items 2, 3, 5, and 6, and they would probably disagree with items 1 and 4. This scheme is not foolproof, however, since those favoring private ownership of firearms may not want small children to be exposed to them. Also, persons who agree that constitutional guarantees mandate private ownership and use of firearms may not agree that when guns are outlawed, only outlaws will have guns or that there is a strong relation between accessibility of firearms and violent crime.

A prevailing belief of researchers is that there is a fairly constant correspondence between the attitudes manifested by people and their behaviors. Therefore, it is often assumed that

$$\text{attitude } X \rightarrow \text{behavior } X'$$

where X is a particular attitude expressed and X' is the behavior that corresponds with that attitude. Thus, if some persons indicate strong prejudicial attitudes toward members of some minority group, it is assumed that they will probably discriminate or act differently toward those minorities. The attitude-action relationship is not consistent, however. Currently, considerable controversy exists about how accurately attitudinal measures forecast behaviors corresponding with those attitudes.

Police Professionalism Scale.   To illustrate the application of Likert scaling, we must begin with a nominal definition of some phenomenon. Suppose we wish to measure police officer professionalism. We might define police officer professionalism nominally as the adoption of a set of attitudes and values by police officers, where those attitudes and values are consistent with a professional ideology (Crank et al., 1987:1). Professionalization has been conceptualized as the process of legitimation an occupation goes through as it endeavors to improve its social status. Crank and his associates indicate that efforts toward conceptualizing police professionalism have focused upon recruitment and training practices as well as management policies of police departments (1987:1).

It is significant to note that a clear, concise nominal definition of police professionalism does not exist in the above paragraph. This is not intended to be critical of Crank et al., since their extensive research efforts have been designed to devise such a concept and measure it. The fact is that many nominal definitions, including the one for police professionalism, are elusive, vague, and nonspecific. We might suspect as much, considering our earlier attempt to define anxiety using the *Webster's New World Dictionary* as our source. Further, this author researched ten separate articles that studied police professionalism and in which that phrase was used in all article titles. No article contained a definition of police professionalism, not even a vague, elusive, or nonspecific one. It was as if everyone knew what it meant and it didn't need to be defined. Nevertheless, these articles discussed police professionalism at length, including factors associated with it, how it develops, and how it influences officer performance in the field.

However, from the statements about police professionalism provided by Crank et al., we can glean that police professionalism has something to do with rigorous selection and training procedures for police officers. Perhaps acquiring more education or achieving high scores on various fitness and situational tests is regarded by many as evidence of police professionalism.

In any case, once we have given a term a nominal definition, the next step is to give the term some substance through the creation of an operational definition. Regoli et al. (1987) attempted this particular task, although they were primarily interested in exploring the relation between police professionalism and cynicism. They devised various statements believed to be indicative of police professionalism, such as the following:

Police Professionalism Scale

1. I systematically read the professional journals (e.g., *Police Chief*).
2. I regularly attend professional meetings at the local level.
3. Although I would like to, I really don't read the police journals (e.g., *Police Chief*) too often.
4. Some other occupations are actually more important to society than mine is.

5. Other professions are actually more vital to society than mine.
6. The importance of being a police officer is sometimes overstressed.
7. There is really no way to judge fellow police officers' competence.
8. There is not much opportunity to judge how another police officer does his or her work.
9. My fellow police officers have a pretty good idea about each others' competence.

Thus, a strict operational definition of police professionalism would be "police professionalism is what the Regoli et al. police professionalism scale measures."

Accompanying each item might be the following responses and numerical weights:

Strongly agree	Agree	Undecided, probably agree	Undecided, probably disagree	Disagree	Strongly disagree
6	5	4	3	2	1

or

Strongly agree	Agree	Undecided, probably agree	Undecided, probably disagree	Disagree	Strongly disagree
1	2	3	4	5	6

These two response patterns are designed to accompany positively worded and negatively worded statements, such as "I like my job" or "I hate my job." Regarding the police professionalism scale above, items 1, 2, and 9 appear favorably worded, while the other items are somewhat negatively worded. If a police officer strongly agrees with statement 1, "I systematically read the professional journals," then we might interpret this response as a sign of the officer's professionalism or commitment to the profession of policing. Also, if the police officer's response is strong disagreement to item 7, "There is really no way to judge fellow officers' competence," this response suggests that "professional" criteria exist whereby officers may be evaluated objectively. We might interpret agreements with items 3, 4, 5, 6, 7, and 8 as indicative of low professionalism, since the importance of the police officer role compared with other professions and occupations is played down, or perhaps objective criteria do not exist to evaluate this role.

The weights associated with each response reflect different intensities of agreement or disagreement with these statements. This particular weight arrangement is a six-point response pattern. The reversed weights shown in the previous example are useful whenever we wish to interrupt the monotony of the same response pattern. Also, those who answer these statements may do so with little interest or enthusiasm. Sometimes, respondents don't read the statements carefully, and they rush through the questionnaire checking the first answers to all questions. A careful inspection of item weights associated with the responses they select may tell the researchers whether their responses are valid or whether they should be questioned. For instance, if someone says "Strongly agree" to the statement, "I love my job," and later, that same person says "Strongly agree" to the statement, "I hate my job," this suggests a problem. Specifically, it suggests a response set or set response, where respondents rush through their questionnaires and check the first responses they encounter. They do this simply to "get it over with quick." For all practical purposes, their responses to the questionnaire are worthless to the researcher, because they didn't take any interest in completing it and in giving truthful responses. This issue will be addressed later in the section dealing with measurement issues.

Returning to our example of police professionalism and the scale items that compose it, we have hypothetically assigned a six-point response pattern to the nine items on pages 340 and 341. This means that the most points one may receive per item answered is 6, while the least number of points is 1. If there are nine items that make up the scale of police professionalism, we may quickly calculate the range of raw scores officers may receive when they respond to these scale items. We may multiply the largest weight, 6, by the number of items on the scale. This is (6)(9 items) = 54. Multiplying the number of scale items by the smallest weight, 1, will give us (1)(9 items) = 9. If we designate 6 to be indicative of a high degree of professionalism and 1 to be indicative of a low degree of professionalism, then the range of responses for this particular set of items will be from 9 (low professionalism) to 54 (high professionalism).

For example, if ten officers respond to these nine items, they might receive the following raw scores: 14, 22, 25, 29, 32, 33, 33, 40, 44, and 49. These are ordinal-level scores, since they were derived from a Likert scale. These raw scores may be grouped into different categories (low professionalism, 9–25; medium or moderate professionalism, 26–35; and high professionalism, 36–54). This categorization is mostly arbitrary, depending upon the number of officers who respond and the overall raw scores they receive for this measure.

So far, what have we done to measure police professionalism?

1. We devised a nominal definition of police professionalism.
2. We created several items or statements that appeared to correlate highly with the nominal meaning of the term.
3. We devised a six-point response pattern for all items.
4. We assigned item weights to the different responses.
5. We administered the set of items to ten police officers.
6. We summed each officer's weights for the nine items and determined their total scores.
7. We devised four intensity categories to portray police professionalism, according to the distribution of their raw scores.

There is nothing magical about any of this. The items that have been created were literally the products of the researchers' thoughts. They formulated items that they believed would closely parallel what they meant by police professionalism. But this doesn't necessarily mean that they derived the best items or the only items.

Numbers of Items. This nine-item scale is only one of many scales we might construct to measure police professionalism or any other attitudinal variable. We might create 35 statements or 100 statements. We might even use one statement to measure this and other phenomena. We might furnish officers with the following statement: "I consider myself a true police professional." The response might be a simple "yes" or "no." Of course, not many police officers are going to say that they are not professional. We will expand the number of items used to measure any phenomenon in order to create a wider range of response over which these officers may be distributed. This will enable us to obtain some meaningful variation on this variable and correlate the raw scores with scores on other variables. There is no limit to the number of items researchers may use whenever they create Likert scales. Of course, larger numbers of items may wear out respondents. They may approach a 50-page questionnaire with apathy or resistance, whereas they might feel more comfortable with a 10-page or shorter questionnaire.

Forms of Response. The particular form of response for Likert scaling is not restricted to the agree-disagree variety. Any response pattern that can be gradated (very strong/very weak, increasing/decreasing, very positive/very negative, more/less) may be adapted to fit the Likert pattern. The most common response pattern is the agree–disagree format shown earlier, however.

There is little uniformity pertaining to the number of response categories, and there is no uniformity regarding the number of statements researchers may use to measure things. Decisions about the number of items and the particular response patterns to be used are made by the researcher. Consideration is made for the size of the group where the measure will be administered. If the researcher's intention is to administer the measure to thousands of people, then more statements will be required to render a desirable degree of precision regarding the raw scores obtained. Perhaps more responses per item will be required as well.

For example, if we expand the number of items from 9 to 25, then our range of response becomes $(1)(25) = 25$ (low) to $(6)(25) = 150$ (high). If we expand the number of items to 50, we have a range of from 50 to 300, using a six-point response pattern. Or we can devise a ten-point response pattern with ten items and have a low score of 10 and a high score of 100 $(1 \times 10$ and $10 \times 10)$.

Sometimes the Likert format may be used to characterize attitudes of persons toward particular issues or programs. Kaci and Tarrant (1988:192) studied the attitudes of prosecuting attorneys and probation departments toward diversion programs for persons charged with spousal abuse in domestic violence cases. They were able to solicit opinions from district attorneys' offices in two California counties concerning various attitudes toward diversion programs. They devised categories such as the following:

Very high rating of diversion, highly effective

Good opinion of diversion, somewhat effective

Guarded opinion of diversion, possibly effective

Totally negative opinion of diversion, ineffective program

No opinion of diversion

The proportion or percentage of responses of district attorneys were charted for each of these categories. Kaci and Tarrant found that a majority of district attorneys rated diversion programs as highly effective or somewhat effective, on the basis of these percentage distributions. This is a type of Likert pattern that appears to have some utility in portraying respondent opinions.

Another version of a Likert-type scale is the Multidimensional Anger Inventory devised by Judith Siegel (1985). Her inventory consists of 38 statements with a five-point response pattern per statement. Each response is weighted as follows: 1 = Completely undescriptive, 2 = Somewhat undescriptive, 3 = Descriptive, 4 = Rather descriptive, 5 = Completely descriptive. Siegel asked respondents to rate themselves on each of the following items:

————— 1. I tend to get angry more frequently than most people.

————— 2. Other people seem to get angrier than I do in similar circumstances.

————— 3. I harbor grudges that I don't tell anyone about.

————— 4. I try to get even when I am angry with someone.

————— 5. I am secretly quite critical of others.

————— 6. It is easy to make me angry.

————— 7. When I am angry with someone, I let that person know.

————— 8. I have met many people who are supposed to be experts who are not better than I.

————— 9. Something makes me angry almost every day.

————— 10. I often feel angrier than I should.

————— 11. I feel guilty about expressing my anger.

————— 12. When I am angry with someone, I take it out on whoever is around.

————— 13. Some of my friends have habits that annoy and bother me very much.

————— 14. I am surprised at how often I feel angry.

————— 15. Once I let people know I'm angry, I can put it out of my mind.

————— 16. People talk about me behind my back.

————— 17. At times, I feel angry for no specific reason.

————— 18. I can make myself angry about something in the past just by thinking about it.

————— 19. Even after I have expressed my anger, I have trouble forgetting about it.

————— 20. When I hide my anger from others, I think about it for a long time.

————— 21. People can bother me just by being around.

————— 22. When I get angry, I stay angry for hours.

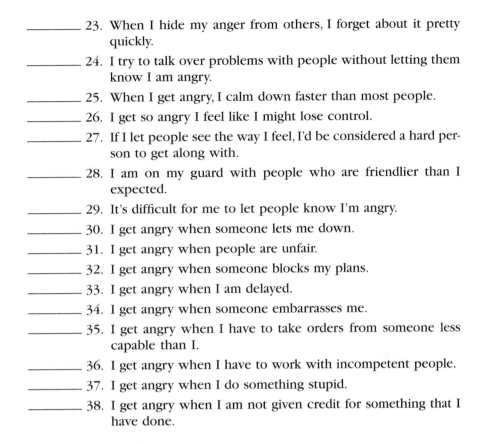

_____ 23. When I hide my anger from others, I forget about it pretty quickly.

_____ 24. I try to talk over problems with people without letting them know I am angry.

_____ 25. When I get angry, I calm down faster than most people.

_____ 26. I get so angry I feel like I might lose control.

_____ 27. If I let people see the way I feel, I'd be considered a hard person to get along with.

_____ 28. I am on my guard with people who are friendlier than I expected.

_____ 29. It's difficult for me to let people know I'm angry.

_____ 30. I get angry when someone lets me down.

_____ 31. I get angry when people are unfair.

_____ 32. I get angry when someone blocks my plans.

_____ 33. I get angry when I am delayed.

_____ 34. I get angry when someone embarrasses me.

_____ 35. I get angry when I have to take orders from someone less capable than I.

_____ 36. I get angry when I have to work with incompetent people.

_____ 37. I get angry when I do something stupid.

_____ 38. I get angry when I am not given credit for something that I have done.

Siegel has devised various subscales on this instrument to measure specific aspects of anger, such as hostile anger and situations that evoke anger. Raw scores received by respondents can be compared with other variables, such as gender, prior record, or probationer/parolee designation. Researchers such as Delores E. Craig-Morehead have used this scale to measure anger levels of inmates. Craig-Morehead found, for instance, that anger levels vary according to the conviction offense of inmates in a large penitentiary in a Midwestern state. Interestingly, property offenders had the highest anger scores compared with other inmates in her study, including those convicted of violent crimes.

Meaning of Raw Scores Derived from Likert Scales.   Provided that the items on a Likert scale are true indicators of the phenomenon to be measured, what do the **raw scores** mean that are yielded? Raw scores by themselves mean relatively little. Raw attitudinal scores are of the greatest value whenever they are compared with one another. Thus, persons who receive raw scores of 50 or lower on some attitudinal scale may be predicted to behave differently in some social situation compared with those who receive raw scores greater than 50.

A hypothetical example illustrates how we might use scores from a Likert scale. Suppose we administer our nine-item police professionalism scale to a random sample of 100 police officers of the Los Angeles Police Department, and that they receive raw scores ranging from 9 to 54. Further suppose that we determine that approximately 50 of these officers have scores of 32 or lower, while the other half of our sample has scores above 32. If we decide to see whether professionalism is associated with the rate of citizen complaints filed against these police officers, we might devise a table such as the one shown in Table 10.2.

Table 10.2 is a hypothetical cross-tabulation of police professionalism with citizen complaint filings against officers. A cross-tabulation occurs when two or more variables are compared in tabular form. One variable is placed across the top of the table, while the other variable is located down the left-hand side. The more influential variable is placed across the top. In this case, police professionalism is believed to effect changes in citizen complaint filings. Thus, it is placed across the top of the table. Police professionalism has been divided or dichotomized into two categories, according to "high" or 33 points or more on the police professionalism scale and "low" or 32 or fewer points on the scale. The number of citizen complaint filings is depicted down the left-hand side. Complaint filings by citizens have been divided into two categories, high and low, based on three or more filings or two or fewer filings.

Researchers looking at this table will understand that police professionalism influences citizen complaint filings. Had we placed citizen complaint filings across the top of the table and police professionalism down the left-hand side, this may have meant that we believe that citizen complaint filings determine or influence one's police professionalism. We are merely following an accepted conventional tabular arrangement here by placing the more influential variable across the top.

According to Table 10.2, we might expect to find that officers with high professionalism scores tend to have low numbers of citizen complaints filed against them, whereas officers with low professionalism scores tend to have high numbers of citizen complaints filed against them. In Table 10.2, 45 out of 50 officers with high professionalism scores have low numbers of citizen complaints filed against them, while 35 out of 50 officers with low professionalism scores have high numbers of citizen complaints filed against them. These find-

TABLE 10.2 Hypothetical Distribution of Citizen Complaints Filed Against Police Officers Who Have High and Low Amounts of Professionalism

	Police professionalism[a]		Totals
	High (33+)	Low (32 or less)	
High citizen complaint filings (3+)	5	35	40
Low citizen complaint filing (2 or fewer)	45	15	60
Totals	50	50	100

[a]Measured by nine-point professionalism scale, where 32 or lower means low professionalism, while 33 or higher means high professionalism.

ings strengthen our belief that we have measured police professionalism with these items. In short, the more professional the police officers, the less likely they will engage in the types of behaviors that cause citizen complaints. This is one way these Likert-type scores can be used and interpreted.

The cutting points we used to determine high and low police professionalism and high and low numbers of citizen complaint filings were not magically determined. If our 100 police officers are distributed widely from scores of 9 to 54, we can use the point that divides them into halves as our cutting point. Perhaps that dividing line is the raw score of 32: half of our officers are below this point and the other half of them are above this point.

Also, suppose we tally the number of complaints for all officers and determine that there is an average of three complaints filed against officers during the year. We might note that some officers have ten complaints filed against them, while some officers have no complaints filed against them. Thus, we might arbitrarily say that those officers who have three or more complaints filed against them will be in the "high complaint" group, while those receiving two or fewer complaints will be in the "low complaint" group. This distinction will enable us to cross-tabulate these results as shown in Table 10.2. Thus, the five officers with high professionalism scores also have high numbers of complaints filed against them, or three or more. The 45 officers with high professionalism scores also have low numbers of complaints filed against them, or two or fewer.

"Don't Know" or "Undecided" Responses. The response scenarios provided in the earlier examples did not contain "Don't know" or "Undecided" response options. The major concession to the "Undecided" category was two middle-of-the-road categories designated as "Undecided, but probably agree" and "Undecided, but probably disagree." This arrangement was deliberate. Typically, many Likert scales contain "Undecided" or "Don't know" categories. Thus, we might see a response pattern like this:

Strongly agree	Agree	Don't know or Undecided	Disagree	Strongly disagree
5	4	3	2	1

Notice that the "Undecided" category has been "weighted" with a "3." The same would be true of a "Don't know" response. Some of the social sciences have reported a general trend in America toward noncommittal responses or middle-of-the-road opinions. Thus, if persons are presented with a "Don't know" or "Undecided" option, they will probably take it. It is a safe response. Unfortunately, it has no weight or value. Persons who honestly don't know or are undecided about some statement are neither in agreement or disagreement with it. When these categories are assigned weights, the resulting point totals or raw scores lose some of their meaning.

Suppose someone responds to a scale with 10 items, where the five-point response pattern shown earlier is used. A possible score range of 10 to 50 exists.

It is possible for someone to obtain a score of 30 strictly on the basis of checking the "Undecided" response category for each of the ten scale items. This score is contrasted with others near it, where persons have received individual item weights of 4, 5, or 2. These other weights are meaningful, reflecting the intensity of attitude og the respondent. Rather than run the risk of winding up with meaningless "30" scores in a scale such as this, the "Undecided, but probably agree" and "Undecided, but probably disagree" options are created. This gives persons an opportunity to say they are undecided, but it also gives them a chance to lean one way or another in terms of their attitudinal intensity.

This means forcing them to make a choice one way or another. While many respondents apparently have no serious objections to these forced choices, a few respondents have been known to write "Don't know" or "Undecided" in capital letters in the margins of their questionnaires, or perhaps a string of profanity in response to these forced-choice scenarios. The presumption made by researchers who study attitudes, however, is that people generally have attitudes, one way or another, about various issues. The "Undecided, probably agree/disagree" choices simply make it easier for them to make a middle-of-the-road decision with some degree of commitment. Further, it permits researchers to give meaningful weights to these middle categories.

Several exotic techniques have been proposed to deal with "Don't know" or "Undecided" responses, such as assigning these items the "average" weight otherwise assigned to the other items where persons actually express "agree" or "disagree" choices. This is tantamount to putting words in the respondents' mouths and creating artificial scores for them. Thus, this alternative is discouraged. It is preferable to provide "forced choice" responses and risk offending a few respondents while obtaining meaningful responses rather than to use "Don't know" categories and assign meaningless weights to these choices.

What do you do when respondents leave certain items blank? First, don't put words in their mouths by creating artificial responses for them based upon their responses to the completed items. There are different kinds of "missing item" situations. Did the respondent skip one item in a ten-page questionnaire? Did the respondent skip one page of a ten-page questionnaire? Did the respondent skip four pages of a ten-page questionnaire? Any respondent who skips one or more pages when completing a questionnaire is rushing through it and probably not taking it seriously. One page skipped may be accidental. Two or more pages skipped represent apathy and carelessness.

The recommended solution when one page is skipped is to survey the contents of the page. If a portion of a scale is printed on the page, then that scale should be dropped from the questionnaire. If *several* key questions are on the page, such as age, years of education, gender, and socioeconomic status, it might be a good idea to throw out the questionnaire completely. It is better not to have the additional questionnaire as a part of your collected data, where strong evidence exists that the respondent did not take the study seriously. Skipped pages or numerous skipped items should tell you something. Dropping such questionnaires from your study makes your study better and more reliable anyway.

The recommended solution when one or two items are skipped is to determine if those items are a part of a scale. If they are part of a scale, drop the scale from the questionnaire. This type of omission frequently accounts for odd sample analyses in articles and reports. A researcher may indicate that 600 persons were surveyed and responded. But a table included in the report may show income averages for 590 persons. This probably means that ten persons did not disclose their incomes to the investigator. The same thing may happen with other variables in other tables. Don't be disturbed when reading reports and different sample sizes are reported for different tabular analyses. Omissions of questions by respondents are common occurrences.

Strengths and Advantages of Likert Scales.   Some of the major advantages of summated rating scales include the following:

1. Likert scales are easy to construct and interpret. Because researchers combine their professional experience with logic to derive items from an abstract theoretical universe of some trait, it is not too difficult to construct a questionnaire as a measure. Researchers are at liberty to word statements derived from theory in any manner they choose, provided that they adhere to some logical standard of continuity between the trait being measured and the items used to measure it. Scoring Likert scales is easy also. Further, statements can be worded negatively or positively, and numerical weights can be assigned to any common Likert response format. It is a simple matter to sum the responses to individual statements and derive a total score or raw score that may be compared with other scores from the same scale. The larger (or smaller) the score, the more (or less) the subject possesses the attribute being measured, according to the logic underlying this scaling procedure.

2. Likert scaling is the most common scaling format used in criminology and criminal justice. Likert summated rating measures are most frequently applied in social research. The ease of application and simplicity of interpretation are factors that make this scaling procedure especially attractive. The popularity of this measurement form is evidenced by its widespread conventional use in criminology and criminal justice.

3. Likert scaling is flexible. The flexibility of these scales is unattained by any other attitudinal scaling procedure yet devised. Researchers are at liberty to include as many or as few items in their measures as they choose. Because each item is presumed to count equally in the measure of some phenomenon, increasing the number of statements or responses to statements will increase the instrument's ability to disclose differences in the trait measured as group size increases.

4. Summated rating scales lend themselves to ordinal-level measurement. Numerous ordinal-level statistical procedures exist for assessing variations and patterns in social and psychological phenomena.

5. Likert scales are similar to other forms of attitude measurement such as Thurstone scaling or Guttman scaling. Inspections of scores derived by other scaling procedures show that Likert scaling yields raw scores that are roughly equivalent with those obtained by alternative means.

Weaknesses of Likert Scales. Weaknesses of Likert scales include the following:

1. There is no consistent meaning that can be attached to the raw scores derived by such measurement. There is little that can be said about raw scores by themselves. Raw scores vary according to the number of statements devised and the extensiveness of response patterns used. This adds to the inconsistency of things as well. Summated rating measures are primarily useful when they permit comparisons to be made between individuals.

2. It is assumed that each item in the measure has identical weight in relation to every other item. This is not necessarily a valid assumption. Certain statements compared with other statements may have greater meaning or relevance to the trait being measured. Different persons may possess a given attitude to the same degree, although they may respond differently to common items on the measure.

3. Persons receiving the same score on a measure do not necessarily possess the trait or attitude to the same degree. This means that our measures are never as precise as they could be. Raw scores are crude estimates of people's locations on intensity continuums.

4. The validity of summated ratings is questionable. Because the process of deducing items from an abstract universe of traits is a logical one, the possibility always exists that some items may be wrongly included in the measuring instrument at any given time. How do we know that we are measuring what we say we are measuring? The validity of our measures is generally determined by comparing score results with manifest behaviors of respondents in prediction situations. This is not an infallible process.

Thurstone Scales and Equal-Appearing Intervals

A second type of measuring technique is **Thurstone scaling.** Another term for it is equal-appearing interval scaling (Thurstone and Chave, 1929). This technique probably rates second in overall social science usage to Likert scaling, although probably fewer than 10 percent of all researchers might be inclined to use it. Thurstone scaling differs from the Likert summated rating format by supplying each attitudinal statement with a specific scale value that stands for the intensity of the statement itself. Thus, instead of deriving a total score from accumulated item weights in the case of Likert scales, Thurstone scales would use intensity values associated with two or three items selected by respondents from a larger list of items. Consider the following five statements:

(10.5) 1. Life imprisonment might be an acceptable punishment for child sexual abusers.

(2.1) 2. Convicted child sexual abusers should be treated like any other convicted felons.

(3.4) 3. Most child sexual abusers suffer from psychological problems and should be hospitalized rather than imprisoned.

(1.8)   4. I would allow former convicted child sexual abusers to work as cus-
todians in large apartment complexes with large numbers of children.

(8.3)   5. Child sexual abuse is itself an aggravating factor in any prosecution for
child sexual abuse.

These five statements are hypothetical items that might be used to measure district attorneys' attitudes toward prosecuting child sexual abusers. These items are designed to reflect different intensities or degrees to which persons hold one view or another toward some idea, issue, person, or group. The values in parentheses are item weights or intensities assigned through a simple, but rather elaborate, judging procedure. In this hypothetical example, the larger the value, the more intense one's position toward the prosecution of child sexual abusers. Persons who would select item 1, for example, would probably press the prosecution of alleged child sexual abusers more vigorously than those who might select item 4.

Consider several statements designed to measure degree of racial prejudice:

1. I would consider living next door to members of race *X*.
2. I would consider marrying a member of race *X*.
3. I would bar members of race *X* from my church.

It is apparent that each of these items reflects a different degree of acceptance or hostility toward members of race *X*. We might consider the most accepting item as 2, where one might agree to marry persons from race *X*. The least accepting item might be 3, where respondents would not permit members of race *X* to belong to their churches.

Therefore, instead of furnishing respondents with a questionnaire consisting of various Likert-type items with which they must agree or disagree, researchers using Thurstone scales would provide them with a list of items from which they would choose two or three that they agree with the most. These items would already have weights assigned that reflect each item's intensity.

How do researchers devise these Thurstone scales? Thurstone recommended that investigators begin by creating a large number of statements that they believe closely correlate with the trait to be measured. Thurstone recommended that about 100 statements should be constructed. Next, at least 25 judges should inspect these items and sort them into various intensity categories. Thurstone recommended 25 judges, although he later indicated that fewer judges could accomplish the task adequately. The intensity categories into which these items might be sorted would consist of seven, nine, or eleven categories.

Who are the "judges" and how are the categories conceived? Originally, Thurstone envisioned using university professors who taught psychology courses as judges. He believed they would be able to sort items of different intensities into appropriate categories, largely because of their training and expertise in attitudinal measurement. Since it was quite difficult to get these individuals to perform such sorting chores, this qualification was later relaxed. Currently, anyone may be a judge and sort these items, including introductory students in criminology courses. Sorting was simplified by providing judges with boxes containing various numbers of slots. Judges would be handed items individually typed on strips of paper. They would be asked to read each item and place it in one of seven, nine, or eleven categories, ranging from "low intensity" to "high intensity." These slots or categories would be numbered, and it would be easy to calculate the average for each item, according to the categories it was assigned by the judges.

Consider the following simplified example. Suppose we were to ask 25 judges to sort 10 statements into seven categories. We might designate each statement by letters, including items A, B, C, D, E, F, G, H, I, and J. We would hand each judge slips of paper containing each statement. Each judge would sort the statements into the various categories or slots, according to each item's intensity (in the judge's opinion or "judgment"). Following is hypothetical statement A and the number of judges who sorted it into various categories.

Statement A

Category	Number of Judges Placing Statement A in Category	Category Multiplied by Number of Judges
1	5	5
2	2	4
3	6	18
4	8	32
5	3	15
6	0	0
7	1	7
Totals	25	81

Hypothetical statement A, whatever it might be, has been rated by 25 judges and placed into one of seven categories as shown. The categories into which it has been placed by these judges are used to "weight" statement A. Thus, category numbers are multiplied by the number of judges placing statement A into those categories. These are the products shown in the far right column. To determine an item's "average weight," we compute a simple average, or $81/25 = 3.2$. Statement A's weight is 3.2.

After all items have been sorted and assigned numerical weights, it is possible to select approximately 20 or 30 of these statements for use in our final questionnaire. Some statements will have weights in the 6 to 7 range, while others will have weights in the 1 to 2 range. The objective in our statement selections is to include statements having weights that span the spectrum of them, from 1 to 7. For instance, suppose we select the following statements shown in Table 10.3 from an original list of 100 statements.

The different weights accompanying the 20 items in Table 10.3 are derived from judges' ratings measured by us earlier. Note that there is a broad diversity of weights ranging from a low of 1.2 to a high of 6.8.

The next step is to ask a sample of respondents to select two or three statements from this list that best reflect their position or attitudes or sentiments.

TABLE 10.3 Twenty Hypothetical Statements Taken from an Original List of 100 Statements, with Item Weights

Statement	Weight	Statement	Weight
1	6.8	11	3.9
2	6.2	12	3.4
3	5.9	13	3.2
4	5.6	14	2.8
5	5.2	15	2.7
6	5.0	16	2.2
7	4.8	17	1.9
8	4.6	18	1.8
9	4.2	19	1.6
10	4.1	20	1.2

Thurstone recommended that respondents should select at least three statements. Theoretically, if these statements are accurate reflections of one's sentiments, then persons will select statements having similar weights. For instance, persons who select item 1 as closest to their opinion about something might also be expected to select items having weights close to that item's weight, or 6.8. These items are nearest the person's attitude. It is unlikely that persons will select item 1, with a weight of 6.8, and item 20, having a weight of 1.2, since these weights are at such different points on the intensity spectrum. According to these different weights, they indicate basically different points of view.

Suppose a female respondent selects items 1, 5, and 6 as the three statements that best suit her. We would take the weights associated with these statements and average them. Respectively, the weights would be 6.8, 5.2, and 5.0. Averaging these values, we would have (6.8 + 5.2 + 5.0)/3, or 17/3 = 5.7. Thus, 5.7 would be the final raw score we would use for this person.

Equal-Appearing Nature of Intervals. Individual raw scores may be compared with one another and are theoretically reflective of differences in the degree or intensity of the attitude expressed. Thurstone believed that the weight assigned each scale item is a better way (e.g., compared with Likert scaling) of assessing attitudinal variations among people and plotting their differences along some attitudinal continuum. One assumption he made was that the resulting weights would enable researchers to approximate the interval level of measurement with the collected data. He used the term **equal-appearing intervals** to describe positions of these points along a continuum. Thurstone's scale of attitudinal intensity would look something like this:

Low 1 ——— 2 ——— 3 ——— 4 ——— 5 ——— 6 ——— 7 High

Subsequently, Thurstone changed his mind about the equal-appearing nature of spacing between items on these scales. He said that the interval level of measurement would be approached or approximated rather than actually achieved by such a scaling method. A subsequent comparison of Likert and Thurstone scales and their relative accuracy for measuring the same variables was made by Edwards (1957). Edwards reported no significant differences in the accuracy of the two scaling methods. Therefore, the greater time and effort required to formulate Thurstone scaling doesn't result in greater accuracy of attitudinal measurement, as Thurstone had originally anticipated. Likert scaling is much easier to administer and has accuracy equivalent with that of Thurstone scaling.

Three points should be made about applying Thurstone scaling in criminological research. First, it is not acceptable to place item weights on questionnaires so that respondents can see them. Many researchers who use Thurstone scaling to measure attitudes often include such weights, since this makes the scoring process much easier for them. But to include these weights conspicuously causes respondents to focus more upon the weights than upon the items. Some bias may be incurred as a result.

A second problem pertains to the items subsequently selected by respondents as most typical of them. There are some disturbing patterns that may result. For instance, suppose persons A and B chose the following items as most typical of them from Table 10.3: 1, 6, and 20. These items have weights of 6.8, 5.0, and 1.2 respectively. These weights sum to 13.0, and the average for persons A and B would be 13/3 = 4.3. Next, suppose persons C and D picked items 8, 9, and 10, with respective weights of 4.6, 4.2, and 4.1. These weights, summed, equal 12.9. The average of these three weights would be 12.9/3 = 4.3. The two average weights for persons A and B and for persons C and D would be 4.3. However, if we compare the actual distribution of weights for both pairs of subjects, it is apparent that there is less homogeneity in response weights among C and D compared with A and B. The greater the differences among item weights selected by various persons, the greater the unreliability of the Thurstone scale. It is presumed that no such wide variations among weights will occur. However, they do occur occasionally.

Finally, when Thurstone scaling is used, some researchers are inclined to believe that they have actually achieved the interval level of measurement with their scales. This is not so. The scale scores are at best ordinal.

Advantages and Strengths of Thurstone Scaling.   Thurstone scales have the following advantages and strengths:

1. Thurstone-derived scales enable researchers to differentiate between large numbers of people regarding their attitudinal positions. When item weights are averaged, a greater variety of attitudinal positions is revealed compared with Likert-type scale values. This would seemingly have the advantage of making more precise distinctions between people according to the attitudes they possess.

2. Another argument in favor of using Thurstone-derived scales is that judges—usually professional persons and sometimes students—have achieved a high degree of agreement on the items used, and hence, they perform a screening function by eliminating the bad or poor items that

produce little or no agreement. Researchers might apply such scales with increased confidence that the items used have a greater claim to reliability than would be the case in Likert scale construction.

Weaknesses of Thurstone Scales. Thurstone scaling procedures have the following weaknesses and limitations:

1. Thurstone scales are time-consuming to construct. Investigators must solicit judges who must take the time to sort numerous items. Then scale values must be determined. Then respondents' item selections must be averaged in order to place them on some attitudinal **intensity continuum.**

2. It is possible to derive identical scores based upon widely divergent attitudinal views. This is the problem noted previously, where two different persons might receive identical scale scores, but where the scores are made up of widely dispersed scale items with different intensity weights. Do these persons with the same scores actually hold the same attitudes to the same degree? We don't know. The fact that greater variation in score values results from one subject compared with another subject would seem to place the validity of this scale in question.

3. There is no way of controlling the influence of a judge's bias in item sorting. The personal biases of judges might interfere with their objectivity in making item categorizations. However, repeatedly Thurstone scaling has yielded a high degree of consistency among judges when attitudinal items have been sorted.

4. In reality, Thurstone scale values are no better at predicting behavior than Likert-based measures. Because Likert measures are so much easier to construct and score, the logical preference would be to use Likert scaling over Thurstone-derived methods.

■ OTHER TYPES OF SCALING PROCEDURES

Several other types of attitudinal scaling procedures exist. It is beyond the scope of this book to cover all other types of procedures, but six alternative procedures will be mentioned here because of their utility in criminology and criminal justice. These include (1) Guttman scaling or the Cornell Technique, (2) the semantic differential, (3) the Q-sort, (4) the Sellin-Wolfgang Index, (5) the Salient Factor Score (SFS 81), and (6) Greenwood's Rand Seven-Factor Index.

Guttman Scaling

Another scaling method is called **Guttman scaling** or cumulative scaling. Other popular terms that refer to it are the **Cornell technique** and **scalogram analysis.** Guttman (1944) devised a method of scaling that permits researchers to determine whether the items they use in their scales are actually unidimensional. **Unidimensionality** means that the instrument items measure the same dimension of the same phenomenon. Thus, a **unidimensional scale** would consist of several items that would assess one, and only one, dimension of an attitude.

By comparison, Likert and Thurstone scales are **multidimensional scales**, since several different dimensions are measured by various items included on these scales. The police professionalism scale, for instance, contained items that tapped whether officers read police journals, whether assessments of officer competence can be made, and whether officers attend professional meetings. These are obviously different dimensions of professionalism, and it is possible for someone to agree with one item but not the others. With Guttman scaling, however, it is assumed that all items reflect a single dimension of the trait measured. Applied to our police professionalism example, items on a Guttman scale of police professionalism might focus upon professional meeting attendance, including such factors as how often such meetings are attended, whether papers are presented at those meetings, whether the police officers hold various positions at those meetings, and so on. All items would focus on one specific dimension of professionalism.

Edwards (1957:172) defines a unidimensional scale as follows: "In the case of attitude statements, we might say that this means that a person with a more favorable attitude score than another person must also be just as favorable or more favorable in his response to every statement in the set than the other person. When responses to a set of attitude statements meet this requirement, the set of statements is said to constitute a *unidimensional scale*" [emphasis in original].

Using aspects of the **Bogardus social distance scale**, suppose we were to ask respondents to either agree or disagree with the following five statements:

1. I would marry a member of race *X*.
2. I would allow a member of race *X* to attend my church.
3. I would allow a member of race *X* to live in my neighborhood.
4. I would allow a member of race *X* to live in my community.
5. I would allow a member of race *X* to live in my country.

All of these statements are indicative of the amount of social distance we will permit or accept between ourselves and members of race *X*. Guttman would argue that if we agree with item 1, it makes sense that we would also agree with items 2, 3, 4, and 5. Guttman said that if we assign a "1" to all agreements, a person's score on this scale of five items would be 5. Knowing the score of 5 would enable us to predict the person's responses to all items. Knowing the score on the scale is 4 would allow us to predict their responses as well. We would probably say that the person with a score of 4 picked items 2 through 5 and disagreed with item 1. Knowing a person's score is 1 would mean agreement with item 5 only. Using these five statements, Guttman scaling or scalogram analysis may be illustrated. Table 10.4 shows these five statements of different attitudinal intensity for 15 persons. We have provided hypothetical responses for all 15 persons according to whether they agree or disagree with each item.

The far left-hand column in Table 10.4 shows each individual, numbered from 1 to 15. The next five columns show x's for either agreement or disagree-

TABLE 10.4 Illustration of the Guttman Cornell Technique[a]

Individual	Statement 1 A	Statement 1 D	Statement 2 A	Statement 2 D	Statement 3 A	Statement 3 D	Statement 4 A	Statement 4 D	Statement 5 A	Statement 5 D	Score
1	x		x		x		x		x		5
2	x		x		x		x		x		5
3		x	x		x		x		x		4
4		x	x		x		x		x		4
5		x		x	x		x		x		3
6		x		x	x		x		x		3
7		x		x		x	x		x		2
8		x		x		x	x		x		2
9		x		x		x		x	x		1
10		x		x		x		x	x		1
11		x		x		x		x	x		1
12		x		x		x		x	x		1
13		x		x		x		x		x	0
14		x		x		x		x		x	0
15		x		x		x		x		x	0

[a]The horizontal lines (dashes) in the body of the table are defined as "cutting points" for each statement.

ment for each of the five items listed across the top of the table. In the far right-hand column of the table are total scale scores, ranging from a "high" of 5 to a "low" of 0. Horizontal lines have been drawn underneath the pattern of agreements for each item. When agreements end, lines are drawn. These are cutting points based upon how these 15 persons have responded to the five items. The statements have been arranged in the table, from left to right, according to "most intense" to "least intense." Thus, persons who agree with item 1 will likely agree with the other four items. This is the case for persons 1 and 2. However, persons 3 and 4 do not agree with items 1 and 2. But they do agree with item 4. They also agree with the remaining items of lesser intensity. When items vary in a gradated fashion, such as those five items in Table 10.4, Guttman calls the scale a perfectly reproducible one. Reproducible scales are those where one's individual item responses can be reproduced fairly accurately with a knowledge of one's overall scale score. A perfect, error-free response pattern is illustrated in Table 10.5.

Few perfectly reproducible scales actually exist in reality, however. Thus, Guttman devised a coefficient of reproducibility, which would enable him to calculate the amount of error involved in reproducing any individual's response pattern to a set of items through **reproducible scales.** This would ultimately tell Guttman whether he was measuring a single dimension of the variable or whether multiple dimensions were being measured. What does a scalogram with

TABLE 10.5 Error-Free Scalogramatic Presentation

	Statement[a]					
	(Most Intense)			(Least Intense)		
Individual	*1*	*2*	*3*	*4*	*5*	Score
1	+	+	+	+	+	5
2	−	+	+	+	+	4
3	−	−	+	+	+	3
4	−	−	−	+	+	2
5	−	−	−	−	+	1

[a]A plus indicates acceptance or agreement with statement; a minus, rejection or disagreement with statement.

errors look like? Table 10.6 shows a pattern of responses with several errors for a sample of two persons.

In this small-scale example, two persons have identical scale scores of 4. However, notice that person 1 has agreed (indicated by a +) with items 1, 2, 4, and 5 but has disagreed with item 3. By the same token, person 2 has agreed with items 1, 3, 4, and 5 but has disagreed with item 2. These are errors, according to Guttman. We have circled them and will later refer to such errors in the computation of the **coefficient of reproducibility:**

$$\text{Coefficient of reproducibility} = 1 - \frac{\text{number of errors}}{\text{number of responses}}$$

where the number of responses = the number of people times the number of statements. A larger-scale example illustrates this computation more clearly. Suppose we observe a response pattern to five items for ten people as shown in Table 10.7, in which three errors have been circled. In order to detect errors, we usually arrange persons by ranking their overall scale scores. Persons who have the same scores can be moved upward or downward among one another in order to minimize errors. Thus, in Table 10.7, persons 2, 3, and 4 can be moved upward or downward in relation to each other to minimize errors. Note what would happen if we switched persons 2 and 3. Two errors in their response pat-

TABLE 10.6 Scalogramatic Presentation of Errors

	Statement[a]					
	(Most Intense)			(Least Intense)		
Individual	*1*	*2*	*3*	*4*	*5*	Score
1	+	+	⊖	+	+	4
2	+	⊖	+	+	+	4

[a]A plus indicates acceptance or agreement; a minus, rejection or disagreement. Circled responses indicate errors.

TABLE 10.7 Error Illustration of Scalogram Analysis

| | Statement[a] | | | | | |
| | (Most Intense) | | | (Least Intense) | | |
Individual	1	2	3	4	5	Score
1	+	+	+	+	+	5
2	+	⊖	+	+	+	4
3	−	+	+	+	+	4
4	−	+	+	+	+	4
5	−	−	+	+	+	3
6	−	−	+	+	+	3
7	−	⊕	−	−	+	2
8	−	−	−	⊕	+	2
9	−	−	−	⊕	−	1
10	−	−	−	−	⊕	1
Errors	0	2	0	2	1	

[a]A plus indicates acceptance or agreement; a minus, rejection or disagreement. Circled responses indicate errors.

terns would occur instead of one. Suffice it to say that the way they are presently arranged yields minimal errors in their response patterns. If we were to draw imaginary horizontal lines underneath each item cutting point, minuses (−) above those lines and pluses (+) below those lines would be errors. These are illustrated in Table 10.7. A total of five errors are shown in this table and have been circled. We may compute the coefficient of reproducibility as follows:

$$\text{Coefficient of reproducibility} = 1 - \frac{5}{(10)(5)}$$
$$= 1 - \frac{5}{50}$$
$$= 1 - 0.10 = .90.$$

The coefficient of reproducibility would be .90 in this case. This would mean that we can reproduce these persons' individual scores with 90 percent accuracy. Guttman believed that 90 percent is an acceptable cut-off point, and that coefficients below 90 percent were simply nonreproducible. Later, he changed his mind somewhat and allowed unidimensionality to be declared if scales could be reproduced with 80 percent accuracy. He called these quasi-reproducible scales. Apparently, not too many researchers were developing unidimensional scales with reproducibility coefficients of .90 or higher and this rigorous standard was relaxed somewhat.

Guttman believed that unidimensional scales are superior to multidimensional scales for several reasons. First, if we really develop a true measure of something, then the scores yielded by the measure should reflect the attribute consistently. Also, if several dimensions are being tapped by the measure, it is entirely possible that items from some other attitudinal universe (the imaginary place from which items are derived or thought of by researchers in their construction of scale items) may be included in our multidimensional scales. Therefore, our multidimensional measures, including Likert and Thurstone scales, may suffer some inaccuracy. This is a debatable point and one beyond the scope of this text.

The reality of the situation suggests that most attitudes are multidimensional anyway. If someone is satisfied with their work, for instance, they usually are satisfied with it because of several desirable features, such as good working hours, long lunch breaks, good supervision, extensive fringe benefits, good work content, challenging tasks, good work associates, and reasonable commuting distances. Presently, it is unknown how extensively Guttman scaling is used in criminology and criminal justice. An inspection of a wide assortment of current criminal justice and criminology journals shows several articles where Guttman scaling procedures are used, however.

Advantages and Strengths of Guttman Scaling. Some of the advantages and strengths of Guttman scaling include the following:

1. Guttman scaling demonstrates the unidimensionality of items in an attitudinal measure. Guttman considers this feature of scalogram analysis desirable, although it remains to be seen whether Guttman scaling yields scores that are any more accurate compared with Likert or Thurstone scale scores.

2. Assuming a scalable set of items used in an attitudinal measure, the researcher is in a good position to identify inconsistencies in responses of subjects and possible untruthful replies. This desirable feature could enhance a researcher's confidence in the quality of information furnished by respondents.

3. Guttman's procedure is relatively easy to use when applied to small numbers of items. However, when the number of items exceeds 12, the technique becomes unwieldy.

4. A person's response pattern may be reproduced with a knowledge of one's total raw score on the scale. Likert and Thurstone scale scores are not reproducible, although this should not detract from their usefulness as attitudinal measures.

Disadvantages and Weaknesses of Guttman Scaling. The following are some of the weaknesses of Guttman scaling:

1. The Guttman scaling technique fails to provide as extensive an attitudinal continuum as the Likert and/or Thurstone methods. Thus, if we were to attempt to apply Guttman scaling to a sample of 100 or more persons, there would be an excessive number of tied scores. The error rate for these tied scores would be quite difficult to determine, and the researcher would not know whether the scale items were truly reproducible.

2. The Guttman procedure is most easily applicable to situations where the researcher has few items with dichotomous responses. Although Guttman scales may be constructed where there are more than two responses, the complexities of scoring such instruments outweigh their usefulness as unidimensional measures.

The Semantic Differential

The **semantic differential** consists of a series of bipolar characteristics, such as hot–cold, popular–unpopular, witty–dull, cold–warm, sociable–unsociable. Osgood (1965) says that the semantic differential is a useful measure of psychological, social, and physical objects to various respondents. According to these researchers, the semantic differential should represent three basic dimensions of a person's attitude toward another person, group, or object. These dimensions are (1) potency, the strength or physical attraction of the object; (2) evaluation, the favorableness or unfavorableness of the object; and (3) activity, the degree of movement of the object. These researchers originally devised a list of 50 pairs of terms, called scales, and arranged them on a continuum, such as:

```
                              Neutral
  Witty  ——————————————————————————————————————  Dull
            1     2     3     4     5     6     7
  Friendly ————————————————————————————————————  Unfriendly
            1     2     3     4     5     6     7
```

and so on. Persons responding to the semantic differential would check the point on each of the continuums which described their particular feelings toward the object or person or group. The marks can be scored easily.

Criminologists might apply the semantic differential and make up terms to suit their particular needs. Studies of juvenile delinquents may make use of the semantic differential to evaluate the desirability or repulsion of school or peer groups. Personality assessments can also be made. Subjects are asked to portray themselves as they believe they are at present, and how they would like to view themselves in the future. Treatment programs in community corrections agencies might benefit from such applications, since insight may be gained about various clients. The primary usefulness of the semantic differential is to assess the subject's perception of the attractiveness of social and personal objects according to several dimensions. This assessment, in turn, may lead to specifying reasons for certain behaviors manifested in relation to those objects or groups or persons, to the extent that attitudes and behaviors coincide with reality.

Q-Sort

The **Q-sort** is a variation of Thurstone scaling. It is seldom used in research. A survey of the *Criminal Justice Abstracts* found four articles in which the Q-sort was used as a methodological tool between 1970 and 1999. Using the Q-sort involves presenting research subjects with a number of slips of paper or cards.

These slips of paper or cards contain descriptors or statements which each respondent is asked to rate. Respondents are asked to sort these descriptors or statements into various categories, ranging from "strong" to "weak" or "high" to "low." Depending upon how the respondents sort the statements or descriptors, individual scores can be assigned to each subject, and they can be differentiated from one another for possible experimental purposes.

An early application of the Q-sort involved a study of juvenile offenders committed to Japanese training schools for short terms. The delinquents were compared with nondelinquents of comparable age. The results of an attitude test indicated that the average test scores for nondelinquents were somewhat higher than those for delinquents. Juveniles were given several items and asked to sort them according to how they were viewed by their parents and others, either positively or negatively. The results of the Q-sort test revealed a significant difference between nondelinquents and delinquents in how they are viewed by their parents and other persons (Hashimoto et al., 1968).

The National Council on Crime and Delinquency (1979) used the Q-sort technique to determine informational needs in juvenile justice. Numerous members of state juvenile advisory groups and related staff or members of analogous ad hoc state groups were given questionnaires and asked to rate 99 different topics on a 5-point Likert scale. Additionally, these members were asked to rank, by means of a Q-sort, 15 major topics according to desire for more information. Based on the rankings generated by these group members, prevention and diversion were selected as the two topics about which most information was needed, followed by information on juvenile status offenders and serious juvenile offenders. The need for information about violent crimes was ranked relatively low.

A more recent application of the Q-sort was by Trevor Josephson and Wally Unruh, who used a Q-sort personality instrument administered to four subgroups of male delinquents. A trait analysis revealed two interpretable factors which were labeled "normal, adjusted, responsible, positive self-concept" versus "abnormal, alienated, psychotic tendency, and outer-directed." The results of the Q-sort led to certain modifications in treatment programming for delinquents with personality disorders (Josephson and Unruh, 1994).

Sellin-Wolfgang Index

Thorsten Sellin and Marvin Wolfgang (1966) established an index of crime seriousness as applied to youthful offenders. The **Sellin-Wolfgang Index** is a rating system that assigns values to different crimes. It generates point values for both offense quality (offense seriousness) and quantity (financial loss attributable to the offense). Sometimes known as the Sellin-Wolfgang Crime-Severity Index, the scale includes different weights for offenses such as homicide or voluntary manslaughter, forcible sexual intercourse, aggravated assault, armed robbery, burglary of an occupied residence, larceny/theft of more than $1,000, auto theft in which the vehicle was not recovered, arson of an occupied building, kidnapping, extortion, or illegal sale of dangerous drugs.

On the basis of scale scores for different offender aggregates, crime seriousness may be tracked over time and compared. Thus, violence escalation and other crime trends might be noted using the Sellin-Wolfgang Index. This crime seriousness index has been used extensively in the research literature. Reliability studies have shown that the measure has considerable stability.

The Salient Factor Score (SFS 81)

The **Salient Factor Score (SFS 81)** is an actuarial device used by the U.S. Parole Commission as an aid in assessing federal prisoners' likelihood of recidivism after release. The SFS was designed to assist parole board members to make fair parole decisions. Departures from these guidelines by parole boards were to be accompanied by written rationales outlining the reasons for such departures. At the federal level, the salient factor score was made up of seven criteria and was refined in 1976. This was referred to as SFS 76. In August 1981, the salient factor scoring instrument underwent further revision and a new, six-factor predictive device, SFS 81, was constructed (Hoffman and Beck, 1985). A comparison of the revised SFS 81 with its previous counterpart (SFS 76) was made according to validity, stability, simplicity, scoring reliability, and certain ethical concerns.

Both instruments appeared to have similar predictive characteristics, although the revised device possesses greater scoring reliability (Hoffman and Beck, 1985). Of even greater significance is that SFS 81 places considerable weight on the extent and recency of an offender's criminal history (Hoffman and Beck, 1985). Seven points can be earned by having no prior convictions or adjudications (adult or juvenile), no prior commitments of more than 30 days, and being 26 years of age or older at the time of the current offense (with certain exceptions). Figure 10.1 shows the six-item federal Salient Factor Score, SFS 81.

Scores on the SFS 81 can range from 0 to 10. The following evaluative designations accompany various score ranges:

Raw Score	Parole Prognosis
0–3	"Poor"
4–5	"Fair"
6–7	"Good"
8–10	"Very Good"

The paroling authority next consults a table of offense characteristics consisting of categories varying in offense severity. Adult ranges in numbers of months served are provided for each category and are cross-tabulated with the four-category parole prognosis above. The SFS 81 retains predictive power when the follow-up period is extended to five years and the definition of recidivism is restricted to cases that sustain a new sentence of imprisonment exceeding one year, an outcome measure that focuses on the most serious type of recidivism.

Greenwood's Rand Seven-Factor Index

Peter Greenwood, a researcher who works for the Rand Corporation in Santa Monica, California, has spent considerable time developing various scales to measure an offender's dangerousness and potential for recidivism. One of the

Salient Factor Score Index

1. Prior convictions/adjudications (adult or juvenile):

   None (3 points)
   One (2 points)
   Two or three (1 point)
   Four or more (0 points)

2. Prior commitments of more than 30 days (adult or juvenile):

   None (2 points)
   One or two (1 point)
   Three or more (0 points)

3. Age at current offense/prior commitments:

   25 years of age or older (2 points)
   20–25 years of age (1 point)
   19 years of age or younger (0 points)

4. Recent commitment free period (three years):

   No prior commitment of more than 30 days (adult or juvenile) or released to the community from last such commitment at least three years prior to the commencement of the current offense (1 point)
   Otherwise (0 points)

5. Probation/parole/confinement/escape status violator this time:

   Neither on probation, parole, confinement, or escape status at the time of the current offense, nor committed as a probation, parole, confinement, or escape status violator this time (1 point)
   Otherwise (0 points)

6. Heroin/opiate dependence:

   No history of heroin/opiate dependence (1 point)
   Otherwise (0 points)

   Total score = _____

FIGURE 10.1 Salient factor score index, SFS 81 [*Source:* U.S. Parole Commission (1985). *Rules and Procedures Manual.* Washington, DC: U.S. Parole Commission.]

measures developed by Greenwood is known as the **Rand Seven-Factor Index.** This index consists of seven items. These include

1. Prior conviction for same charge
2. Incarcerated more than 50 percent of preceding two years
3. Convicted before age 16
4. Served time in state juvenile facility
5. Drug use in preceding two years

6. Drug use as a juvenile

7. Employed less than 50 percent of preceding two years (Greenwood and Abrahamse, 1982)

Using a simple yes–no answer format, a score is derived which ranges from 0 to 7. A score of 7 for any offender indicates that the offender poses the greatest risk, while a score of 0 means that the offender poses the least amount of risk. Risk refers to one's success potential for either probation or parole.

Greenwood's seven-factor scale has been constructed on the basis of actuarial information about chronic recidivists. For instance, it is widely known that recidivists often have problems with alcohol and/or drugs. Furthermore, unemployment is frequently associated with committing new offenses. Most scales purporting to predict one's risk or dangerousness use percentage of employment preceding one's arrest and conviction as a predictor variable. Also, the earlier the onset of criminal behavior, the more serious it is regarded. This is probably why Greenwood included information about one's juvenile record on the scale. If certain adult offenders were previously adjudicated as delinquent offenders prior to age 16, this is a serious concomitant of future adult offending. Greater weight is given to the earlier onset of delinquency or criminal conduct.

Essentially, a profile of specific criminals is devised using the seven-factor index. Therefore, a prediction is made about the potential of any given offender for recidivating in the future. Parole boards and judges can consider information from the Rand Seven-Factor Index as one of several criteria for evaluating offenders for parole or probation eligibility. The index serves as a "successfulness forecast"; that is, the score is indicative of future conduct.

■ SOME ISSUES OF MEASUREMENT

Several measurement issues are discussed in this section. These include (1) the attitude-action relation, (2) social desirability as a contaminating factor, (3) response sets and validity, and (4) the level of measurement-statistical choices relation.

Attitude-Action Relation

Social scientists presume that behind every action is an attitude related to it. The logic is that if these attitudes can be identified in advance and measured accurately, then actions or behaviors can be predicted or anticipated. Sounds easy, doesn't it? It isn't. Unfortunately, the attitude-action relation is far from certain. For example, it is possible for persons to possess certain attitudes and not express behaviors consistent with those attitudes. Those who may be prejudiced toward certain racial or ethnic groups may not discriminate against those groups, since discrimination is prohibited by law. Also, persons may behave in certain ways that suggest they possess certain attitudes when they don't possess them.

Criminologists do not terminate their investigations of factors that explain criminal behavior or delinquent conduct or spousal assault simply because there

Box
10.2

Lloyd Klein
Medgar Evers College

Statistics: Ph.D. (sociology), City
University of New York

Interests: I am a sociologist through academic training and possess a criminal justice background. My current research interests are Megan's Law and restorative justice.

My doctoral thesis examined social control within the growth of the consumer credit industry and the larger society. The thesis is the basis for a recently published book on credit cards. My interests in criminal justice were stimulated years earlier after taking a graduate course in 1974 with Richard Quinney. My first research efforts during the mid-1970s were rooted in understanding social policy with a focus on privacy issues.

A chance meeting with Joan Luxenburg stimulated subsequent research interests. We eventually worked together on various projects from 1980 to 1996. Most significant, I became part of an important professional network that still sustains my continuing professional research and intellectual development. Joan was also influential because she introduced me to the Academy of Criminal Justice Sciences and the American Society of Criminology. Our first project during those early years (1980–1984) concentrated on studying transcripts generated from citizen's band radio transmissions. We examined numerous theoretical approaches, the role of the criminal justice system, and portrayed a subcultural world relatively unexplored at that point in time.

Consideration of deviant behavior issues associated with CB radio led to research on pornography and telephone sex (two separate topics engendering much controversy during the mid-1980s). A synthesis of those two factors attracted an invitation from the 1985 Meese Commission to contribute some telephone sex materials.

Public policy issues opened a new path in my research. I became fascinated with crime prevention and would produce approximately a dozen papers on the crime control model and community co-production of public safety. Several publications on neighborhood watch, drug policy initiatives, and community control over public safety would follow. Research work with Joan and others during that time featured the first efforts at analyzing crimestopper programs (1983) and an early criminal justice scenario, setting the stage for Megan's Law (1988–1989). I was among the early pioneers studying the linkage between crime and mass media. Some of the early papers on *America's Most Wanted* and extensions of the media as educational and law enforcement tools were also well received.

The mid-1990s featured my most productive research period. I became associated with two topics that occupy my present research agenda—Megan's Law and restorative justice. The focus on Megan's Law developed out of the papers about the Larry Singleton case and merged into debates in Washington state and New Jersey. Since that time, I have presented over a dozen papers on the topic and published an important article on Megan's Law.

The restorative justice theme developed out of my interest in alternatives to the punitive justice model. An e-mail communication with John Wilmerding yielded an invitation to participate on a United Nations working group devoted to restorative justice. Subsequently, I worked with John's group and presented numerous papers on restorative justice. Participation in a Quaker meeting house discussion on restorative justice was one of the highlights of my work.

In essence, my career was shaped through personal curiosity about the relationships between certain subcultural groups and deviant behaviors and specific questions about evolving criminal justice philosophies. Much of this work came in stages. My intellectual life expanded through the elaboration of research themes and a quantum leap from one research thread into a related or trendy topic. My work is guided by intuitive judgments and luck in both meeting stimulating people and jumping on trendy topics.

I would like to think that my observations on crime control, restorative justice, Megan's Law, and other issues did make a difference. Numerous researchers and students regularly request copies of my written work. My research on Megan's Law stands out in the relatively sparse literature on the topic. Surprises never cease when researchers find their name in print: Bill Chambliss's American Society of Criminology presidential address cited my paper on children-turned-informants during President Reagan's early War on Drugs in the 1980s.

Advice to Students: My advice to students is relatively simple. Keep an open mind and go where your curiosity beckons. An innocuous item on the local news or a television program like "Judge Judy" may pique your interest and produce unpredictable lines of intellectual discourse. Data is all around us—just look closely and question the processes of the criminal justice system and everyday life rather than taking information for granted. Go beyond the obvious and add your own observations to ordinary events. I am already in the middle of a personal intellectual journey—but just think of all the wonderful opportunities awaiting you through future interaction with teachers or colleagues and recognition of the wider social world.

are questions about the attitude-action relation. The attitude-action controversy actually began many decades ago. An early article about the relation between attitudes persons express and their accompanying actions was written by Richard LaPiere (1934). LaPiere was interested in determining whether people behave in ways consistent with the attitudes they express. He planned a research project where he traveled throughout various parts of the country. He questioned hotel and restaurant owners about whether they would serve certain minorities, such as blacks and Orientals. Overwhelmingly, the hotel and restaurant owners indicated to LaPiere and his assistants that they would not serve such persons. Several months later, LaPiere instructed black and Oriental couples to travel to these same hotels and restaurants and attempt to be served. LaPiere expected that in most instances, they would be refused accommodations or food services because of their minority status. Interestingly, over 90 percent of the minority couples said that they were served or accommodated without incident. This finding caused LaPiere and others to critically evaluate their earlier thoughts about attitudes and how behaviors might be affected or influenced by their presence or absence.

Despite the uncertainty of the attitude-action relation, a prevalent belief among criminologists and others is that attitudes should be studied. A majority of empirical investigations in criminology and criminal justice reveal attitudinal factors that appear related to actions or behaviors observed. However, replication research or repeating studies under different conditions and in different time periods contributes to our knowledge stockpile. As we learn more about people and their behaviors, we refine our instrumentation and theoretical schemes to more sophisticated levels. Interestingly, several complex statistical tools have been useful in helping us to understand how numerous variables affect behavior. **Multiple correlation, path analysis,** and other correlational techniques have proved valuable in assisting us in building our theories of criminal behavior.

If attitudes precede certain types of social conduct, then it is imperative that we develop sound measures of these attitudes. Not only must we identify those attitudes most relevant in explaining certain behaviors, but we must measure these attitudes accurately and reliably. The validity of measures, or the extent to which our instruments actually measure what we say they are measuring, as well as the reliability of measures, or their consistency for applications over time, are discussed in the following chapter. Several conventional procedures will be described that enable researchers to demonstrate whether their instruments are accurate and consistent attitudinal measures.

Because we deal largely with quantities that cannot be observed directly, many of our attitudinal measures are challenged by competing instruments. It is not unusual to see numerous ways of conceptualizing and measuring police officer professionalism, or burnout and stress among probation officers. Every researcher is potentially capable of devising new instruments to measure virtually any attitudinal phenomenon. However, some attitudinal instruments have acquired some popularity and are used frequently to measure certain attitudinal dimensions. In the area of personality assessment, for instance, criminologists and others rely heavily on measures of personality such as the Minnesota Multiphasic Personality Inventory or MMPI, or Cattell's 16 Personality Factor Inventory, or 16 PF. Subparts of both of these personality assessment devices have been used by many researchers to assess one's ego strength, self-concept, self-assurance, and other personality dimensions for selected purposes. Treatment programs in community-based corrections agencies, mental hospitals, and prisons often rely on such measures for preliminary assessments of patients or inmates. Some of these devices are used for classification purposes, in order to segregate more potentially violent patients and prisoners from less violent ones.

Because there is no single device to measure any attitudinal phenomenon that has 100 percent acceptance in criminal justice and criminology, we must constantly be aware of the strengths and weaknesses of all measures as we use or develop them. Better instruments stand the test of time, through repeated applications. Few, if any, professionals are prepared to declare a moratorium on questionnaire construction and instrumentation. The field is expanding rapidly and maturing. Experimentation is vital to its growth, and we must constantly subject our devised theories and created measures to empirical testing.

Social Desirability as a Contaminating Factor

When attitudinal measures are constructed, we rely upon the honesty of respondents to provide us with truthful information about themselves. The more sensitive the questions, however, the more difficult it may be for others to disclose their personal thoughts and feelings to us. An example of measuring anxiety was provided earlier. That example contained excerpted items from Janet Taylor's Manifest Anxiety Scale. Some of these items were personal statements about one's bowel and bladder habits. Some items required that persons disclose things about their dreams or worries or manners of sleep. All of these personal items are, to one extent or another, related to anxiety. However, respondents may be inhibited and hesitate to give honest responses about themselves. Who wants to say that their sleep is fitful and disturbed, that the palms of their hands perspire frequently, or that they have bowel or bladder trouble frequently? These traits are undesirable. Few persons want to be undesirable. Therefore, people may say things about themselves that are not true but desirable. Methodologists refer to this behavior as **social desirability.**

Social desirability is saying things or disclosing things about yourself in writing that you want others to hear or see or that are favorable or self-serving. Social desirability is perhaps the most important contaminating factor affecting any attitudinal measure. We have no way of preventing social desirability. No foolproof remedies exist to detect it. Some standardized personality assessment tools have built-in "lie" factors that seek to detect the influence of social desirability. Thus, persons are suspected of giving socially desirable responses when they deny behaviors or thoughts that most persons experience at one time or another. Asking people whether they worry about things or think about trivial matters may prompt some respondents to deny that they worry about things or think about trivial matters. Almost everyone worries about things from time to time, and it is rare for anyone to avoid thinking about trivial things occasionally. The thinking behind the inclusion of such items on personality assessment devices is that if people lie about commonplace traits, they will probably lie about less commonplace traits, such as frequent bowel or bladder trouble or frequent fitful and disturbed sleep.

Therefore, any measure of attitudinal phenomena must be considered a candidate for **contamination of data** by social desirability the more it delves into deeply private and personal matters and opinions. Giving responses that you think the researcher wants to hear or that make you look good tend to detract from the accuracy and reliability of measures.

Response Sets and Validity

Another contaminating factor is the response set or set response. Set responses occur whenever respondents check all "agree" or "disagree" responses or use some other systematic response pattern in a self-administered questionnaire, regardless of statement or question content. Therefore, if respondents were presented with obviously contradictory statements, such as "My job completely lacks challenge and intrinsic interest" and "My job is intellectually rewarding, challenging, and intrinsically interesting," a response set would be indicated if "Strongly agree" were checked for both items. Usually, with a response set there is a systematic response pattern throughout the entire questionnaire. A male respondent, for instance, may check "Female," if "Female" is the first space to be checked among the information items included in the questionnaire. The best thing to do with questionnaires in which response sets are strongly suspected is to throw them out. The researcher's concerns should be about the quality, not the quantity, of data collected. Detecting response sets whenever they occur is fairly easy if researchers have constructed their questionnaires creatively. This usually means that they have interrupted phrasings of items that purportedly measure the same thing with reverse phraseology suggested by the two previous items. The decision to reject questionnaires or data because of the strong likelihood of set responses rests with the individual researcher and is a judgment call that depends on each situation.

The Level of Measurement–Statistical Choices Relation

Much has been made of levels of measurement and a researcher's efforts to measure attitudinal phenomena at the highest measurement levels. This is because we normally convert our collected data into numerical quantities for subsequent analysis. We want our analyses of collected data to be legitimate analyses. The scientific community has generally agreed upon the rules by which the scientific game should be played. If one or more of those rules are violated in the course of our research efforts, then our research is perhaps weakened in terms of its scientific contribution and significance.

The most typical rule violation relating to attitudinal measurement is the use of certain statistical procedures that involve particular arithmetic operations, such as summing and averaging. The facts are simple. Regarding the data you have collected and how you measured the different variables, you either have achieved the required level of measurement to conduct these arithmetic operations or you haven't achieved the required level of measurement. The following hypothetical scenario illustrates a common occurrence in the social sciences whenever attitudinal variables are investigated.

Suppose researchers study two samples and collect data about certain attitudes they possess. Suppose that Likert-type scales have been used to operationalize each of the attitudes investigated. At best, these researchers have achieved the ordinal level of measurement by using Likert scaling. They now have numerous raw scores over some range from low to high. How should these scores be analyzed?

Perhaps these data have been coded and stored in a computer. A subsequent statistical program package is run for these data, and much descriptive material about the two samples is generated. Since the computer package usually features programming that computes assorted statistical values for the data to be analyzed, the results of the analysis may be the equivalent of data overload. In other words, even if the researchers are interested in only one particular computation, the computer package churns out all sorts of additional information not otherwise requested or desired by these researchers. They didn't ask for additional data analyses, but the computer gave it to them anyway.

Perhaps they scan the data analyzed by the computer and notice that the program computed sample means or averages for all variables, including the attitudinal ones. Of course, the computer also computed modes, medians, ranges, standard deviations, and other miscellaneous descriptors for the same data. It is sometimes difficult to resist the temptation to do something with the additional data not originally requested from the computer.

Suppose that Attitude X was measured according to Likert scaling and became a part of the data the computer analyzed. Subsequently, Attitude X for the two samples was examined, and the researchers determined the following about Attitude X:

Attitude X		Group 1	Group 2
Mean (Average)	=	55.2	51.6
Mode	=	50.0	49.3
Median	=	54.7	52.1
Standard Deviation	=	4.6	4.9
Range	=	29.0	31.0

The first three values reported are called measures of central tendency, because they describe points around which scores in the distribution tend to focus. The standard deviation and range are measures of dispersion or variability because they depict how the scores are distributed around those central points. The mean or average for each sample on Attitude X is shown, together with the mode and median respectively. These are other central tendency measures that reflect different information about the central tendency of distributions. For instance, the mode indicates which scores are most popular or occur most frequently. The median defines that point separating the distribution of scores into two equal parts. In the previous example, the median for group 1 of 54.7 divides group 1 into two equal parts, so that 50 percent of sample 1 is below 54.7 while 50 percent of sample 1 is above 54.7.

Now, how does this relate to rule violations? Likert scaling procedures produce ordinal-level raw scores. These are rankables, where raw scores may be placed along an intensity continuum from low to high. Scores at one point on the continuum are either higher or lower than other scores, but we cannot say how much higher or lower. If we wanted to say how much higher or lower these scores were from others, we would need to achieve the next highest level of measurement with these scores, or the interval level of measurement. If we had achieved the interval level of measurement for Attitude *X,* then it would be arithmetically permissible to say how much higher or lower these scores were from each other. Unfortunately, we have only achieved the ordinal level of measurement with these scores using our Likert-type instrument to measure Attitude *X.* The central tendency measure of choice should be the median. The median fits ordinal-level data well. The mean doesn't fit, because averaging ordinal-level scores is meaningless, something similar to averaging Social Security numbers.

As the researchers examine their data, they observe arithmetic similarities between the means and medians of scores for these two groups on Attitude *X.* For group 1, for instance, the mean of 55.2 isn't much different from the median of 54.7. Likewise, the average of 51.6 for group 2 isn't all that different from the median of 52.1. Since there is an obvious similarity in the two values, and since other investigators are more likely to be familiar with the mean or average rather than median, it might be considered harmless to report the means for these groups instead of the medians.

If researchers regard this as harmless, they might also regard as harmless the idea of using a "difference between means" test to evaluate the significance of differences between these two groups, particularly now that they have two means to work with. There is such a test, and it, too, requires that researchers have interval-level data at their disposal. Thus, bending the rules in one instance may lead to other instances of rule-breaking.

How important is all of this for the measurement of attitudes? There are mixed opinions among professionals about this matter. Some researchers do not consider these data treatments as serious. In a conventional sense, considerable rule-breaking can be detected in many professional journals. Thus, if we gauge the incidence of this type of rule-breaking according to what professional researchers do, then we will conclude that it is generally acceptable. Convention often compels us to follow procedures that have been used by others. Beyond this, some professionals contend that if we were to comply fully with all requirements for statistical applications, we would never be able to do research. This is because our investigations are imperfect in various respects. Seldom are all requirements of tests and procedures actually achieved. Therefore, some information (where some rules are violated) is better than no information (where no rules are violated). In sum, the importance of this section is that it cautions us to recognize the various limitations of our data collection and instrumentation and to view our findings accordingly.

■ KEY TERMS

Bogardus social distance scale	Empirical referent
Categorical variable	Epistemic correlates
Coefficient of reproducibility	Equal-appearing intervals
Constructs	Guttman scaling
Contamination of data	Index
Cornell technique	Intensity continuum

Interval level of measurement
Item weights
Likert scale
Method of summated ratings
Multidimensional scales
Multiple correlation
Nominal definition
Nominal level of measurement
Operational definition
Operationalization
Ordinal level of measurement
Path analysis
Q-sort

Rand Seven-Factor Index
Ratio level of measurement
Raw scores
Reproducible scales
Salient Factor Score (SFS 81)
Scalogram analysis
Sellin-Wolfgang Index
Semantic differential
Social desirability
Thurstone scaling
Unidimensional scale
Unidimensionality
Weighting

■ QUESTIONS FOR REVIEW

1. What is measurement? Identify and discuss briefly several important functions of measurement.

2. What are Likert scales? Briefly describe their construction. What are some general strengths and limitations of Likert scales?

3. What are Thurstone scales? Compare their accuracy with Likert scales of the same attitudinal phenomena. Which scales seem more accurate to you? Why?

4. What are some general limitations and strengths of Thurstone scales?

5. Differentiate between concepts and constructs. How do these terms relate to operationalization?

6. Distinguish between an operational definition and a nominal definition. What are the purposes of each in social research? Explain.

7. What are three important issues relating to measurement? Discuss each issue briefly, noting why it is important and is considered an issue.

8. What are Guttman scales? What is meant by the coefficient of reproducibility?

9. Contrast multidimensional and unidimensional scales. Which scales seem more realistic and easier to construct? Why?

10. What are the respective contributions of nominal and operational definitions in theory construction, verification, and hypothesis testing?

11. What are four levels of measurement? Which levels of measurement permit averaging and division?

12. Why are levels of measurement important in relation to statistical applications to collected data? How can misapplications of statistical procedures influence the meaningfulness of scientific findings? Give two hypothetical examples from your own reading in criminal justice.

13. What are two major contaminating factors in self-administered question-naires? How does each factor function as a contaminating factor? Of the two factors, which is probably more important and why?

14. What is the semantic differential? What are some possible applications of it in criminology? Give two examples.

15. How can social desirability be detected in a questionnaire? How can a set response be detected? Explain.

chapter 11

Validity and Reliability of Measures

■ INTRODUCTION

How do we know if our measures of criminological phenomena are accurate and consistent? This chapter examines various methods for determining the accuracy of the instruments we construct to measure attitudinal phenomena. The accuracy of any measure is known as its validity. Also, several ways of assessing a measure's consistency are described. The consistency of an attitudinal measure is known as its reliability. These particular properties of measuring instruments are vital to theory verification and to the entire research enterprise. If we use measures that lack either validity or reliability, we are unsure of what we are measuring. Our tests of hypotheses will lack credibility, and it will be doubtful whether we can successfully test our theories if attitudinal dimensions are included.

First, four methods of assessing validity are examined. These methods use either logic or statistical procedures as a means of determining whether instruments are reflecting accurately the variables purportedly assessed. Next, several procedures for determining a measure's reliability are presented. These procedures include both internal and external methods that seek to determine whether the raw scores we generate through our instrumentation may be consistently interpreted. It will become apparent that of the two test properties, validity is the more elusive, since a measure's validity can only be inferred indirectly and is not provable. In contrast, reliability assessments may be made directly, and the reliability of measures is provable.

■ VALIDITY DEFINED

Validity is the property of a measuring instrument that allows researchers to say that the instrument is measuring what they say it is measuring (Selltiz et al., 1959). If we say that an instrument measures trait X, an attitudinal variable, then our measuring instrument is valid to the extent that it truly measures trait X. If our instrument measures trait Y and not trait X, then it is not a valid measure of trait X, even though we might think it is. Thus, it is possible for instruments to be valid indicators of certain other unknown variables when they are not particularly valid indicators of those variables we wish to define.

Measuring instruments are created by people. For example, our standard measures of weight and length are previously agreed upon standards. In early times, primitive cultures used the distance from the tip of one's thumb to the first thumb joint as a length standard. However, it was soon apparent that some people's thumbs were longer than other's. More objective measures were subsequently employed to measure length and weight. Currently, rulers are universally used to measure feet, inches, meters, and millimeters; assorted weights and scales are used to measure pounds, ounces, and grams.

The use of such objective measures leaves little room for dispute among most people. They have agreed that certain measuring instruments will be used to take into account various properties of objects, such as length and weight. We say that a ruler is a valid measure of feet to the extent that it is patterned after some commonly agreed upon standard that has been determined to measure feet. If the ruler is constructed of wood and if the wood gets wet, there is the possibility that shrinkage and warping of the instrument will affect its accuracy. All of our measuring instruments, without exception, are vulnerable to contamination from various sources outside (external) or inside (internal) to the instrument itself. Various weights may become worn, and their precision as measures will be affected. The validity of any measure, therefore, is a variable property.

Validity is a relative term, inasmuch as there are serious doubts among some social scientists that there is anything such as absolute validity. Rather, we determine the degree of validity, and validity has little meaning apart from particular operations by which it is determined. Some measures have higher validity, some have moderate validity, and some have lower validity, relative to other measures.

Assessing the validity of weights and measures is accomplished rather easily, since it is not difficult to compare certain instruments with those already in existence and accepted as standards. If certain rulers and weights correspond to the accepted standard measures, then we conclude that our measuring instruments are valid. In criminology and other social sciences, however, it is somewhat more difficult to establish the validity of instruments that assess nonempirical phenomena such as attitudes, prestige, power, or peer group pressure. Because many types of attitudes are said to be important in predicting human behavior in various social contexts, it is necessary for social scientists to devise measures of these attitudes so that their usefulness as predictors can be assessed empirically.

Once a measure has been constructed for some attitude, there is usually no objective standard whereby it may be evaluated. We have no universally acceptable measure of burnout and stress, or of police officer professionalism. If we devise scales for these variables, what good would it do to compare them with other scales of these phenomena already in existence? These other measures must also be assessed in their own right, in terms of the degree of validity they happen to manifest. How do criminologists know whether their measures possess validity?

Before we examine several ways of tapping this elusive instrument property, we need to consider the relation between the items included on a paper-pencil questionnaire measure and the theoretical universe of traits and items that may be used to measure that phenomenon. Figure 11.1 shows a theoretical universe of items that measure some variable, in this case, trait X. The universe of items does not exist in the real world. It is merely an abstraction. Thus, it comprises an infinite universe of items and traits for any variable that has been nominally defined. Also, theoretically, abstract universes of items and traits exist for all other variables that currently remain unknown or that we have not, as yet, nominally defined.

Consider the illustration in Figure 11.1. Researchers extract items from this abstract universe, almost wholly arbitrarily, although logic is an integral feature involved in their method of item or trait selection. Researchers have no way of proving that those items extracted are indeed from the universe of items that theoretically measures trait X. Thus, investigators are in the difficult position of attempting to illustrate to others that the measures they have devised actually

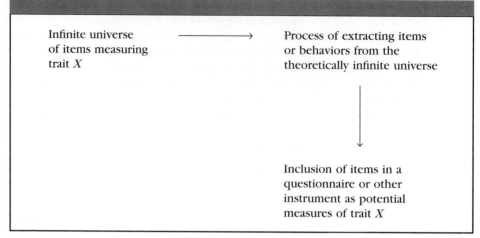

FIGURE 11.1 An illustration of the process of extracting items from an abstract and infinite universe of traits measuring phenomenon *X*.

measure what they say they are measuring. The main arguments they cite supporting the validity of their instruments are founded almost entirely on logic and/or statistical support.

■ TYPES OF VALIDITY

There are four major methods for establishing a test's validity: (1) face or content validity, (2) predictive validity, (3) concurrent validity, and (4) construct validity. The labels applied to these types of validity are not uniformly used throughout the social sciences. Alternative terms are sometimes used, such as criterion validity and pragmatic validity. Where appropriate, alternative terms will be noted when they might be substituted for some of the labels used to describe types of validity here.

Content Validity

Content validity or **face validity** is based upon the logical inclusion of a sampling of items taken from the universe of items that measure the trait in question. Sometimes such scales are known as **arbitrary scales,** since they are developed on the basis of individual discretion. The only way content validity can be demonstrated is by examining the test or instrument items and comparing them with the universe of items that could theoretically be included, if known. Researchers judge, on the basis of the items that make up the instrument, whether the test or instrument is valid according to its representative content. On the basis of the contents of the measure or on the face of it, do the items included seem logically related to the trait measured?

Content or face validity is exclusively a logical type of validity that any given measuring instrument may possess. For example, in the construction of verbal or quantitative tests, such as the Graduate Record Examination (GRE), it is important that these tests have content validity. For example, it is essential that the items included on the GRE should reflect the abilities and achievements of the persons taking the test or their personal experience and professional background. If the examination were to emphasize a rather narrow treatment of mathematical skills rather than cover a broad spectrum of mathematical items (e.g., if the emphasis were on trigonometry rather than algebra, calculus, and/or simple arithmetic), then the content validity of the measure as an index of general mathematical knowledge would be called into question. Specifically, we would challenge the test as a valid measure of general quantitative aptitude. And accordingly, if the verbal portion of the GRE emphasized only grammatical rules exclusive of reading comprehension and word understanding, we would seriously question whether it was a valid measure or indicator of verbal aptitude.

Therefore, for any given test or measuring instrument to have content validity, researchers must endeavor to ensure that the instrument contains a logical sampling of items from the so-called universe of items that presumably reflects the characteristic to be measured and that the instrument corresponds with this universe in some consistent fashion. In the classroom, for example, students might rationalize a poor performance on an examination by arguing that the instructor selected test items from book chapters that were not emphasized as important in class. If the test is supposed to cover the first five chapters of a book but only chapter 1 has questions drawn from it, then the test lacks content validity. It fails to have a representative sampling of items from the **universe of items** that could be utilized in the test's construction; that is, it fails to have text material from the other four chapters that the students have studied.

Applied to attitudinal measures, face or content validity would be applied by simply inspecting a measure's content. Does the measure contain logical items that seem related to whatever the instrument purports to measure? If work satisfaction of probation officers is being assessed, the following items might appear on such an instrument administered to probation officers:

1. I would recommend this probation agency to my friends as a good place to work.
2. I would like to continue my present work arrangement for an indefinite time period.
3. If I had the opportunity, I would leave this work to work in another organization doing entirely different things.
4. It would take a sizable change in pay to get me to move from my present position.
5. I don't get along well with my work associates.
6. I like my job more than most of my work associates like theirs.
7. My work assignments are boring and repetitious.
8. There are many things about my job that should be changed to make it more interesting to me.

9. There are many things about my job that I don't like.

10. My work is challenging and interesting.

It is apparent on the face of this instrument that these items are directed at work satisfaction and at different dimensions of the work environment. These are just a few of the items that could be selected from the universe of items that purportedly measure job satisfaction. Our direct inspection of these items suggests that the instrument has at least content validity. This is a strictly logical analysis and conclusion.

Criticisms of Content Validity. The fact that a measure appears to have content validity doesn't necessarily mean that we are indeed measuring the trait. In the previous chapter, problems occurred relative to social desirability and response sets as contaminating factors in attitudinal measurement. Certainly these factors may be involved to varying degrees with the administration of any attitudinal scale, and we must expect a certain amount of social desirability to influence one's personal responses. If measures contain items that are so obvious about what they measure, it is relatively easy for respondents to fake their responses to these items or alter them in favorable ways. Therefore, some researchers resort to indirect means of assessing certain attitudinal variables. For instance, rather than asking persons if they are afraid of being confined in small places or of heights, they might ask persons whether they would like to be either a forest ranger or an accountant working in a small office. The indirect nature of this and other similar questions enables researchers to prevent respondents from knowing what the researchers are trying to measure. But the more indirect the questions or items, the greater the chance that some universe of items will be tapped other than the one associated with the variable to be measured. This criticism is discussed in a later section dealing with construct validity.

Another criticism of content validity is that it is subjectively determined. Because content validity is dependent to a large extent upon the subjective professional judgment of the researcher, what one person regards as high content validity might be regarded by another as low content validity. Consider the divergent views of teachers and students about the content validity of the same examination. The teacher may believe strongly that the test has high content validity, but the student may take issue with this belief.

Content validity depends heavily upon the quality of judgment of researchers. Whoever devises the measuring instrument must be careful to include as many as possible of a representative set of items that will measure the particular trait, whether it be verbal or quantitative aptitude, degree of anxiety, or socioeconomic level.

Another criticism concerns the reality of defining the universe of items from which the measuring instrument will be constructed. The universe of items may consist of all facts included in specific chapters of some textbook students have been assigned. Or the universe of items may consist of all biological, social, and/or psychological features of anxiety. How does one go about identifying all of these features? For all practical purposes, anxiety has an infinite number of physiological, psychological, and social factors that may be extracted and included on an anxiety scale. Again, the judgment of researchers permits them to draw reasonably representative sets of items that measure the trait.

It is difficult to argue that a test does not have content validity, primarily because there is usually some resemblance of the items in the test to the trait that the test is presumably measuring. Few measuring instruments, if any, are perfectly valid indicators of social and psychological traits. The general content validity of any test rests to a great extent on the skill and judgment of the constructor of the test. If poor judgment has been exercised (always a possibility), then the test or measure will likely have low content validity or no validity at all.

Pragmatic Validity

Perhaps the most useful and popular indicators of validity are **predictive validity** and **concurrent validity,** both forms of **pragmatic validity.** Pragmatism suggests that the validity of something can be assessed by whether or not it works. Does a particular attitudinal measure work in assessing a specific attitude? Two ways of demonstrating whether a measure works are to use the measure to forecast some future behavior consistent with scores on the instrument (predictive validity), or to correlate these instrument scores with some other activity at the same point in time (concurrent validity).

Predictive Validity. Predictive validity, also known as **criterion validity,** is based upon the measured association between what an instrument predicts behavior will be and the subsequent behavior exhibited by an individual or group (Magnusson, 1967). For example, if we obtain attitudinal scores that purportedly reflect the degree of prejudice toward minority group members (written expressions of what subjects might do if placed in a social situation requiring interactions with minorities), the relationship between their scores on the measuring instrument and their subsequent behaviors toward minority group members will provide us with the necessary evidence of the predictive validity of the measure. If their scores indicate discriminatory behaviors and then these subjects exhibit discriminatory behaviors toward one or more minority group members, this is evidence that the test is measuring what we say it measures.

Suppose we devise a measure of male chauvinism among personnel officers of several companies and find that some officers possess male chauvinistic attitudes to a high degree while others possess this characteristic to a low degree. A comparison of their subsequent hiring practices and their respective chauvinism scores might disclose much about the predictive utility of our measure. If those officers with high chauvinism scores have hiring records that show some gender discrimination (e.g., low numbers of female hires), and if those officers who have low chauvinism scores have hiring records showing more equitable hiring practices, then our measure of male chauvinism would seem to have predictive validity. Predictive validity is the simple correlation of predicted behavior with subsequent exhibited behavior. A high correlation or relationship between the predicted behavior and the behavior exhibited means that the measure possesses predictive validity.

Concurrent Validity. Concurrent validity differs from predictive validity in that the scores of predicted behavior are obtained simultaneously with the exhibited behavior. For instance, if we obtained manual dexterity and work efficiency scores from drill press operators in a factory, we might also obtain from their supervisors their productivity records. We can compare directly their productivity records with their manual dexterity and work efficiency scores to determine if there is concurrent validity. Again, as in the case of predictive validity, a high correlation or relation between the dexterity scores and high–drill press productivity suggests that our measure has concurrent validity. Therefore, predictive validity forecasts expected behaviors in some future time period, while concurrent validity is assessed by comparing test results with some simultaneous behavior. Consider some hypothetical scores in Table 11.1.

In the example of hypothetical scores shown in Table 11.1, two measures have been obtained from a sample of delinquent boys. One measure we have presumably constructed is self-esteem, while the other is perceived peer pressure. Wishing to validate our self-esteem scale, we might predict that those boys with lower amounts of self-esteem might be more receptive to peer pressures. Accordingly, we might suspect that as their scores on self-esteem increase, their perceived peer pressure scores might decrease. Also, as their self-esteem scores decrease, their perceived peer pressure scores might increase. Table 11.1 has been deliberately configured to demonstrate this. If these were actual scores of self-esteem and perceived peer pressure, we would consider this relation supportive of our theorizing. Also, our measure of self-esteem would appear to be validated by its correlation with perceived peer pressure.

Both predictive and concurrent validity are determined largely by statistical correlations, although we might conclude that our measures have these types of validity by visually inspecting the patterns of scores such as those displayed in Table 11.1. If there is a logical relation between these sets of scores, this is logical evidence of predictive and/or concurrent validity.

Criticisms of Predictive and Concurrent Validity. One criticism of predictive and concurrent validity is that simply observing a numerical association be-

TABLE 11.1 Self-Esteem and Peer Pressure Scores for Ten Delinquent Boys

Delinquent	Self-Esteem	Perceived Peer Pressure
1	42	28
2	45	27
3	47	25
4	49	24
5	52	23
6	55	21
7	56	20
8	58	20
9	59	19
10	61	16

tween a test score and some actual individual or group behavior is no guarantee that the measuring instrument is a valid indicator of the trait we have nominally defined. It could be, for example, that our measure really is a valid indicator of something else closely related with the phenomenon we are investigating. Therefore, we might be led to suspect that our instrument is a valid measure of what we say it is, when in fact it may be a measure of something else. This problem always exists, whenever attitudinal measures are constructed. There is no way we can ever be sure that we are measuring what we say we are measuring regarding attitudinal scales. However, we do consider as evidence of the potential validity of the instrument the relationship between the predicted and the observed behavior in question. This should actually serve as a caution. Researchers must always be aware of the potential limitations of their measures. They should not be overconfident that they are measuring what they say they are measuring, strictly on the basis of high correlations between predicted and observed behaviors.

In the case of gender and racial discrimination, another criticism is apparent. Since it is illegal to discriminate on the basis of gender and race, it is entirely possible to tap a gender or racial prejudice dimension with our devised instruments but not observe discriminatory behaviors. Thus, people may have an amount of gender or racial prejudice, but they may not exhibit illegal behaviors of discriminating against persons because of their race or gender. Even if certain behaviors are not prohibited by law, social constraints exist to prevent certain discriminatory behaviors from being observed.

Another criticism of pragmatic validity is the researcher's interpretation of exhibited behaviors by respondents as representing the predicted behavior. Some attitudinal measures are so abstract that several different kinds of interpretations of given behavior patterns could be made according to a variety of social researchers who define the situation. Again, the judgment of the researcher is a crucial element in determining the degree of pragmatic validity that exists.

Construct Validity

Construct validity is both a logical and a statistical validating method. Also known as factorial validity, construct validity is useful for measuring traits for which external criteria are not available, such as latent aggressiveness. This type of validity is determined through the application of **factor analysis.** Factor analysis is a statistical technique designed to determine the basic components of a measure (Blalock, 1972:97–102). For example, if we were to factor analyze a measure of police professionalism, we might find that the variable consists of three predominant factors: formal educational attainment, supervisory expectations, and promotional ambitions. Factor analysis is beyond the scope of this text, although we can discuss briefly what it does. If we devised a police officer professionalism scale that consisted of 50 items, the application of factor analysis might cause our scale to factor into three major parts corresponding to educational attainment, supervisory expectations, and promotional ambitions. Thus, we could see three distinct clusters of items that focus around these dimensions. An inspection of the individual items within each cluster should bear directly

Box 11.1

Peter J. Benekos
Mercyhurst College

Statistics: B.S. (social science), Clarion University of Pennsylvania; M.A. (sociology), University of Cincinnati; Ph.D. (sociology/criminology), University of Akron.

Interests: From earlier interest in victimology and theoretical explanations of crime, my attention shifted to crime control policies and criminal justice system responses to crime and criminals. Recent projects include evaluations of juvenile justice policy, intermediate punishment programs, and drug court initiatives.

The "sociological imagination" described by C. Wright Mills captured my attention as an undergraduate student and helped focus my interest and academic career in sociology. While the substantive areas of deviance and criminology were especially absorbing and presented interesting questions for research, professional work in prisons and community-based programs shifted my attention to questions regarding program effectiveness, system responses, and policy development. In addition, the politics of crime and the politicalization of criminal justice policy raised timely questions about *how* policy decisions are determined and what *impact* they have on crime. As a result of working with criminal justice programs and committees, and becoming involved in related community initiatives, I gained some insights into the challenges and issues confronting juvenile justice and criminal justice practitioners. In this regard, questions about the effectiveness of electronic monitoring, intermediate punishment programs, group home placement, and alternatives to incarceration are concerns not only for program directors and policymakers but also for the community as well.

With these interests, and with the recent focus on youth crime, juvenile justice system reforms, and budget constraints, I became involved in a local collaboration with community and agency leaders which resulted in (1) identifying a policy-oriented research agenda on children and youth, (2) developing a college-community partnership to secure funding to support the research, and (3) establishing a college "institute"—Institute for Child and Family Policy—to conduct ongoing policy-relevant research. As a result, my current research is focused on collecting data on local delinquency and crime trends and on sentencing and corrections outcomes. The data are used to inform local justice policy decisions, to evaluate offender intervention strategies, to provide timely information to policymakers, and to promote effective criminal and juvenile justice policies. This represents an effort to involve academic, community, court, and agency leaders in data-driven policy decisions and to present quantitative information in a useful format. In contrast to theory testing, this research is evaluation-oriented and policy-focused in nature.

Aside from being timely and interesting professional work, this research provides (1) an opportunity to have input into system reform, (2) access to data and agency information (which is integrated into classroom presentations), (3) opportunities for student involvement and applied research experience (e.g., theses, senior projects, part-time, grant-funded employment), and (4) collaboration between academics and practitioners. This research approach is also consistent with guidelines from federal and state criminal justice funding sources, which emphasize collaborative projects and outcome-based evaluations. In the context of "what works?" in a given situation, this type of research attempts to inform policy decisions and to improve criminal justice initiatives. From a pedagogical perspective, it provides excellent opportunities to mentor students interested in applying and developing the research skills presented in methods texts.

Essentially, this is applied research that permits ongoing information exchange and networking with criminal justice professionals. It facilitates academic-practitioner relations, offers insights into criminal justice policies and practices, and provides relevant information to decision makers and community leaders.

Advice to Students: Students interested in developing research relationships with criminal justice agencies have several opportunities to establish credibility and to work with agency staff in identifying mutual research interests and also in securing funding. As program evaluations, especially funded programs, become imperative, the role of research becomes more significant. Cooperative relationships with agency administrators can be initiated and enhanced by becoming involved in related community projects, visiting agencies and learning about their programs, developing an understanding of agency networks, and helping to define and design the research questions. In addition, as more agencies collaborate in applying for grants for new programs or evaluations (e.g., partnerships among schools, juvenile probation, and treatment providers to target at-risk youth), academic researchers can be invaluable in developing the methodology for the project and in ensuring appropriate evaluation measures.

Doing research is an on-going learning process. It requires (1) keeping informed of the literature and substantive information, (2) applying and developing research skills, (3) connecting theory and practice, and (4) using interpersonal skills.

upon those particular factors. We could determine this relation in much the same way that we would use content or face validity to evaluate the contents of a scale.

A popular personality assessment device is Raymond Cattell's 16 Personality Factor Inventory, developed at the Institute for Personality and Abilities Testing in Champaign, Illinois. Designated as the "16 PF," Cattell's inventory purportedly measures sixteen separate personality dimensions. When factor analysis is applied to this measure, which consists of 187 questions, it factors into sixteen separate parts, with sixteen separate clusters of items. This is evidence of **factorial validity.** More advanced sources may be consulted for how factor analysis might be applied.

Some Criticisms of Construct Validity.   Construct validity can be used to demonstrate whether or not a measuring instrument is, in fact, measuring a particular phenomenon. If a measure is supposed to reflect only one dimension, and if factor analysis shows that more than one dimension of the variable is being measured, then this raises serious questions about the instrument's validity.

Another criticism is that construct validity requires a rather sophisticated statistical background on the part of the researcher in order to apply it manually. While statistical programs exist and have been adapted for computer use to facilitate computations, we must still possess interpretive skills to make sense out of what has been computed.

Further, because construct validity pertains almost exclusively to traits that are not directly observable, there is a greater risk that the instrument is actually measuring some other phenomenon closely related to the trait being investigated rather than the actual trait itself. Compared with predictive validity, for instance, there is no direct means to correlate actual behaviors with test scores as a way of demonstrating the construct validity of the instrument.

It was mentioned earlier that researchers will often devise items that are indirect indicators of the traits they investigate. Thus, rather than asking persons whether or not they like their work, researchers may ask them whether they would recommend the job to others as an indirect way of assessing their own job contentment or work satisfaction. For more deep-seated personality characteristics such as acrophobia (fear of heights) or claustrophobia (fear of small, enclosed places), indirect items are preferable. The use of indirect items is to discourage respondents from making socially desirable responses. We might ask someone if they are anxious or claustrophobic, for instance. It is likely that they will not be perfectly honest with us, and that they will say things that are socially desirable instead. This is a case of the test-taker trying to outwit the tester. However, if we ask indirect questions, they cannot easily determine what it is we are trying to assess. Indirect questions involve the tester attempting to outwit test-takers. Consider the following item as an example:

121. I would rather:

(A) grow flowers, (B) add columns of numbers, (C) something else.

Presumably, an inference might be made if someone selects (A) and prefers growing flowers over adding numbers. Since "growing flowers" is a largely out-of-doors activity and "adding columns of numbers" is associated with in-door work, we might use this item to assess claustrophobic tendencies, if any. Bear in mind that we do not limit our inferences about behaviors to one such item. We might use multiple items, perhaps as many as 15 or 20, in order to ensure that our behavioral and attitudinal inferences are more valid. We are not going to conclude that because someone likes to grow flowers, that person must be claustrophobic.

But the further we depart from the actual traits or characteristics we want to measure with the items we construct, the more likely it is that we might be tapping variables closely related to those we are investigating. Thus, our indirect indicators of variables are helpful in the sense that they discourage test-takers from making socially desirable responses, but they are detrimental in the sense that we may be losing touch with the variables purportedly measured.

RELIABILITY DEFINED

Another important test property is reliability. **Reliability** is the ability of a measuring instrument to consistently measure whatever it is designed to measure (Selltiz et al., 1959). Suppose we develop a measure of police professionalism. We believe our measure is reliable. If we administer our police professionalism scale to a sample of police officers in time 1 and record their scores, and then if we wait a month and measure these same officers again on our police professionalism scale in time 2, the officers' scale scores should be the same or very similar between the two time periods. This fact presumes that nothing happens to these officers between the two time periods that might otherwise change their scores. No differences between officers' scores between the time 1 and time 2 administration of our police professionalism scale is evidence of the reliability of this measure.

WHY IS IT IMPORTANT TO HAVE RELIABLE MEASURES?

It is important to have reliable measures for at least two reasons: (1) reliability is a prerequisite for a measuring instrument's validity, and (2) researchers want to assess the impact of certain variables on other variables. Reliable measuring instruments will enable researchers to draw tentative conclusions about causal relationships between variables.

Reliability as a Prerequisite for Validity. In order for a measuring instrument to be valid, it must be demonstrably reliable. Any measuring instrument that does not reflect some attribute consistently has little chance of being considered a valid measure of that attribute. For example, suppose persons have conservative political views. A measure of conservatism would be regarded as unreliable if, after repeated measures for the same persons, widely different conservatism scores were reported. This assumes, of course, that other variables did not intervene to cause changes in their score results.

Determining Whether One Variable Affects Other Variables. If it can be reasonably determined that individuals are relatively uninfluenced by extraneous variables that are a part of their environment from one instrument administration to the next, then the chances for a measure to be considered unreliable are greatly increased if significant score differences are observed. The reliability of a measuring instrument is seldom, if ever, determined by examining responses from a single individual to that measure. Most often, evidence of reliability is gathered from large aggregates of persons.

Scores on a reliable measuring instrument will fluctuate only in response to some independent factor or condition causally associated with it directly or indirectly. Caution should be exercised in interpreting apparent relationships between two or more variables as causal relationships. If researchers observe a change in a person's score on some attitudinal dimension from one time period to the next, they want to be able to say that the score change is empirical evidence of the potential effect of one variable upon the other.

Generally, if a factor X is introduced between two time periods, then theoretically, certain changes in specific attitudinal dimensions that relate meaningfully to factor X should occur. For example, in many police departments in the United States, films and videotapes dealing with human relations skills are shown to units of officers as a part of their training and to enhance their interactions with the public. If officers manifest poor human relations skills in dealing with the public prior to seeing these films or videotapes, and then they are much improved in this respect after viewing the films and videotapes, this is considered to be tacit support for the assumption that the audiovisual aides helped to account for their behavioral change. Taken by itself, this does not prove that the audiovisual aides caused the changes in human relations skills, but it is nevertheless strong support for this contention. Figure 11.2 illustrates a conventional independent-dependent variable pattern, where one variable purportedly causes changes to occur in another variable.

Whereas Figure 11.2 shows only one score, most real-world applications use many scores in before-and-after research. In this hypothetical example, however, measures are taken in time 1 (t_1) and time 2 (t_2). Score differences are noted in a column to the far right. In this case, one score of 50 is observed for the dependent variable Y in time 1 and the score of 25 is recorded on the same measure of Y administered in time 2. The score difference of -25 is recorded. Between the two time periods, an experimental variable X is introduced. The score difference of -25 is presumed attributable to the introduction of variable X, if our measure of Y is reliable. Again, some caution must be exercised when drawing causal inferences among variables. Several other factors may have ac-

FIGURE 11.2 The effect of an experimental variable X on factor Y.

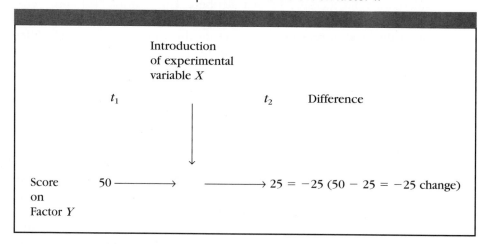

counted for this score difference. We will examine several phenomena that influence a measure's reliability and validity in a later section of this chapter.

TYPES OF RELIABILITY

Four methods for assessing an instrument's reliability are presented here. These are divided into internal and external reliability checks or methods. Internal checks establish reliability by examining the internal consistency of items, while external checks use the measure against itself over time or a comparison of two or more equivalent measures of the same phenomenon. **Internal reliability checks** include the split-half method and item discrimination analysis. **External reliability checks** include test-retest and parallel forms of the same test.

Internal Reliability Checks

One way of attacking the reliability problem of instruments is to examine the **internal consistency** of items used to construct them. Items that measure the same phenomenon should logically cling together in some consistent pattern. Persons who like their jobs are unlikely to give responses that would typify persons who don't like their jobs. The argument is that persons with particular traits will respond predictably to items affected by those traits.

Suppose we were to construct a measure of some attitude and include 20 items in our instrument. These 20 items are statements with Likert-type agree-disagree responses. Ten of the items are positively worded, whereas the other 10 statements are negatively worded. Persons who have the attitude to either a high degree or a low degree should respond to all 20 items consistently, provided that each of these items has been extracted from the same attitudinal universe. Examining the internal consistency of the instrument enables researchers to determine which items are not consistent with the rest in measuring the phenomenon under investigation. The object is to remove those inconsistent items from the measure to improve its internal consistency. One preliminary caution is in order, however. Since most of our attitudinal measures are multidimensional, it may be possible for respondents to give positive responses to some items and negative responses to others. They might like their income but not their work associates. Thus, internal consistency may be more or less difficult to create, depending upon the potential for these complex variations in item responses. Two categories of internal checks for reliability include the split-half method and item discrimination analysis.

Split-Half Method.   The **split-half method** or **technique** is designed to correlate one half of the test items with the other half. For instance, if we devised a 30-item scale, a suitable procedure for establishing the internal consistency of the test would be to divide the items into two equal parts and correlate them. Some researchers recommend numbering the items from 1 to N, and then correlating the odd-numbered items with the even-numbered ones.

There are no conventional standards that prescribe how to interpret the results of these correlations. One rule-of-thumb that might be applicable is to regard correlations of .90 or higher as indicative of high test reliability. The Kuder-Richardson 20 procedure may be applied here. Step-by-step directions for applying this advanced statistical procedure are presented in Magnusson (1967).

Applied to Likert-type scaling, recall that item weights are assigned on five- or six-point response patterns from "Strongly agree" to "Strongly disagree." If we took one half of all test items and correlated them with the other half of the test, we would be correlating item weights with one another. Theoretically, if a person receives lots of "6's" and "5's" on one half of the test, then there should be lots of "6's" and "5's" on the other half of the test, if it is internally consistent. The Kuder-Richardson 20 procedure produces a correlation coefficient of the magnitude of relation between these two test halves.

Item Discrimination Analysis. The second internal method of determining a test's reliability is called **item discrimination analysis,** sometimes simply **item analysis.** It is relatively simple to illustrate and understand, and complex statistical manipulations of data are not required.

For instance, let's assume that researchers have administered an attitudinal instrument to 100 persons. Further assume that the instrument contains 10 items, each having a six-point Likert-type response pattern of attitudinal intensity (i.e., Strongly agree; Agree; Undecided, probably agree; Undecided, probably disagree; Disagree; and Strongly disagree). If we weigh each response per item according to a 1, 2, 3, 4, 5, and 6 intensity pattern (or, 6, 5, 4, 3, 2, and 1 in the case of negatively worded items), it would be possible for a person to obtain a maximum high score of $10 \times 6 = 60$ and a minimum low score of $10 \times 1 = 10$. This would be the number of items times the largest weight for a single item. The scoring range would be between 10 and 60.

Logically, persons with larger overall scores on the instrument (e.g., 60, 59, 58, 56, and so on) would tend to respond to each item in such a way that the weight assigned each item response would probably be either a 4, 5, or 6. Persons with smaller overall scores of 10, 12, 15, and so on would probably have small weights of 1, 2, or 3 associated with particular item responses. Sometimes, persons with overall larger scores will respond to an item and receive a 1, 2, or 3 instead of a 4, 5, or 6. By the same token, those with overall smaller scores might receive an item weight of 4, 5, or 6 instead of 1, 2, or 3. These response deviations are inconsistencies. If there are too many inconsistencies in any given response pattern for particular items, then those items become suspect. An inconsistent item may not be from the same universe as the other items. Possibly the inconsistent item may be excluded from the rest in order to improve the internal consistency of the measure and thereby improve its reliability. To illustrate item inconsistencies, consider the hypothetical response patterns of 12 research participants to 10 items in a questionnaire designed to measure variable X. These are shown in Table 11.2.

The body of Table 11.2 consists of weights assigned to each of the 10 items. Each column consists of the response pattern of different individuals to the ten items. Note the consistency of subject 1 to all items except item 5. Note also the consistency of subject 2 (with opposite response patterns and indicat-

TABLE 11.2 Example of Item Discrimination Analysis

Item	Subject											
	1	2	3	4	5	6	7	8	9	10	11	12
1	6	1	3	2	5	1	6	4	1	4	1	6
2	5	1	2	1	5	1	6	4	1	4	1	6
3	6	2	2	1	5	2	6	4	1	5	2	5
4	6	1	3	1	4	2	6	4	1	4	2	6
5	2	5	6	4	2	4	2	2	5	2	4	3
6	6	2	1	1	5	2	6	4	1	3	2	5
7	6	1	2	2	6	2	5	4	2	5	1	6
8	5	1	3	3	5	2	5	4	3	5	2	4
9	5	1	3	1	5	2	6	4	1	6	2	5
10	6	1	2	1	5	1	6	4	3	6	2	4

ing low attitudinal intensity) to all items except 5. Subject 3 is equally consistent in responses with the exception of item 5. When certain items stand out from the rest as being inconsistent, this may be considered evidence to challenge not only the reliability of the particular item, but also its validity. If items are to be discarded and total attitudinal scores are recalculated on the basis of the new item composition and arrangement, the resulting score would be considered a more reliable estimate of the person's attitude X.

It is important to note that items having consistently inconsistent response patterns such as item 5 in Table 11.2 may not be unreliable items. If they are consistently inconsistent, we must examine the weight pattern we have assigned them. It may be that we mistakenly applied the 6, 5, 4, 3, 2, and 1 pattern to this item weight pattern when it should have received a 1, 2, 3, 4, 5, and 6 pattern. The wording of the item should be considered in relation to the weights we have assigned. In short, we may have a reliable item. It may be that we simply assigned the wrong weight to it.

Another way of spotting inconsistent items is to deal with the discriminatory power of each item and reject those items that fail to discriminate between individuals possessing the attitudinal trait to a high or a low degree respectively. This method is as follows. We would first obtain responses from N individuals and rank them according to their total raw scores on the measuring instrument from high to low, or from the largest to smallest scores. Next, we would divide the total scores into the upper and lower quartiles. The upper quartile would contain the upper 25 percent of all raw scores, while the lower quartile would contain the lower 25 percent of all raw scores. Those individuals in the center of the distribution, the central 50 percent of it, would be excluded from further consideration according to this particular internal consistency procedure. The argument favoring their exclusion is that if the item discriminates, then it is most observable in the case of extreme attitudinal intensity scores.

We now have two groups of respondents representing both extremes of attitudinal intensity. As one example, suppose we evaluated the hypothetical data presented in Table 11.2. Taking one item at a time on the measure, we could construct a table identifying the response weights of all individuals in the upper and lower quartiles. In Table 11.3, all responses to item 1 have been recorded for two groups of subjects in the upper and lower quartiles, considering their overall scores. This table has been constructed, based upon an overall sample of 40 persons. Thus, the upper and lower quartiles would consist of 10 persons each, since $10/40 = 25$ percent. In this particular instance, note that the weights of persons in the upper quartile are considerably larger collectively compared with the weights shown for the subjects in the lower quartile. This is what we would expect logically for an item that discriminates between individuals possessing varying degrees of some attitudinal characteristic.

On the basis of the total scores persons receive for a set of attitudinal items, we may infer that their response for each item should be consistent with their overall responses. Therefore, persons identified as belonging to the upper quartile should have consistently larger weights assigned their responses for each item in the questionnaire, and those who belong to the lower quartile on the basis of their total score should have consistently smaller weights assigned their responses for each item. In the case illustrated in Table 11.3, item 1 (any item taken from the set of items in our measure of some attitude) appears to discriminate. We must verify this statement further, however.

The next step is to determine the average weight for item 1 among the subjects of the upper and lower quartiles. Averaging the weights of both groups, we have a mean or $\overline{X}_1$ (the average score for the upper quartile on item 1) = 5.1. The mean or $\overline{X}_2$ for the lower quartile on the same item is 2.4. A visual inspection of the difference between the means of both groups would reveal that the item appears to discriminate between those who possess the trait to a high degree and those who possess it to a low degree.

TABLE 11.3 Illustration of Item Discrimination Analysis for a Single Item: Responses of Upper and Lower Quartiles to Item 1

$N_1 = 10$ Upper Quartile	$N_2 = 10$ Lower Quartile
6	1
5	3
4	2
5	3
4	4
5	3
6	4
6	1
5	2
5	1
Sum of item scores = 51	Sum of item scores = 24
$\overline{X}_1 = 5.1$	$\overline{X}_2 = 2.4$

We may continue our item analysis by selecting item 2, recording the response weights for all individuals in the upper and lower quartiles, determining the average response for both groups, and so on. Finally, we would generate a table containing the means and mean differences of the upper and lower quartiles of subjects for all 10 items as is shown in Table 11.4.

In Table 11.4, the column to the far right contains mean differences between the average weights of the upper and lower quartiles of respondents based upon total scores to a measure of attitude X. Notice that items 1, 4, 5, 7, 8 and 9 appear to discriminate between the two groups to varying degrees. These averages are consistent with what we would expect them to be. Note also that items 2, 3, and 6 do not appear to discriminate at all. In fact, item 6 contradicts slightly the way the average weights should logically be arranged in relation to one another. Predictably, averages for each item among the upper quartile of respondents should be larger than the averages of item weights for members of the lower quartile. Finally, observe that item 10 discriminates, but it does so in reverse!

There are several reasons why the item fails to discriminate as predicted. First, it could be a poor item and should not be included with the other items. It does not measure the phenomenon under investigation. Second, it may be that the researchers assigned the wrong weights to that particular statement. They must double-check the statement and response pattern assigned to it before throwing the item out altogether. It can be observed that if response weights have been assigned inappropriately to that item, then a correction will reinstate the item as a discriminating one. The function of item discrimination analysis is to improve the reliability of a test by eliminating those items that are inconsistent with the other items.

If researchers were to use item discrimination analysis, it would be advisable to begin by including a large number of items, at least in excess of 20. When item analysis is completed, several of the statements will be eliminated from the list because of their inability to discriminate between those individuals possessing vari-

TABLE 11.4 Comparison of the Upper and Lower Quartiles

Item	Upper Quartile $\bar{X}_1$	Lower Quartile $\bar{X}_2$	Mean Difference $\bar{X}_1 - \bar{X}_2$
1	5.1	2.4	+2.7
2	4.6	4.5	+0.1
3	3.3	3.3	0.0
4	5.5	3.1	+2.4
5	4.8	1.8	+3.0
6	3.9	4.1	−0.2
7	5.0	4.0	+1.0
8	4.8	2.5	+2.3
9	4.9	2.8	+2.1
10	1.3	5.4	−4.1

able amounts of the attitudinal trait under investigation. As a result of eliminating items, the range of response that is possible to achieve is narrowed. Considering the previously given response pattern of 6, 5, 4, 3, 2, and 1, a 20-item questionnaire would yield a total response range of from 20 to 120. Decreasing the number of items from 20 to 10 will narrow the range of response of from 10 to 60. Decisions to eliminate items are based in part on the following considerations:

1. The degree to which the item discriminates
2. The number of individuals to whom the instrument is administered
3. The degree to which precision is desired by researchers in their attempt to measure the attitudinal phenomenon

If researchers reject too many items, the likelihood of larger numbers of tied scores among respondents is increased. This narrows the latitude of flexibility in the data analysis stage and will affect tabular construction and significantly eliminate statistical test options. On the other hand, if too many items are retained, then the chance of including items that discriminate poorly increases.

Choices as to which items should be retained and which ones should be excluded are almost always made arbitrarily by the researcher. Again, no specific conventional guidelines exist for making these kinds of decisions. Some researchers have advocated conducting statistical tests of significance of difference between two means as a way of introducing probability theory into their decisions to accept or reject specific attitudinal statements, but this is not recommended. Nevertheless, in Table 11.4, for example, items 1, 4, 5, 8, and 9 would probably be included in the final form of the measure of attitude X. The other items would either be excluded entirely or modified and reexamined within another subject situation. The decision to include specific items from Table 11.4 was based on a purely arbitrary mean difference of + 2.00 or greater in the expected direction.

When the final items are chosen, it is possible to rescore the entire sample according to the remaining items. The results for all persons involved should be more reliable than before item analysis was applied. At least the internal consistency of the instrument has been significantly improved. And to that extent, the overall reliability of the instrument was strengthened.

A question may arise about why the middle 50 percent of persons was excluded from the original item analysis. The reason is that the upper and lower quartiles represent the extreme attitudinal intensities in either direction. Those persons in the middle of the distribution in terms of their overall scores are more likely to have response weights of 3 or 4 associated with each item. Thus, the discriminatory ability of each item would be obscured by using these middle-of-the-road persons and their scores.

Strengths and Weaknesses of Item Discrimination Analysis. One advantage of item discrimination analysis is that it assists researchers in eliminating those unreliable items that are inconsistent with the rest and the internal consistency of any measure is strengthened. On the negative side, item discrimination analysis may result in the exclusion of items that truly measure the trait investigated. Some of those excluded items may be among the best indicators of the trait measured.

External Reliability Checks

External reliability checks utilize cumulative test results against themselves as a means of verifying the reliability of the measure. Test results for a group of people are compared in two different time periods, or two sets of results from equivalent, but different, tests groups are compared. Two major methods of determining the reliability of a test by external consistency are test–retest and parallel forms of the same test.

Test-Retest.   The method of **test–retest** as a reliability measure is perhaps the most popular of all procedures discussed in this section. To determine the reliability of a measuring instrument using test–retest, an attitudinal measuring instrument is administered to a sample of persons at a given point in time. After a given time interval lapses (perhaps two to four weeks), the instrument is administered again to the same persons. The two sets of test results are correlated, and the resulting correlation coefficient is a measure of the reliability of the attitudinal measure. The higher the correlation between the two sets of scores, the more reliable the instrument. All of this assumes that nothing intervenes to influence test scores of these subjects between the two time periods. The logic is that if the measure is reliable, the score results should be equivalent or nearly equivalent in both time periods.

A reliable measure will reflect the characteristic to the same degree over two different time periods where no intervening variables can interfere significantly with test scores. A high correlation or similarity between the two sets of scores for the same individuals is considered as evidence of the instrument's reliability. Then, if researchers wish to use the instrument in an experimental situation, in which some experimental variable is anticipated to elicit changes among respondents, then the use of the reliable measure may yield score differences between the two time intervals that will most likely be attributable to the experimental variable rather than to the unreliability of the instrument.

The test-retest reliability method is useful primarily in stable social situations in which it is unlikely that the environment will change significantly from one test administration to the next (particularly over relatively short time periods such as a few months). Ideally, for a measuring instrument to be demonstrably reliable, the researcher expects a situation similar to that shown in Table 11.5.

In Table 11.5, scores are shown in the upper half of the table for 10 individuals in a test–retest situation with no intervening variable occurring between the two test administrations. There are no differences between scores comparing the two time periods. In the lower half of the table, score changes over two time periods are illustrated. Researchers want the measure to be reliable so that any observed score differences following the introduction of the experimental variable can tentatively be attributable to it. Score differences from one time period

TABLE 11.5 Scores for Ten Individuals on Measure of Attitude A

Individual	t_1	t_2	Difference in Scores $t_1 - t_2$
Experimental variable absent			
1	45	45	0
2	35	35	0
3	27	27	0
4	50	50	0
5	46	46	0
6	31	31	0
7	29	29	0
8	30	30	0
9	41	41	0
10	45	45	0
Experimental variable present			
1	45	20	−15
2	35	18	−17
3	27	22	− 5
4	50	31	−19
5	46	40	− 6
6	31	22	− 9
7	29	26	− 3
8	30	29	− 1
9	41	40	− 1
10	45	38	− 7

to the next should reflect actual differences in the trait being measured rather than the result of some chance fluctuation of an unreliable instrument.

Advantages and Criticisms of the Test–Retest Reliability Method.   One of the major strengths of the test-retest method for determining reliability is that it permits instruments to be compared directly against themselves. An instrument that performs unreliably in a test-retest situation may require some kind of item-by-item analysis, such as item discrimination analysis, in order to determine which items discriminate between those who possess the trait to varying degrees. Test-retest also most directly reveals the continuity of the measure over time. It is easier to use in an external reliability check than other methods designed to perform the same function. Test-retest is quick and easy to apply, and it offers researchers the greatest degree of control over extraneous factors that might otherwise interfere with the instrument's reliability.

On the negative side, test-retest means that respondents will be able to see the same items again and perhaps recall how they originally responded. There is often a strain for consistency among respondents, and therefore, even if they really feel differently in another time period, they will attempt to recreate their original responses from the first instrument administration. There is little researchers can do to prevent respondents from recalling their original responses to questions. One way of dealing with this problem is to lengthen the time interval between test administrations to several months. However, changes might occur among these persons over time as the result of natural causes and **maturation.** Conventionally, two to four weeks is considered an appropriate time interval between test administrations when applying the test–retest reliability check, but there is no prescribed time interval that is universally accepted by all criminologists.

Another weakness of test–retest is that it is not foolproof. It is difficult for researchers to assess the impact of extraneous factors that might otherwise affect scores in two time periods. A high correlation between two sets of scores is not absolute proof of the test's reliability, since consistencies may be the result of chance fluctuations. Also, when researchers enter social settings to administer their instruments, their entry into these settings acts as an intervening variable that must be considered. Sometimes, after persons have had an opportunity to observe questionnaires and scales, they may not be receptive to reentry at a later date to complete the second phase of the test–retest sequence.

Parallel Forms of the Same Test.   A second major reliability check is the use of **parallel forms of the same test.** When researchers use parallel forms of the same test, they actually devise two separate measures of the same phenomenon. Previously mentioned was the 16 PF, a personality inventory developed by Raymond Cattell. This instrument has two versions, Form A and Form B. Both versions consist of 187 questions, and both purportedly measure 16 different personality dimensions. Both versions of the 16 PF are considered equivalent. Whenever factor analyses of these instruments are conducted, they "factor" into 16 different parts. Interestingly, those items on Form A that purportedly measure certain personality dimensions factor into the same areas as those items on Form B that supposedly measure the same dimensions. Thus, the two versions of the measure help to validate each other as well as to verify the reliability of each.

Advantages and Criticisms of the Parallel Forms of the Same Test.   The chief advantage of devising two separate tests of the same attitudinal variable is that the instruments may be administered to the same audiences over different time periods without having to worry about recalling previous responses. The two versions of these measures are made up of entirely different items. It is impossible to recall how you responded to items you haven't seen. Further, it is unnecessary to have "waiting periods" between test administrations in order to evaluate the measure's reliability. Basically, two forms of the measure are administered and their results are correlated.

On the negative side, it is quite difficult and time-consuming to create two separate measures of the same attitudinal phenomenon. Some researchers have difficulty creating one measure. Doubling the number of items compounds, the problems of establishing test validity and reliability. Finally, it is difficult to establish the equivalency of two instruments that purportedly measure the same phenomenon. What if the two measures correlate highly? Does this mean the measures are reliable? What if they measure different attitudes, although those different attitudes may be related to a degree? One test may measure factor *X*, while the other measures factor *Y*. A high correlation between the two measures doesn't automatically mean that the two instruments are measuring identical phenomena.

■ SOME FUNCTIONAL RELATIONSHIPS BETWEEN VALIDITY AND RELIABILITY

Of the two properties of measuring instruments, validity and reliability, the more important is reliability. There are several reasons for this. Before we examine these reasons, four general statements about the relation between validity and reliability may be made:

1. *Valid instruments are always reliable instruments.* This statement says that if you *really are* measuring whatever you say you are measuring, then you are also measuring it consistently. All valid measures are also reliable measures.

2. *Instruments that are not valid measures of a specific variable may or may not be reliable.* This means that if you are not really measuring variable *X*, then you *may* or *may not* be measuring something else, such as variable *Y*. If we say we are measuring variable *X*, such as job burnout, but in fact, we are *really* measuring variable *Y*, which may be job stress, then we don't have a valid measure of *X* (burnout) but we *do* have a valid measure of *Y* (stress). We just don't know that we have a valid measure of *Y* (stress).

3. *Reliable instruments may or may not be valid for measuring specific variables.* What this means is that if we are measuring something consistently such as variable *X* (job stress), then the instrument is a valid measure of job stress. However, the instrument may actually be measuring something else, such as job burnout. We don't know we're measuring job burnout, since we think the instrument is measuring job stress. In short, we really don't know what we're measuring, but at least it is significant. We can rely on it. The same thing is true about reliability. If our instrument exhibits reliability, we are measuring something. We may or may not be measuring what we think we are measuring, but we are definitely measuring something consistently.

4. *Unreliable instruments are never valid.* If we do not have a reliable measure, then we most definitely do not have validity either. Reliability is fundamental to an instrument's validity. Reliability is the more important measure characteristic, therefore, since validity is very much dependent on the instrument's reliability. If any measure lacks reliability, then it also lacks validity. However, any measure that lacks validity for measuring a specific phenomenon may or may not lack reliability.

■ FACTORS THAT AFFECT VALIDITY AND RELIABILITY

Thus far, we have examined validity and reliability in considerable detail and have considered several ways these instrument properties may be assessed or determined. In this section, we focus upon several factors and conditions that significantly affect the validity and reliability of measures. These factors are as follows: (1) the instrument and its contents, (2) environmental factors, (3) personal factors, (4) researcher interpretations, (5) the testing (pretest) effect, (6) selection bias, (7) experimental mortality, (8) the halo effect, (9) the placebo effect, and (10) diffusion of treatment with control and experimental groups.

The Instrument and Its Contents

Whenever the validity and reliability of attitudinal measures are assessed, the first aspect to be critically scrutinized is the list of items included in the instrument. Are the items valid? Have they been drawn from the universe of traits and characteristics that measure the phenomenon under investigation? If the researcher has been careless and included items from a universe other than the one consistent with the variable designated in the theoretical scheme, the validity of the test will be seriously undermined. Apart from the logical and theoretical connection between the items included in the measure and the trait to be measured, other aspects of the test emerge as crucial as well. Some of these factors are (1) the length of the test, (2) the cultural date of the test, (3) open-ended versus fixed-response questions, and (4) mechanical factors.

1. *The length of the test.* A lengthy instrument will sometimes cause respondents to give answers based on convenience rather than how they really feel about things. Longer tests may become boring, and respondents begin to check the first responses they come to, as is the case with set responses.

2. *The cultural date of the test.* A test that uses words or phrases not used conventionally becomes increasingly unreliable and, hence, not a valid indicator of the trait in question. Using a term such as "ice box" to refer to "refrigerators" may create a misunderstanding between the meaning intended by the statement (defined by the researcher) and the way it is understood by respondents. The American Correctional Association and the American Jail Association have done much in recent years to improve the professional image of correctional officers who work in jails and prisons. In recent years, the term *guard,* used earlier to refer to those who perform jail duties and monitor inmates, has been rejected as archaic and derogatory. In its place, the term *jail officer* is considered more respectful and dignified. The use of the word *guard* on a questionnaire to be administered to jail officers may be considered offensive by them. Thus, unwittingly, researchers may evoke hostility from respondents because of the terms they use to characterize the respondents and their work.

3. *Open-ended versus fixed-response questions.* Measures that utilize open-ended questions (questions that have respondents furnish written answers rather than check specific fixed alternatives) place a strong emphasis on the ability of respondents to express themselves in writing. Respondents' educational sophistication then becomes an important consideration. Because the type of response provided to open-ended questions determines the degree of intensity of some attitude possessed by respondents, it is clear that the ability to express themselves may seem to reflect differences in attitudes by persons of varying educational backgrounds when actually there are no differences.

4. *Mechanical factors.* Mechanical factors refer to instrument problems, including misspelled words, illegible words, missing pages, and poorly phrased items. All of these mechanical factors may cause some misunderstanding of instrument content, and this misunderstanding will detract from the instrument's validity and reliability. The same is true of face-to-face interviews. If researchers leave certain statements off their list of questions or if they use alternative words at random, the information solicited becomes less reliable, since respondents may make different interpretations of the questions asked. Ideally, the same administration conditions should prevail for each respondent. This uniformity would tend to minimize the possibility of errors due to differences in the way various subjects are approached by the investigator. Usually, pretests of instruments in smaller-scale pilot studies help to eliminate most of the mechanical deficiencies of measures.

Environmental Factors

Environmental factors describe the conditions under which instruments are administered. These include face-to-face interviews versus self-administered questionnaires and the clarity of instructions for completing the instrument.

1. *Face-to-face interviews versus self-administered questionnaires.* Varying the degree of anonymity or confidentiality under which the instrument is administered may generate score differences for the same person under various test administration conditions. Persons sometimes report feelings to an interviewer face-to-face that are quite different from those feelings they would otherwise disclose in a more confidential, self-administered questionnaire situation in which considerable anonymity exists.

2. *The clarity of instructions for completing the instrument.* If investigators fail to clarify the procedures to be followed in the completion of the instrument, there is a good chance that subjects will provide misleading information unintentionally.

Personal Factors

Some of the more relevant personal characteristics that impinge upon the validity and reliability of measures include (1) the socioeconomic status of the respondent; (2) the age, gender, and maturity level of the respondent; (3) the respondent's ethnic and racial background; (4) the respondent's memory or recall ability; and (5) the social desirability sought by the respondent.

1. *Socioeconomic status of respondents.* Occupation, educational level, income, and race/ethnicity are primary components of socioeconomic status. These factors may influence performance on any attitudinal instrument. Researchers should attempt to construct their questionnaires and other measures to closely approximate the socioeconomic level of the audiences they investigate. The cultural aspects of any measuring instrument will limit the generalizability and utility of it to particular social aggregates.

2. *Age, sex, and maturity level.* Like socioeconomic status, age and gender are important considerations in any instrument administration. Closely associated with age and gender are differences in maturity levels among respondents. The maturity level of intended respondents may influence the manner in which researchers are accepted and the degree of cooperation and interest demonstrated by participating subjects.

3. *Ethnic and racial background.* Although ethnicity and race are conventionally regarded as a part of socioeconomic status, it is worthwhile to note that ethnic background may account for certain misunderstandings pertaining to word choices in questionnaires. Different words may have different meanings and convey different ideas to people from different ethnic backgrounds as well as to persons of different socioeconomic statuses. In testing and measurement, researchers are increasingly moving toward the development of culture-free measures. They are learning more and more to appreciate the fact that tests often have built-in cultural biases that significantly affect our interpretations of results for different ethnic audiences.

4. *Memory or recall.* The ability of subjects to recall earlier responses on a before-and-after test administration may elicit responses consistent with earlier ones, regardless of whether or not the respondent's beliefs are the same in both time periods. Parallel forms of the same test are used frequently to overcome the effects of memory or recall in test–retest situations, particularly if the span of time between test administrations is short.

5. *Social desirability.* Many questionnaires have social desirability measures incorporated into them to ascertain the effect of this important variable on a subject's overall response pattern. Social desirability, or responding in accordance with what subjects believe to be a desirable set of traits rather than what might be true of them, frequently contaminates questionnaires and obscures how respondents really feel about things. There is no way to prevent social desirability from occurring.

Researcher Interpretations

Another important consideration in assessing an instrument's validity and reliability is the kind of interpretation made of instrument results by researchers. This includes the coding procedure and the interpretations of raw scores.

Box
11.2

Lanette Dalley
Minot State University

Statistics: B.S. (sociology), Montana State University; M.S.W. (social work), Washington University of St. Louis, MO; Ph.D. (criminology), Indiana University of Pennsylvania.

Interests: My current research interests are female inmates and their children, domestic violence, juvenile justice, and law and mental illness. I considered focusing my doctoral studies on juvenile delinquency, although I subsequently decided to study female offenders and their children after reading an earlier study involving this population.

My bachelor's degree was from Montana State University, and I soon became a juvenile probation officer for the state of Utah. Eventually I obtained an M.S.W. from Washington University in St. Louis. My concentration was on children and youth, as well as family therapy. I worked as a psychiatric social worker for an in-patient psychiatric facility for adolescents as well as at a community mental health center.

During the time I was collecting data for my doctoral dissertation at Indiana University of Pennsylvania, I found that most studies had investigated the mother–child relation only during imprisonment. These studies suggested that the mother–child relationship was strained because of enforced separation. However, based on my experience as a social worker and probation officer, I questioned the quality of the mother–child relationship *before* imprisonment. I found that the majority of the relationships were strained long before maternal imprisonment because of other separations, parental addiction and neglect, domestic violence, and poor parenting skills and knowledge. Unfortunately, my study found that because of the weakened relationship before imprisonment, reunification of the mother and child can be extremely difficult and at times hopeless. Thus, the study provided valuable data regarding who these women and children really were, as opposed to how we would like to envision them. However, on the positive side, my study ultimately provided the foundation for proactive policies in terms of addressing the intergenerational cycle of incarceration. Moreover, by understanding the reality of the situation, steps could be taken to resolve the underlying and preexisting problems with the mother–child relationship, thereby making reunification at least possible in many cases.

Advice to Students: Students who have an interest in studying female offenders need to consider a variety of things. First, because many female offenders experience illiteracy, cognitive delays, and mental health problems, questionnaires should be researcher administered in order for the women to understand the questions and provide more accurate data. Second, **quantitative data** need to be combined with **qualitative data** when examining sensitive topics, such as addictions, parenting styles, parental and children's rights, and physical and sexual abuse. Third, students need to have training and experience dealing with individuals who have these types of characteristics, including an understanding of child development, addictions, crisis intervention, and assessment. Fourth, students will need to be able to withstand hearing the often traumatic and disheartening details of these women's lives. If at all possible, students will need to debrief with a colleague or chairperson during the research process in order to maintain a perspective and prevent burnout. Finally, although research in this area may be disconcerting, successful application in this area allows the greatest possible satisfaction for the researcher: making a true difference in the lives of women and their children, those who are most in need of realistic assistance.

1. *Coding procedures.* Researchers may code their information any way they wish. The validity and reliability of instruments often hinge, in part, on the coding pattern followed by investigators. It is possible for researchers to code their information in such ways as to increase the chances of supporting one particular theoretical perspective or another. Objectivity in coding is encouraged, and it is recommended that researchers compare their own coding procedures with those used by other researchers who investigate similar phenomena. This will not guarantee that their coding procedures will be foolproof, but at least researchers can minimize the possibility that their own values and biases will enter the picture significantly when data are interpreted.

2. *Interpretation of raw scores.* Raw scores on any attitudinal measure are seldom meaningful apart from their comparison with other scores on the same scale. When researchers extract raw scores, they run the risk of assigning meanings to scores that are quite different from the practical meanings those scores have in a comparative sense. Single-score interpretations should be made conservatively and tentatively. Sometimes previous norms exist for specific instrument applications to certain types of audiences. These norms may be used for evaluations of scores on subsequent administrations, although researchers should not rely too much on such previous norms. It is likely that each test administration is somewhat different from previous test administrations, and that the norms applicable in one setting may not be applicable to another setting.

Testing (Pretest) Effect

Respondents who are given the same self-administered questionnaires over several different time periods may be influenced by the fact that they have previous experience with or exposure to the same questionnaire. For instance, suppose you wanted to chart or track the influence of a type of counseling intervention for juvenile offenders over time. Your intent is to see whether juvenile offenders develop more positive self-concepts as the result of exposure to an innovative counseling method. Therefore, you administer a self-concept questionnaire to these youths in time 1, prior to the counseling, and then again at successive time intervals throughout the duration of the counseling, which may be six months. Each month you administer the same self-concept questionnaire to these juveniles. Each month they are exposed to the same questionnaire items. After the counseling therapy, you compare the juvenile offenders' scores across the different time periods to see if there are marked improvements in their self-concepts.

Now you may or may not find differences in these youths' self-concept scores from the different questionnaire administrations. After all, these youths have been given the same self-concept questionnaire at least six or seven times. You presume that each time they have responded to the same questionnaire, they have been truthful. If there have been improvements in their self-concepts, these changes should be evident from the different test or questionnaire administrations. Few changes or small changes in self-concept may be the effects of repeated testing.

Investigators label these effects as **pretest effects** or **pretest bias.** Interestingly, under repeated questionnaire administrations, many respondents in different studies have reported changes in their attitudes and behaviors. However, sometimes respondents do not report changes in their behaviors or attitudes even though they have actually changed. When asked about *why* they don't report changes in their behaviors on these questionnaires, some respondents reply that they wanted to be consistent with how they responded in earlier questionnaire administrations. This strain for consistency seems illogical to researchers who expect respondents to tell the truth and report differences in their behaviors and attitudes as they occur over time. Despite our best efforts to elicit truthful answers from respondents, the fact is that they may not be truthful for various reasons. This fact is attributable to pretest bias or the **testing effect.**

Selection Bias

Selection bias refers to deliberately designating two groups for comparison when the two groups are not equivalent in various salient characteristics. For instance, if an investigator wished to study the effects of electronic monitoring, two samples of probationers might be selected for comparison. Beforehand, the investigator knows that 100 probationers differ according to a risk assessment instrument they have been given. The risk-assessment instrument measures their potential dangerousness and community risk (i.e., the risk the community is exposed to by these probationers). The researcher divides the probationers into two groups of 50 probationers each according to those receiving the highest and those receiving the lowest risk scores. Those with the highest risk scores are monitored in the community for one year under standard supervision, which involves minimal probationer/client contacts with the probation office. Those with the lowest risk scores are placed on electronic monitoring for one year and are otherwise expected to comply with other standard probation conditions. At the end of one year, the different samples of probationers are compared according to their recidivism rates and numbers of program infractions. The sample of electronically monitored probationers has a much lower rate of recidivism and fewer program infractions than the sample of standard probationers who were not electronically monitored. The researchers conclude that electronic monitoring caused the lower recidivism rates and fewer numbers of program rule infractions.

Do you believe that this comparison is a legitimate one? Don't you think it is peculiar that the high-risk offenders would be placed on standard probation, while the low-risk offenders would be placed on electronic monitoring? We are not dealing with a level playing field here. This comparison is flawed. The researcher deliberately contrived a situation for comparison in which those *least likely to reoffend,* those with low risk scores, were placed in an electronic monitoring program, where their whereabouts could be verified 24 hours a day. However, the high-risk group of probationers was virtually *unsupervised* much of the time, reporting perhaps monthly to the probation office. Thus, the high-risk group of probationers was far more likely to recidivate than the low-risk group. In fact, we would have *expected* the high-risk probationers to reoffend at a greater rate and have more program infractions compared with the low-risk group. This is known as "creaming" in the probation profession, where only the best candidates are selected for inclusion in client community management programs, such as electronic monitoring. These are the very persons *who do not need to be electronically monitored.* Thus, it is very unclear whether the fact of electronic monitoring resulted in lower recidivism rates and fewer program infractions, or whether the fact of the low-risk nature of the probationer sample resulted in lower recidivism rates and fewer program infractions. More legitimate comparisons of groups require that the groups should be equivalent. Selection bias should be eliminated in order for valid comparisons and evaluations to be made.

Experimental Mortality

In any experiment, especially a longitudinal study over time, the same sample of respondents may be studied. The researcher's intent is to compare these respondents at different time periods to determine the effects of an experimental variable. But experimental mortality may occur. This means that some attrition occurs among the sample of respondents. Fewer respondents exist in later time periods than in earlier time periods. **Experimental mortality** may occur for a variety of reasons. Persons may move away, be transferred, or refuse to participate in subsequent experimental periods. In fact, some respondents may die.

Suppose an investigator were studying the effects of a new inmate management method for elderly inmates in a federal prison. Elderly inmates were previously housed in isolated cells. Many of these inmates were morose and moody, depressed, with low self-esteem levels. Under a new inmate management method, elderly inmates were transferred to dormitory-like housing, where they were celled in pairs. Investigators believed that these new accommodations, especially for elderly offenders, would result in improved self-esteem, and that fewer elderly inmates would be depressed, moody, and morose. Researchers planned to study elderly inmate attitudes over a two-year transition period. They started out with 200 elderly inmates in 1996, but by 1998, only 124 of the original elderly inmates were still housed in the federal prison. Attrition resulted in a reduction of 66 inmates compared with the original sample. Attrition was caused by 40 inmate deaths from old age or fatal diseases, and 26 other inmates were paroled.

But experimental mortality occurs in other ways besides death and disease. Suppose you are studying a sample of 500 male delinquents in Compton, California. These are adjudicated delinquents who are gang members. You plan to study these 500 delinquents over a one-year time period. Your experiment contemplates exposing these youths to a Big Brother program, in which each youth is assigned to an adult male who will work with that youth on a one-to-one basis. As a part of the program, the Big Brother will take the youth to sports events and to other activities on weekends. The intent of the experiment is to decrease delinquent propensities by providing social alternatives to delinquency. Further, the Big Brothers are supposed to provide a caring and interpersonally supportive environment for these youths.

At the beginning of the year, 500 male delinquents are designated by the Compton Juvenile Court, and Big Brothers are assigned each of these youths. However, by the end of the year, only 260 of the youths are still participating in the Big Brother program. The remaining 240 youths moved away from Compton to other cities or out of the state and could not be located. This is an example of experimental mortality.

Experimental mortality poses a serious problem for researchers. In our example, the characteristics of those who drop out of the study are unknown, other than the scant information from the superficial juvenile records that have been maintained about them. Had these juveniles remained in the Big Brother program, then the significance of the Big Brother program as a delinquency prevention mechanism could be more adequately assessed. With about half of the delinquents remaining in the program, we are able to report on the successfulness of the Big Brother program for only 260 delinquents. Therefore, experimental mortality causes the same difficulty for researchers that nonresponse to mailed questionnaires poses. We don't know who the nonrespondents are. We have no way of calculating the impact of the nonrespondents on our final results and study findings, for they have not been included in our data analysis. The same is true about the dropout effect in experimental mortality. We have no way of assessing the impact of the study on these persons, since they were not a part of our final data analysis. Researchers can exert little or no control over experimental mortality. Rather, they must make the best of study findings based on those respondents who are present throughout the entire research process.

Halo Effect

The **halo effect** is the bias toward observed subjects based upon preconceived opinions of the observer. Perhaps a researcher has been advised that there are two groups of inmates. One group, group A, has participated in a self-help GED program and other prison educational and vocational services while incarcerated. The other group, group B, has not made use of the self-help GED program or the other prison educational and vocational services. If the researcher knows who the individual inmates are from both groups and later conducts experiments between the two groups, some bias may exist toward group A. If the investigator must rate the two groups of inmates later on some variable, such as improvement in self-esteem or self-worth, group A inmates may be designated as having improved more than group B inmates. In fact, neither group has changed in self-esteem or self-worth during the investigator's experiment. The halo effect occurs when the researcher attributes greater self-worth and self-esteem to a group of inmates known to have participated in self-help prison programs.

Another example of the halo effect might be a study of police officers in a precinct where citizen complaints against the police are low or infrequent. The investigator perceives that the police officers in the precinct must be better, on the average, compared with officers in other precincts, since they have fewer citizen complaints filed against them. Later, when the investigator observes these officers as they implement a community policing program and attempt to foster better public relations between themselves and community residents, the investigator may believe that these officers are superior to or more effective than officers in other precincts where community policing and public relations improvements are attempted. In reality, the officers of all precincts are equivalent in their community policing and public relations effectiveness. However, because one precinct has the lowest numbers of citizen complaints, its effectiveness is rated more highly. The researcher simply believes that these officers are inherently better than other officers. The investigator's perception of their effectiveness will carry over and influence their performance in other tasks.

The halo effect is a dangerous phenomenon, since it can nullify the objectivity of any experimental situation. Researchers must guard against such preconceived opinions about any group they study. In Knoxville, Tennessee, for example, the Knox County Sheriff's Department had a volunteer auxiliary unit known as the Organized Reserve. The Organized Reserve was an unpaid organization, and it performed valuable work such as guard duty at the Knox County Jail. Some Organized Reserve officers performed cruiser work and assisted regular sheriff's deputies in their patrols. However, because these Organized Reserve officers were volunteers, they were regarded as second-class citizens in the sheriff's department. Their uniforms differed from regular deputies' uniforms only by the inclusion of "OR" on the county sheriff patch worn at the shoulder. There was no basis for these biased perceptions from regular deputies, since Organized Reserve officers went through officer training and participated in numerous law enforcement exercises regularly. Had any experiment been conducted involving police professionalism, comparing Organized Reserve officers with regular sheriff's deputies, it is likely that Organized Reserve officers would have been downgraded in their professionalism despite the existence of few if any differences in the two groups of officers. The halo effect compromises the validity and reliability of any study in which preconceived biases exist about the groups to be studied.

Placebo Effect

The **placebo effect** originated with biochemical experiments on human subjects. A **placebo** is a harmless, nonmedicinal substance. In experiments, placebos are used as controls in order to test the efficacy of another medicinal substance. Groups receiving placebos are control groups and are usually matched with another group, the experimental group, that receives the actual medication intended to produce a specific result. In experiments comparing two groups on motor skills, for instance, one group receives a stimulant drug designed to accelerate reaction time, while the other group receives a pill, the placebo, containing no stimulant. The placebo has no effect whatsoever on body chemistry. However, researchers instruct both groups that they are being given drugs to accelerate their motor skills.

Later, the two groups are compared on some motor-skill activity. Accelerated motor activity is detected among the experimental group members who actually received the drug. However, the control group, the group receiving the placebo, exhibits little or no change in motor-skill behavior. However, there may be *some* improvement in their motor-skill behaviors, simply because these persons *believe* they have received a drug to accelerate their motor skills. Thus, a placebo can have an effect even though it is not intended to do so.

The placebo effect may obscure the effects of social experiments, since both persons in the experimental and control groups may exhibit changes in their behaviors and attitudes. Sometimes persons have been given placebos that were described as hallucinogenic drugs, such as LSD. They have reported feeling "funny" and having distorted perceptions of their surroundings, similar to someone who has taken LSD. In fact, these persons were given absolutely nothing to cause distortions in their perceptions.

Placebos are not always tangible "sugar-coated" pills. Sometimes placebos may be suggestions or instructions. When criminologists conduct experiments with two or more groups, control groups may be given certain instructions or suggestions. These instructions may be that as a result of exposure to some educational course or experience, group members should experience certain feelings or have noticeably increased skills. Subsequently the control group is exposed to a mundane lecture about general leadership skills. Afterwards, the group members report that they have the increased skills or feeling anticipated by the researcher. Thus, these control subjects are conforming their behaviors to fit researchers' expectations. The validity and reliability of studies are impaired to the extent that a placebo effect exists among control groups.

Diffusion of Treatment with Control and Experimental Groups

Sometimes diffusion of treatment may occur between the experimental and control groups. **Diffusion of treatment** occurs whenever the experimental stimulus is partially or totally adopted by both the experimental and control groups. The likelihood for diffusion of treatment is heightened to the extent that the experimental and control groups are in close proximity and may interact.

Suppose researchers study the effects of more frequent face-to-face visits of probation officers with their probationer/clients. Perhaps two probation departments in communities of equal size in the same state are studied. The probation officers from both probation departments in the two cities, Probation Department A and Probation Department B, are involved in an experiment to determine whether greater frequency of face-to-face visits reduces recidivism and improves program success of probationer/clients. In Probation Department A, probation officers are instructed to have five face-to-face visits with 30 different probationers for a period of one year. In Probation Department B, probation officers are instructed to conduct their visits with probationers as usual, meaning perhaps one face-to-face visit per month. At the end of the one-year study, recidivism rates and program success measures will be obtained from probationers in both communities. It is expected that more face-to-face visits will reduce probationer recidivism and improve their program success.

However, suppose probation officers in Probation Department B determine that the experiment is some sort of evaluation of their performance as officers. If they make this determination, they may decide to outperform the probation officers in Probation Department A. They can do this by visiting their own probationers at least as often or more often than the probation officers in Probation Department A. Therefore, for the next year, probation officers in Probation Department B conduct seven face-to-face visits with their probationers. At the end of one year, the investigators compare the recidivism and success rates of the two aggregates of probationers in the two communities and find that there are no differences. They conclude, erroneously, that increasing the number of face-to-face visits with certain probationers has no effect on their recidivism or success rates. In fact, the probation officers in Probation Department B have obscured the study results by deliberately competing with Probation Department A. This is a clear case of diffusion of the treatment variable, the number of face-to-face visits with probationers, and the results of our study of face-to-face interviews on probationer recidivism or program success rates are confounded. When diffusion of treatment occurs, we cannot rely on our study results as valid indicators of the impact of the experimental variable.

The numbers and types of factors that can influence the validity and reliability of studies are endless. Maturational changes in juveniles may cause many of them to grow out of delinquency between the ages of 15 and 17. Studies of delinquency career escalation may be affected by maturational changes. Personality changes or significant disruptions in the social lives of experimental or control group members may cause changes in their reactions to experiments that are not expected or anticipated.

■ OTHER MEANINGS OF VALIDITY

The discussion of validity and reliability in this chapter has been directed largely at the nature and construction of measures used to assess the existence of attitudinal variables. Validity is used in another sense. Sometimes researchers refer to external validity and internal validity in relation to the characteristics of *studies* they conduct.

External Validity

External validity refers to the generalizability of study findings to other samples and populations. The major question raised by external validity is how representative or typical the sample that was used in the study is. Investigators want to know how the sample was selected, how large the sample was, and what evidence exists that reflects favorably on sample representativeness. Generally, we know that probability samples are more often more representative of the populations from which they were drawn than nonprobability samples. But then we also know that certain nonprobability samples, such as saturation or dense samples, contain such a large proportion of the population, as much as 50 percent or more, that they are somewhat representative as well.

The fact is that we never know how representative any sample is unless the entire population is studied. And this event, studying entire populations, defeats the economizing purpose of sampling. Such analytical methods as meta-analysis can enhance a study's external validity to the extent that it seems consistent with the findings of similar studies.

Internal Validity

Internal validity refers to the theoretical and methodological integrity of the study itself. Internal validity assesses the study design and construction of instruments. Theoretical adequacy and the soundness of derived hypotheses are integral parts of a study's internal validity. Any criticism of one's research plan and its implementation is a criticism of the internal validity of a study.

If the validity and/or reliability of the measures used in a study are faulted for any reason, these faults will degrade the study's internal validity. If there is significant nonresponse, social desirability, and set response, internal validity is adversely affected. All of the potential problems that can affect instrument reliability and validity are also problems that can hamper a study's internal validity.

It is desirable for investigators to conduct studies exhibiting both external and internal validity. However, these study properties cannot be guaranteed. No study is perfect. Investigators can enhance the likelihood of a study's external and internal validity by following conventional research strategies and avoiding any situation that might undermine the integrity of the research plan.

■ KEY TERMS

Arbitrary scales	Experimental mortality
Concurrent validity	External reliability checks
Construct validity	External validity
Content validity	Face validity
Criterion validity	Factor analysis
Diffusion of treatment	Factorial validity
Environmental factors	Halo effect

Internal consistency
Internal reliability checks
Internal validity
Item analysis
Item discrimination analysis
Maturation
Parallel forms of the same test
Placebo
Placebo effect
Pragmatic validity
Predictive validity

Pretest bias
Pretest effects
Qualitative data
Quantitative data
Reliability
Selection bias
Split-half method or technique
Testing effect
Test-retest
Universe of items
Validity

■ QUESTIONS FOR REVIEW

1. What is reliability? How is it measured or determined? Describe two internal reliability methods.

2. What are four general relationships between validity and reliability? Discuss each briefly.

3. What is validity? How is it measured or determined? Identify four different methods for determining test validity. Is validity provable? Why or why not? Explain.

4. What are two external methods for determining a test's reliability? Discuss each.

5. Write a short essay on the importance of social desirability and how it might influence test results. How are reliability and validity influenced by social desirability?

6. What is meant by environmental factors that impinge on a test's validity and reliability? Discuss two of these factors.

7. What are five personal factors that influence the validity and reliability of tests?

8. Is it possible to have a valid test that is not reliable? Why or why not?

9. What is meant by a mechanical factor as it pertains to questionnaire construction?

10. How would the cultural dating of a test or measure influence its validity or reliability? Give an example.

11. Compare and contrast test–retest and parallel forms of the same test as reliability checks. What are the respective weaknesses and strengths of each?

12. What is meant by diffusion of treatment?

13. Distinguish between external and internal validity. How can internal validity be improved?

14. What is experimental mortality?

15. What is the placebo effect?

chapter 12

Data Coding, Presentation, and Descriptive Techniques

■ INTRODUCTION

This chapter is about coding, tabulating, and presenting data. Researchers must code or assign numerical values to the different variables used in their research. **Coding** *facilitates the data analysis process. If statistical applications are intended, then coding data in certain ways enables investigators to apply quantitative methods to their collected information.*

Any introduction to criminology or a criminal justice course will expose students to diverse forms of graphic presentation. Graphic presentation includes charts, tabular materials, drawings with lines or bars, pie charts, and other visual material that assists us in describing what we have found. The idea that "a picture is worth a thousand words" is appropriate here. The Uniform Crime Reports, compiled by the FBI and published by the Department of Justice, is filled with graphic material about crime and crime trends. One glance at a well-constructed graph or table can tell you much about whether certain crimes have increased or decreased over different time intervals.

Graphs and tabulated data presentations are not limited to scientific research journals. Popular periodicals, such as U.S. News & World Report, Time, Newsweek, or The Reader's Digest, feature numerous illustrations that inform us about such things as drug flow from South American countries, illegal immigration, violence among juveniles, prison and jail overcrowding, and public opinion or sentiment. Thus, these tables, graphs, charts, figures, and diagrams enhance our understanding of written material. Further, our efforts to build theories and test hypotheses are enhanced by the strategic use of these materials.

This chapter describes several popular graphic techniques and methods that are used to illustrate published material in criminal justice and criminology. We should learn about this material for at least two reasons. First, we will be exposed to a great deal of written material using illustrations to highlight important points. We need to be informed about how these illustrative materials should be interpreted and how they enhance our understanding of subject matter. Second, we will be preparing reports, articles, and other writings ourselves. We want to maximize the reader's understanding of our own work, and graphic materials can assist us in achieving this objective.

Various types of graphs, including line drawings and figures known as pie charts, bar graphs, histograms, and frequency polygons are described. Tabular construction is also discussed. Often we create tables consisting of differing numbers of rows and columns. When our data are distributed in various tables we have created, they become amenable to certain statistical test applications, through which we can evaluate the significance of what we have found. Throughout this chapter, conventional rules guide much of our graphic and tabular construction. Further, each of these illustrative techniques and methods has accompanying strengths and weaknesses.

CODING VARIABLES

Whenever we construct a questionnaire or design an interview, we need to code the questions or statements as well as the responses. Even if we are conducting content analyses or investigating secondary sources for new information, we usually devise a code to give some structure to our analysis. In order to facilitate our processing of information, we often precode our data collection instruments. Perhaps we have a questionnaire that includes the following:

1. ID_____[For research use only]
2. What is your gender? [Check one] _____ Male _____ Female
3. What is your age? [Check one]

    _____ Under 21
    _____ 21–23
    _____ 24–25
    _____ 26–28
    _____ 29 or over

4. What is your education? [Check one]

    _____ Some elementary school, not completed
    _____ Completed elementary school
    _____ Some high school, not completed
    _____ Completed high school
    _____ Some college, not completed
    _____ Completed college
    _____ Graduate work or degree

5. What is your political affiliation? [Check one]

    _____ Democrat
    _____ Republican
    _____ American-Independent
    _____ Other

These are four simple questions. We want to know the respondent's gender, age, educational level, and political affiliation. The "ID" refers to an identifying number we will assign to the questionnaire. This information as it is presented is uncoded. If we were to code the information, we might have something like the following:

Column	Item
1,2,3	1. ID [For research use only] <u>0</u> <u>0</u> <u>1</u>
4 <u>1</u>	2. What is your gender? [Check one]
	1 <u> X </u> Male
	2 _____ Female
5 <u>3</u>	3. What is your age? [Check one]
	1 _____ Under 21
	2 _____ 21–23
	3 <u> X </u> 24–25
	4 _____ 26–28
	5 _____ 29 or over
6 <u>5</u>	4. What is your education? [Check one]
	1 _____ Some elementary school, not completed
	2 _____ Completed elementary school
	3 _____ Some high school, not completed
	4 _____ Completed high school
	5 <u> X </u> Some college, not completed
	6 _____ Completed college
	7 _____ Graduate work or degree
7 <u>2</u>	5. What is your political affiliation? [Check one]
	1 _____ Democrat
	2 <u> X </u> Republican
	3 _____ American Independent
	4 _____ Other

The identified columns are categories designated to contain each variable. Notice that the first three columns, **1, 2, 3,** are used for the respondent's identification: "001" refers to the first person who completes the questionnaire. The next column, **4,** is for recording gender. We have recorded a "1" to indicate that the person checked the "male" subcategory of gender. The next column, **5,** is for recording age. The person indicated "24–25," and so we coded this response with a "3." The next column, **6,** is for recording the person's education. We have recorded a "5" for column **6,** since the person answered "Some college, not completed." For column **7,** we record a "2" to stand for "Republican," the choice indicated by the respondent.

For more complicated coding, such as coding a scale that measures anger intensity or police professionalism, we might have a set of statements with Likert-type responses. For a ten-item scale and a six-point response pattern (Strongly agree = 1; Agree = 2; Undecided, probably agree = 3; Undecided, probably disagree = 4; Disagree = 5; Strongly disagree = 6), we would have possible responses from a low of 10 to a high of 60 (e.g., $1 \times 10 = 10; 6 \times 10 = 60$). We might record the raw score in *two* columns, such as columns **8** and **9**. The score might be "36." Or we might decide to code the *range of responses* to our anger intensity or police professionalism scales, such as:

10–15 = 1
16–20 = 2
21–25 = 3
26–30 = 4
31–35 = 5
36–40 = 6
41–45 = 7
46–50 = 8
51–55 = 9
56–60 = 0

Coding a scale in this way enables us to use a single column, such as column **8,** for the scale score. Thus, a "3" on column **8** means a raw score of 21–25. A "0" on column **8** would mean a raw score of 56–60. Let's assume the person responded with a raw score of "28," and therefore we will code column **8** with a "4." So far, we may have coded eight columns as follows:

Columns

1	2	3	4	5	6	7	8	9	10	11	12	13	14	15 . . .
0	0	1	1	3	5	2	4	?	?	?	?	?	?	?

We may assign one or more columns to each variable in our study. There are no restrictions on the numbers of variables we can measure; however, it is unusual for studies to contain more than 50 variables. Besides sociodemographic and personal information, several attitudinal scales, and other included measures, there is not a whole lot more that investigators can include in their questionnaires and interviews. In most cases, researchers are interested in explaining criminological phenomena by limiting their analyses to those variables that have the greatest explanatory power. Even complex research designs will yield fewer than 10 explanatory variables that have the greatest predictive power.

Another consideration is that as we add more variables to our study, we increase the length of our questionnaires and stand a greater chance of wearing out our respondents. Few persons want to sit down and fill out a 100-page questionnaire. Some novice researchers want to add as many variables as possible to their questionnaires, thinking that certainly something significant will emerge from all of those variables. Some persons refer to this as "shotgunning." Fortunately, we have the guidance of criminological theory. Theories tend to limit our explanations of criminal behaviors, attitudes, and social events to several key variables.

Developing a Coding Manual. After we have constructed our questionnaire or interview schedule, we may want to construct a **coding manual** or code book. A coding manual contains all the columns we are going to use and the information to be recorded in each column. The coding manual explains exactly how each column is to be coded and how the codes are to be interpreted. Our coding manual for the variables coded earlier might be as follows:

Column	Variable	Question #s	Code
1,2,3	Respondent ID	1	As indicated
4	Gender	2	1 = male
			2 = female
			9 = no answer
5	Age	3	1 = under 21
			2 = 21–23
			3 = 24–25
			4 = 26–28
			5 = 29 or over
			9 = no answer
6	Education	4	1 = Some elementary school, not completed
			2 = Completed elementary school
			3 = Some high school, not completed
			4 = Completed high school
			5 = Some college, not completed
			6 = Completed college
			7 = Graduate work or degree
			9 = no answer
7	Political Affiliation	5	1 = Democrat
			2 = Republican
			3 = American Independent

```
                                                        4 = Other
                                                        9 = no answer
    8           Police Professionalism      6           1 = 10–15
                                                        2 = 16–20
                                                        3 = 21–25
                                                        4 = 26–30
                                                        5 = 31–35
                                                        6 = 36–40
                                                        7 = 41–45
                                                        8 = 46–50
                                                        9 = 51–55
                                                        0 = 56–60
    9 ...
```

It is apparent from this abbreviated version of the coding manual that we may construct our manual as simply as we choose. The purpose of this manual is to enable us or anyone else to review the column codes and determine what specific numbers mean. If we administer our questionnaire to 100 persons, then we would have coded information for these 100 persons transferred to coding sheets. Coding sheets contain all of the columns we are using in our research. Coding sheets summarize the numbers assigned, based on each respondent's answers.

The coding sheet contains the answers for the first respondent to our questionnaire. In this coding sheet, we have used 22 columns. The coding manual enables us to determine what the number in each column means. Notice that the first 24 persons in our sample have been identified in the first three columns. As we record information for each of our respondents, the coding sheet will fill with values. Later, the numbers from the coding sheet can be entered into various statistical computer programs, such as the Statistical Package for the Social Sciences, or **SPSS.** Once this information has been entered into our SPSS program, various kinds of statistical analyses are possible. For the time being, it is important to know how to transmit data from our questionnaires and interview schedules/guides to the coding sheets and how to develop a coding manual.

What to Do About "Don't Know" Responses or No Responses.   In a perfect world, everyone we contact about completing our questionnaires will do so happily and will be truthful in their responses. Additionally, they will fill out the questionnaires completely. All questions will be answered. All scales will be completed. Unfortunately, it is not a perfect world. Bad things happen to researchers. Some information on questionnaires is missing. Some items are skipped. We have noted some of these problems in earlier chapters. How should these situations be handled when we are coding data?

In our example, digits ranging from "1" to "0" were used to represent different responses for each variable. If someone leaves the "gender" item blank or refuses to tell us their political or religious affiliation, there isn't much we can do

1	2	3	4	5	6	7	8	9	10	11	12	13	14	15	16	17	18	19	20	21	22
0	0	1	1	3	5	2	4	6	4	2	1	7	3	6	5	3	4	2	4	2	3
0	0	2																			
0	0	3																			
0	0	4																			
0	0	5																			
0	0	6																			
0	0	7																			
0	0	8																			
0	0	9																			
0	1	0																			
0	1	1																			
0	1	2																			
0	1	3																			
0	1	4																			
0	1	5																			
0	1	6																			
0	1	7																			
0	1	8																			
0	1	9	2	3	2	9	0														
0	2	0																			
0	2	1																			
0	2	2																			
0	2	3																			
0	2	4																			

about it. When there is no response to a given item, or when a scale measuring some variable is incomplete, we need to indicate this in some way in our coding manual. Sometimes, investigators will use either "9" or "0" to indicate "No response," "Not ascertained," or "Not given." Notice that the police professionalism scale used a "9" as well as a "0" for different score intensities. If we decided to use

"9" or "0" to indicate "No response" or "Not ascertained," then we could code this and other scales in a way that would utilize only eight or fewer categories. Perhaps we could code our police professionalism scale as follows:

10-19 = 1
20-29 = 2
30-39 = 3
40-49 = 4
50-60 = 5
No response or
incomplete response = 9 (or "0")

Accordingly, we could expand our categories for gender, education, political affiliation, and other variables to allow for nonresponse. Thus, gender would be

1 = male
2 = female
9 = not ascertained

Our political affiliation responses would be coded as follows to allow for nonresponse:

1 = Democrat
2 = Republican
3 = American Independent
4 = Other
0 = Not ascertained

Therefore, either "9" or "0" functions as an indication that there was no response to that particular item, or a scale score could not be calculated. For instance, on a ten-item scale, if the respondent failed to answer one or more items, we could not calculate a meaningful raw score for the variable, such as police professionalism. We would record a "9" or a "0" in the column designated for that variable. Notice respondent 19. Hypothetical entries have been made in several columns. Columns **7** and **8** contain "9" and "0," indicating that the person either did not respond to the item or failed to give responses to all of the items making up the scale.

VERIFICATION AND CLEANING DATA

Data-cleaning and **verification** refer to the close examination of all numerical information taken from questionnaires or interviews to determine that it is accurate. Thus, data-cleaning is an error-detection process, most often used in connection with questionnaire data and data coding sheets. Once researchers and their assistants have entered data on coding sheets, called **data entry,** this information will be transmitted to some type of computer software program for statistical analysis. The type of program to be used is unimportant at this point. The fact is that data are transmitted to a computer. There are possible errors that may occur during the transmittal process. For instance, suppose one or more mistakes were made when entering data and numerical information on the coding sheets. Suppose erroneous numbers were entered on these sheets. Instead of entering a "1" for "male," the coder may have entered a "2," meaning "female," in error. Or perhaps an entry of "5" was given for this variable. There is no gender as "5," but the "5" appears anyway. Suppose other numerical errors occurred as information was copied from questionnaires to the coding sheets. If left undetected, these errors will be transmitted to computer programs. Once computer programs have erroneous information, the results these programs produce will be somewhat unreliable, depending upon the nature and extent of the erroneous information entered.

Erroneous information can be minimized by following a few simple steps. These steps are not foolproof, but errors can be detected in data entries and corrected easily. The first step is to be particularly careful if you are copying information from questionnaires to coding sheets. Second, have another coder examine your copied information and authenticate it. The numerical information recorded by you is double-checked by another person. If the transmitted information survives two inspections, you have fairly accurate data recorded.

Some computer software programs, such as SPSS, require that users first create the categories into which data will be recorded. All variable titles are created as well as the subclasses of all variables. The subclasses for "male" and "female," the "1" and "2," will be recorded by the program. Later, if the researcher attempts to enter a digit other than a "1" or "2" (or a "9" or "0" in the case of no response) into that particular category, an error message will appear, questioning the possibly erroneous entry. But not all software programs for analyzing data have this capability.

There is nothing particularly complicated about cleaning data. Basically it is a process of verifying the accuracy of recorded information. In the event that coded information is erroneous but was not detected, sometimes clues about errors appear when data have been tabulated. If researchers prepare a distribution of age categories for their sample of respondents, the expected range is "1" through "5" (or a "9" or "0" for no answer). Perhaps the distribution shows the following:

1 = 22
2 = 32
3 = 15
4 = 26
5 = 16
7 = 1
8 = 1
9 = 3

Box
12.1

Xiaogang Deng
University of Massachusetts at Boston

Statistics: Ph.D. (criminal justice), SUNY
at Buffalo.

Interests: Research methods, statistics, social control, and deviance.

My early life in China was difficult. I could not complete my middle school education because all school systems in China were shut down during the Cultural Revolution. I worked in a steel factory for eight years. Later when Chinese universities admitted students, I went to college and earned my B.A. degree.

I now conduct research in two areas: identifying significant motivational factors that influence criminal and deviant behavior by testing self-control, labeling, and reintegrative shaming theories; and using a comparative perspective to study crime and social control in China.

When I was a graduate student, my mentor, Dr. Simon Singer, asked me to assist him in the annual evaluation of a shoplifting prevention program in Buffalo, New York. Annually more than 1,000 shoplifters entered the prevention program. We did the annual evaluation for several years. Gradually I found that shoplifting was a very interesting offense to study. First, people from all walks of life become shoplifters and many social factors may contribute to their decisions to steal. Many important theories could be empirically tested. Second, it is also interesting to study the historical development of shoplifting by using historical documents, and to see how the society has defined and reacted to this offense in different historical periods. And so I designed a questionnaire that incorporated some measures of self-control theory, differential association theory, and strain theory. I first pretested the questionnaire among college students and then conducted the survey of the shoplifters.

My research is significant in several respects. First, my work on self-control theory empirically tests two important questions that have not been adequately addressed in previous research: (1) whether self-control reflects a general criminal propensity that can predict all kinds of criminal and deviant acts (the versatility hypothesis); and (2) whether self-control as an invariant general construct can predict criminal and deviant acts over time (the stability hypothesis). Using a sample of first-time arrested property offenders, my study indicates that self-control is not only a good predictor of past criminal/delinquent acts, but also is a good predictor of projected behavioral intention to shoplift after these offenders received their initial sanction. This study provides further evidence for Gottfredson's and Hirschi's self-control theory.

Comparative studies can expand our intellectual horizons and cultural appreciation of non-Western crime control alternatives. Social control in China has unique characteristics that are not emphasized in the Western formulation of criminological theories. My comparative work mainly focuses upon drastic social and structural changes during China's transition from state socialism to state capitalism on social control and crime. My study of social control and crime raises questions which are fundamental to extending the scope of criminology toward Western capitalist nations. For me, the most interesting part of research is the intellectual challenge to conduct research that can contribute to our further understanding of our complicated social world. We can then share our findings with other scholars through our publications.

Advice to Students: Although research methods can be a very demanding course, you will find it rewarding later on in your career. There is a Chinese saying that the most difficult thing is usually the right thing to do. Personally I have greatly benefited from research methods courses—more so than from any other courses I took in my entire graduate career. As a tool, research methods is a very empowering skill to have. Do not be afraid of temporary setbacks or failures in your pursuit of knowledge. Persistence and patience will reward you handsomely in the long run. You have to firmly believe that there is always room for improvement. Keep your eyes on the latest theoretical and methodological developments in the field by reading major criminological journals such as *Criminology* and *Justice Quarterly.*

This distribution says that 22 persons answered with a response that was coded with a "1," 32 persons answered and were coded with a "2," and so on. But our attention is immediately directed to categories "7" and "8." These categories simply don't exist. The age range went up to "5," and after that a "9" or "0" was used for no response. Thus, the two responses of "7" and "8" are errors. Once detected, these errors are corrected and the data can be analyzed. These types of errors are fairly common, especially if there are large numbers of respondents being analyzed.

■ SIMPLE DATA PRESENTATION

Researchers have lots of options when reporting their findings. The most frequent option is to prepare a written account of what was done. The investigator can write an article about the research, what was studied, and what was found. This written account can be 20 or more pages. The style of the report varies greatly depending upon the intended purpose of the written work. If the work is submitted to a professional journal for publication, the journal's guidelines will dictate the format to be followed. This format indicates how to list citations and bibliographical entries and other information. If the work is a report to a federal agency or some other organization providing funds for the research, the researcher will prepare it differently from a report prepared for a journal. Many studies are originally submitted and published as technical reports to different organizations or agencies. Appendix C contains additional descriptions of various types of papers and reports that are prepared by persons who do different types of research and writing.

The written word provides much enriching detail about one's study and its findings. However, supplemental charts, tables, and graphs can help to illustrate results in creative ways. If the research involves extensive analysis of data and statistical computations, some of this information may be tabled or graphed to enhance reader interest. Some numerical information, such as crime rates and population ratios, can be reported as a part of the written document.

■ MEASURES OF CRIME AND CRIME RATES

An important dimension of measurement of variables pertains to charting crime, delinquency, and other criminological phenomena over time and describing diverse components of the criminal justice system.

Crime Rate

The crime rate in the United States is reported by the FBI in the *Uniform Crime Reports* and other sources. It is given for different states, cities and towns, counties, and rural and urban areas. It is also provided for different types of crime and for crime generally. The **crime rate** is computed as follows:

$$\text{Crime Rate} = \frac{\text{Number of Crimes}}{\text{Population}} \times 100,000$$

For example, in 1999 there were 245,807,000 persons in the United States. During that year, there were 12,356,865 property crimes, including burglary, larceny, and vehicular theft reported to the FBI. Using these figures, we have

$$12,356,865/245,807,000 \times 100,000 = .0502706 \times 100,000 = 5027.06$$

This means that there were approximately 5,027 crimes against property per 100,000 persons in 1999. In the same year, 20,675 murders were reported. Therefore, $20,675/245,807,000 \times 100,000 = .00084 \times 100,000 = 8.4$ murders per 100,000 persons.

Caution should be exercised when interpreting any official statistics such as crime rates. The limitations and strengths of these statistical compilations are extensively documented elsewhere. Most introductory criminal justice texts summarize the pitfalls of such measures. There are seasonal variations in different types of crime. Crime varies from city to city and from state to state. Reported crime does not reflect the amount of unreported crime, which is known to be extensive from independent victimization reports. Large numbers of arrests do not represent large numbers of convictions. Crime waves may be politically created. When law enforcement agencies report crime to the FBI annually, only the most serious crime is reported, even if more than one crime was committed during a particular incident. These are only a few of the sources of error that interfere with the accuracy of these crime figures.

Suppose we wished to determine whether particular types of crime were increasing or decreasing from one year to the next. Hypothetically suppose that in 1995 there were 11,722,700 property crimes reported in the United States. Also, there were 241,077,000 persons in the United States, as provided by Bureau of the Census estimates. What was the increase in property crime between 1995 and 1999? We can calculate the percent of change by using the following formula:

$$\text{Percent change} = \frac{(\text{quantity at time 2}) - (\text{quantity at time 1})}{(\text{quantity at time 1})} \times 100$$

$$= \frac{12,356,865 - 11,722,700}{11,722,700} \times 100$$

$$= \frac{634,165}{11,722,700} \times 100$$

$$= .054 \times 100 = 5.4 \text{ percent}$$

There was a 5.4 percent increase in reported property crimes from 1995 to 1999. Was this increase equivalent with the general population increase during the same time period? The same formula may be used to answer this question. The population of the United States in 1995 was estimated to be 241,077,000. In 1999, it was estimated to be 245,807,000. Therefore,

$$\text{General Population Increase} = \frac{245,807,000 - 241,077,000}{241,077,000} \times 100$$

$$= \frac{4,730,000}{241,077,000} \times 100$$

$$= .0196 \times 100 = 1.96 \text{ percent}$$

Thus, between 1995 and 1999, the general population was estimated to increase slightly less than 2 percent, or 1.96 percent. Compared with the 5.4 percent increase in property crimes, it would appear that property crimes increased at a greater rate than the growth of the general U.S. population between 1995 and 1999. At least the *reporting* of property crimes increased at a greater rate than U.S. population growth.

Ratios

Ratios are commonly used by criminal justice professionals and others for various purposes. Suppose we wished to determine the ratio of prison inmates to prison correctional officers. If the prison population consisted of 1,500 prisoners and there were 500 correctional officers, the ratio of prisoners to correctional officers would be

[1,500 to 500] to 1 or 1500/500 to 1 or = 3 to 1

Thus, there would be three prisoners per correctional officer. This might also be expressed as 3:1. Reversing this ratio, we might consider the number of correctional officers to prisoners or [500 to 1500] to 1, or 500/1500 to 1 or .33:1. A 1:1 ratio would mean one correctional officer per prisoner. If this type of arrangement actually existed, which it doesn't, it would be found in a close custody, maximum-security facility. In 1999 there was an average of six inmates per corrections officer in all jails and prisons in the United States.

GRAPHIC PRESENTATION

Graphic presentation consists of all tables, charts, illustrations, figures, and line drawings that depict how collected data are distributed or arranged. Usually, graphics are limited to the most important features of studies, those that deserve to be highlighted. Charts and graphs can show trends over time regarding the incidence of different types of crime and other variables. The "spread" or distribution of frequencies throughout tables can show the influence of certain variables on other variables, and whether associations exist. Informative summaries of statistical information, such as the proportionate distribution of race, gender, age, and type of offense associated with jail or prison inmate populations, enable researchers to design their own studies more effectively by isolating the most crucial factors for investigation. Following is a summary of some of the more important functions of graphic presentation.

FUNCTIONS OF GRAPHIC PRESENTATION

The major functions of graphic presentation include (1) enhancing articles, reports, and data summaries; (2) testing hypotheses derived from theories; (3) illustrating relationships between variables; (4) depicting trends and proportionate distributions; (5) influencing statistical test selections and applications; and (6) influencing policy decision making.

Enhancing Articles, Reports, and Data Summaries. It is helpful to provide line drawings and other illustrations to highlight the written words in technical reports. Those who read articles often analyze charts and graphs before digesting the written material. Much can be gained by paying attention to how variables are distributed. Readers may quickly grasp whether certain variables are important as explanatory factors and deserve to be studied further.

Testing Hypotheses Derived from Theories. Data are often presented by researchers in tabular form for the purpose of testing hypotheses derived from theories. Depending upon how graphs and tables are constructed and arranged, investigators may be able to influence the significance of whatever they find. As we will see, it is fairly easy to "lie with statistics," and the manipulation of the same data in graphs and tables by two different researchers may yield opposite and contradictory results when analyzed. Several objective rules or conventional procedures have been established to minimize the bias that may be introduced by the different vested interests of researchers. However, not everyone adheres strongly to convention when presenting data to others. At appropriate points in this chapter, conventional guidelines that are calculated to enhance the objectivity of data presentation are discussed.

Illustrating Relationships Between Variables.   Tabular materials may illustrate relationships or associations between two or more variables. Thus, we may be able to point at the distribution of tabular frequencies to show that one or more variables are related in meaningful ways. Statistical tests may be applied to furnish independent numerical objectivity to our visual interpretations of tabular material.

Depicting Trends and Proportionate Distributions.   Certain line drawings and graphs help to show whether variables change in certain directions over time. Is crime in the United States increasing? What is the proportion of mentally ill inmates among the entire U.S. jail population? How does the incidence of property crimes compare with violent crimes over time in specific cities or geographical regions? Which states have the highest execution rates? Graphic presentation illustrates this material easily.

Influencing Statistical Test Selections and Applications.   In order for certain statistical tests to be applicable for our data analyses, various assumptions about score distributions may be required. Some statistical procedures require that the sample data be distributed in the form of a bell-shaped curve or normal distribution. If our line drawings of raw scores show curves or distributions other than "normal" ones, then we have failed to meet at least one statistical test assumption. Our choices of central tendency and dispersion or variability measures often depend upon how our data are distributed or arranged as well. If some raw scores among our collected data are quite different from the others or are "deviant scores" (e.g., most of 100 scores in some hypothetical distribution fluctuate between 10 and 30, but three of these scores are 80, 85, and 90 and are considered "deviant scores"), then we would want to apply the central tendency measure that works best with these deviant scores. Otherwise, applications of the other central tendency measures to our data with deviant scores would be distorted or misleading. Visually inspecting the distribution in graphic form influences our statistical test selections.

Influencing Policy Decision Making.   Intervention programs that are intended to change behavior may be adopted on a large scale by communities if positive results can be illustrated by investigators. For example, researchers may believe that a particular elementary school juvenile counseling and therapy method for youths considered "at risk" is useful for reducing their inclination to become delinquent. Graphic presentations of samples of high-risk youths exposed to the intervention program or therapy may eventually illustrate low numbers of delinquent youths over time. Thus, the community may adopt the intervention in schools as a general policy. Or a graphic illustrating low recidivism rates among parolees and probationers attributable to lower probation and parole officer caseloads and more intensive supervision may influence policymakers. Therefore, attempts may be made to keep parole officer caseloads low in an effort to decrease recidivism among clients.

■ TYPES OF GRAPHIC PRESENTATION

The following types of graphic presentation are illustrated: (1) pie charts, (2) bar graphs, (3) frequency distributions, (4) histograms and frequency polygons, (5) other types of graphic presentation, and (6) cross-tabulation and complex variable interrelationships.

Pie Charts

Pie charts are circular graphs that portray either portions of 100 percent of some aggregate or the frequency of incidents. Figures 12.1 shows a crime clock of the incidence of robbery occurring every 360 seconds in the United States, while Figure 12.2 illustrates the proportion of minimum-, medium-, and maximum-security U.S. state prisons.

The FBI has considered dropping **crime clocks** from its publication, the *Uniform Crime Reports,* because it is possible to easily misinterpret them. When certain crimes are represented as occurring every few minutes, this refers to the total number of those crimes during the year divided into the total number of minutes in that same time interval. It does not mean that if there is a rape every 20 minutes in the United States, then rapes occur every 20 minutes in Denver, Colorado, or Sioux Falls, South Dakota. Rather, *national* figures are portrayed. There are *seasonal fluctuations* in these crime rates as well. More rapes occur in warm, summer months than in cold, winter months. One reason is that less clothing is worn by potential rape victims in summer months, making the victims more attractive to attackers.

Few restrictions exist pertaining to the construction and application of pie charts. Their major shortcoming is the number of segments into which they may be conveniently divided. Too many segments create a "cluttered" pie chart. A rule of thumb governing the maximum number of divisions used for portraying data would be to use no more than six. Beyond six divisions, it is difficult for re-

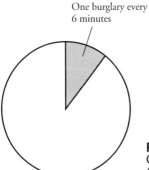

One burglary every 6 minutes

FIGURE 12.1
Crime clock. [*Source:* From the *FBI Uniform Crime Report Bulletin* (Washington, DC: U.S. Government Printing Office).]

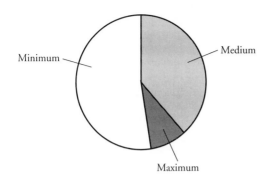

FIGURE 12.2
Pie chart showing proportion of minimum-, medium-, and maximum-security state prisons in the United States.

searchers to label each sector in the chart adequately. Pie charts may be used with virtually any variable and its subdivisions.

Bar Graphs

Bar graphs contain either vertical or horizontal bars that portray the frequency of values on some variable. Figure 12.3 shows a bar graph of state and federal correctional facilities that were operating over their original design capacities in 1995.

Bar graphs can be used to illustrate trends, such as increases or decreases in crime rates over time. An imaginative use of bar graphs is the portrayal of various forms of delinquent conduct for both males and females. Figure 12.4 shows hypothetical proportionate distributions of male and female juveniles for overall delinquency and for specific types of offenses within uniformly drawn horizontal bars. Much like pie charts, the area within each bar represents 100 percent of each type of offense. Shaded areas are used to represent proportions of either males or females within each offense category.

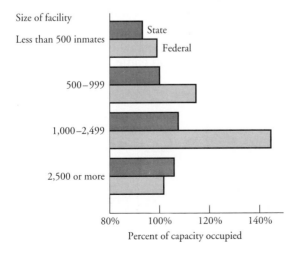

FIGURE 12.3
State facilities were operating at 3% above capacity; federal facilities, 24% above, 1995.
(*Source:* Stephan, 1997:2)

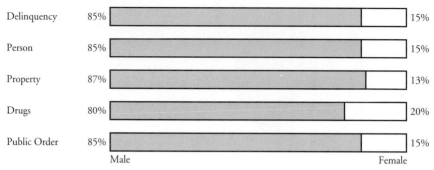

FIGURE 12.4 Offense characteristics of delinquency cases by gender.

Bar graphs do not need to consist of uniformly drawn bars. For example, we might construct a bar graph such as the one shown in Figure 12.5 to depict the incidence of crime across various social classes. In this instance, we have simply constructed vertical and horizontal axes, with high and low crime rates illustrated on the vertical axis, and with social class, arranged from low to high, across the horizontal axis. The widths of the vertical bars in this case reflect either smaller or larger proportions of persons in different social classes. The wide flexibility of bar graphs and their lack of restrictions for any particular measurement level (e.g., nominal, ordinal, interval, or ratio) make them attractive illustrative devices in research reports and articles.

Frequency Distributions

Constructing Frequency Distributions. One of the more important illustrative tools available to researchers is the frequency distribution. **Frequency distributions** are arrangements of raw scores from high to low, according to intervals of a designated size. The construction of frequency distributions is one of the first items on a researcher's agenda after data have been collected. Investigators organize their data in some meaningful way in order to make sense out of it. Suppose an investigator conducted interviews with fifteen probation officers.

FIGURE 12.5 Bar graph reflecting social class and crime.

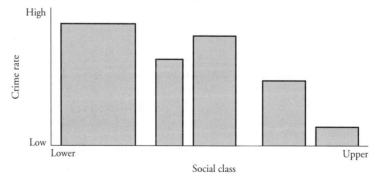

The investigator determined from interviews that the ages of the probation officers were as follows: 35, 49, 62, 55, 41, 40, 35, 31, 30, 26, 29, 39, 39, 36, and 48. Taken as an aggregate, these ages are diverse and don't tell us much about these officers. Some organization of these ages is necessary. Perhaps the investigator decides to arrange these ages as shown here:

Age Category	Number of Officers (Frequency) f
25–29	2
30–34	2
35–39	5
40–44	2
45–49	2
50–54	0
55–59	1
60–64	1
Total (N)	$15 = \Sigma f$ (Sum of frequencies)

These data have been arranged into a frequency distribution of various age categories, and the **frequency** of each age has been placed in the appropriate category created. We can gain a better impression of the age distribution of these officers and see that the most common age category is 35–39. Few officers are over age 50.

Depending upon the size of the sample, we treat the data as either ungrouped or grouped. **Ungrouped data** analyses involve dealing directly with raw scores, without any attempt to order or arrange them from low to high or high to low. **Grouped data** analyses are arrangements of data into **intervals** of various sizes for better data management. A rule of thumb applied to making the ungrouped/grouped data decision is to group the data whenever the sample size is 25 or larger ($N \geq 25$, read as "N is equal to or greater than 25"). For sample sizes less than 25 (indicated as $N < 25$), treating data in ungrouped or grouped form is optional for the researcher, although it is probably best to deal with smaller samples in ungrouped fashion. The logic underlying grouping larger sample sizes is that the data are made more manageable for purposes of description, analysis, and statistical test applications. After arranging many scores into a frequency distribution, researchers can inspect the spread of scores or their distribution properties visually. Particular statistical tests and descriptive measures are suggested by different types of distribution arrangements.

In the previous example, in which probation officers' ages were arranged into several age categories, only fifteen ages were involved. While it was helpful to organize these data into several age categories to enable us to see the spread of raw age scores, we could have left these scores as they were and computed various descriptive measures such as the "average" or mean. This would be following the rule of thumb noted earlier, that is, to deal with samples smaller than 25 in ungrouped form. As we will see in later chapters, statistical procedures are often designed for application to samples of specified sizes. Usually, statistical procedures have operating ranges of certain sample sizes that maximize their meaningfulness and application. Thus, there are statistical tests for small-sample situations and for large-sample applications. Further, various descriptive techniques have alternative formulas for their application to data in either ungrouped or grouped form. Because of the diversity of studies that are conducted in criminal justice and criminology, it is important for researchers to be familiar with both types of data management, whenever large or small samples are encountered. A larger sample example will illustrate the greater ease of data management whenever raw scores are grouped.

Table 12.1 shows 82 hypothetical scores on an achievement test administered to prison inmates who are enrolled in a GED program. The larger the score, the higher the performance on the achievement test. Table 12.1 doesn't make a lot of sense as shown. The raw scores are in disarray. We might profit by arranging the individual scores from high to low, but because of the large sample size, $N = 82$, this would be time-consuming. Our decision is to arrange these data into a certain number of intervals of some size so that we can manage the data more easily. We will follow the steps below to create a frequency distribution for these data:

1. Identify the largest and smallest raw scores in the distribution. In this case, an inspection of Table 12.1 shows that the largest score is 390, while the smallest score is 322.

2. Divide the difference between the largest and the smallest scores by 15. The difference in the scores, 390 and 322, is $390 - 322 = 68$. Dividing 68 by 15, we would have $68/15 = 4.5$. We divide the score difference by 15 because of a conventional rule that we should construct frequency distributions that contain from 10 to 20 intervals of some size. Frequency distributions with fewer than 10 intervals compact our data into too few categories, and we cannot evaluate clearly how the scores are distributed. Frequency distributions with more than 20 intervals are spread out too thinly, and again, we cannot evaluate clearly how the scores are distributed. The figure 15 is selected as a happy medium, an arbitrary number between 10 and 20 intervals. Dividing the distance between the largest and smallest scores in the distribution by 15 gives us a value, 4.5, which is near a desirable **interval size,** either 4 or 5.

We may evoke another conventional rule about our interval size choice. Conventional interval sizes are 1, 2, 3, 4, 5, 10, 20, 30, 40, 50, 100, 200, 300, 400, 500, and so forth. If we are dealing with decimals, rates, or proportions, our interval sizes may be .1, .2, .3, .4, .5, .01, .02, .03, .04, .05, and so on. In the previous exam-

TABLE 12.1 An Ungrouped Listing of 82 Hypothetical Achievement Test Scores for Prison Inmates

326	322	349	358	343	390	345	322	333	335	338	338	339
349	350	351	365	371	356	344	355	345	344	340	359	351
356	381	375	371	370	360	365	378	390	349	341	346	362
324	381	327	348	367	368	369	371	382	369	387	345	330
327	346	344	332	330	330	344	348	354	358	366	366	367
389	388	324	322	339	368	373	378	377	382	383	345	365
345	369	340	358									

ple, the value 4.5 is midway between an interval size of 4 and an interval size of 5. If we choose the interval size 5, then we will have fewer intervals of size 5. If we choose 4, then we will have more intervals of size 4. It is unusual and unconventional to have intervals of size 4.5, 7, 9, 13, or some number other than those noted here. This doesn't mean that unusual interval sizes cannot be chosen, but our computational work and general data management will be somewhat more complicated. In this case, let's use the interval size 5 to create a frequency distribution for the data (raw scores) in Table 12.1.

3. The next step is to decide where to begin our intervals and which numbers to use. It is conventional to construct our first interval so that the first number in it is a multiple of the interval size and the largest or smallest score is included in the interval. Since our interval size is 5, examples of multiples of size 5 would be 5, 10, 15, 20, 320, 330, 345, and 365. We examine our data and determine that the smallest score is 322. The largest score is 390. Therefore, we may begin our interval construction with either 320–324 or 390–394. Both of these intervals begin with a multiple of size 5, and each contains either the smallest or largest values among the scores in Table 12.1. The interval 320–324 contains the smallest scores in the distribution and is considered the "bottom" of it. The interval 390–394 is the "top" of the distribution, since it contains the largest scores. Suppose we decide to begin with the interval 320–324.

4. Our next step is to establish all intervals beginning with 320–324 and continue constructing intervals until we have reached and included 390–394. This is illustrated in Table 12.2.

TABLE 12.2 Frequency Distribution of 82 Achievement Scores for Prison Inmates, Constructed from Raw Scores in Table 12.1

Interval	f	
320–324	5	("bottom" of distribution)
325–329	3	
330–334	5	
335–339	5	
340–344	8	
345–349	12	
350–354	4	
355–359	7	
360–364	2	
365–369	12	
370–374	5	
375–379	4	
380–384	5	
385–389	3	
390–394	2	("top" of distribution)
	$\Sigma f = 82$	

5. The fifth step is to enter the numbers of raw scores from Table 12.1 into their appropriate intervals in Table 12.2. A raw score of 369 belongs in the interval, 365–369, whereas the raw score 370 belongs in the interval, 370–374. These frequencies have been entered into their appropriate intervals as shown. Finally, we sum the frequencies as a check on our work to see that we have tabulated them correctly.

The rationale for beginning our intervals with a multiple of the interval size is simple. We may easily check the accuracy of our interval construction by scanning the first numbers in all intervals. Each is a multiple of the interval size of 5. Had we made one interval 365–370, our next interval would have been 371–374. Both of these intervals are improper because they are the wrong size. The interval 365–370 might look as though it is of size 5, but it is of size 6. The scores 365, 366, 367, 368, 369, and 370 are included in it. The other interval, 371–374, only has four scores: 371, 372, 373, and 374. We can easily detect our error, since 371 is not a multiple of our interval size, 5. Another reason for verifying the consistency among the intervals we have constructed is that the interval size, i, is often a key term in descriptive and inferential statistical formulae. Therefore, if we are careless about how our intervals are constructed, we will eventually obtain erroneous statistical results. The importance of accuracy in the construction of frequency distributions cannot be overestimated. If in doubt about the size of any interval, some advice from a late statistics professor is relevant here: Use your fingers and count how many scores are contained in it.

Now we may examine Table 12.2 and determine several things. First, we have 15 intervals. Had we used the interval size 4 in constructing our intervals, there would have been more than 15 intervals. Also, the first interval constructed would have been 320–323. The value 320 is a multiple of the interval size 4, and the interval 320–323 is of size 4 and contains the smallest score of 322. Our next interval would have been 324–327. Another feature of Table 12.2 is that two intervals, 345–349 and 365–369, contain the most frequencies. Later, when we construct a line drawing of the scores shown in Table 12.2, two high peaks will be observed, reflecting the two intervals that contain the most frequencies. As mentioned earlier, this feature of the distribution will influence our choice of descriptive measures and statistical tests.

It is important to note that we have two options for arranging our data. We can arrange them as shown in Table 12.2, where the interval containing the smallest scores (the "bottom" of the distribution) is physically at the top of the page, or we can reverse our arrangement so that the "bottom" of the distribution is at the bottom of the page. Table 12.3 shows a reversal of information shown in Table 12.2.

This particular point is important, since many students lock themselves into one way or the other of constructing these intervals. This is like trained incapacity—someone becomes proficient at solving problems only one way and cannot cope with other easy strategies for problem solving. Later, when these persons encounter distributions of scores that are arranged differently from what they have learned, they may make procedural mistakes associated with the computational requirements of certain inferential and descriptive statistical pro-

TABLE 12.3 An Interval Rearrangement from the Data in Table 12.2

Interval	f
390–394	2 ("top" of distribution)
385–389	3
380–384	5
375–379	4
370–374	5
365–369	12
360–364	2
355–359	7
350–354	4
345–349	12
340–344	8
335–339	5
330–334	5
325–329	3
320–324	5 ("bottom" of distribution)
	$\sum f = 82$

cedures. Either way of presenting data is acceptable here. Certain formulae applied to the same information arranged in either Table 12.2 or Table 12.3 will yield different results if we fail to take into account how the data are arranged. Thus, it is important for us to know which is the top and bottom of any distribution we examine.

Some Characteristics of Frequency Distributions.   In order to solve various problems, including determining central tendency or dispersion values, such as means or standard deviations, it is imperative to acquire a familiarity with different aspects of frequency distributions. It is necessary to understand how to determine interval upper and lower limits as well as their midpoints. This assumes that the data are treated as though they are measured according to an interval scale, although frequency distributions may be created for data measured according to lower levels of measurement (e.g., nominal and ordinal).

Technically, intervals in frequency distributions extend from their lower limits to their upper limits. For example, the interval 335–339 technically extends from 334.5 (its lower limit) to 339.5 (its upper limit). Thus, if we subtract the lower limit from the upper limit of any interval, our result will be the interval size, or $339.5 - 334.5 = 5$. Midpoints of intervals are those points within intervals that divide the intervals into two equal parts. If the interval is of size 5, then a point within the interval is the midpoint, where 2.5 values are on one side and 2.5 values are on the other. We determine interval midpoints easily by taking one-half of the interval size and either adding it to the lower limit of the interval or subtracting it from the upper limit of the interval. Thus, if our interval is 335–339, we take one-half of the interval size of 5, $5/2 = 2.5$, and add this

TABLE 12.4 Interval Sizes, Upper and Lower Limits, and Midpoints

Interval	Lower Limit	Upper Limit	Midpoint	Interval Size
15–19	14.5	19.5	17	5
500–509	499.5	509.5	504.5	10
.21–.23	.205	.235	.22	.03
1460–1479	1459.5	1479.5	1469.5	20
.0058–.0071	.00575	.00615	.00595	.0004

amount to 334.5 (the lower limit), or $334.5 + 2.5 = 337$. The alternative is to subtract one-half the interval size from the interval upper limit, or $339.5 - 2.5 = 337$. Thus, 337 is the interval midpoint. Table 12.4 shows some examples of intervals of different sizes, **upper** and **lower limits of intervals,** and **interval midpoints,** as well as the actual interval sizes for each interval shown.

Upper and lower limits of intervals are particularly meaningful when we deal with data that are continuously distributed. All too often we deal with scores in whole number form, such as 10, 200, 85, or 350, although data are sometimes presented in decimal form, such as 10.3, 200.889, 85.0035, and so on. If we had an array of values expressed in decimal form, we would need to have some system whereby these scores could be assigned to one interval or another in our frequency distribution. For instance, if we observed the value 324.7, would this value belong in the interval 320–324, or in the interval 325–329? We may examine the upper and lower limits of these two intervals, which would be 319.5–324.5 and 324.5–329.5. Notice that the upper limit of the interval 320–324 is identical with the lower limit of the interval 325–329 (324.5). In the case of our score of 324.7, it would belong in the interval, 325–329, since the interval technically extends from 324.5 to 329.5.

If we encounter values that occur directly on the line between one interval or another, such as the value 324.5, does it belong in the interval 320–324 or in the interval 325–329? At this point we will invoke a **rounding rule,** which means that if our value is located exactly between two other values or is an equal distance from each, we will round the value either upward or downward, in favor of one of the values. The **rounding** procedure followed in this book is to round our values in the direction of the nearest even number. Thus, 324.5 would be rounded to 324 rather than 325, since 324 is the nearest even number. There is nothing sacred about this rounding rule. It is simply a matter of author preference in this case. It is important that we agree at the outset about our rounding rule, since answers to numerical questions at chapter ends have been rounded in the direction of the nearest even number. Student answers will more likely match those in the textbook if this rounding rule is followed. The answer itself is not more right or more wrong if rounded in the other direction, however. Some examples of rounding according to the nearest even number follow:

Value	Rounded to:
324.5	324 (nearest even number)
329.5	330 (nearest even number)
324.4	324 (324.4 is closer to 324 than to 325)
329.4	329 (329.4 is closer to 329 than to 330)
329.6	330 (329.6 is closer to 330 than to 329)

We would engage in such rounding merely to determine in which interval to locate our raw scores that may be in decimal form. Most researchers express raw scores in whole numbers, although from time to time, decimal values occur and we must have a rule for dealing with them.

Interval midpoint values are important because they express the average value found in each interval. For example, the intervals 320-324 and 330-334 have interval midpoints equal to 322 and 332. These are the representative values of any frequency found in those intervals. For instance, in Table 12.2 these two intervals contained five scores each. When grouped data are presented, it is assumed that the interval midpoints typify the scores found in the intervals. Therefore, all five scores in each of the intervals are regarded as 322 and 332 respectively.

This feature highlights an important drawback of grouping data into intervals such as those in Table 12.2. Whenever data are grouped into intervals, a certain amount of precision is lost in our resulting calculations. What if the interval 320-324 had five scores in it equal to 320? And what if the interval 330-334 had five scores equal to 334? In the first instance, we would be overestimating the average values of interval frequencies with 322. In the second instance, we would be underestimating the average values of interval frequencies with 334. This imprecision is a common feature of grouped data. Statisticians believe that for any given frequency distribution, most of the imprecision is cancelled out by overestimating and underestimating such as that shown here. Obviously, the most precise calculations would be to deal directly with raw scores and not group them into intervals. But our data management would become unwieldy. Imagine dealing with 82 raw scores directly, or 300 scores, or 500 scores! It is considered a fair trade-off, whereby we lose a certain amount of precision in our numerical calculations of such values as means and standard deviations, but we gain by rendering our data in a more manageable form for making such calculations. We also gain by being able to inspect the distribution of scores and by making informed statistical test choices.

Cumulative Frequency Distributions.   Before we leave the subject of frequency distributions, several additional operations must be described. For instance, we may create a **cumulative frequency distribution** from any frequency distribution we have constructed. Table 12.5 is a cumulative frequency distribution constructed for the data in Table 12.2.

As can be seen from Table 12.5, cumulative frequency distributions are simply distributions of frequencies in which the frequencies from successive inter-

TABLE 12.5 A Cumulative Frequency Distribution for the Data in Table 12.2

Interval	f	cf
320–324	5	5
325–329	3	8 (3 frequencies added to previous 5)
330–334	5	13 (5 frequencies added to previous 8)
335–339	5	18 (5 frequencies added to previous 13)
340–344	8	26 (8 frequencies added to previous 18)
345–349	12	38 (12 frequencies added to previous 26)
350–354	4	42 (4 frequencies added to previous 38)
355–359	7	49 (7 frequencies added to previous 42)
360–364	2	51 (2 frequencies added to previous 49)
365–369	12	63 (12 frequencies added to previous 51)
370–374	5	68 (5 frequencies added to previous 63)
375–379	4	72 (4 frequencies added to previous 68)
380–384	5	77 (5 frequencies added to previous 72)
385–389	3	80 (3 frequencies added to previous 77)
390–394	2	82 (2 frequencies added to previous 80)
	$\sum f = 82$	$cf = 82$

vals are added to those totaled from previous intervals. This operation has been illustrated. Cumulative frequency distributions assist researchers in determining the accuracy of their computations. They provide an independent means for showing that all frequencies have been counted. A knowledge of the total frequencies can be used to locate easily the point most central to the distribution. In Table 12.5, for instance, there are 82 frequencies. Half of these frequencies would be 82/2 = 41 frequencies. This sum of 41 frequencies is closest to 42 frequencies, located in the interval, 350–354. Thus, the central point in the distribution is probably near the midpoint of that interval, or 352. This would be the approximate point at which the entire distribution of 82 scores is separated into two roughly equal parts.

Centiles, Deciles, and Quartiles.   Additional features of frequency distributions are points that separate those distributions into different proportions. A **proportion** is determined by dividing a part of the sum of frequencies by the sum of frequencies. For example, if we wanted to know what proportion 20 scores were of 50, we would divide 20 by 50 or 20/50 = .40. In this case, .40 is the proportion of scores that 20 is of 50. If we multiply this proportion, .40, by 100, we can easily convert the proportion to a percentage. Therefore, (100)(.40) = 40 percent or 40%. Twenty scores equal 40 percent of 50 scores. We can also accomplish this by moving the decimal point two spaces to the right and adding the word *percent.* Thus, .40 becomes 40.0 *percent.* Conventionally, in article and report writing, *percent* is usually spelled out rather than using the % sign. If we wanted to determine those points below or above which a certain proportion of scores would be found, we would compute centiles, deciles, or quartiles.

In any frequency distribution, there are points below and above which a certain proportion (or percentage) of scores will be found. A specific point in a distribution below which a given proportion of scores will be found is called a **centile** and is designated symbolically by the letter C. Centiles divide distributions of scores into increments of 1 percent. Particular subscripts are added to C to indicate the specific centile. For example, C_{18} is the 18th centile, and 18 percent of all scores in the distribution would be located below it. C_{35} is the 35th centile, and 35 percent of all scores in the frequency distribution would be found below it. Another way of dividing the distribution of scores into different parts is to use **deciles,** designated symbolically by the letter D. Deciles divide distributions of scores into increments of 10 percent. D_2 is the 2nd decile, and 20 percent of the scores in the distribution would be located below this point. D_8 would be the 8th decile, and 80 percent of the scores would be located below it. Conversely, 20 percent of all scores would be located above it.

The third way of dividing frequency distributions is according to **quartiles,** designated symbolically by the letter Q. Quartiles divide distributions into increments of 25 percent. Q_3 is the third quartile, and 75 percent of all scores in the distribution lie below it. Conversely, 25 percent of the scores lie above this point. Table 12.6 illustrates centiles, deciles, and quartiles, their relation with one another, and the percentages of scores below various points.

TABLE 12.6 Centiles, Deciles, and Quartiles in a Hypothetical Distribution of Scores, Equivalencies, and Proportions of Scores Below Particular Points

Interval	Quartiles	Deciles	Centiles
Highest scores	$Q_4 =$	D_{10}	$= C_{100}$(point leaving 100% of scores below it)
		D_9	$= C_{90}$ (point leaving 90% of scores below it)
		D_8	$= C_{80}$ (point leaving 80% of scores below it)
	Q_3		$= C_{75}$ (point leaving 75% of scores below it)
		D_7	$= C_{70}$ (point leaving 70% of scores below it)
		D_6	$= C_{60}$ (point leaving 60% of scores below it)
	$Q_2 =$	D_5	$= C_{50}$ (point leaving 50% of scores below it)
		D_4	$= C_{40}$ (point leaving 40% of scores below it)
		D_3	$= C_{30}$ (point leaving 30% of scores below it)
	Q_1		$= C_{25}$ (point leaving 25% of scores below it)
		D_2	$= C_{20}$ (point leaving 20% of scores below it)
		D_1	$= C_{10}$ (point leaving 10% of scores below it)
Lowest scores			

Centiles, deciles, and quartiles are computed easily and will be useful for understanding various central tendency and dispersion measures. They are also useful for other methodological operations as well. Their computation will be illustrated by using the cumulative frequency distribution shown in Table 12.5.

Suppose we wished to compute the 5th decile, D_5. An examination of Table 12.6 shows that this point is also equivalent with the 50th centile, C_{50}, and the second quartile, Q_2. We begin our computations by determining the proportion of 82 scores in Table 12.5 occurring below the 5th decile. This figure is determined by multiplying 82 by 0.50, or $(82)(0.50) = 41$ scores. Therefore, there are 41 scores below D_5. We will examine Table 12.5 and determine the sum of scores below and closest to 41. There are 38 scores in the interval 345–349. The next interval, 350–354, contains the scores we need to acquire our 41 scores. However, the interval contains four frequencies. We need only three of them. We may apply the following formula to complete our computations:

$$LL' + fn/ff(i),$$

where LL' = the lower limit of the interval entered to obtain the frequencies needed

fn = the frequencies we need

ff = the frequencies found in the interval

i = the interval size

Determining D_5, we have:

$$D_5 = 349.5 + 3/4(5)$$
$$= 349.5 + 3.8$$
$$= 354.3$$

The 5th decile is 354.3. This is also the 50th centile, C_{50}, and the 2nd quartile, Q_2. Fifty percent of all scores in the distribution are located below 354.3.

Suppose we wanted to compute C_{80}, or that point below which 80 percent of all scores is found. We would first determine how many scores are below the 80th centile, or $(82)(.80) = 65.6$. We need to find that point leaving 65.6 scores below it. We determine from the cumulative frequency distribution in Table 12.5 that 63 scores are found in the interval 365–369, the cumulative frequencies that are below and closest to 65.6 desired frequencies. The next interval, 370–374, contains five frequencies. We need 2.6 of these five frequencies to obtain our desired 65.6 frequencies. We may calculate C_{80} as follows:

$$C_{80} = 369.5 + 2.6/5(5)$$
$$= 369.5 + 2.6$$
$$= 372.1.$$

The 80th centile, C_{80}, is equal to 372.1. There are 80 percent of all scores in the distribution located below 372.1. This point is also the equivalent of the 8th centile, D_8. At the end of this chapter are various problems that can be worked for practice and to enhance your understanding of the concepts presented here. Answers to all numerical questions are found in Appendix D, pages 668–669.

In each of these examples, the frequencies we sought for the 80th centile were rounded to the nearest *tenth* (65.6) rather than to the nearest *whole* number (66). Most numerical problems at the chapter ends have been rounded to the nearest tenth, unless other instructions have been given. In order to maximize the meaningfulness of centile, decile, and quartile computations, it is preferable that researchers have interval-level data at their disposal. However, these values are frequently computed for data measured according to ordinal scales, such as attitudinal phenomena.

Histograms and Frequency Polygons

Histograms and **frequency polygons** are graphic portrayals of data that have been presented in frequency distributions. Figure 12.6 is a histogram of the frequencies shown in Table 12.2. The horizontal axis in the histogram marks off various intervals, commencing with 320–324 in the far left corner and ending with 390–394 to the far right. Graph paper is useful for such drawings and interval designations. The vertical axis to the left represents the number of frequencies found in each interval in Table 12.2. Vertical bars similar to those found in bar graphs have been drawn for each interval, and the height of each vertical bar is determined by the number of frequencies found. Notice in Figure 12.6 that the vertical bars have been drawn in such a way that the centers of the bars are interval midpoints. The height of the first vertical bar to the far left is "5," since there are five

FIGURE 12.6 Histogram of the data in Table 12.2.

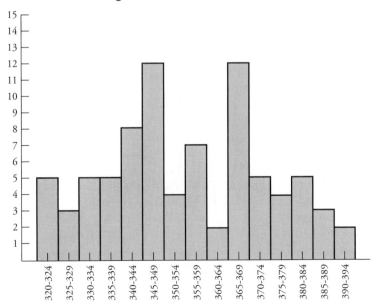

Intervals

frequencies found in the interval 320–324. The height of the bar in the interval 345–349 is "12," since there are twelve frequencies found in that interval.

Figure 12.7 shows a frequency polygon drawn from the histogram in Figure 12.6 and from the data originally presented in Table 12.2. In the case of the frequency polygon in Figure 12.7, points at the centers and tops of the vertical bars of the histogram shown in Figure 12.6 have been connected by straight lines. Note also that the ends of the frequency polygon to the far left and far right have been tied down to the horizontal axis at fictitious interval midpoints in the extremes of the distribution. While there are no intervals 315–319 or 395–399, the frequency polygon is nevertheless tied down to the horizontal axis at the midpoints of these next intervals progressing to the left and to the right for the purpose of completion.

The distribution of scores in Table 12.2 contained two intervals with frequencies of 12 each. It was suggested then that a subsequent histogram or frequency polygon would show at least two high peaks reflecting these large numbers of frequencies. Both the histogram in Figure 12.6 and the frequency polygon in Figure 12.7 show these prominent points.

Both histograms and frequency polygons provide readers with rapid visual inspections of how data are distributed in frequency distributions. Thus, the distribution of scores shown in Table 12.2 is not approximately bell shaped or "normal." Our inspection of the drawings of this distribution of scores shown in Figure 12.7 would, therefore, rule out the application of certain statistical tests, since bell-shaped distributions of scores are required for some of these applications. Also, certain measures of central tendency and dispersion would be pre-

FIGURE 12.7 Frequency polygon for the data in Figure 12.6.

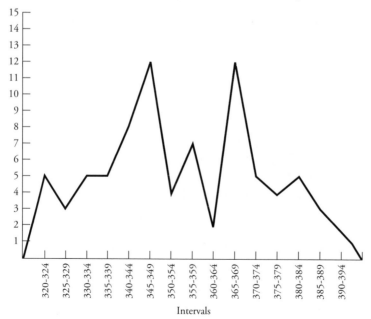

ferred over others, given the spread or dispersion of these scores that we can see graphically portrayed.

If we were to construct a frequency polygon for cumulative frequency distributions, we would create what is known as an **ogive curve.** An example of an ogive curve is shown for some fictitious data in Figure 12.8. The construction of an ogive curve for the cumulative frequency distribution shown in Table 12.5 is left as an exercise. The shape of this distribution should resemble that in Figure 12.8.

Ogive curves are useful for illustrating how rapidly scores increase from low to high over a designated range. Sometimes, offenders are charted over time according to how many months or years lapse between their probation or parole and their commission of new crimes (recidivism). Ogive curves may also be superimposed upon one another, and we might learn, for instance, whether parolees recidivate more or less rapidly than probationers. The horizontal axes in such curves would consist of months lapsing since probation or parole, while the vertical axis would portray the frequency of new crimes of probationers or parolees who recidivate. Of course, these figures may be presented in some other tabular form. But ogive curves provide an immediate visual impression and comparison.

Other Types of Graphic Presentation

Stick figures, drawings of persons of different sizes, and dollar signs are also used by social scientists to illustrate population increase, gross national products, expenditures for justice purposes, or prison–jail inmate population comparisons. Creative graphics may be used in various combinations to illustrate trends, such as the escalation of the number of inmates on death rows throughout the United States. Figure 12.9 shows a distribution of the number of persons under sentence of death between 1953 and 1997.

FIGURE 12.8 Ogive curve for cumulative frequency distribution of fictitious data.

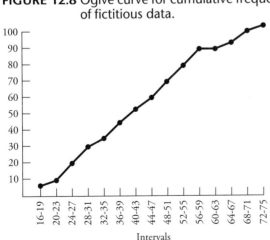

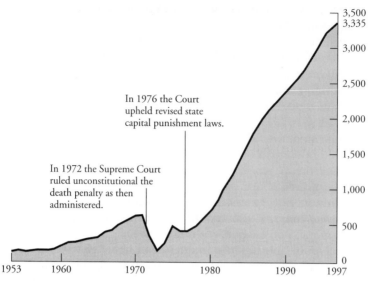

FIGURE 12.9 Persons in the United States under sentence of death, 1953–1997. [*Source:* Tracy L. Snell. (1998). *Capital Punishment 1997.* Washington, DC: Bureau of Justice Statistics. p. 2.]

■ TABULAR PRESENTATION AND CROSS-TABULATION

Tables and How to Read Them

Tabular presentation is the most popular method of presenting data in research articles and reports. Tables may be small or large, simple or complex, depending upon the research purposes of investigators and the elaborateness of the data they are presenting. Tables consist of various rows (r) and columns (c), designated as size $r \times c$. These **rows** and **columns** are designated variables, and the particular divisions on the rows and columns depict the *subclasses* of these variables. If the variable is *gender,* then the two subclasses on the gender variable are *male* and *female.* If the variable is *political affiliation,* then several subclasses on this variable might be *Republican, Democrat,* and *American Independent.* If the variable is *police professionalism,* the variable subclasses may be *high, moderately high, moderately low,* and *low.*

The smallest tables used in research contain either one row or one column, divided into two subclasses, and are either of size 2×1 or 1×2. For illustrative purposes, some fictitious data have been presented that portray the distribution of conviction offenses for a sample of state prison inmates. Tables $12.7c_1$ and 12.8 show examples of these smallest table sizes. In Table 12.7, one column is used to show inmates divided according to property or violent conviction offenses. The column represents the numbers of inmates in each of the conviction offense categories. The two rows show whether the conviction offense is a property crime (r_1) or a violent crime (r_2).

Table 12.8 is arranged differently. In this table, the two types of conviction offenses are in different columns with a single row. The row r_1 shows the num-

TABLE 12.7 The Distribution of a Hypothetical Sample of State Prison Inmates, by Conviction Offense, Illustrated with a 2 × 1 Table

	Conviction Offense	Column (c_1) N	Row numbers
Rows	Property	250 (68.4%)	r_1
	Violent	115 (31.6%)	r_2
	Total	$N = 365$ (100.0%)	

ber of persons in each conviction offense category. The two columns c_1 and c_2 represent the two conviction offense categories.

Notice that for each of these tables, percentages have been calculated for the property and violent inmate categories. An inspection of articles and reports in a wide array of professional journals discloses several stylistic differences in how data are arranged in tabular form. While each journal has specific requirements about how to construct tabular material, a convention is often followed regarding how to percentage the data. This convention is to percentage in the direction of the independent variable. In Tables 12.7 and 12.8, only one variable has been portrayed—conviction offense. In one-variable tables, it makes little difference whether we percentage in one direction or the other. However, for larger tables where **cross-tabulations** are involved, it does make a difference. There are a few conventional rules that most researchers follow. These are explained subsequently.

Cross-tabulations of Variables. **Cross-tabulations of variables** represent arrangements of two or more variables in tables of size 2 × 2 or larger, and in which one of the variables has been designated as independent. Table 12.9 shows some fictitious data arranged in a **2 × 2 table**.

In Table 12.9, gender has been cross-tabulated with type of delinquent offense and has been designated as the independent variable. Notice also that the table has been percentaged in the direction of the independent variable, gender. Had the table been so constructed that type of delinquent offense had been

TABLE 12.8 A Distribution of a Sample of State Prison Inmates, by Conviction Offense, Illustrated with a 1 × 2 Table

	Conviction Offense		Totals
	Property	Violent	
Column numbers	c_1	c_2	
Row (r_1) N's =	250 (68.4%)	115 (31.6%)	$N = 365$ (100%)

TABLE 12.9 Example of a 2 × 2 Table

Dependent variable		Independent variable (Gender)		Totals
		Males	Females	
(Type of delinquent offense)	Property	30a (17%)	120b (75%)	150 (44%)
	Violent	150c (83%)	40d (25%)	190 (56%)
	Totals	180 (100%)	160 (100%)	340 (100%)

placed across the top of the table and gender down the left-hand side of it, type of delinquent offense would be treated as influencing gender. As Table 12.9 is currently presented, however, gender is the variable used to account for variation on the type of delinquent offense variable. This particular presentation of the data is conventional and makes more sense, although not all researchers follow such a convention. A scam of several professional journals would disclose a variety of tabular styles, although a majority of the styles would probably be consistent with the conventional independent–dependent variable layout as shown in Table 12.9. Thus, following this particular convention permits readers to make easier and more systematic interpretations of tabular material. Again, not all researchers follow this tabular style.

Table 12.9 also shows that four table cells have been identified with the letters *a, b, c,* and *d*. This is because several statistical tests and measures of association are constructed especially for data presented in 2 × 2 tabular form, and these letters have symbolic significance in various statistical formulae. When reading Table 12.9, we can see that our 340 juveniles are almost evenly distributed according to gender (180 males and 160 females). Property offenders account for 44 percent of our sample, while violent offenders account for 56 percent of it. However, we have percentaged in the direction of the independent variable, gender, and, therefore, we can say that 83 percent of our male juveniles are violent offenders, whereas 75 percent of our female juveniles are property offenders. Our initial impression is that our sample of female juveniles commits more property offenses than violent offenses. Just the opposite impression is drawn about our sample of male juveniles, in which most appear to have committed violent offenses. Tentatively, gender appears to explain whether or not one will tend to be a violent or property offender.

Although caution has been recommended about drawing conclusions about cause-effect relationships between **variables,** we may at least infer that some causality exists between gender and type of delinquent offense, as shown in Table 12.9. Our rationale for making this inference about a possible relation between these two variables is based on the particular arrangement of frequencies throughout the cells in this table. Notice that the largest numbers of **cell frequencies** are found in cells *b* and *c*. The fewest frequencies are found in cells *a* and *d*. This **diagonal distribution of frequencies** is important as well as desirable, since it permits us to make direct inferences about how the variables might be related to each other. The other desirable diagonal arrangement that would permit such relational inferences would be for the largest numbers of the cell frequencies to accumulate in cells *a* and *d.* Using the 2×2 tabular case to illustrate desirable and undesirable distributions of frequencies, we have the following two desirable distributions:

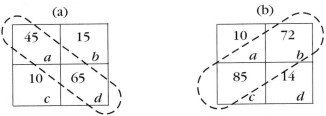

These distributions are considered desirable, not only because tentative causal inferences between variables may be drawn, but because of the direction of the relationship between variables may be determined. In the case of the data distributed in table (*a*) above, cells *a* and *d* contain the most frequencies. If these frequencies were placed in Table 12.9, we would conclude tentatively that male juveniles and property offenses appear related, while female juveniles and violent offenses appear related. Note that the distribution of frequencies in table (*b*) is more similar to the actual distribution shown in Table 12.9, in which the largest numbers of frequencies are found in cells *b* and *c.*

The following four tabular arrangements of frequencies are less desirable:

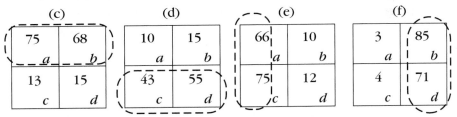

The primary reasons these four tabular arrangements are undesirable are that the largest numbers of frequencies are found in the **subclasses** of either the independent or dependent variables, and the direction of the relationship between the two variables cannot be determined easily. Thus, there is little variation on either the independent or dependent variables. For instance, in the first table (*c*), the largest numbers of frequencies are found in the first subclass of the dependent variable, cells *a* and *b*. In the table (*d*), the largest numbers of frequencies are found in the second subclass of the dependent variable in cells *c* and *d.* In the latter two tables (*e*) and (*f*), the largest numbers of frequencies are found in either the first or second subclasses of the independent variables (cells *a* and *c* and cells *b* and *d*, respectively).

This lack of variation in either the dependent or independent variable fails to provide us with an adequate opportunity to evaluate the impact of either variable on the other. This would be the same as commencing a study by declaring that we want to observe the impact of an intensive supervised probation program on recidivism among probationers rather than a program involving standard probation. We might obtain a large sample of probationers, but in creating our tables for these probationers and identifying their degree of recidivism, we may find that only a small proportion of probationers is involved in intensive supervised probation programs. Alternatively, we might find that the particular sample we have collected exhibits a low rate of recidivism across the board. Thus, it is imperative for researchers to ensure that ample representations of elements will be available to have more desirable tabular distributions. Statisticians recommend that proportionate breakdowns on the independent variable should be approximately 50–50, or close to it. Equal divisions on the dependent variable are also desirable, although dependent variables are often more difficult to control than independent variables.

Whenever less desirable tabular distributions of frequencies are encountered, and the preponderance of frequencies is found on one or the other subclasses of independent or dependent variables such as those illustrated earlier, researchers may make proportionate analyses of their data and determine whether greater proportions of persons with specific characteristics share other designated attributes. For example, suppose we investigated two samples of 100 first-degree murderers each in selected states that use the death penalty as the maximum punishment. One sample consists of convicted offenders who killed police officers during the commission of their crimes, whereas the other sample consists of convicted offenders who killed store clerks, innocent bystanders, or relatives during the commission of their crimes. We observe the results of jury deliberations in all cases and cross-tabulate both samples of convicted murderers with the nature of punishment imposed. Keeping our problem simplified, suppose only two punishment options exist—life without parole and the death penalty. Perhaps our belief is that those convicted of murdering police officers will be more likely to receive the death penalty than those convicted of killing others. Our data might appear as follows:

| | | Victim of Convicted Murderer | | |
		Police Officer	Non/Police Officer	Totals
Punishment imposed by jury	Life without parole	14	26	40
	Death penalty	86	74	160
	Totals	100	100	$N = 200$

Perhaps we are disappointed at first because there is no diagonal relation between the punishment imposed and whether the murder victim was a police officer. For both samples, the death penalty was imposed, and our cell frequencies accumulated on the second subclass of the dependent variable, the death penalty as punishment. However, we can examine the proportionate distribution of the imposition of the death penalty and see whether or not those convicted of murdering police officers received it more frequently than the other sample of convicted murderers. In the table shown, we can see that 86 percent of those convicted of murdering police officers received the death penalty, whereas only 74 percent of those convicted of murdering nonpolice received it. This is an obvious proportional difference and is generally consistent with what we originally anticipated, despite the fact that both samples of murderers tended to receive the death penalty anyway. Statistical tests may be applied to this table to determine whether 86 percent is significantly different from 74 percent. After all, this difference may be due to chance, and not to whether police officers were the murderer's victims. In this case, a statistical test, the Z test for differences between two proportions, discussed elsewhere (Champion, 1981:227–230; Siegel, 1956), could be used as a numerical measure of the significance of difference between these two proportions in a statistical sense. Thus, if diagonal relations between variables are nonexistent, we can usually adopt "Plan B" methods to evaluate proportionate differences. Alternative problem solutions are useful whenever tables such as (c), (d), (e), and (f) are encountered.

It is relatively easy to illustrate direction and association between variables by using the 2 × 2 tabular case for our example. However, when tables larger than 2 × 2 are constructed, it becomes increasingly difficult to detect relations between variables or to infer the direction of an association. An example of this more difficult chore might be illustrated by a 5 × 5 table. Consider the following hypothetical table, in which data have been distributed across five rows and five columns:

| | Independent Variable | | | | | |
	(Low) Col. 1	Col. 2	Col. 3	Col. 4	(High) Col. 5	Totals
Dependent Variable (Low)						
Row 1	18	28	36	15	19	116
Row 2	31	22	19	45	28	145
Row 3	16	18	18	14	21	87
Row 4	31	29	20	15	12	107
Row 5	16	19	30	40	60	165
(High) Totals	112	116	123	129	140	620

It is quite difficult to determine whether any directional relation exists between the independent and dependent variables in this table. The frequencies appear scattered and do not seem to occur in any patterned relation. Not all larger tables exhibit this much disarray, however. Below is a 5 × 5 table where direction is more visually apparent:

| | Independent Variable | | | | | |
	(Low) Col. 1	Col. 2	Col. 3	Col. 4	(High) Col. 5	Totals
Dependent Variable (Low)						
Row 1	6	15	19	30	50	120
Row 2	8	16	20	28	31	103
Row 3	10	6	20	16	15	67
Row 4	30	16	12	10	8	76
Row 5	70	40	20	16	3	149
(High) Totals	124	93	91	100	107	515

In this particular 5 × 5 tabular scenario, we can see that as we move across the five columns on the independent variable from left to right, there are few frequencies in the first few columns, but these frequencies increase in successive columns as we move to the right (e.g., 6, 15, 19, 30, and 50 as frequencies across row 1; and 8, 16, 20, 28, and 31 as frequencies across row 2). However, in row 3, there is an inconsistent pattern in the distribution of frequencies across the five columns (10, 6, 20, 16, and 15, moving from left to right). In rows 4 and 5, however, there are initially larger numbers of frequencies to the far left, although these frequencies systematically decrease as we move to the right across other columns (30, 16, 12, 10, and 8 in row 4; and 70, 40, 20, 16, and 3 in row 5, moving from left to right).

We would be able to say that for this particular table, higher scores on the independent variable are associated with lower scores on the dependent variable, while lower scores on the independent variable are associated with higher scores on the dependent variable. A rough line has been drawn around the preponderance of frequencies in the table, showing an approximately diagonal relation. Unfortunately, relationships between variables in many of these larger tables are not seen as clearly whenever real data are presented and discussed in articles, reports, or research summarizations.

When we increase the number of variables to be cross-tabulated, we make it possible to control for the influence of these additional variables on the remaining variables. We may observe a tentative association between some hypothetical variables in the following 2 × 2 table:

		Status of mother		Totals
		Works	Does Not Work	
Status of children	Delinquent	100	50	150
	Nondelinquent	50	100	150
	Totals	150	150	300

When we first inspect this table, it seems that it makes a difference whether mothers work or do not work and whether their children are or are not delinquent. While it is entirely possible that the working/nonworking status of mothers affects whether their children become delinquent, we may wish to explore other factors to evaluate their potential impact on our initial observation. Perhaps we want to consider the influence of *continuous adult supervision* on the incidence of delinquency among the children involved in this research. Maybe research suggests that continuous adult supervision of children is a more important determinant of a youth's delinquency or nondelinquency rather than the working/nonworking status of mothers. We can reconstruct the previous data in the following rearranged table:

		Continuous Adult Supervision of Children				Totals
		Yes		No		
		Mother works	Mother does not work	Mother works	Mother does not work	
Status of children	Delinquent	0	0	100	50	150
	Nondelinquent	50	100	0	0	150
	Totals	50	100	100	50	300

Now, an entirely different pattern of the role of working mothers in relation to the delinquency/nondelinquency of their children emerges. After we added the third variable, *continuous adult supervision,* it seems that the more important factor is whether the children are continuously supervised by adults, regardless of whether their mothers work. This also illustrates spuriousness, or the presence of a supposed association between two variables that is actually the result of a third, perhaps unknown, variable. Notice that all of the delinquent children are found under the category in which children are not continuously supervised by adults, and that all of the children who are not delinquent are under the *continuous adult supervision* category. Although this finding does not prove a relation between the continuity of adult supervision and delinquency/nondelinquency, it nevertheless seems to rule out the status of working/nonworking mothers as an explanatory factor.

In the event that our tables are too large and unwieldy, such as our first 5 × 5 table containing 620 frequencies in disarray, it is possible to collapse such tables to create smaller and more meaningful ones. **Collapsing tables** means to reduce either the number of rows or the number of columns or both and to combine the total frequencies into smaller numbers of cells. Suppose that the column designations for the first 5 × 5 table were "Strongly agree," "Agree," "Undecided, probably agree," "Disagree," and "Strongly disagree." Further suppose that the row designations were "Very favorable," "Favorable," Undecided, probably favorable," "Unfavorable," and "Very unfavorable." We could collapse the data into a 3 × 3 table to see whether our results are more meaningful. We might decide to collapse the columns as follows: place the "old" columns 1 and 2 into "new" column 1, the "old" column 3 into a "new" column 2, and the "old" columns 4 and 5 into a "new" column 3. Further, we might decide to collapse our rows as follows: combine our "old" rows 1, 2, and 3 into a "new" row 1, "old" row 4 into a "new" row 2, and the "old" row 5 into a "new" row 3. These collapsed data follow (the old row and column totals are shown in parentheses in each of the nine cells of the new, collapsed 3 × 3 table):

(Collapsed table)
or
Independent variable

	(Agree) Col. 1	Col. 2	(Disagree) Col. 3	Totals
Dependent variable				
(Favorable) Row 1	(18+28+31 +22+16+18) = 133	(36+19+18) = 73	(15+19+45 +28+14+21) = 142	348
Row 2	(31+29) = 60	= 20	(15+12) = 27	107
Row 3 (Unfavorable)	(16+19) = 35	= 30	(40+60) = 100	165
Total	= 228	= 123	= 269	= 620

	or Independent variable			
Dependent variable	Agree		Disagree	Total
(Favorable)	133	73	142	348
	60	20	27	107
Unfavorable	35	30	100	165
Total	228	123	269	= 620

This pattern has simplified the task of perceiving any relationships between these variables. However, an inspection of the distribution of frequencies shows no meaningful pattern. There are 133 elements (persons) who tend to "agree" on the independent variable, while they are "favorable" on the dependent variable. However, 142 persons who "disagree" on the independent variable also are "favorable" on the dependent variable. It is possible that we might collapse these data differently and generate more meaningful patterns of frequencies. But collapsing of categories on either the independent or dependent variables should be done in a logical fashion. It would be illogical, for instance, to combine "unfavorables" with "favorables" on the dependent variable or to combine "agrees" with "disagrees" on the independent variable.

Other Forms of Tabular Presentation

Many other forms of tabular presentation exist. Often, these tables illustrate trends or present informative figures. *The Sourcebook of Criminal Justice Statistics 1997* (Maguire and Pastore, 1998) contains hundreds of tables about all aspects of the criminal justice system, including crime trends and case information. For example, Table 12.10 shows the average and median number of days between arrest and sentencing for various crimes disposed of by state courts for 1994.

An inspection of Table 12.10 breaks these data into cases by type of offense and method of conviction (i.e., whether a jury or bench trial was conducted, and whether a guilty plea was entered through plea bargaining). Both average (mean) and median figures are presented, expressed in numbers of days from arrest to conviction. Explanatory notes in the table indicate the meaning of the median for purposes of reading the table. For bench trials, murder cases seem to take the longest to resolve, with an overall average of 398 days from arrest to sentencing. Also for bench trials, aggravated assault accounts for those cases most rapidly resolved, taking an average of 146 days from arrest to conviction. In almost every type of criminal case, the mean number of days to dispose of each case was higher than the median number of days. Averages are influenced greatly by deviant scores or, in this case, a few extraordinarily long, drawn-out trials.

Tables may present **trend information,** such as the rates associated with the use of plea bargaining over time, or the proportion of civil and criminal cases in federal courts across several decades. The *Uniform Crime Reports* publishes tabular information about index crimes in most U.S. cities and counties on an annual basis.

TABLE 12.10 Average and Median Number of Days Between Arrest and Conviction for Felony Cases Disposed by State Courts

By offense and method of conviction, United States, 1994

(In days)

	NUMBER OF DAYS BETWEEN ARREST AND CONVICTION FOR CASES DISPOSED BY:		
	Trial		
Most serious conviction offense	*Jury*	*Bench*	*Gulity plea*
Average number of days			
All offenses	273	235	165
Violent offenses	285	252	203
Murder	356	398	307
Rape	295	347	214
Robbery	263	218	193
Aggravated assault	245	214	201
Other violent	346	262	178
Property offenses	249	229	158
Burglary	263	219	151
Larceny	205	229	155
Fraud	320	259	171
Drug offenses	271	232	155
Possession	245	218	142
Trafficking	279	242	163
Weapons offenses	279	215	159
Other offenses	231	236	159
Median number of days			
All offenses	219	167	116
Violent offenses	233	185	148
Murder	309	364	253
Rape	254	247	159
Robbery	232	167	151
Aggravated assault	173	146	144
Other violent	319	219	122
Property offenses	200	154	111
Burglary	200	154	110
Larceny	175	167	107
Fraud	224	154	114
Drug offenses	202	162	108
Possession	181	159	98
Trafficking	202	164	112
Weapons offenses	203	161	120
Other offenses	191	181	113

The median marks the point below which and above which 50% of all cases fall. The grand total column includes all cases, whether or not conviction type was known. Some estimates are based on as few as one case and are therefore unreliable.

Source: U.S. Department of Justice, Bureau of Justice Statistics, *State Court Sentencing of Convicted Felons, 1994,* NCJ-164614 (Washington, DC: U.S. Department of Justice, 1998), p. 52.

DECIDING HOW BEST TO PRESENT YOUR INFORMATION

There are no definitive guidelines about how much graphic material is best for any research report or article. One guideline is that such materials should not appear to be thrown in or frivolous. Editors of professional journals generally favor shorter publications rather than longer ones. Excess graphic presentation and use of tabular materials may be distracting. Many articles are written without any graphic material in them. Qualitative research projects rely heavily on interpretations of social actions and descriptions of attitudes. In short, it is not a requirement of social scientific writing that such materials must always be supplemented with tables or graphs.

Decisions about the inclusion of graphs or tabular materials depend, in large part, on the nature of one's research. If samples of elements are studied and described, summary tables are helpful for portraying various features of the sample, including average age, prior record, educational training, gender, and a host of other factors. This material is also presented in written form, as authors describe the essential aspects of their graphic and tabular presentations. Studies that investigate trends, such as whether there is a rise in juvenile violence or female criminality over time, might profit from including summary tables of crime rates across several years.

KEY TERMS

Bar graphs
Cell frequencies
Centiles
Coding
Coding manual or code book
Collapsing tables
Control of variables
Crime clocks
Crime rate
Cross-tabulations
Cross-tabulations of variables
Cumulative frequency distribution
Data cleaning
Data entry
Deciles
Diagonal distribution of frequencies
Frequency
Frequency distributions
Frequency polygons
Graphic presentation
Grouped data

Histograms
Interval midpoints
Intervals
Interval size
Ogive curve
Pie charts
Proportion
Quartiles
Ratios
$r \times c$
Rounding; rounding rule
Rows and columns
SPSS
Subclasses
Tabular presentation
Trend information
2×2 table
Ungrouped data
Upper and lower limits of intervals
Variables
Verification

QUESTIONS FOR REVIEW AND PROBLEMS TO SOLVE

1. Under what conditions might a researcher benefit from treating a set of scores in grouped fashion in a frequency distribution?

2. What guidelines exist for constructing frequency distributions and determining the sizes of intervals?

3. Construct a frequency polygon for the following frequency distribution:

Intervals	f
10–14	6
15–19	7
20–24	13
25–29	8
30–34	6
35–39	10
40–44	19
45–49	15
50–54	7
55–59	3
60–64	9
65–69	12
70–74	13
75–79	5

$$\Sigma f = 133$$

4. Determine upper and lower limits for the following intervals:

   (a) 90–100   (b) 1500–1599   (c) .20–.29
   (d) .0055–.0059   (e) 136–139   (f) 200–249

5. Given the following array of scores, construct a frequency distribution, beginning with the interval 30–39:

```
33    44    57    39    92   111   103   152   188   159    57    45    50  60
70    42    79    68    62   165   158    35    49    82    95    99   102
91    94    39    40   110   115    56    84   137   126   145   176   164
138  156   148   186    67    58    92    30    49    90    54    87    96  76
 94  100   103   100   105   110   110   182   167   173   128   119
177  115   115    83    49    68    58   190   187   154   139   150   112
```

6. For the data you have arranged into a frequency distribution in Problem 5, determine the following centiles, deciles, and quartiles:

   (a) C_{27} (b) Q_3 (c) D_8 (d) C_4
   (e) D_5 (f) Q_1 (g) C_{90} (h) D_3

7. Given the following information, construct a pie chart.

Larceny—35 percent
Burglary—42 percent
Rape—20 percent
Homicide—3 percent

What are some major restrictions governing the use of pie charts? What are some of their intended applications?

8. Convert the following proportions to percentages:

(a) .0036   (b) .1560   (c) .9700
(d) .1158   (e) .5550   (f) .0004

9. Identify interval midpoints for the frequency distribution you constructed in Problem 5.

10. What is an ogive curve? Construct an ogive curve for the data presented in the frequency distribution in Problem 5.

11. What are desirable distributions of frequencies in 2 × 2 tables? Give two examples different from those in this book, using hypothetical variables.

12. What are some conventional rules governing the construction of $r \times c$ tables?

13. What is meant by spuriousness? How can it be detected?

14. Collapse the following information into a 2 × 2 table, using a logical collapsing procedure:

Variable X

		Very strong	Strong	Weak	Very weak
	Very high	30	20	15	10
Variable Y	High	20	15	10	5
	Low	10	20	30	40
	Very low	5	15	20	60

Illustrate your new table. Briefly explain the rationale for collapsing your table into a 2 × 2 form. Is there any kind of direction apparent as the result of the collapsed 2 × 2 table? What interpretation can you make of the relation between variables X and Y?

chapter 13

Hypothesis Testing
and
Theory Verification

INTRODUCTION

This chapter examines hypotheses, or various testable statements that are derived from our theories. Hypotheses are the means whereby our theories are tested. Hypotheses vary in their complexity and wording, and thus several different kinds of hypotheses are described. Conventional use of hypotheses in research suggests that these statements should be implicitly or explicitly presented in pairs or in hypothesis sets. Hypothesis sets, including the conventional pairing of research and null hypotheses, are examined and several examples from the research literature are provided.

Hypotheses perform several important functions. Their use in criminological research signifies more elaborate or sophisticated research plans, wherein investigators are interested in description and experimentation. Hypotheses may contain one or several variables. As we add variables to hypothesis statements, these statements become increasingly complex and more difficult to test. Both one- and k-variable hypothesis statements are illustrated.

Although it is possible to verify or refute theories without deriving hypotheses from them to test, it is a widely accepted practice to use hypotheses for theory verification purposes. Also, whenever hypotheses are subject to empirical tests, researchers use probability theory as a means of minimizing guesswork and subjectivity when interpreting scientific results. Hypothesis test outcomes are evaluated in terms of the adequacy of the theory from which they were derived, the quality of instrumentation and sample selected, and other factors. Several considerations relevant for interpreting the results of hypothesis tests are presented and examined.

HYPOTHESES AND THEORY

Hypotheses are tentative statements about something, the validity of which is generally unknown. For example, to declare that "upper-class people have fewer delinquent children than lower-class people" might be construed as a hypothesis concerning the effect of social class on delinquent behavior. Whether or not this is a statement of fact or a hypothesis depends upon how much we know about the social class–delinquency relation and whether the declarer actually knows if the statement is true. If the statement reflects the investigator's "hunch" about the social class–delinquency relation, then the statement is largely a hypothetical one. However, if census data exist to show clearly that large proportions of delinquents are found in lower-class families and small proportions of them are found in upper-class families, then these data provide empirical support for the authenticity of the statement.

Many facts that we know today were hypotheses in earlier times. For example, we know a great deal more about marijuana today than we did in the 1930s. Some persons believed that marijuana caused irreversible mental illness and insanity. Others believed that it led to sexual promiscuity. Today, although it is unlawful to use marijuana in any U.S. jurisdiction, we understand that it impairs our judgment and depth-perception, although it doesn't appear to cause irreversible mental illness, insanity, or sexual promiscuity.

Another example pertains to the relation between broken homes and delinquency. Children from broken homes (either by desertion or divorce) were believed to be likely candidates for delinquency. Religious leaders promoted the importance of family stability and unity as a way of preventing children in those families from acquiring delinquent behaviors and characteristics. Single-parent adoptions of children were unheard of in most jurisdictions, because the conventional, two-parent family was believed most therapeutic for children. Today, however, several states permit single-parent adoptions of children, since the evidence that single-parent families are unhealthy for child-rearing has been inconclusive and contradictory.

Many of our present beliefs have been shaped by previous verifications of theories. Much uncertainty remains about different types of behaviors and social events, however. Following are examples of hypotheses that might be tested in criminological and criminal justice research today:

1. *Female correctional officers have the same stress levels compared with male correctional officers.*
2. *Crime rates in neighborhoods decrease as police visibility increases.*
3. *Criminal court judges in the South are more lenient in sentencing elderly offenders than criminal court judges in the North.*
4. *The greater the numbers of correctional officers supervising prisoners, the fewer the numbers of inmate disturbances.*
5. *Jurors are more sympathetic to female defendants than they are to male defendants.*
6. *Increasing the punitive fines for committing crimes will decrease the crime rate.*
7. *Felons who participate in community-based correctional programs will have lower rates of recidivism than will incarcerated felons who are paroled.*
8. *Crime rates vary inversely with the amount of money spent on crime prevention.*
9. *Females charged with felonies have a better chance of obtaining pretrial release than males charged with the same crimes and having similar criminal histories.*
10. *Offenders on probation with electronic monitoring will have fewer program violations than will offenders on standard probation.*

Hypotheses may pertain to anything. Hypotheses do not necessarily have to be true, however. In fact, the truth of many hypotheses formulated by researchers is often unknown. Hypotheses, therefore, are tentative statements about things that researchers wish to support or refute.

The ten hypotheses listed here have been studied and subjected to verification by various researchers in recent years. Some of these statements have

Box 13.1

Barry C. Feld
University of Minnesota

Statistics: B.A. (psychology), University of Pennsylvania; J.D., University of Minnesota Law School; Ph.D. (sociology), Harvard University.

Interests: While at Harvard, I served as Research Project Director at the Harvard Law School's Center for Criminal Justice (1970–1972). Between 1974 and 1978, I was a reporter for the American Bar Association's Juvenile Justice Standards Project, and I co-authored a volume entitled *Rights of Minors* (1980). I worked as a prosecutor in criminal and juvenile courts in Hennepin County (Minneapolis) from 1975 to 1978. During 1987 to 1988, the Office of Juvenile Justice and Delinquency Prevention (OJJDP), U.S. Department of Justice, selected me as the first Visiting Fellow at the National Center for Juvenile Justice in Pittsburgh, Pennsylvania, to do research on the delivery of legal services in juvenile courts. I have written six books and more than 40 major law review and criminology articles on juvenile justice administration, with special emphases on serious young offenders, procedural justice in juvenile court, youth sentencing policy, and the future of the juvenile court.

Serendipity characterizes my career as one research interest has led to the next. My initial interests in crime and urban policy led me to Harvard to study criminology with Lloyd Ohlin. In turn, Ohlin's ongoing research with the Massachusetts Department of Youth Services resulted in my dissertation research on juvenile correctional institutions, which I have published as *Neutralizing Inmate Violence* (1977).

As the result of studying juvenile training schools, after I joined the University of Minnesota faculty, I consulted closely with the Minnesota Department of Corrections to develop programs for serious and chronic young offenders. The correctional administrative problems posed by serious young offenders, in turn, directed my research toward the processes and policies that led authorities to waive some serious young offenders to criminal courts for prosecution as adults. My ongoing empirical, criminological, and legal research and writing on the transfer of youths to criminal courts and their sentencing as adults has dominated the waiver literature for more than two decades. My scholarship has led to fundamental jurisprudential and legal changes in states' waiver policies throughout the nation.

In another research area, the profound differences between the quality of procedural justice in juvenile courts and in criminal courts impressed me when I worked as a prosecutor in both justice systems and, in turn, led to my extensive research on juvenile court administrative practices. For example, while writing footnotes for a law review article on juveniles' waivers of *Miranda* rights in the mid-1980s, I discovered that virtually no research existed on juveniles' access to or waiver of counsel in delinquency prosecutions. I conducted research on the delivery and impact of legal representation in juvenile court and produced three articles and a book, *Justice for Children: The Right to Counsel and the Juvenile Courts* (1993), dealing with juvenile courts' continuing reluctance to provide youths with effective representation.

My research, scholarship, and speeches have helped to shape state and national juvenile justice policy debates. As a result of my research on procedural justice and access to counsel, in 1992 the United States Senate, Committee on the Judiciary, Juvenile Justice Subcommittee, held hearings on "Juvenile Courts: Access to Justice," in conjunction with the reauthorization of the federal Juvenile Justice and Delinquency Prevention (JJDP) Act. The 1992 JJDP law required the General Accounting Office (GAO) to evaluate youths' access to counsel; the GAO replicated my research and findings in a separate publication. The JJDP reauthorization also mandated OJJDP to fund proposals to improve the delivery and quality of legal services in juvenile courts. OJJDP funded the American Bar Association's Juvenile Justice Due Process Committee, on which I served, that issued *A Call for Justice* (1995). The 1994 Minnesota legislature enacted this task force's recommendations and revised the juvenile code's provisions on counsel and procedural justice, transfer of serious offenders to criminal courts, and the sentencing of youths in juvenile courts.

I am probably the most severe critic of juvenile justice administration in the country. I began my research career studying juvenile corrections, and I immediately recognized that juvenile courts punish youths in euphemistically sanitized youth prisons. Because I worked as a prosecutor in both juvenile and criminal courts, I realized that juvenile courts used a procedural regime to which few adults facing the prospect of confinement would consent to be tried. The rise of youth violence and homicide in the late-1980s and the increased punitiveness of juvenile justice policies have prevented juvenile courts from realizing their original rehabilitative mission. I contend that the punitiveness of juvenile justice policies reflects broader social, structural, and racial demographic changes in American society. I have called for the abolition of the juvenile court, the trial of all offenders in one integrated juvenile justice system, with special sentencing provisions to recognize youthfulness as a mitigating factor in sentencing young offenders.

Advice to Students: As an academic scholar, it is extremely rewarding and satisfying to see criminological research and policy proposals enacted into laws with real-world consequences. Those contemplating a professional research career should initially attempt to identify what the coming "hot" policy issues will be. One useful way to do so is through involvement or collaboration with the justice system administrators who have to deal with those problems on a daily basis. In framing a research agenda, make your research, findings, and recommendations relevant to policy and decision makers. As you design and conduct your research, keep in mind what you will tell justice system administrators or law-makers about the nature of the problem and the alternative solutions. And emphasize why your proposed recommendation is preferable to the others.

been investigated more often than others. Thus, our degree of certainty about any given statement is based, in part, upon the amount of confirming evidence we can compile about it. Also, each of these statements is derived from a larger theoretical scheme. If we are examining the effectiveness of various probation programs, for instance, we might theorize about the amount of control exerted over probationers by using home confinement and/or electronic monitoring as means of verifying their whereabouts and otherwise keeping track of their movements. One statement we might test would be whether those on standard probation might be more likely to commit new crimes than those subject to more intensive monitoring, especially electronic monitoring.

It might also be believed that fining offenders might function to reduce their recidivism. Currently, the Internal Revenue Service and Drug Enforcement Administration, together with the U.S. Department of Justice, seize the assets of drug dealers and those who traffic in illegal drugs. These assets might include automobiles, boats, airplanes, homes, and other types of property, in addition to large sums of money used for illicit drug transactions. In 1991, for instance, the Department of Justice claimed that several billion dollars had been used to improve law enforcement effectiveness, and that much of this money was from illegal drug transactions and property seizures. It might be hypothesized, therefore, that hitting drug dealers in their pocketbooks might have a deterrent effect on their propensity to violate the law.

Each hypothesis is closely connected with a theoretical scheme that provides an explanatory and predictive framework for it. A hypothesis is like an advance forecast, since a certain outcome is anticipated or expected. The theoretical rationale is such that it explains how it came to be so that the hypothesis might be true.

■ TYPES OF HYPOTHESES, HYPOTHESIS CONSTRUCTION, AND HYPOTHESIS SETS

There are several different kinds of hypotheses used in criminological research. The primary types of hypotheses examined here are (1) research hypotheses, (2) null hypotheses, and (3) statistical hypotheses.

Research Hypotheses

Hypotheses that are derived from the researcher's theory are called either **research hypotheses** or **working hypotheses.** Social scientists believe that their research hypotheses are true, since they are derived logically from theoretical schemes constructed by these researchers. These hypotheses are believed true to the extent that the theories from which they were derived are true.

Because theories are, in a sense, suppositions about the true nature of things and thus considered tentative statements about reality until they have been verified to the scientist's satisfaction, the hypotheses derived from a theory must also be regarded as tentative suppositions until they have been tested. Testing hypotheses means to subject them to some type of empirical confirmation or disconfirmation. For example, testing the hypothesis "The average income expectation of boys in a poverty area is $1,000 per month as adults" might be done by entering a poverty area, obtaining a sample of male youths, and asking them questions about their monthly income expectations as adults. If most of the boys tell us that their income expectation is around $1,000 per month, then our hypothesis about their income expectation is confirmed, at least in this instance. If their reports are substantially more or less than $1,000, then our hypothesis is disconfirmed, refuted, or not supported, again in this instance. It is important to understand that hypothesis tests under any condition or in any situation, regardless of the magnitude, are not conclusive proof of the truthfulness of the hypothesis. Replication research is advised, which repeats research again and again, under different circumstances and in different geographical areas. If sufficient samples of boys continue to report income expectations of $1,000 as adults, then our hypothesis gradually becomes a factual statement. In time, there will be no further need to test it.

Null Hypotheses

In a sense, **null hypotheses** are the reverse of research hypotheses, although this is not entirely accurate. Null hypotheses are also statements about the reality of things, except that they serve to refute or deny whatever is explicitly stated in a given research hypothesis. To continue with our example, if investigators state in their research hypothesis that "the average income expectation of boys in a poverty area is $1,000 as adults," then the appropriate null hypothesis to accompany this research hypothesis is "the average income expectation of boys in a poverty area is not $1,000 as adults." If investigators subsequently find out that boys in a poverty area have income expectations considerably more (or less) than $1,000 as adults, then the null hypothesis can be rejected and the research hypothesis will be supported.

Another way of looking at research and null hypotheses is that both statements are directly contradictory and cannot coexist as true. Therefore, if one of the statements is true, then the other statement must be false. If one of the statements is false, then the other statement must be true. If we show that the statement "the average income expectation of boys in a poverty area is not $1,000 as adults" is false, then this statement can be rejected. Then we conclude that it must be true that "the average income expectation of boys in a poverty area is $1,000 as adults" is true and should be supported. Confirming one statement denies the other. Denying one statement confirms the other.

Null hypotheses are usually paired with specific research hypotheses, as is illustrated by the ten statements that follow. These ten research hypotheses have been recreated, and null hypotheses have been devised for each of them. Notice the wording of both hypotheses in these **hypothesis sets.**

Hypothesis Set 1

1. *Research Hypothesis: Female correctional officers have the same stress levels compared with male correctional officers.*

1'. *Null Hypothesis: Female correctional officers have different stress levels compared with male correctional officers.*

Hypothesis Set 2

2. *Crime rates in neighborhoods decrease as police visibility increases.*

2'. *Crime rates in neighborhoods either increase or remain the same as police visibility increases.*

Hypothesis Set 3

3. *Criminal court judges in the South are more lenient in sentencing elderly offenders than criminal court judges in the North.*

3'. *Criminal court judges in the South are equally lenient or less lenient in sentencing elderly offenders than criminal court judges in the North.*

Hypothesis Set 4

4. *The greater the numbers of correctional officers supervising prisoners, the fewer the numbers of inmate disturbances.*

4'. *The greater the numbers of correctional officers supervising prisoners, the numbers of inmate disturbances will either remain the same or be greater.*

Hypothesis Set 5

5. *Jurors are more sympathetic to female defendants than they are to male defendants.*

5'. *Jurors are equally sympathetic or less sympathetic to female defendants than they are to male defendants.*

Hypothesis Set 6

6. *Increasing the punitive fines for committing crimes will decrease the crime rate.*

6'. *Increasing the punitive fines for committing crimes will either increase the crime rate or exert no effect upon it.*

Hypothesis Set 7

7. *Felons who participate in community-based correctional programs will have lower rates of recidivism than will incarcerated felons who are paroled.*

7'. *Felons who participate in community-based correctional programs will have the same rates of recidivism or higher rates of recidivism than will incarcerated felons who are paroled.*

Hypothesis Set 8

8. *Crime rates vary inversely with the amount of money spent on crime prevention.*

8′. *Crime rates either vary directly or do not vary at all with the amount of money spent on crime prevention.*

Hypothesis Set 9

9. *Females charged with felonies have a better chance of obtaining pretrial release than males charged with the same crimes and having similar criminal histories.*

9′. *Females charged with felonies have either the same chance or a poorer chance of obtaining pretrial release than males charged with the same crimes and having similar criminal histories.*

Hypothesis Set 10

10. *Offenders on probation with electronic monitoring will have fewer program violations than will offenders on standard probation.*

10′. *Offenders on probation with electronic monitoring will either have the same or greater program violations than will offenders on standard probation.*

In each of these hypothesis sets, the null hypothesis was constructed *directly from the wording of the research hypothesis.* Notice that if we refute any of the null hypotheses, then the accompanying research hypothesis will be true, at least under those specific test circumstances. Why should we do all of this in the first place? After all, we have a perfectly good theory that we have constructed. We have extracted various hypothesis statements from it to test. Why not test them and let it go at that?

Before these questions are answered, we must also accept the fact that null hypotheses are strictly hypothetical models used to test research hypotheses indirectly. Thus, in reality, they were never intended to exist, on their own. We make up null hypotheses directly from research hypotheses. Then, we test null hypotheses. As the result of our tests of null hypotheses, we make decisions about research hypotheses. Rejecting a specific null hypothesis, or throwing it out, or refuting it, or disconfirming it, means that we support the specific research hypothesis that was used originally to construct that null hypothesis. If we fail to reject a null hypothesis, we fail to support the specific research hypothesis from which that null hypothesis was created. We never accept or support or confirm null hypotheses, because they do not exist in reality, except as indirect tests of the real research hypotheses we have formulated. The following relation is helpful in understanding what is meant by rejecting or by failing to reject null hypotheses, and these two alternative consequences for specific research hypotheses:

Our decision about the null hypothesis is:	**Our decision about the research hypothesis is:**
Reject It ⟶	Support It
Fail to Reject It ⟶	Fail to Support It

Many students want to know why criminologists bother with null hypotheses: Why don't they just test their research hypotheses directly and be content with that? There are four reasons why null hypothesis models are used, most of which may not answer these questions to your satisfaction. These reasons are the following:

1. Because criminologists and other social scientists define their roles as being more detached and objective about phenomena than laypeople, it would appear as though they were not behaving objectively if they sought to prove true those statements that they believed to be true initially. Therefore, attempting to show the truthfulness of research hypotheses would imply some bias toward trying to confirm one's suppositions and possibly ignoring facts or findings that refute one's beliefs. Null hypotheses assist researchers, therefore, because such hypotheses are denials of what is believed to be true. If investigators are able to reject or refute null hypotheses, then their case for supporting their research hypotheses is strengthened as a result.

2. It seems easier to prove a statement false than to prove it true. There are those who contend that it is easier to find fault with something (i.e., an idea, belief, or hypothesis) than to look for facts or evidence that would support it. Whatever the merits of this argument, the null hypothesis is assumed to be true until proven otherwise.

3. It is *conventional* to use null hypotheses in criminological and criminal justice research. The key word here is *convention*. It is conventional in social research of any kind to use null hypotheses in conjunction with research hypotheses. Most social scientists use null hypotheses in their own research and in their articles published in professional journals.

4. Null hypotheses fit the probability model underlying hypothesis testing. This is the best of the four reasons. Under a probability theoretical model, hypotheses have a likelihood of being either true or false. The null hypothesis is an expression of one possible alternative outcome of our social observations. The probability model specifies that the null hypothesis may be either true or false, but not both simultaneously. Another **alternative hypothesis** about our social observations is the research hypothesis. Research hypotheses are "grounded" in and derived from theory. Research hypotheses also have a probability of either being true or false. Thus, the null hypothesis is a statement that may or may not be true, but is subject to empirical verification or refutation. Neither the research hypothesis nor the null hypothesis is absolutely true or false for any given test conducted. There is always a probability that both types of hypotheses are true or false.

Statistical Hypotheses

A third type of hypothesis is known as a statistical hypothesis. **Statistical hypotheses** are statements about statistical populations that, on the basis of information obtained from observed data, one seeks to support or refute (Winer,

1962). Statistical populations refer to either people or things. It is generally the case when testing hypotheses that our observations about people or things are reduced in some way to numerical quantities and symbolic expressions. For instance, suppose we are concerned about age differences between two groups of persons. We hypothesize that one group is older than the other. In order to test our research hypothesis, which might be "group 1 is older than group 2," we first create a null hypothesis, which becomes "group 1 is the same age as or younger than group 2."

To subject these hypotheses to an empirical test, we would obtain age values for groups 1 and 2, average the ages, and assess the average age difference by applying a statistical test of significance. In effect, we are transforming both our research and null hypotheses into statistical hypotheses so that they can be tested by numerical means.

A statistical hypothesis concerning the difference in average ages between groups 1 and 2 can be represented symbolically. Following are both verbal and statistical expressions of the previous hypotheses:

Verbal expression:

Null Hypothesis, H_0: Group 1 is the same age as or younger than group 2.
Research Hypothesis, H_1: Group 1 is older than group 2.

Statistical expression:

Null Hypothesis, H_0: $\overline{X}_1 \leq \overline{X}_2$
Research Hypothesis, H_1: $\overline{X}_1 > \overline{X}_2$
where H_0 is the symbol for the null hypothesis
H_1 is the symbol for the research hypothesis
$\overline{X}_1$ (read as "X bar sub one") is the mean or average age of group 1
$\overline{X}_2$ (read as "X bar sub two") is the mean or average age for group 2

The symbols, $>$ and $\leq$ mean "greater than" and "equal to or less than."

In this example, H_0 denotes the null hypothesis that says that the mean or average age of group 1 is equal to or less than the mean or average age of group 2. The research hypothesis, H_1, says that the average age of group 1 is greater than the average or mean age for group 2. Sometimes, the designations H_1 and H_2 are used to signify the null and research hypotheses. The notation systems or symbolic portrayals of statistics such as the average or mean, and even research and null hypothesis designations, differ from one textbook to the next. Most books use the H_0 and H_1 designation, however; and this format is considered conventional.

Notice in the previous example that the null hypothesis does not say simply that group 1 is younger than group 2. Rather, it says that group 1 is either younger or the same age as group 2. Think about which hypothesis would be supported if an investigator rejected a null hypothesis that said, "Group 1 is younger than group 2." If this statement were not true, then it would be true that either group 1 is older than group 2 *or* that group 1 is the same age as group 2. In order to prevent this imprecision, the null hypothesis is carefully worded as follows: "Group 1 is the same age or younger than group 2." This is an "equal to or less than" type of arrangement between the two samples, and thus the symbol $\leq$ (equal to or less than) is used. If this statement is rejected, the single remaining option is that "group 1 is older than group 2," and the symbol $>$ (greater than) would be used.

Two conventional symbol combinations used by criminologists and others are intended to illustrate direction and nondirection. Direction is intended to signify that one value is greater or less than another, whatever the values happen to be. Anytime the "greater than" ($>$) or "less than" ($<$) signs are used in any hypothesis set, it can be safely assumed that a directional test of some hypothesis is being made. That is, the researcher is interested in saying whether or not two or more values differ in specified directions. If the hypothesis set contains "equal to" ($=$) or "not equal to" ($\neq$) signs, this means the hypothesis test is nondirectional. In this case, investigators are interested only in whether differences exist among observed values, not in whether they differ in any particular direction. Thus, in the previous hypothesis set relating to the average ages of two groups, the hypothesis set was directional, since "greater than" ($>$) and "less than" ($<$) signs were used. A nondirectional hypothesis set is the following:

H_0: The average age of group 1 is equal to group 2.

H_1: The average age of group 1 is different from group 2.

Symbolically expressed, these hypotheses become

$$H_0: \overline{X}_1 = \overline{X}_2$$
$$H_1: \overline{X}_1 \neq \overline{X}_2$$

Nondirectional hypothesis tests are also known as **two-tailed tests,** while a **directional hypothesis test** is designated as a **one-tailed test.** The *tails* refer to areas of sampling distributions of statistics and are reserved for more extensive discussion later. Statistical hypotheses are usually established to indicate (1) differences between two or more groups regarding some trait or characteristic that they possess, (2) associations between two or more variables within one group or between several groups, and (3) point estimates of certain population characteristics such as average values.

Summarizing briefly, three classifications of hypotheses are important to us. These are research hypotheses, null hypotheses, and statistical hypotheses. Research hypotheses are derived as a result of theorizing. Null hypotheses are established conventionally in accordance with how various research hypotheses are stated. Null hypotheses are hypothetical models established so that research hypotheses may be tested indirectly. Numerical and symbolic expressions of research and null hypotheses are called statistical hypotheses. Statistical hypotheses are those ultimately subjected to some sort of empirical test. On the basis of one's observations and the test of statistical hypotheses, tentative conclusions are reached about null hypotheses, and ultimately, about research hypotheses. If certain null hypotheses are not refuted by evidence found by researchers, then certain accompanying research hypotheses are not supported. However, if certain null hypotheses are rejected by evidence found by investigators, then certain accompanying research hypotheses are supported. Evidence supporting any research hypothesis derived from some theory is considered partial support for that theory.

Hypotheses are composed of variables. Hypotheses may contain a single variable, two variables, or k (meaning more than two) variables. Hypotheses containing more than two variables are considered complex hypotheses and are more difficult to test because the interrelatedness of more than two variables acting simultaneously is more difficult to assess quantitatively and theoretically. Table 13.1 shows the general relation between research, null, and statistical hypotheses.

Where Do Hypotheses Come From?

Scanning various professional journals exposes any student to a wide variety of studies, each with its array of hypotheses and theories. People often ask where hypotheses come from. Quite simply, hypotheses come from our thoughts about things. Hypotheses are generated in graduate student "bull sessions," conversations, and discussions between students and faculty; from random observations and reflections about life as people go to and from work; and of course, from theory. Because of the diverse circumstances under which hypotheses are formulated, it stands to reason that there will be a wide variation in the quality of hypotheses.

Also, criminologists employ various standards to determine whether hypotheses are good or bad, useful or not useful. It is possible, for example, for two different researchers working independently to derive similar hypotheses from a common theory, although they might word their hypotheses differently and/or they might select different circumstances under which to conduct their empirical tests. The evaluation of hypotheses is quite often a relative matter. What one social scientist might regard as a good hypothesis might be judged as bad by another social scientist. We don't want to convey the impression that social science advances purely on the whims and personal preferences of criminologists or

TABLE 13.1 Relation Between Research, Null, and Statistical Hypotheses

H_1	H_0	H_1 and H_0
Research Hypothesis	Null Hypothesis	Statistical Hypothesis (Symbolically Expressed)
Two groups differ according to age.	Two groups do not differ regarding age.	H_0: $\overline{X}_1 = \overline{X}_2$ H_1 $\overline{X}_1 \neq \overline{X}_2$
↓	↓	↓
(Derived from theory)	(Created from research hypothesis)	If conclusion is to reject null hypothesis, research hypothesis is supported.

criminal justice professionals. What is important to understand here is that flexibility and latitude enable social investigators to design studies in unique ways and to give hypotheses the wording of their personal styles. Further, investigators may design their studies any way they wish and specify the empirical tests to be conducted in accordance with their personal and professional standards. Although personal standards of researchers vary, conventional guidelines are followed by most investigators. And so despite the diversity in methodological inquiry, there is a high degree of uniformity regarding the application of certain methodological guidelines.

Hypothesis Formulation: Good, Better, and Best

The informative value of any particular hypothesis is dependent upon the circumstances of the theory from which it was derived. One way of evaluating hypotheses is in terms of the amount of information they specify about phenomena. Consider the following example of three statements, each stating a simple relationship between two variables, X and Y.

Hypothesis A: X and Y are related.
Hypothesis B: X is related to Y.
Hypothesis C: As X increases, Y decreases.

Notice that for hypothesis A, a simple statement of relationship is provided. Nothing else is indicated about the relationship other than the fact that X and Y are associated. From the way this statement is worded, we know little or nothing about *which* variable, X or Y, has more of an impact on the other in a causal sense. Anyway, we are cautious about making statements of a causal nature, since causality is so difficult to establish in any type of social research. Clues about which variables tend to influence others may, of course, be found in the theoretical scheme. This explanatory framework shows linkages among variables and specifies how each relates with the others. However, examining hypothesis A gives us no clue as to which variable might be independent or dependent.

Statement B, X is related to Y, is more informative, since it mildly implies that Y influences values of X. If we wished to mildly imply that X influences Y, we might rephrase this hypothesis, Y is related to X. Statement B is considered an improvement over statement A. Statement C, however, is the most informative of the three statements. This statement indicates that increasing values of X seem to elicit changes on the Y variable; namely, Y values decrease as X values increase.

Which of these hypotheses is best? Ordinarily, we might choose the most informative hypothesis, if the specific direction of the relationship between the two variables is indicated. The objectives of the research come into play here as well. If the research is primarily exploratory or descriptive, then statements A or B might be suitable, given our immediate lack of awareness of how X and Y are related to one another. However, if extensive investigations have been conducted of variables X and Y, then statement C would be best, since it is the most informative. Investigators would tend to select hypothesis statements such as statement C, since their research designs would be more experimental in nature.

FUNCTIONS OF HYPOTHESES

Theories are relatively elaborate tools we use to explain and predict events. Social scientists develop theories to account for social and psychological phenomena, and then they devise a means whereby these theories can be tested and subjected to verification or refutation. Seldom do researchers actually test their entire theories directly. Most of the time, they conduct tests of specific hypotheses derived from theory. These hypotheses pertain to different parts of the theory, and if they test out and are supported by the evidence researchers find, then the researchers' theories are supported in part.

Usually, it takes many tests of different hypotheses derived from the theory in order to adequately test the theory and determine its predictive value and its adequacy as a tool of explanation for events. One major function of hypotheses, therefore, is to make it possible to test theories. In this regard, an alternative definition of a hypothesis is a statement of theory in testable form. All statements of theory in testable form are called hypotheses.

Sometimes, certain hypotheses are not associated with any particular theory. It could be that as a result of some hypothesis, a theory eventually will be devised or constructed. Consequently, another function of hypotheses is to suggest theories that may account for some event. Although it is more commonplace that research proceeds from theories to hypotheses, occasionally the reverse is true. Social investigators may have some idea about why a given phenomenon occurs, and they hypothesize several things that relate to it. They judge that some hypotheses have greater potential explanatory value than others, and as a result, they may construct a logical system of propositions, assumptions, and definitions linking their explanation of the event to the event itself. In other words, they create a theory. Working from hypotheses back to some theory is not necessarily poor methodology. Eventually, investigators are going to have to subject their resulting theory to empirical test anyway to determine its accuracy. The predictive value of the theory may be evaluated at that time.

Hypotheses also perform a descriptive function. Each time hypotheses are tested empirically, they tell us something about the phenomena they are associated with. If the hypothesis is supported, then our information about the phenomenon increases. Even if the hypothesis is refuted, the test tells us something we did not know before about the phenomenon. Even the inventor who discovers 600 ways of doing something wrong learns something as a result of these frustrating experiences. The accumulation of information as a result of hypothesis testing reduces the amount of ignorance we may have about why certain social events occur in given ways. For criminologists, therefore, the major functions of hypotheses are that they (1) test theories, (2) suggest theories, and (3) describe social phenomena.

Several secondary functions of hypotheses may be mentioned. As one result of testing certain hypotheses, social policies may be formulated in communities, penal institutions may be redesigned or revamped, teaching methods may be altered or improved, solutions to various kinds of social problems may be suggested and implemented, delinquents and criminal offenders may be treated differently, and supervisory practices may be changed in organizations. Testing

Box 13.2

Todd R. Clear
John Jay College of Criminal Justice

Statistics: Ph.D. (criminal justice), University of Albany.

Interests: I am professor and dean, John Jay College of Criminal Justice. I have written on topics of correctional policy and justice system reform, including the recent books *Harm in American Penology* and *The Community Justice Ideal: Preventing Crime and Achieving Justice.* Previous books include *Controlling the Offender in the Community* and *American Corrections.* Other published research covers the topics of correctional classification, prediction methods in correctional programming, community-based correctional methods, intermediate sanctions, and sentencing policy. My current research includes religion and crime, the correctional implications of "place," and the concept of "community justice." I have served as a programming and policy consultant to justice agencies in over 40 states and five nations, and I have received awards from the Rockefeller School of Public Policy, the American Probation and Parole Association, and the International Association of Paroling Authorities.

In September 1971, while I was in my first semester of graduate work at the University of Albany, a few miles down the road, the prison at Attica erupted in revolt. Watching the events of Attica unfold changed my life. When I first began graduate school, I had hoped for a career as a prison warden, but the close proximity to the Attica revolt and its aftermath convinced me that I should dedicate my career to challenging the legitimacy of incarceration as a solution to the problem of crime. For 28 years, I have kept that focus.

My work has been an abject failure. In 1971, when I made a vow to work to reduce the use of incarceration, there were fewer than 200,000 prisoners in the United States, and the incarceration rate was under 100 (per 100,000 citizens). Today as I write, there are 1.3 million prisoners and the incarceration rate exceeds 500. Among African American males aged 20 to 40, the imprisonment rate is an astounding 7,000+. No other nation on earth—none in history—has produced such a stunning policy of locking up its citizens. Here and there, I have made contributions toward better, more humane, more rational correctional policy, through my work on classification and offender case management in the community (stemming from my doctoral thesis, which was completed in 1977), and through advocacy for correctional reform. Taken as a whole, however, my work on penal justice has helped a few individuals in isolated programs, but it has had only negligible impact on the field. Cynicism and resentment dominate the thinking of penal policymakers and the subjects of their efforts, alike, in the empty hopes that a proliferation of harms against one another might help each of us achieve some measure of a good life. I have no regrets regarding the focus of my work; a person can choose no more noble life work than to improve the prospects of those least advantaged by the social lottery. Certainly, I have had more fun at this life's work than anyone has a right to ask, and I have received far more back from these endeavors than I have contributed to them. I merely regret that the work has had so little in the form of objective consequences for the better.

Advice to Students: Be true to your most cherished beliefs. Follow the golden rule: treat others (including—especially—the subjects of your research) as you would want to be treated. Never turn down an opportunity that has been placed before you simply because of the risks it seems to entail. Choose enjoyable work partners. Do not worry about deadlines. Allow yourself to be changed by what you learn as your work progresses.

hypotheses refutes certain "common sense" notions about human behavior, raises questions about the explanations we presently use to account for things, and most generally alters our orientation toward our environment in various ways. All hypotheses relate to our knowledge of things, and, as this knowledge changes, we change also.

■ SINGLE-VARIABLE, TWO-VARIABLE, AND *K*-VARIABLE HYPOTHESES

Hypotheses are distinguished according to whether they contain single variables, two variables, or *k* variables (i.e., more than two variables).

Single-Variable Hypotheses

Single-variable hypotheses are often known as **point estimate hypotheses.** Researchers are interested in forecasting certain values associated with populations of elements. This is known as **point estimation.** They might predict various population values, such as the average age of some population. This predicted average age is known as a **point estimate.** Subsequently, they might obtain a sample of persons from that population and make a comparison of their sample mean with the hypothesized population mean. These are single-variable hypotheses, since the only variable is the predicted mean value for the population. An example of a single-variable hypothesis might be

The average age of the inmate population of prisons is increasing.

Two-Variable Hypotheses

If we add a second variable and construct new statements, we will have two-variable hypotheses. All of the ten hypotheses presented earlier in this chapter are examples of **two-variable hypotheses.** If we wanted to make a two-variable hypothesis out of the one-variable hypothesis just given, we might differentiate inmates according to whether they are in prisons or jails. Our new two-variable hypothesis might be

> *The average age of jail inmates is decreasing, while the average age of prison inmates is increasing.*

Another way of phrasing this is

> *Jail inmates tend to be younger than prison inmates,*

or

> *The average age of jail inmates is less than the average age of prison inmates.*

However, these last two statements are not exactly equivalent with the first statement. The first statement indicates a trend in inmate age—upward for prison inmates and downward for jail inmates. But the last two statements merely indicate average age differences between prison and jail inmates, not trends over time.

K-Variable Hypotheses

Hypotheses with three or more variables are designated as **k-variable hypotheses.** The letter *k* technically means "two or more." In this book, however, we will use *k* to mean "three or more," since there are so many specific statistical tests for *two* samples and so many measures of association for *two* variables. Distinctions are subsequently made, therefore, between two- and *k*-sample tests and between two-variable and *k*-variable hypotheses. In the general case, *k*-variable hypotheses are very difficult to test. For example, we might have the following *k*-variable hypothesis:

> *Correctional officer job effectiveness varies according to job satisfaction, which varies inversely with the closeness of supervision that officers receive from their correctional officer supervisors.*

This hypothesis is difficult to test for several reasons. First, we may find that job effectiveness and job satisfaction may be related as we have predicted. However, it may be that the type of supervision may have nothing to do with job satisfaction or with job effectiveness. To solve the problem of testing this hypothesis, it is recommended that this hypothesis should be broken down into two separate hypotheses, and then each can be tested independently. These two hypotheses would be

> *Correctional officer job effectiveness and job satisfaction are related.*

> *Correctional officer job satisfaction varies inversely with the closeness of supervision that officers receive from correctional officer supervisors.*

If a third hypothesis is desirable to link job effectiveness with closeness of supervision, we can state:

Correctional officer job effectiveness varies inversely with the closeness of supervision received from correctional officer supervisors.

■ HYPOTHESIS TESTING

Hypothesis testing, means that we subject hypotheses to some kind of empirical scrutiny to determine if they are supported or refuted by collected evidence. If we are testing hypotheses about delinquents, we usually will need to go out and study a sample of delinquents to collect evidence relative to our hypotheses about them. If we are studying correctional officers or probationers, we will need to obtain samples of correctional officers from a prison or prisons or probationers from one or more probation programs. Actually, testing hypotheses involves several tasks:

1. A real social situation is needed that will provide a reasonable testing ground for the hypotheses. Testing grounds are actual social settings where data exist pertaining to the hypotheses to be tested. These "grounds" may be probation agencies, jails, community corrections agencies, city or county courts, or any other location containing people with the information we need to test our hypotheses.

2. Investigators must make sure that their hypotheses are testable. This means that only empirical phenomena should be selected for study. It makes no sense to ask questions that cannot be answered with our present instrumentation. Hypotheses containing variables that cannot be measured are also not amenable to empirical tests. For example, if we hypothesize that "evil spirits cause delinquency," this statement is incapable of being refuted. It cannot be supported either, but it cannot be refuted. This and similar statements are outside of the realm of scientific inquiry, because one or more variables are simply not amenable to empirical measurement.

For instance, in 1947, Hans Von Hentig wrote about western outlaws and observed that some of them had red hair. Von Hentig presented some spectacular observations about red hair and lawbreaking behavior to a convention of psychologists, and he claimed to identify an internal motivator that, he said, precipitated abnormal and even criminal behavior. This phenomenon, he said, was "accelerated motor innervation," some mystical central nervous system phenomenon that seemed closely associated with red scalp and body hair. However, Von Hentig never outlined clearly how accelerated motor innervation could be measured or taken into account by other scientists. Thus, there was no way to refute Von Hentig's claims.

Many social scientists regarded Von Hentig's research as far-fetched, and some even suggested that his work might even aggravate the unfavorable stereotype

Box
13.3

Meda Chesney-Lind
University of Hawaii-Manoa

Statistics: B.A. (sociology), Whitman
College; M.A., Ph.D., University
of Hawaii-Manoa.

Interests: My interests include girls and women in the criminal justice system; the juvenile justice system and services available to juvenile females; and the rise in women's imprisonment and alternatives to incarceration.

I can still recall vividly hearing a male researcher who, reporting on fertility rates at a population meeting in Seattle, referred to his subjects using male pronouns throughout his presentation. Since his subjects were female (we are after all the only ones who can give birth), I was puzzled. I was a graduate student attending my first national meeting. At the break, I asked him about his word choice. He informed me that "I say 'he or him' because to say 'she or her' would trivialize my research." I learned that for years, criminology had this same problem. Criminology was viewed as incontrovertibly male, a "macho" field. In fact, some researchers have characterized crime as the ultimate form of masculinity. In Albert Cohen's words, "the delinquent is a rogue male" whose behavior no matter how it is condemned on moral grounds "has at least one virtue: it incontestably confirms, in the eyes of all concerned, his essential masculinity." The criminological fascination with male deviance and crime, which I had dubbed the "Westside Story Syndrome," is not as some might contend simply a reflection of the American crime problem. The question is whether theories of delinquency and crime, which were admittedly developed to explain male behavior, can be used to understand female crime, delinquency, and victimization. Will the "add women and stir" approach to criminological theory be sufficient? Are there really, despite their origins, general theories, as some have argued?

About fifteen years ago when I was reading files compiled on youth referred to Honolulu's family court during the first half of this century, I discovered a bizarre pattern. Over half of all girls were referred to court for immorality, and another third were charged with being wayward. I found that this meant that all young women were suspected of being sexually active. Virtually all files contained gynecological examinations. Doctors would routinely note the condition of the hymen on the form, writing "admits intercourse, hymen ruptured," "no laceration," as well as comments about whether the "laceration" looks new or old. Harsh sanctions from juvenile court judges would follow adjudications of guilt for these offenses. Thus, despite the chivalrous attitude toward female offenders found in the research literature, at least twice as many girls than boys referred to juvenile court were being detained and institutionalized. Girls were three times more likely than boys to be placed in training schools.

It occurred to me that girls were being treated in this fashion as criminology was developing. Thus, while mostly male criminologists were paying a lot of attention to male delinquency, large numbers of girls were being processed, punished, and incarcerated in most jurisdictions. One of the classic excuses given by juvenile justice personnel for this discriminatory treatment of juvenile females was that their numbers were so few. However, girls make up about half of all juveniles committed to Hawaii training schools well into the 1950s.

One reason for the neglect of girls by researchers was the inability of investigators to identify with their problems or situations. By contrast, I was unable to distance myself from the lives of female juveniles. The women's movement was becoming an increasingly important part of my life, and I began to see patterns of abuse among officials who processed juvenile females. Female researchers in Honolulu and elsewhere were beginning to realize that what we were discovering was both personal and political. I knew firsthand about physical examinations, and I could imagine how a 13-year-old female would feel who was taken to a detention center and forcibly examined by a doctor she didn't know. I would also read of legal cases in which girls were placed in solitary confinement for refusing to be examined, and I would talk to women who had these experiences as girls. Their comments and experiences confirmed the degradation and personal horror of this experience. From what I was able to reconstruct, I came to the conclusion that a feminist revision of delinquency was in order and that a feminist criminology should emerge. But there would be numerous personal and professional impediments to delay this change.

In my graduate work, I was thwarted repeatedly whenever I attempted to study female delinquency. The sociology department where I completed research for my master's thesis failed to recognize the importance of these data. I was forced to abandon my work on women and crime and venture into population research. That's how I got to Seattle and the population conference.

Subsequently and gradually, feminist criminology has become widely accepted and plays a major role in maintaining the place of women in male society. Feminist research is making it clear that gender stratification in a patriarchal society is as powerful a system as class. Efforts must be undertaken to understand female and male deviance and conformity in the context of a ubiquitous system of male control and power over women's labor and sexuality. Delinquency research may need to be revised. Early thinking was such that if female juveniles didn't fit particular delinquency theories, the females were eliminated from the study. Now, it seems more logical to revisit the theory and revise it to explain juvenile female delinquency patterns as well as male delinquency patterns.

Over the years I have devoted much attention to women's issues and female delinquency. My books include *Girls, Delinquency and Juvenile Justice* (1992), awarded the American Society of Criminology's Michael J. Hindelang Award for "outstanding contribution to criminology," *Girls and Gangs in America* (Lakeview Press), and *Female Offender: Girls, Women and Crime* (Sage, 1988). My research in feminist criminology has resulted in several awards, including the Donald Cressey Award from the National Council on Crime and Delinquency, the Paul Tappan Award for "outstanding contributions to the field of criminology" (awarded by the Western Society of Criminology), and the University of Hawaii Board of Regent's Medal for Excellence in Research. I have served as vice president of the American Society of Criminology and president of the Western Society of Criminology. Thinking back on what I have done, I don't think I'd change much other than to do it sooner and push my mentors to allow me to pursue less popular research subjects.

Advice to Students: I would urge students to be passionate about their work and extremely diligent in their search for the truth (with a small "t"). I would also suggest that they spend time with the data that they have collected, sifting through things; nothing important comes quickly. They should also listen to their gut when they sense that they've found something significant. That's what I did. Initially, it took a bit of convincing to make others understand that what I found was important, but in the end, I feel very fortunate to have been one of the first to study girls' pathways into delinquency.

of the "hot-tempered redhead." Von Hentig's work clearly rested outside the realm of scientific inquiry. This does not mean that we can never discover ways of measuring accelerated motor innervation empirically. For the time being, however, we must reject his explanation, since it lies outside of the realm of **empiricism.** The lesson to be learned here is to confine theorizing to only those phenomena that can be taken into account empirically.

3. Investigators should devise and use measures of the phenomena of interest so that these phenomena may be quantified easily. Each variable must be operationalized in order that objective, numerical assessments may be made of the hypothesis's worth. An assortment of statistical tests exists for hypothesis-testing purposes.

■ INTERPRETING THE RESULTS OF HYPOTHESIS TESTS

Whenever hypotheses are tested, it is usually the case that several hypotheses, rather than a single-hypothesis, are either confirmed or refuted. There is no fixed number of hypotheses that researchers must test, since different theories vary in their detail and sophistication. Some theories are more elaborate than others and yield more testable hypotheses. An extreme might include tests of 100 or more hypotheses in a single study. More often, however, are situations involving tests of ten or fewer hypotheses. Again, there are no conventional rules about how many hypotheses we should test.

In order to illustrate how we might judge the results of hypothesis tests in the general case, let's assume that we are testing ten hypotheses from a given theory in our research project. We have constructed a theory to explain relationships between certain variables, we have collected relevant data, and on the basis of our analysis of that data, we have tentatively concluded certain things about our findings. Since hypotheses are predictions of what we believe will be found, based upon the validity of our previous theorizing about phenomena, either some or all of our hypotheses may test out and be supported, or some or all may not test out and be refuted.

Three possible outcomes or scenarios might be anticipated:

1. All of our hypotheses tested are supported by whatever we find.
2. None of the hypotheses we are testing are supported by whatever we find.
3. Some of the hypotheses we are testing are supported by our findings, while the remaining hypotheses are not supported.

Neophyte researchers will probably make the following interpretations of these outcomes:

Outcome 1: If all hypotheses being tested are supported, it might be assumed that the theory from which the hypotheses were derived is also supported.

Outcome 2: If none of the hypotheses tested are supported, it might be assumed that the theory from which these hypotheses were derived is refuted, or at least, not supported.

Outcome 3: The most perplexing outcome, partial support of the theory through supporting some hypotheses and refuting others, might be interpreted as "faulty theorizing." Perhaps our theory is faulty in certain respects, particularly those respects relevant to those research hypotheses that were refuted rather than supported.

We must be careful not to attach too much significance to our hypothesis-test outcomes. After all, we are testing our hypotheses, using various samples of elements that may or may not be representative of the general population about which we seek information. Some researchers blindly claim that their theories are valid if all of their hypotheses are supported. Other researchers "throw in the towel" and proclaim their theories "untrue" if all their hypotheses are refuted. Neither of these conclusions is warranted because so many factors influence hypothesis-test outcomes. The adequacy of one's theory is only one factor. We may have a perfectly good theory but poor methodology. We may have perfectly good theory, perfectly good methodology, but a poor, unrepresentative sample. We may have perfectly good theory, perfectly good methodology, a perfectly good sample, but poor instrumentation and measures of our phenomena. We may choose the wrong statistical tests to apply when analyzing our data. We may apply interpretive standards that are too rigorous. Suffice it to say that we may unintentionally commit any number of errors or experience any number of problems in the course of implementing our research plans.

If you turn to various professional journals and inspect the contents of different articles, you will often find that the authors of those articles have incorporated various safeguards into their studies. These warnings are similar to product liability statements, in which manufacturers tell consumers, in advance, whether their products contain substances that have been known to produce adverse side effects, whether some assembly is required, or whether there are sharp edges that might be harmful to children. Product liability–type statements in criminological research warn "consumers" or readers about a study's flaws. Some common phrases are "These findings should be cautiously viewed," "Further study is recommended," or "Some suggestions for future research include . . ." Specific drawbacks of the research or study limitations are cited, such as "The sample analyzed in the present study consisted of only 35 percent of the original 500 persons selected randomly, and therefore there is a question about how reliable the sample is in relation to its parent population." Or, "Evidence emerged to indicate that our measures lacked reliability, and further research is needed in which more precise indicators of these phenomena can be constructed and applied." These writers are calling our attention to one or more "faults" of their studies. This is acceptable, since no study is perfect.

The point is that we should not attach too much importance to any specific study, regardless of its magnitude. It is best to interpret research findings from any particular study in a more general context. Thus, how do these study results compare with the findings of other similar studies? Considering several studies of the same topic, how does any new study support, refute, or modify what is generally believed about the phenomena under investigation? Regardless of the outcome of any given test of hypotheses (i.e., outcomes 1, 2, and 3 previously given), therefore, researchers should always raise questions about each of the following problem areas: theory, sampling, measurement, data collection, statistics, and participant involvement. Raising such questions will enable researchers to

1. Improve the quality and meaning of the interpretation of any hypothesis test
2. Evaluate the relative importance of a given hypothesis test for theory building
3. Determine the degree to which the study supports the work of others
4. Determine the reliability of the explanation of events that are either explicitly or implicitly stated by the hypotheses.

Theoretical Considerations

Judging the results of one's hypothesis tests involves evaluating the adequacy of the theory from which the hypotheses were derived. Was the theory coherent, logical, and meaningful? Did it include measurable phenomena? Was it too broad or too narrow? Was the theory comprehensive enough to take into account certain intervening variables, but narrow enough to be fruitful as a predictive tool? Was the theorizing consistent with what has been found in the research literature on the subject? Were the hypotheses formulated correctly and did they contain variables that were included in the theory?

Sampling Considerations

How representative was the sample of the population from which it was drawn? If questionnaires were mailed to respondents, was there any nonresponse? How much? What importance would nonresponse have on the hypothesis test outcomes, if any? Was the sample adequately selected? Did sample elements possess the necessary information relative to the hypothesis tests and theoretical questions?

Measurement Considerations

Were the measures used valid and reliable? What tests were conducted by the investigators to demonstrate the reliability and validity of the measures and other instrumentation? How closely connected were the operational definitions of terms to the nominal definitions devised in the theory?

Data Collection Procedures as a Consideration

Were the data collection procedures necessarily the best ones to use, given the problem investigated? Would other data collection methods have yielded more fruitful results? If secondary sources were used, how reliable were those secondary sources? Was any triangulation employed by investigators to improve their data accuracy and validity?

Statistical Considerations

Were appropriate statistical tests selected for data description and analysis, given the quality and randomness of the sample obtained? Was the level of significance appropriate, given the sample size and generalizability desired? Were all statistical assumptions satisfied so that the meaning of the measures applied was maximized?

Participant Observation as a Consideration

Were respondents coerced into participating in the study or was their involvement voluntary? What degree of anonymity was provided by researchers to enhance response objectivity? Was there anything unusual about how respondents were questioned, observed, or otherwise studied that might interfere with our appraisal of the findings?

■ KEY TERMS

Alternative hypothesis
Directional hypothesis test
Empiricism
H_0
H_1
Hypothesis sets
Hypothesis testing
k-variable hypotheses
Nondirectional hypothesis test
Null hypotheses

One-tailed test
Point estimate
Point estimate hypotheses
Point estimation
Research hypotheses
Single-variable hypotheses
Statistical hypotheses
Two-tailed tests
Two-variable hypotheses
Working hypotheses

1. What is a hypothesis? How are hypotheses used in social research?

2. What are some major functions of hypotheses?

3. Identify and describe three different kinds of hypotheses. What is a hypothesis set? Give three examples different from those in this book and selected from your inspection of the research literature.

4. What is the relationship between hypotheses and theory? Discuss.

5. Where do hypotheses come from?

6. What is the basic rationale for using null hypotheses instead of testing research hypotheses directly?

7. Does any particular study stand as the definitive work in any given subject area? Why or why not? Explain.

8. Describe how research hypotheses should be interpreted if
   (a) particular null hypotheses are rejected.
   (b) particular null hypotheses are not rejected.
   Why don't we "accept" null hypotheses? Explain.

9. What are three kinds of statistical hypotheses? Give some examples.

10. Using X and Y as two variables, describe three different kinds of relationships between X and Y that reflect three different degrees of knowledge about their relation.

11. Several research hypotheses follow. Write null hypotheses for each.
    (a) The mean for group 1 equals or exceeds 20.
    (b) Two groups differ in their average age.
    (c) Probation officers have higher job satisfaction than parole officers.
    (d) Suicide rates are the same between jail inmates and prison inmates.
    (e) Suicide rates vary inversely with social cohesion.
    (f) As variable X increases, variable Y decreases.
    (g) There is a positive relation between variables X and Y.

12. Construct three complex hypotheses, relating any three variables of your choice. Indicate in a subsequent discussion why such hypotheses are more difficult to test than either one-variable or two-variable hypotheses.

13. Why was Hans Von Hentig's research on western outlaws generally rejected by the scientific community? What is the significance of Von Hentig's study for hypothesis testing and empiricism? Discuss.

14. What are some major considerations that must be made regarding outcomes of hypothesis tests? Discuss each briefly.

chapter 14

Statistics in Criminal Justice and Criminology
Some Descriptive Applications

■ INTRODUCTION

Between 1986 and 1999, robberies in the United States decreased by about 22 percent. Also in 1999, property crimes outnumbered violent crimes by 9 to 1. Further, between 1986 and 1999, rapes in the United States increased by about 38 percent. Studies also show that approximately 10 to 20 percent of those defendants on pretrial release are arrested again for other crimes while awaiting trial. In 1995, there was one adult probationer for every 109 adults in the United States. By 1999, this figure had risen to 1 adult on probation for every 94 persons in the nation. Between 1984 and 1999, the one-day count of all juveniles in custody rose by 20 percent in relation to the average national daily adult population increase of 16 percent during the same period. In 1999, females made up only 7 percent of all incarcerated state prison inmates. And 65 percent of the state prisons in the United States in 1999 were designed to house fewer than 500 inmates.

You have just been deluged by statistics. All of the statements in the previous paragraph reflect statistical information about prisoners, juveniles, incarcerated female offenders, probationers, and crime rates. The Uniform Crime Reports and National Crime Victimization Survey, together with the Sourcebook of Criminal Justice Statistics, the source from which the above information was taken, are compendiums of statistical information about criminals, crime rates, and victims of crime. This chapter introduces you to the field of statistics, although you will soon discover that the word statistics has several different meanings. Statistics have extensive applications in criminological and criminal justice research beyond the descriptive statements presented earlier. First, statistics will be explored according to the different functions it performs in the research process. Beyond merely describing things, statistics extends to a wide variety of tests and measures that help us to make decisions about whatever we observe. Accordingly, there are assumptions we must address that underlie statistical applications.

Criminal justice experts and criminologists ordinarily study samples of persons in their investigations. These samples are often described through the use of statistical information such as that mentioned earlier. In addition, researchers seek information about entire populations (e.g., all probation officers, all police officers, all state prison inmates, all female juvenile offenders), and they frequently use samples of persons drawn from these populations to make inferences about the populations from which they were drawn. Thus, statistics performs both descriptive and inferential roles. Additionally, correlations are investigated between different combinations of variables. Many correlation techniques are available to criminologists and others for drawing causal inferences between different variables selected for investigation. Therefore, this chapter is an overview of the various meanings of statistics, how statistics function to benefit us in our research endeavors, and how they might be applied to solve various problems in criminal justice and criminology.

Another part of this chapter examines descriptive statistical measures. Two types of descriptive measures include **central tendency** *and* **dispersion** *or* **variability.** *Measures of central tendency describe the points in a distribu-*

tion of scores around which other scores tend to focus. Three measures of central tendency discussed here include the mode, the median, and the mean. Measures of dispersion or variability describe the manner or way in which scores are focused around some central tendency measure we have used. Some of these measures describe distances over which an array of scores is spread. The variability measures presented are the range, the average deviation, the variance, and the standard deviation.

WHAT ARE STATISTICS?

Statistics is the body of methods and procedures used to assemble, describe, infer something from, or make decisions about the distribution of numerical data. Numerical data refer to any information we might collect about people and their characteristics (e.g., age, gender, religion, race, ethnicity, socioeconomic status, criminality, probationary status, and crime patterns). An examination of these data by persons skilled in data analysis and interpretation will yield statistical information or results that can be presented to others for their consideration and/or action.

All of us are consumers of statistical information in one form or another, and some of us are also generators of statistical information, as we do research and conduct scientific investigations of criminological phenomena. We learn about statistics in our early years, as we compile batting averages of our favorite baseball players and yardage gained by our favorite football players, as well as our own performance characteristics in various sports. We learn to evaluate things on the basis of statistical information. We might choose not to purchase certain automobiles because of poor statistics demonstrated by performance tests conducted by independent consumer agencies. We may or may not be admitted to colleges or universities depending upon our grade point averages and entrance examination scores compared with national norms. Most of us are quite familiar with what statistics can do in describing phenomena. Only some of us are familiar with what statistics can do for us in helping us make decisions about the social or psychological events we observe. Some preliminary distinctions are in order.

Statistics as Characteristics

One way of viewing statistics is to compare samples in relation to populations. Populations refer to a broad class of persons about which we seek information. Sometimes we use the term *element* to refer to all persons in the population. Actually, *element* may refer to either people or things. Thus, 90 elements may mean that we have 90 light bulbs. For our present purposes, however, *elements* will always refer to persons. Populations of relevance to those conducting criminal justice or criminological research might include all correctional officers in the United States, all county jail officers, all police officers in municipalities, all federal judges, all district attorneys and their assistants, all defense attorneys, all probation or parole officers, all robbers, all rapists, or all murderers.

Seldom do we investigate all elements in the population, however. It would be unwieldy for even the most financially endowed organizations or corporations to study all probation officers in the United States at any given point in time. Even the U.S. Bureau of the Census fails to study every family in the United States from one decade to the next. Rather, we find it more convenient (and less expensive) to study samples of elements. Samples consist of proportions of any given population. Thus, rather than study all probation officers in the United States, we might elect to study a sample of probation officers taken from the states of Georgia, Florida, Alabama, Pennsylvania, and New Jersey. Our investigation objectives, personal or agency resources, and other practical criteria will dictate how large our samples of elements will be. Our intent is to obtain samples that are representative of the populations from which they were drawn, according to certain relevant characteristics. Unfortunately, there are no means whereby we can guarantee the representativeness of any sample we choose to study. Thus, we are left with statements such as, "Our sample seems to have these characteristics; therefore, it is possible or likely that the population has these same or similar characteristics as well." Of course, much depends upon how a sample is drawn from its population initially.

Population Parameters and Sample Statistics.   Population **parameters** are characteristics of populations. In criminal justice and criminology, for instance, population parameters might be the average annual caseload of all probation officers in the United States, the average age of all state inmates, the offense profile of all juvenile delinquents adjudicated delinquent within a given time period, or the average salaries of all municipal police officers nationally. The list of population parameters and accompanying population characteristics is limited only by our imaginations.

Sample statistics are characteristics of samples. Therefore, the average annual caseload of a sample of California probation officers, the average age of a sample of Louisiana prison inmates, the offense profile of a sample of Detroit juvenile delinquents, or the average salaries of a sample of Decatur, Georgia, police officers are statistics or sample characteristics.

We determine the scale of our investigations. We may wish to limit our analyses to all persons of a certain type in a single community or part of the community. Or we may wish to study the national population of persons possessing certain characteristics. The important thing is that we decide or determine how broad our population base will be. In turn, the size of our target population will help us determine our sample size.

Functions of Statistics

Statistics that we have mentioned thus far have been largely descriptive. But there are other functions of statistics beyond simple description. One useful way of viewing statistics is to regard them as a set of tools to be used for various purposes. While some of these purposes may include description, others may be to enable us to make inferences about population parameters by using sample statistics as estimates of them. Also, there are statistical procedures that disclose how closely related two or more variables happen to be. These are correlation measures, and within limits, they permit us to infer causal connections between things. However, we must be cautious regarding statements of causality. Correlations between two or more phenomena imply causality but do not prove its existence. Finally, another purpose of statistics is aiding us in decision making about differences we observe between groups of elements.

Description and Inference. The descriptive function of statistics is well known. We can learn much about samples of elements based upon descriptive statistical information obtained about them. For example, if we know about some of the more relevant characteristics of certain types of prison inmates, we might be able to determine with greater accuracy the type of intermediate punishment program they should eventually be assigned. We might make strategic changes in police patrol styles in given cities as the result of learning which patrol styles seem to influence crime prevention the most. Such information would pertain to fluctuations in crime rates in relation to different police patrol styles. Thus, **description** not only informs, it also influences policy decisions by various criminal justice agencies. Studying the use of electronic monitoring and home confinement on a sample of Nebraska delinquent youths and their relative avoidance of delinquent activity, for instance, might prompt us to make the use of electronic monitoring of delinquent youths more widespread.

Another important function of statistics is **inference.** We may infer things about populations by studying samples taken from them. Of necessity, our inferences are not absolutely perfect, since we do not ordinarily have access to the entire population of elements we study. However, if we use certain types of sampling plans such as probability sampling, we can make statements, couched in a probabilistic context, about certain populations based upon our sample statistics. Thus we say, "There is a 95 percent likelihood that the population of police officers in Newark, New Jersey, is similar in certain characteristics shared by a sample of Newark police officers." Inferences about populations made from sample estimates are never made with absolute certainty.

Correlation and Causality: What Appears to Be May Not Be So. Certain statistical procedures are correlational, in that they demonstrate apparent relationships or associations between two or more variables. Suppose we are interested in devising a risk assessment instrument to be used by parole boards in determining an inmate's early release potential. We may assemble statistical data about a large sample of parolees and determine that those who return to prison because of one or more parole program violations also share certain characteristics. We might find, for instance, that a majority of these parolee-recidivists are younger, male, black, unemployed or underemployed, alcohol and/or drug abusers, and of lower socioeconomic status and have earlier histories as juvenile offenders. Should we conclude from these findings that these variables "cause" recidivism? And should we deny parole in the future to those inmates who possess these characteristics? No. Further analysis may show that many "successful" parolees also have these same characteristics. There are any number of variables that may be used to explain recidivism behavior of designated parolees. We are only scratching the surface by referring to a limited number of social and personal traits as possibly causally related to recidivism. Obviously, if two variables are unrelated statistically, then no causal relation exists between them. However, it is important to establish an initial connection between variables as a basis for establishing an eventual causal relation.

Depending upon how certain variables are measured and the level of measurement that may be assumed to underlie them, certain correlational techniques are more useful or appropriate than others. We will learn to identify which correlational procedures are most appropriate for specific two-variable and multi-variable situations. Other criteria exist for assessing the utility of particular measures of association for our research problems. Assorted assumptions, weaknesses and strengths, and/or advantages and disadvantages of these procedures obligate us to make choices for particular correlational applications. These are discussed in conjunction with each procedure described.

Tests of Significance and Statistical Decision Making. One of the most useful functions of statistics relates to decisions about what we have found. Statistical tests are procedures we use to assist us in making objective appraisals of the significance of the data we have collected. Perhaps we might examine labor turnover among paraprofessionals in several community corrections agencies. In certain agencies with higher labor turnover, we may discover that the agency administrators obligate staff to complete extensive paperwork and comply rigidly with program requirements. In other agencies with lower turnover, we may find less demanding administrators who expect less compliance with agency rules from their subordinates. Do significant differences exist in labor turnover among paraprofessionals in the different agencies, controlling for type of administrative style? While we may observe different rates of paraprofessional turnover, certain statistical procedures may be applied to provide us with a numerical appraisal to accompany our subjective opinions about these differences.

How do we know whether intensifying face-to-face contacts between probation officers and their clients will have any appreciable effect on probationer recidivism? We might view recidivism rates of two or more different probation programs and note differences among them. Is the difference we observe "significant"? We may "think" or "believe" or have a "gut feeling" that the differences we observe are significant, but a statistical procedure applied to these data will provide independent numerical evidence to confirm or refute our feelings or views. These statistical decision-making procedures are not substitutes for good thinking. Rather, they perform "supporting roles" in the research enterprise.

All statistical decision making involves probability theory. A common example illustrating probability theory is flipping a coin. When a coin is flipped, the result will be "heads" or "tails." There is a 50–50 chance that a "head" will occur or that a "tail" will occur. If the coin is flipped 100 times, it is expected by chance that there will probably be 50 heads and 50 tails. However, if the 100 flips yielded 51 heads and 49 tails, this would not be a substantial departure from our "expected" 50–50 split. We might expect or anticipate this outcome and would not be particularly disturbed by it. What if we observed 99 heads and 1 tail? Would this result be expected? Probably not. This is a departure not expected according

Box 14.1

J. Mitchell Miller
University of South Carolina

Statistics: B.S. (criminal justice), Middle Tennessee State University; M.C.J. (criminal justice), Middle Tennessee State University; Ph.D. (sociology), University of Tennessee

Interests: Drug enforcement, drug control policy, and drug subcultures.

My research interests in drug enforcement, drug control policy, and drug subcultures originated from an internship on a domestic marijuana eradication team. I was fascinated with this clandestine underworld, its jargon, rules, and subcultural value system. When I received training in research methods and criminological theory during my doctoral program at the University of Tennessee, I realized that the world of vice offered unbroken research ground.

During my graduate program, I was fortunate to be the graduate research assistant for the Society of the Study of Social Problems, where I had the opportunity to interact with Albert Cohen and Bill Chambliss. I was already developing a critical criminological orientation from Donald Clelland at the University of Tennessee, and so I began to couple conflict and subcultural perspectives to examine unintended consequences of the war on drugs.

My advocacy of alternative qualitative designs, particularly covert participant observation, was a natural course for examining the drug subculture. I find it especially troubling that there is a methodological training bias that essentially bans covert research. This is really quite hypocritical when you think that society largely endorses undercover measures to address crime but rejects utilization of covert strategies to study the esoteric world of undercover. Covert observation and similar strategies are our only way of gaining entry to some areas of concern to criminologists and enabling the most complete ethnographic account of what transpires within the immediate context of crime, as opposed to more traditional approaches, such as surveys or in-depth interviews, that are after-the-fact translations.

Advice to Students: My advice to students regarding research methods would be to develop a broad understanding of both quantitative and qualitative methods so that the research arsenal is sufficiently equipped to choose the method appropriate for the research question at hand. It seems that too many research questions are constructed toward research design when the nature of the data should drive analysis. One way to ensure a well-rounded approach is to become familiar with a variety of techniques, rather than quickly identifying with one or two methods. The best way to learn research methods is to get involved beyond the classroom. The real meaning of multicollinearity, for example, doesn't become clear until one is involved in its remedy in an actual project.

to chance. At some point, we need to decide when these departures are "significantly different" from our chance expectations of 50–50. Is a 60–40 split significant? Is a 75–25 split significant? Where should this line be drawn? The statistical procedures we apply to assess the differences we observe between groups on certain measured characteristics simply tell us whether the differences are "chance differences" or likely attributable to something else. The "something else" might be administrative differences as in the previous paraprofessional labor turnover example or different amounts of intensively supervised probation accounting for variations in recidivism rates among samples of probationers.

But statistical significance isn't everything. Frankly, statistical significance is often overrated by researchers, since certain findings may be statistically significant, but at the same time, they may not mean much to us in any practical sense. Increasing our sample sizes does much to influence the significance of whatever we observe. If our sample sizes are large enough, any differences we observe will be statistically significant. For instance, if we were to study 10,000 probationers, 5,000 involved in Probation Program A and 5,000 involved in Probation Program B, it may be that Program A has a 29.9 percent recidivism rate, while Program B has a 30.1 percent recidivism rate. This minor variation, 0.2 percent, may be judged statistically significant according to specific tests we apply. But most, if not all, researchers would conclude that for all practical purposes, the two programs are the same regarding their recidivism rates. Thus, there is substantive or practical significance that we must consider in addition to the significance associated with statistical tests. In short, we don't want to be in the position of saying "It is statistically significant, but it doesn't mean anything."

Meeting the Assumptions: Elements, Sample Size, Randomness, Levels of Measurement

All statistical procedures, even descriptive ones, have various assumptions that must be met before they may be applied appropriately. It is much the same as playing a game with rules decided in advance. If one or more players chose to ignore certain rules of the game, the outcome would be questionable, possibly meaningless. All statistics are data-sensitive, in a sense. That is, they depend on how the data are measured and distributed, among other things, in order for them to be maximally efficient in serving their intended purpose. However, there are diverse points of view about the importance of meeting all assumptions associated with particular tests before they are applied.

For example, suppose I wished to describe the proportionate distribution of male and female inmates of county jails. I could simply determine the proportion of males and the proportion of females, convert this information to percentages, and present this as a part of a larger report on jail conditions. However, someone might wish to describe this same information differently. Or a computer program might print out unwanted information such as the "average gender" in county jails. After all, computers aren't in the position of "knowing" what numbers stand for that are used to express subclasses on different variables. Computers are "number-crunchers," and they process any information they are fed. It makes no difference to computers if a "1" stands for a male, a "2" for a female, and so forth. If the operating computer program is designed to produce averages or means for each variable, then it might generate a 1.2 as the "average gender" of county jail inmates. What does this average mean? Nothing.

The two extreme points of view relating to meeting the assumptions are as follows. First, there are the purists who contend that no statistical test or descriptive procedure should be applied if one or more assumptions of the procedure are not met. If we had some attitudinal data measured according to an ordinal scale, and if we wanted to apply a statistical test requiring interval-level data, then we would not be able to apply the interval-level test to ordinal-level data. Purists would reject the interval-level test and seek other tests for which ordinal-level data were required.

At the other extreme are those investigators who completely ignore the assumptions associated with statistical tests and measures, throwing caution to the wind, and applying any test they wish to any data. The term **robustness** is used to describe statistical test applications in which certain assumption violations occur. Robustness is the ability of any particular statistical test to yield reliable results despite one or more assumption violations. Statistical tests are robust to the extent that they yield results under assumption violations that are somewhat consistent with results obtained when assumptions are not violated. Thus, the assumption violation may not be particularly important in affecting the outcome of the test.

These extreme points of view have supporting evidence. Philosophically and realistically, it is likely that even under the most ideal research conditions, not all of the assumptions of a given statistical test will be met fully. For instance, randomness is required to enhance the representativeness of a sample in relation to its population. Most researchers report some amount of nonresponse, however, if certain persons originally selected as a part of a random sample did not respond to their questionnaires or interviews. What should we call a sample of a random sample? We do know that we cannot call the sample *random*. Yet, many researchers report their studies in major journals or present papers at professional meetings and repeatedly refer to their "random samples." Over the years, it has become conventional in various professions to use the term *random sampling* rather loosely. Everyone recognizes the problems created by nonresponse in research, yet this fact is often glossed over hurriedly in presentations and publications.

Considering these opposing views, the best advice would be to do the most with your data under the circumstances, acknowledging the limitations of your study as you become aware of them. The research process is an ongoing enterprise, and hundreds of thousands of studies on different subjects will be conducted over time. It is through the accumulation of literature on a given topic that we move toward certainty about the topics we investigate. Regardless of particular methodological pitfalls in any specific study, repeated research over time discloses trends or the most viable solutions to criminological questions. In the following section, we highlight certain ideal considerations and assumptions that should precede a test's application. There almost always will be a gap between what researchers *ought to do* and what they *actually do* in their research enterprise. We will learn certain ideal ways to proceed, although we realize that often the reality of research is far from ideal. Three assumptions associated with most statistical tests and procedures include (1) sample size, (2) randomness, and (3) level of measurement. Other assumptions besides these may be applicable for certain statistical procedures.

Sample Size.   Most statistical procedures were originally designed for samples of certain sizes. Some procedures are designed for small group research in which the sample sizes of two groups are 12 or fewer. For many researchers, these small-sample tests are not particularly useful, since their applications for larger samples are inappropriate. Other procedures have been designed for large-sample applications, where sample size is 200 or larger. There are no standards that differentiate large samples from small ones. Some research organizations study 15,000 or 20,000 persons in a survey. These organizations would consider samples of 2,500 or 1,000 as small. Other researchers may regard samples of 100 as large. Thus, the sample size recommendations in this book are crude indicators of a test's usefulness for certain types of data analysis. These recommendations are "rules of thumb." Rules of thumb are not precise and rigidly enforced. Rather, they are guidelines for applying tests in ways that maximize their application.

One rule of thumb about sample size is that the sampling fraction should be approximately $\frac{1}{10}$th. This means that ideally, if our population size is 1,000, we should draw $\frac{1}{10}$th of 1,000 or 100 for our desired sample size. This $\frac{1}{10}$th sampling fraction rule of thumb breaks down when our population size is enormous. If the population size is 15 million, for instance, we would never be expected to obtain a sample size of 1.5 million. We can usually accomplish our research objectives with samples much smaller than $\frac{1}{10}$th of the population, especially if our population is large. The $\frac{1}{10}$th rule of thumb is generally applicable up to a population size of 2,500. This would mean that we would attempt to obtain 250 persons in our resulting sample. Considering the nonresponse expected, we would probably end up with fewer elements than 250. Beyond a population size of 2,500, however, researchers should use their own judgment. In this book, at least, large sample sizes are 100 or more, although this figure is purely arbitrary.

Randomness.   Randomness is the primary means of control for obtaining probability samples. All statistical procedures relating to statistical inference require (ideally) the assumption of randomness associated with the sample selected. However, this is a key assumption that is frequently violated. Depending upon the degree of the violation, it is up to the researcher to provide an appropriate, preferably conservative, interpretation of test results. Nonresponse affects the representativeness of the sample in relation to the population from which it was drawn. The greater the nonresponse, the greater the nonrepresentativeness of the sample.

Much research is published in leading criminal justice and criminology journals in which nonresponse (to mailed questionnaires, for instance) has been as high as 70 percent or more. This means that only 30 percent of the original sample responds. In a mailed questionnaire situation, this would mean a 30 percent return rate. If 100 questionnaires are mailed to a random sample of respondents, only 30 questionnaires might be returned. Is this sample of 30 random? No. Unfortunately, we have no way of knowing how the representativeness of any given sample is affected by varying amounts of nonresponse.

Levels of Measurement.   Conventional **levels of measurement** are the nominal, ordinal, interval, and ratio levels. Each statistical test, both descriptive and inferential, as well as all correlational procedures, assumes a particular level of measurement. For all practical purposes, we may ignore the ratio level of measurement, since no statistical procedure in this book requires it. For each statistical procedure or correlational technique, therefore, it is important that we know in advance the recommended level of measurement associated with the ideal test application.

For the most part, statistical tests have stringent assumptions underlying their ideal application. However, certain of these stringent assumptions are relaxed or are not required at all in an array of procedures. Many of these tests are designed to perform equivalent functions to those in which stringent assumptions are required. Thus, choices may be made among tests according to different kinds of assumptions associated with them. It has often been said that statistics is an art in the sense that statistical test selections are made according to several important criteria. Broad applications of specific tests to *every* data analysis situation are seldom seen or warranted. Rather, researchers must search for the most appropriate procedures that fit the data they have collected.

Other Assumptions.   Besides sample size requirements or limitations, the level of measurement assumption, and randomness, some tests have one or more additional assumptions. It is a requirement of some procedures that if two or more samples are being compared on some measured characteristic, then their variances should be similar. This is referred to as *homogeneity of variances.* There are statistical tests or procedures that determine whether homogeneity of variances exists for particular samples studied.

Another assumption for some statistical tests is that the scores observed should be distributed in a **bell** or **bell-shaped** or **normal curve.** Bell-shaped distributions have many scores near the central point, and fewer scores tapering off toward the low and high ends of the score distribution. All assumptions for each statistical test will be presented where appropriate.

■ OVERVIEW OF STATISTICS AND THEIR APPLICATION IN CRIMINAL JUSTICE AND CRIMINOLOGY

Criminal justice and criminology use statistical procedures extensively. Applications of statistical procedures in these disciplines include their use in descriptions of samples or entire populations of elements, inferential work, decision making about differences among samples investigated, and correlational computations. The *Uniform Crime Reports, National Crime Victimization Survey,* and *Sourcebook of Criminal Justice Statistics* are only a few of the many publications distributed annually by government agencies about crime and criminals in the

United States. The U.S. Department of Justice and Bureau of Justice Statistics distribute large amounts of material monthly about different dimensions of crime, criminals, juveniles, and victims. Many of these reports are summaries of research conducted by persons working under the auspices of government research grants.

Among the many topics these publications address are prisoners and prisoner characteristics, probationers and parolees in the United States, criminal victimization figures, criminal defense for the poor or indigent, felony laws among the states, drug law violators, drug use and crime, drunk driving, elderly victims, households touched by crime, jail inmates and their characteristics, juvenile records and record-keeping systems, population density in state prisons, recidivism of young parolees, seasonality of crime victimization, setting prison terms, sentencing outcomes in felony courts, federal civil justice systems, time served in prison and on parole, the tracking of white-collar offenders, sentencing and time served, sentencing practices in various states, the prosecution of felony arrests, pretrial release, detention, bail reform, public access to criminal history record information, historical statistics on prisoners in state and federal institutions, and international crime rates. The Rand Corporation, the Vera Institute, and other private organizations distribute vast amounts of informative material as well concerning crime, criminals, victims, and crime patterns.

Those who conduct research in criminal justice and criminology are often affiliated with universities or colleges in professorial capacities. These professionals are often expected to do research in addition to teaching courses. However, many investigators are employed as researchers for governmental or private corporations and agencies. These individuals identify problems for investigation, design research plans, collect data, analyze collected information, and publish their findings in articles, books, or technical reports. Often, these researchers extend statistical applications to tests of hypotheses and theories. Samples of elements are selected or designated, and certain of their characteristics are described and/or measured. Depending upon the interests of the researcher, any topic may become a target for criminological inquiry or an object of interest to criminal justice professionals.

Those interested in juvenile delinquency, for instance, may wish to explore plausible explanations of delinquency through analyses of samples of delinquents and nondelinquents in a given jurisdiction. Their theories may suggest that delinquents possess certain characteristics not ordinarily possessed by nondelinquents. Or these designated characteristics may be more prevalent among delinquents compared with nondelinquents. Statistical tests of significance can answer questions about differences among samples according to these and other measured characteristics.

Certainly those interested in devising inmate classification schemes and risk prediction instruments want to know which factors or characteristics are highly correlated with a criminal subject's future dangerousness. Correlational procedures or measures of association may be used to provide numerical evidence of such relationships.

We have already alluded to the use of statistical procedures in evaluation research, in which the effectiveness of various programs, including home confine-

Box
14.2

Suman Kakar
Florida International University

Statistics: M.S. (criminology), Ph.D.
(criminology), University of Florida.

Interests: I have written extensively concerning the nature of the relationship between family environment and juvenile delinquency. I have focused upon the development of a body of knowledge on understanding the etiology, intergenerational transmission, and developmental sequelae of child abuse in terms of its relationship with juvenile delinquency, which can be used to develop effective prevention and control programs. This interest in the relationship between child abuse and delinquency has led me to study family environment as a whole and its impact on children and juveniles. I have also written on other topics such as the role of law enforcement in delinquency prevention. The focus is upon understanding the causes of delinquency and developing a body of knowledge to devise effective and efficient prevention strategies.

I got interested in research early when, as an undergraduate, I took my first course in criminology. As a novice in criminology and criminological theory, I felt anxious to learn the empirical challenges to theory. I felt that criminological theories in the absence of empirical data verifying or refuting them were meaningless. Even as an undergraduate student, I felt compelled to use data to test criminological theories. As I progressed in my studies, I took several courses in research, statistics, and research methods. After obtaining my master's degree, I started conducting research using statistics to scientifically understand the relationship between various criminological concepts proposed by theories. While working on my Ph.D., I took several courses in advanced statistics and specialized in juvenile delinquency and research methods.

My research has contributed to the base of knowledge in criminology and criminal justice in several ways. The majority of my research has been focused on the development of a clear understanding of the connection between child abuse and delinquency. Whereas earlier research assumed a direct and inevitable relationship between abuse and delinquency, my research identifies interim variables—the factors that exacerbate and the factors that mitigate the adverse effects of childhood victimization. Thus, it suggests that the intervention and prevention efforts must focus not only on child maltreatment but also on what happens between the time of abuse and the manifestation of the adverse effects of childhood experiences.

My research is empirical and theoretically grounded. It utilizes conceptual frameworks to develop research hypotheses that are later tested using empirical data. Thus, one of my major contributions would be to encourage students to see a relationship between theory and research and research methods. This will help students understand the practical usage of learning theories and research methods. My research utilizes both qualitative and quantitative research methodologies and emphasizes the interdependence of both research methodologies. Each of the techniques is presented as complementary to the other in order to conduct research in the best possible manner. Next, my research is based on rigorous sample selection methods, taking into consideration sample size, sampling error, and other related issues. This aspect of my research is expected to emphasize that all stages of conducting research are equally important. Researchers must be methodological, articulate, meticulous, objective, insightful, and analytical from the very first step to the last. My research also emphasizes that researchers must maintain the highest professional integrity. Despite the fact that all of my research is empirical and theoretical, I do not forget to show the practical policy implications of all of my research. Thus, another major contribution of this research is that all research affects practical aspects of life. I also underscore the fact that researchers should be engaged in continuous quality improvement, since no research is error-free.

Advice to Students: My advice to students would be to be analytical and insightful. Take nothing for granted and make no speculations. Use data to validate or challenge your hypotheses. Use experimental or quasi-experimental designs and comparison groups to establish baselines for comparisons to prove or support your point. Above all, my advice to students would be to think clearly, form research questions, and test your research ideas. My first advice to all my students is that clear thinking is the first and most essential ingredient for research.

ment or house arrest, electronic monitoring, furloughs, work release, halfway houses, intensive supervised probation programs, and a host of other community-based correctional services may be measured by particular statistical applications. Recidivism is often used to determine whether one program is more successful than another. Other criteria are used as well. For example, how effective is a community-based correctional agency for assisting parolees and others in finding employment? Effectiveness in placing clients in various types of jobs might be one way of measuring whether certain types of programs are working. Again, statistical tests may be used to answer these questions and to furnish confirming numerical evidence to support our personal beliefs. But as we have seen in past chapters, the research we conduct and statistical tests we subsequently apply in data analyses may refute our personal beliefs. Thus, we should retain a high degree of objectivity in our investigations and interpret whatever we find according to objective criteria. Statistical tests help us to maintain our objectivity.

■ DESCRIPTIVE STATISTICS

Descriptive statistics include any statistical measure that characterizes persons, their behaviors, or things that happen to them, according to particular variables. Some of the many variables investigated by criminologists and criminal justice professionals include age, gender, race/ethnicity, socioeconomic status, prior record, type of crime, juvenile adjudicatory dispositions, peer-group influence, cultural deprivation, achievement motivation, family stability, recidivism rates, religious affiliation, religiosity, degree of alcohol and/or drug abuse, political affiliation, employment status, burnout and stress, professionalism, type of sentencing scheme, police officer discretion, force used in effecting arrests, probation or parole officer caseloads, crime trends, jury size, type of criminal trial, risk assessment scores, inmate adjustment, style and intensity of police patrol, sentencing disparities, length of prison terms, and speedy trial provisions of different states.

Descriptive statistics may be used to describe samples of elements at a single point in time. They may also be used to chart various trends over many time periods, as in the case of changing crime rates annually reported in the *Uniform Crime Reports (UCR)*. As we have seen, the *UCR* utilizes many forms of graphic presentation to illustrate crime and crime trends, including pie charts, crime clocks, bar graphs, and histograms. Numerical information, such as crime rates and the actual incidence of crime, is also extensively included in these reports. Researchers make various uses of this information. Some investigators analyze it further, as a means of testing certain theories they have devised about crime control or prevention. Two types of descriptive measures—measures of central tendency and measures of dispersion or variability—follow.

Ungrouped and Grouped Data

Data are either ungrouped or grouped. *Ungrouped data* refers to the raw scores collected from various subjects. Working as ungrouped data is relevant for a sample size of 25 or less. In this case, no attempt is made by investigators to arrange the data into a frequency distribution with intervals of a specified size.

Grouped data refers to placing data into intervals of a specified size when more than 25 respondents are studied. Grouping data into intervals of a fixed size enables researchers to describe the data more easily. Different statistical formulae exist for both ungrouped and grouped data situations. Thus, when the investigator has ungrouped data, one particular formula for measures of central tendency or dispersion is used. For grouped data, an alternative formula is used.

Measures of Central Tendency

In a sense, measures of central tendency are ill-named, since it is expected that they disclose central points in a distribution of scores. Only one of three measures of central tendency presented here has this property: the median. The median is a value representing the midpoint or halfway mark in a listing of scores from low to high. The other measures, the mode and mean, may or may not reflect the centrality of these same scores. Measures of central tendency reflect points around which other scores tend to focus.

Modes, Medians, and Means

Modes, medians, and means are the most common measures of central tendency, and each has a different significance for us. The following sections explain the significance of each. First, each of these measures is illustrated for both ungrouped and grouped data applications. Then, a summary is provided, highlighting each measure's underlying assumptions, weaknesses, strengths, and possible applications. To conclude each section, we examine briefly the grand mean or mean of means, applicable whenever we want to average two or more means.

The Mode. For data in ungrouped form, the **mode** is defined as the value or values occurring most frequently in a distribution. In the following distribution of raw scores,

$$10\ 10\ 11\ 12\ 14\ 14\ 14\ 15\ 15\ 15\ 15\ 16\ 16\ 16\ 17\ 18\ 19\ 20$$

the value 15 would be designated as the mode, since it occurs more than any other value or four times. While the values 14 and 16 occur three times each, they do not occur as frequently as 15. However, suppose we were to observe a variation such as the one that follows:

$$10\ 10\ 11\ 14\ 14\ 14\ 14\ 15\ 15\ 15\ 15\ 16\ 16\ 16\ 16\ 17\ 18\ 19$$

We would designate the values 14, 15, and 16 as modes, since each occurs most frequently in the distribution of scores. Conventionally, there is a limit placed on the numbers of values that are designated as modes. If there are two modes, the distribution of scores is a **bimodal distribution.** We may define up to three values as modes, but if more than three values occur in a distribution (e.g., if there were four 10's, four 11's, four 12's, four 13's, four 14's), then we would simply say that there is no mode. This is a conventional rule of thumb that is followed by many researchers.

If we have grouped data in which our scores are arranged into a frequency distribution, the mode would be defined as the midpoint of the interval containing the most frequencies. Again, we would apply the conventional rule of thumb used for ungrouped data, meaning that we would identify up to three interval midpoints as being modes, but if there were more than three intervals containing the most frequencies, we would declare that there is no mode for these data. Table 14.1 is a distribution of scores grouped into intervals of size 5: Note that the interval 75–79 contains 12 frequencies. Thus, the interval mid-

TABLE 14.1 A Frequency Distribution with One Mode

Interval	f
45–49	7
50–54	3
55–59	5
60–64	3
65–69	7
70–74	2
75–79	12

TABLE 14.2 A Frequency Distribution Showing Three Modes

Interval	f
45–49	12
50–54	5
55–59	7
60–64	12
65–69	3
70–74	6
75–79	12

point, 77, would be the mode for these data. This also illustrates what was mentioned earlier, that central tendency measures are not necessarily "centrally located" within the distribution. In this instance, the interval 75–79 is at the far end of this distribution rather than in the center of it. The mode defines the most popular value, therefore, and not necessarily the most central one. If we observed a variation of this distribution, as shown in Table 14.2, several modes would be defined.

In this instance, there are three intervals that contain the most frequencies, and thus their interval midpoints, 47, 62, and 77, respectively, would be reported as the modes for this distribution. Also, if more than three intervals contained the most frequencies, we would simply say that there is no mode for these data.

The Median. The **median** is the halfway point in a distribution of scores. It is defined as the point that divides a distribution of scores into two equal parts. For ungrouped data such as the following 17 scores:

15 16 17 18 19 20 21 22 23 24 25 26 27 28 29 30 31

the median would be the middle score of 23. If several values near the center of the distribution are identical, such as in the following array:

15 16 17 18 19 20 21 22 22 22 25 26 27 28 29 30 31

we would simply designate 22 as the median for these data. If we were to change the largest score from 31 to 100, we would have

15 16 17 18 19 20 21 22 22 22 25 26 27 28 29 30 100

In this new arrangement, the median is still 22, since the central arrangement of scores is unaffected by the deviant score of 100 compared with the other scores. Generally, deviant scores have no impact on median values.

For grouped data, the median is the point dividing a distribution into two equal parts. However, the median is somewhat more complicated to compute where grouped data are involved. An illustration of the median for grouped data is shown in Table 14.3.

TABLE 14.3 The Median for Grouped Data

Interval	f	Cf
500–509	8	8
510–519	17	25
520–529	14	39
530–539	3	42
540–549	10	52
550–559	11	63
560–569	12	75
570–579	15	90
580–589	12	102
590–599	9	111
600–609	13	124
610–619	15	139
620–629	12	151

$$\Sigma f = 151$$

In order to compute the median for the grouped data in Table 14.3, we might want to construct a cumulative frequency distribution. In a cumulative frequency distribution, the frequencies in previous intervals are added to successive intervals. The third column, *Cf*, shows the cumulative frequency distribution based upon the distribution of frequencies in the second column (f). The cumulative frequency distribution assists us in determining which interval contains the median or central point in this distribution of scores. We must divide our total number of frequencies by 2, or $151/2 = 75.5$. This indicates that our median value divides our distribution of scores such that 75.5 scores are above that value and 75.5 scores are below that value. Examining Table 14.3 we see that 75.5 is slightly above the cumulative frequencies shown in the interval 560–569. We may seek our median in the next interval 570–579. We proceed as follows.

First, we enter that interval from the lower limit of it, 569.5. We add to that value the frequencies we need, .5 (one-half of one frequency), divided by the number of frequencies found in that interval, 15, and multiply the result by the interval size, 10. The formula is

$$\text{Median} = LL' + (\,fn/ff\,)(i)$$

where LL' = the lower limit of the interval we must enter
to obtain the frequencies we need to acquire
half of them

fn = the frequencies we need in the interval

ff = the frequencies found in the interval

i = the interval size

Thus, using the values from Table 14.3, the median computation is as follows:

$$\text{median} = 569.5 + .5/15(10)$$
$$= 569.5 + 5/15$$
$$= 569.5 + .3$$
$$= 569.8$$

The median for these data is 569.8. This is the point that divides the distribution into two equal parts. Note that had we wished to compute a mode for the same data in Table 14.3, it would have been the midpoint of the interval containing the most frequencies, in this case, 510–519, which contains 17 frequencies. The midpoint of this interval is 514.5. Observe that the mode is quite different in magnitude compared with the median, and that it is well away from the center of the distribution, not particularly representative of the central tendency of it.

The Mean. The most popular and familiar measure of central tendency is the **mean.** The mean is the arithmetic average of all scores in a distribution. The mean is the sum of the scores divided by the number of scores. Thus, if we observed the following array of 11 scores in ungrouped form:

15 16 17 18 19 20 21 22 23 24 25

the mean would be the sum of these scores, 220, divided by the number of scores, 11, or 220/11 = 20. In this particular situation, the median would also be 20, since it is the point dividing the 11 scores into two equal parts, precisely located in the center of the distribution. There is at least one important difference between the median and the mean, however. Suppose we were to change the score of 25 to 250. While this would continue to have no effect on the median (either extremely large or small scores), the mean would be "pulled" upward, toward the deviant score of 250. The new sum of scores would be 445. Dividing this new sum by the number of scores would be 445/11 = 40.4. This would be the true average or mean, although the mean of 40.4 would be atypical of any score in that distribution. The presence of deviant scores tends to distort the mean depending upon their magnitude. Therefore, whenever deviant scores are present in a distribution, the median would be preferred, since it is nearly immune to distortions resulting from such deviant scores.

The mean for grouped data is slightly more complicated to compute. The computation of the mean for grouped data is illustrated by using the information in Table 14.4, which shows a frequency distribution containing 116 scores and the arbitrary reference point method for mean computation. The **arbitrary reference point** method involves selecting an interval, normally one near the "center" of the distribution, as the one designated as containing the arbitrary reference point. In this instance, the interval 295–299 is selected. There is nothing sacred about this selection. It is simply an interval near what appears to be the center

TABLE 14.4 The Arbitrary-Reference-Point Method of Mean Computation with an Array of 116 Scores

Interval	f	x'	fx'
325–329	6	6	36
320–324	10	5	50
315–319	11	4	44
310–314	3	3	9
305–309	12	2	24
300–304	2	1	2
295–299	6	0	0
290–294	10	−1	−10
285–289	9	−2	−18
280–284	4	−3	−12
275–279	8	−4	−32
270–274	15	−5	−75
265–269	11	−6	−66
260–264	9	−7	−63
	$\Sigma f = 116$		$\Sigma fx' = -111$

of the distribution. Virtually any interval could have been selected, since the arbitrary reference point procedure is self-correcting and yields the same mean value each time. However, an interval near the center of the distribution is selected primarily to minimize our mathematical computations. We may designate the midpoint of this interval, 297, as the MP' or arbitrary reference point.

Notice in Table 14.4 that two additional columns have been constructed. These columns are labeled as x' and fx' respectively. The x' column designates a "0" placed adjacent to the interval we selected originally as that containing the arbitrary reference point. We may number away from 0 in both directions (toward the top and bottom of the distribution) as follows: −1, −2, −3, −4, and so on, until the bottom of the distribution is reached (i.e., the interval containing the smallest scores). Also, we number 1, 2, 3, 4, and so on, until the top of the distribution is reached (i.e., the interval containing the largest scores). It is important to take into account how the intervals have been arranged so that we do not erroneously number the x' column −1, −2, −3, and so on, toward the "top" of the distribution, and 1, 2, 3, and so on, toward the "bottom" of the distribution.

Once these x' values have been placed adjacent to each interval, the interval frequencies, f, are multiplied by the x' values as shown in a column labeled fx'. The negative sum of products is offset by the positive sum of products to yield $\Sigma fx'$. In this instance, the sum is −111, since the negative sum of products is greater than the positive sum. Using the information from Table 14.4, we may apply the following formula:

$$\overline{X} = MP' + (\Sigma fx'/N)(i),$$

where MP' = the midpoint of the interval we selected as the arbitrary reference point

$\Sigma fx'$ = the sum of products of frequencies and their adjacent values

N = sample size

i = interval size

With this information, we have

$$\overline{X} = 297 + \frac{-111}{116}(5)$$

$$= 297 + \frac{-555}{116}$$

$$= 297 - 4.8$$

$$= 292.2$$

The mean for these data in Table 14.4 is 292.2. Again, it makes no difference which interval we select as the one containing the arbitrary reference point, since the computational formula is self-correcting. Changing the location of the arbitrary reference point either upward or downward will modify the resulting $\Sigma fx'$ value as well as the MP'. However, the formula is self-correcting depending upon the interval chosen for the arbitrary reference point.

The Grand Mean. Occasionally, researchers may wish to average several means for various purposes and determine a **grand mean** or **mean of means.** They may be interested in whether several different groups of employees in a police agency vary in their work output from overall employee productivity. If certain groups are below agency standards or norms, officials may wish to improve the group's productivity by implementing new incentive systems or different types of supervision or leadership. Averaging two or more means is also a step involved in the computation of certain statistical tests of significance, such as the *F* **test for analysis of variance.** Thus, for at least these two reasons, it is important to understand grand mean computations. The mean of means or grand mean is easily illustrated below. Suppose we observed the following means for three groups of 10 employees each:

Groups	Means
1	15
2	12
3	9
	$\Sigma \overline{X}_i = 36$

In this example, the sum of the individual means = 36. We may simply divide the sum of means by 3, or 36/3 = 12. The grand mean or $\overline{X}_T = 12$. However, if the groups contain unequal numbers of elements or are of different sizes, we must take into account each group's size before completing our computational work. For instance, if group 3 above consisted of 25 employees, but group 1 consisted of only 5 employees, our original grand mean would be erroneous, since we would be giving equal weight to the means of groups consisting of 25 and 5, respectively. We would seriously underrepresent group 3 and overrepresent group 1 in our calculations. The correct procedure would be to multiply each mean by the number of elements in the sample. Once these products were determined, we would sum the products and divide by the sum of all sample elements. For instance, given the same information above, but changing the sample N's, we would have the following:

Group	N_i	$\overline{X}_i$	$(N_i)(\overline{X}_i)$
1	5	15	75
2	10	12	120
3	25	9	225
	$\Sigma N_i = 40$		$\Sigma(N_i)(\overline{X}_i) = 420$

The grand mean would be $420/40 = 10.5$. This smaller grand mean or mean of means is correct, since it takes into account the proportionate weight of each sample size. Thus, because there are considerably more persons in group 3, the smallest mean of 9 receives greater weight. Accordingly, the least weight is given the first group mean of 15, since there are only five persons in group 1. This is known as weighting. We have weighted each mean according to its sample size.

Comparing the Mode, Median, and Mean.   Applying the mode, median, and mean correctly is governed by several factors. First, the level-of-measurement assumption should be met for each measure. Accordingly, the nominal, ordinal, and interval levels of measurement are respectively required for computing the mode, median, and mean. Thus, the mean is subject to the most rigorous test of an interval scale underlying the attribute or characteristic measured. The mode is least rigorous, applicable to data measured according to nominal scales. Since virtually all attitudinal scales devised thus far are measurable according to an ordinal measurement scale at best, the median is perhaps most appropriate for situations in which attitudes are investigated. Age, years of educational attainment, income, and sentence lengths in months or years are examples of variables that may be assessed readily by an interval scale.

As measures of central tendency, the mode, median, and mean have different advantages. Some of these have already been illustrated by examples. The mode is indicative of the most popular value, although we know this popular value may not be located near the center of the distribution. The median is the central value, identifying a point dividing the distribution of scores into two equal parts. The mean is the average value, although it is easily influenced upward or downward by the presence of deviant large or small scores. If deviant scores existed in a distribution, the median would be preferred over the mean. Therefore, in this sense, the median is more stable than the mean.

However, another connotation of stability gives the mean greater standing than the mode or median. Suppose researchers analyzed data from multiple samples of elements. For instance, investigators might have sets of scores from ten groups. Thus, they could compute ten sample modes, ten sample medians, and ten sample means. If we were to examine the variation among the sample modes, medians, and means, the *least* amount of variation would occur among the sample means. This means that there would be greater similarity among means. Since the mean has this characteristic of stability, it is often preferred as the central tendency measure of choice for statistical inference.

■ MEASURES OF DISPERSION OR VARIABILITY

Measures of dispersion or variability describe how scores are distributed around certain central tendency values. Consider the following example in which two sets of scores are presented. The means are the same for both distributions, but the scores are distributed differently, more or less scattered around the same point:

Distribution 1: 55 56 57 58 59 60 61 62 63 64 65

Distribution 2: 10 20 30 40 50 60 70 80 90 100 110

In both distributions, the means = 60. However, the scores in distribution 1 are more closely distributed around the mean of 60, while the scores in distribution 2 are more sparsely distributed around 60. In order to maximize our descriptive information about any array of scores, we must know both the central tendency and its dispersion. Useful measures of dispersion include the range and standard deviation. Other measures exist and some are discussed briefly in this section. One of these other measures is the average deviation. While the average deviation is seldom used today in criminological research, it illustrates the concept of a **deviation score.** This concept is important for understanding the meaning of the standard deviation. Subsequently, we will find that the standard deviation is the preferred measure of variability in much the same sense as the mean is the preferred measure of central tendency.

Ranges. The **range** is the distance over which certain proportions of scores are distributed. There are several different types of ranges. For ungrouped data, the range or true range is the distance between the lower limit of the smallest score and the upper limit of the largest score. If we observed the following distribution of scores:

11 12 13 14 15 16 17 18 19 20

the true range would be $20.5 - 10.5 = 10$. Sometimes, investigators compute the range as the largest score minus the smallest score plus 1, or $20 - 11 + 1 =$

9 + 1 = 10. This method also takes upper and lower limits of scores into account by combining each into the 1. The range defines the distance over which all scores (100 percent) in the distribution are spread. The use of upper and lower limits of scores is only meaningful when the researcher has data measured according to an interval scale.

For grouped data, the range is either the distance between the midpoints of extreme intervals or the distance between the upper limit of the interval containing the largest scores and the lower limit of the interval containing the smallest scores. Table 14.5 shows a hypothetical distribution and the range computation using both methods.

Note that for method 1, midpoints of the extreme intervals (those containing the largest and smallest scores) are identified, and the difference computed, yielding a range = 18. The second method is the difference between the two upper and lower limits of the extreme intervals, or 47.5 − 26.5 = 21. Either 18 or 21 is reported as the range. Sometimes investigators compute both as a check on their work. The difference between them will always be the equivalent of the interval size, in this case "3."

Besides the **true range,** which is the distance over which 100 percent of the scores are distributed, other ranges are the **10–90 range** or **interdecile range,** and the **interquartile range.** The 10-90 range is the distance between the 10th (C_{10} or D_1) and 90th (C_{90} or D_9) centiles, and it describes the distance over which the central 80 percent of all scores is spread. The interquartile range is the difference between the first (Q_1) and third (Q_3) quartiles and is the distance over which the middle 50 percent of the scores is spread.

The major reason for using these alternative ranges rather than the range itself is that, sometimes, deviant scores in a distribution may distort the true range value. This distortion may cause researchers to think that most of the scores are distributed over a large distance. In reality, however, most scores might be closely grouped near one another, with only a few deviant scores far away from the rest. For example, if we had 100 scores, and 98 scores were between 15 and 35 and two additional scores of 95 and 96 were found, this

TABLE 14.5 A Distribution of Scores and Two Range Computations

Interval	f	
45–47	5	Range (Method 1) = 46 − 28 = 18
42–44	7	
39–41	8	
36–38	4	
33–35	3	Range (Method 2) = 47.5 − 26.5 = 21
30–32	5	
27–29	6	
$\Sigma f = 38$		

would mean a true range of 82. Close inspection of the distribution of scores would show that most of our scores were within a range of 21, not 82. Thus, some compensation is made for these deviant scores. Thus, when deviant scores are encountered, researchers may decide to report other distances over which the middle 80 or 50 percent of scores are spread. These alternative ranges are more reliable and stable indicators of the spread of scores, compared with the true range, which may give misleading information about the score distribution.

Average Deviation and Deviation Scores. The **average deviation** is the average variation of scores about the mean of the distribution. This is illustrated by the following simple example:

15 16 17 18 19 20 21 22 23 24 25

These 11 scores have a mean = 20. Each score departs or deviates from the mean of 20, either positively or negatively, a certain distance. This distance is measured by a deviation score or x'. For these 11 scores, x' values have been computed as follows:

Score	x'
15	−5
16	−4
17	−3
18	−2
19	−1
20	0
21	+1
22	+2
23	+3
24	+4
25	+5
	$\Sigma x' = 0$

Note that the x' for the score of 15 = −5, since 15 is 5 points below the mean of 20. The score of 24 has an x' value = +4, since 24 is 4 points above 20, and so on. The score of 20, which occurs at the same point where the mean is found, has an $x' = 0$, since there is no deviation from the mean. As a check on one's work, the sum of the x' values always equals 0, provided we begin our computations with a correct mean value.

In order to compute the average deviation for these data, we must ignore the signs (+ or −) associated with each deviation score, and compute the sum of the absolute (| |) departures from the mean. These absolute deviations from the mean are illustrated here:

Score	$|x'|$
15	5
16	4
17	3
18	2
19	1
20	0
21	1
22	2
23	3
24	4
25	5

$$\Sigma|x'| = 30$$

The absolute departures of all scores from the mean, summed, would be $5 + 4 + 3 + 2 + 1 + 0 + 1 + 2 + 3 + 4 + 5 = 30$. We must divide this sum by the total number of scores, N, in order to obtain the average deviation. With an $N = 11$, this becomes $30/11 = 2.7$. The scores fluctuate about the mean of 20 an average of 2.7 points. This is what is meant by the average deviation.

For many years, the average deviation was believed to be an approximation of the standard deviation. It seems that researchers wanted an approximation of the standard deviation without having to formally compute it. Instead, values with little meaning, such as the average deviation, were often erroneously reported as approximations of the standard deviation. There is no mathematical equivalence between the average deviation and standard deviation. It was presented here merely to illustrate the meaning of deviation scores.

The Variance and Standard Deviation. With our knowledge of the average deviation and the meaning of deviation scores, the **standard deviation** is determined by following a simple series of steps. As we work from our original data used in the earlier average deviation problem, our series of steps will take us first through a solution of the **variance.** Once the variance has been determined, we may take the square root of this value. The result is the standard deviation. Using the information from the average deviation example and extending our computational work to square each deviation score and sum these squared scores, we have

Scores	$|x'|$	$|x'|^2$
15	5	25
16	4	16
17	3	9

18	2	4
19	1	1
20	0	0
21	1	1
22	2	4
23	3	9
24	4	16
25	5	25
$N = 11$	$\Sigma|x'| = 30$	$\Sigma|x'|^2 = 110$

Knowing the number of scores, $N = 11$, and the sum of the squared deviation scores, $\Sigma x'^2$, we can calculate the variance, s^2, by dividing the sum of the squared deviation scores by N. We may use the following expression:

Variance, $s^2 = \Sigma x^2/N$

where $\underline{\Sigma}x^2$ = the sum of the squared deviation scores

and N = the number of sample elements

Carrying out this computation yields $110/11 = 10$. The variance is 10.

The square root of the variance is the standard deviation, s. Thus, $\sqrt{10} = 3.2$.

A short-cut for computing the standard deviation for ungrouped data is as follows. This method eliminates the necessity of first determining the sample mean and then determining deviation scores. We may work directly with the raw scores and the squares of the raw scores. For the preceding data, we would have the following:

X_i	X_i^2
15	225
16	256
17	289
18	324
19	361
20	400
21	441
22	484
23	529
24	576
25	625
Sums $\Sigma X_i = 220$	$\Sigma X_i^2 = 4510$
$N = 11$	

For these data, we may apply the following formula to compute our sum of squared deviation scores or Σx^2:

$$\Sigma x^2 = \Sigma X^2 - (\Sigma X_i)^2/N$$

Substituting these values for formula symbols, we have

$$\Sigma x^2 = 4510 - (220)^2/11$$
$$= 4510 - 48,400/11$$
$$= 4510 - 4400$$
$$= 110$$

Again, the sum of squared deviation scores = 110. The same result was obtained when the mean and actual deviation scores were used. The main advantages of this latter method are that we do not need to compute a mean first, we avoid possible rounding error in the event our mean is not a whole number, and our computational work is greatly simplified. Using the sums of scores and the sums of the squared scores is recommended. The Table of Squares and Square Roots, Table A1 in Appendix A, pages 610–619, may be used to expedite the computation of standard deviations for ungrouped data.

For data in grouped form, the standard deviation procedure appears considerably more complex than it really is. Actually, we perform all functions used for computing the mean for grouped data presented earlier in this chapter. In addition, we add another column as illustrated in Table 14.6.

TABLE 14.6 Data from Table 14.4 Recast to Illustrate the Arbitrary
Reference Point Method of the Standard Deviation
Computation with an Array of 116 Scores

Interval	f	x'	fx'	$(x')(fx')$
325–329	6	6	36	216
320–324	10	5	50	250
315–319	11	4	44	176
310–314	3	3	9	27
305–309	12	2	24	48
300–304	2	1	2	2
295–299	6	0	0	0
290–294	10	−1	−10	10
285–289	9	−2	−18	36
280–284	4	−3	−12	36
275–279	8	−4	−32	128
270–274	15	−5	−75	375
265–269	11	−6	−66	396
260–264	9	−7	−63	441
	$\Sigma f = 116$		$\Sigma fx' = -111$	$\Sigma fx'^2 = 2141$

The final column in Table 14.6 eliminates the minuses from our computational work. Actually, we multiply each value in the column, x', by the adjacent values in the fx' column. These computations have been illustrated. Next, we sum these products. We use the following formula to derive the sum of squared scores:

$$\Sigma x^2 = (i)^2 \left[\Sigma fx'^2 - \frac{(\Sigma fx')^2}{N} \right],$$

where

i = interval size

$\Sigma fx'^2$ = sum of products of the fx' and x' columns

$\Sigma fx'$ = sum of products of the f and x' columns

N = sample size

From the information in Table 14.6, we have

$$\Sigma x^2 = (5)^2 \, [2141 - (-111)^2/116]$$
$$= 25 \, [2141 - 14{,}462/116]$$
$$= 25 \, [2141 - 124.7]$$
$$= 25 \, (2016.3)$$
$$= 50{,}407.5$$

In order to compute s, we apply an earlier formula, $s = \sqrt{s^2} = \sqrt{\dfrac{\Sigma x^2}{N}}$

$$s = \sqrt{50{,}407.5/116}$$
$$= \sqrt{434.5} \text{ (also the variance, } s^2) = 20.8$$

The standard deviation for these data is 20.8.

The principal reason why the standard deviation is the best measure of variability, especially in inferential work, is that under most circumstances it has a consistent meaning from one distribution to the next. One standard deviation value of 5.1 for one distribution of scores means the same thing as 15.3 means for another distribution of scores. A standard deviation of 200 in a third distribution of scores would have an equivalent meaning as well. This property of consistency of interpretation makes the standard deviation distinctive among other variability measures.

When applied to any distribution of raw scores, the standard deviation usually refers to a given distance on either side of the mean, which will include a specific proportion of scores. Thus, if we knew that the mean for a distribution of scores was 100 and the standard deviation was 10, then a specific proportion of scores would be included between the mean of 100 and one standard deviation above or below the mean, or from 90 to 100 and from 100 to 110. A knowledge of the mean and standard deviation for most distributions of scores permits us to determine the likely or expected proportion of scores between any pair of points in that distribution. For instance, we could determine the proportion of scores between 85 and 120, between 60 and 62, or between 140 and 175. For the present, it is important only to recognize the importance of this property of consistency.

All measures of dispersion or variability discussed in this section assume the interval level of measurement associated with the variable under investigation. The range is a useful computation for establishing the size of intervals in the construction of frequency distributions for grouped data. However, it fluctuates according to the presence of deviant or especially large or small scores in any distribution. Thus, in this sense it is considered an unstable measure of variability. Researchers have attempted to compensate for the presence of deviant scores by moving into distributions from their upper and lower extremes and by calculating distances over which a certain proportion of the central scores are spread. These adjustments or compensations are the 10–90 range and the interquartile range. Respectively, they reflect distances over which the central 80 percent and 50 percent of scores are spread.

Measures such as the average deviation have been created primarily as less cumbersome methods for approximating standard deviation values. However, there is no mathematical relation between the standard deviation and the average deviation. The average deviation serves an important function, however, in that it illustrates the meaning of deviation scores. Utilizing deviation scores helps us to understand such computations as the variance and standard deviation.

Ordinarily, the usefulness of the variance is largely related to other tests of statistical significance, such as the F test for **analysis of variance.** The square root of the variance is the standard deviation. This measure of variability is important because it has a consistent interpretation and is maximally useful when combined with the mean in statistical inference problems. In order to obtain a more complete understanding of the standard deviation and what it can do for researchers in such problems, we must first consider particular distributions of scores and how these distributions occur around central tendency points.

■ KEY TERMS

Analysis of variance
Arbitrary reference point
Average deviation
Bell or bell-shaped normal curve
Bimodal distribution
Central tendency
Description
Descriptive statistics
Deviation score
Dispersion or variability
F test for analysis of variance
Grand mean
Inference
Interdecile range

Interquartile range
Levels of measurement
Mean
Mean of means
Median
Mode
Parameter
Range
Robustness
Standard deviation
Statistics
10–90 range
True range
Variance

1. Given the following information, compute the values requested.

Interval	f
640–643	8
644–647	10
648–651	3
652–655	2
656–659	9
660–663	14
664–667	12
668–671	11
672–675	9
676–679	15
680–683	14
684–687	12
688–691	5

$$\Sigma f = 124$$

(a) The variance and standard deviation

(b) The 10–90 range

2. Given the following information, determine the values requested.

Interval	f
550–554	2
545–549	3
540–544	6
535–539	8
530–534	4
525–529	6
520–524	19
515–519	0
510–514	0
505–509	4
500–504	5

$$\Sigma f = 57$$

(a) The mode

(b) The median

(c) The mean

3. For the following ungrouped data, determine the mode, median, and mean.

$$8\ 9\ 10\ 11\ 12\ 13\ 14\ 14\ 15\ 20$$

4. Given the following information, determine the mode, median, and mean.

$$15\ 17\ 17\ 18\ 22\ 68\ 120\ 15\ 60\ 45\ 13\ 19$$

$$26\ 31\ 28\ 15\ 22\ 29\ 41\ 95$$

5. In what sense is the median more stable as a measure of central tendency than either the mode or mean? In what sense is the mean more stable than the median?

6. Given the following information, determine the grand mean.

Sample	N_k	$\overline{X}_i$
1	52	47.8
2	65	28.3
3	29	52.5
4	70	40.1
5	10	65.3
6	23	55.4

7. Given the following information, determine the mean and standard deviation.

$$55\ 75\ 82\ 41\ 28\ 41\ 55\ 67\ 69\ 75\ 78\ 75$$

$$55\ 24\ 38\ 42\ 46\ 49\ 57\ 76$$

8. Given the following information, determine the mode, median, mean, and standard deviation.

Interval	f
115–119	5
120–124	10
125–129	11
130–134	15
135–139	10
140–144	9
145–149	10
150–154	7
155–159	8
160–164	13
165–169	3
170–174	6
175–179	4
$\Sigma f = 111$	

9. Compute the range and standard deviation for the following distribution of scores:

2 5 7 8 8 8 9 12 13 13 13 14 15 15 16

10. Compute the standard deviation and range for the following distribution:

3 8 12 14 9 16 12 29 58 22 4 14 14

11. Determine the standard deviation for the distribution below:

Interval	f
900–909	3
910–919	7
920–929	13
930–939	14
940–949	15
950–959	4
960–969	10
970–979	15
980–989	10
990–999	11
1000–1009	5
1010–1019	10
	$\Sigma f = 117$

12. Given the following information, determine the range and standard deviation:

21 21 35 36 38 39 40 41 42 42 43

55 66 66 67 67 67 71 75 78

13. What is meant by the term *statistics*? Briefly describe at least two uses of the term for those interested in criminal justice and criminology.

14. Distinguish between statistic and parameter. Write a short paragraph about the relation between statistics and parameters in research work. Relate this discussion to inference.

15. How is sample size related to statistical test assumptions?

16. Why is it important that researchers obtain random samples of elements in their research work? Explain briefly.

20. What are four general functions of statistical procedures? Describe each briefly.

chapter 15

The Normal Curve and Sampling Distributions

INTRODUCTION

Criminologists and criminal justice professionals are interested in generalizing their studies of samples of elements to larger populations of them. When sampling plans were discussed in an earlier chapter, our attention was drawn to different types of sampling plans used in social scientific research. Some of these plans are better than others for statistical inference. These plans, known as probability sampling plans, are especially useful because they permit us to generalize about the characteristics of populations of elements from the distribution of sample characteristics. These sampling plans include simple random sampling, proportionate and disproportionate stratified random sampling, and cluster, area, or multistage sampling. These sampling plans enhance the likelihood of drawing samples that are representative or typical of their populations. While no sampling plan guarantees that any sample will be perfectly representative of the population from which it is drawn, the use of probability sampling plans increases this likelihood.

Whenever probability sampling plans are used for research purposes, investigators wishing to make inferences about population values may be able to utilize the unit normal distribution for some of their generalizations. Over the years, social scientists have found that many distributions of characteristics based upon probability samples tend to resemble the unit normal distribution. In fact, they have been able to use several features of unit normal distributions in their research work for making inferential statements about population parameters within a probabilistic context. For instance, it has been found that if the unit normal distribution is approximated by several different distributions of raw scores, those scores may be standardized and compared with one another by using the unit normal distribution as the objective, comparative standard.

This chapter examines the unit normal distribution and describes this important comparative feature. The unit normal distribution yields a **normal distribution** *or bell-shaped curve representing the total area encompassed by any set of scores. It has been found that different areas of the unit normal distribution include constant proportions of curve area, and that these constant proportions of curve area may have applications for certain distributions of raw scores. Standardized values associated with the unit normal distribution have been derived and tabled so that social scientists can easily understand and apply them.*

One distribution assumption discussed earlier pertained to arrangements of raw scores that we might analyze. Specifically, some of our statistical tests require that our raw scores should be distributed in a fashion similar to the unit normal distribution or bell-shaped curve. If our distributions of scores do not resemble this bell-shaped curve, then we cannot use the standardized properties of unit normal distributions profitably in our own data analyses. If we use a probability sampling plan, in which elements have an equal and independent chance of being included, this action will enhance the likelihood that our sample characteristics will approximate the unit normal distribution. The more our distributions of scores approximate the unit normal distribution in form, the more we can use this distribution for generalizing or inferential purposes.

The **unit normal distribution** *is also approximated by sampling distributions of statistics. If we use specific statistics, such as the mean, which have sampling distributions approximating normality, then our inferential work is improved and our generalizations about population parameters are more meaningful. The concept of a sampling distribution of a statistic is illustrated and discussed. Finally, the use of unit normal distributions extends to hypothesis testing. Certain types of hypotheses about population parameters have* **decision rules** *that influence our judgments and inferences. We examine decision rules and see how they relate to sampling distributions of statistics.*

■ THE NORMAL CURVE

The unit normal distribution does not exist in the real world. Rather, it is a theoretical distribution. Statisticians and mathematicians have created the unit normal distribution theoretically by using the following formula:

$$Y = \left(\frac{1}{\sigma\sqrt{2\pi}}\right)\epsilon^{-\frac{1}{2}\left(\frac{X-\mu}{\sigma}\right)^2}$$

where $\pi = 3.1416$

$\epsilon = 2.7183$

σ = parameter equal to the standard deviation of the distribution

μ = parameter equal to the mean of the distribution

X = abscissa—measurement of score marked on the horizontal axis

Y = ordinate—height of the curve at a point corresponding to an assigned value of X

Figure 15.1 illustrates the unit normal distribution derived by the given formula. Because the curve drawn for this distribution appears bell-shaped, it is sometimes known as the bell curve. Other names for the unit normal distribution are the normal distribution, the **standard normal distribution,** or simply, the normal curve. In this chapter, the term *unit normal distribution* will apply specifically to this mathematically derived curve.

Since other distributions of raw scores may resemble the unit normal distribution by their bell-curve shape, these other distributions of scores are often said to be *normal in form.* Frequently researchers refer to their raw score distributions as normal or having the characteristics of the normal distribution. Whenever they make these statements, they want to show that their distributions of raw scores approximate the unit normal distribution in their shape or form. Thus, it may be said that there is only *one* unit normal distribution, the one that is theoretically derived. But an *infinite* number of normal distributions of raw scores may exist where they appear to approximate the unit normal distribution with their form.

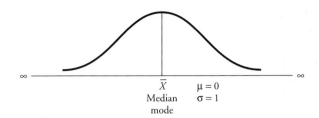

FIGURE 15.1
Unit normal distribution.

$\overline{X}$ $\mu = 0$

Median $\sigma = 1$

mode

Characteristics of the Unit Normal Distribution

Several important features of the unit normal distribution include the following:

1. The curve of the unit normal distribution, known as the normal curve, is bell-shaped and perfectly symmetrical. The highest point of the curve is at its center, and the ends of the curve or the tails taper off in opposite directions in an identical manner.

2. The tails of the curve, extending to the left and right, continuously approach the horizontal axis, but they never touch it. Thus, these tails extend toward infinity. A close examination of Figure 15.1 reveals this feature of the curve. This is known as the **asymptotic property** of the unit normal distribution and discloses one departure of this theoretical distribution from actual distributions of raw scores. In the real world, actual distributions of raw scores have low and high points or limits. There are lowest and highest scores in a distribution, and thus the horizontal axis is reached at both ends by the tapering tails of curves drawn for distributions of raw scores.

3. The mean, median, and mode all occur at the same point on the unit normal distribution, which is at its precise center or highest point. Thus, these central tendency measures calculated for the unit normal distribution are exactly equal to one another.

4. Because the median is located at the center of the unit normal distribution, and because the unit normal distribution is perfectly symmetrical, the distribution is divided into two equal parts, with the area to the left of the median equaling the area to the right of it. These two areas are each equal to one half of the total area under the normal curve, or 50 percent of it.

5. The total area under the curve is equal to unity or 1.0000 or 100 percent. Various proportions of curve area located either to the left or right of the mean are equal to various portions of 1.0000, such as .4000, .3425, or .2618. Four-place decimal values representing various proportions of curve area are used because Table A.3 of Appendix A on page 624, Areas Under the Normal Curve, are proportionately expressed to four places.

6. The two parameters or characteristics of the unit normal distribution are the mean, μ (the Greek letter pronounced "mew"), which is equal to "0" and the standard deviation, σ (the Greek letter pronounced "sigma"), which is equal to "1." Because the curve is perfectly symmetrical and the mean is

located where the median occurs that divides the distribution into two equal parts, identical standard deviation values to the left or right of the mean cut off identical portions of curve area in opposite directions.

■ STANDARD SCORES AND THEIR INTERPRETATION

Because the unit normal distribution is central to discussions of many statistical tests and statistical inference generally, considerable attention will be given to working with the Table of Areas Under the Normal Curve, Table A.3, on page 624. In fact, much of the work pertaining to determining normal curve areas presented here is for the purpose of increasing your facility in using Table A.3, not only for purposes of statistical inference, but also for purposes of statistical decision making.

While the unit normal distribution exists only in theory, criminologists and others have found over the years that the distributions of a wide variety of variables often approximate the unit normal distribution in their central tendency and dispersion. For instance, police professionalism might be approximately normally distributed in given samples of law enforcement officers, with most officers exhibiting a moderate amount of professionalism and a few officers exhibiting very high and very low degrees of it. Various attitudes that have been converted into numerical quantities appear to be normally distributed in various samples. Distribution of scores that approximate several of the characteristics of the unit normal distribution are said to be normally distributed. And statements that can be made about the unit normal distribution can also be applied to distributions of scores that approximate it. In short, if we have a distribution of attitudinal scores that is approximately normal in form (e.g., resembling the form of the curve illustrated in Figure 15.1), we can say things about the distribution of attitudinal scores that can also apply to the unit normal distribution. The functional utility of the unit normal distribution is illustrated in the following discussion.

Standard Scores

Various points along the horizontal axis of the unit normal distribution cut off various portions of curve area. These points are referred to as **standard values** or **standard scores.** They are most often designated by *Z;* hence, they are known also as **Z scores** or **Z values.** Standard scores or *Z* values depict both the direction and distance of a given point along the horizontal axis of the unit normal distribution in relation to its mean, $\mu = 0$. This distance is measured in terms of standard deviation units of 1 because one of the parameters of this distribution is $\sigma = 1$. Figure 15.2 shows the unit normal distribution with various *Z* values depicted.

Each of the *Z* values in Figure 15.2 cuts off a constant proportion of curve area. Each of these values is a given distance from the $\mu = 0$ expressed in σ's of 1. Each of these *Z* values may be translated as shown in Table 15.1.

Further, we can identify the curve area proportions cut off by given *Z* values by turning to Table A.3 of Appendix A. In Table A.3, the left-hand column con-

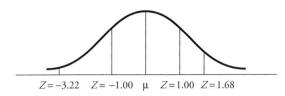

FIGURE 15.2
Unit normal distribution with Z values depicted.

$Z=-3.22$ $Z=-1.00$ μ $Z=1.00$ $Z=1.68$

tains Z values expressed to the nearest tenth. Values across the top of the table provide additional precision to the nearest hundredth. Therefore, if we are looking up a Z value of 1.68 in this table, we must first find 1.6 down the left-hand column and then .08 across the top of the table. Where these values intersect in the body of the table identifies the proportion of curve area lying between $\mu = 0$ and a Z value of 1.68, or .4535. This proportion also may be expressed as a percentage. In other words, approximately 45 percent of the curve area lies between the mean of 0 and a Z of 1.68 (which is 1.68σ's above the mean). The proportion .4535 represents the amount of curve area between these two points, as is illustrated in Figure 15.3.

In Figure 15.3, an additional Z value of -1.68 has been provided to illustrate that because of the symmetry of the unit normal distribution, identical Z values lying in opposite directions away from the $\mu = 0$ cut off identical proportions of curve area. Thus, the $Z = -1.68$ cuts off .4535 of the curve area to the left of μ just as a $Z = 1.68$ cuts off .4535 of the curve area to the right of μ. Generally, all negative Z values occur below or to the left of the mean, μ, while all positive Z values occur to the right of or above μ. A Z value that occurs directly on the mean would be a $Z = 0.00$. Z values are ordinarily expressed to the nearest hundredth, as the Z values in Table A.3 are presented. In fact, it a useful rule of thumb that in any subsequent statistical application, statistical results are ordinarily expressed to the nearest place commensurate with values shown in various statistical tables in Appendix A. Therefore, if we want to identify the proportion of curve area cut off by any Z value, regardless of whether it is above (positive) or below (negative) the mean, we simply examine the absolute Z value shown in Table A.3. A Z value of 1.00 cuts off .3413 of the curve area, while a Z value of -1.00 cuts off the same amount of curve area, .3413, in the opposite direction. Additional examples of Z values of different magnitudes and in different directions from μ are shown in Table 15.2.

TABLE 15.1 Direction and Distance of Z Values from Mean of Unit Normal Distribution

Z Value	Direction and Distance from $\mu = 0$ in Sigmas Equal to 1
1.00	1.00 σ's or 1.00 σ above the mean
-1.00	-1.00 σ's or 1.00 σ below the mean
1.68	1.68 σ's or 1.68 σ's above the mean
-3.22	-3.22 σ's or 3.22 σ's below the mean

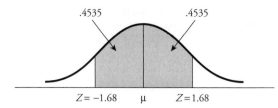

.4535   .4535

Z= −1.68   μ   Z=1.68

FIGURE 15.3
Z values of the unit normal distribution.

The proportions of the curve area shown in Table 15.2 are constant proportions that have been derived from the proportions tabled in Table A.3. They are constant proportions included between μ = 0 and some designated number of sigmas (σ's) above or below the mean. Another way of looking at these is to regard them as standard proportions. These standard proportions always exist for each sigma (σ) departure from the mean of the unit normal distribution. If we encounter distributions of scores in our research that are approximately normally distributed, we can make fairly reliable estimates about the proportion of scores included within a given distance of the mean, whatever it might be, in terms of standard deviation units or values.

Suppose we were to draw a random sample of elements from a population and construct a frequency distribution of ages for the sample. Table 15.3 shows a frequency distribution of ages for a sample of 199 elements. These age values have also been arranged into a curve of ages shown in Figure 15.4.

Figure 15.4 is nothing more than a frequency polygon for these data, and we have merely smoothed out the lines connecting the various frequencies in each interval. It will be observed that the curve for these data is bell-shaped and appears normal in form. Statements that can be made about the unit normal distribution may also apply to this distribution of 199 ages to the extent that this distribution is also approximately normal in form. How do we know whether our distributions of raw scores are normal? Some preliminary computations for the data in Table 15.3 will show that the mean, mode, and median are identical, or 52. The standard deviation for these data, s, is 20.8. Knowing the mean and standard deviation of any distribution that is approximately normally distributed will enable us to determine several important things about the distribution. For

TABLE 15.2 Proportions of Curve Area Cut Off by Various Z Values

Z Value	Proportion of Curve Area from Mean to Z Value
2.26	.4881
−2.26	.4881
−3.14	.4992
.03	.0120
1.45	.4265
1.96	.4750
2.33	.4901
−2.33	.4901

TABLE 15.3 Frequency Distribution of Ages for 199 Elements

Interval	f
5–9	2
10–14	3
15–19	7
20–24	9
25–29	12
30–34	13
35–39	14
40–44	15
45–49	16
50–54	17
55–59	16
60–64	15
65–69	14
70–74	13
75–79	12
80–84	9
85–89	7
90–94	3
95–99	2
	$\Sigma f = 199$

instance, we can determine the approximate proportion of ages that occurs between the mean, 52, and one standard deviation of 20.8 above or below 52. Given an $\overline{X} = 52$ and $s = 20.8$, we will know that .3413 or approximately 34 percent of all 199 ages should probably occur between 52 and 20.8 points above or below 52. We know this because (1) our distribution of ages is approximately normally distributed, and because (2) .3413, or the curve area for the unit normal distribution lies between a $\mu = 0$ and 1σ to either the left or right of μ.

A Z value of $+1.00$ or -1.00 cuts off .3413 of the curve area or approximately 34 percent of it. Therefore, a point in our distribution of ages that is one

FIGURE 15.4 Curve drawn for the data in Table 15.3.

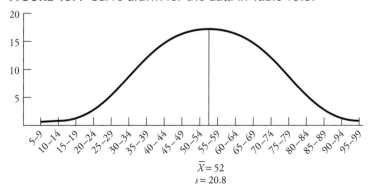

$\overline{X} = 52$
$s = 20.8$

standard deviation (*s*) above or below the mean *X* will cut off and include an identical proportion of .3413 or 34 percent. The point of −1.00 on the unit normal distribution is analogous to the point 31.2 on the distribution of ages, which is 1 standard deviation (1*s*) of 20.8 below the mean of 52 (i.e., 52 − 20.8 = 31.2). The *Z* value of −1.00 is 1σ below the mean of 0, whereas the value, 31.2, is 1 standard deviation of 20.8 (1.00*s*) below the mean of 52. Thus, 31.2 is at the same point along the horizontal axis of its distribution as −1.00σ is along the horizontal axis of the unit normal distribution. If we were to superimpose the two distributions upon one another, these points, −1.00*s* and −1.00σ, would be identical. This statement holds to the extent that our distribution of scores is normal in form or approximates the unit normal distribution with its characteristics.

Referring to the information in Table 15.3, if we know that a given person's age is 75, for instance, we can determine the proportion of persons in the sample who are between the ages of 52 and 75. First, we must convert our age "score" of 75 to a standard score or *Z* value. Once we have made this conversion, we can determine easily the amount of curve area lying between the mean, 52, and the observed age, 75. This is accomplished with the following *Z* formula:

$$Z = (X_i - \overline{X})/s,$$

where X_i = any raw score in a frequency distribution

$\overline{X}$ = the mean of the distribution

s = the standard deviation of the distribution

Given an $\overline{X}$ = 52 and s = 20.8, we compute the *Z* score for our age of 75 as follows:

$$Z = (75 - 52)/20.8$$
$$= 23/20.8$$
$$= 1.11$$

The *Z* value associated with our raw score (age) of 75 is 1.11. Turning to Table A.3, we determine that .3665 of the unit normal curve area lies between 0 (the mean) and a *Z* = 1.11. Thus, nearly 37% of our sample of 199 ages occurs between 52 and 75. In the general case, raw scores for any distribution may be converted to *Z* scores by using the *Z*-score formula above. Once we have converted raw scores to *Z* scores, we can use Table A.3, as a way of knowing about where our raw scores might be located in any distribution.

Comparisons of Standard Scores Using the Unit Normal Distribution

One of the major uses of *Z* scores is to make comparisons of persons of different abilities and skills. Criminologists might wish to compare elementary and secondary school students who either have or have not committed prior delin-

TABLE 15.4 Four Test Scores

Test	Raw Score
A	25
B	3000
C	150
D	15

quent acts. Self-report information can disclose profiles of offending juveniles, even if they have never had direct contacts with police. Different aptitude tests that measure totally different attributes, such as mathematical or verbal skills, can be compared, and educational contrasts between different categories of children may be made. Analyses of scores that reflect different aptitudes and skill levels may enable interventionists to make a difference in children's lives. Perhaps special programs might be devised to assist children to improve in areas in which they appear deficient.

For example, suppose we subjected a single student to a battery of four different aptitude tests. It is assumed that these four aptitude tests have also been administered to large classes of students in the school, although we are now focusing our interest on the performance of a single student. Suppose the students' scores on these four tests, labeled tests A, B, C, and D, are those shown in Table 15.4.

It is apparent from a preliminary examination of these scores that the best score for the student, 3,000, was achieved on test B, while the worst score was received on test D (15). But our preliminary appraisal would be in error. We cannot make such direct comparisons of test scores from different tests, since each test may be quite different from the others in terms of difficulty, conditions of administration, ability level of other students taking the test, the score range, and several other factors. In order to obtain a crude appraisal of our student's test performances, we must convert all four test scores into standard scores or Z scores. But in order to make this conversion, we must first know the means and standard deviations of all four tests. Table 15.5 shows the student's raw scores on tests A, B, C, and D, together with the class means and standard deviations on all four tests. Additional information in Table 15.5 are Z scores that have been calculated for each raw score.

TABLE 15.5 Tests, Raw Scores, Z Scores, Standard Deviations, and Means

Test	Raw Score	Mean	Standard Deviation	Z Score
A	25	20	5	1.00
B	3,000	3,300	300	−1.00
C	150	165	7.5	−2.00
D	15	12	1	3.00

To determine the person's standard scores for the four tests, the Z-score formula presented earlier is used. Using this formula,

$$Z = (X_i - \overline{X})/s$$

we can determine the Z values shown in Table 15.5 as follows:

Test A: $(25 - 20)/5 = 5/5 = 1.00 = Z_1$

Test B: $(3000 - 3300)/300 = -300/300 = -1.00 = Z_2$

Test C: $(150 - 155)/7.5 = -15/7.5 = -2.00 = Z_3$

Test D: $(15 - 12)/1 = 3/1 = 3.00 = Z_4$

Next, we can place each of these Z scores on the unit normal distribution as shown in Figure 15.5. A visual inspection of Figure 15.5 discloses that the student did best on test D, having a standard score (Z score) of 3.00. The student did worst on test C, receiving a standard score (Z score) of −2.00. Thus, the student did best, relative to other class members, on test D, although this test had the smallest raw score of 15. The student's "worst" performance, compared with other students who took the test, occurred on test C. Specifically, the Z score of 3.00 tells us that the raw score of 15 was three standard deviations of 1 above the mean of 12. We can now see, with the other means and standard deviations for comparison, that the score of 3,000 was actually below the mean of its distribution for test B, 3,300, by 1 standard deviation of 300. This raw score of 3,000 received a standard score or Z score of −1.00. Since test C showed that the student's score, 150, was actually 2 standard deviations of 7.5 below the class mean of 155, we might persuade the student to remedy this deficiency by means of a special curriculum or counseling. These test scores are not the only criteria we would use in advising students or diagnosing their weaknesses and strengths. Such diagnoses are more complicated than that. But, at least, these scores are of some assistance in helping us to highlight a person's skill levels and deficiencies.

This is the comparative function served by the unit normal distribution. We may convert any raw scores from any distribution into Z scores for comparative purposes. The unit normal distribution is the common denominator for all distributions of scores that tend to approximate it in form. Additionally, once we have determined Z scores for any set of raw scores, it is possible to determine other interesting information as well. For instance, we will be able to determine the amount of curve area above or below (to the right or left of) given Z values and the amount of curve area lying between two Z values.

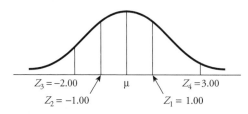

FIGURE 15.5
Unit normal distribution showing four Z scores.

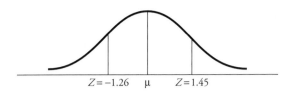

FIGURE 15.6
Unit normal distribution showing two *Z* values.

$Z=-1.26$ μ $Z=1.45$

Determining Curve Area to the Left or Right of a *Z* Value.   Two *Z* values of 1.45 and −1.26 are shown in Figure 15.6. Suppose that we want to know how much curve area lies below (or to the left of) each of these *Z* values. For the *Z* value of 1.45, we first determine the amount of curve area (from Table A.3) between the mean, 0, and a *Z* = 1.45. The amount of curve area between the mean, 0, and the *Z* = 1.45 is equal to .4265. Since we are concerned about all of the curve area lying to the left of a *Z* = 1.45, we must not ignore the entire left half of the curve which contains .5000 of curve area. Remember that the unit normal distribution is divided into two perfectly equal parts of .5000 each. Thus, we should add .5000 to .4265, giving us .9265, the total amount of curve area lying to the left of the *Z* = 1.45. This is the shaded portion of curve area shown in Figure 15.7.

For the *Z* = −1.26, this *Z* value lies to the left of the mean, 0. We want to know how much curve area lies to the left of this *Z* value. Again, we must first determine how much of the curve area lies between the *Z* score of −1.26 and the mean, 0. From Table A.3, we determine that the proportion is .3962. We are now ready to solve this problem. Since .3962 is the known proportion of curve area lying between this point and the mean, 0, and since we know that the total amount of curve area lying to the left of the mean, 0, is .5000 or half of the distribution, we simply solve for the unknown. This means subtracting .3962 from .5000, or .5000 − .3962 = .1038. This is the shaded portion of curve area shown in Figure 15.8.

As additional examples, suppose we are interested in determining the amount of curve area to the right of the same *Z* scores above, *Z* = 1.45 and *Z* = −1.26. These presently unknown areas of the unit normal distribution are shown as shaded portions in Figures 15.9 and 15.10.

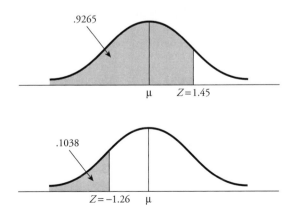

.9265

μ $Z=1.45$

FIGURE 15.7
Unit normal distribution showing the curve area to the left of *Z* = 1.45.

.1038

$Z=-1.26$ μ

FIGURE 15.8
Unit normal distribution showing the curve area to the left of *Z* = −1.26.

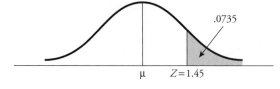

FIGURE 15.9
Unit normal distribution showing the curve area to the right of $Z = 1.45$.

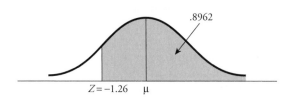

FIGURE 15.10
Unit normal distribution showing the curve area to the right of $Z = -1.26$.

Using our knowledge of the unit normal distribution, we must determine the amount of curve area lying between each of the Z values. This is simple, since these are the same proportions of curve area that we determined earlier, or .4265 between the mean, 0, and a $Z = 1.45$, and .3962 between the mean, 0, and a $Z = -1.26$. In order to find how much curve area lies to the right of a $Z = 1.45$, we subtract the area, .4265 from .5000, or $.5000 - .4265 = .0735$. This is the amount of curve area lying to the right of a $Z = 1.45$. Again, we are taking what we know and solving for the unknown. For the second task of finding the curve area to the right of a $Z = -1.26$, we add .3962 to .5000, the total amount of curve area lying to the right of the mean, 0. This becomes $.5000 + .3962 = .8962$. Thus, about 7 percent of the curve area is found to the right of a $Z = 1.45$, while about 90 percent of the curve area lies to the right of a $Z = -1.26$.

Determining Proportions of Curve Area Between Two Z Values. If we wanted to determine the amount of curve area between two Z values, we would first determine the amount of curve area between each and the mean, 0. Suppose we had the Z values of -1.55 and 1.86 respectively. The amount of curve area included between the mean, 0, and -1.55 is equal to .4394 (from Table A.3). The amount of curve area between the mean, 0, and 1.86 is .4686. Summing these two proportions will give us the total amount of curve area between the two Z scores. This is the shaded portion shown in Figure 15.11, or .9080.

If the two Z scores happen to both occur to the right or left of the mean, 0, we would again determine for each the amount of curve area between them

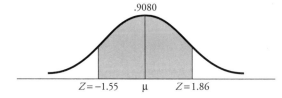

FIGURE 15.11
Unit normal distribution showing the curve area between the Z values -1.55 and 1.86.

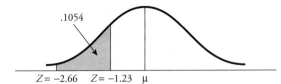

.1054

$Z = -2.66$ $Z = -1.23$ μ

and the mean, 0. Thus, if we had Z scores of -1.23 and -2.66, we would again determine the proportionate amount of curve area between each and the common mean of 0. The Z value, -1.23, cuts off .3907 of curve area, while the Z value, -2.66, cuts off .4961 of curve area. In this case, to find the proportion of scores between the two Z values, simply determine the difference between these proportions. Here, we have .4961 $-$ .3907 $=$ .1054. Almost 11 percent of the curve area occurs between Z scores of -1.23 and -2.66. This is the shaded portion of the unit normal distribution shown in Figure 15.12.

Converting Z Scores into Raw Scores.   What if we are reading a research report and discover that the author has presented only Z scores for samples of elements rather than raw score information? What if we want to know what the sample raw scores happen to be in order to compare them with our own samples of elements? This operation would involve converting Z scores or standard scores back into raw score form.

The conversion of Z scores into raw scores is relatively easy. We might wish to make this conversion if those who read our material are not familiar with standard scores. In order to transform Z scores into raw scores, we must know the original mean, $\overline{X}$, and the original standard deviation, s. With these two pieces of information, any Z score from that distribution may be converted back into its original raw score form. The formula we would use is illustrated as follows:

X_i (raw score) $= \overline{X} + (Z)(s)$
where $\overline{X} =$ the original mean

$s =$ the original standard deviation

$Z =$ the standard score to be transformed into a raw score.

For instance, suppose that one of our sample elements had a Z score of 1.50. If the mean and standard deviation of the distribution where that Z score was obtained were 65 and 4 respectively, we could determine that person's original raw score as follows:

$X_i = 65 + (1.50)(4)$

$= 65 + 6$

$= 71$

The person's original raw score would be 71. If someone else had a Z score of -2.75, we would determine his or her original raw score the same way. The computation would be

$$X_i = 65 + (-2.75)(4)$$
$$= 65 + (-11)$$
$$= 65 - 11$$
$$= 54$$

The person's original raw score is 54. In the second raw score computation, note that we had to subtract the product from the mean of the distribution, since we had a negative Z value associated with the original raw score. This negative Z value meant that the person's raw score occurred below the mean. What if another person's Z score were 0.00? No computation would be necessary, since a Z score of 0.00 lies directly on the mean of the distribution. In this case, if the mean of the original distribution were 65, the raw score would also be 65. This could be figured by inspection.

Standard Scores and Nonnormal Distributions

When investigators can assume normality when comparing different distributions of raw scores, the mean and standard deviation are always used to provide systematic and consistent interpretations of raw scores among distributions. Unfortunately, researchers cannot always assume **normality** for the data they have collected. From time to time, some types of score arrangements are not normal in form. Two kinds of conditions may exist that cause distributions of scores to be nonnormal. These conditions are skewness and kurtosis. **Skewness** refers to score arrangements that "bunch up" to the far left or right of the distribution rather than spreading out in a bell-shaped fashion. **Kurtosis** refers to curve peakedness, with the scores accumulated near the center of the distribution, spread out too thinly, or distributed irregularly so that they yield a bulged appearance. Normal distributions are relatively free of both skewness and kurtosis. The best way to appreciate the meaning of skewness and kurtosis is to look at distributions where they exist.

Figures 15.13 and 15.14 show two types of skewed distributions. Figure 15.13 shows **positive skewness**, while Figure 15.14 shows **negative skew-**

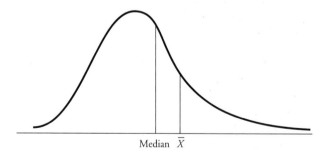

Median $\overline{X}$

FIGURE 15.13
Distribution that is positively skewed.

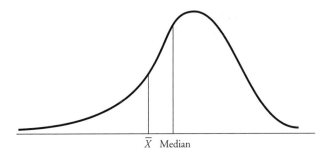

FIGURE 15.14
Distribution that is
negatively skewed.

$\overline{X}$ Median

ness. Note that in Figure 15.13, the scores appear to bunch up toward the left end of the distribution, and the tail of the curve tapers off toward the right. In Figure 15.14, the scores appear to be accumulated toward the right end of the distribution, and the curve tail tapers off toward the left. In Figure 15.13, the mean is larger than the median, while in Figure 15.14, the mean is smaller than the median.

How do we know if any distribution of scores is skewed? Can skewness be measured? Skewness for any distribution may be computed as follows:

$$\text{Skewness} = \frac{(3)(\overline{X} - \text{Mdn})}{s}$$

where $\overline{X}$ = the mean of the distribution

Mdn = the distribution median

s = the distribution standard deviation.

3 = a constant value

If the mean for a distribution were 30, the median were 27, and the standard deviation were 2, skewness for the distribution would be computed as follows:

$$\text{Skewness} = \frac{(3)(30 - 27)}{2} = \frac{(3)(3)}{2} = \frac{9}{2} = +4.50$$

Skewness for this distribution is +4.50. The distribution is positively skewed, and we know that it probably looks much like the distribution shown in Figure 15.13. We know that some amount of skewness exists, since the mean and median are different. But how much skewness is too much skewness? Since perfectly normal distributions have no skewness (the mean and median are identical in the unit normal distribution, since they occur at the same point on the horizontal axis of it), an arbitrary rule of thumb exists that if skewness for any distribution exceeds +1.00 or −1.00, then too much skewness exists for the distribution to be considered normal. If too much skewness exists, then our statements about Z scores and the proportions of curve area they represent are inaccurate. Skewed distributions do not permit accurate use of Table A.3. For example, if we defined two identical distances of 2 standard deviations from the mean of a skewed distribution in opposite directions, the area cut off

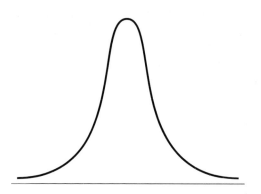

FIGURE 15.15
Leptokurtic distribution.

from the mean to a $Z = -2.00$ would not be identical to the curve area cut off from the mean to a $Z = +2.00$.

Kurtosis refers to curve peakedness. The three types of kurtosis are (1) leptokurtosis, (2) platykurtosis, and (3) mesokurtosis. **Leptokurtic** distributions are tall distributions; **platykurtic** distributions are flat distributions; and **mesokurtic** distributions, although the most normal-appearing of the three, have irregular distributions of frequencies and appear bulgy. These three types of distributions are illustrated in Figures 15.15, 15.16, and 15.17.

As in the case of skewness, any attempt to apply the table of areas of the normal curve, Table A.3, would be unsuccessful and misleading, since these distributions are not normally distributed. Thus, if a researcher calculated the curve area lying 1σ to the left or right of the mean of the unit normal distribution, the result would be .3413 as shown in Table A.3. This is the area cut off by a Z score of + or − 1.00. However, a skewed distribution or one exhibiting substantial kurtosis would not contain .3413 of curve area from the mean to a Z value of + or − 1.00. The curve areas in these nonnormal distributions would be unequal to .3413.

Under certain conditions, distributions may appear to have one type of kurtosis or another, but in fact, they may be normal in form. Thus, we must be careful to distinguish between leptokurtic-appearing, mesokurtic-appearing, and platykurtic-appearing normal distributions and those distributions that are truly leptokurtic, mesokurtic, or platykurtic. The latter distributions are not normal ones, whereas the former distributions might be normal. If researchers suspect that substantial kurtosis exists for any given distribution of scores so that normality may not be assumed, direct tests may be made. Direct counts of raw scores lying between two points in the distribution of scores can determine whether the actual area of the curve matches the tabled area for the unit normal distribution as shown in Table A.3. Thus, the researcher can count the number of scores within one standard deviation on either side of the mean. The total area within a $Z = -1.00$ and a $Z = 1.00$ is .3413 + .3413 = .6826 or about 68 per-

FIGURE 15.16 Platykurtic distribution.

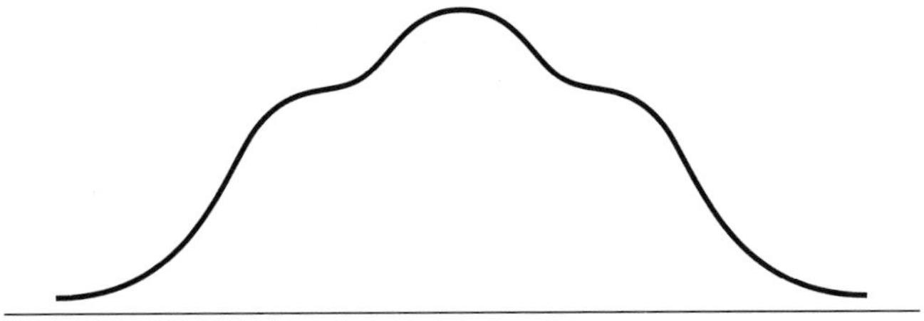

FIGURE 15.17
Mesokurtic distributions.

cent of the total curve area on the unit normal distribution. The researcher's distribution of raw scores should have about 68 percent of all scores within one standard deviation on either side of the actual mean. If the mean is 50 and the standard deviation is 10, then about 68 percent of all scores should occur between 40 and 60, points exactly one standard deviation below and above the mean of 50. You can count the number of scores and see if they represent 68 percent of the scores. Minor departures from 68 percent won't necessarily disqualify the distribution from being designated as normal. However, if there is an appreciable discrepancy, then kurtosis and/or skewness probably exists.

Applying the Normal Curve in Criminological Research.   In research projects in criminal justice and criminology, the unit normal distribution is used for comparing scores taken from different distributions. These scores may be aptitude scores, attitudinal scores, test results involving the effectiveness of rehabilitative or treatment programs, recidivism statistics, or any other measured variable.

Another application of the unit normal distribution is for statistical inference and decision making about hypotheses. In addition to being useful for comparative purposes in educational testing and diagnostic activities, the unit normal distribution serves a probability function. Proportions of curve area can be interpreted as probabilities. Scores that occur within one standard deviation on either side of the mean have a 68 percent chance of occurring within this general area. Thus, the proportions of curve area encompassed by any standard score or Z value can be translated into probabilities. Scores found in the extremes of the distribution (i.e., in the tails to the left or to the right) are less plentiful than scores near the center of the distribution, and therefore there is a much lower probability associated with their occurrence.

For some of the statistical procedures presented in later chapters, a Z value will be the result of a statistical test application. We will evaluate each Z value according to where it is located on the unit normal distribution. A probability will be assigned that will tell us how significant the Z value is within a chance or probability context.

■ DECISION RULES

Whenever statistical tests are made of any hypothesis set, the results of those tests are interpreted by researchers. The results may lead the investigator to believe that the null hypothesis is not true and ought to be rejected. Or the result may indicate that the null hypothesis cannot be rejected. Guiding the investigator's decision making about the outcomes of these statistical tests and how such outcomes should be interpreted are decision rules.

Decision rules consist of a set of conditions specified in advance of statistical tests that define how test outcomes should be properly interpreted. If investigators were to proceed with hypothesis testing without using a set of decision rules, the results would be subject to any interpretation the investigator would care to make. One researcher's interpretation of a test outcome would be just as valid as any other researcher's interpretation of it. This is because no standards would exist to function as objective or impartial arbiters about what is found and how it should be interpreted. Decision rules are employed, therefore, to minimize the subjectivity and guesswork that might otherwise exist. Following the canons of scientific inquiry, researchers are obligated to abide by certain decision rules when judging hypothesis test results or outcomes. Decision rules include the following: (1) the sampling distribution of statistics, (2) the level of significance, and (3) the critical region or region of rejection.

Sampling Distributions of Statistics

All known statistics have a **sampling distribution.** Therefore, all statistics presented thus far, including the mode, median, mean, standard deviation, interquartile range, and range, have sampling distributions. A **sampling distribution of a statistic** is a distribution of all possible values a given statistic may assume when computed for samples of specified sizes drawn from populations of specified sizes. This concept is a very important one and this discussion must be followed carefully.

If an investigator had a population of 300 elements and drew a random sample of 20 elements from that population, this would be only one sample of many samples that could be drawn from that population. We can calculate how many possible samples of a given size could be drawn from a population of a given size by using the following formula:

$$N^n$$

where N = the population size

n = the sample size

Using this formula, given a population size (N) = 300 and a sample size (n) = 20, we would have 300^{20} samples. We can appreciate this better by using a smaller-scale example. Suppose the researcher had a population of 10 and a sample size of 3. Under this condition, how many possible samples of size 3 could be drawn from a population of 10? This is worked out as follows:

$$10^3 = (10)(10)(10) = 1,000 \text{ samples}$$

Thus, 1,000 samples of size 3 could be drawn from a population of 10. Of course, throughout this book we have been discussing sample sizes of several hundred persons taken from populations numbering in the thousands or millions. Imagine how many samples of size 500 could be drawn from a population of 100,000? This would be $100,000^{500}$, or $(100,000)(100,000)(100,000)$ . . ., until 500 products had been obtained. This staggers the imagination to contemplate just how many different samples of 500 could conceivably be drawn from that original population of 100,000!

But returning to our smaller-scale example of drawing all possible samples of size 3 from a population of 10 persons, we know that we would be able to draw 1,000 samples of size 3. Let us assume that for each sample of size 3 drawn from this population of 10, we compute a mean, median, a standard deviation, and a range. Therefore, after we obtain all 1,000 of our samples, we would have 1,000 means, 1,000 medians, 1,000 standard deviations, and 1,000 ranges. Now, if we were to arrange all of these values into frequency distributions, we would have a frequency distribution of 1,000 means, 1,000 medians, 1,000 standard deviations, and 1,000 ranges. Each of these four frequency distributions would be called sampling distributions of these statistics. In other words, the frequency distribution of all 1,000 means we computed would be the sampling distribution of the mean. The frequency distribution of all 1,000 standard deviations we computed would be the sampling distribution of the standard deviation, and so on.

In each of the cases just described, researchers have arranged all observed statistical values into a frequency distribution. The sampling distribution of means is the distribution of all possible values that the mean can be for samples of a specified size (in this case, 3) drawn from a specified population (in this case, 10). The sampling distribution of standard deviations is the distribution of all possible values that the standard deviation can be for samples of a specified size (again, 3) drawn from a specified population (again, 10).

These sampling distributions can be illustrated, especially using a small-scale example, by the following illustration. Suppose we had a population of six probation officers from an intensive supervision probation program and caseloads for each officer. We might designate each of these officers by a different letter, such as A, B, C, D, E, and F. To the right of each probation officer, caseloads are indicated. Caseloads refer to the number of probationers each probation officer supervises. Table 15.6 shows these probation officers and their respective caseloads. Officer A has a caseload of 10, officer B has a caseload of 11, and so on. Also indicated is the population mean, $\mu = 12.5$.

Now, although in the present case we know all of the population values as well as the actual population mean, most of the time in actual research projects

TABLE 15.6 Caseloads for a Population of Six Probation Officers

Officer	Caseload	
A	10	
B	11	
C	12	$\mu = 12.5$
D	13	
E	14	
F	15	

these facts are unknown. The main reason we sample from larger populations is to learn about the characteristics of these populations and to estimate these characteristics without having to study entire populations. In this case, however, our intent is to illustrate how a sampling distribution is constructed and how it appears.

Suppose we wish to draw a sample of size 2 from this population of six officers. Using the earlier formula, the possible numbers of samples of $n = 2$ that could be drawn from a population of $N = 6$ would be N^n or $(6)^2 = 36$ possible samples. Using the different letter combinations from Table 15.6, the following sample combinations may be generated:

AA	BA	CA	DA	EA	FA
AB	BB	CB	DB	EB	FB
AC	BC	CC	DC	EC	FC
AD	BD	CD	DD	ED	FD
AE	BE	CE	DE	EE	FE
AF	BF	CF	DF	EF	FF

After these 36 samples of size 2 have been drawn, the researcher computes all of the sample means. These means would be symbolically portrayed as $\overline{X}_1$, $\overline{X}_2$, and so on, until $\overline{X}_{36}$ is reached. These are illustrated here. Notice that there are letter combinations of AA, BB, CC, DD, EE, and FF. This is possible because of sampling with replacement, in which elements once selected for inclusion in a sample are replaced in the population and may be drawn again. Sampling with replacement permits such samples and includes them in the possible number of different samples of a given size that can be drawn from a population of a given size. Sampling with replacement is a necessary assumption underlying random sampling, since it enables researchers to assume that their population elements have had an equal and an independent chance of being selected. To the far right of these mean symbols are the actual mean values computed for all samples. The smallest mean is $\overline{X}_1 = 10.0$, while the largest mean is $\overline{X}_{36} = 15.0$.

$\overline{X}_1$	$\overline{X}_2$	$\overline{X}_3$	$\overline{X}_4$	$\overline{X}_5$	$\overline{X}_6$	10.0	10.5	11.0	11.5	12.0	12.5
$\overline{X}_7$	$\overline{X}_8$	$\overline{X}_9$	$\overline{X}_{10}$	$\overline{X}_{11}$	$\overline{X}_{12}$	10.5	11.0	11.5	12.0	12.5	13.0
$\overline{X}_{13}$	$\overline{X}_{14}$	$\overline{X}_{15}$	$\overline{X}_{16}$	$\overline{X}_{17}$	$\overline{X}_{18}$	11.0	11.5	12.0	12.5	13.0	13.5
$\overline{X}_{19}$	$\overline{X}_{20}$	$\overline{X}_{21}$	$\overline{X}_{22}$	$\overline{X}_{23}$	$\overline{X}_{24}$	11.5	12.0	12.5	13.0	13.5	14.0
$\overline{X}_{25}$	$\overline{X}_{26}$	$\overline{X}_{27}$	$\overline{X}_{28}$	$\overline{X}_{29}$	$\overline{X}_{30}$	12.0	12.5	13.0	13.5	14.0	14.5
$\overline{X}_{31}$	$\overline{X}_{32}$	$\overline{X}_{33}$	$\overline{X}_{34}$	$\overline{X}_{35}$	$\overline{X}_{36}$	12.5	13.0	13.5	14.0	14.5	15.0

Next, the researcher constructs a simple frequency distribution of these sample means as shown in Table 15.7. The resulting frequency distribution of sample means is called the sampling distribution of the mean for samples of size 2 drawn from a population of size 6. It is possible for the researcher to determine any other statistic desired for these samples of size 2 and arrange those statistical values obtained into a similar frequency distribution of them. In these cases, the researcher would have sampling distributions of whatever statistic has been

TABLE 15.7 Sampling Distribution of $\bar{X}$'s for Samples of Size 2 from a Population of Size 6

Observed $\bar{X}$'s	f	Proportion	Probability
10.0	x	$\frac{1}{36}$	0.03
10.5	x x	$\frac{2}{36}$	0.06
11.0	x x x	$\frac{3}{36}$	0.08
11.5	x x x x	$\frac{4}{36}$	0.11
12.0	x x x x x	$\frac{5}{36}$	0.14
12.5	x x x x x x	$\frac{6}{36}$	0.16
13.0	x x x x x	$\frac{5}{36}$	0.14
13.5	x x x x	$\frac{4}{36}$	0.11
14.0	x x x	$\frac{3}{36}$	0.08
14.5	x x	$\frac{2}{36}$	0.06
15.0	x	$\frac{1}{36}$	0.03
	$\Sigma f = 36$	$\frac{36}{36}$ or 1.00	1.00

computed, such as "the sampling distribution of the standard deviation," "the sampling distribution of the median," or "the sampling distribution of the mode."

The sampling distribution of the mean shown in Table 15.7 has several desirable properties. For one thing, this distribution is approximately normal in form, in that it resembles the unit normal distribution. In the example shown in Table 15.7, these frequencies have been plotted into a curve shown in Figure 15.18. Although in this small-scale example the smoothed curve is more triangular than normal, this curve actually becomes smoother, more bell-shaped, and approaches normality as larger sample sizes are drawn from larger population bases.

Generally, whenever one's sample size is greater than 30, the normality approximation is quite close. In fact, the mean is the only statistic presented in this book that has a sampling distribution that is normal in form or approximates the unit normal distribution. This means that the sampling distributions of the standard deviation, mode, median, variance, or average deviation are not normal in form.

Another characteristic of the sampling distribution of means is that its mean or average (in this case, the average of all 36 sample means) is equal to the original population mean, μ. Notice in Table 15.6 that the probation officer population mean caseload = 12.5. Computing a mean for the means shown in Table 15.7 also yields a mean = 12.5. Thus, it can be said generally that the mean of the sampling distribution of the means is equal to the population mean. This is an important statement. No other statistic we have presented can make this claim. For example, the mean of the sampling distribution of standard deviations is not equal to the population standard deviation. The mean of the sampling distribution of sample modes is not equal to the population mode.

Whenever a statistic has a sampling distribution whose mean (expected value) is equal to the parameter it is designed to estimate, we say that the statis-

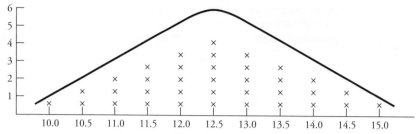

FIGURE 15.18 Curve drawn for the data presented in Table 15.7.

tic is an **unbiased estimate** of its population parameter. The statistic, the mean, is an unbiased estimate of the population parameter, μ, because the mean has a sampling distribution whose mean is equal to the population mean. However, the standard deviation is not an unbiased estimate, since it has a sampling distribution whose **expected value** (mean) is not equal to the population standard deviation. In fact, most sample standard deviations are smaller than the expected value of the sampling distribution of standard deviations. This is because the sampling distribution of the standard deviations is positively skewed. The standard deviation as a **biased estimator** of the population standard deviation consistently underestimates it.

The sampling distribution of the sample means has two parameters. It has a mean and a standard deviation. But because we are discussing sampling distributions of statistics and not simply sample distributions of raw scores, we give special names to these parameters. These are called the expected value and **standard error,** respectively. Thus, expected values are means of sampling distributions of statistics. **Standard errors of statistics** are standard deviations of sampling distributions of statistics. Therefore, whenever you see terms such as *expected value* or *standard errors,* you know that sampling distributions of statistics are being discussed.

Looking at these terms another way, the expected value of the mean is the mean of the sampling distribution of sample means. The expected value of the standard deviation is the mean of the sampling distribution of sample standard deviations, and so on. The expected value of the sampling distribution of means is simply equal to μ, the same notation we use to denote the population mean.

Standard error terms are somewhat more complicated to define. As we have seen, standard errors are standard deviations of sampling distributions of statistics. The **standard error of the mean,** $s_{\bar{x}}$, is the standard deviation of the sampling distribution of sample standard deviations. In order to compute the standard error of the mean, $s_{\bar{x}}$, we may use the following formula:*

---

*Sometimes, the standard error of the mean is described in statistics books as $\sigma_{\bar{x}}$. This particular expression assumes that we somehow have a knowledge of the actual population standard deviation. Thus, we might be able to compute $\sigma_{\bar{x}}$ by using the formula, $\sigma/\sqrt{N}$ where σ is the known population standard deviation and N is the sample size. However, since we are attempting to estimate these values by using sample statistics, it is unlikely that we will ever know the population standard deviation and not know the population mean we are attempting to estimate. Thus, for the sake of reality, we will use only the symbol, $s_{\bar{x}}$.

$$s_{\bar{x}} = \frac{s}{\sqrt{n-1}}$$

where s = the sample standard deviation

n = the sample size

In the illustration of six probation officers, if we had the sample of two elements, A and F, for example, with caseloads of 10 and 15, respectively, the resulting $s_{\bar{x}}$ would be equal to 2.5, as an example. (You can prove this as an exercise.)

The sampling distribution of sample means is therefore normal in form and has the parameters μ and $s_{\bar{x}}$. In the general case, it may be illustrated by Figure 15.19. Note the two parameters, μ and $s_{\bar{x}}$. Almost always, the sampling distribution of means is bell-shaped, symmetrical, and approximates the unit normal distribution. It is also a **probability distribution.** Referring to Table 15.7, for example, the observed mean of 10.0 occurs once in 36 times. The observed mean of 12 occurs five times out of 36 times. These occurrences of various means have been illustrated as proportions to the center right, and ultimately, as probabilities to the far right. These probability values are the likelihoods that samples of size 2 will be drawn, having those means associated with them. Thus, the probability of drawing a random sample of size 2 (from that original population of size 6) with a mean = 10.0 is .03 or 3 times in 100 times. The probability of drawing a random sample of size 2 (from that original population of size 6) with a mean = 12.5 is .15 or 15 times in 100 times.

Continuing to refer to Table 15.7, what would be the probability of drawing a sample of size 2 from that original population of 6, where the mean would be either 10.0, 10.5, or 11.0? To answer this question, we would simply sum the individual probabilities associated with the occurrence of each value. In this case, .03 + .06 + .08 = .17. The probability of getting a sample of size 2 from that population of 6, where the mean would be either 10, 10.5, or 11 would be 17 times in 100 times or 17 percent. Another way of saying this would be that the odds of getting a 10, 10.5, or an 11 as a mean for a sample of size 2 drawn from that population of size 6 would be 17 times in 100.

Notice that the means occurring most frequently in the distribution shown in Table 15.7 are those at or near the population mean of 12.5. This is called the area of high probability. If you were a betting person, you would expect that in any random draw of 2 elements from the original population of 6, you would probably get a mean whose value was somewhere close to the population mean of 12.5, rather than draw one of those extreme samples with a mean of either 10 or 15. Those means in the tails of the distribution occur in low probability areas.

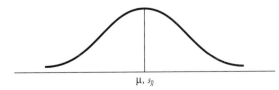

$\mu, s_{\bar{x}}$

FIGURE 15.19
Sampling distribution of means.

Up to now, we have been dealing with a small-scale example, a situation in which we know all about the population characteristics as well as the values of all possible statistics for samples of a given size that could be drawn from it. Fine. But what about the real world? When are we ever going to know all about the population and all possible samples that could be drawn from it? We will never know, unless of course we study the entire population of elements. The fact is, we will draw only one sample in most of our research investigations, not 36 or 10,000 of them, and we will have absolutely no idea of whether our sample mean is close to or far away from the population mean or the expected value of the sampling distribution of means.

But at this point, we may take advantage of what we have learned about the unit normal distribution and apply it to our sampling distribution of sample means. What have we learned? First, a table exists showing that the unit normal distribution has standard Z scores that cut off certain proportions of curve area. For instance, we know that within 1 standard deviation, σ, on either side of the mean, μ, is located .3413 of curve area on the unit normal distribution. Since our sampling distribution of means is also normal in form, let's superimpose it over the unit normal distribution and see what happens. Figure 15.20 shows our sampling distribution of sample means superimposed over a unit normal distribution. However, we have substituted the standard error of the mean, $s_{\bar{x}}$, for the standard deviation term, σ, on the unit normal distribution.

The standard error of the mean functions precisely the same way on the sampling distribution of the mean as the standard deviation does on the unit normal distribution. Whereas the standard deviation on the unit normal distribution cuts off a portion of curve area that contains a proportion of raw scores, the standard error of the mean cuts off curve area on the sampling distribution of means that contains a proportion of all sample means. In the case of the sampling distribution of the mean, if we move one standard error of the mean to the left and to the right of the population mean, μ, we will cut off .3413 + .3413 = .6826 or about 68 percent of all sample means. The terms $-1.00s_{\bar{x}}$ and $+1.00s_{\bar{x}}$ on the sampling distribution of the means are analogous to -1.00σ and $+1.00\sigma$ on the unit normal distribution. This fact underscores the similarity between the unit normal distribution and the sampling distribution of means. It also is indicative of why researchers often prefer to compute means in their statistical inference and estimation work rather than use other statistics. The fact that the unit normal distribution principles can apply to sampling distributions of means supplies researchers with an important advantage which they would not have if other sampling distributions of statistics were used.

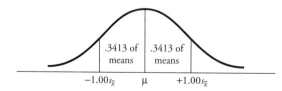

FIGURE 15.20
Sampling distribution of means superimposed over unit normal distribution.

Levels of Significance

As a second decision rule, the **level of significance** is the probability a researcher assigns to the decision made about any hypotheses tested. The researcher is interested in rejecting null hypotheses and supporting research hypotheses. Research hypotheses have usually been derived from theoretical schemes that are believed to be reasonably sound explanations of phenomena. If research hypotheses are supported or confirmed by observed data, then there is a good chance that the theories from which those hypotheses were derived are also confirmed or supported by the researcher's findings. But as we have seen in an earlier discussion, it is conventional to test null hypotheses directly and to infer support or lack of support for some alternative research hypothesis as the result of rejecting or failing to reject some null hypothesis counterpart. The probability of being wrong, P, can only be increased or decreased. It can never be eliminated completely.

Type I and Type II Errors and Hypothesis Tests

Table 15.8 provides a more complete picture of statistical decision making and the probable implications of these decisions for hypothesis tests. We always make the assumption that the null hypotheses being tested are potentially both true or false. We must make this assumption, since we never know absolutely that our collected data or samples are perfectly representative of their populations or the phenomena we are investigating. The investigations we usually conduct are simply single instances of tests of theories. We lack the certainty of knowing that our particular research represents a true picture of reality. Therefore, a probability must always exist that any hypotheses we test may or may not be true, regardless of the outcomes of such hypothesis tests and the decisions we make about those outcomes.

If we decide on the basis of collected data that the null hypothesis we are testing should be rejected, there is always some likelihood that we are wrong in our decision. This is one source of error known as **Type I error** or **Alpha error** (α), shown in Table 15.8. Therefore, Type I error is the probability of rejecting a null hypothesis when it is true and should not be rejected. This is also the level

TABLE 15.8 Type I and Type II in Statistical Decision-making Situations

Decision is to:	H_0 is: True	H_0 is: False
Reject H_0	Type 1 error, α	$1 - \beta$
Fail to reject H_0	$1 - \alpha$	Type II error, β

of significance at which our hypotheses are tested, or the P or probability we have designated.

A second type of error exists as well. This is known as **Type II error**, or **Beta error (β).** What if we test the null hypothesis and fail to reject it? What if it is false and ought to be rejected? In this case, we have committed the error of failing to reject a false hypothesis. Type II or Beta error is the probability of failing to reject the null hypothesis when it is false and ought to be rejected. The computation of Type II error is complicated and beyond the scope of this text. Nevertheless, we can consider its relevance for hypothesis-testing.

Our objective is to minimize both Type I and Type II errors whenever we test hypotheses. We can minimize Type I error simply by reducing the level of significance to a smaller value, from .05 to .01. But when we do this, we influence the amount of Type II error we will incur. Usually, whenever Type I error is lowered, Type II error is raised. There is not a perfect one-to-one relationship between these types of error, however. Type II error is only indirectly influenced by Type I error. But the general nature of this influence is to increase Type II error whenever Type I error is lowered.

The conventional significance levels of .05 and .01 have been selected by many researchers because they offer reasonable amounts of error (Type I error) and keep Type II error to a minimum. However, we can influence Type II error another way besides changing the amount of Type I error. We can increase our sample size. Generally, as our sample sizes are increased, the amount of Type II error decreases, regardless of what our **significance level** happens to be. Sample sizes of 500 have less Type II error associated with them than samples of size 50. This occurs because of the amount of sampling error involved in our research projects. Usually, larger N's have smaller sampling error, and smaller sampling error usually means less Type II error.

An examination of Table 15.8 also shows $1 - \alpha$ values and $1 - \beta$ values. These are probabilities we wish to maximize in our research work. The probability, $1 - \alpha$, is the probability of failing to reject the null hypothesis when it is true and should not be rejected. The probability, $1 - \beta$, is the probability of rejecting the null hypothesis whenever it is false and ought to be rejected. $1 - \beta$ is also known as the measure of the power of any statistical test. The power of a statistical test is the ability of the test to reject false null hypotheses. It makes sense that if we can reduce Type II or β error by increasing our sample size, then we can also increase accordingly the power of any statistical test by using precisely the same strategy. This follows as the result of the β error/$1 - \beta$ error relation. Decreases in one probability will result in increases in the other probability. The **power of tests** is often used as a basis for selecting certain tests over others. When data are analyzed, several statistical tests might be applicable. However, each test differs regarding its power to reject false null hypotheses. Thus, among other things, researchers usually attempt to use the most powerful statistical procedures when testing hypotheses. However, given the many circumstances that accompany hypothesis testing, other considerations may be more important than test power (e.g., the level of measurement assumed, the type of sample, the sample size, and the arrangement of data or how they are presented).

Regions of Rejection in Hypothesis Tests

A third decision rule is the specification of a **critical region** or **region of rejection,** which is an area on the sampling distribution of sample means. The sampling distribution of means is used here because our hypothesis test deals with observed sample means; other sampling distributions of statistics would be used if other sample statistics were used in hypothesis tests. The area designated as the critical region on our sampling distribution of means is determined directly by our choice of the level of significance for hypothesis tests. If we have selected the .05 level of significance (also known as $\alpha = .05$ or the amount of Type I error), then 5 percent of the sampling distribution of means will comprise the critical region. If the .01 level of significance has been chosen, then 1 percent of the sampling distribution of means will make up the critical region or region of rejection.

These critical regions or regions of rejection are located in the "tails" or extremes of sampling distributions. Consider the following hypothesis set as an illustration of how we would identify critical regions on the sampling distribution of means:

$$H_0: \mu = 75$$
$$H_1: \mu \neq 75$$
$$P \leq .05 \text{ (also, } \alpha = .05)$$

H_0, the null hypothesis, says that the population mean is equal to 75. The research hypothesis, H_1, says that the population mean is not equal to 75. The level of significance is set at .05. Here, the mean of 75 is actually a guess, or more accurately, our estimate of the population mean, μ. Since the mean of the sampling distribution of means (the expected value) is also equal to μ, H_0 is also specifying that the expected value of the mean is equal to 75. Figure 15.21 shows a sampling distribution of sample means with our guessed or estimated $\mu = 75$ at its center as illustrated. Interestingly, we do not need to know the value of all sample means to construct our sampling distribution of means. We know that in most cases it will be normal in form.

An area on the sampling distribution of means will be designated as the critical region. We know that 5 percent of the area of this distribution will be set aside as the critical region. This is because we set the significance level at .05. We also know that the area will be located in either one or both tails of the distribution. Notice that the null hypothesis says that the population mean is equal to 75, and that our research hypothesis is that the population mean is not equal to 75. Thus, we conceivably could reject the null hypothesis by finding a sample

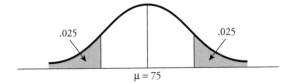

.025   .025

$\mu = 75$

FIGURE 15.21
Sampling distribution of means showing critical regions.

mean that is substantially higher or lower than 75. Since we are not concerned about the direction of the departure of our sample mean from the hypothesized population mean, we will establish critical regions in both tails of the distribution to the far left and far right. This is easily accomplished by halving our level of significance, .05, and placing each half, .025, in both of the extreme tails. This has been done in Figure 15.21. These shaded areas that contain .025 each of the total amount of curve area are our critical regions or regions of rejection. If we find that our sample mean is in either of these shaded areas, we will reject the null hypothesis and conclude, with some amount of error (Type I error), that the population mean is not equal to 75. This is why these regions are called "regions of rejection," because they result in rejecting null hypotheses. Any sample mean occurring in either of these regions is considered significantly different from the hypothesized μ value.

But how do we know whether our observed sample mean is significantly different from the hypothesized μ value? When do we know whether our observed sample means lie in the critical regions of sampling distributions we have specified? Again, we will use our knowledge of the unit normal distribution to answer these questions. We will proceed systematically with a hypothetical research problem to illustrate the solution to our apparent dilemma.

Suppose researchers are conducting a study of stress among correctional officers and are specifically interested in the influence of intervention methods whereby stress can be reduced. In this hypothetical situation, researchers have identified a population of correctional officers in a large Midwestern state, where a popular stress index has been administered to officers on an annual basis. During the previous year, correctional officers in the state were exposed to an educational program designed to equip them with coping strategies to combat stress. The educational program, a three-week course, is highly experimental, and no previous information is available about it and whether it has been found effective in other settings. Because the researchers have access to previously published reports about all state correctional officers and their stress levels for previous years, they know that the stress level, as measured by the popular stress index, has averaged about 100 for the population. Believing that the educational experience will change stress levels among officers for the current year, the researchers decide to draw a random sample of current officers who have had the educational course in order to see whether there are significant differences in their stress levels compared with previous years. The researchers decide to test the following hypothesis set:

$H_0: \mu = 100$

$H_1: \mu \neq 100$

$P \leq .05$

The research hypothesis says that the mean stress level for correctional officers will not be equal to 100. The null hypothesis, therefore, is that the average stress level for officers will be equal to 100. The level of significance used for this hypothesis test is .05. Suppose that the researcher obtains a random sample of 50 correctional officers from the state roster and calculates the average stress score for the sample. In this case, suppose the sample mean, $\bar{X}$, is 108. The question to be answered is whether 108 is significantly different from the hypothesized μ of 100. We know that 108 is different from 100. But is 108 significantly different from 100 so that it lies in the region of rejection on the sampling distribution of the sample means?

A sampling distribution of means is constructed by the researcher. The hypothesized μ under H_0 is supplied and critical regions for the distribution indicated. These regions are shown in Figure 15.22. In order to determine whether our observed mean of 108 lies in either of the rejection regions of this distribution, we must assign 108 a Z score. Also, we must assign Z values to those points along the horizontal axis of the sampling distribution of means that identify the critical regions of it.

First, each of the critical regions of our sampling distribution of means contain .025 of curve area, or one half of .05, the level of significance chosen. Since the unit normal distribution is also approximated by this sampling distribution, we may apply what we have learned about it to solve this particular part of our problem. The question becomes, what Z value cuts off a proportion of curve area from the mean to some point to the left or right of the mean, that leaves 2.5 percent of the curve area in the tails of the distribution? We know that 50 percent or .5000 of the curve area of the unit normal distribution is found on either side of the mean of it. Therefore, if we know that 2.5 percent or .0250 of curve area lies in either tail, then .4750 (.5000 − .0250 = .4750) is the amount of curve area between the mean, 0, and those particular points to the left and right of μ. We can examine Table A.3 of Appendix A, page 624, and find a proportion in the body of the table that corresponds most closely to .4750. In this case, we find .4750 exactly. We note the Z value that intersects this proportion and determine it is 1.96. Therefore, our Z values corresponding to the critical values along the horizontal axis of our unit normal distribution are ± 1.96. In other words, on the unit normal distribution, we would move 1.96σ's of 1 to reach a point to the left and right of μ = 0 that would cut off .4750 of the curve area, leaving .0250 in each tail. On the sampling distribution of sample means, we would move along the horizontal axis of the distribution in terms of standard error of the mean units. Thus, moving ± 1.96$s_{\bar{x}}$'s would define points to the left and right of our μ = 100 that mark off the two critical regions. These points are illustrated in Figure 15.22, and the shaded areas are the two critical regions. Also, these points are referred to as critical values of Z, since they identify critical regions of sampling distributions.

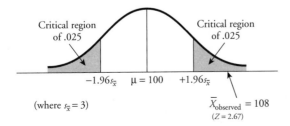

FIGURE 15.22
Sampling distribution of means showing critical values.

Assigning our observed mean of 108, a Z value requires that we have a knowledge of the value of the standard error of the mean. Assume that we have already determined the sample standard deviation, s, and that $s = 21$. With an $s = 21$ and an $n = 50$, the standard error of the mean, $s_{\bar{x}}$, is equal to:

$$s_{\bar{x}} = \frac{s}{\sqrt{n-1}}$$

$$= \frac{21}{\sqrt{50-1}}$$

$$= \frac{21}{\sqrt{49}}$$

$$= \frac{21}{7}$$

$$= 3$$

The $s_{\bar{x}} = 3$. Using this standard error term, we can convert our observed mean of 108 into a Z value by using a formula similar to the one used to convert raw scores into Z scores. In this case, we can give our observed sample mean a Z score as follows:

$$Z = \frac{\overline{X}_{obs} - \mu}{s_{\bar{x}}}$$

where $\overline{X}_{obs}$ = observed sample mean

μ = hypothesized population mean

$s_{\bar{x}}$ = standard error of the mean

Using this information, the Z value for our observed mean of 108 becomes:

$$Z = \frac{108 - 100}{3}$$

$$= \frac{8}{3}$$

$$= +2.67$$

The Z value associated with our observed mean of 108 is 2.67. This is also known as our observed value of Z. Since this Z value of 2.67 equals or exceeds the absolute critical value of Z, ± 1.96, we may reject the null hypothesis and support the research hypothesis that the population mean is different from 100. Of course, there is a 5 percent chance that we are wrong in making this conclusion, because .05 was our chosen level of significance (Type I error).

Generally, the values of Z that identify critical regions on sampling distributions are called critical values of Z. Any time an observed Z value (associated with an observed $\overline{X}$ value) equals or exceeds the critical value of Z (as established by the level of significance or α), the null hypothesis being tested can be rejected at the level of significance indicated. The amount of error we incur in this decision is equal to or smaller than the level of significance we originally selected.

The foregoing problem was solved by translating our observed mean into a Z value and comparing that Z value with a critical value of Z established to identify the critical regions on the sampling distribution of means. We can also solve this problem by translating critical values of Z into a form that can be compared directly with our observed mean of 108. For instance, the critical values of Z for the .05 level of significance in the earlier problem were -1.96 and $+1.96$ respectively. These Z values are a given distance from the hypothesized μ value of 100. Specifically, these points are 1.96 standard errors of the mean above and below the hypothesized mean of 100. If our standard error of the mean $= 3$, then these points are $(1.96)(3)$ above and below 100. Thus, if $s_{\bar{x}} = 3$, then $100 \pm (1.96)(3) = 100 +$ or $- 5.88$, or 94.12 and 105.88. The value, 94.12, is 1.96 standard errors of the mean (of 3) below 100, while 105.88 is 1.96 standard errors of the mean (of 3) above 100. Does our observed mean of 108 fall below 94.12 or above 105.88? Yes. In the general case, the following formula may be used to identify these critical points:

$$\mu \pm (s_{\bar{x}})(Z)$$

where μ = hypothesized population mean under H_0

$s_{\bar{x}}$ = standard error of the mean

Z = critical value of Z identifying critical regions

This example involved a prediction of stress levels of correctional officers, for which the researchers were not concerned about the direction of difference between the observed sample mean and the hypothesized population mean. This situation is called a two-tailed hypothesis test, since two tails of the sampling distribution of the mean are involved as critical regions. The two-tailed nature of the statistical test was made, in large part, because the educational program these researchers studied was a highly experimental one. No one could anticipate whether it would have negative or positive results. Thus, simple differences were predicted. What if these researchers believed that the educational program would reduce stress? Perhaps the program had been used previously by other states as a part of their program of correctional officer training. Under this circumstance, and anticipating that the educational program might actually reduce officer stress levels, these researchers might make a one-tailed or directional prediction instead of a two-tailed, nondirectional one. An example of a one-tailed test application follows.

Suppose that all information from the original problem is the same in this case, except that these researchers observe a sample mean of 90 instead of 108 for these 50 officers. Prior to drawing the sample of officers, however, these researchers construct the following hypothesis set:

$H_0: \mu \geq 100$

$H_1: \mu < 100$

$P \leq .05$

Notice in this hypothesis set that the notation is different regarding the prediction made about μ. In this case, the null hypothesis says that "the population mean is equal to or larger than 100," while the research hypothesis says that "the population mean is less than 100." Because this hypothesis set indicates the direction of difference expected, it is a one-tailed test rather than a two-tailed one. We still have the .05 level of significance as our P, only this time, instead of halving this value, we will place all of it in one tail of the curve or the other. Which tail of the sampling distribution will contain the critical region in a one-tailed test situation? Our H_1 will answer this question. Always look at the research hypothesis to ascertain which tail of the curve will be used for the critical region, whenever a one-tailed test of a hypothesis is being made. In this case, the research hypothesis says that the population mean will be "less than 100," and so we will place all 5 percent of the level of significance in the left tail of the sampling distribution. This is illustrated in Figure 15.23.

Again, we place our hypothesized μ of 100 on the sampling distribution of means as shown in Figure 15.23. However, this time we are dealing with only one tail of the curve—the left tail. Notice in Figure 15.23 that .05 of the curve area occurs in the shaded area or critical region. We can again apply some of our knowledge about the unit normal distribution to solve our problem. We know that 50 percent or .5000 of curve area on the unit normal distribution lies to the left of the mean of 0, and that .0500 remains in the left tail (the shaded portion from Figure 15.23). Thus, from the mean of the unit normal distribution to this point cuts off .5000 − .0500 = .4500 of curve area. Looking at Table A.3 of Appendix A, page 624, we are interested in the Z value that cuts off .4500 of curve area, leaving .0500 in the left tail of the curve. We attempt to find the closest proportion to .4500. This presents us with an instructive problem here. Notice in the body of Table A.3 that there is no .4500. However, two proportions are found that are identical distances from .4500. We find .4495 and .4505. These are associated with Z values of 1.64 and 1.65 respectively. Which one should we choose? When we are the same distance from the desired proportion we are seeking in Table A.3, always select the Z value that ends in an even digit. Again, this is an arbitrary selection, but it will make your answers correspond with various normal curve exercises at chapter ends. In this case, we will pick the Z value associated with .4495, since it is 1.64, an even Z value.

In Figure 15.23, the critical value of Z, −1.64, has been located to the left of the mean of 100. The Z value carries a minus (−) sign since the Z value is to the left of or below μ. Next, we must assign a Z value to our observed mean =

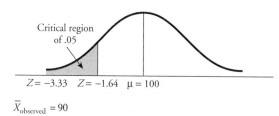

$Z = -3.33$ $Z = -1.64$ $\mu = 100$

$\bar{X}_{observed} = 90$

FIGURE 15.23
Sampling distribution for one-tailed test.

90. In this case, we will use the same Z score formula as in our earlier two-tailed problem:

$$Z = (90 - 100)/3 = -10/3 = -3.33$$

Our observed Z value is -3.33. If the critical value of Z, -1.64, is equalled or exceeded by our observed Z value, then we may reject the null hypothesis and support the research hypothesis, that the population mean is less than 100. Clearly, -3.33 is to the left of -1.64, and we may say that 90 is significantly different from 100. We run a 5 percent risk of being wrong in making this statement, according to the significance level we have used.

Again, we may convert our critical Z value into a form that will enable us to compare it directly with the observed mean of 90. Our critical Z value is -1.64, which means that it is 1.64 standard errors of the mean below the hypothesized μ of 100. If our "standard error of the mean" term is 3, then the critical region is 1.64 of these 3's below 100. Accordingly, $(1.64)(3) = 4.92$. Then, $100 - 4.92 = 95.08$. The critical value (expressed in terms similar to mean values) is 95.08. Is our observed mean of 90 equal to or smaller than 95.08? Obviously it is smaller. Therefore, there are two ways of resolving this problem and testing our hypotheses.

All hypothesis tests that utilize the signs, "less than" ($<$) or "greater than" ($>$) are directional or one-tailed tests. All hypothesis tests that use the signs "equal to" ($=$) or "not equal to" ($\neq$) are two-tailed or nondirectional tests. In all two-tailed tests, the critical region is dispersed evenly in both tails of the sampling distribution. In one-tailed tests, the critical region is determined by the direction predicted under the research hypothesis. If the research hypothesis uses "greater than," then the right tail of the sampling distribution will contain the critical region. If the research hypothesis uses "less than," then the left tail of the curve contains the critical region.

Sample Size Considerations

Increasing sample size through any probability sampling procedure generally decreases the amount of sampling error incurred. In turn, the amount of statistical test power increases, and Beta error or Type II error is reduced. Chapter 16 discusses statistical tests of significance. The significance of any observed numerical value associated with any statistical test is, in part, a function of the sample size. Generally, the larger the sample size, the more significant the findings will be statistically. Thus, it will be important for researchers to distinguish between statistical significance and substantive significance or "practical" significance.

It is entirely possible that if the sample sizes are large enough, all reported statistical values will be significant, at least in a probabilistic sense. Therefore, we should not be overly impressed with large sample sizes and lengthy discussions of their statistical significance. The sheer magnitude of samples will cause significance to occur, although it will not be that meaningful. The statement "What we have observed is statistically significant, but it doesn't mean anything" applies here. We must evaluate both the statistical significance of whatever we find and the practical significance our findings have for social applications.

Sample-size considerations are relevant for the present discussion of sampling distributions of statistics, since larger sample sizes decrease the size of standard errors of means. Since standard errors of means are the units of measurement along the horizontal axes of sampling distributions of means, the significance of observed means is evaluated according to how many standard errors of the mean they are apart from hypothesized means. The larger the sample, the smaller the standard error of the mean, and the more "significant" the difference between the observed and hypothesized means.

In our previous examples, in which population means of 100 were hypothesized regarding stress levels of correctional officers, observed means of 90 and 108 were used. In each of these cases, reported Z values associated with these means were considered significantly different from the hypothesized population means. If our sample sizes were inflated from 50 to 50 million, as an exaggerated illustration, then observed means of 100.1 or 99.9 would be significantly different from the hypothesized mean of 100 as well. However, we wouldn't pay much attention to these negligible differences. Again, we might observe statistical significance associated with our results, but it may not mean anything of any practical significance.

■ KEY TERMS

Alpha error (α)	Positive skewness
Asymptotic property	Power of tests
Beta error (β)	Probability distribution
Biased estimator	Region of rejection
Critical region	Sampling distribution
Decision rules	Sampling distribution of a statistic
Expected value	Significance level
Kurtosis	Skewness
Leptokurtic	Standard error
Leptokurtosis	Standard error of the mean
Level of significance	Standard errors of statistics
Mesokurtic	Standard normal distribution
Mesokurtosis	Standard values or standard score
Negative skewness	Type I error
Normal distribution	Type II error
Normality	Unbiased estimate
Platykurtic	Unit normal distribution
Platykurtosis	Z scores, or Z values

■ QUESTIONS FOR REVIEW AND PROBLEMS TO SOLVE

1. Determine the proportion of curve area lying to the right of the following Z values:

   (a) 1.45   (b) −2.33   (c) 0.00
   (d) −.40   (e) 1.99   (f) 1.00

2. Determine the proportion of curve area lying between the following pairs of Z values:

   (a) −1.95 and −1.26   (b) −1.66 and 1.66
   (c) 2.11 and .04   (d) 2.33 and 2.44

3. Convert the following raw scores to Z scores, where $\overline{X} = 115$ and the standard deviation = 10:

   (a) 156   (b) 115   (c) 100   (d) 85

4. Convert the following Z scores to raw scores, where $\overline{X} = 220$ and $s = 15$:

   (a) −5.55   (b) 1.44   (c) 3.11   (d) .00

5. Determine the proportion of curve area lying to the left of the following Z values:

   (a) .32   (b) −2.18   (c) .99
   (d) −.03   (e) 1.11   (f) 2.23
   (g) −.81   (h) 1.00

6. Determine the raw score associated with each of the following Z values, given an $\overline{X} = 40$ and an $s = 4.2$ (round your raw scores to the nearest whole number):

   (a) −1.09   (b) .11   (c) .99
   (d) −6.00   (e) 0.00   (f) −2.26

7. Determine the amount of curve area lying between the following Z values:

   (a) .26 and 1.21   (b) 1.09 and −2.18
   (c) .00 and 1.00   (d) 1.45 and −1.02
   (e) 2.32 and 2.33   (f) 2.88 and −1.18
   (g) 1.86 and −1.23   (h) −.09 and −1.10

8. Transform the following raw scores into standard scores, given an $\overline{X} = 400$ and an $s = 32$:

   (a) 442   (b) 496   (c) 448
   (d) 411   (e) 465   (f) 480

9. With an $\overline{X} = 60$ and an $s = 4$, what proportion of scores theoretically lies above the following values:

   (a) 64   (b) 49   (c) 46   (d) 55

10. If the $\sigma_x = 3$ and the hypothesized $\mu = 68$, what would be the Z value associated with the following observed sample means:

   (a) 68   (b) 90   (c) 55   (d) 65   (e) 40

11. Differentiate between Type I and Type II errors. Who determines each type of error? How can these types of errors be minimized? Explain.

12. How does the level of significance we select relate to critical regions on sampling distributions?

13. For the following six population scores, construct a sampling distribution of means, based upon samples of size 2:

Person	Score
A	20
B	22
C	24
D	26
E	28
F	30

   Construct a frequency distribution of your sample means.

14. Under what circumstances are both tails of sampling distributions of statistics used in hypothesis testing? Explain.

15. Why is the critical region also known as the "region of rejection"? Explain.

chapter 16

Inferential Statistics, Tests of Significance, and Correlation

INTRODUCTION

Criminologists and others investigating the characteristics of samples usually want to generalize their results beyond those samples studied. Studies of prison inmates, juvenile delinquents, correctional officers, judges, district attorneys, public defenders, halfway house volunteers, or those working in private, community-based facilities are generally conducted for purposes beyond mere description. While describing the characteristics of samples is an important task of researchers, a general objective of social scientists is to expand their knowledge so that statements may be made about the population generally. Whatever investigators find relating to a sample of public defenders in Columbus, Ohio, for example, might be applicable to studies of public defenders throughout the remainder of the state. As we have seen, researchers cannot guarantee the representativeness or typicality of any sample they study in relation to the population from which the sample was drawn, but they can enhance the likelihood that it is generalizable to the population through the use of probability sampling plans and randomness in element selection.

There are two types of statistical inference: point estimation and interval estimation. The chapter begins by describing both types of inference, together with a rationale for their use by criminal justice professionals and others. Examples from the criminological literature are used to enhance the meaningfulness of these procedures. Several tests of significance are presented. These tests are applied to samples of elements, and they vary in their application according to the type of data collected by researchers as well as the nature of the samples studied. Two broad divisions of statistical tests are parametric and nonparametric. These are defined and described. Each division has certain strengths and weaknesses. Sample applications of these procedures are illustrated from the research literature in criminology and criminal justice.

The chapter concludes with an examination of correlation. Investigators are interested in establishing causal relations between variables. A preliminary step in this process is determining whether an association exists between variables. Correlation involves assessing the degree to which two or more variables are associated. Numerical coefficients are yielded, and these coefficients express both the strength and direction of association between variables. The chapter also describes how coefficients of association are interpreted.

STATISTICAL INFERENCE

Statistical inference is the process of estimating population parameters with sample statistics. Ideally, populations are identified in advance and samples of elements are drawn from populations. Researchers hypothesize about the parameters of the population and test these hypotheses by investigating sample characteristics and comparing them with hypothesized estimates using **inferential statistics.**

■ PURPOSES OF STATISTICAL INFERENCE

The purposes of statistical inference are to (1) test unlimited numbers of hypotheses about population values, (2) determine likely limits within which population parameters occur, and (3) advance our knowledge about population characteristics.

Types of Statistical Inference

Two alternative forms of estimation are point estimation and interval estimation. Both types of estimation involve sample statistics or information generated from samples. However, **point estimation** involves a forecast or prediction about some hypothesized population parameter, while **interval estimation** uses an observed sample statistic to generalize about several population parameters. For several reasons discussed subsequently, point estimation is relatively unpopular compared with interval estimation and receives less coverage in most texts where both types of estimation are discussed. Nevertheless, it provides a convenient illustration of hypothesis-testing and relates directly to several tests of significance.

Point Estimation. Point estimation is the process of forecasting or predicting the value of a population parameter and then comparing the sample statistic with it. For instance, we might predict that the population $\mu = 100$. Then a sample of elements is drawn and the sample mean is compared with the population mean. The degree of discrepancy between our observed $\overline{X}$ and the hypothesized μ will indicate the accuracy of our inference or **estimation.** In short, we will estimate a point at which we believe the population mean, μ, occurs. This is a point estimate and will be compared with the observed sample mean, $\overline{X}$, to determine the accuracy of the estimate. Accordingly, estimates are made about population standard deviations, modes, medians, and/or 10–90 ranges. Sample standard deviations, modes, medians, and 10–90 ranges are used as our observed sample statistics to compare with our predictions of population parameters.

The primary problems with point estimation are that we must make guesses in advance about what the population parameter will be, and unless we know a great deal about the population we are studying, we will have little basis for justifying the guesses we make. Earlier, a guess was made about the stress levels of a population of correctional officers, and a statistic from a sample of correctional officers was compared with this estimate. The basis for this guess was previous information about known stress levels of correctional officers from prior years. If we had no previous information about the population or if our general knowledge about it were limited, we would have no logical basis for our predictions. Actually, using information about correctional officer stress levels from previous years doesn't truly legitimize our estimates for later years. Each year is a new year, and whatever levels of stress existed in prior years are no longer relevant for later years. Therefore, point estimates are almost pure guesswork. Nevertheless, in the absence of any other information, information about a population for previous years is better than no knowledge at all.

The purpose of statistical inference is to learn about population parameters by studying samples drawn from them. Initially, we assume no knowledge of the population or its characteristics. This is why point estimation is troublesome for so many researchers, because the question always exists as to the source of our point estimates. More often than not, the population parameters about which we seek information are unknown. We draw samples of elements from populations in order to learn more about certain population parameters. It is no coincidence that we use the sample mean as an estimate of the population mean, since the mean has a sampling distribution that is normal in form. The principles of the unit normal distribution apply to it, and we can benefit from this knowledge.

We know that the sampling distribution of means is generally normal in form. It is perfectly symmetrical. Most statements that can be made about the unit normal distribution can also apply to any normal distribution of scores, including certain distributions of sample statistics such as the sampling distribution of the mean. While the horizontal axis of the unit normal distribution is measured according to standard deviation (σ) units of 1 as they depart from the μ of 0, the sampling distribution of means is measured according to standard errors of the mean, $s_{\bar{x}}$, in relation to the population mean, μ. We know that means of sampling distributions of statistics are called expected values, and standard deviations on these distributions are called standard errors.

Finally, we know that whenever the expected value of any statistic equals the population parameter that that statistic is intended to estimate, the statistic becomes an unbiased estimate of that population parameter. All sample statistics have corresponding population parameters. We know that the mean of the sampling distribution of means, μ, is always equal to the actual population mean, μ. Therefore, the sample mean, $\bar{X}$, is an unbiased estimate of the population μ. All other statistics we have presented are not unbiased estimates of their respective population parameters, because, despite the fact that they all have sampling distributions, they do not have sampling distributions with means equal to those corresponding parameters.

Point estimation is illustrated by the following problem. Suppose investigators wish to study the influence of new sentencing guidelines on reductions in sentencing disparities that have previously been attributed to gender, race, ethnicity, and socioeconomic factors. Sentencing disparities exist whenever several convicted offenders in the same jurisdiction are sentenced to widely different prison terms by the same judge, despite the similarity of their conviction offenses and prior records. A blatant example is sentencing two convicted male robbers, one black and one white, to terms of 10 years and 5 years respectively. Both offenders have similar criminal records and are about the same age, and the circumstances of their respective offenses are nearly identical. Yet, the black offender receives a sentence twice as harsh (10 years) as that of the white offender (5 years).

Suppose a jurisdiction is selected in which indeterminate sentencing has been used to sentence offenders. Indeterminate sentencing is a sentencing scheme that permits wide judicial discretion in imposing sentence lengths. In the most recent year, suppose this jurisdiction has implemented new guidelines for sentencing convicted offenders. These guidelines provide a range of months within which judges should sentence offenders, depending upon the seriousness of their acts and prior records. The prevailing belief among officials in that jurisdiction is that the new guidelines will minimize previous sentencing disparities that were considered discriminatory.

Previous information available from this fictitious jurisdiction shows that sentencing disparities according to race averaged about 12 months, or one year. In other words, sentences for black offenders who were convicted of the same crimes as white offenders received an average of 12 additional months as punishment compared with the incarcerative terms imposed on convicted whites. Using this "previous information" as the basis for our current estimate, we obtain a sample of black and white convicted offenders in that jurisdiction and determine their conviction offenses and sentences imposed under the new guidelines. Under point estimation, we predict as our projected amount of sentencing disparity the following, as illustrated by our hypothesis set:

$H_0: \mu \geq 12$ months

$H_1: \mu < 12$ months

$\quad P \leq .05$ (one-tailed test)

The research hypothesis says that the average sentencing disparity between black and white offenders in this jurisdiction will be less than 12 months. Based upon this research hypothesis, we derive a null hypothesis that says that the average sentencing disparity will either equal or exceed 12 months. A one-tailed hypothesis test is being made here, since we reasonably expect disparities in sentences between black and white convicted offenders to be minimized under the new sentencing guidelines.

Further information available, based upon the samples of offenders we have selected, is given: the observed $\overline{X} = 6.5$, which represents the current amount of sentencing disparity under the new guidelines; and a standard error of the mean, $s_{\overline{x}} = 2.00$, based upon the magnitude of the standard deviation and sample size obtained.

First, the hypothesis set tested is using the .05 level of significance, and a one-tailed or directional prediction is being made. Therefore, we would follow these steps to test our hypothesis:

1. Construct a sampling distribution of means.
2. Place the population mean of 12 months at the center of this sampling distribution.
3. Identify the critical region in the left tail of this distribution as containing the 5 percent of error consistent with the .05 level of significance used. The left tail is chosen because under the research hypothesis, the direction of difference hypothesized is below or to the left of 12 months.
4. Identify a Z value from Table A.3, Appendix A, page 624, that corresponds with the .05 level of significance or which leaves 5 percent of the curve area in the left tail of the sampling distribution. In this case, the Z value

leaving 5 percent of the curve area in the left tail of the curve also cuts off .4500 of curve area from the mean of 12 to that point, or $Z = -1.64$. This becomes our critical value of Z for the .05 level of significance, making a one-tailed test.

5. Assign our observed mean of 6.5 a Z value, using the standard error of the mean term, 2.00. This Z value will represent the distance 6.5 is from the forecast mean of 12. The computational work is simple, consisting of

$$\text{observed } Z = \frac{(\overline{X} - \mu)}{s_{\overline{x}}}$$

where $\overline{X}$ = observed sample mean

μ = hypothesized population mean

$s_{\overline{x}}$ = the standard error of the mean

or $(6.5 - 12)/2.00 = -5.5/2 = -2.75$. The observed $Z = -2.75$.

6. Compare the observed mean with the hypothesized mean and evaluate its significance. Since our observed Z value, -2.75, is in the predicted direction under H_1 and equals or exceeds the critical value of $Z = -1.64$, we may reject H_0 and support the research hypothesis. In this case, although disparities in sentencing continue to exist, they appear to have minimized significantly, at least according to these test results. Also, there is a 5 percent chance we are wrong (the α level or level of significance chosen) in making this conclusion based upon these findings. This concludes our point estimate test.

Interval Estimation and Confidence Intervals. Interval estimation can be used to answer the same question raised in the point estimation example. However, for various reasons described later, interval estimation is superior to point estimation. The logic of interval estimation is as follows. If we obtain a sample of elements (by using a probability sampling plan) and compute various statistics for it, there is a strong likelihood that our sample statistics are close to their parametric counterparts in the population. For example, a sample $\overline{X}$ is probably near the true population μ value on the sampling distribution of sample means. A sample median is probably near the true population median value. In fact, for any random sample of elements we select, any mean we compute is more likely to be closer to the population mean than far away from it.

Recalling the nature of the sampling distribution of means, we may say with considerable assurance (and confidence) that there are far more sample means occurring in and around the center of the distribution than occur in its extremes. We might designate the general area near the center of the sampling distribution of means as an area of high probability. Similarly, we may designate the tails of the sampling distribution of means as areas of low probability. The area of high probability near the center of the distribution is where a majority of sample means are located. Relatively few means are found in the extremes of the distribution. Utilizing what we know about the sampling distribution of means and the unit normal distribution it approximates, about 68 percent of the sample means lie within $\pm 1.00 s_{\bar{x}}$ on either side of the population μ. This is because approximately 68 percent of the normal curve area lies between -1.00σ and $+1.00\sigma$ on either side of μ on the unit normal distribution.

To make this statement, we do not have to know the value of μ for the sampling distribution of means. We merely need to know that the sampling distribution of means is normal in form. A given distance to the left or to the right of the unknown μ value will cut off a certain amount of curve area, which is also equivalent to a portion of mean values occurring there. Therefore, whenever we draw a random sample of elements from a designated population, the probability is in our favor of obtaining a sample with an $\bar{X}$ that is nearer μ than far away from it. It is logical to assume that if we place our observed $\bar{X}$ value on the horizontal axis of the sampling distribution of sample means, it will probably be near μ, the true population mean. Furthermore, if we advance a short distance to the left and to the right of our observed $\bar{X}$, it is probable that the true μ value will be overlapped. In short, an interval can be created around our observed value which will probably include or overlap the population μ at some point. The interval created around an observed $\bar{X}$ value is referred to as a **confidence interval** and is the subject of interval estimation.

Confidence intervals are designated distances above and below an observed sample $\bar{X}$ value that have a specified likelihood of overlapping the true μ value at some point. Confidence intervals are labeled as 95 percent confidence intervals, 90 percent confidence intervals, or 99 percent confidence intervals, and so forth. These percentage values refer to the likelihood that any given confidence interval we determine will overlap the true population mean, μ.

Since the true population mean is almost always unknown, we are never absolutely sure that any confidence interval we construct will truly overlap μ. As a way of illustrating the logic of confidence interval construction, imagine that researchers were to draw all possible samples of size 50 from a population of 2,000. As we have discussed earlier, there would be N^n or $2,000^{50}$ samples that could be drawn. Furthermore, suppose that researchers were to compute a mean for each of the samples drawn. Obviously, this would require much work, but eventually, researchers would have $2,000^{50}$ $\bar{X}$'s.

Next, imagine that a 95 percent confidence interval were to be constructed around each and every one of the $2,000^{50}$ sample means. There would be $2,000^{50}$ confidence intervals constructed. Since all of these would be 95 percent confidence intervals, we could say with certainty that 95 percent of these confidence intervals would overlap the true population μ at some point. We could also say with certainty that 5 percent of these confidence intervals would not overlap μ.

Had we created 99 percent confidence intervals for all observed mean values, we would have $2,000^{50}$ 99 percent confidence intervals. We could say that 99 percent of them would overlap μ at some point, and that 1 percent of them would not overlap it. Had we created 80 percent confidence intervals for all of our observed $\bar{X}$ values, then 80 percent of those confidence intervals would overlap the population mean and 20 percent of them would fail to overlap it. The confidence interval that we designate defines the number of confidence intervals that would overlap the true population mean value if we were to construct such intervals for all possible $\overline{X}$ values that could be computed.

What does the researcher do in reality? Usually, one random sample is drawn rather than 10 samples or 1,000 samples. The researcher observes a single $\overline{X}$ rather than $2,000^{50}$ of them. A single confidence interval of some magnitude is created around that single observed $\overline{X}$. The researcher then specifies the likelihood associated with that confidence interval (e.g., 99 percent, 90 percent, 95 percent) of overlapping the true (and unknown) population μ value. The researcher is never in the position of knowing which sample has been drawn from all of the possible samples that could be drawn. Therefore, the researcher cannot possibly know which mean has been obtained from all possible means that could have been computed. Again, probability works in the researcher's favor here. We do know that the random draw of a single sample will stand a better chance of being near the population mean rather than far away from it, on the sampling distribution of sample means. The probability that our sample mean lies near the population mean is in our favor. Therefore, a confidence interval we construct around that mean will be more likely to overlap μ at some point than not overlap it.

Suppose the researcher has drawn a random sample of 226 elements and has observed a sample $\overline{X} = 25$ and a sample $s = 5$. Further suppose that the researcher wants to construct a 90 percent confidence interval about the observed $\overline{X}$ of 25. The 90 percent confidence interval is constructed as follows:

90 percent confidence interval $= \overline{X}_{obs} \pm (s_{\bar{x}})(Z)$

where $\overline{X}$ = observed sample mean

$s_{\bar{x}}$ = standard error of the mean

Z = standard score associated with cutting off one-half of the confidence interval percent (in this case, 90 percent/2 = 45 percent or .4500)

Using the information provided by the hypothetical example above, we have:

$$90 \text{ percent confidence interval} = 25 \pm \left(\frac{5}{\sqrt{226 - 1}} \right)(1.64)$$

$$= 25 \pm \left(\frac{5}{15} \right)(1.64)$$

$$= 25 \pm (.33)(1.64)$$

$$= 25 \pm .54$$

$$= 24.46 \text{ to } 25.54$$

The 90 percent confidence interval around the observed mean of 25 extends from 24.46 to 25.54 and has a 90 percent chance of overlapping the population μ at some point. We used the sample size and standard deviation to derive our standard error of the mean value.

In the general case, if we wish to construct any confidence interval around any observed $\overline{X}$, the following formula could be used:

? percent confidence interval $= \overline{X}_{obs} \pm (s_{\overline{x}})(Z)$

where $\overline{X}_{obs} =$ observed mean

$\qquad s_{\overline{x}} =$ standard error of the mean

$\qquad Z =$ standard score associated with cutting off normal curve area equal to one-half of whatever percent the confidence interval happens to be

To determine which Z value should be used in this formula, we must first divide the percent of the confidence interval desired by 2. If we are computing the 90 percent confidence interval, we would divide 90 percent by 2 or 90 percent/2 $= 45$ percent (.4500). If we are computing the 80 percent confidence interval, we would divide 80 percent by 2 or 80 percent/2 $= 40$ percent (.4000), and so on. Once we have determined this result, we may look up the equivalent Z value in Table A.3 of Appendix A, p. 624. This is the Z value cutting off one-half of the confidence interval percentage we have designated. The Z value cutting off .4500 (from the mean of 0 to that point) is 1.64, while the Z value cutting off .4000 (from the mean of 0 to that point) is 1.28.

Given an observed $\overline{X} = 25$ and $s_{\overline{x}} = .33$, we could determine the following confidence intervals as shown:

95% confidence interval $= 25 \pm (.33)(1.96)$
$\qquad\qquad\qquad\qquad = 24.35$ to 25.65

99% confidence interval $= 25 \pm (.33)(2.58)$
$\qquad\qquad\qquad\qquad = 24.15$ to 25.85

80% confidence interval $= 25 \pm (.33)(1.28)$
$\qquad\qquad\qquad\qquad = 24.58$ to 25.42.

In each of these cases, we have added to and subtracted from the observed mean the product of the $s_{\overline{x}}$ and the Z value associated with cutting off one-half of whatever the confidence interval percent happens to be. The 95 percent confidence interval above means that there is a 95 percent chance that the true and unknown population μ lies somewhere between 24.35 and 25.65. The 99 percent confidence interval means that there is a 99 percent chance that the true and unknown population μ lies somewhere between 24.15 and 25.85. And finally, the 80 percent confidence interval means that there is an 80 percent chance or likelihood that the true and unknown population mean lies somewhere between 24.58 and 25.42.

It will be observed that the confidence interval gets larger as the percentage increases. Also, the confidence interval decreases in magnitude as the percentage decreases. This reflects either an increase or decrease in our "confidence" that the population mean will be found within any given confidence interval. Thus, we are provided with another reason for the use of the term *confidence interval.*

Confidence intervals have the distinct advantage over point estimation of providing a range wherein the population μ might occur. We begin our estimation with an observed $\overline{X}$ value and create an interval around it which likely overlaps μ. This is superior to the method of guessing a population mean value in advance, with little or no information, and then comparing a sample mean with our point estimate.

It is helpful to compare point estimation with interval estimation on a problem we have already solved involving forecasts of population values. Regarding the hypothetical problem of sentencing disparities discussed earlier under point estimation, we forecast a population mean of 12 months, indicating the disparity in sentence lengths between convicted black and white offenders. Under a new sentencing guidelines scheme, it was anticipated that sentence lengths would be more equivalent as disparities likely due to racial factors diminished. A one-tailed test was made which predicted that under new guidelines, disparities in sentence lengths between black and white offenders would be less than 12 months.

In the following scenario, let's assume the same information as given in the original problem, where our predicted μ = 12 months, observed $\overline{X}$ = 6.5 months, and the $s_{\overline{x}}$ = 2.00. However, we will generate the following two-tailed hypothesis set, where direction is not forecast:

H_0: μ = 12 months

H_1: $\mu \neq$ 12 months

$P \leq$ .05 (two-tailed test)

The research hypothesis says that the average length of sentencing disparity (measured in months) will be different from 12 months, while the null hypothesis says the average disparity will be equal to 12 months. This forecast is based upon previous information about sentencing in the jurisdiction studied. The same level of significance, .05, is used in this case. But because the direction of difference is not predicted, a two-tailed or nondirectional test is conducted. This means that we will have to split our significance level of .05 into two equal parts and place each part in the two tails of our sampling distribution of means. This will require that we locate a Z value that cuts off .4750 of curve area in both directions from the mean, leaving .0250 in each tail of the curve as the regions of rejection or critical regions. This Z value is $\pm$ 1.96 and is designated as our critical value of Z for the .05 level of significance, using a two-tailed test.

Since we already know that our observed $\overline{X}$ = 6.5 months and has an observed Z value associated with it of -2.75, we need only ask whether -2.75 equals or exceeds the critical values of $\pm$ 1.96. Yes, the $Z = -2.75$ is in the region of rejection to the far left of -1.96. Thus, we may reject the null hypothesis and conclude (with 5 percent error) that the sentencing disparity in that jurisdiction is not equal to 12 months.

Interval estimation may be used to answer the same question of whether the new guidelines have had any impact on sentencing disparities between convicted black and white offenders. In this case, we will not hypothesize anything. Rather, we will obtain our sample, compute our mean of 6.5, our standard error of the mean = 2.00, and construct a confidence interval around our observed $\overline{X}$ = 6.5. In order to make a test commensurate with the .05 level of significance used in the point estimate problem, we select a percent confidence interval that corresponds with the probability of .05. In this case, the probability is 95 percent. Therefore, we are seeking the 95 percent confidence interval around the observed $\overline{X}$ = 6.5. Taking our given information, we have

$$95\% \text{ confidence interval} = 6.5 \pm (2.00)(1.96)$$
$$= 6.5 \pm 3.92$$
$$= 2.58 \text{ to } 10.42$$

Our 95 percent confidence interval extends from 2.58 to 10.42. We may say, with 95 percent confidence, that the population mean is overlapped by this interval 95 percent of the time. Notice that our original population mean of 12 months is outside of this confidence interval. Any population mean that occurs outside of confidence interval ranges is considered significantly different from the sample mean. We are answering essentially the same question about differences in sentence lengths, except that we are solving this problem by using alternative strategies.

Further note that the Z value chosen for our 95 percent confidence interval problem was the same value that was selected for a two-tailed hypothesis test at the .05 level of significance. This is the general relation between point estimation and interval estimation. Two-tailed point estimation is the functional equivalent of interval estimation, where the same levels of significance are involved. Levels of significance and confidence interval percentages are linked as follows:

90 % confidence interval = .10 level of significance, two-tailed test

95 % confidence interval = .05 level of significance, two-tailed test

80 % confidence interval = .20 level of significance, two-tailed test

99 % confidence interval = .01 level of significance, two-tailed test

Summary Comparison of Point and Interval Estimation. Summarizing the basic differences between point and interval estimation, point estimation involves making a prediction about an unknown population parameter, drawing a random sample, determining the appropriate corresponding statistic, and making a comparison of this statistic with what was hypothesized as the population mean. Interval estimation involves no advance prediction of population values. Rather, interval estimation involves drawing a random sample of elements, computing sample statistics, and establishing likely ranges within which the population parameters will occur. Interval estimation deals with what is known, namely, the values of sample statistics. Point estimation involves dealing with what is unknown, namely, population parameters. The main function of point estimation in recent years is to illustrate hypothesis testing and the meaningfulness of statistical significance and critical regions on sampling distributions.

■ PARAMETRIC AND NONPARAMETRIC STATISTICAL TESTS AND DECISION MAKING IN CRIMINAL JUSTICE

Tests of significance, sometimes known as **tests of significance of difference,** may apply to cases involving single samples of elements. Two or more samples of elements may be involved for two-sample and k-sample statistical tests. Further, in the two- and k-sample cases, specialized tests of significance have been designed to work with independent samples as well as related samples.

What does *difference* refer to in tests of significance of difference? The term *difference* refers to the discrepancy between what researchers observe and what might be expected according to chance. In single-sample situations, researchers want to know whether their observed sample values or statistics differ from some hypothesized population parameter. When we were concerned in the hypothetical situation above about whether sentencing disparities were reduced under a sentencing guidelines scheme, we wanted to know whether 6.5 months was significantly different from 12 months as hypothesized. This difference of 5.5 months appeared significant. Whether or not we realized it, we applied a statistical test of significance of difference (a Z test in this case) to our point estimation problem. We evaluated the significance of the difference between our sample observation and the hypothesized population mean, 5.5 months, and determined that it was significant statistically, with a 5 percent chance of being in error.

What if we observed several different samples of elements? What if we observed public defenders from several different cities, and we were concerned with whether they varied significantly in their general competence when representing indigent clients. A statistical test of significance of difference could be applied here. Provided we had a reasonable measure of attorney competence, we could determine if several samples of public defenders differed significantly on the competency variable. Numerical values resulting from our statistical test application could be assessed, and we could conclude, with some error, whether the different samples of attorneys actually differed significantly in their degree of competency.

The questions of whether one sample differs from what we hypothesize or whether two or more samples of elements differ according to selected measured variables are not the questions we attempt to answer when we apply statistical tests of significance of difference. We can see whether or not samples differ from one another. We can see whether 6.5 months differs from 12 months, or whether our competency measures for several different samples of public defenders yield different values. These observed differences are obvious or apparent. The questions we want answered pertain to the statistical significance of the differences in the scores we observe. Therefore, we may observe differences in competency ratings between two or more groups of public defenders, but these differences may not be significant statistically. We may see differences in months reflecting sentencing disparity from one type of sentencing scheme to another, but these differences may not be significant statistically. The decision rules we formulate also function as guidelines whereby we can evaluate the significance of whatever we find. We normally and conventionally establish decision rules in advance of any hypothesis test we make, and on the basis of our decision rules, we decide to reject or fail to reject null hypotheses and support or fail to support corresponding research hypotheses.

Two major categories of statistical tests of significance of difference exist: parametric and nonparametric. **Parametric statistical tests** are those that either require or have (1) randomness or a probability sampling plan, (2) a normal distribution underlying the characteristic or variable measured, (3) the interval level of measurement associated with the measured variable, and (4) sample sizes of 30 or larger. They are further characterized as having high test power relative to rejecting false null hypotheses.

Because many variables studied by criminologists, criminal justice professionals, and social scientists do not generally achieve the interval level of measurement for selected variables or have normally distributed samples of elements to study, parametric statistical test choices may often be inappropriate ones. For instance, attitudes are popular investigative topics. Do probation officers with high client caseloads have higher or lower burnout scores than probation officers with lower client caseloads? Does police chief cynicism vary according to years in grade as chief? Do attitudes of delinquents change over time as the result of various intervention programs? All of these studies and thousands of others are concerned, at least in part, with attitudes of sample elements. Judging from reviews of recent criminological literature, since the most popular measures of attitudes today are Likert or summated rating scales (e.g., "Strongly agree,"–"Strongly disagree"), Thurstone scales (equal-appearing interval scales), Guttman scales (i.e., the Cornell technique, unidimensional scaling), and the semantic differential, all of these scaling methods yield scores measured at best according to the ordinal level of measurement.

Also, many of the samples investigated by criminal justice professionals exhibit distributions of scores that depart markedly from normality and do not approximate the characteristics of the unit normal distribution. Examples of parametric statistical tests include the t test and Z tests for significance of difference between means, the F test for analysis of variance, and the Newman-Keuls procedure.

A second major category of statistical procedures consists of nonparametric statistical tests. **Nonparametric statistical tests** assume or require randomness or a probability sampling plan. They are characterized as being applicable to situations where sample sizes may be quite small, where the level of measurement is usually, though not always, nominal or ordinal, and where normality is not assumed to exist regarding distributions of raw scores. Compared with parametric tests that are designed to answer similar questions, they are less powerful regarding rejections of false null hypotheses.

Sometimes, nonparametric tests are called **distribution-free statistics.** This does not mean that there are *no* distributional assumptions underlying these tests. As we have seen, all statistics have sampling distributions. Distribution-free means that the normal distribution assumption is not required. Generally, nonparametric tests do not require that researchers have distributions of sample scores that are normally distributed. Another designation of many of these tests is that they are "goodness-of-fit" procedures. The "goodness-of-fit" label means the "fit" between some chance occurrence or what would be expected according to chance and whatever scores happen to be observed. Flipping a coin 100 times, for instance, might be expected to yield 50 tails and 50 heads. However, a real distribution of 100 coin flips may yield 55 tails and 45 heads. Is the 55–45 difference different from what would be expected according to chance, namely, 50–50? "Goodness-of-fit" tests assess the significance of such differences. A popular goodness-of-fit test is the chi square test.

Advantages and Disadvantages of Parametric and Nonparametric Tests

Parametric tests of significance or statistical procedures are well known. In fact, they are so well known that they have often obscured the importance of utilizing more appropriate nonparametric tests under certain study conditions. Parametric tests are more sensitive regarding statistical observations. Therefore, if researchers were to simultaneously apply parametric and nonparametric procedures to the same sets of scores for two or more samples of elements, they would be more likely to reject false null hypotheses with their parametric test results rather than with their nonparametric test results. This reflects the general difference that parametric tests are more powerful than nonparametric tests. However, the significance of this difference in test power between parametric and nonparametric procedures is often exaggerated.

Several nonparametric statistical procedures have power levels that are almost equivalent to those associated with parametric tests. Since a test's power may be increased by increasing sample size, it is possible to make certain nonparametric test applications approximately as powerful as their parametric counterparts. Nonparametric tests have fewer restrictive assumptions associated with their application. Most are rapid to compute and easy to apply to a wide variety of social and psychological investigations. The use of nonparametric statistics in the social sciences generally has been increasing steadily over the years. Our increased familiarity with such procedures and a greater recognition of the tasks they can potentially accomplish accounts for such increased usage of them in criminal justice and criminology.

Nonparametric statistical tests are more conservative procedures than their equivalent parametric counterparts. Thus, if serious questions are raised about whether one or more assumptions have been violated during the application of certain parametric tests, a conservative step would be to use a similar nonparametric procedure.

SOME EXAMPLES OF PARAMETRIC TESTS

Z and t Tests for Single Samples

The *t* test is perhaps the *best* single-sample test of significance of difference where data are measured according to an interval scale. *Both* the Z test and the *t* test share the *same* formula:

$$Z \text{ or } t = \frac{\overline{X}_{\text{obs}} - \mu}{\sigma_{\bar{x}}}$$

where $\overline{X}_{\text{obs}}$ = observed sample mean

μ = hypothesized population mean

σ = standard error of the mean estimated by

$$\frac{S}{\sqrt{N-1}}$$

where s = sample standard deviation

N = sample size

A distinction between the Z and *t* tests is that the Z test requires a knowledge of the *population standard deviation,* whereas the *t* test requires only a knowledge of the *sample standard deviation.* Since it is unlikely that estimates about population means will ever be made when the population standard deviation is *known, either* the Z or *t* test is applied conventionally using the *sample standard deviation* for both applications. One additional difference is that for Z test applications, the *unit normal distribution* is used for interpretive purposes. For *t* test applications, the *t distribution* is used to interpret observed *t* values. Whenever the sample size being examined exceeds 120, *both* of these distributions are identical, meaning that the Z and *t* **critical values** for different levels of significance and for both one- and two-tailed tests are the same. But for situations involving analyses of *smaller* sample sizes, critical values yielded by the *t* test are generally *larger than* those derived by the Z test. A special *t* table has been provided in Table A.5, Appendix A, p. 626, for easy interpretation. The meanings of both *t* and Z values will be illustrated by the following example.

MacKenzie and Shaw (1990) studied inmate adjustment and change resulting from a Louisiana shock incarceration program known as the *Intensive Motivational Program of Alternative Correctional Treatment (IMPACT).* The program consists of two phases, in which offenders are placed in shock incarceration from 90 to 180 days in a "rigorous boot-camp atmosphere" in the first phase (p. 127), and in an intensive supervised parole program for the second phase. Among other things, the shock incarceration experience conducted by "drill instructors" was designed to modify inmate behaviors and provide them with positive reinforcement and prosocial attitudes.

Suppose that MacKenzie and Shaw wanted to determine if the prosocial attitudes and social adjustment of a sample of inmate IMPACT participants tended to be *higher* than the general prison population not exposed to IM-PACT. Such a finding might prove valuable in showing the effectiveness of IM-PACT for the subsequent adjustment of inmates to life outside of prison through supervised parole. Suppose a measure of prosocial attitudes and social adjustment exists, the Prosocial Attitude and Adjustment Scale (PASSAC), and that it *has been applied* to populations of Louisiana prison inmates in *previous years.* Further assume that in previous years, the population mean on PASSAC has been 64, a relatively low degree of prosocial attitudes and social adjustment. This *previous information* will be used by MacKenzie and Shaw to use as a *standard* against which to compare their own inmate sample. They believe that their own sample of inmates will exhibit higher scores on the attitude scale than previous samples of inmates studied by others. The following hypothesis set is constructed:

$H_0: \mu \leq 64$

$H_1: \mu > 64$

$P \leq .05$ (one-tailed test)

This hypothesis set says the following: The null hypothesis, H_0, is that the population mean, μ, on PASSAC will be *equal to or smaller than* 64, whereas the research hypothesis is that the population mean, μ, will be *greater than* 64. A *directional prediction* is made under H_1 that for an observed sample of IMPACT participants, their prosocial attitudes and social adjustment will be higher than the predicted population mean of 64. It will be assumed that a significant difference of scores in the predicted direction under the research hypothesis will signify the effectiveness of the IMPACT program. Suppose the following information has been obtained, based upon a sample of 41 IMPACT inmates: $\overline{X}_{obs} = 68.5, s = 12.2,$ and $N = 41$.

A *t* test is conducted, yielding the following t_{obs}:

$$t_{obs} = \frac{68.5 - 64}{12.2 \sqrt{41 - 1}}$$

$$= \frac{4.5}{1.94}$$

$$= 2.320$$

The observed value of *t* is $2.320 = t_{obs}$.

In order to determine the statistical significance of our observed *t* value, we must turn to Table A.5, Appendix A, page 626. This table contains *critical values* of the *t* statistic that must be *equaled* or *exceeded* by our observed *t* values in order for our observed *t* values to be significant at the levels of probability indicated across the top of the table. Note that in Table A.5, *both one-* and *two-tailed* probabilities are provided. Since our hypothesis test is being made at the .05 level of significance for a *one-tailed* or *directional* test, we locate the .05

one-tailed probability across the top of the table. Next, we must determine **degrees of freedom.***

Degrees of freedom, *df,* are located down the left-hand side of Table A.5. We determine the appropriate *df* for one-sample tests by the formula, $N - 1$, where N = the sample size. In this case, degrees of freedom are $N - 1$ or $41 - 1 = 40$ *df.* Where $df = 40$ and the .05 level of significance for a one-tailed test *intersect* in the body of the table defines the *critical value of t* which we must *equal or exceed* with our *observed t value.* The critical value found where these values intersect is 1.684.

Does our observed $t = 2.320$ *equal or exceed* the critical value of 1.684? Yes. Therefore, we may reject H_0 and conclude that the sample mean, 68.5, is larger than and significantly different from the hypothesized population mean of 64. It appears that the IMPACT program may be influential in increasing inmate prosocial attitudes and social adjustment or PASSAC scores. However, there is also a 5 percent chance that we might be *wrong* in rejecting H_0. This is because we set the level of significance (*P*) at .05 prior to making our test. Also, we made a directional or one-tailed prediction. (A two-tailed or nondirectional test of the same hypothesis set would have required equaling or exceeding a critical value of $t = \pm 2.021$. See if you can find this critical value in Table A.5.)

If we had we applied the *Z* test to the above problem, we would have used the unit normal distribution or values of *Z* from Table A.3, page 624. How would we know which *Z* value to use as our *critical value of Z?* Again, our observed *t* value, 2.320, would be treated precisely as a *Z* value and interpreted accordingly. Since the .05 level of significance is being used in this hypothesis test, and a one-tailed or directional test is involved, we would identify a *Z* value that would cut off *45 percent of the curve area in one direction or the other,* leaving 5 percent of the curve area in one tail of the curve. Under the research hypothesis specified in the above problem, the *right tail* of the unit normal distribution would contain the critical region. The critical value of *Z* would be 1.64, which is the *Z* value that cuts off 45 percent of the curve area between the mean of 0 and a *Z* value = 1.64. If our observed *Z* is equal to or larger than the critical *Z* value of 1.64, we may reject the null hypothesis and conclude H_1. In this case, an observed $Z = 2.320$ *does* equal or exceed the critical value of $Z = 1.64$. Conventional levels of measurement are .05 and .01. Critical values of *Z* for one- and two-tailed hypothesis test applications are shown in Table 16.1 for the .05 and .01 significance levels.

Notice *two* important points about what we have done in our applications of *t* and *Z* tests. The first point is that we have carried out the observed *t* value *three places,* to *2.320.* This was done because the critical *t* values in Table A.5 are also expressed to three places. Thus, our comparisons are conveniently made, without having to worry about rounding. In this hypothesis test situation, rounding wouldn't have made any difference to our decision whether to reject or fail

---

*Degrees of freedom are frequently used for the purpose of entering statistical tables and determining critical values. They are almost always designated as *df* and refer to *the number of values in a set of them which are free to vary.* Different ways of determining degrees of freedom are calculated whenever tabular distributions of frequencies are analyzed.

TABLE 16.1 Conventional .05 and .01 Levels of Significance and Critical Values of Z or t.[a]

	Levels of Significance	
	.05	.01
One-tailed Z or t values $=$	1.64	1.96
Two-tailed Z or t values $=$	2.33	2.58

[a]When $N = \infty$, critical values of t and Z are identical; for all practical purposes, whenever $N > 150$, t and Z values are identical.

to reject H_0. In other tests of hypotheses, however, borderline decisions often have to be made. It is best to express your observed statistical values to *the same number of places* as those same critical values are expressed in all appropriate Appendix A tables.

The second point is to note the similarity between the t and Z critical values. The critical value of t was 1.684, while the critical Z value was 1.64. Remember that t critical values will tend to be larger than Z critical values whenever samples are smaller than 120. In this case, our hypothetical sample size of IMPACT inmates was 41. Had the sample size been 121, then $N - 1 = 120$ would have been our *df* for the same problem above, using the t table. The critical t value would have been 1.658, somewhat closer to Z than was found when *df* equaled 40. Notice also that the infinity (∞) line in Table A.5 virtually equals Z values for equivalent significance levels. In the infinity case, the t value becomes 1.645, approximately what our critical Z value would be if the unit normal distribution is used instead of the t distribution.

In the *df* column in Table A.5, precise degrees of freedom between points 30 and 40, 40 and 60, and 60 and 120 are *not* provided. Thus, if you do not have the exact *df* as shown in the table, *always* choose the *smaller df* point in the table rather than the larger one. This is a *conservative step* and yields slightly *larger* critical t values to equal or exceed with observed t values. You are actually making it slightly more difficult for yourself to reject null hypotheses.

Table A.5 provides only one side of the t distribution. Like the unit normal distribution, the distribution of t is perfectly symmetrical and has a $\mu = 0$. Because of this symmetry, both sides of the t distribution are identical. We may assign negative $(-)$ t values to those values below the mean of 0 or to the left of it, and positive t values occurring above 0 or to the right of it. This is especially important whenever one-tailed hypothesis tests are made.

Coming or Not Coming from the Same Populations

Sometimes, interpretations of statistical test results are phrased in seemingly unusual language. This unusual language might go something like this: "We reject the null hypothesis and conclude that our sample comes from a different population." Another way of saying this is that "The two means (i.e., $\overline{X}$ and μ) come from different populations." Both of these phrases are confusing to beginning students. Remember that statistical inference is the process of saying something about a population of elements based upon a sample drawn from the population. The sample mean, $\overline{X}$, is considered the best estimate of the hypothesized population mean, μ. When we conduct t or Z tests and find that the two $\overline{X}_k$'s differ from one another, saying that *one mean is not from the same population as the other* is the same as saying that the two means are different in a statistically significant sense.

This phraseology is illustrated easily with a two-sample example. If we were to draw samples from two classes of sociology students, one class from the University of California at Irvine (UCI) and the other from the University of Kentucky (UK), the two samples of students would obviously be *independent* from one another. Measuring these students on some variable, such as their "knowledge of history of sociology" or their "level of sociology aptitude" would probably yield different average scores for the two samples. If we designate the UCI class as N_1 and the UK class as N_2, and their respective means as $\overline{X}_1$ and $\overline{X}_2$, it is assumed that these respective $\overline{X}$'s are estimates of the two populations of UCI and UK scores on these measured variables. Thus, $\overline{X}_1$ is an estimate of μ_1, and $\overline{X}_2$ is an estimate of μ_2.

Since we are dealing with sample means, however, we are using them as estimates of their respective population means to help us to determine whether the population μ's differ from one another. If the sample $\overline{X}$'s differ, then it will be assumed that the populations from which the samples were derived *also* differ. Thus, we will say that the two samples *come from different populations* on their average "knowledge of sociology history" scores or their "sociology aptitude" score averages. However, if our test of significance shows that the two $\overline{X}_k$'s (where k = the different samples) do *not* differ from one another significantly, then we say that the two samples *come from the same population* regarding the distributions of those variables, namely, their "knowledge of sociology history" or their "sociology aptitude." Obviously, the UCI and UK students come from different *school* populations, but their history or aptitude score distributions are sufficiently similar (or different) to conclude that the population distributions of those scores are similar (or different.)

Assumptions, Advantages, and Disadvantages of Z and t Tests

The assumptions of the **Z and t tests** include (1) randomness, (2) the interval level of measurement underlying the characteristic measured, and (3) a normal distribution associated with the observed scores. The primary advantages of the t and Z tests are (1) they are easy to use, (2) tables of critical t and Z values exist for quick and convenient interpretations of observed t and Z values, (3) there are no sample-size restrictions, (4) these tests are well-known and conventionally applied in social scientific work, and (5) these tests have high power at rejecting false null hypotheses. However, there are some strong disadvantages associated with t and Z test applications. Popular attitudinal scales, such as Likert, Thurstone, and Guttman scaling, yield scores measured according to ordinal scales. Thus, applications of t and Z tests to attitudinal information should be interpreted with caution.

Another disadvantage of these tests is the normality assumption. While few researchers actually take the time to verify whether the scores they have collected from a sample are normally distributed, it is unlikely that normality is achieved in a substantial number of these score distributions. Also, complete randomness is seldom achieved because of nonresponse. Thus, we must consider that there may be multiple assumption violations whenever these parametric tests are applied. However, these tests are popular and frequently applied despite any assumption violations. These tests are conventional tests.

Another weakness is that applications of t or Z are unreliable whenever there are deviant scores present in distributions of raw scores. This is because of the distorting effect of deviant scores on the mean. There are no serious sample-size restrictions regarding the application of t or Z. However, it is recommended that you use the t table, Table A.5, whenever your sample sizes are 120 or less. Use either Table A.5 or Table A.3 whenever your sample sizes exceed 120 appreciably. However, for extremely large samples of elements, perhaps N's of 500 or larger, standard error terms in statistical formulae are grossly inflated. This means that whatever we observe using the t or Z tests will probably be statistically significant, but the substantive meaning of such results may be minimal.

Two-Sample t Test

The t test for differences between means is a **two-sample t test** similar to the single- sample t test described in the previous section. Therefore, almost all assumptions, advantages, and disadvantages underlying this procedure are the same as those that apply to single-sample applications. An example of the t test for differences between means follows. Since we have already examined a hypothetical problem based upon an actual study of inmate prosocial behaviors in Louisiana conducted by MacKenzie and Shaw (1990), it might continue to serve as a useful comparison to show how the t test may be extended to two-sample analyses. These researchers studied the influence of an Inmate Motivational Program of Alternative Correctional Treatment (IMPACT) on prosocial attitudes and social adjustment of a sample of prison inmates exposed to shock incarceration ranging from 90 to 180 days in prison. The influence of IMPACT was predicted to be therapeutic, in that those inmates exposed to IMPACT would theoretically have higher prosocial attitudes and social adjustment scores measured on some Prosocial Attitude and Social Adjustment Scale (PASSAC).

In the actual study, MacKenzie and Shaw studied two samples of offenders: those inmates exposed to IMPACT and designated as the "shock sample" (1990:131) and those inmates who may have been eligible for inclusion in the IMPACT program but were subject to regular prison incarceration instead, designated as the "incarcerated sample." Both samples were given the PASSAC as well as other instruments designed to measure various factors associated with their adjustment to prison life and their potential for successful supervised parole. These researchers believed that IMPACT would facilitate the inmate participants' adjustment by reducing their levels of aggressive behavior as measured by the magnitude of the PASSAC scores. The lower the scores on the PASSAC, the lower the aggressiveness exhibited by the respective inmate samples.

Suppose these researchers had obtained measures for both the shock and incarcerated samples on the hypothetical PASSAC instrument after the IMPACT program had been completed. Suppose that the incarcerated sample consisted of 305 participants ($N_1 = 305$), while 50 inmates were included in the IMPACT sample ($N_2 = 50$). (The substantially smaller sample of IMPACT inmates might be due to the highly experimental nature of the IMPACT program and the selectivity standards used by officials when participants are included.) PASSAC scores for both samples might be averaged and compared, using the t test. Do the two samples, the incarcerated sample and the shock sample, come from the same population on the PASSAC instrument or do they come from different populations? Do the two samples have similar average PASSAC scores or do their score averages differ significantly? The t test for significance of difference between two means may be used. Since it was believed that the shock sample would have higher PASSAC scores than the incarcerated sample, a one-tailed hypothesis test was made. The following hypothesis set was tested:

H_0: Incarcerated inmates will have the same mean PASSAC scores as IMPACT (shock) inmates; if there is a difference, incarcerated inmates will have higher PASSAC scores than the sample of IMPACT (shock) inmates.

H_1: Incarcerated inmates will have lower mean PASSAC scores than IMPACT (shock) inmates.

$P \le .01$ (one-tailed test)

The wording of these hypotheses is important. The null hypothesis must be worded in such a way so that if it is rejected, a specific research hypothesis believed true by these researchers will be supported. The level of significance was set at .01. PASSAC scores were averaged for both groups and means were computed, where $\overline{X}_1$ was the mean for the incarcerated sample, while $\overline{X}_2$ was the mean for the IMPACT inmate sample. In symbolic terms, the true hypotheses being tested pertained to the population means of PASSAC scores, where two sample means were estimates of their respective population parameters. The following hypothesis set illustrates the hypothesis set actually tested:

H_0: $\mu_1 \ge \mu_2$ estimated by $\overline{X}_1 \ge \overline{X}_2$

H_1: $\mu_1 < \mu_2$ estimated by $\overline{X}_1 < \overline{X}_2$

$P \le .01$ (one-tailed test)

The following hypothetical information is available from collected data:

$\overline{X}_1 = 61.71$	$s_1 = 7.46$	$N_1 = 305$
$\overline{X}_2 = 69.38$	$s_2 = 5.16$	$N_2 = 50$

With this information, a t test for the significance of difference between means is applied by using the following formula:

$$t = \frac{\overline{X}_1 - \overline{X}_2}{s_{\overline{x}_1 - \overline{x}_2}}$$

where $\overline{X}_1$ = mean for the first sample

$\overline{X}_2$ = mean for the second sample

$s_{\overline{x}_1} - _{\overline{x}_2,}$ = standard error of the difference between the two means

or

$$t = \frac{\overline{X}_1 - \overline{X}_2}{\sqrt{\dfrac{s_1^2}{N_1} + \dfrac{s_2^2}{N_2}}}$$

where N_1 and N_2 are the two sample sizes; $\overline{X}_1$ and $\overline{X}_2$ are the two sample means; and s_1^2 and s_1^2 are the two sample variances

The **standard error of the difference between two means,** $s_{\overline{x}_1 - \overline{x}_2}$, functions in precisely the same way as does the standard error of the mean for a single sample. In this case, there are two samples being compared. Thus, there are two sources of sampling error. Sampling error comes from samples 1 and 2 and is combined or pooled into a denominator term. Using the given values from the present problem, we can now solve for t:

$$t = \frac{61.71 - 69.39}{\sqrt{\dfrac{(7.46)^2}{305} + \dfrac{(5.16)^2}{50)}}}$$

$$t = \frac{-7.67}{\sqrt{\dfrac{55.6}{305} + \dfrac{26.6}{50}}}$$

$$= \frac{-7.67}{\sqrt{.71}}$$

$$= -7.67/.84$$

$$= -9.13$$

The resulting t observed is -9.13.

We may review Table A.5, Appendix A, page 626 to determine the statistical significance of this observed t value. Since we are dealing with *two* samples instead of one, degrees of freedom are computed somewhat differently. In this case, degrees of freedom (*df*) are computed as follows:

Degrees of freedom for two-sample case (*df*) = $(N_1 - 1) + (N_2 - 1)$

In this instance, we have $(305 - 1) + (50 - 1) = 304 + 49 = 353$ df. With a df this large, we may use either the infinity line (∞) in Table A.5 or the 120 df line down the left-hand side to determine our critical value of t. We locate the level of significance, $P \leq .01$, for a one-tailed test across the top of the table, and where this intersects with df of infinity in the body of the table defines the critical value of t which we must *equal or exceed* with our observed value. This critical t value (t_{cv}) $= -2.326$. Examining our research hypothesis, it was predicted that $\overline{X}_1$ would be less than $\overline{X}_{2}$, and this directional prediction occurred in the present hypothesis test. Thus, a negative t value resulted. This is good, since this is what was predicted. This is also why a negative critical value of t has been designated.

Does -9.13 equal or exceed (in magnitude) -2.326? Yes. Thus, we may reject the null hypothesis and conclude that at least for these samples, IMPACT inmates have significantly higher PASSAC scores than those inmates in the incarcerated sample. In other words, the two means are different and the samples do not come from the same population regarding their respective distributions of PASSAC scores. We could be wrong 1 percent of the time, considering the level of significance at which the hypothesis was tested ($P \leq .01$).

Had a two-tailed, nondirectional test been made of the same hypothesis set, the new critical value of t would be -2.576, slightly larger than the one-tailed t critical value of -2.326. See if you can locate this value in the body of Table A.5. Again, the null hypothesis would have been rejected in view of the magnitude of our observed $t = -9.13$ in excess of the critical value required.

Assumptions, Advantages, and Disadvantages of the Two-Sample t Test. The assumptions of the t test for differences between means are: (1) both samples are selected randomly, (2) the analyzed scores must be measured according to an interval scale, (3) the samples must be independent of one another, (4) both sets of scores should be normally distributed, and (5) the sample variances should be similar. The assumption concerning the similarity of sample variances is often relaxed whenever this test is applied. An alternative formula discussed elsewhere (Champion, 1981) may be applied in the derivation of the standard error of the difference between two means. This formula adjusts for large variance (s^2) differences in the two samples and yields slightly smaller (more conservative) observed t values. In most instances, these adjustments are negligible and seldom influence the final hypothesis test outcome seriously.

The advantages of this test are that (1) it is well-known and widely applied, (2) it is quick and easy to interpret using tabled values, (3) it has no sample size restrictions, and (4) it is the most powerful test in tests of hypotheses about two independent samples, for which the variable under investigation is measured according to an interval scale. In fact, the t test for differences between means is used as the standard against which several nonparametric tests are compared.

Among the t test's disadvantages are the fact that the interval level of measurement is often difficult to achieve in criminological investigations. As we have seen, attitudinal information is often measured at best according to ordinal scales. The requirement, often ignored, that the sample variances should be similar is sometimes difficult to achieve. However, this requirement is often relaxed.

One important point should be illustrated relative to interpretations of observed values of t. When our observed t values are significant, this means that the two sample means are different. The inference is that the two population means, μ_1 and μ_2, which the two sample means are intended to estimate, are also different. This may or may not be true. Much depends upon how representative our samples are of the populations from which they were drawn. And we are never in the position of knowing how representative our samples are in any absolute sense. Thus, if our sample means are not, in fact, representative of their respective population means, we may make erroneous conclusions about the population mean differences. A graphic illustration is provided.

Suppose we had information relative to two sampling distributions with different μ's, distributed as shown in Figure 16.1. Notice that two μ values have been indicated for the two population means. There is also some overlap of the two distributions. Bear in mind that we do not know these values and are unlikely to ever know them. Notice also that two sample means are identified. These are close to one another on these two sampling distributions, but are located in the extremes of their respective curves. Thus, for the sampling distribution with μ_1, the sample mean we might select, $\overline{X}_1$, occurs in the far right tail of it, in an area of "low probability." In contrast, we have drawn a second mean, $\overline{X}_2$, that occurs in the far left tail of its distribution with μ_2. In each case, the sample means are purportedly representative of their population means. But we can see that these sample means are far from representative of their respective μ values. If we were to use the t test and determine that the two sample means were the same, it is likely that we would *fail to reject* the null hypothesis that might state that *the population means do not differ.* Obviously, with the special information we have, we can see such a decision would be wrong. But the researcher doesn't have this information or insight. These two sample means are "chance" occurrences, and while they are unlikely and in "low probability" areas of their respective sampling distributions, they may still occur.

The other scenario illustrating possible estimation errors on our part is shown in Figure 16.2. In this case, two sampling distributions have been drawn in such a way so as to be almost the same. Two population μ values have been identified that are the same for all practical purposes. But notice that the sample means have been selected from the extremes of both distributions. In the case of $\overline{X}_1$ as an estimate of μ_1, it has occurred in the far left tail of the first curve,

FIGURE 16.1 Two different population means with sample means as estimates shown close together.

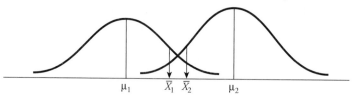

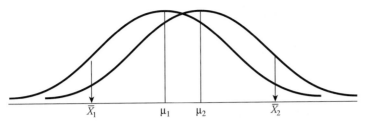

FIGURE 16.2 Two similiar population means with sample means as estimates shown far apart.

again in a low probability area. Also, $\overline{X}_2$ as an estimate of μ_2 occurs in the far right tail of its curve. Both sample means are poor estimates of their respective population parameters. However, researchers are never in the position of having prior knowledge about the true values of these respective μ's. In this case, a test of differences between these two sample means would lead researchers to believe that the two population means are probably different when, in fact, they are not.

These examples for the two-sample case are good reasons for why caution is recommended when making interpretations of our test results. We never know when our sample mean values are truly representative of their population parameters. If either of these cases exist, as illustrated by Figures 16.1 and 16.2, then we are in trouble and don't know it. We conclude our hypothesis tests with erroneous conclusions. But we use our levels of significance as the probability of being wrong in making these decisions about mean differences. These examples show why we use levels of significance, as well as why there must always be *some* error in any type of statistical inference. For the *k*-sample case, the problems illustrated in Figures 16.1 and 16.2 are simply compounded. The *F* test for analysis of variance exhibits this same type of problem. Only in the case of the *F* test, more than two means are involved.

The *F* Test for Analysis of Variance

The **F test for analysis of variance (ANOVA)** is a procedure that examines *k* groups and determines whether a significant difference exists between them on some interval-level characteristic. In a sense, it is an extension of the *t* test discussed in an earlier section of this chapter. Therefore, when the researcher has more than two samples of elements and is examining differences among them on some interval-level characteristic, one possible option might be to examine differences between two groups at a time with the *t* test. But researchers would be faced with multiple applications of the *t* test in order to examine all of these differences between pairs of sample means. For example, if investigators were examining differences among eight groups, there would be the following number of separate two-sample *t* tests required:

$$k(k - 1)/2$$

where k = number of sample means

Therefore, there would be $(8)(8 - 1)/2 = 56/2 = 28$ different t tests to be computed. The results of 28 separate t tests would tell researchers *which* groups differed from one another, but a great amount of time would be spent in tedious computational work. Fortunately, a procedure is available that examines all mean differences simultaneously. This procedure is the F test. The F test answers the following question: Does a significant difference exist anywhere among k samples on the variable measured? The answer to the question raised by the F test is equally simple: Yes, a difference exists somewhere, or No, a difference does not exist. Note that the F test doesn't specify *where* differences between groups are found, just that there are differences or no differences among the groups. An example of the application of the F test follows.

Silverman and Vega (1990) were interested in studying the amount of stress exhibited by correctional officers of several different types of prison environments in Florida. Suppose that through the Florida Department of Corrections, they obtained three samples of correctional officers from the following facilities: (1) Hillsborough Correctional Institution (HLCI) in Balm, (2) Indian River Correctional Institution (IRCI) in Vero Beach, and (3) the Sumter Correctional Institution (SCI) in Bushnell. The HLCI and IRCI facilities in Balm and Vero Beach, Florida, are considered minimum- and medium-security facilities, with inmate populations from 225 to 325. The SCI facility, housing about 850 offenders, includes all levels of custody, including maximum-security offenders. All three facilities house youthful (under age 25) first-offender felons, although those housed in SCI are considered most violent or dangerous compared with those housed in either HLCI or IRCI.

Suppose Silverman and Vega administered four inventories to three samples of correctional officers at the three institutions. These included a State-Trait Personality Inventory, an Anger Expression Scale, a Stress Stimuli Scale, and a Stress Reaction Scale. Among other things, these researchers might want to know whether correctional officer stress would be higher in more dangerous inmate settings (i.e., maximum-security) than less dangerous ones (i.e., minimum- or medium-security). On the basis of staff to inmate ratios, IRCI had 1.5 staff for every 2 inmates, whereas HLCI and SCI had one staff member for every 2 inmates.

Hypothetically, suppose we were to add a *fourth* institution, the Lancaster Correctional Institution (LCI) at Trenton (a minimum- and medium-security institution for youthful offenders with a staff-inmate ratio of 1.5:3) and arrange all four institutions ranging from most dangerous to least dangerous. Dangerousness might be decided partly on the basis of levels of custody and partly on the smaller ratios of staff to inmates. Higher levels of custody would suggest more dangerous institutions, while lower staff-inmate ratios would also reflect greater dangerousness, since there would be fewer staff to oversee more inmates. Conceivably, we might arrange these institutions as follows:

Most Dangerous   **Least Dangerous**

SCI _____ LCI _____ IRCI _____ HLCI

Further suppose that we administer a Stress Index (SI) to correctional officers at all four facilities. The SI results in a maximum of 30 points as indicative of high stress levels, while 0 points is indicative of either no stress or low stress levels. Based upon our theorizing about stress levels of these officers and the dangerousness of the institutions to which they are assigned, we might hypothesize the following:

H_0: There is no difference in stress levels among four samples of correctional officers assigned to correctional institutions that vary according to their dangerousness for officers.

H_1: There is a difference in stress levels among four samples of correctional officers assigned to correctional institutions that vary according to their dangerousness for officers.

$P \leq .01$ (two-tailed test)

Table 16.2 shows hypothetical distributions of correctional officers from each of these institutions, where $N_1 = 18, N_2 = 19, N_3 = 14$, and $N_4 = 15$. Individual or raw scores on the SI measure are designated for each of the samples, together with the computation of the four sample means as shown. Additional computational work in Table 16.2 includes determining the sums of scores and sums of all squared scores for the four samples. Finally, a grand mean or mean of means has been calculated.

A preliminary inspection of the different sample means in Table 16.2 shows that stress scores apparently decrease from one correctional facility to the next, moving from left to right, which is consistent with Silverman and Vega's presumptions about stress and facility dangerousness. The main question to be answered by the *F* test is whether there is a significant difference statistically in SI scores somewhere among these four samples of correctional officers? In order to answer this question, we must construct an analysis-of-variance summary table such as that shown in Table 16.3.

An examination of the ANOVA Summary in Table 16.3 discloses that there are two sources of variation in the scores that we have observed. These two sources are "between-group variation" and "within-group variation." **Between-group variation** *occurs whenever differences in scores exist between samples.* The fact that there are mean differences means that there is between-group score variation. If all of the four group means happened to be *identical,* there would be *no* between-group variation. This is seldom, if ever, the case in the real world of attitudinal scores and measurement. **Within-group variation** exists whenever scores within *any given sample differ from one another.* We can see by inspection that the individual raw scores in Table 16.2 vary within each group. Not everyone in the same group has the same score, and therefore, *some* within-group variation exists. In this case, the different samples of correctional officers exhibit variations in scores within each group. It is peculiar and highly unlikely for everyone in every group to have identical scores. This would mean that *all* persons in Group 1 would have identical scores; all

TABLE 16.2 Hypothetical Distribution of Correctional Officers from Four Different Correctional Institutions and Stress Index Scores

				INSTITUTION				
	SCI		LCI		IRCI		HLCI	
	$(N_1 = 18)$		$(N_2 = 19)$		$(N_3 = 14)$		$(N_4 = 15)$	
X_i	X^2_i	X_i	X^2_i	X_i	X^2_i	X_i	X^2_i
22	484	19	361	19	361	3	9
19	361	14	196	18	81	9	81
14	196	13	169	12	144	12	144
24	576	22	484	12	144	9	81
21	441	28	784	14	196	7	49
20	400	17	289	12	144	18	324
24	576	14	196	10	100	7	49
23	529	15	225	7	49	9	81
17	289	12	144	9	81	14	196
16	256	9	81	11	121	10	100
29	841	19	361	12	144	9	81
15	225	22	484	21	441	8	64
26	676	20	400	11	121	8	64
23	529	19	361	13	169	10	100
23	529	17	289			11	121
28	784	11	121				
21	441	14	196				
25	625	17	289				
		17	289				

$\Sigma X_1 = 390$ $\Sigma X^2_1 = 8758$ $\Sigma X_2 = 319$ $\Sigma X^2_2 = 5719$ $\Sigma X_3 = 181$ $\Sigma X^2_3 = 2539$ $\Sigma X_4 = 144$ $\Sigma X^2_4 = 1544$

$\overline{X}_1 = 21.7$ $\overline{X}_2 = 16.8$ $\overline{X}_3 = 12.9$ $\overline{X}_4 = 9.6$

$\overline{X}_T = 15.7$

TABLE 16.3 Analysis-of-Variance (ANOVA) Summary Table

Source of Variation	SS	df^a	MS	F_{obs}^b
Between Groups	1329.0 (SS_{bet})	3 (df_{bet})	443.0 (MS_{bet})	26.69
Within Groups	1031.7 (SS_{within})	62 (df_{within})	16.6 (MS_{within})	
Total	2360.7 (SS_{total})	65 (df_{total})		

[a] Between-groups $df = k - 1$, where k = number of groups; within-groups $df = \Sigma(N_k - 1)$, where N_k = each sample size; and total $df = \Sigma N_k - 1$.
[b] $F_{obs} = MS_{bet}/MS_{within} = 443/16.6 = 26.69$.

persons in Group 2 would have identical scores, and so forth. If either no variation between groups or no variation within groups had been observed, both of these values would be zero. This phenomenon is rare, however, since most k-sample comparisons exhibit both between- and within-group variation. For both between- and within-group variation, there are respective *sums of squares* (*SS*), degrees of freedom (*df*), and mean squares (*MS*) to be computed. After computing these values, we determine an **F ratio,** which is found in the upper right-hand corner of the ANOVA Summary in Table 16.3. This F ratio becomes our F_{observed} for purposes of making a decision about whether there are differences among the four samples of officers. There is much to do before reaching that point, however.

With the computations we have made and our knowledge of the four sample means, the grand mean, and individual sample sizes from Table 16.2, we may solve for the various values across the top of Table 16.3. We will solve for these values systematically, moving from left to right, across the top of the table. The first set of values we must determine is in a column, *SS*. *SS* means *sums of squares*. Notice that we must calculate the sums of squares for *both* between- and within-groups. These are designated respectively as SS_{bet} and SS_{within}. Once we have calculated these values, their sum will be SS_{total}. Each of these values is calculated as shown below. Sums of squares for between-groups is:

$$SS_{\text{bet}} = \Sigma N_k(\overline{X}_k - \overline{X}_T)^2$$

where N_k = sample size for the kth sample

$\overline{X}_k$ = mean for the kth sample

$\overline{X}_T$ = grand mean for all elements

Within-group variation is

$$SS_{\text{within}} = \Sigma(X_{ik} - \overline{X}_k)^2$$

where X_{ik} = each individual score across k samples (i.e., the ith score, kth sample)

$\overline{X}_k$ = kth sample mean

Total variation, SS_{total}, is the sum of both SS_{bet} and SS_{within}. A formula for this value is

$$SS_{\text{total}} = \Sigma(X_{ik} - \overline{X}_k)^2$$

where X_{ik} = ith score in the kth sample

$\overline{X}_T$ = grand mean

The SS_{bet} and SS_{within} values are critical to our problem solution, determining our observed F value. The SS_{total} is not an essential formula component, although it does enable us to *check our computational accuracy* through the so-called *short method* for determining each of the sums of squares. This short method is illustrated as follows. We must compute three numerical terms:

(1) $(\Sigma X_T^2)/\Sigma N_k$

where ΣX_T = sum of all scores across all groups

ΣN_k = sum of all sample sizes

(2) ΣX_k^2 or the sums of all squared scores across all samples

(3) $\Sigma\ [(\Sigma X_k)^2/N_k]$

where ΣX_k = sum of scores for each sample

N_k = sample size for each sample

Carrying out these computations for these three terms from the data we have computed in Table 16.2, we have

(1) $(390 + 319 + 181 + 144)^2/(18 + 19 + 14 + 15) = (1034)^2/66$

$$= 1,069,156/66$$

$$= 16,199.3$$

(2) $(8758 + 5719 + 2539 + 1544) = 18,560$

(3) $(390)^2/18 + (319)^2/19 + (181)^2/14 + (144)^2/15$

$$= 152,100/18 + 101,761/19 + 32,761/14 + 20,736/15$$

$$= 8450 + 5355.8 + 2340.1 + 1282.4$$

$$= 17,528.3$$

With these three terms calculated, we can solve for SS_{bet}, SS_{within}, and SS_{total} as follows:

SS_{bet} = (3) − (1) = 17,528.3 − 16,199.3 = 1329.0

SS_{within} = (2) − (3) = 18,560 − 17,528.3 = 1031.7

SS_{total} = (2) − (1) = 18,560 − 16,199.3 = 2360.7

Rounding error may result in slight differences in values when using the longer method compared with the shorter method. These differences are not crucial and will not affect our resulting F value significantly.

After determining the sums of squares, our next step is to determine degrees of freedom. Notice in the ANOVA Summary, Table 16.3, that there are degrees of freedom for between-group variation (df_{bet}), degrees of freedom for within-group variation (df_{within}), and degrees of freedom for total variation (df_{total}). The degrees of freedom for each of these sources of variation are computed as follows: df for between groups is simply $k - 1$, where k = the number of groups. Thus, with four groups, $4 - 1 = 3$ df. For within-group variation df, we must subtract "1" from each sample size and sum these results, or $(N_1 - 1)$

$+ (N_2 - 1) + (N_3 - 1) + (N_4 - 1)$. For the information in Table 16.3, we have $(18 - 1) + (19 - 1) + (14 - 1) + (15 - 1) = 17 + 18 + 13 + 14 = 62$ *df*. Thus, we have 62 *df* for within-group variation. We place these degrees of freedom in Table 16.3 as shown. Total *df* is calculated only as a computational check on our accuracy. We may obtain this value two ways. One is to sum the *df* for between- and within-group variation. Thus, $3 + 62 = 65$. The other way is to sum all sample sizes and subtract 1, or $18 + 19 + 14 + 15 = 66$, and $66 - 1 = 65$ for our total degrees of freedom. Degrees of freedom computational formulae are provided in a footnote to Table 16.3 for easy reference.

The fourth column, *MS*, stands for *mean square*. Mean squares for between-groups and within-groups are determined by dividing their respective *df*'s into their sums of squares or *SS*'s. These calculations are illustrated as follows:

$$
\begin{aligned}
MS_{bet} &= SS_{bet}/df_{bet} \\
&= 1329/3 \\
&= 443 \\
MS_{within} &= SS_{within}/df_{within} \\
&= 1031.7/62 \\
&= 16.6
\end{aligned}
$$

There is no such thing as MS_{total}, and, therefore, there is no need to make such a computation.

We are now ready to determine our observed value of F or $F_{observed}$. This is the ratio of our MS_{bet} to MS_{within}, or $443/16.6 = 26.69$ as shown in Table 16.3. We must now take our $F_{observed}$ to the table of critical values of F in Appendix A, Table A.6, pages 627–630. We must either *equal* or *exceed* the critical value of F, $F_{critical\ value}$, shown in the body of Table A.6 with our $F_{observed}$ value. Determining which critical value of F we must equal or exceed is accomplished by finding where our between- and within-group degrees of freedom intersect in the body of the table. Entering Table A.6 with *df*'s of 3 and 62 respectively (between- and within-group *df*), we first find our between-group *df* = 3 across the top of the table. Down either the left-hand or right-hand side of the table are various values of within-group degrees of freedom.

Inspecting this table shows no *df* = 62. The *closest* degrees of freedom to 62 provided in this table are for 60 *df* and 65 *df*, respectively. Whenever we are between *df* points in this table, we will *always* select the *smaller df*, since smaller *df* values yield slightly *larger* critical values of $F_{critical\ value}$, which we must equal or exceed with our $F_{observed}$. Thus, this is a *conservative decision*. Thus, where 3 *df* and 60 *df* intersect in the body of the table defines two critical values of F. Values shown in boldface are for the .01 level of significance, whereas other values are for the .05 level of significance. We are limited to these two significance levels when using this table. Incidentally, this is one reason why the significance levels of .05 and .01 have been conventionalized: *If we use these interpretive tables, these are the only two significance levels we can choose.*

However, if other statistics textbooks are available, sometimes a greater variety of significance levels and F critical values is provided.

With 3 df and 60 df respectively at the .01 level of significance, the $F_{critical\ value}$ which we must equal or exceed with our $F_{observed} = 4.13$. If our $F_{observed}$ equals or exceeds 4.13, then there is a significant difference in stress levels among these four samples of correctional officers. Our $F_{observed} = 26.69$ which is decidedly larger than 4.13. There is a difference in stress levels among these groups of correctional officers on the SI measure. Again, we could be wrong in rejecting H_0 and supporting H_1 about 1 percent of the time. For subsequent applications of the F test, Table A.6 contains a useful headnote that includes explanations of how degrees of freedom apply in determining critical values of F and how the levels of significance are designated.

It should be noted that a two-tailed test of the hypothesis set was made above. In almost all situations involving the F test of differences between k samples of elements, researchers are interested in whether the k samples *differ* on the measured characteristic. If it is important that direction be known or assessed, this can usually be done by inspecting the arrangement of means across the k samples. For example, moving from left to right in Table 16.3, each sample of correctional officers has a lower mean value on their SI scores. This means that directionally, at least, as we move from more dangerous facilities (SCI and LCI) to less dangerous ones (IRCI and HLCI), there appears to be less correctional officer stress indicated by these SI scores.

Assumptions of the F Test. The assumptions underlying the F test are (1) randomness, (2) independent samples, (3) the interval level of measurement underlying the trait measured, (4) normal distribution for each distribution of scores analyzed, and (5) **homogeneity of variances** or equal variances. The Hartley F_{max} test is one procedure that can be used to determine whether homogeneity of variance exists. It is discussed elsewhere (Champion, 1981).

Advantages and Disadvantages of the F Test. The F test is the most powerful measure of differences between k samples. In a sense, it is an extension of the t test and has equivalent power. It is not particularly difficult to apply. Rather, it may be a tedious more than a difficult application for large N's. However, because of its stringent assumptions, it is likely that more than one of these assumptions will be violated when applying this test. But like the t test, the F test is popular and has widespread conventional usage in social research. There are no sample size restrictions associated with this test.

■ GOODNESS-OF-FIT AND NONPARAMETRIC STATISTICAL TESTS

A majority of the statistical procedures presented in this chapter are known as goodness-of-fit tests. **Goodness of fit** refers to the similarity between what is observed and what might be expected according to chance. Another way of viewing goodness of **fit** is the similarity between **observed** and **expected** frequencies. An extreme hypothetical situation serves to illustrate what is meant by goodness of fit. Suppose we possessed information about a sample of 100 convicted rapists in North Dakota. Further suppose that we knew absolutely nothing about the characteristics of rapists, including their probable gender.

Expected frequencies are often defined by the number of categories into which they are arranged. For instance, if we distributed 300 persons across three categories, we might expect 100 persons to be in each of the categories. Our expected frequencies would be defined by taking the number of persons, N, and dividing this by the number of categories into which they are dispersed, k, or N/k. If $N = 300$ and $k = 3$, then $300/3 = 100$ frequencies. Thus, we would expect 100 persons to be found in each of the three categories. Applying N/k to the present hypothetical example of North Dakota rapists, we may wish to disperse them into two categories, *male* and *female*. In order to determine how many male and female rapists would be expected to occur according to chance, we would apply N/k or $100/2 = 50$ to yield the following:

Expected Number of Male and Female Rapists

Male	Female	
50	50	$N = 100$

Thus, it would appear from these expected frequencies that there would be 50 male and 50 female rapists *according to chance*. Again, chance is defined according to the number of categories into which our data have been divided and our sample size, or N/k. When we tabulate the actual numbers of North Dakota rapists who are male and female, we might observe the following distribution:

Observed Number of Male and Female Rapists

Male	Female	
90	10	$N = 100$

These frequencies are known as our **observed frequencies,** since they are what we actually observe when we tabulate our collected information. The goodness of fit is the discrepancy between what is observed and what is expected according to chance. Therefore, we would compare the expected 50–50 split with our observed 90–10 split to see the degree of goodness of fit. Obviously, there is poor goodness of fit between these observed and expected cell frequencies. *The greater the discrepancy between what we expect and what we observe, the more significant are our observations statistically.* This is important. In the above instance, we would likely conclude that disproportionately more of our North Dakota rapists are males rather than females. And if we had applied a goodness-of-fit test to evaluate the discrepancy between the expected and observed cell frequencies, our test results would probably have been statistically significant.

The Chi Square Test

The **chi square test**, χ^2, is the most popular goodness-of-fit statistic used in social science literature today. An example from criminal justice literature illustrates the test application. Reed Adams and Ron Vogel (1986) investigated prostitution, sentencing patterns of those arrested and convicted for the crime, and citizen awareness of its incidence in a North Carolina jurisdiction. Among other objectives, the researchers sought to determine whether there were significant differences between first-offenders (arrested prostitutes) and the frequency with which warnings/releases, fines, or probation were used as optional punishments. First-offenders are often treated leniently by judges, although the type of leniency/punishment might vary. Using this idea for our example and a hypothetical sample of 192 convicted prostitutes in a particular North Carolina jurisdiction, we might generate the following hypothesis set:

H_0: There is no difference in the type of punishment imposed on first-offender prostitutes.

H_1: There is a difference in the type of punishment imposed on first-offender prostitutes.

$P \leq .001$ (two-tailed test)

This is a two-tailed or nondirectional test, since no attempt is made to predict the direction of difference associated with the three punishment categories. Table 16.4 shows a hypothetical sample of 192 arrested prostitutes according to whether they have been given warnings by judges and released, whether they have been convicted and ordered to pay fines, or whether they have been convicted and granted probation. This table has been constructed so as to show both the observed and expected frequencies distributed throughout the three punishment categories.

In Table 16.4, both the observed and expected frequencies are presented. The expected frequencies for the three categories have been determined by using N/k, where N is the sample size of numbers of prostitutes ($N = 192$) and k = the number of punishment categories (i.e., whether these prostitutes received warnings and were released, were convicted and fined, or convicted and received probation). In this case, the expected frequencies were determined as

TABLE 16.4 Observed and Expected Frequencies for a Hypothetical Sample of 192 North Carolina Prostitutes According to Punishment Severity

First-Offenders	Warning Release	Fine	Probation	Totals
Observed frequencies	121	40	31	$N = 192$
	(63%)	(21%)	(16%)	100%
Expected frequencies	64	64	64	$N = 192$

192/3 = 64 frequencies per category as illustrated. The formula for the chi square test for a single sample is as follows:

$$\chi^2 = \Sigma \frac{(O_k - E_k)^2}{E_k}$$

where O_k = the observed frequencies in the kth cell

E_k = the expected frequencies in the kth cell

For the data in Table 16.4, we may carry out our computations as follows:

$$\chi^2 = (121 - 64)^2/64 + (40 - 64)^2/64 + (31 - 64)^2/64$$
$$= (57)^2/64 + (24)^2/64 + (33)^2/64$$
$$= 3249/64 + 576/64 + 1089/64$$
$$= 50.766 + 9.000 + 17.016$$
$$= 76.782.$$

The observed chi square (χ^2) value = 76.782.

To determine the significance of this observed χ^2, we turn to Table A.4, Appendix A, page 625. Across the top of the table are both one- and two-tailed probabilities. Down the left-hand side of the table are degrees of freedom, df. For the single-sample application of χ^2, $df = k - 1$, where k = the number of categories into which the sample has been divided. In this case, $k = 3$, and so $df = k - 1$ or $3 - 1$ or 2 df. Entering Table A.4 with 2 df at the .001 level of significance with a two-tailed test of the hypothesis, we determine where these values intersect in the body of the table. This defines the critical value of χ^2, or 13.815. If our observed χ^2 value equals or exceeds 13.815, then we can reject H_0 and support H_1. Since our observed χ^2 value of 76.782 equals or exceeds the critical value in Table A.4, we support H_1 that there is a difference among first-offender prostitutes and the type of punishment they receive.

Headnote instructions in Table A.4 are useful for using the table for one-tailed hypothesis tests. Whenever one-tailed χ^2 applications are desired for single-sample tests, it is necessary to inspect the observed distribution of frequencies to see whether the distribution is in the direction predicted under H_1. Had we predicted that first-offender prostitutes would tend to receive warnings rather than fines or probation, for instance, then our data would have been in the predicted direction under H_1. One-tailed tests always require careful inspection of the distribution of observed cell frequencies to make sure they are in the predicted direction as specified in our H_1's.

Assumptions, Advantages, and Disadvantages of the Chi Square Test. Three assumptions of the chi square test are (1) randomness, (2) the nominal level of measurement, and (3) a sample size of 25 or larger. The chi square test is easy to apply and interpret. It has both one- and two-tailed applications and may be applied to any data in categorical form. An interpretive table (Table A.4 in Appendix A) exists for a rapid determination of critical values of this statistic. A major weakness of the chi square test is the sensitivity of the test to very small and very large samples. The reasonable operating range for this test is sample size variation from 25 to 250.

An example of the influence of sample size changes on the magnitude of the observed chi square value may be provided by doubling the observed frequencies in Table 16.4. Thus, instead of having observed frequencies of 121, 40, and 31 respectively, we would have 242, 80, and 62. We would still have $k = 3$, but we would now be dealing with a sample size double that of 192 or (2)(192) = 384. This would mean that our calculated expected cell frequencies would be 384/3 = 128. If we were to carry out our chi square computations on this enlarged sample size, the original observed χ^2 of 76.782 would double to 153.564. (The truthfulness of this statement is left for you as a mathematical exercise).

If you entered Table A.4 in Appendix A with this new value, 153.564, this result may appear impressive. This is because the largest critical value in the entire table is 59.703, in the lower right-hand corner. Precisely the same proportionate distribution of frequencies exists in the new situation, where the frequencies have been doubled, compared with the original distribution of frequencies. However, our new result seems more significant statistically. In reality, an inflated chi square value occurred because of the doubled frequencies. There is no true change in the proportionate distribution of frequencies. This demonstrates chi square sensitivity to changes in sample size. When the chi-square test is applied to samples appreciably larger than 250, the distortion on the χ^2 value makes it unreliable as a test of significance.

Two additional recommendations are made. First, percentages have been computed for the observed frequencies in Table 16.4. Sometimes researchers have applied the chi square test to percentages. This is incorrect. Using the chi square test on percentages is like treating the data as though the sample size were 100 (i.e., 100 percent). Every time χ^2 is computed for percentages, the sample size for each variable subclass changes to 100, consistent with 100 percent. *Do not chi square percentages.* Also, the chi square test should not be applied whenever one or more expected cell frequencies is less than 5. The reason for not applying it is the same as before—you will obtain a distorted chi square value that may be misinterpreted as significant when no such significance exists.

Chi Square for Two or *K* Independent Samples

The chi square test for two or k independent samples is similar to the one-sample chi square test and is actually an extension of it. This chi square application is perhaps the most popular, since data are cross-tabulated according to one independent variable and one dependent variable. Cross-tabulations of variables are expressed in tables of various sizes. Table sizes are expressed as $r \times c$, where $r =$ the number of rows and $c =$ the number of columns. Conventionally, the column variable is independent, while the row variable is dependent. Also, the independent variable subclasses or number of divisions on the independent variable express the number of samples investigated. Thus, for the two-sample case, our chi square statistic would apply to any $r \times 2$ case. This means that we always would have two columns, while the number of rows might vary. However, r will never be smaller than 2 for this particular chi square application. The most common is $r \times c = 2 \times 2$ or two rows and two columns. This is the conventional 2×2 table. An example from criminology literature illustrates both the application of chi square and the use of 2×2 tables.

Crank et al. (1986) have extensively investigated cynicism among police chiefs and factors that appear to influence such cynicism. Cynicism is described in various ways, but these researchers characterize it by "three interlocking sentiments: diffuse feelings of hate, envy, and hostility" (pp. 345-346). Cynicism among police chiefs appears to vary according to how long these chiefs have been in their present positions. The longer they remain on the job as chiefs, the greater the likelihood for the onset of cynicism. One reason is that during their early years as chiefs, their policies and recommendations are often followed by subordinates. However, the longer they remain in their positions, the more likely certain subordinates are to oppose subsequent policies and changes that these chiefs recommend. What are basically satisfying and rewarding experiences in one's early years as a police chief gradually shift to dissatisfying and unrewarding experiences. Cynicism is gradually acquired. These authors note that another factor contributing to such cynicism is that departmental personnel "may be protected by civil service or union statutes, and therefore [may be] able to deflect much of a chief's authority" (pp. 348-349).

Suppose we were to obtain a sample of 128 police chiefs from various police departments in the Midwest. Further assume that we could divide these chiefs according to whether they were "tenured" or "untenured," where tenure is granted after these persons have served as chiefs satisfactorily for at least six years or longer. We might also devise a measure of "police cynicism" and create a dichotomous distinction of those who have either "high" or "low" cynicism. The fact that "years of service" and "high and low cynicism" are measurable according to higher scales than nominal is irrelevant whenever a quantity is expressed as a **dichotomous variable.** When variable subclasses are dichotomized, any ordinal or interval features associated with them is immediately eliminated. Thus, we might as well be examining discrete subclasses such as "male" and "female," "Democrat" and "Republican," or "Catholic" and "Protestant" and "Jewish." We might observe the following cross-tabulation of nontenured–tenured police chiefs and high and low cynicism as shown in Table 16.5.

TABLE 16.5 Nontenured–Tenured Status of 128 Midwestern Police Chiefs and Cynicism

Tenured Status of Police Chiefs

		Untenured		Tenured		Totals
	High	29	*a*	34	*b*	63
Cynicism						
	Low	43	*c*	22	*d*	65
	Totals	72		56		$N = 128$
		(N_1)		(N_2)		

The following hypothesis set is suggested for test:

H_0: There is no difference between police chiefs with or without tenure and their degree of cynicism.

H_1: There is a difference between police chiefs with or without tenure and their degree of cynicism.

$P \le .05$ (two-tailed test)

In order to compute our observed χ^2 for the data shown in Table 16.5, the following procedure is applied. We must first determine the expected cell frequencies. In the 2×2 table in Table 16.5, each cell has been labeled as a, b, c, and d. To determine the expected frequency for each cell, multiply the row total in which the cell is found by the column total in which that cell is found and divide by the total N. The following computations illustrate how each expected cell frequency is determined:

Cell:

$a = (63)(72)/128 = 4536/128 = 35.4$

$b = (63)(56)/128 = 3528/128 = 27.6$

$c = (65)(72)/128 = 4680/128 = 36.6$

$d = (65)(56)/128 = 3640/128 = 28.4$

With these expected cell frequencies determined, we may compute the observed χ^2 value as follows:

$$\text{Observed } \chi^2 = \frac{(O_k - E_k)^2}{E_k}$$

where O_k = the observed cell frequency for the kth cell

E_k = the expected cell frequency for the kth cell

The computational work for determining our observed χ^2 value is shown in Table 16.6.

The computation in Table 16.6 yields an observed χ^2 value = 5.202. We may now turn to Table A.4 in Appendix A, page 625, and interpret this χ^2 value. Table A.4 contains both one- and two-tailed probabilities across the top of the table. Down the left-hand side are degrees of freedom, df. For the two-sample case, df are determined by the formula $(r - 1)(c - 1)$, where r = the number of rows and c = the number of columns. In the 2×2 tabular case, $df = (2 - 1)$ $(2 - 1) = (1)(1) = 1 \ df$. Where 1 df intersects with the .05 level of significance (used for testing the hypothesis set) for a two-tailed test is found the critical value of $\chi^2 = 3.841$. If our observed value equals or exceeds the critical value, then we may reject the null hypothesis and support H_1. Since 5.202 equals or ex-

TABLE 16.6 Computation of Chi Square for a 2 × 2 Table

Cell	O_k	E_k	$(O_k - E_k)^2$	$(O_k - E_k)^2/E_k$
a	29	35.4	40.96	$40.96/35.4 = 1.157$
b	34	27.6	40.96	$40.96/27.6 = 1.484$
c	43	36.6	40.96	$40.96/36.6 = 1.119$
d	22	28.4	40.96	$40.96/28.4 = 1.442$
Total				Observed $\chi^2 = 5.202$

ceeds 3.841, we may reject H_0 and support the hypothesis that there is a difference between these untenured and tenured police chiefs and their degree of cynicism. Because this was a two-tailed, nondirectional test, we were simply interested in determining whether there was a difference among the chiefs rather than projecting a difference among them in a specific direction.

If a one-tailed interpretation of chi square is desired and direction specified in the hypothesis set, we may use the one-tailed probability levels shown in Table A.4 in Appendix A. The headnote in Table A.4 elaborates on how the table can easily be used. In the one-tailed directional case, we should first inspect our distribution of observed frequencies in Table 16.5 to make sure that the cell frequencies bunch up in the desired direction as specified by the research hypothesis. For instance, if we say that police chiefs without tenure will have less cynicism than chiefs with tenure, then large numbers of chiefs without tenure will also have low cynicism. Also, those chiefs with tenure will be expected to have a high degree of cynicism. An inspection of Table 16.5 shows that the frequencies bunch up in the right direction, where 34 chiefs with tenure have high cynicism and where 43 chiefs without tenure have low cynicism.

Assumptions, Advantages and Disadvantages of the Chi Square Test. The assumptions underlying the appropriate application of the chi square test for two samples are (1) randomness, (2) independent samples, and (3) data measured according to a nominal scale. With the exceptions of how degrees of freedom and expected cell frequencies are determined, the chi square test for two independent samples is the same as the single-sample application of it. This includes the recommendation that it should be applied when the researcher has sample sizes ranging from 25 to 250. Appreciably smaller or larger sample sizes would seriously distort the resulting observed chi square value, and we might likely misinterpret the significance of our tabular distributions of data. The test is easy to apply, an interpretive table exists for a rapid determination of critical values and the significance of χ^2, and there are few restrictive assumptions governing its appropriate application. Finally, the two-sample procedure may be extended to apply to k samples in tables of *any $r \times c$* size.

■ CORRELATIONS, ASSOCIATIONS, AND RELATIONSHIPS

The numerical expression of the degree to which two variables are in step or fluctuate with each other is known as a **coefficient of association.** A procedure that yields these coefficients is called a **measure of association.** Tests of theory or theoretical schemes often involve **measures of association.** To what extent do two variables vary one from the other? To what extent does a **relationship** exist between one variable and another? For instance, it might be believed that an association exists between poverty and crime. It may appear that those in lower socioeconomic statuses have higher arrest rates than those in higher socioeconomic statuses. An association would be said to exist between poverty and crime.

In another instance, it might be believed that increasing the number of street lights in a given section of a city will decrease the amount of crime in that section. Subsequently, if researchers observe that well-lighted sections of the city have proportionately fewer crimes committed compared with poorly lit city sections, one conclusion drawn might be that an association exists between the incidence of crime and the amount of city lighting.

A measure of **association,** also known as **relationship** and **correlation,** furnishes the platform for making causal statements about variables. Although the terms *relationship, correlation,* and *association* are used interchangeably in criminological research, there are some subtle differences between them. The term *association* is preferred because it has the least connotation of causality. Relationship and correlation have a stronger implication of causality.

Associations between variables may be described according to (1) the strength of association, (2) the direction of association, (3) the statistical significance of an association, and (4) the predictive utility of the association.

Strength of Association

There are several ways of describing associations between variables. One way is to discuss variable associations in terms of the **strength of association.** A strong association between variables or **direct relationship** is gauged according to how closely we approach either +1.00 (a perfect positive association) or −1.00 (a perfect negative association). No association or an absence of an association is indicated by 0. Association coefficients are either positive or negative and are conventionally expressed to the nearest hundredth. From a conventional standpoint, coefficients of association of ±.30 or larger are considered strong in the criminological literature. The following guide may be used to assess the general strength of association coefficients:

± 0.00 to .25 = no association or low association (weak association)

± .26 to .50 = moderately low association (moderately weak association)

± .51 to .75 = moderately high association (moderately strong association)

± .76 to 1.00 = high association (strong association) up to perfect positive or negative association

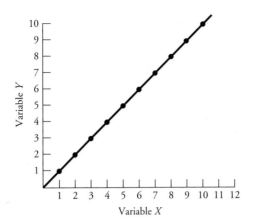

FIGURES 16.3
Perfect positive association between variables *X* and *Y*.

Figures 16.3 and 16.4 illustrate (1) a perfect positive association between variables *X* and *Y*, and (2) a perfect negative association between variables *X* and *Y*. In Figure 16.3, a unit increase in variable *X* is followed by a unit increase in variable *Y*. Plotting the intersection points as shown enables us to draw a straight line representing the perfect association between these hypothetical variables. Since this line is fairly straight, it is also considered as **linear. Linearity** is a straight-line relation between variables. For example, if a new crime occurs in a given neighborhood for each street light we remove, there will be a linear relation between the number of street lights and the amount of crime. If we observe a one-inch growth in a plant for each quart of water we give it, then a linear relation exists between the amount of water fed to a plant and the amount of its growth. Figure 16.4 shows that for each unit increase in variable *Y*, a unit decrease occurs in variable *X*. Plotting the intersecting points in this figure also shows a straight line, but in the opposite direction to that shown in Figure 16.3. This is also a linear association, but in this case, it is a perfect negative or *inverse* association.

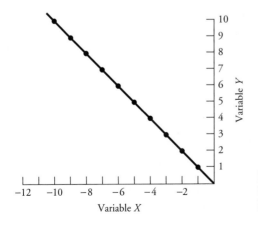

FIGURES 16.4
Perfect negative (inverse) association between variables *X* and *Y*.

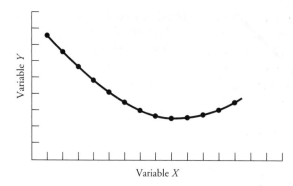

FIGURES 16.5
Curvilinear association between variables *X* and *Y*. Values on variable *Y* tend to decrease for a time as the values on variable *X* increase. While *X* continues to increase, the values on *Y* begin to increase after a time as well.

Nonlinear associations between variables are represented by lines drawn from intersection points that are not aligned in a straight-line fashion. Figure 16.5 represents a *curvilinear association* between variables *X* and *Y*. It is probably true that few, if any, variable interrelationships in criminology and criminal justice are truly linear. But for certain measures of association, such as the well-known Pearson *r*, linearity between variables is assumed. Thus, if linearity does not exist, then at least one assumption of the Pearson *r* is not met, and the application of the *r* to one's data would be questionable.

Direction of Association

We can also discuss association in terms of the **direction of association.** If we were to discuss both the strength and direction of .32, for example, then this would be a moderately low (moderately weak) positive association. An association coefficient of −.55 would be a moderately strong (moderately high) negative or inverse association.

Statistical Significance of Association

Another way of discussing association is the **statistical significance of association.** Each measure of association can be evaluated in terms of how significant the observed coefficient is from 0. All measures of association have tests of significance to determine the significance of the observed coefficient from zero or no association. For instance, if researchers observe a coefficient of .83, they might conclude that this coefficient is significant at the .05 level. But as we will soon see, tests of significance applied to measures of association are frequently misleading and inappropriate. A measure's significance depends in large part upon one's sample size. Larger sample sizes affect interpretations of the significance of correlation coefficients in the same way that larger sample sizes affect the interpretation of other tests of significance, such as the *t* test, *Z* test, or *F* test.

An example of how the statistical significance of a measure of association can be badly misinterpreted is the hypothetical case of observing a coefficient = .01, the amount of association between variables *X* and *Y*. This means that there is almost no association between the two variables. Using our crude interpretive table above, we might say there is a low positive association between the two variables. Suppose our sample size is 2000. A sample size this large may reduce our sampling error to the extent that when we assess how different .01 is from 0.00, we may conclude that our association coefficient of .01 is significant at the .05 level of significance. So what? This is an example of statistical significance that doesn't mean anything. We can maximize the interpretation of our correlation coefficients by using the proportional reduction in error.

Proportional-Reduction-in-Error (PRE), Explanation, and Prediction

We are interested in the predictive power or explanatory utility of certain variables related to others. For instance, if we want to explain juvenile delinquency, what is the importance of knowing about socioeconomic status or peer-group pressure and the possible influence of these variables upon delinquency? What kind of association exists between delinquency and broken homes?

These prediction situations involve associations between variables. But our interest is in making accurate forecasts of individual and social behaviors based on our previous knowledge of other crucial variables. We would like to be able to say, "If X, then Y." Certainly a juvenile delinquency rehabilitation center would like to cure all delinquents who participate in the center's program. But this example assumes *perfect* prediction. Unfortunately, there are few instances of perfect prediction in any science. Whatever we fail to predict accurately is called **error.** Therefore, we devote much time to identifying, measuring, and using variables that will minimize errors in our prediction scenarios.

Using certain measures of association in our research will often serve the function of telling us how much error we have accounted for in predicting particular behavioral outcomes. Suppose we are interested in the association between delinquency and whether children are or are not continuously supervised by adults. We may believe that children who are continuously supervised by adults will have little or no opportunity to commit delinquent acts. Those youths who do not have continuous adult supervision may be in a better position to commit delinquent acts if they choose to do so. Therefore, we predict initially that delinquency will depend on whether or not children are under continuous adult supervision. We expect to find the association between these two variables, *delinquency* and *degree of adult supervision,* as shown in Table 16.7.

TABLE 16.7 Error-free Relation Between Delinquency and Continuity of Adult Supervision Over Youths

	Continuous Adult Supervision	
	Yes	No
Delinquent	0	50
Nondelinquent	50	0

In Table 16.7, we have samples of 50 delinquents and 50 nondelinquents. We cross-tabulate these delinquents and nondelinquents according to whether they are continuously supervised by adults. Under an error-free model, we would find *all* delinquent youths without continuous adult supervision, while *all* nondelinquent youths would have continuous adult supervision. There are no errors in this type of model. But what we if we observe a distribution that is less-than-perfect, such as the cross-tabulation shown in Table 16.8?

Table 16.8 contains 15 "errors." Errors occur when delinquents and nondelinquents fall into cells where they are not expected to fall. For instance, there are five youths who are delinquent but who are also continuously supervised by adults. These are unexpected and therefore "errors." There are also ten nondelinquent youths who are not supervised continuously by adults. Together, these 15 youths are "errors," in that they do not fall into the categories we expected as forecast in Table 16.7. Although our knowledge of whether the youths are continuously supervised by adults did not result in perfect prediction in this situation, we *did* manage to account for a large amount of the error we would otherwise have without this knowledge. We accounted for 85 of the cases of delinquents and nondelinquents by knowing whether they were or were not continuously supervised by adults, but we failed to account for the remaining 15 cases.

If we had predicted that *all* youths in our sample of 100 were delinquent, then we would have been wrong 50 times, since 50 of these youths turned out to be nondelinquent. Accordingly, had we predicted that all 100 youths would be nondelinquent, we would have made 50 errors, since 50 of the youths turned out to be delinquent. With a knowledge of continuous or noncontinuous supervision, however, we have minimized our prediction error as follows:

$$\frac{\text{original error} - \text{error with continuous adult supervision variable}}{\text{original error}} (100)$$

$$= \frac{50 - 15}{50} (100)$$

$$= \frac{35}{50} (100)$$

$$= 70 \text{ percent}$$

TABLE 16.8 Imperfect Relation Between Delinquency and Continuity of Adult Supervision

	Continuous Adult Supervision	
	Yes	No
Delinquent	5	40
Nondelinquent	45	10

By using the adult supervision variable, we have reduced our error in predicting delinquency for these 100 youths by 70 percent. Instead of committing 50 errors as we did originally, we only commit 15 errors using a predictor variable such as adult supervision. We have reduced the actual number of errors from 50 to 15, a 70 percent error reduction. This **proportional reduction in error** is conventionally labeled **PRE.** Some measures of association have *PRE* interpretations, whereas other measures do not have them. Generally, measures of association having *PRE* interpretations are preferred over those not having such interpretations. Thus, whether measures have *PRE* interpretations becomes one of the criteria we use to select our measures of association to apply in our analysis of data.

PRE is perhaps the most important criterion used for discussing coefficients of association. We may compare variables to see which are better predictors of phenomena than other variables. In most cases, those measures of association that have *PRE* interpretations and that are discussed in subsequent sections usually have *symmetric PRE* interpretations. This means that whether we use variable *X* as a predictor of variable *Y* or variable *Y* as a predictor of variable *X,* both scenarios will yield identical coefficients of the same magnitude. In a few cases, some measures of association have **symmetric** and **asymmetric** *PRE* **interpretations.** When measures have asymmetric interpretations, this means that we can determine which variable is the better predictor of the other. For instance, if we use variable *X* as a predictor of *Y,* and then use variable *Y* as a predictor of *X,* coefficients of different magnitudes will be yielded by our computations. This occurrence is from a measure of association with an asymmetric interpretation. One such measure is lambda (λ), the coefficient of predictability. It has both asymmetric or directional and symmetric or nondirectional interpretations.

In popular statistical programs and software packages, such as the *Statistical Package for the Social Sciences for Windows* or *SPSSWIN,* perhaps as many as 30 different measures of association may be calculated. Not all of these measures are suitable for a particular research problem, however. As is the case with different tests of significance, each measure of association has advantages, disadvantages, assumptions, and limited applications. Depending upon the data we have collected, we may or may not be able to apply certain measures.

■ SELECTED MEASURES OF ASSOCIATION

Two Nominal-Level Variables

When researchers want to determine the association between two variables measured according to a nominal scale, there are several measures that may be selected. At least six measures are available, including (1) Pearson's *C*; (2) Guttman's coefficient of predictability, lambda, λ; (3) Cramer's *V*; (4) Tschuprow's *T*; (5) the phi coefficient, ϕ.; and (6) tetrachoric *r.* All of these measures are discussed elsewhere (Champion, 1981). Two of them are featured here for a brief discussion: Pearson's *C* and Guttman's lambda, λ.

Pearson's C. **Pearson's C** is derived directly from a chi square value. Suppose we have some data from 91 parole-eligible prison inmates. An inspection of inmate records reveals that these prisoners have committed various numbers of prison infractions and have been written up by correctional officers during the period of their confinement. Suppose we divide these 91 inmates according to whether they have "many" write-ups and "few" write-ups, where "many" is defined as 4 or more write-ups and "few" is 3 or fewer write-ups. We determine that 43 inmates have "many" write-ups, while 48 inmates have "few" write-ups.

Next, we observe these inmates' parole hearings and determine which of these 91 inmates are granted parole or early release. We note that 48 inmates are granted parole, while 43 inmates are denied parole. If we cross-tabulate inmate write-ups or infractions with their parole decision, we might have a table such as shown in Table 16.9.

A preliminary inspection of Table 16.9 shows that 26 inmates who have many write-ups or infractions are denied parole, whereas 31 inmates with few write-ups of infractions or write-ups are granted parole. A chi square test of goodness of fit yields a $\chi^2 = 6.227$, which is significant at the .05 level (1 *df*). This test of significance is important because it says that the distribution of frequencies in Table 16.9 is different from what would be expected by chance. There is a definite difference between those inmates with many and those with few write-ups as to whether they are granted or denied parole. Our inspection of the table seems to support the idea that those inmates with few infractions tend to be granted parole, while those inmates with many infractions tend to be denied parole. However, the chi square test does not say what correlation exists between these two variables. We must apply some correlation measure to answer this question. Pearson's C might be applied, since it can be determined easily and directly from a knowledge of the chi square value. The formula for Pearson's C is as follows:

$$C = \sqrt{\frac{\chi^2}{N + \chi^2}}$$

where N = sample size

χ^2 = observed chi square value

TABLE 16.9 Inmate Parole Decision and Number of Infractions

Inmate infractions or write-ups

		Many	Few	Totals
Parole Granted	Yes	17	31	48
	No	26	17	43
Totals		43	48	91

Inserting our N and χ^2 values in the formula, we have

$$C = \sqrt{\frac{6.227}{91 + 6.227}}$$

$$C = \sqrt{.0640}$$

$$C = .25$$

The resulting Pearson's $C = .25$. This is a moderately low positive association between the number of write-ups or infractions and whether inmates are granted parole.

Strengths and Weaknesses of Pearson's C.
The primary strengths of Pearson's C are that it can be computed directly from a chi square value and interpreted easily. The significance of the C value itself is measured by the magnitude of the original chi square value. Chi square is the test of significance for C. If the chi square value is significant, then the Pearson's C is also significant. In this instance, we have a significant C value, but it is a moderately low correlation between the two variables.

On the negative side, Pearson's C is merely an index number. It can never achieve 1.00 or perfect correlation, because of inherent computational limitations. In fact, the maximum C value that could be obtained for this table, even if *all* paroled inmates had few infractions and *all* nonparoled inmates had many infractions would be .71. Thus, the $C = .25$ is somewhat misleading. A correction factor can be applied in order to bolster the magnitude of the observed C value. This correction factor is discussed elsewhere and is contingent upon table size (Champion, 1981:309–310). In the present example, the correction factor is .707 and is used as a denominator term. A corrected C value, or $\overline{C}$ is yielded. In this case, the corrected C or $\overline{C} = C/.707 = .25/.707 = .35$. This corrected C value is an improvement over the original C value of .25, but nevertheless, we still have a moderately low correlation between the two variables.

An additional problem with C values is that they cannot be compared directly with one another. If we had different C values for different samples of elements, these coefficients could not be compared directly. Finally, Pearson's C has no *PRE* interpretation. We do not know how much variation in either variable is explained by using the two variables as mutual predictors.

Guttman's Coefficient of Predictability, Lambda, λ.
Guttman's coefficient of predictability, lambda, (λ), is the best measure of association whenever we have two variables measured according to a nominal scale. Lambda has a *PRE* interpretation and enables us to determine how much variation is explained by using the two variables as predictors. Lambda is a substantial improvement over Pearson's C. Suppose we were to apply lambda to the data in Table 16.9. We would use the following formula for lambda:

$$\lambda = \frac{\Sigma f_r + \Sigma f_c - (F_r + F_c)}{2N - (F_r - F_c)}$$

where f_r = largest frequency occurring in a row

$\quad f_c$ = largest frequency occurring in a column

$\quad F_r$ = largest marginal frequency occurring among the rows

$\quad F_c$ = largest marginal frequency occurring among the columns

$\quad N$ = number of observations for the table

Using information from Table 16.9, we would compute lambda as follows:

$$\lambda = [(31 + 26) + (26 + 31) - (48 + 48)]/[(2)(91) - (48 + 48)]$$

$$= (114 - 96)/(182 - 96)$$

$$= 18/86 = .21.$$

Our λ = 21. Using this lambda of .21, we can say that 21 percent of the variation between the two variables (write-ups or infractions and parole granting or denial) is explained by the two variables used as mutual predictors. Again, this is a low correlation between the two variables if we were to interpret lambda according to its strength. Conversely, we can say that 79 percent of the variation between the two variables is unexplained.

Strengths and Weaknesses of Lambda. The primary strengths of lambda include the fact that it has a *PRE* interpretation. Lambda values computed for different samples may be compared directly with one another. Lambda can achieve perfect association of 1.00. There are no table size limitations governing when lambda can be applied. Although lambda is designed for two variables measured according to a nominal scale, it may be applied to data where higher levels of measurement are achieved. There are no significant weaknesses of lambda.

The lambda we determined for the data in Table 16.9 is interpreted as a symmetric **PRE measure.** This means that *both* variables, write-ups or infractions and parole granting or denial are used as mutual predictors of one another. If we wanted to determine which variable was the *better* predictor of the other, we could use an alternative lambda formula for this purpose. We would have to rearrange our table so that the dependent variable, parole granting or denial, would be placed in the independent variable position across the table. We would interchange these variables as independent ones and compute two separate lambdas. The two lambdas will differ in magnitude. Hypothetically, if we used parole granting or denial as the independent variable and write-ups or infractions as the dependent variable, we might observe a lambda of .17. When we reverse these variables and use the number of write-ups or infractions as the independent variable, we might yield a lambda of .25.

In this hypothetical case, we would interpret these lambdas as follows: We are able to explain 25 percent of the variation in parole granting or denial by using numbers of write-ups or infractions as a predictor. However, we are only able to explain 17 percent of the variation in write-ups or infractions when we use parole granting or denial as a predictor. Thus, the number of write-ups or infractions is the better predictor variable. It predicts 25 percent of the variation, whereas parole granting or denial only explains 17 percent of the variation. These are asymmetric *PRE* interpretations, meaning that different lambda coefficients are yielded depending upon which variable is used as the independent one. The asymmetric formula for lambda is discussed elsewhere (Champion, 1981:319–320).

Two Ordinal-Level Variables

When the investigator has two variables measured according to an ordinal scale, there are several correlational procedures available. Three such measures are (1) **Kendall's tau** (τ), (2) **Somers' *d***; and (3) **Goodman and Kruskal's gamma** coefficient of ordinal association (γ). These are discussed at length elsewhere (Champion, 1981:323–331). The best measure of the three for general purposes is Goodman and Kruskal's gamma. An example follows.

Goodman and Kruskal's Gamma (γ). Suppose we have some information about public defenders in a large city. We have a sample of 150 public defenders and are interested in learning whether their caseloads somehow influence their work satisfaction. Perhaps we have previous information showing that where public defenders have higher caseloads, this situation creates greater stress and lower work satisfaction. We devise two measures, one for size of caseload, and the other for work satisfaction. We create three categories for each variable, classifying these public defenders as high, medium, or low. Table 16.10 shows our sample of 150 public defenders distributed for the two variables. Notice in Table 16.10 that letters have been assigned to each cell in the 3 ×3 table. These letters are useful for designating components of the formula for **gamma,** γ which is:

$$\gamma = \frac{\Sigma f_a - \Sigma f_i}{\Sigma f_a + \Sigma f_i}$$

where Σf_a = frequency of agreements

Σf_i = frequency of inversions

TABLE 16.10 Work Satisfaction and Caseload Size for 150 Public Defenders

		Size of Caseload			
		High	Medium	Low	Totals
	High	25a	18b	10c	53
Work Satisfaction	Medium	12d	13e	15f	40
	Low	8g	17h	32i	57
	Totals	45	48	57	150

The frequency of agreements is determined by starting in the upper left-hand corner of the table in cell a and multiplying cell a by the sum of all cell values below and to the right of a. Then we move to cell b and multiply cell b by the sum of all cell values below and to the right of b. We continue moving to each cell and performing this procedure. The Σf_a is determined as follows:

$$\Sigma f_a = (a)(e + f + h + i) + (b)(f + i) + d(h + i) + (e)(i)$$

$$= (25)(13+15+17+32) + (18)(15+32) + (12)(17+32) + (13)(32)$$

$$= 1925 + 846 + 588 + 416$$

$$= 3775$$

The Σf_i is determined by starting in the upper right-hand corner of the table and multiplying cell c by all cell values below and to the left of c. Then we move to cell b and multiply this cell value by the sum of all cell values below and to the left of b and so on. Thus, Σf_i is calculated as follows:

$$\Sigma f = (c)(d + e + g + h) + (b)(d + g) + (f)(g + h) + (e)(g)$$

Substituting values from Table 16.10 for these letters, we have

$$\Sigma f_i = (10)(12+13+8+17) + (18)(12)(8) + (15)(8+17) + (13)(8)$$

$$= 500 + 360 + 375 + 104$$

$$= 1339$$

Once these two values have been determined, Σf_a and Σf_i, then we can solve for gamma. The gamma coefficient is:

$$\lambda = (3775 - 1339)/(3775 + 1339)$$

$$= 2436/5114$$

$$= .48$$

Gamma for the data in Table 16.10 is .48. Although we can say that this is a moderately low gamma value, we can also say that 48 percent of the variation in the two variables has been explained or accounted for by their mutual predictability. This is because gamma is a symmetric *PRE* measure. An inspection of Table 16.10 shows that high caseloads appear to be associated with low work satisfaction, while low caseloads appear associated with high work satisfaction. The gamma value is evidence of the correlation or relation between the two variables.

Strengths and Weaknesses of Gamma. The primary strengths of **Goodman and Kruskal's gamma** are that it is directly interpretable as a *PRE* measure and can achieve perfect positive or negative association of ± 1.00. There are no table size restrictions. Further, no correction factor is required. Sometimes, however, gamma may yield perfect positive or negative correlations when perfect association doesn't exist. This is because of peculiar distributions of cell frequencies. Fortunately, this situation occurs infrequently. Otherwise, gamma is an excellent measure of association whenever the researcher has two variables measured according to ordinal scales.

Two Interval-Level Variables

When investigators have two variables measured according to an interval scale, the best measure available is the **Pearson r**. Known as the Pearson product-moment correlation coefficient, the Pearson r was the researcher's measure of choice for many decades. In fact, if all of its assumptions are met by one's data, the Pearson r is the best correlational measure available.

Suppose we have some data relating to police department size and the size of the department's administrative component. The administrative component would be the ratio of administrative personnel (A) to the number of full-time personnel (P) in the department. An A/P ratio might be determined, where A = administrators and P = full-time personnel. Thus, if the number of administrators in a police department were 20 and there were 100 personnel, the A/P ratio would be 20/100 = .20. Twenty percent of the personnel in the police department are administrators. An A/P ratio of .15 would mean that 15 percent of the personnel in a police department are administrators, and so on. If we simply use percentage of administrative personnel as our A/P measure, and if we identify the total personnel in the police organization, we can study a sample of police departments and determine the correlation between organizational size (number of personnel) and the A/P ratio. A study of 15 police departments might yield data shown in Table 16.11.

Table 16.11 has been constructed as follows. We enter all police department personnel sizes in the first column, Variable X. Next, we enter the administrative components or A/P ratios in the second column, Variable Y. The third and fourth columns are the squares of the first two columns. The last column, XY, consists of the products of the first two columns of values (e.g., $125 \times 20 = 2,500$, $128 \times 18 = 2,304$, and so on). Once we have these values and sums determined, we can apply the following formula for calculating the Pearson r:

$$r = \frac{N\Sigma XY - (\Sigma X)(\Sigma Y)}{\sqrt{[N\Sigma X^2 - (\Sigma X)^2][N\Sigma Y^2 - (\Sigma Y)^2]}}$$

Substituting our table values for formula terms, we have the following:

$$r = \frac{(15)(29,147) - (1,521)(296)}{\sqrt{[(15)(162,659) - (1,521)^2][(15)(6,018) - (296)^2]}}$$

$$r = \frac{427,205 - 450,216}{\sqrt{(126,444)(2654)}}$$

$$r = -13,011/18,318.9$$

$$r = -.71$$

TABLE 16.11 Police Organization Size and Proportionate Size of Administrative Component

	Organization size (Variable X)	A/P ratio (Variable Y)	X^2	Y^2	XY
1.	125	20	15,625	400	2,500
2.	128	18	16,384	324	2,304
3.	130	16	16,900	256	2,080
4.	95	22	9,025	484	2,090
5.	82	24	6,724	576	1,968
6.	140	15	19,600	225	2,100
7.	65	22	4,225	484	1,430
8.	59	21	3,481	441	1,239
9.	75	25	5,625	625	1,875
10.	88	23	7,744	529	2,024
11.	100	15	10,000	225	1,500
12.	120	14	14,400	196	1,680
13.	110	18	12,100	324	1,980
14.	105	20	11,025	400	2,100
15.	99	23	9,801	529	2,277
	$\Sigma X = 1,521$	$\Sigma Y = 296$	$\Sigma X^2 = 162,659$	$\Sigma Y^2 = 6,018$	$\Sigma XY = 29,147$

The Pearson $r = -.71$. Regarding the strength of association, we can say that there is a moderately high negative association between the size of the organization (number of personnel) and the A/P ratio. It would seem that organizational size and the size of the administrative component vary inversely.

The Pearson r has a *PRE* interpretation, which is r^2. In this case, $r^2 = (-.71)^2 = .50$. We can say that 50 percent of the variation between the two variables has been accounted for or explained by their mutual predictability.

Strengths and Weaknesses of the Pearson r. The primary strengths of the Pearson r include the fact that it has a *PRE* interpretation and is well known. In fact, the Pearson r is used most often in advanced correlational problems, including path analysis and multiple **regression.** The Pearson r is a standard feature of every statistical software package. It can achieve perfect positive or negative association and requires no correction factor.

On the negative side, the Pearson r is one of the most abused measures of association. This is because it has five rather stringent assumptions. Besides randomness and the interval level of measurement, the Pearson r requires that the scores for both variables should be normally distributed. This is referred to as the bivariate normal assumption. A fourth assumption is that the relation between the two variables should be linear. Straight-line associations between variables, especially variables commonly examined in the social sciences, are not frequently observed. Thus, if two variables were related in a curvilinear fashion, then the resulting r value would be misleading. **Curvilinearity** causes distortion in the magnitude of the Pearson r value, and this distortion would cause it to be misinterpreted. Finally, if the two variables were to be graphed with intersectional points on a grid, these intersectional points between the two variables are assumed to form an ellipse around the **regression line,** which resembles a football. This feature is known as **homoscedasticity.** Any other type of distribution of intersection points would not be homoscedastic, and therefore, this assumption would be violated. Thus, if the researcher has randomness, two variables measured according to the interval level of measurement, a **bivariate normal distribution,** linearity, and homoscedasticity, then the Pearson r may be applied. Most researchers do not perform routine tests of their data to determine if these various distributional requirements are met. In most cases, such assumptions are not met but conventional applications of the Pearson r are made anyway. An alternative measure of association is **Spearman's rho,** ρ_{ss}. This measure is discussed elsewhere (Champion, 1981:331–334).

Other Specialized Measures of Association

The measures of association we have just examined are useful whenever researchers have two variables that are measured according to a common level of measurement, such as two interval-level variables, two ordinal-level variables, or two nominal-level variables. There are occasions when researchers will have two variables of different measurement levels. For instance, a researcher may wish to correlate income with work satisfaction (an interval-level variable with an ordinal-level variable), or the variables may be gender (nominal-level) and social class (ordinal-level). When there are different measurement levels associated with the two variables, it was common practice in the 1940s and 1950s to reduce the higher-level variable to the lower-level variable and compute a two-nominal-level-variable measure of association, such as lambda. This would mean, for instance, that we would treat social class as though it were a nominal-level variable and correlate it with gender. In short, we would be using the nominal-level-of-measurement properties of social class and ignoring the ordinal-level features of this variable. If we had income and work satisfaction, we would reduce income (measured according to an interval scale) to the ordinal level and carry out a two-ordinal-level-variable measure such as gamma. This procedure is proper, but it wastes information because the full interval-level properties of income cannot be taken into account.

Several solutions were established through the creation of specialized measures of association for different variable combinations. Thus, when researchers have one variable measured according to a nominal scale and one variable measured according to an ordinal scale, the best measure of association would be **Wilcoxon's theta,** θ. Theta is designed for a nominal-ordinal variable combination. If the two variables are ordinal and interval, then **Jaspen's M** would be used. If the two variables are nominal and interval, then **eta, the correlation ratio,** η, would be used. Each of these specialized measures preserves the original level of measurement achieved by each variable. A discussion of these measures is beyond the scope of this text but can be found elsewhere (Champion, 1981:341–354). The fact is that we now have measures of association for virtually every research purpose. The task for investigators is to select the most appropriate measures for analyzing their data according to which measures do the best job at yielding useful information.

WHICH TESTS SHOULD YOU USE?

The artful nature of criminological research is such that blanket generalizations about statistical applications that cover all types of situations are unwarranted. Choices of statistical tests for particular applications should be made carefully, in part, by weighing both the strengths and weaknesses of different procedures under consideration. Compared with procedure A, for example, procedure B may be more powerful. But procedure B may require normality of distribution, whereas procedure A has no such prerequisite. Procedure A may be easier to apply directly to raw scores, whereas procedure B may require that data should be transformed into ranks or different kinds of categories. Procedure B may yield distorted results if sample sizes are too small or too large, whereas procedure A may be applicable to samples of diverse sizes without incurring substantial distortion effects.

In many cases, statistical tests have been tailor-made for particular kinds of research problems. But you must pay attention to the assumptions underlying each test before deciding whether it can be applied. Researchers run certain risks by applying tests where the assumptions of those tests have not been fully satisfied.

KEY TERMS

Association
Between-group variation
Bivariate normal distribution
Chi square test
Coefficient of association
Confidence interval
Correlation
Cramer's V
Critical values
Curvilinearity
Degrees of freedom
Dichotomous variable
Direction of association
Direct relationship
Distribution-free statistics
Error
Estimation
Eta, the correlation ratio, η
Expected frequencies

Fit
F ratio
F test for analysis of variance (ANOVA)
Gamma, γ
Goodman and Kruskal's gamma
Goodness of fit
Guttman's coefficient of predictability, lambda (λ)
Homogeneity of variances
Homoscedasticity
Inferential statistics
Interval estimation
Jaspen's M
Kendall's tau
Lambda λ
Linear
Linearity
Measure of association

Nonparametric statistical tests
Observed frequencies
Parametric procedures
Parametric statistical tests
Pearson's C
Pearson r
Phi coefficient, ϕ
Point estimation
PRE measure
Proportional-reduction-in-error (*PRE*)
Regression
Regression line
Relationship
Somers' d
Spearman's rho, ρ_s
Standard error of the difference between two means

Statistical inference
Statistical significance of association
Strength of association
Symmetric and asymmetric *PRE* interpretations
t test
Tschuprow's T
Tests of significance
Tests of significance of difference
Theta, coefficient of differentiation, θ
Two-sample t test
Wilcoxon's theta, θ
Within-group variation
Z test

QUESTIONS FOR REVIEW AND PROBLEMS TO SOLVE

1. Differentiate between parametric and nonparametric statistical tests. What are some identifying characteristics of each?

2. What is a confidence interval? Give an example.

3. What is the difference between point estimation and interval estimation? Which method of estimation is preferred and why?

4. Given that $s_{\bar{x}} = 2.55$, $N = 108$, and $\overline{X}_{obs} = 100$, determine the following:
   (a) 90 percent confidence interval
   (b) 80 percent confidence interval
   (c) 99 percent confidence interval

5. With an $\overline{X}_{obs} = 100$, $N = 65$, and $s = 24$, determine the following:
   (a) 95 percent confidence interval
   (b) 80 percent confidence interval
   (c) 85 percent confidence interval

6. Determine the confidence intervals for each of the following, where $\overline{X}_{obs} = 330$, $s = 25$, and $N = 145$:
   (a) 88 percent confidence interval
   (b) 95 percent confidence interval
   (c) 70 percent confidence interval

7. On the basis of the magnitudes of the confidence intervals you established in problem 6 above, what can be said generally about increasing and decreasing the percentages of confidence intervals you have determined and

the likelihood that the population mean is overlapped? Explain.

8. Identify the Z values you chose for solving problems 5 and 6.

9. With an $s = 15, N = 220$, and an $\overline{X}_{obs} = 122$, determine the following:
   (a) 85 percent confidence interval
   (b) 95 percent confidence interval
   (c) 65 percent confidence interval

10. You have the following information: $\overline{X}_{obs} = 25, s_{\overline{x}} = 3$. You have previously hypothesized the population mean to be 30. Using the .01 level of significance, conduct a two-tailed test to see whether 25 is significantly different from 30 at the .01 level. Next, construct a confidence interval around the observed $\overline{X} = 25$. What Z value did you use for this confidence interval? What is the relation between two-tailed hypothesis tests of point estimation and confidence interval problems relating to the same sample means and identical significance levels?

11. Given the following means, variances, sample sizes, and other pertinent information, carry out an analysis of variance test and supply the missing values below:

Information:

Means = $19, 21, 24, 25, 26, 28, 30$

Standard deviations = $3.3, 2.6, 5.7, 2.3, 4.5, 2.9, 2.2$

N's = $10, 4, 15, 8, 9, 11, 15$

$SS_{within} = 420.3, MS_{bet} = 32.8$, and $P \leq .01$

Hint: Set up an ANOVA summary table and fill in the values given above. Solve for the unknown values by first determining your degrees of freedom and then multiplying MS_{bet} by df_{bet} to obtain SS_{bet}, and then dividing SS_{within} by df_{within} to obtain MS_{within}. Once you have determined these values, you can solve for the other unknown values.

a. df_{within}
b. df_{bet}
c. df_{total}
d. MS_{within}
e. SS_{bet}
f. F_{obs}
g. $F_{critical\ value}$

appendix A

Statistical Tables

TABLE A.1 Table of Squares and Square Roots, 1–1000 (compiled by the author)

n	n^2	$\sqrt{n}$	n	n^2	$\sqrt{n}$
1	1	1.0000	51	2601	7.1414
2	4	1.4142	52	2704	7.2111
3	9	1.7321	53	2809	7.2801
4	16	2.0000	54	2916	7.3485
5	25	2.2361	55	3025	7.4162
6	36	2.4495	56	3136	7.4833
7	49	2.6458	57	3249	7.5498
8	64	2.8284	58	3364	7.6158
9	81	3.0000	59	3481	7.6811
10	100	3.1623	60	3600	7.7460
11	121	3.3166	61	3721	7.8102
12	144	3.4641	62	3844	7.8740
13	169	3.6056	63	3969	7.9373
14	196	3.7417	64	4096	8.0000
15	225	3.8730	65	4225	8.0623
16	256	4.0000	66	4356	8.1240
17	289	4.1231	67	4489	8.1854
18	324	4.2426	68	4624	8.2462
19	361	4.3589	69	4761	8.3066
20	400	4.4721	70	4900	8.3666
21	441	4.5826	71	5041	8.4261
22	484	4.6904	72	5184	8.4853
23	529	4.7958	73	5329	8.5440
24	576	4.8990	74	5476	8.6023
25	625	5.0000	75	5625	8.6603
26	676	5.0990	76	5776	8.7178
27	729	5.1962	77	5929	8.7750
28	784	5.2915	78	6084	8.8318
29	841	5.3852	79	6241	8.8882
30	900	5.4772	80	6400	8.9443
31	961	5.5678	81	6561	9.0000
32	1024	5.6569	82	6724	9.0554
33	1089	5.7446	83	6889	9.1104
34	1156	5.8310	84	7056	9.1652
35	1225	5.9161	85	7225	9.2195
36	1296	6.0000	86	7396	9.2736
37	1369	6.0828	87	7569	9.3274
38	1444	6.1644	88	7744	9.3808
39	1521	6.2450	89	7921	9.4340
40	1600	6.3246	90	8100	9.4868
41	1681	6.4031	91	8281	9.5394
42	1764	6.4807	92	8464	9.5917
43	1849	6.5574	93	8649	9.6437
44	1936	6.6332	94	8836	9.6954
45	2025	6.7082	95	9025	9.7468
46	2116	6.7823	96	9216	9.7980
47	2209	6.8557	97	9409	9.8489
48	2304	6.9282	98	9604	9.8995
49	2401	7.0000	99	9801	9.9499
50	2500	7.0711	100	10000	10.0000

n	n^2	$\sqrt{n}$		n	n^2	$\sqrt{n}$
101	10201	10.0499		151	22801	12.2882
102	10404	10.0995		152	23104	12.3288
103	10609	10.1489		153	23409	12.3693
104	10816	10.1980		154	23716	12.4097
105	11025	10.2470		155	24025	12.4499
106	11236	10.2956		156	24336	12.4900
107	11449	10.3441		157	24649	12.5300
108	11664	10.3928		158	24964	12.5698
109	11881	10.4403		159	25281	12.6095
110	12100	10.4881		160	25600	12.6491
111	12321	10.5357		161	25921	12.6886
112	12544	10.5830		162	26244	12.7279
113	12769	10.6301		163	26569	12.7671
114	12996	10.6771		164	26896	12.8062
115	13225	10.7238		165	26225	12.8452
116	13456	10.7703		166	27556	12.8841
117	13689	10.8167		167	27889	12.9228
118	13924	10.8628		168	28224	12.9615
119	14161	10.9087		169	28561	13.0000
120	14400	10.9545		170	28900	13.0384
121	14641	11.0000		171	29241	13.0767
122	14884	11.0454		172	29584	13.1149
123	15129	11.0905		173	29929	13.1529
124	15376	11.1355		174	30276	13.1909
125	15625	11.1803		175	30625	13.2288
126	15876	11.2250		176	30976	13.2665
127	16129	11.2694		177	31329	13.3041
128	16384	11.3137		178	31684	13.3417
129	16641	11.3578		179	32041	13.3791
130	16900	11.4018		180	32400	13.4164
131	17161	11.4455		181	32761	13.4536
132	17424	11.4891		182	33124	13.4907
133	17689	11.5326		183	33489	13.5277
134	17956	11.5758		184	33856	13.5647
135	18225	11.6190		185	34225	13.6015
136	18496	11.6619		186	34596	13.6382
137	18769	11.7047		187	34969	13.6748
138	19044	11.7473		188	35344	13.7113
139	19321	11.7898		189	35721	13.7477
140	19600	11.8322		190	36100	13.7840
141	19881	11.8743		191	36481	13.8203
142	20164	11.9164		192	36864	13.8564
143	20449	11.9583		193	37249	13.8924
144	20736	12.0000		194	37636	13.9284
145	21025	12.0416		195	38025	13.9642
146	21316	12.0830		196	38416	14.0000
147	21609	12.1244		197	38809	14.0357
148	21904	12.1655		198	39204	14.0712
149	22201	12.2066		199	39601	14.1067
150	22500	12.2474		200	40000	14.1421

n	n^2	$\sqrt{n}$	n	n^2	$\sqrt{n}$
201	40401	14.1774	251	63001	15.8430
202	40804	14.2127	252	63504	15.8745
203	41209	14.2478	253	64009	15.9060
204	41616	14.2829	254	64516	15.9374
205	42025	14.3178	255	65025	15.9687
206	42436	14.3527	256	65536	16.0000
207	42849	14.3875	257	66049	16.0312
208	43264	14.4222	258	66564	16.0624
209	43681	14.4568	259	67081	16.0935
210	44100	14.4914	260	67600	16.1245
211	44521	14.5258	261	68121	16.1555
212	44944	14.5602	262	68644	16.1864
213	45369	14.5946	263	69169	16.2173
214	45796	14.6287	264	69696	16.2481
215	46225	14.6629	265	70225	16.2788
216	46656	14.6969	266	70756	16.3095
217	47089	14.7309	267	71289	16.3401
218	47524	14.7648	268	71824	16.3707
219	47961	14.7986	269	72361	16.4012
220	48400	14.8324	270	72900	16.4317
221	48841	14.8661	271	73441	16.4621
222	49284	14.8997	272	73984	16.4924
223	49729	14.9332	273	74529	16.5227
224	50176	14.9666	274	75076	16.5529
225	50625	15.0000	275	75625	16.5831
226	51076	15.0333	276	76176	16.6132
227	51529	15.0665	277	76729	16.6433
228	51984	15.0997	278	77284	16.6733
229	52441	15.1327	279	77841	16.7033
230	52900	15.1658	280	78400	16.7332
231	53361	15.1987	281	78961	16.7631
232	53824	15.2315	282	79524	16.7929
233	54289	15.2643	283	80089	16.8226
234	54756	15.2971	284	80656	16.8523
235	55225	15.3297	285	81225	16.8819
236	55696	15.3623	286	81796	16.9115
237	56169	15.3948	287	82369	16.9411
238	56644	15.4272	288	82944	16.9706
239	57121	15.4596	289	83521	17.0000
240	57600	15.4919	290	84100	17.0294
241	58081	15.5242	291	84681	17.0587
242	58564	15.5563	292	85264	17.0880
243	49049	15.5885	293	85849	17.1172
244	59536	15.6205	294	86436	17.1464
245	60025	15.6525	295	87025	17.1756
246	60516	15.6844	296	87616	17.2047
247	61009	15.7162	297	88209	17.2337
248	61504	15.7480	298	88804	17.2627
249	62001	15.7797	299	98401	17.2916
250	62500	15.8114	300	90000	17.3205

n	n^2	$\sqrt{n}$	n	n^2	$\sqrt{n}$
301	90601	17.3494	351	123201	18.7350
302	91204	17.3781	352	123904	18.7617
303	91809	17.4069	353	124609	18.7883
304	92416	17.4356	354	125316	18.8149
305	93025	17.4642	355	126025	18.8414
306	93636	17.4929	356	126736	18.8680
307	94249	17.5214	357	127449	18.8944
308	94864	17.5499	358	128164	18.9209
309	95841	17.5784	359	128881	18.9473
310	96100	17.6068	360	129600	18.9737
311	96721	17.6352	361	130321	19.0000
312	97344	17.6635	362	131044	19.0263
313	97969	17.6918	363	131769	19.0526
314	98596	17.7200	364	132496	19.0788
315	99225	17.7482	365	133225	19.1050
316	99856	17.7764	366	133956	19.1311
317	100489	17.8045	367	134689	19.1572
318	101124	17.8326	368	135424	19.1833
319	101761	17.8606	369	136161	19.2094
320	102400	17.8885	370	136900	19.2354
321	103041	17.9165	371	137641	19.2614
322	103684	17.9444	372	138384	19.2873
323	104329	17.9722	373	139129	19.3132
324	104976	18.0000	374	139876	19.3391
325	105625	18.0278	375	140625	19.3649
326	106276	18.0555	376	141376	19.3907
327	106929	18.0831	377	142129	19.4165
328	107584	18.1108	378	142884	19.4422
329	108241	18.1384	379	143641	19.4679
330	108900	18.1659	380	144400	19.4936
331	109561	18.1934	381	145161	19.5192
332	110224	18.2209	382	145924	19.5448
333	110889	18.2483	383	146689	19.5704
334	111556	18.2757	384	147456	19.5959
335	112225	18.3030	385	148225	19.6214
336	112896	18.3303	386	148996	19.6469
337	113569	18.3576	387	149769	19.6723
338	114244	18.3848	388	150544	19.6977
339	114921	18.4120	389	151321	19.7231
340	115600	18.4391	390	152100	19.7484
341	116281	18.4662	391	152881	19.7737
342	116964	18.4932	392	153664	19.7990
343	117649	18.5203	393	154449	19.8242
344	118336	18.5472	394	155236	19.8494
345	119025	18.5742	395	156025	19.8746
346	119716	18.6011	396	156816	19.8997
347	120409	18.6279	397	157609	19.9249
348	121104	18.6548	398	158404	19.9499
349	121801	18.6815	399	159210	19.9750
350	122500	18.7083	400	160000	20.0000

n	n^2	$\sqrt{n}$		n	n^2	$\sqrt{n}$
401	160801	20.0250		451	203401	21.2368
402	161604	20.0499		452	204304	21.2603
403	162409	20.0749		453	205209	21.2838
404	163216	20.0998		454	206116	21.3073
405	164025	20.1246		455	207025	21.3397
406	164836	20.1494		456	207936	21.3542
407	165649	20.1742		457	208849	21.3776
408	166464	20.1990		458	209764	21.4009
409	167281	20.2237		459	210681	21.4243
410	168100	20.2485		460	211600	21.4476
411	168921	20.2731		461	212521	21.4709
412	169744	20.2978		462	213444	21.4942
413	170569	20.3224		463	214369	21.5174
414	171396	20.3470		464	215296	21.5407
415	172225	20.3715		465	216225	21.5639
416	173056	20.3961		466	217156	21.5870
417	173889	20.4206		467	218089	21.6102
418	174724	20.4450		468	219024	21.6333
419	175561	20.4695		469	219961	21.6564
420	176400	20.4939		470	220900	21.6795
421	177241	20.5183		471	221841	21.7025
422	178084	20.5426		472	222784	21.7256
423	178929	20.5670		473	223729	21.7486
424	179776	20.5913		474	224676	21.7715
425	180625	20.6155		475	225625	21.7945
426	181476	20.6398		476	226576	21.8174
427	182329	20.6640		477	227529	21.8403
428	183184	20.6882		478	228484	21.8632
429	184041	20.7123		479	229441	21.8861
430	184900	20.7364		480	230400	21.9089
431	185761	20.7605		481	231361	21.9317
432	186624	20.7846		482	232324	21.9545
433	187489	20.8087		483	233289	21.9773
434	188356	20.8327		484	234256	22.0000
435	189225	20.8567		485	235225	22.0227
436	190096	20.8806		486	236196	22.0454
437	190969	20.9045		487	237169	22.0681
438	191844	20.9284		488	238144	22.0907
439	192721	20.9523		489	239121	22.1133
440	193600	20.9762		490	240100	22.1359
441	194481	21.0000		491	241081	22.1585
442	195364	21.0238		492	242064	22.1811
443	196249	21.0476		493	243049	22.2036
444	197136	21.0713		494	244036	22.2261
445	198025	21.0950		495	245025	22.2486
446	198916	21.1187		496	246016	22.2711
447	199809	21.1424		497	247009	22.2935
448	200704	21.1660		498	248004	22.3159
449	201601	21.1896		499	249001	22.3383
450	202500	21.2132		500	250000	22.3607

n	n^2	$\sqrt{n}$		n	n^2	$\sqrt{n}$
501	251001	22.3830		551	303601	23.4734
502	252004	22.4045		552	304704	23.4947
503	253009	22.4277		553	305809	23.5160
504	254016	22.4499		554	306916	23.5372
505	255025	22.4792		555	308025	23.5584
506	256036	22.4944		556	309136	23.5797
507	257049	22.5167		557	310249	23.6008
508	258064	22.5389		558	311364	23.6220
509	259081	22.5610		559	312481	23.6432
510	260100	22.5832		560	313600	23.6643
511	261121	22.6053		561	314721	23.6854
512	262144	22.6274		562	315844	23.7065
513	263169	22.6495		563	316969	23.7276
514	264196	22.6716		564	318096	23.7487
515	265225	22.6936		565	319225	23.7697
516	266256	22.7156		566	320356	23.7908
517	267289	22.7376		567	321489	23.8118
518	268324	22.7596		568	322624	23.8328
519	269361	22.7816		569	323761	23.8537
520	270400	22.8035		570	324900	23.8747
521	471441	22.8254		571	326041	23.8956
522	272484	22.8473		572	327184	23.9165
523	273529	22.8692		573	328329	23.9374
524	274576	22.8910		574	329476	23.9583
525	275625	22.9129		575	330625	23.9792
526	276676	22.9347		576	331776	24.0000
527	277729	22.9565		577	332929	24.0208
528	278784	22.9783		578	334084	24.0416
529	279841	23.0000		579	335241	24.0624
530	280900	23.0217		580	336400	24.0832
531	281961	23.0434		581	337561	24.1039
532	283024	23.0651		582	338724	24.1247
533	284089	23.0868		583	339889	24.1454
534	285156	23.1084		584	341056	24.1661
535	286225	23.1301		585	342225	24.1868
536	287296	23.1517		586	343396	24.2074
537	288369	23.1733		587	344569	24.2281
538	289444	23.1948		588	345744	24.2487
539	290521	23.2164		589	346921	24.2693
540	291600	23.2379		590	348100	24.2899
541	292681	23.2594		591	349281	24.3105
542	293764	23.2808		592	350464	24.3311
543	294849	23.3023		593	351649	24.3516
544	295936	23.3238		594	352836	24.3721
545	297025	23.3452		595	354025	24.3926
546	298116	23.3666		596	355216	24.4131
547	299209	23.3880		597	356409	24.4336
548	300304	23.4094		598	357604	24.4540
549	301401	23.4307		599	358801	24.4745
550	302500	23.4521		600	360000	24.4949

n	n^2	$\sqrt{n}$	n	n^2	$\sqrt{n}$
601	361201	24.5153	651	423801	25.5147
602	362404	24.5337	652	425104	25.5343
603	363609	24.5561	653	426409	25.5539
604	364816	24.5764	654	427716	25.5734
605	366025	24.5967	655	429025	25.5930
606	367236	24.6171	656	430336	25.6125
607	368449	24.6374	657	431649	25.6320
608	369664	24.6577	658	432964	25.6515
609	370881	24.6779	659	434281	25.6710
610	372100	24.6982	660	435600	25.6905
611	373321	24.7184	661	436921	25.7099
612	374544	24.7386	662	438244	25.7294
613	375769	24.7588	663	439569	25.7488
614	376996	24.7790	664	440896	25.7682
615	378225	24.7992	665	442225	25.7876
616	379456	24.8193	666	443556	25.8070
617	380689	24.8395	667	444889	25.8263
618	381924	24.8596	668	446224	25.8457
619	383161	24.8797	669	447561	25.8650
620	384400	24.8998	670	448900	25.8844
621	385641	24.9199	671	450241	25.9037
622	386884	24.9399	672	451584	25.9230
623	388129	24.9600	673	452929	25.9422
624	389376	24.9800	674	454276	25.9615
625	390625	25.0000	675	455625	25.9808
626	391876	25.0200	676	456976	26.0000
627	393129	25.0400	677	458329	26.0192
628	394384	25.0599	678	459684	26.0384
629	395641	25.0799	679	461041	26.0576
630	396900	25.0998	680	462400	26.0768
631	398161	25.1197	681	463761	26.0960
632	399424	25.1396	682	465124	26.1151
633	400689	25.1595	683	466489	26.1343
634	401956	25.1794	684	467856	26.1534
635	403225	25.1992	685	469225	26.1725
636	404496	25.2190	686	470596	26.1916
637	405769	25.2389	687	471969	26.2107
638	407044	25.2587	688	473344	26.2298
639	408321	25.2784	689	474721	26.2488
640	409600	25.2982	690	476100	26.2679
641	410881	25.3180	691	477481	26.2869
642	412164	25.3377	692	478864	26.3059
643	413449	25.3574	693	480249	26.3249
644	414736	25.3772	694	481636	26.3439
645	416025	25.3969	695	483025	26.3629
646	417316	25.4165	696	484416	26.3818
647	418609	25.4362	697	485809	26.4008
648	419004	25.4558	698	487204	26.4197
649	421201	25.4755	699	488601	26.4386
650	422500	25.4951	700	490000	26.4575

n	n^2	$\sqrt{n}$		n	n^2	$\sqrt{n}$
701	491401	26.4764		751	564001	27.4044
702	492804	26.4953		752	565504	27.4226
703	494209	26.5141		753	567009	27.4408
704	495616	26.5330		754	568516	27.4591
705	497025	26.5518		755	570025	27.4773
706	498436	26.5707		756	571536	27.4955
707	499849	26.5895		757	573049	27.5136
708	501264	26.6083		758	574564	27.5318
709	502681	26.6271		759	576081	27.5500
710	504100	26.6458		760	577600	27.5681
711	505521	26.6646		761	579121	27.5862
712	506944	26.6833		762	580644	27.6043
713	508369	26.7021		763	582169	27.6225
714	509796	26.7208		764	583696	27.6405
715	511225	26.7395		765	585225	27.6586
716	512656	26.7582		766	586756	27.6767
717	514089	26.7769		767	588289	27.6948
718	515524	26.7955		768	589824	27.7128
719	516961	26.8142		769	591361	27.7308
720	518400	26.8328		770	592900	27.7489
721	519841	26.8514		771	594441	27.7669
722	521284	26.8701		772	595984	27.7849
723	522729	26.8887		773	597529	27.8029
724	524176	26.9072		774	599076	27.8209
725	525625	26.9258		775	600625	27.8388
726	527076	26.9444		776	602176	27.8568
727	528529	26.9629		777	603729	27.8747
728	529984	26.9815		778	605284	27.8927
729	531441	27.0000		779	606841	27.9106
730	532900	27.0185		780	608400	27.9285
731	534361	27.0370		781	609961	27.9464
732	535824	27.0555		782	611524	27.9643
733	537289	27.0740		783	613089	27.9821
734	538756	27.0924		784	614656	28.0000
735	540225	27.1109		785	616225	28.0179
736	541696	27.1293		786	617796	28.0357
737	543169	27.1477		787	619369	28.0535
738	544644	27.1662		788	620944	28.0713
739	546121	27.1846		789	622521	28.0891
740	547600	27.2029		790	624100	28.1069
741	549081	27.2213		791	625681	28.1247
742	550564	27.2397		792	627264	28.1425
743	552049	27.2580		793	628849	28.1603
744	553536	27.2764		794	630436	28.1780
745	555025	27.2947		795	632025	28.1957
746	556516	27.3130		796	633616	28.2135
747	558009	27.3313		797	635209	28.2312
748	559504	27.3496		798	636804	28.2489
749	561001	27.3679		799	638401	28.2666
750	562500	27.3861		800	640000	28.2843

n	n^2	$\sqrt{n}$		n	n^2	$\sqrt{n}$
801	641601	28.3019		851	724201	29.1719
802	643204	28.3196		852	725904	29.1890
803	644809	28.3373		853	727609	29.2062
804	646416	28.3549		854	729316	29.2233
805	648025	28.3725		855	731025	29.2404
806	649636	28.3901		856	732736	29.2575
807	651249	28.4077		857	734449	29.2746
808	652864	28.4253		858	736164	29.2916
809	654481	28.4429		859	737881	29.3087
810	656100	28.4605		860	739600	29.3258
811	657721	28.4781		861	741321	29.3428
812	659344	28.4956		862	743044	29.3598
813	660969	28.5132		863	744769	29.3769
814	662596	28.5307		864	746496	29.3939
815	664225	28.5482		865	748225	29.4109
816	665856	28.5657		866	749956	29.4279
817	667489	28.5832		867	751689	29.4449
818	669124	28.6007		868	753424	29.4618
819	670761	28.6182		869	755161	29.4788
820	672400	28.6356		870	756900	29.4958
821	674041	28.6531		871	758641	29.5127
822	675684	28.6705		872	760384	29.5296
823	677329	28.6880		873	762129	29.5466
824	678976	28.7054		874	763876	29.5635
825	680625	28.7228		875	765625	29.5804
826	682276	28.7402		876	767376	29.5973
827	683929	28.7576		877	769129	29.6142
828	685584	28.7750		878	770884	29.6311
829	687241	28.7924		879	772641	29.6479
830	688900	28.8097		880	774400	29.6648
831	690561	28.8271		881	776161	29.6816
832	692224	28.8444		882	777924	29.6985
833	693889	28.8617		883	779689	29.7153
834	695556	28.8791		884	781456	29.7321
835	697225	28.8964		885	783225	29.7489
836	698896	28.9137		886	784996	29.7658
837	700569	28.9310		887	786769	29.7825
838	702244	28.9482		888	788544	29.7993
839	703921	28.9655		889	790321	29.8161
840	705600	28.9829		890	792100	29.8329
841	707281	29.0000		891	793881	29.8496
842	708964	29.0172		892	795664	29.8664
843	710649	29.0345		893	797449	29.8831
844	712336	29.0517		894	799236	29.8998
845	714025	29.0689		895	801025	29.9166
846	715716	29.0861		896	802816	29.9333
847	717409	29.1033		897	804609	29.9500
848	719104	29.1204		898	806404	29.9666
849	720801	29.1376		899	808201	29.9833
850	722500	29.1548		900	810000	30.0000

n	n^2	$\sqrt{n}$		n	n^2	$\sqrt{n}$
901	811801	30.0167		951	904401	30.8383
902	813604	30.0333		952	906304	30.8545
903	815409	30.0500		953	908209	30.8707
904	817216	30.0666		954	910116	30.8869
905	819025	30.0832		955	912025	30.9031
906	820836	30.0998		956	913936	30.9192
907	822649	30.1164		957	915849	30.9354
908	824464	30.1330		958	917764	30.9516
909	826281	30.1496		959	919681	30.9677
910	828100	30.1662		960	921600	30.9839
911	829921	30.1828		961	923521	31.0000
912	831744	30.1993		962	925444	31.0161
913	833569	30.2159		963	927369	31.0322
914	835396	30.2324		964	929296	31.0483
915	837225	30.2490		965	931225	31.0644
916	839056	30.2655		966	933156	31.0805
917	840889	30.2820		967	935089	31.0966
918	842724	30.2985		968	937369	31.1127
919	844561	30.3150		969	938961	31.1288
920	846400	30.3315		970	940900	31.1448
921	848241	30.3480		971	942841	31.1609
922	850084	30.3645		972	944784	31.1769
923	851929	30.3809		973	946729	31.1929
924	853776	30.3974		974	948676	31.2090
925	855625	30.4138		975	950625	31.2250
926	857476	30.4302		976	952576	31.2410
927	859329	30.4467		977	954529	31.2570
928	861184	30.4631		978	956484	31.2730
929	863041	30.4795		979	958441	31.2890
930	864900	30.4959		980	960400	31.3050
931	866761	30.5123		981	962361	31.3209
932	868624	30.5287		982	964324	31.3369
933	870489	30.5450		983	966289	31.3528
934	872356	30.5614		984	968256	31.3688
935	874225	30.5778		985	970225	31.3847
936	876096	30.5941		986	972196	31.4006
937	877969	30.6105		987	974169	31.4166
938	879844	30.6268		988	976144	31.4325
939	881721	30.6431		989	978121	31.4484
940	883600	30.6594		990	980100	31.4643
941	885481	30.6757		991	982081	31.4802
942	887364	30.6920		992	984064	31.4860
943	889249	30.7083		993	986049	31.5119
944	891136	30.7246		994	988036	31.5278
945	893025	30.7409		995	990025	31.5436
946	894916	30.7571		996	992016	31.5595
947	896809	30.7734		997	994009	31.5753
948	898704	30.7896		998	996004	31.5911
949	900601	30.8058		999	998001	31.6070
950	902500	30.8221		1000	1000000	31.6228

TABLE A.2 Random Numbers

10097 32533	76520 13586	34673 54876	80959 09117	39292 74945
37542 04805	64894 74296	24805 24037	20636 10402	00822 91665
08422 68953	19645 09303	23209 02560	15953 34764	35080 33606
99019 02529	09376 70715	38311 31165	88676 74397	04436 27659
12807 99970	80157 36147	64032 36653	98951 16877	12171 76833
66065 74717	34072 76850	36697 36170	65813 39885	11199 29170
31060 10805	45571 82406	35303 42614	86799 07439	23403 09732
85269 77602	02051 65692	68665 74818	73053 85247	18623 88579
63573 32135	05325 47048	90553 57548	28468 28709	83491 25624
73796 45753	03529 64778	35808 34282	60935 20344	35273 88435
98520 17767	14905 68607	22109 40558	60970 93433	50500 73998
11805 05431	39808 27732	50725 68248	29405 24201	52775 67851
83452 99634	06288 98083	13746 70078	18475 40610	68711 77817
88685 40200	86507 58401	36766 67951	90364 76493	29609 11062
99594 67348	87517 64969	91826 08928	93785 61368	23478 34113
65481 17674	17468 50950	58047 76974	73039 57186	40218 16544
80124 35635	17727 08015	45318 22374	21115 78253	14385 53763
74350 99817	77402 77214	43236 00210	45521 64237	96286 02655
69916 26803	66252 29148	36936 87203	76621 13990	94400 56418
09893 20505	14225 68514	46427 56788	96297 78822	54382 14598
91499 14523	68479 27686	46162 83554	94750 89923	37089 20048
80336 94598	26940 36858	70297 34135	53140 33340	42050 82341
44104 81949	85157 47954	32979 26575	57600 40881	22222 06413
12550 73742	11100 02040	12860 74697	96644 89439	28707 25815
63606 49329	16505 34484	40219 52563	43651 77082	07207 31790
61196 90446	26457 47774	51924 33729	65394 59593	42582 60527
15474 45266	95270 79953	59367 83848	82396 10118	33211 59466
94557 28573	67897 54387	54622 44431	91190 42592	92927 45973
42481 16213	97344 08721	16868 48767	03071 12059	25701 46670
23523 78317	73208 89837	68935 91416	26252 29663	05522 82562
04493 52494	75246 33824	45862 51025	61962 79335	65337 12472
00549 97654	64051 88159	96119 63896	54692 82391	23287 29529
35963 15307	26898 09354	33351 35462	77974 50024	90103 39333
59808 08391	45427 26842	83609 49700	13021 24892	78565 20106
46058 85236	01390 92286	77281 44077	93910 83647	70617 42941
32179 00597	87379 25241	05567 07007	86743 17157	85394 11838
69234 61406	20117 45204	15956 60000	18743 92423	97118 96338
19565 41430	01758 75379	40419 21585	66674 36806	84962 85207
45155 14938	19476 07246	43667 94543	59047 90033	20826 69541
94864 31994	36168 10851	34888 81553	01540 35456	05014 51176
98086 24826	45240 28404	44999 08896	39094 73407	35441 31880
33185 16232	41941 50949	89435 48581	88695 41994	37548 73043
80951 00406	96382 70774	20151 23387	25016 25298	94624 61171
79752 49140	71961 28296	69861 02591	74852 20539	00387 59579
18633 32537	98145 06571	31010 24674	05455 61427	77938 91936

Source: The Rand Corporation, *A Million Random Digits* (New York: The Free Press, 1955). By permission of the publishers.

74029 43902	77557 32270	97790 17119	52527 58021	80814 51748
54178 45611	80993 37143	05335 12969	56127 19255	36040 90324
11664 49883	52079 84827	59381 71539	09973 33440	88461 23356
48324 77928	31249 64710	02295 36870	32307 57546	15020 09994
69074 94138	87637 91976	35584 04401	10518 21615	01848 76938
09188 20097	32825 39527	04220 86304	83389 87374	64278 58044
90045 85497	51981 50654	94938 81997	91870 76150	68476 64659
73189 50207	47677 26269	62290 64464	27124 67018	41361 82760
75768 76490	20971 87749	90429 12272	95375 05871	93823 43178
54016 44056	66281 31003	00682 27398	20714 53295	07706 17813
08358 69910	78542 42785	13661 58873	04618 97553	31223 08420
28306 03264	81333 10591	40510 07893	32604 60475	94119 01840
53840 86233	81594 13628	51215 90290	28466 68795	77762 20791
91757 53741	61613 62269	50263 90212	55781 76514	83483 47055
89415 92694	00397 58391	12607 17646	48949 72306	94541 37408
77513 03820	86864 29901	68414 82774	51908 13980	72893 55507
19502 37174	69979 20288	55210 29773	74287 75251	65344 67415
21818 59313	93278 81757	05686 73156	07082 85046	31853 38452
51474 66499	68107 23621	94049 91345	42836 09191	08007 45449
99559 68331	62535 24170	69777 12830	74819 78142	43860 72834
33713 48007	93584 72869	51926 64721	58303 29822	93174 93972
85274 86893	11303 22970	28834 34137	73515 90400	71148 43643
84133 89640	44035 52166	73852 70091	61222 60561	62327 18423
56732 16234	17395 96131	10123 91622	85496 57560	81604 18880
65138 56806	87648 85261	34313 65861	45875 21069	85644 47277
38001 02176	81719 11711	71602 92937	74219 64049	65584 49698
37402 96397	01304 77586	56271 10086	47324 62605	40030 37438
97125 40348	87083 31417	21815 39250	75237 62047	15501 29578
21826 41134	47143 34072	64638 85902	49139 06441	03856 54552
73135 42742	95719 09035	85794 74296	08789 88156	64691 19202
07638 77929	03061 18072	96207 44156	23821 99538	04713 66994
60528 83441	07954 19814	59175 20695	05533 52139	61212 06455
83596 35655	06958 92983	05128 09719	77433 53783	92301 50498
10850 62746	99599 10507	13499 06319	53075 71839	06410 19362
39820 98952	43622 63147	64421 80814	43800 09351	31024 73167
59580 06478	75569 78800	88835 54486	23768 06156	04111 08408
38508 07341	23793 48763	90822 97022	17719 04207	95954 49953
30692 70668	94688 16127	56196 80091	82067 63400	05462 69200
65443 95659	18288 27437	49632 24041	08337 65676	96299 90836
27267 50264	13192 72294	07477 44606	17985 48911	97341 30358
91307 06991	19072 24210	36699 53728	28825 35793	28976 66252
68434 94688	84473 13622	62126 98408	12843 82590	09815 93146
48908 15877	54745 24591	35700 04754	83824 52692	54130 55160
06913 45197	42672 78601	11883 09528	63011 98901	14974 40344
10455 16019	14210 33712	91342 37821	88325 80851	43667 70883

12883 97343	65027 61184	04285 01392	17974 15077	90712 26769
21778 30976	38807 36961	31649 42096	63281 02023	08816 47449
19523 59515	65122 59659	86283 68258	69572 13798	16435 91529
67245 52670	35583 16563	79246 86686	76463 34222	26655 90802
60584 47377	07500 37992	45134 26529	26760 83637	41326 44344
53853 41377	36066 94850	58838 73859	49364 73331	96240 43642
24637 38736	74384 89342	52623 07992	12369 18601	03742 83873
83080 12451	38992 22815	07759 51777	97377 27585	51972 37867
16444 24334	36151 99073	27493 70939	85130 32552	54846 54759
60790 18157	57178 65762	11161 78576	45819 52979	65130 04860
03991 10461	93716 16894	66083 24653	84609 58232	88618 19161
38555 95554	32886 59780	08355 60860	29735 47762	71299 23853
17546 73704	92052 46215	55121 29281	59076 07936	27954 58909
32643 52861	95819 06831	00911 98936	76355 93779	80863 00514
69572 68777	39510 35905	14060 40619	29549 69616	33564 60780
24122 66591	27699 06494	14845 46672	61958 77100	90899 75754
61196 30231	92962 61773	41839 55382	17267 70943	78038 70267
30532 21704	10274 12202	39685 23309	10061 68829	55986 66485
03788 97599	75867 20717	74416 53166	35208 33374	87539 08823
48228 63379	85783 47619	53152 67433	35663 52972	16818 60311
60365 94653	35075 33949	42614 29297	01918 28316	98953 73231
83799 42402	56623 34442	34994 41374	70071 14736	09958 18065
32960 07405	36409 83232	99385 41600	11133 07586	15917 06253
19322 53845	57620 52606	66497 68646	78138 66559	19640 99413
11220 94747	07399 37408	48509 23929	27482 45476	85244 35159
31751 57260	68980 05339	15470 48355	88651 22596	03152 19121
88492 99382	14454 04504	20094 98977	74843 93413	22109 78508
30934 47744	07481 83828	73788 06533	28597 20405	94205 20380
22888 48893	27499 98748	60530 45128	74022 84617	82037 10268
78212 16993	35902 91386	44372 15486	65741 14014	87481 37220
41849 84547	46850 52326	34677 58300	74910 64345	19325 81549
46352 33049	69248 93460	45305 07521	61318 31855	14413 70951
11087 96294	14013 31792	59747 67277	76503 34513	39663 77544
52701 08337	56303 87315	16520 69676	11654 99893	02181 68161
57275 36898	81304 48585	68652 27376	92852 55866	88448 03584
20857 73156	70284 24326	79375 95220	01159 63267	10622 48391
15633 84924	90415 93614	33521 26665	55823 47641	86225 31704
92694 48297	39904 02115	59589 49067	66821 41575	49767 04037
77613 19019	88152 00080	20554 91409	96277 48257	50816 97616
38688 32486	45134 63545	59404 72059	43947 51680	43852 59693
25163 01889	70014 15021	41290 67312	71857 15957	68971 11403
65251 07629	37239 33295	05870 01119	92784 26340	18477 65622
36815 43625	18637 37509	82444 99005	04921 73701	14707 93997
64397 11692	05327 82162	20247 81759	45197 25332	83745 22567
04515 25624	95096 67946	48460 85558	15191 18782	16930 33361

83761 60873	43253 84145	60833 25983	01291 41349	20368 07126
14387 06345	80854 09279	43529 06318	38384 74761	41196 37480
51321 92246	80088 77074	88722 56736	66164 49431	66919 31678
72472 00008	80890 18002	94813 31900	54155 83436	35352 54131
05466 55306	93128 18464	74457 90561	72848 11834	79982 68416
39528 72484	82474 25593	48545 35247	18619 13674	18611 19241
81616 18711	53342 44276	75122 11724	74627 73707	58319 15997
07586 16120	82641 22820	92904 13141	32392 19763	61199 67940
90767 04235	13574 17200	69902 63742	78464 22501	18627 90872
40188 28193	29593 88627	94972 11598	62095 36787	00441 58997
34414 82157	86887 55087	19152 00023	12302 80783	32624 68691
63439 75363	44989 16822	36024 00867	76378 41605	65961 73488
67049 09070	93399 45547	94458 74284	05041 49807	20288 34060
79495 04146	52162 90286	54158 34243	46978 35482	59362 95938
91704 30552	04737 21031	75051 93029	47665 64382	99782 93478

TABLE A.3 Areas Under the Normal Curve: Fractions of Unit Area from 0 to Z

The Z values are expressed to the nearest hundredth. The left-hand column contains the first two digits of the Z value. The values across the top of the table are third digits. To determine the proportion of curve area from the mean to a Z = 1.45, find 1.4 down the left-hand column. Next, find .05 across the top of the table. Where these values intersect in the body of the table defines the proportion of curve area. In the case of a Z = 1.45, the proportion of curve area is .4265.

Z	0.00	0.01	0.02	0.03	0.04	0.05	0.06	0.07	0.08	0.09
0.0	0.0000	0.0040	0.0080	0.0120	0.0160	0.0199	0.0239	0.0279	0.0319	0.0359
0.1	.0398	.0438	.0478	.0517	.0557	.0596	.0636	.0675	.0714	.0753
0.2	.0793	.0832	.0871	.0910	.0948	.0987	.1026	.1064	.1103	.1141
0.3	.1179	.1217	.1255	.1293	.1331	.1368	.1406	.1443	.1480	.1517
0.4	.1554	.1591	.1628	.1664	.1700	.1736	.1772	.1808	.1844	.1879
0.5	.1915	.1950	.1985	.2019	.2054	.2088	.2123	.2157	.2190	.2224
0.6	.2257	.2291	.2324	.2357	.2389	.2422	.2454	.2486	.2517	.2549
0.7	.2580	.2611	.2642	.2673	.2704	.2734	.2764	.2794	.2823	.2852
0.8	.2881	.2910	.2939	.2967	.2995	.3023	.3051	.3078	.3106	.3133
0.9	.3159	.3186	.3212	.3238	.3264	.3289	.3315	.3340	.3365	.3389
1.0	.3413	.3438	.3461	.3485	.3508	.3531	.3554	.3577	.3599	.3621
1.1	.3643	.3665	.3686	.3708	.3729	.3749	.3770	.3790	.3810	.3830
1.2	.3849	.3869	.3888	.3907	.3925	.3944	.3962	.3980	.3997	.4015
1.3	.4032	.4049	.4066	.4082	.4099	.4115	.4131	.4147	.4162	.4177
1.4	.4192	.4207	.4222	.4236	.4251	.4265	.4279	.4292	.4306	.4319
1.5	.4332	.4345	.4357	.4370	.4382	.4394	.4406	.4418	.4429	.4441
1.6	.4452	.4463	.4474	.4484	.4495	.4505	.4515	.4525	.4535	.4545
1.7	.4554	.4564	.4573	.4582	.4591	.4599	.4608	.4616	.4625	.4633
1.8	.4641	.4649	.4656	.4664	.4671	.4678	.4686	.4693	.4699	.4706
1.9	.4713	.4719	.4726	.4732	.4738	.4744	.4750	.4756	.4761	.4767
2.0	.4772	.4778	.4783	.4788	.4793	.4798	.4803	.4808	.4812	.4817
2.1	.4821	.4826	.4830	.4834	.4838	.4842	.4846	.4850	.4854	.4857
2.2	.4861	.4864	.4868	.4871	.4875	.4878	.4881	.4884	.4887	.4890
2.3	.4893	.4896	.4898	.4901	.4904	.4906	.4909	.4911	.4913	.4916
2.4	.4918	.4920	.4922	.4925	.4927	.4929	.4931	.4932	.4934	.4936
2.5	.4938	.4940	.4941	.4943	.4945	.4946	.4948	.4949	.4951	.4952
2.6	.4953	.4955	.4956	.4957	.4959	.4960	.4961	.4962	.4963	.4964
2.7	.4965	.4966	.4967	.4968	.4969	.4970	.4971	.4972	.4973	.4974
2.8	.4974	.4975	.4976	.4977	.4977	.4978	.4979	.4979	.4980	.4981
2.9	.4981	.4982	.4982	.4983	.4984	.4984	.4985	.4985	.4986	.4986
3.0	.4987	.4987	.4987	.4988	.4988	.4989	.4989	.4989	.4990	.4990
3.1	.4990	.4991	.4991	.4991	.4992	.4992	.4992	.4992	.4993	.4993
3.2	.4993	.4993	.4994	.4994	.4994	.4994	.4994	.4995	.4995	.4995
3.3	.4995	.4995	.4995	.4996	.4996	.4996	.4996	.4996	.4996	.4997
3.4	.4997	.4997	.4997	.4997	.4997	.4997	.4997	.4997	.4997	.4998
3.6	.4998	.4998	.4999	.4999	.4999	.4999	.4999	.4999	.4999	.4999
3.9	.5000									

Source: Harold O. Rugg, *Statistical Methods Applied to Education* (Boston: Houghton Mifflin Company, 1917), Table III, pp. 389–390. With the permission of the publishers. Reprinted by permission from *Statistical Methods,* 6th edition, by George W. Snedecor and William G. Cochran, © 1967 by the Iowa State University Press, Ames, Iowa.

TABLE A.4 Distribution of χ^2

Degrees of freedom are defined as $k - 1$ for single samples, where $k =$ the number of categories into which the data are divided. For 2×2 tables or larger, $df = $ (rows $- 1$) (columns $- 1$). Probabilities for a two-tailed test are shown across the top of the table. For one-tailed test interpretations, simply halve the probability shown; i.e., .10 (two-tailed) becomes .10/2 = .05 for a one-tailed probability.

df	.99	.98	.95	.90	.80	.70	.50	.30	.20	.10	.05	.02	.01	.001
1	.03157	.03628	.00393	.0158	.0642	.148	.455	1.074	1.642	2.706	3.841	5.412	6.635	10.827
2	.0201	.0404	.103	.211	.446	.713	1.386	2.408	3.219	4.605	5.991	7.824	9.210	13.815
3	.115	.185	.352	.584	1.005	1.424	2.366	3.665	4.642	6.251	7.815	9.837	11.345	16.268
4	.297	.429	.711	1.064	1.649	2.195	3.357	4.878	5.989	7.779	9.488	11.668	13.277	18.465
5	.554	.752	1.145	1.610	2.343	3.000	4.351	6.064	7.289	9.236	11.070	13.388	15.086	20.517
6	.872	1.134	1.635	2.204	3.070	3.828	5.348	7.231	8.558	10.645	12.592	15.033	16.812	22.457
7	1.239	1.564	2.167	2.833	3.822	4.671	6.346	8.383	9.803	12.017	14.067	16.622	18.475	24.322
8	1.646	2.032	2.733	3.490	4.594	5.527	7.344	9.524	11.030	13.362	15.507	18.168	20.090	26.125
9	2.088	2.532	3.325	4.168	5.380	6.393	8.343	10.656	12.242	14.684	16.919	19.679	21.666	27.877
10	2.558	3.059	3.940	4.865	6.179	7.267	9.342	11.781	13.442	15.987	18.307	21.161	23.209	29.588
11	3.053	3.609	4.575	5.578	6.989	8.148	10.341	12.899	14.631	17.275	19.675	22.618	24.725	31.264
12	3.571	4.178	5.226	6.304	7.807	9.034	11.340	14.011	15.812	18.549	21.026	24.054	26.217	32.909
13	4.107	4.765	5.892	7.042	8.634	9.926	12.340	15.119	16.985	19.812	22.362	25.472	27.688	34.528
14	4.660	5.368	6.571	7.790	9.467	10.821	13.339	16.222	18.151	21.064	23.685	26.873	29.141	36.123
15	5.229	5.985	7.261	8.547	10.307	11.721	14.339	17.322	19.311	22.307	24.996	28.259	30.578	37.697
16	5.812	6.614	7.962	9.312	11.152	12.624	15.338	18.418	20.465	23.542	26.296	29.633	32.000	39.252
17	6.408	7.255	8.672	10.085	12.002	13.531	16.338	19.511	21.615	24.769	27.587	30.995	33.409	40.790
18	7.015	7.906	9.390	10.865	12.857	14.440	17.338	20.601	22.760	25.989	28.869	32.346	34.805	42.312
19	7.633	8.567	10.117	11.651	13.716	15.352	18.338	21.689	23.900	27.204	30.144	33.687	36.191	43.820
20	8.260	9.237	10.851	12.443	14.578	16.266	19.337	22.775	25.038	28.412	31.410	35.020	37.566	45.315
21	8.897	9.915	11.591	13.240	15.445	17.182	20.337	23.858	26.171	29.615	32.671	36.343	38.932	46.797
22	9.542	10.600	12.338	14.041	16.314	18.101	21.337	24.939	27.301	30.813	33.924	37.659	40.289	48.268
23	10.196	11.293	13.091	14.848	17.187	19.021	22.337	26.018	28.429	32.007	35.172	38.968	41.638	49.728
24	10.856	11.992	13.848	15.659	18.062	19.943	23.337	27.096	29.553	33.196	36.415	40.270	42.980	51.179
25	11.524	12.697	14.611	16.473	18.940	20.867	24.337	28.172	30.675	34.382	37.652	41.566	44.314	52.620
26	12.198	13.409	15.379	17.292	19.820	21.792	25.336	29.246	31.795	35.563	38.885	42.856	45.642	54.052
27	12.879	14.125	16.151	18.114	20.703	22.719	26.336	30.319	32.912	36.741	40.113	44.140	46.963	55.476
28	13.565	14.847	16.928	18.939	21.588	23.647	27.336	31.391	34.027	37.916	41.337	45.419	48.278	56.893
29	14.256	15.574	17.708	19.768	22.475	24.577	28.336	32.461	35.139	39.087	42.557	46.693	49.588	58.302
30	14.953	16.306	18.493	20.599	23.364	25.508	29.336	33.530	36.250	40.256	43.773	47.962	50.892	59.703

Source: Ronald A. Fisher and Frank Yates, *Statistical Tables for Biological, Agricultural and Medical Research*, published by Longman Group Ltd. London (previously published by Oliver & Boyd, Edinburgh). By permission of the authors and publishers: Table V. Reprinted from *Basic Statistical Methods* (2nd ed.), N. M. Downie and R. W. Heath, Harper & Row, 1965.

TABLE A.5 Distribution of *t*

Degrees of freedom (*df*) are defined as $N - 1$ for a single sample. For two-sample tests, $df = (N_1 - 1) + (N_2 - 1)$, where the *N*'s are the respective sample sizes. When the exact *df* cannot be located down the left-hand side of the table, use the smaller *df* for locating significant *t* values. For example, if the researcher has $df = 110$, use 60 *df* for entering the table. This renders the decision somewhat more conservative. Any observed *t* value that equals or exceeds the value shown in the body of the table for any df is significant statistically at the probability level shown at the top of the table.

df	Level of significance for one-tailed test					
	.10	.05	.025	.01	.005	.0005
	Level of significance for two-tailed test					
	.20	.10	.05	.02	.01	.001
1	3.078	6.314	12.706	31.821	63.657	636.619
2	1.886	2.920	4.303	6.965	9.925	31.598
3	1.638	2.353	3.182	4.541	5.841	12.941
4	1.533	2.132	2.776	3.747	4.604	8.610
5	1.476	2.015	2.571	3.365	4.032	6.859
6	1.440	1.943	2.447	3.143	3.707	5.959
7	1.415	1.895	2.365	2.998	3.499	5.405
8	1.397	1.860	2.306	2.896	3.355	5.041
9	1.383	1.833	2.262	2.821	3.250	4.781
10	1.372	1.812	2.228	2.764	3.169	4.587
11	1.363	1.796	2.201	2.718	3.106	4.437
12	1.356	1.782	2.179	2.681	3.055	4.318
13	1.350	1.771	2.160	2.650	3.012	4.221
14	1.345	1.761	2.145	2.624	2.977	4.140
15	1.341	1.753	2.131	2.602	2.947	4.073
16	1.337	1.746	2.120	2.583	2.921	4.015
17	1.333	1.740	2.110	2.567	2.898	3.965
18	1.330	1.734	2.101	2.552	2.878	3.922
19	1.328	1.729	2.093	2.539	2.861	3.883
20	1.325	1.725	2.086	2.528	2.845	3.850
21	1.323	1.721	2.080	2.518	2.831	3.819
22	1.321	1.717	2.074	2.508	2.819	3.792
23	1.319	1.714	2.069	2.500	2.807	3.767
24	1.318	1.711	2.064	2.492	2.797	3.745
25	1.316	1.708	2.060	2.485	2.787	3.725
26	1.315	1.706	2.056	2.479	2.779	3.707
27	1.314	1.703	2.052	2.473	2.771	3.690
28	1.313	1.701	2.048	2.467	2.763	3.674
29	1.311	1.699	2.045	2.462	2.756	3.659
30	1.310	1.697	2.042	2.457	2.750	3.646
40	1.303	1.684	2.021	2.423	2.704	3.551
60	1.296	1.671	2.000	2.390	2.660	3.460
120	1.289	1.658	1.980	2.358	2.617	3.373
∞	1.282	1.645	1.960	2.326	2.576	3.291

Source: Abridged from Ronald A. Fisher and Frank Yates, *Statistical Tables for Biological, Agricultural and Medical Research,* published by Longman Group Ltd., London (previously published by Oliver & Boyd, Edinburgh). By permission of the authors and publishers. Table III. Reprinted from Sidney Siegel, *Nonparametric Statistics for the Behavioral Sciences* (McGraw-Hill Book Company, 1956) by permission of the publishers.

TABLE A.6 5 Percent (Lightface Type) and 1 Percent (Boldface Type) Points for the Distribution of F

Across the top of the table are degrees of freedom (df) for "Between-Group" variation. The far left- and far right-hand columns contain df for "Within-Group" variation. Where these values intersect in the body of the table define critical values of F that must be equaled or exceeded for statistical significance at the .05 or .01 levels. The lightface type are .05 critical values, while the boldface type are .01 critical values. If the exact df for either "Between-Group" variation or "Within-Group" variation cannot be found, the smaller df points should be used for a conservative hypothesis test. For example, if "Within-Group" $df = 280$, we would use the $df = 200$ for entering the table.

f_1 Degrees of Freedom (for greater mean square)

f_2	1	2	3	4	5	6	7	8	9	10	11	12	14	16	20	24	30	40	50	75	100	200	500	∞
1	161 **4,052**	200 **4,999**	216 **5,403**	225 **5,625**	230 **5,764**	234 **5,859**	237 **5,928**	239 **5,981**	241 **6,022**	242 **6,056**	243 **6,082**	244 **6,106**	245 **6,142**	246 **6,169**	248 **6,208**	249 **6,234**	250 **6,261**	251 **6,286**	252 **6,302**	253 **6,323**	253 **6,334**	254 **6,352**	254 **6,361**	254 **6,366**
2	18.51 **98.49**	19.00 **99.00**	19.16 **99.17**	19.25 **99.25**	19.30 **99.30**	19.33 **99.33**	19.36 **99.36**	19.37 **99.37**	19.38 **99.39**	19.39 **99.40**	19.40 **99.41**	19.41 **99.42**	19.42 **99.43**	19.43 **99.44**	19.44 **99.45**	19.45 **99.46**	19.46 **99.47**	19.47 **99.48**	19.47 **99.48**	19.48 **99.49**	19.49 **99.49**	19.49 **99.49**	19.50 **99.50**	19.50 **99.50**
3	10.13 **34.12**	9.55 **30.82**	9.28 **29.46**	9.12 **28.71**	9.01 **28.24**	8.94 **27.91**	8.88 **27.67**	8.84 **27.49**	8.81 **27.34**	8.78 **27.23**	8.76 **27.13**	8.74 **27.05**	8.71 **26.92**	8.69 **26.83**	8.66 **26.69**	8.64 **26.60**	8.62 **26.50**	8.60 **26.41**	8.58 **26.35**	8.57 **26.27**	8.56 **26.23**	8.54 **26.18**	8.54 **26.14**	8.53 **26.12**
4	7.71 **21.20**	6.94 **18.00**	6.59 **16.69**	6.39 **15.98**	6.26 **15.52**	6.16 **15.21**	6.09 **14.98**	6.04 **14.80**	6.00 **14.66**	5.96 **14.54**	5.93 **14.45**	5.91 **14.37**	5.87 **14.24**	5.84 **14.15**	5.80 **14.02**	5.77 **13.93**	5.74 **13.83**	5.71 **13.74**	5.70 **13.69**	5.68 **13.61**	5.66 **13.57**	5.65 **13.52**	5.64 **13.48**	5.63 **13.46**
5	6.61 **16.26**	5.79 **13.27**	5.41 **12.06**	5.19 **11.39**	5.05 **10.97**	4.95 **10.67**	4.88 **10.45**	4.82 **10.29**	4.78 **10.15**	4.74 **10.05**	4.70 **9.96**	4.68 **9.89**	4.64 **9.77**	4.60 **9.68**	4.56 **9.55**	4.53 **9.47**	4.50 **9.38**	4.46 **9.29**	4.44 **9.24**	4.42 **9.17**	4.40 **9.13**	4.38 **9.07**	4.37 **9.04**	4.36 **9.02**
6	5.99 **13.74**	5.14 **10.92**	4.76 **9.78**	4.53 **9.15**	4.39 **8.75**	4.28 **8.47**	4.21 **8.26**	4.15 **8.10**	4.10 **7.98**	4.06 **7.87**	4.03 **7.79**	4.00 **7.72**	3.96 **7.60**	3.92 **7.52**	3.87 **7.39**	3.84 **7.31**	3.81 **7.23**	3.77 **7.14**	3.75 **7.09**	3.72 **7.02**	3.71 **6.99**	3.69 **6.94**	3.68 **6.90**	3.67 **6.88**
7	5.59 **12.25**	4.74 **9.55**	4.35 **8.45**	4.12 **7.85**	3.97 **7.46**	3.87 **7.19**	3.79 **7.00**	3.73 **6.84**	3.68 **6.71**	3.63 **6.62**	3.60 **6.54**	3.57 **6.47**	3.52 **6.35**	3.49 **6.27**	3.44 **6.15**	3.41 **6.07**	3.38 **5.98**	3.34 **5.90**	3.32 **5.85**	3.29 **5.78**	3.28 **5.75**	3.25 **5.70**	3.24 **5.67**	3.23 **5.65**
8	5.32 **11.26**	4.46 **8.65**	4.07 **7.59**	3.84 **7.01**	3.69 **6.63**	3.58 **6.37**	3.50 **6.19**	3.44 **6.03**	3.39 **5.91**	3.34 **5.82**	3.31 **5.74**	3.28 **5.67**	3.23 **5.56**	3.20 **5.48**	3.15 **5.36**	3.12 **5.28**	3.08 **5.20**	3.05 **5.11**	3.03 **5.06**	3.00 **5.00**	2.98 **4.96**	2.96 **4.91**	2.94 **4.88**	2.93 **4.86**
9	5.12 **10.56**	4.26 **8.02**	3.86 **6.99**	3.63 **6.42**	3.48 **6.06**	3.37 **5.80**	3.29 **5.62**	3.23 **5.47**	3.18 **5.35**	3.13 **5.26**	3.10 **5.18**	3.07 **5.11**	3.02 **5.00**	2.98 **4.92**	2.93 **4.80**	2.90 **4.73**	2.86 **4.64**	2.82 **4.56**	2.80 **4.51**	2.77 **4.45**	2.76 **4.41**	2.73 **4.36**	2.72 **4.33**	2.71 **4.31**
10	4.96 **10.04**	4.10 **7.56**	3.71 **6.55**	3.48 **5.99**	3.33 **5.64**	3.22 **5.39**	3.14 **5.21**	3.07 **5.06**	3.02 **4.95**	2.97 **4.85**	2.94 **4.78**	2.91 **4.71**	2.86 **4.60**	2.82 **4.52**	2.77 **4.41**	2.74 **4.33**	2.70 **4.25**	2.67 **4.17**	2.64 **4.12**	2.61 **4.05**	2.59 **4.01**	2.56 **3.96**	2.55 **3.93**	2.54 **3.91**
11	4.84 **9.65**	3.98 **7.20**	3.59 **6.22**	3.36 **5.67**	3.20 **5.32**	3.09 **5.07**	3.01 **4.88**	2.95 **4.74**	2.90 **4.63**	2.86 **4.54**	2.82 **4.46**	2.79 **4.40**	2.74 **4.29**	2.70 **4.21**	2.65 **4.10**	2.61 **4.02**	2.57 **3.94**	2.53 **3.86**	2.50 **3.80**	2.47 **3.74**	2.45 **3.70**	2.42 **3.66**	2.41 **3.62**	2.40 **3.60**
12	4.75 **9.33**	3.88 **6.93**	3.49 **5.95**	3.26 **5.41**	3.11 **5.06**	3.00 **4.82**	2.92 **4.65**	2.85 **4.50**	2.80 **4.39**	2.76 **4.30**	2.72 **4.22**	2.69 **4.16**	2.64 **4.05**	2.60 **3.98**	2.54 **3.86**	2.50 **3.78**	2.46 **3.70**	2.42 **3.61**	2.40 **3.56**	2.36 **3.49**	2.35 **3.46**	2.32 **3.41**	2.31 **3.38**	2.30 **3.36**
13	4.67 **9.07**	3.80 **6.70**	3.41 **5.74**	3.18 **5.20**	3.02 **4.86**	2.92 **4.62**	2.84 **4.44**	2.77 **4.30**	2.72 **4.19**	2.67 **4.10**	2.63 **4.02**	2.60 **3.96**	2.55 **3.85**	2.51 **3.78**	2.46 **3.67**	2.42 **3.59**	2.38 **3.51**	2.34 **3.42**	2.32 **3.37**	2.28 **3.30**	2.26 **3.27**	2.24 **3.21**	2.22 **3.18**	2.21 **3.16**

Source: By permission from *Statistical Methods*, 6th Edition, by George W. Snedecor and William G. Cochran. © 1967 by the Iowa State University Press, Ames, Iowa. The function, $F = e$ with exponent $2z$, is computed in part from Fisher's Table VI. Additional entries are by interpolation, mostly graphical.

f₁ Degrees of Freedom (for greater mean square)

f_2	∞	500	200	100	75	50	40	30	24	20	16	14	12	11	10	9	8	7	6	5	4	3	2	1	f_2
14	2.13 / 3.00	2.14 / 3.02	2.16 / 3.06	2.19 / 3.11	2.21 / 3.14	2.24 / 3.21	2.27 / 3.26	2.31 / 3.34	2.35 / 3.43	2.39 / 3.51	2.44 / 3.62	2.48 / 3.70	2.53 / 3.80	2.56 / 3.86	2.60 / 3.94	2.65 / 4.03	2.70 / 4.14	2.77 / 4.28	2.85 / 4.46	2.96 / 4.69	3.11 / 5.03	3.34 / 5.56	3.74 / 6.51	4.60 / 8.86	14
15	2.07 / 2.87	2.08 / 2.89	2.10 / 2.92	2.12 / 2.97	2.15 / 3.00	2.18 / 3.07	2.21 / 3.12	2.25 / 3.20	2.29 / 3.29	2.33 / 3.36	2.39 / 3.48	2.43 / 3.56	2.48 / 3.67	2.51 / 3.73	2.55 / 3.80	2.59 / 3.89	2.64 / 4.00	2.70 / 4.14	2.79 / 4.32	2.90 / 4.56	3.06 / 4.89	3.29 / 5.42	3.68 / 6.36	4.54 / 8.68	15
16	2.01 / 2.75	2.02 / 2.77	2.04 / 2.80	2.07 / 2.86	2.09 / 2.98	2.13 / 2.96	2.16 / 3.01	2.20 / 3.10	2.24 / 3.18	2.28 / 3.25	2.33 / 3.37	2.37 / 3.45	2.42 / 3.55	2.45 / 3.61	2.49 / 3.69	2.54 / 3.78	2.59 / 3.89	2.66 / 4.03	2.74 / 4.20	2.85 / 4.44	3.01 / 4.77	3.24 / 5.29	3.63 / 6.23	4.49 / 8.53	16
17	1.96 / 2.65	1.97 / 2.67	1.99 / 2.70	2.02 / 2.76	2.04 / 2.79	2.08 / 2.86	2.11 / 2.92	2.15 / 3.00	2.19 / 3.08	2.23 / 3.16	2.29 / 3.27	2.33 / 3.35	2.38 / 3.45	2.41 / 3.52	2.45 / 3.59	2.50 / 3.68	2.55 / 3.79	2.62 / 3.93	2.70 / 4.10	2.81 / 4.34	2.96 / 4.67	3.20 / 5.18	3.59 / 6.11	4.45 / 8.40	17
18	1.92 / 2.57	1.93 / 2.59	1.95 / 2.62	1.98 / 2.68	2.00 / 2.71	2.04 / 2.78	2.07 / 2.83	2.11 / 2.91	2.15 / 3.00	2.19 / 3.07	2.25 / 3.19	2.29 / 3.27	2.34 / 3.37	2.37 / 3.44	2.41 / 3.51	2.46 / 3.60	2.51 / 3.71	2.58 / 3.85	2.66 / 4.01	2.77 / 4.25	2.93 / 4.58	3.16 / 5.09	3.55 / 6.01	4.41 / 8.28	18
19	1.88 / 2.49	1.90 / 2.51	1.91 / 2.54	1.94 / 2.60	1.96 / 2.63	2.00 / 2.70	2.02 / 2.76	2.07 / 2.84	2.11 / 2.92	2.15 / 3.00	2.21 / 3.12	2.26 / 3.19	2.31 / 3.30	2.34 / 3.36	2.38 / 3.43	2.43 / 3.52	2.48 / 3.63	2.55 / 3.77	2.63 / 3.94	2.74 / 4.17	2.90 / 4.50	3.13 / 5.01	3.52 / 5.93	4.38 / 8.18	19
20	1.84 / 2.42	1.85 / 2.44	1.87 / 2.47	1.90 / 2.53	1.92 / 2.56	1.96 / 2.63	1.99 / 2.69	2.04 / 2.77	2.08 / 2.86	2.12 / 2.94	2.18 / 3.05	2.23 / 3.13	2.28 / 3.23	2.31 / 3.30	2.35 / 3.37	2.40 / 3.45	2.45 / 3.56	2.52 / 3.71	2.60 / 3.87	2.71 / 4.10	2.87 / 4.43	3.10 / 4.94	3.49 / 5.85	4.35 / 8.10	20
21	1.81 / 2.36	1.82 / 2.38	1.84 / 2.42	1.87 / 2.47	1.89 / 2.51	1.93 / 2.58	1.96 / 2.63	2.00 / 2.72	2.05 / 2.80	2.09 / 2.88	2.15 / 2.99	2.20 / 3.07	2.25 / 3.17	2.28 / 3.24	2.32 / 3.31	2.37 / 3.40	2.42 / 3.51	2.49 / 3.65	2.57 / 3.81	2.68 / 4.04	2.84 / 4.37	3.07 / 4.87	3.47 / 5.78	4.32 / 8.02	21
22	1.78 / 2.31	1.80 / 2.33	1.81 / 2.37	1.84 / 2.42	1.87 / 2.46	1.91 / 2.53	1.93 / 2.58	1.98 / 2.67	2.03 / 2.75	2.07 / 2.83	2.13 / 2.94	2.18 / 3.02	2.23 / 3.12	2.26 / 3.18	2.30 / 3.26	2.35 / 3.35	2.40 / 3.45	2.47 / 3.59	2.55 / 3.76	2.66 / 3.99	2.82 / 4.31	3.05 / 4.82	3.44 / 5.72	4.30 / 7.94	22
23	1.76 / 2.26	1.77 / 2.28	1.79 / 2.32	1.82 / 2.37	1.84 / 2.41	1.88 / 2.48	1.91 / 2.53	1.96 / 2.62	2.00 / 2.70	2.04 / 2.78	2.10 / 2.89	2.14 / 2.97	2.20 / 3.07	2.24 / 3.14	2.28 / 3.21	2.32 / 3.30	2.38 / 3.41	2.45 / 3.54	2.53 / 3.71	2.64 / 3.94	2.80 / 4.26	3.03 / 4.76	3.42 / 5.66	4.28 / 7.88	23
24	1.73 / 2.21	1.74 / 2.23	1.76 / 2.27	1.80 / 2.33	1.82 / 2.36	1.86 / 2.44	1.89 / 2.49	1.94 / 2.58	1.98 / 2.66	2.02 / 2.74	2.09 / 2.85	2.13 / 2.93	2.18 / 3.03	2.22 / 3.09	2.26 / 3.17	2.30 / 3.25	2.36 / 3.36	2.43 / 3.50	2.51 / 3.67	2.62 / 3.90	2.78 / 4.22	3.01 / 4.72	3.40 / 5.61	4.26 / 7.82	24
25	1.71 / 2.17	1.72 / 2.19	1.74 / 2.23	1.77 / 2.29	1.80 / 2.32	1.84 / 2.40	1.87 / 2.45	1.92 / 2.54	1.96 / 2.62	2.00 / 2.70	2.06 / 2.81	2.11 / 2.89	2.16 / 2.99	2.20 / 3.05	2.24 / 3.13	2.28 / 3.21	2.34 / 3.32	2.41 / 3.46	2.49 / 3.63	2.60 / 3.86	2.76 / 4.18	2.99 / 4.68	3.38 / 5.57	4.24 / 7.77	25
26	1.69 / 2.13	1.70 / 2.15	1.72 / 2.19	1.76 / 2.25	1.78 / 2.28	1.82 / 2.36	1.85 / 2.41	1.90 / 2.50	1.95 / 2.58	1.99 / 2.66	2.05 / 2.77	2.10 / 2.86	2.15 / 2.96	2.18 / 3.02	2.22 / 3.09	2.27 / 3.17	2.32 / 3.29	2.39 / 3.42	2.47 / 3.59	2.59 / 3.82	2.74 / 4.14	2.98 / 4.64	3.37 / 5.53	4.22 / 7.72	26

f_1 Degrees of Freedom (for greater mean square)

f_2	1	2	3	4	5	6	7	8	9	10	11	12	14	16	20	24	30	40	50	75	100	200	500	∞	f_2
27	4.21 **7.68**	3.35 **5.49**	2.96 **4.60**	2.73 **4.11**	2.57 **3.79**	2.46 **3.56**	2.37 **3.39**	2.30 **3.26**	2.25 **3.14**	2.20 **3.06**	2.16 **2.98**	2.13 **2.93**	2.08 **2.83**	2.03 **2.74**	1.97 **2.63**	1.93 **2.55**	1.88 **2.47**	1.84 **2.38**	1.80 **2.33**	1.76 **2.25**	1.74 **2.21**	1.71 **2.16**	1.68 **2.12**	1.67 **2.10**	27
28	4.20 **7.64**	3.34 **5.45**	2.95 **4.57**	2.71 **4.07**	2.56 **3.76**	2.44 **3.53**	2.36 **3.36**	2.29 **3.23**	2.24 **3.11**	2.19 **3.03**	2.15 **2.95**	2.12 **2.90**	2.06 **2.80**	2.02 **2.71**	1.96 **2.60**	1.91 **2.52**	1.87 **2.44**	1.81 **2.35**	1.78 **2.30**	1.75 **2.22**	1.72 **2.18**	1.69 **2.13**	1.67 **2.09**	1.65 **2.06**	28
29	4.18 **7.60**	3.33 **5.42**	2.93 **4.54**	2.70 **4.04**	2.54 **3.73**	2.43 **3.50**	2.35 **3.33**	2.28 **3.20**	2.22 **3.08**	2.18 **3.00**	2.14 **2.92**	2.10 **2.87**	2.05 **2.77**	2.00 **2.68**	1.94 **2.57**	1.90 **2.49**	1.85 **2.41**	1.80 **2.32**	1.77 **2.27**	1.73 **2.19**	1.71 **2.15**	1.68 **2.10**	1.65 **2.06**	1.64 **2.03**	29
30	4.17 **7.56**	3.32 **5.39**	2.92 **4.51**	2.69 **4.02**	2.53 **3.70**	2.42 **3.47**	2.34 **3.30**	2.27 **3.17**	2.21 **3.06**	2.16 **2.98**	2.12 **2.90**	2.09 **2.84**	2.04 **2.74**	1.99 **2.66**	1.93 **2.55**	1.89 **2.47**	1.84 **2.38**	1.79 **2.29**	1.76 **2.24**	1.72 **2.16**	1.69 **2.13**	1.66 **2.07**	1.64 **2.03**	1.62 **2.01**	30
32	4.15 **7.50**	3.30 **5.34**	2.90 **4.46**	2.67 **3.97**	2.51 **3.66**	2.40 **3.42**	2.32 **3.25**	2.25 **3.12**	2.19 **3.01**	2.14 **2.94**	2.10 **2.86**	2.07 **2.80**	2.02 **2.70**	1.97 **2.62**	1.91 **2.51**	1.86 **2.42**	1.82 **2.34**	1.76 **2.25**	1.74 **2.20**	1.69 **2.12**	1.67 **2.08**	1.64 **2.02**	1.61 **1.98**	1.59 **1.96**	32
34	4.13 **7.44**	3.28 **5.29**	2.88 **4.42**	2.65 **3.93**	2.49 **3.61**	2.38 **3.38**	2.30 **3.21**	2.23 **3.08**	2.17 **2.97**	2.12 **2.89**	2.08 **2.82**	2.05 **2.76**	2.00 **2.66**	1.95 **2.58**	1.89 **2.47**	1.84 **2.38**	1.80 **2.30**	1.74 **2.21**	1.71 **2.15**	1.67 **2.08**	1.64 **2.04**	1.61 **1.98**	1.59 **1.94**	1.57 **1.91**	34
36	4.11 **7.39**	3.26 **5.25**	2.86 **4.38**	2.63 **3.89**	2.48 **3.58**	2.36 **3.35**	2.28 **3.18**	2.21 **3.04**	2.15 **2.94**	2.10 **2.86**	2.06 **2.78**	2.03 **2.72**	1.98 **2.62**	1.93 **2.54**	1.87 **2.43**	1.82 **2.35**	1.78 **2.26**	1.72 **2.17**	1.69 **2.12**	1.65 **2.04**	1.62 **2.00**	1.59 **1.94**	1.56 **1.90**	1.55 **1.87**	36
38	4.10 **7.35**	3.25 **5.21**	2.85 **4.34**	2.62 **3.86**	2.46 **3.54**	2.35 **3.32**	2.26 **3.15**	2.19 **3.02**	2.14 **2.91**	2.09 **2.82**	2.05 **2.75**	2.02 **2.69**	1.96 **2.59**	1.92 **2.51**	1.85 **2.40**	1.80 **2.32**	1.76 **2.22**	1.71 **2.14**	1.67 **2.08**	1.63 **2.00**	1.60 **1.97**	1.57 **1.90**	1.54 **1.86**	1.53 **1.84**	38
40	4.08 **7.31**	3.23 **5.18**	2.84 **4.31**	2.61 **3.83**	2.45 **3.51**	2.34 **3.29**	2.25 **3.12**	2.18 **2.99**	2.12 **2.88**	2.07 **2.80**	2.04 **2.73**	2.00 **2.66**	1.95 **2.56**	1.90 **2.49**	1.84 **2.37**	1.79 **2.29**	1.74 **2.20**	1.69 **2.11**	1.66 **2.05**	1.61 **1.97**	1.59 **1.94**	1.55 **1.88**	1.53 **1.84**	1.51 **1.81**	40
42	4.07 **7.27**	3.22 **5.15**	2.83 **4.29**	2.59 **3.80**	2.44 **3.49**	2.32 **3.26**	2.24 **3.10**	2.17 **2.96**	2.11 **2.86**	2.06 **2.77**	2.02 **2.70**	1.99 **2.64**	1.94 **2.54**	1.89 **2.46**	1.82 **2.35**	1.78 **2.26**	1.73 **2.17**	1.68 **2.08**	1.64 **2.02**	1.60 **1.94**	1.57 **1.91**	1.54 **1.85**	1.51 **1.80**	1.49 **1.78**	42
44	4.06 **7.24**	3.21 **5.12**	2.82 **4.26**	2.58 **3.78**	2.43 **3.46**	2.31 **3.24**	2.23 **3.07**	2.16 **2.94**	2.10 **2.84**	2.05 **2.75**	2.01 **2.68**	1.98 **2.62**	1.92 **2.52**	1.88 **2.44**	1.81 **2.32**	1.76 **2.24**	1.72 **2.15**	1.66 **2.06**	1.63 **2.00**	1.58 **1.92**	1.56 **1.88**	1.52 **1.82**	1.50 **1.78**	1.48 **1.75**	44
46	4.05 **7.21**	3.20 **5.10**	2.81 **4.24**	2.57 **3.76**	2.42 **3.44**	2.30 **3.22**	2.22 **3.05**	2.14 **2.92**	2.09 **2.82**	2.04 **2.73**	2.00 **2.66**	1.97 **2.60**	1.91 **2.50**	1.87 **2.42**	1.80 **2.30**	1.75 **2.22**	1.71 **2.13**	1.65 **2.04**	1.62 **1.98**	1.57 **1.90**	1.54 **1.86**	1.51 **1.80**	1.48 **1.76**	1.46 **1.72**	46
48	4.04 **7.19**	3.19 **5.08**	2.80 **4.22**	2.56 **3.74**	2.41 **3.42**	2.30 **3.20**	2.21 **3.04**	2.14 **2.90**	2.08 **2.80**	2.03 **2.71**	1.99 **2.64**	1.96 **2.58**	1.90 **2.48**	1.86 **2.40**	1.79 **2.28**	1.74 **2.20**	1.70 **2.11**	1.64 **2.02**	1.61 **1.96**	1.56 **1.88**	1.53 **1.84**	1.50 **1.78**	1.47 **1.73**	1.45 **1.70**	48

f_1 Degrees of Freedom (for greater mean square)

Each cell lists two values (upper / lower).

f_2	1	2	3	4	5	6	7	8	9	10	11	12	14	16	20	24	30	40	50	75	100	200	500	∞
50	4.03 / 7.17	3.18 / 5.06	2.79 / 4.20	2.56 / 3.72	2.40 / 3.41	2.29 / 3.18	2.20 / 3.02	2.13 / 2.88	2.07 / 2.78	2.02 / 2.70	1.98 / 2.62	1.95 / 2.56	1.90 / 2.46	1.85 / 2.39	1.78 / 2.26	1.74 / 2.18	1.69 / 2.10	1.63 / 2.00	1.60 / 1.94	1.55 / 1.86	1.52 / 1.82	1.48 / 1.76	1.46 / 1.71	1.44 / 1.68
55	4.02 / 7.12	3.17 / 5.01	2.78 / 4.16	2.54 / 3.68	2.38 / 3.37	2.27 / 3.15	2.18 / 2.98	2.11 / 2.85	2.05 / 2.75	2.00 / 2.66	1.97 / 2.59	1.93 / 2.53	1.88 / 2.43	1.83 / 2.35	1.76 / 2.23	1.72 / 2.15	1.67 / 2.06	1.61 / 1.96	1.58 / 1.90	1.52 / 1.82	1.50 / 1.78	1.46 / 1.71	1.43 / 1.66	1.41 / 1.64
60	4.00 / 7.08	3.15 / 4.98	2.76 / 4.13	2.52 / 3.65	2.37 / 3.34	2.25 / 3.12	2.17 / 2.95	2.10 / 2.82	2.04 / 2.72	1.99 / 2.63	1.95 / 2.56	1.92 / 2.50	1.86 / 2.40	1.81 / 2.32	1.75 / 2.20	1.70 / 2.12	1.65 / 2.03	1.59 / 1.93	1.56 / 1.87	1.50 / 1.79	1.48 / 1.74	1.44 / 1.68	1.41 / 1.63	1.39 / 1.60
65	3.99 / 7.04	3.14 / 4.95	2.75 / 4.10	2.51 / 3.62	2.36 / 3.31	2.24 / 3.09	2.15 / 2.93	2.08 / 2.79	2.02 / 2.70	1.98 / 2.61	1.94 / 2.54	1.90 / 2.47	1.85 / 2.37	1.80 / 2.30	1.73 / 2.18	1.68 / 2.09	1.63 / 2.00	1.57 / 1.90	1.54 / 1.84	1.49 / 1.76	1.46 / 1.71	1.42 / 1.64	1.39 / 1.60	1.37 / 1.56
70	3.98 / 7.01	3.13 / 4.92	2.74 / 4.08	2.50 / 3.60	2.35 / 3.29	2.23 / 3.07	2.14 / 2.91	2.07 / 2.77	2.01 / 2.67	1.97 / 2.59	1.93 / 2.51	1.89 / 2.45	1.84 / 2.35	1.79 / 2.28	1.72 / 2.15	1.67 / 2.07	1.62 / 1.98	1.56 / 1.88	1.53 / 1.82	1.47 / 1.74	1.45 / 1.69	1.40 / 1.62	1.37 / 1.56	1.35 / 1.53
80	3.96 / 6.96	3.11 / 4.88	2.72 / 4.04	2.48 / 3.56	2.33 / 3.25	2.21 / 3.04	2.12 / 2.87	2.05 / 2.74	1.99 / 2.64	1.95 / 2.55	1.91 / 2.48	1.88 / 2.41	1.82 / 2.32	1.77 / 2.24	1.70 / 2.11	1.65 / 2.03	1.60 / 1.94	1.54 / 1.84	1.51 / 1.78	1.45 / 1.70	1.42 / 1.65	1.38 / 1.57	1.35 / 1.52	1.32 / 1.49
100	3.94 / 6.90	3.09 / 4.82	2.70 / 3.98	2.46 / 3.51	2.30 / 3.20	2.19 / 2.99	2.10 / 2.82	2.03 / 2.69	1.97 / 2.59	1.92 / 2.51	1.88 / 2.43	1.85 / 2.36	1.79 / 2.26	1.75 / 2.19	1.68 / 2.06	1.63 / 1.98	1.57 / 1.89	1.51 / 1.79	1.48 / 1.73	1.42 / 1.64	1.39 / 1.59	1.34 / 1.51	1.30 / 1.46	1.28 / 1.43
125	3.92 / 6.84	3.07 / 4.78	2.68 / 3.94	2.44 / 3.47	2.29 / 3.17	2.17 / 2.95	2.08 / 2.79	2.01 / 2.65	1.95 / 2.56	1.90 / 2.47	1.86 / 2.40	1.83 / 2.33	1.77 / 2.23	1.72 / 2.15	1.65 / 2.03	1.60 / 1.94	1.55 / 1.85	1.49 / 1.75	1.45 / 1.68	1.39 / 1.59	1.36 / 1.54	1.31 / 1.46	1.27 / 1.40	1.25 / 1.37
150	3.91 / 6.81	3.06 / 4.75	2.67 / 3.91	2.43 / 3.44	2.27 / 3.14	2.16 / 2.92	2.07 / 2.76	2.00 / 2.62	1.94 / 2.53	1.89 / 2.44	1.85 / 2.37	1.82 / 2.30	1.76 / 2.20	1.71 / 2.12	1.64 / 2.00	1.59 / 1.91	1.54 / 1.83	1.47 / 1.72	1.44 / 1.66	1.37 / 1.56	1.34 / 1.51	1.29 / 1.43	1.25 / 1.37	1.22 / 1.33
200	3.89 / 6.76	3.04 / 4.71	2.65 / 3.88	2.41 / 3.41	2.26 / 3.11	2.14 / 2.90	2.05 / 2.73	1.98 / 2.60	1.92 / 2.50	1.87 / 2.41	1.83 / 2.34	1.80 / 2.28	1.74 / 2.17	1.69 / 2.09	1.62 / 1.97	1.57 / 1.88	1.52 / 1.79	1.45 / 1.69	1.42 / 1.62	1.35 / 1.53	1.32 / 1.48	1.26 / 1.39	1.22 / 1.33	1.19 / 1.28
400	3.86 / 6.70	3.02 / 4.66	2.62 / 3.83	2.39 / 3.36	2.23 / 3.06	2.12 / 2.85	2.03 / 2.69	1.96 / 2.55	1.90 / 2.46	1.85 / 2.37	1.81 / 2.29	1.78 / 2.23	1.72 / 2.12	1.67 / 2.04	1.60 / 1.92	1.54 / 1.84	1.49 / 1.74	1.42 / 1.64	1.38 / 1.57	1.32 / 1.47	1.28 / 1.42	1.22 / 1.32	1.16 / 1.24	1.13 / 1.19
1000	3.85 / 6.66	3.00 / 4.62	2.61 / 3.80	2.38 / 3.34	2.22 / 3.04	2.10 / 2.82	2.02 / 2.66	1.95 / 2.53	1.89 / 2.43	1.84 / 2.34	1.80 / 2.26	1.76 / 2.20	1.70 / 2.09	1.65 / 2.01	1.58 / 1.89	1.53 / 1.81	1.47 / 1.71	1.41 / 1.61	1.36 / 1.54	1.30 / 1.44	1.26 / 1.38	1.19 / 1.28	1.13 / 1.19	1.08 / 1.11
∞	3.84 / 6.64	2.99 / 4.60	2.60 / 3.78	2.37 / 3.32	2.21 / 3.02	2.09 / 2.80	2.01 / 2.64	1.94 / 2.51	1.88 / 2.41	1.83 / 2.32	1.79 / 2.24	1.75 / 2.18	1.69 / 2.07	1.64 / 1.99	1.57 / 1.87	1.52 / 1.79	1.46 / 1.69	1.40 / 1.59	1.35 / 1.52	1.28 / 1.41	1.24 / 1.36	1.17 / 1.25	1.11 / 1.15	1.00 / 1.00

appendix B

Using Computers in Criminal Justice

INTRODUCTION

Data analysis in criminal justice and criminology has become increasingly complex and sophisticated, although the mechanics of analyzing data have been made easier through the creation of software programs available for **personal computers (PCs).** *Today most students are familiar with personal computer applications of various kinds, through Internet exploration or word processing for term papers. Appropriate software exists for virtually every kind of statistical application known. This short appendix is designed to acquaint students with SPSS for Windows and its use for data analysis and computational work.*

CALCULATORS AND COMPUTERS

In the 1960s and 1970s, most students relied upon hand calculators in order to calculate statistical formulae and perform simple arithmetic operations, such as adding, subtracting, multiplying, dividing, and calculating squares and square roots. While hand calculators continue to be used, the advent of computers and accompanying statistical software packages has done much to change how we think about data analysis and actually carry out analysis functions.

Computers and computer systems are now an integral part of our lives in many different ways. We have learned to "surf the net," exploring an unlimited number of sites on the Internet. We use computers today for doing some of our research. Databases from both public and private sources can be accessed by computer. We can learn much from different informational sources at an increasing number of Internet sites.

In the past we often relied upon university computer centers to code and analyze our data sets. We waited patiently, sometimes for a week or longer, while university computers, known as mainframe computers, were at work, printing numerous tables and charts filled with volumes of data. For the most part, those days are gone. Now we have access to our own software programs, in which we can enter data for analysis and then analyze it using complex statistical tools. We have many options available to us, depending upon the statistical software program we choose. We can perform data analyses in a matter of minutes, and the output or products of our data analysis are available in seconds. We are becoming used to instantaneous data retrieval. Our computer systems are running faster, and our calculations of statistical tests and other functions are now performed with blinding speed.

COMPUTER SOFTWARE FOR DATA ANALYSES

During the 1980s and 1990s, numerous statistical software packages were created and marketed to simplify social scientific data analyses. Virtually every known statistical test and measure of association can be computed by using one or more of these existing software programs.

Essentially, data collected from questionnaires are entered into the selected computer program. Once variables have been identified and data recorded for the research subjects, then relatively simple instructions can be followed by students or others to examine different aspects of one's data and perform basic statistical operations. Data can be tabulated and descriptive statistics can be computed, including the mean, mode, median, range, and standard deviation. Tests of significance, such as the t test for differences between means or the F test for analysis of variance, can be applied easily by following simple instructions contained in these canned programs. Measures of association can also be computed, depending upon the researcher's needs. Also available are more complex analytical procedures, including multivariate analysis, path analysis, and different types of regression analysis.

THE STATISTICAL PACKAGE FOR THE SOCIAL SCIENCES (SPSS)

One of the most popular statistical software programs is the *Statistical Package for the Social Sciences (SPSS)*. There are several different versions of SPSS on the market today. In 1999, SPSS, Inc., in Chicago created a new SPSS version known as SPSS 9.0 for Windows. This version and its predecessors (e.g., SPSS 7.5 for Windows, SPSS 6.0 for Windows) use Windows 3.1, Windows 95, and/or Windows 98. If these programs are already installed on one's computer, then SPSS for Windows in its different versions can be used effectively.

What SPSS Does

SPSS for Windows is a comprehensive and flexible statistical analysis and data management system. It can accept data from almost any type of file and use them to generate tabulated reports, charts, and plots of distributions and trends, descriptive statistics, and complex statistical analyses (Norusis, 1993:iii). The capabilities of SPSS for Windows are such that there are thousands of variables and large data sets. Most criminological or criminal justice applications would not involve elaborate analyses of thousands of variables. More realistically, researchers might wish to examine up to 40 or 50 variables in any investigation. Many studies reported in conventional research outlets, such as *Criminology, Justice Quarterly, Journal of Crime and Justice, Journal of Research on Crime and Delinquency*, or *Journal of Criminal Justice,* involve samples of subjects of 1,000 or fewer. Some research organizations, such as the National Opinion Research Center at the University of Chicago or the Survey Research Center at the University of Michigan, frequently investigate opinions and attitudes of 15,000 to 25,000 persons or more. SPSS for Windows is capable of handling such data analyses. Thus, it is difficult to conceive of a project for which SPSS for Windows would *not* be an appropriate means for data analyses.

SPSS for Windows uses easy-to-understand dialog boxes so that statistical commands can be given without reference to or use of complex syntax. Investigators can enter data into a data file and then perform various tests and descriptive procedures by following easy instructions.

SPSS for Windows consists of a Base System that contains a wide variety of statistical tests and graphic functions. Students can perform the following functions with the Base System:

1. Establish data sets, data entry, specification of variables, and identification of subclasses on variables
2. Transform data from one form to another, recode data, merge files, and re-sort cases for selected analyses
3. Select a random sample for a designated list of elements, assign weights to cases
4. Create frequency distributions, histograms, frequency polygons, percentiles, and frequencies statistics
5. Cross-tabulate data and calculate percentages
6. Perform cross-tabulation statistics, such as the chi square test
7. Perform difference-between-means tests, including t test, F test for analysis of variance, and one- and two-way analysis of variance procedures
8. Measure linear association, partial correlation and multiple linear regression analysis, and curve estimation
9. Perform numerous nonparametric statistical tests, including the Mann-Whitney U test; Kolmogorov-Smirnov one- and two-sample tests; runs test; and one-sample, two-sample, and k-sample tests
10. Create scatterplots and three-dimensional matrices

Several add-on modules are also available for more advanced and specialized analyses. These modules include

1. SPSS Professional Statistics: techniques to measure the similarities and differences in data, data classification, cluster, k-means cluster, discriminant, factor, multidimensional scaling, proximity, and reliability
2. SPSS Advanced Statistics: loglinear analysis; logistic regression; multivariate analysis of variance; constrained nonlinear regression; probit analysis; Cox regression; Kaplan-Meier and actuarial survival analysis
3. SPSS Tables: creates complex stub-and-banner tables and displays multiple-response data; creates a variety of presentation-quality tabular reports
4. SPSS Trends: performs comprehensive forecasting and time series analyses with multiple curve-fitting models, smoothing models, and methods for estimating autoregressive functions
5. SPSS Categories: performs conjoint analysis and optimal scaling procedures, including correspondence analysis
6. SPSS CHAID: simplifies tabular analyses of categorical data, develops predictive models, screens out extraneous predictor variables, and produces easy-to-read tree diagrams that segment a population into subgroups that share similar characteristics
7. SPSS LISREL: analyzes linear structural relations and simultaneous equation models (Norusis, 1993:iii–iv)

It is unlikely that most students would ever want to perform statistical functions beyond those contained in the SPSS Base System. However, these other modules are available if more complex statistics and analyses are desired.

How to Transform Data Sets for SPSS Operations

When investigators have collected their data from research subjects, the data must be transmitted to a file on the computer for storage. Before data are transmitted to computer, they are coded. The variables and their subclasses are defined. Numerical information, usually taken directly from questionnaires, is entered into a data file for the SPSS for Windows program. It is assumed that SPSS for Windows has been installed on one's computer and is ready to access.

The SPSS program begins with a data editor window. This window is very important since it is the initial point at which data from your questionnaires are entered. Figure B.1 shows a data window. This window is actually inside an output window, which is also inside an application window. When the default settings are accepted when starting an SPSS session, the window displayed in Figure B.1 automatically appears.

The data editor window displays across the top "Newdata." New data files can be created at this stage, or if data already exist, they can be modified. The Newdata window shows columns and rows. The columns designate variables as "var." Each of the rows contains the coded responses from research subjects. When an investigator is starting out with this SPSS program, all of these cells are blank. The first step is to define the variables used in the study. If there are 25 variables, these will take up 25 columns. If there are 10 variables, 10 columns will be used. Column labels are usually abbreviated in relation to a variable. For

FIGURE B.1 SPSS application, output, and data editor windows.

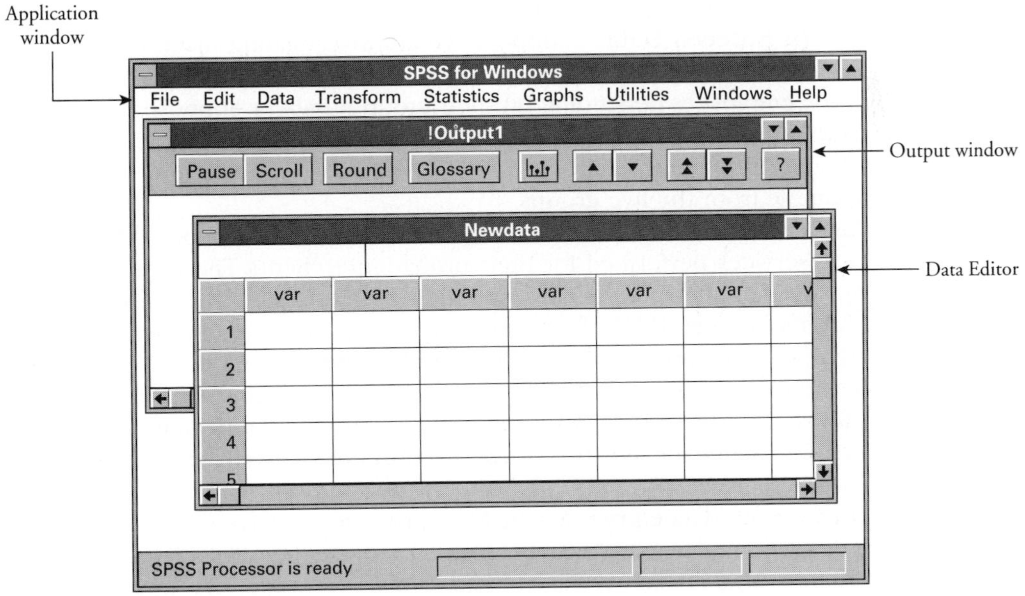

instance, below is a listing of random variables and some abbreviations for them:

Age	=	age
Gender	=	gend
Years of Education	=	educa
Prior Record	=	priorrec
Drug Abuse	=	drgabuse
Alcohol Abuse	=	alcabuse

Notice in this listing that three characters are used for Age, while eight characters are used for Alcohol Abuse. With the SPSS program, a maximum number of eight characters can be used for variable definitions. These abbreviations for variables should be included as a permanent part of the coding manual for easy reference. Subsequently, when data analyses of different kinds are conducted, the researcher will be asked in various dialog boxes which variables are to be controlled or manipulated. *The variables will be displayed in these dialog boxes according to how they have been abbreviated.* Thus, a defined variable listing would be the following:

age

gend

educa

priorrec

drgabuse

alcabuse

Example of Entered Data. Suppose we are investigating five groups of probation officers in different probation agencies. We can assign a 1, 2, 3, 4, or 5 to each of the employees depending on their group numbers. Suppose we have 11 persons in group 1, 12 persons in group 2, 11 persons in group 3, 15 persons in group 4, and 19 persons in group 5. This gives us a total of 68 persons in our overall sample from the five groups.

Further suppose that we have asked these 68 persons about their stress levels and services performed for their probationer/clients. These variables may be designated simply as "stress" and "productivity." Perhaps we have a stress scale as well as a scale measuring their productivity (e.g., average number of contact hours with clients during a six-month period). Suppose both scales have possible low and high values of 10 and 50 respectively. In our actual sample of 68 probation officers, we observe a low productivity score of 10 and a high productivity score of 45, while for our stress scale, we observe a low stress score of 10 and a high stress score of 45.

Thus, for our data entry with the SPSS program, we have defined three variables: (1) the group to which each probation officer belongs, (2) productivity, and (3) stress. This means we have created three columns, one for each of the variables. Next, we have entered scores for our 68 probation officers in each of the three columns. Column 1, *group*, contains the number of the group to which each probation officer belongs, ranging from 1 to 5. Column 2, *producti* (productivity), contains the raw scores from the productivity scale we have administered to these officers. These scores range from 10 to 45. In Column 3, *stress*, we have entered the stress scores for all 68 probation officers, ranging from 10 to 45. Figure B.2 shows these columns and rows with the raw scores entered.

FIGURE B.2 Columns and rows for 68 probation officers.

	group	producti	stress		group	producti	stress
1	1.00	24.00	13.00	35	4.00	35.00	23.00
2	1.00	35.00	12.00	36	4.00	50.00	27.00
3	1.00	22.00	14.00	37	4.00	34.00	27.00
4	1.00	25.00	15.00	38	4.00	38.00	30.00
5	1.00	34.00	23.00	39	4.00	39.00	31.00
6	1.00	22.00	12.00	40	4.00	40.00	32.00
7	1.00	23.00	12.00	41	4.00	41.00	34.00
8	1.00	25.00	14.00	42	4.00	43.00	32.00
9	1.00	26.00	15.00	43	4.00	43.00	19.00
10	1.00	27.00	12.00	44	4.00	28.00	22.00
11	1.00	23.00	12.00	45	4.00	37.00	26.00
12	2.00	25.00	15.00	46	4.00	39.00	27.00
13	2.00	27.00	13.00	47	4.00	49.00	30.00
14	2.00	27.00	13.00	48	4.00	40.00	30.00
15	2.00	29.00	10.00	49	4.00	39.00	32.00
16	2.00	31.00	23.00	50	5.00	38.00	32.00
17	2.00	32.00	23.00	51	5.00	49.00	35.00
18	2.00	32.00	21.00	52	5.00	49.00	32.00
19	2.00	32.00	21.00	53	5.00	59.00	27.00
20	2.00	34.00	20.00	54	5.00	49.00	25.00
21	2.00	35.00	15.00	55	5.00	49.00	28.00
22	2.00	35.00	15.00	56	5.00	49.00	36.00
23	2.00	32.00	14.00	57	5.00	45.00	37.00
24	3.00	35.00	16.00	58	5.00	45.00	36.00
25	3.00	35.00	17.00	59	5.00	44.00	38.00
26	3.00	37.00	18.00	60	5.00	43.00	39.00
27	3.00	23.00	22.00	61	5.00	43.00	40.00
28	3.00	34.00	21.00	62	5.00	42.00	45.00
29	3.00	37.00	21.00	63	5.00	42.00	43.00
30	3.00	38.00	19.00	64	5.00	42.00	34.00
31	3.00	40.00	15.00	65	5.00	45.00	34.00
32	3.00	41.00	30.00	66	5.00	43.00	36.00
33	3.00	41.00	21.00	67	5.00	44.00	36.00
34	3.00	34.00	22.00	68	5.00	45.00	35.00

Notice in these columns that groups are identified as 1.00, 2.00, 3.00, 4.00, and 5.00. Also, productivity and stress scores contain 10.00 through 45.00 values. The ".00" is a default setting accepted by the researcher when beginning the SPSS program. It is not important for most applications. In criminal justice and criminology, most variables are expressed as whole numbers. In some instances where rates or proportions are reported, the decimal places used in these numbers may be relevant.

Once all of the data have been entered from whatever sources (e.g., questionnaires, observation notes, interview records), the data are given a file name that is saved within the SPSS program. The investigator titles the file and saves it by following simple instructions in the window box. In the case of these 68 probation officers, the data have been saved in a file labeled "dummy.sav." We could just as easily save this file as "proboff.dat," meaning "probation officer data." The choice of file name is a matter of personal preference by the researcher. Researchers may use up to eight characters for the file name, not including the three-character extension. If the researcher exits from the SPSS program, a prompt asks whether the data should be saved, and if so, under which file designation. When the investigator returns to work with the data, the dialog box will display the saved file, "dummy.sav." Simply placing the cursor on this file and pushing the mouse button will activate the file for subsequent statistical analysis.

One good thing about SPSS is that it displays "error" messages whenever data have been entered incorrectly. If you are entering gender information and somehow enter a "3" or "8" by mistake instead of a "1" or "2," the SPSS program will detect this potential error and call your attention to it. It is not likely that there is a third or eighth gender out there, and thus you can remedy the problem immediately by reentering the correct code for the particular research subject or case. This feature of SPSS for Windows should give researchers added confidence whenever they transmit raw data to computer files for storage and subsequent analysis.

Analyzing Data from an Established File. Once a file has been created and data entered into it, the data in the file can be analyzed in different ways. For instance, suppose we want to know how many persons are in each group of probation officers and some general descriptive information about these different groups. Under "Statistics" in the dialog box, we can activate a menu that will tabulate and display the different groups, with a count of the number of persons in each group. The display will also show the means for the different groups, standard deviation, standard error, and other information. This displayed information is in accordance with our previous instruction to display a particular variable, such as stress. Perhaps we merely wish to know how many persons are in each group and what are the stress group means. Not only are we provided with this information, but we are also provided with additional unwanted information (e.g., standard deviation, standard error, 95 percent confidence interval). Table B.1 shows such a display for the information recorded in Figure B.2.*

---

*This table and Tables B.2 to B.4 have been compiled by the author using SPSS for Windows–Release 6.0.

TABLE B.1 Frequencies, Means, and Other Values for Data in Figure B.2

Group	Count	Mean	Standard Deviation	Standard Error	95 Pct Conf Int for Mean
Grp 1	11	14.0000	3.2249	.9723	11.8335 to 16.1665
Grp 2	12	16.9167	4.4202	1.2760	14.1082 to 19.7251
Grp 3	11	20.1818	4.0698	1.2271	17.4477 to 22.9160
Grp 4	15	28.1333	4.2572	1.0992	25.7758 to 30.4909
Grp 5	19	35.1579	5.0251	1.1528	32.7359 to 37.5799
Total	68	24.5441	9.1886	1.1143	22.3200 to 26.7682

Group	Minimum	Maximum
Grp 1	12.0000	23.0000
Grp 2	10.0000	23.0000
Grp 3	15.0000	30.0000
Grp 4	19.0000	34.0000
Grp 5	25.0000	45.0000
Total	10.0000	45.0000

Notice also in Table B.1 that we have also been given the minimum and maximum stress score values for persons in the different groups. Group 1 ranges in stress scores from 12 to 23; group 2 ranges from 10 to 23; group 3 ranges from 15 to 30, and so on. A total range is also expressed for all samples, showing a low score of 10 to a high score of 45. Again, this is probably more information than we want or originally requested. But this is the nature of computer programs. Most often we will obtain more information than that originally requested. The important thing is to separate what we need from what we don't need.

Statistical Computations for Entered Data. Now suppose we look at the data in Table B.1 and determine that we would like to compute a difference-between-means t test for two of the samples on the stress variable. We highlight the "Statistics" designation across the bar in the dialog box and follow explicit instructions on what we want. We will be asked which variable we want to examine and which groups will be compared. Suppose we say "productivity" and "groups 1 and 2." The results of our request of the SPSS program are displayed in Table B.2.

Table B.2 displays the two groups, the N's for each group, the means, standard deviations, and standard error terms. Notice also that the mean difference, -4.9167, is displayed. At the bottom of the table are two t values, one for equal variances and one for unequal variances. In both cases, two-tailed and nondirectional t test results are displayed together with actual probability levels. The actual significance levels are considerably more significant than the .01 level that we may have used (e.g., $P = .006, .008$). We are also given information we don't

TABLE B.2 Showing *t* Tests for Independent Samples and Productivity

Variable	Number of Cases	Mean	SD	SE of Mean
PRODUCTI				
GROUP 1	11	26.0000	4.494	1.355
GROUP 2	12	30.9167	3.260	.941

Mean Difference = −4.9167

Levene's Test for Equality of Variances: F = .442   P = .513

	t-test for Equality of Means				95%
Variances	*t*-value	*df*	2-Tail Sig	SE of Diff	CI for Diff
Equal	−3.02	21	.006	1.627	(−8.300, −1.533)
Unequal	−2.98	18.14	.008	1.650	(−8.384, −1.450)

need, including Levene's Test for Equality of Variances. Confidence interval results are also displayed, and this is also information we didn't request.

Beginning students may be confused with such overwhelming information. You ask for one statistical test or one type of display, and not only do you get it, but you also get several other bits of information you didn't request. Why did the computer program generate this excess information or excess baggage? It was programmed to give you this information, but you are not required to use all of it. Novice researchers sometimes exclaim, "Well, the information generated by this computer program must be important! Why else would they give it to us?" We need to separate ourselves from this way of thinking about computer output. Much of it is not relevant for us, and we are under no obligation to use all of the information the computer has produced for us.

Once Around the Block with Probation Officer Stress.   Let's try one additional example. Suppose we want to learn about differences between these five groups of probation officers and their respective stress levels. Is there a significant difference between the five samples on the stress variable? Again, we activate the "Statistics" bar in our dialog box and request a one-way analysis of variance *F* test for these five samples, using "stress" as our dependent variable. The results are shown in Table B.3.

In the present example, an ANOVA Summary Table has been generated, showing between-group and within-group variation. An *F* ratio has been calculated, $F = 58.9438$. Also, a probability level has been generated, $P = .0000$. The string of zeros in the probability value indicates that our observed *F* value is highly significant. If we are using the .01 level of significance for our *F* test, then this significance level has been achieved.

But the *F* test for analysis of variance does not indicate *which* means are significantly different from one another. The *F* test merely answers the question, does a significant difference between means exist somewhere? In this case, a sig-

TABLE B.3 Analysis of Variance for Stress for Five Groups

Source	D.F.	Sum of Squares	Mean Squares	F Ratio	F Prob.
Between-Groups	4	4464.0550	1116.0137	58.9438	.0000
Within-Groups	63	1192.8127	18.9335		
Total	67	5656.8676			

nificant difference exists. In order to find out *where* these mean differences are and *which* mean differences are significant, we *could* instruct our computer program to perform separate *t* tests for all variable combinations. Or we can instruct the computer to give us a *post mortem* comparison which will evaluate *all* mean differences simultaneously. One procedure which we did not cover in earlier chapters was the Newman-Keuls procedure. This is sometimes referred to as the Student-Newman-Keuls test. This test can also be accessed easily by activating the "Statistics" selection on the bar in the dialog box. Once activated, this procedure yields results such as those shown in Table B.4.

The information displayed in Table B.4 shows the results of comparisons of all mean differences for the five groups of probation officers. The groups are indicated across the top of the table as well as down the left-hand side. The means for the different groups are displayed to the far left. Asterisks (*) are shown for different mean comparisons. All asterisks indicate significant mean differences at

TABLE B.4 Student-Newman-Keuls Test with Significance Level .05

The difference between two means is significant if
MEAN(J)-MEAN(I)   >= 3.0768 * RANGE * SQRT(1/N(I) + 1/N(J))
with the following value(s) for RANGE:

Step	2	3	4	5
RANGE	2.84	3.39	3.73	3.97

(*) Indicates significant differences which are shown in the lower triangle

		Group
		1 2 3 4 5
Mean	GROUP	
14.0000	Grp 1	
16.9167	Grp 2	
20.1818	Grp 3	*
28.1333	Grp 4	* * *
35.1579	Grp 5	* * * *

the .05 level, according to information provided in the table printout. Thus, the significant differences occur between the following groups:

3-1
4-1
4-2
4-3
5-1
5-2
5-3
5-4

Had we computed separate t tests for each of these mean differences, we would have achieved similar results.

SPSS Output and What to Do with It

It is quite apparent that SPSS for Windows can do much for researchers who wish to analyze their data. SPSS programs can not only provide tables and statistical summaries of data, but graphic material can also be generated. Bar graphs, pie charts, frequency polygons, and other graphic information can be displayed easily, based on the data files researchers create.

The skill of the researcher is important in helping to distinguish between needed and unneeded information generated by these computer programs. Once tabular displays have been generated, it is a sign of a seasoned researcher to know how best to use this information in report preparation. Report-writing and discussing study results requires some familiarity with statistical tests and their assumptions. Graphic materials can add much to the written word.

■ CAN COMPUTERS DO EVERYTHING FOR YOU?

Computers cannot do everything for you. As tools, computers can help us do many things with the data we have collected. Print-outs from computers contain considerable useful information. This information is sometimes interpreted by the computer in the sense that probabilities are provided or statements about statistical significance are made. However, it is up to individual researchers to make decisions about the usefulness of the available information and how best to interpret it.

Some people believe that if computers print it out, it must be significant. But the decision-making capabilities of computer programs are limited. Computer programs lack imagination. In short, computers do precisely what they are instructed to do and whatever they are capable of doing. This means that they will literally do whatever they are programmed to do, depending upon the software used and the functions to be performed. Frequently, computers will perform certain functions, in a literal sense, that make absolutely no common sense to us. An example of such literal functioning is provided next.

Suppose we were to enter data into an SPSS program. We might enter information that would identify each of our elements. For instance, if we had 200 persons in our sample, we would number each 001, 002, 003, up to 200 to identify particular persons. Other than serving to differentiate these persons from one another, these ID numbers have no other value. Further suppose that we enter information about race/ethnicity, gender, educational level, prior criminal record, six or eight personality characteristics, occupational/professional affiliation, years on the job, job satisfaction, self-concept, religion, socioeconomic status, political affiliation, and ten or so other variables. As we have seen from the previous discussion, we would create variable labels and values for each variable subclass. Thus, our data entry would consist of entering numbers into our SPSS program that refer to a wide variety of variables, ranging from a person's ID to years of education.

Next, we run certain statistical analysis programs. For example, we might command that the computer determine means or averages for all variables. This indicates that means will be computed literally for all variables, including gender and race/ethnicity. If we assign a "1" to males and a "2" to females, what does an average gender of 1.3 mean? Accordingly, if we assign "1" to black, "2" to white, "3" to Hispanic, and "4" to "other," what would an average race/ethnicity of 2.4 mean? Is this someone who is somewhere between white and Hispanic? Such calculations are nonsense.

Computer programs such as SPSS for Windows don't discriminate. For any computer program, numbers are numbers are numbers are numbers. Researchers designate different variables (variable labels) and subclasses for those variables. They assign numerical quantities to these subclasses. Computer programs manipulate these numbers. Computers do not understand that "1's" and "2's" in some cases refer to males and females and should not be averaged. Computers only understand that they should average all numbers on each variable category, *regardless of whatever the numbers represent*. Researchers must examine these numbers and interpret them appropriately. As one might suspect, researchers acquire considerably more information than they really want or need from computer programs. While it is possible to analyze specific variable interrelations, it is sometimes easier to use the shotgun approach and have the computer program correlate *all* variables.

In their own ways, computer programs are designed to be helpful to researchers. For instance, investigators who wish to have computers print out cross-tabulated tables will run the appropriate programs. Some computer programs not only print out the tables requested, but they will also collapse these tables and give different, condensed versions of the original tables. One reason some computer programs do this is that the requirements of certain statistical tests mandate a minimum number of frequencies in the cells of a cross-tabulated table. A hypothetical example follows.

Jane Smith, a criminologist, has some data pertaining to job satisfaction and years of education for a sample of correctional officers. These data are shown in Table B.5. Both variable subclasses have been numbered to show what the computer "sees."

TABLE B.5 Job Satisfaction and Years of Education
for 100 Correctional Officers

Job Satisfaction	Years of Education			
	12 or less (1)	13–14 (2)	15–16 (3)	17 or more (4)
Very satisfied (1)	3	0	5	2
Satisfied (2)	2	0	0	4
Undecided, probably satisfied (3)	0	2	0	8
Undecided probably dissatisfied (4)	4	11	0	7
Dissatisfied (5)	0	0	8	5
Very dissatisfied (6)	11	10	8	9

This is the table Smith wanted. But she notices that the computer has printed out a second table, the one shown in Table B.6. Smith notices that this independently generated table represents a collapsing of the first three education subclasses into one category, while the fourth subclass is in a category by itself. For the job satisfaction variable, the first five subclasses have been combined into one general category, while the sixth subclass is in a category by itself. Smith scratches her head in bewilderment. The computer has just combined apples with oranges. Notice that the new categorization on the job satisfaction variable has combined both "satisfied" and "dissatisfied" subclasses. This is meaningless.

The point of Table B.6 is that while computers can and will do much for you, they cannot think independently and interpret your findings for you. Researchers must still perform this task.

The Seductive Powers of Computer Output: Garbage In, Garbage Out

The fact that computer programs offer so much information to researchers is seductive. We are attracted to the ease with which computations are completed and statistical analyses are conducted. But the computer output varies in quality from very meaningful to meaningless. The best computer programs cannot transform a poorly conceived research project into a good one. If we have unreliable

TABLE B.6 Collapsed Version of Table B.5

Job Satisfaction	Years of Education	
	16 or less	17 or more
	(1-3)	(4)
(1) through (5)	35	26
(6)	30	9

measures of variables, or if there are significant omissions in our research, no statistical program can remedy these problems.

Some persons refer to this problem as "garbage in, garbage out," meaning that computers cannot improve on the quality of information available. Therefore, if a researcher enters data that are deficient in any respect, these deficiencies cannot be remedied by computer manipulation.

More than a few researchers are awed by computer output. Complex tables are generated and formulae calculated. Elaborate displays of numerical data seem impressive. The fact is that over the years, some investigators have masked poorly conceived and implemented research designs with overwhelming statistical manipulations of data. In some cases, research articles consist almost entirely of graphs, tables, and exotic diagrams intended to portray correlations between variables that are at best weak. Readers should be wary of articles that emphasize matrices of intercorrelation, multivariate analyses, and path diagrams. There should be enough substance in these articles to carry them independently—without complex diagrams and tables. Statistics play a supporting role in the drama of the research enterprise. We should not be impressed first by the complexity of formulae and methods, and only second by the theoretical scheme, sampling plan, and other more important research features. This is why we say that computers are seductive in a sense. The sophistication of computer output may lull us into a false sense of security, where we believe we have produced research of greater significance than it really is.

When investigators prepare their research for public consumption, ideally they should make every effort to point out the deficiencies of the study. This doesn't mean that researchers must dwell only on the negative aspects, but rather, they should balance their coverage by noting instances where problems may have arisen or concepts were not fully conceived or measured. Adhering to the objectivity standard will enhance one's reputation among other professionals. No one should disguise the limitations of a study with powerful statistics and impressive-looking tables and graphs.

■ HUMAN INTELLIGENCE AND COMPUTER POWERS: A PRODUCTIVE SYNTHESIS

Using any computer software program, such as SPSS for Windows, should be a productive synthesis between what the investigator knows and what the computer program can do to simplify data analysis and produce useful results. Before data are analyzed by any computer software program, it is imperative that the investigator should familiarize himself or herself with several analytical options or statistical alternatives. Knowing which tests to apply in advance of applying them saves a lot of time. The researcher should be able to go directly to the SPSS for Windows program and, following data entry, be able to analyze the data according to preconceived statistical tests or procedures.

It is equally important for investigators to know the advantages and limitations of any statistical procedure or correlational technique. This includes a knowledge of when particular tests or procedures should be applied and what conditions might render a particular application unsuitable. Again, the synthesis between human intelligence and computer applications is quite important. Computers do only what they have been instructed to do. Human intervention is almost always necessary when interpreting computer output. Computer programs do not discriminate between numbers based on whether they are measured according to nominal, ordinal, interval, or ratio scales. We are reminded of the nonsense of averaging numbers representing different genders. If we assign a "1" to a male and "2" to a female, what does an "average gender" of 1.4 mean for a sample of 50 persons? Unfortunately, we can't blame the computer for doing literally what we programmed it to do. Human intervention is necessary here in order to separate meaningful numerical expressions from meaningless ones.

Writing Papers and Research Reports

INTRODUCTION

Criminology and criminal justice research involves a great deal of writing. Professors expect students to write term papers and undertake other projects for various courses. At important points in their pursuit of graduate degrees, many students will become involved in more elaborate research projects. These projects result in master's theses and/or doctoral dissertations. This chapter examines the nature and types of writing undertaken by persons who take classes or complete work toward graduate degrees. Several types of writing are examined, including term papers, literature reviews, position papers, theses, and dissertations.

An important part of any writing project is to cite or footnote properly. There are several standard footnoting styles. It is beyond the scope of this book to examine all of these styles, but a few styles will be illustrated. Each professor, academic department, and university or college has differing expectations about the citation style students should use in their written work. Some generic citation styles are described.

Because some of the work done by criminologists and criminal justicians involves legal research and writing, some examples of legal citations are provided. Sources of legal cases for both the states and federal system are listed and described.

TYPES OF PAPERS AND RESEARCH REPORTS

Term Papers

The most common form of writing in university settings is the term paper. Term papers are more or less lengthy documents. Usually students who write term papers will focus upon a particular topic, such as community policing, the use of K-9s in law enforcement, deadly force, probation officer turnover, or correctional officer burnout and stress. Instructors' expectations of students vary from class to class. Some professors demand that students follow specific styles, including observance of rigid formatting (e.g., number of lines per page; left, right, top, and bottom margins; type style; letter spacing; type of justification). Other professors merely ask students to be consistent in their formatting.

The topics for term papers are unlimited. Usually professors attempt to guide students in particular directions for their papers by suggesting different topics. These topics are usually narrowed to the class subject matter and focus upon such topics as policing, courts and judges, or corrections. During the 1998 school year, I kept track of all topics selected by my students for term papers. They included juvenile waivers, jury selection, hot pursuit, deadly force, domestic violence, judicial bias, police stress/burnout, jury selection, drug enforcement, terrorism, police discrimination, probation and parole, female police officers, deinstitutionalization of status offenders, probation and parole officer training, personality and crime, juvenile rehabilitation, suicide, Indian tribal law, prison gangs, electronic monitoring, home confinement, jail and prison suicides, death penalty, prison industries,

K-9s in law enforcement, serial killers, Royal Canadian Mounted Police, police history, boot camps, British female inmates, Mexican prisons, police brutality, probation officers and firearms, child sexual abusers, police misconduct, women and stress in law enforcement, court watchers, female prison inmates, spousal abuse, aging offenders, asset forfeiture, hate crimes, missing children, private counsel, police personality, victim and witness participation in sentencing, sentencing hearings, juvenile rights, juvenile death penalty, ineffective assistance of counsel, police patrol styles and effectiveness, prison violence, delinquency, FBI training, juvenile risk assessment, police professionalism, police cautioning, selective incapacitation, jury size and deliberations, habitual offenders, and the war on drugs.

The length and detail required in term papers also varies greatly. Term papers can be short, from 5 to 10 pages, or quite lengthy, 25 pages or more. There is no reliable average paper length to be given. Different class requirements dictate that a certain paper organization should be followed.

Term papers usually involve library research, where books and periodicals are examined for background information about the topic. Professors may specify certain numbers of sources. Thus, an acceptable term paper might include ten or more sources. These sources may be specified as well, such as "only research articles from professional journals." This specification means that students cannot rely exclusively on textbooks for their term paper information.

Term papers are largely descriptive. Except under unusual circumstances, it is unrealistic for professors to expect that their students will generate original data and analyze it in a research report. Sometimes this is done for certain types of classes, such as in courses on research methods. A research methods class may carry out a limited research project, in which questionnaires are constructed and administered. Later during the semester, data are tabulated and analyzed. These analyses are often superficial. Each student might be expected to write his or her version of what is found and its significance. Each student is also responsible for finding selected references relevant to the problem examined.

Generally, term papers are not particularly elaborate. Ten or fifteen sources are consulted and pulled together. If the topic is deadly force, it might be appropriate to describe different kinds of deadly force and the circumstances under which deadly force is applied. Some leading cases about deadly force may be mentioned and discussed. Different authorities raise several interesting issues about deadly force and its use by law enforcement officers, and a term paper might highlight several of these issues. The student preparing the paper might consider summarizing these issues and expressing an opinion about the topic. Some substance is usually expected whenever personal opinions are expressed. Thus, it is insufficient to say, "Deadly force shouldn't be used." Rather, some compelling argument should be presented in defense of the position taken on the subject. This exposition of opinions about a given topic makes the paper interesting.

Reviews of the Literature

Some papers are called literature reviews or reviews of the literature. For example, if a paper is written on sentencing disparities and the factors that influence such disparities, then the relevant literature pertaining to this topic will be reviewed. This means that students must hunt down articles and papers written about sentencing disparities and find out what others have written about it. Reviews of literature are very important, since they can disclose convergences of opinion and/or differences of opinion about the incidence of sentencing disparities and which factors seem most influential in triggering disparities.

It is common to discover certain inconsistencies in the literature. For instance, we might find that one study reports considerable sentencing disparity attributable to race and socioeconomic status. Another study may report that sentencing disparity occurs because of gender and is not related to socioeconomic status. Yet another study may report that sentencing disparities are attributable to the type of attorney used. Thus, in sentencing decision making, judges may impose harsher sentences on convicted offenders if they are represented by public defenders instead of private counsel. What should be made of these inconsistencies?

Some studies contain contradictory information. Contradictions or inconsistencies in the research literature provide the foundation for some interesting writing. Students may attempt to explain these contradictions or inconsistencies. Sometimes experimentation helps. Articles expressing one view or finding may be grouped together, while those expressing a contrary or inconsistent view may be grouped together. Perhaps the definitions of sentencing disparity are different. Different definitions of the same terms may help to explain why there are inconsistencies or contradictions in the literature.

Basically, literature reviews examine what is known about a particular topic. Some topics are more popular than others and therefore larger numbers of articles may exist about them. Some topics are less popular, and therefore there is less research literature generated. If a popular topic is selected, such as electronic monitoring, 100 articles or more may be available. It may be necessary to limit the literature review to the most recent five-year or ten-year interval. It is important for the literature review to be current or up-to-date. This means that only the most recent journals and written work should be consulted. By "recent," we might refer to articles, books, and other materials written within the last ten years.

Critical Essays and Position Papers

A critical essay or position paper is essentially the same as a term paper that contains an assessment or evaluation of some issue. Perhaps the writer wishes to produce a critical essay about some criminological theory or explanation of delinquency. Suppose a researcher wanted to write a critical essay about differential association theory or strain theory. The essay itself would vary in length, depending upon the amount of detail provided by the writer and/or the length and format requirements of the professor. If the article is prepared for a journal or some other publication, then certain requirements must be observed.

The critical essay would examine the contents of the theory and would present an objective evaluation of the theory's efficacy for explaining crime or delinquency. Criticisms may include both positive and negative statements. Examples from the literature may be used to support one position or another.

Perhaps the critical essay or position paper is about capital punishment. Suppose the writer opposes capital punishment. If the position taken is opposition to the death penalty, then objective thoroughness would require an examination of all possible issues surrounding the death penalty and its application. An argument could be made against the death penalty, and supporting information for this position could be gleaned from the research literature.

Research Papers

A research paper differs from term papers and position papers or critical essays in that some original data collection is involved. A project is outlined with specific research goals. In more than a few research methods classes, professors engage the students in collecting data from a sample of students or community residents. These are easy research targets, largely because they are accessible. Once information has been collected, usually by questionnaires, the data are coded and tabulated. Students are then expected to write up their version of an analysis of the data and what they mean.

Research papers involve brief literature reviews and an exposition of what the literature says about the research problem under investigation. Research papers for classes may vary from 10 to 30 or more pages, again depending upon the course requirements and professor's expectations. Usually a certain format is required. Often the intent is to enable students to acquire research report writing skills. The professor may follow up these research papers with a discussion of the significance of the project and what different students said about it in their own writing.

Master's Theses and Doctoral Dissertations

A master's thesis or doctoral dissertation in criminal justice or criminology is a comprehensive study, an elaborate research project, a creative enterprise, and a significant undertaking designed to investigate a researchable problem in any substantive area (e.g., criminal justice, sociology, psychology) for the purpose of testing a theory and hypotheses derived from that theory.

A thesis/dissertation is *not*

1. A term paper
2. A general literature review of some topic (e.g., delinquency and poverty, racism in the United States, the death penalty)
3. A throwing together of some hastily prepared questions distributed to the first 100 students you can find, with a summary of the results of your findings
4. A purely descriptive piece about your thoughts on some issue
5. A lengthy conjecture about your personal beliefs about unfairness in our city, county, state, or nation
6. Some document intended to prove some obscure point you happen to think about and which is of concern to you

What is the proper length for thesis proposals? Thesis and/or dissertation proposals range in length from 10 to 100 pages. There is no optimum length for a thesis proposal. This decision depends upon your research problem, how much literature exists about the problem, how sophisticated the theory is that you are testing, how many hypotheses you are deriving for testing, how sophisticated your methodology is, and so on. It is probably the case that a good thesis proposal is going to range in length from 20 to 30 pages (double-spaced, typed), including all of the relevant components described next.

What does a thesis/dissertation proposal do? A thesis proposal is a blueprint for your research work. It shows, in great detail, what you plan to do; why it is significant, both theoretically and substantively; what your major (and minor) objectives are; where you will get your sample; how you will collect data; how you will analyze your data; what tabular presentations you will make; what statistics you will choose for your analyses; what sorts of things you will be able to say as the result of conducting your study; and what the study's shortcomings are.

What is the role of thesis/dissertation advisor? Thesis advisors assist students in the selection of manageable and important research problems; give them feedback on their thinking; guide them to articles or books where relevant materials about their problem can be found; and criticize their work and offer constructive criticisms about data collection, data analysis, and theoretical scheme development and hypothesis formulation.

What level of statistical sophistication is appropriate for theses/dissertations? All appropriate statistical procedures cannot be learned in a few statistics courses. Those who teach statistics attempt to convey selected procedures that students might find useful for their own research. Often a foundation is provided for doing some elementary independent study. But statistical learning does not end in the classroom. Graduate work of any kind, whether it is a doctoral dissertation or master's thesis, must show initiative and originality.

Where can students find good examples of statistical analysis of data? Examining articles in leading criminal justice or criminology journals will provide good examples of statistical analysis and use. *Criminology, Justice Quarterly, Journal of Crime and Justice, Journal of Crime and Delinquency, Journal of Criminal Justice, Law and Society Review, Criminal Justice Review, Journal of Contemporary Criminal Justice, Judicature, Journal of Criminal Law and Criminology, Journal of Quantitative Criminology,* and *Journal of Criminal Justice Education* are some of the leading journals containing sophisticated statistical techniques applied to criminological data. The university library contains an index of all periodicals available.

What if these articles contain methodological and statistical techniques beyond what students have studied? Sometimes, students will need to familiarize themselves with new methodological techniques and statistical strategies in order to make meaningful interpretations of studies they find in the criminology literature.

The research proposal is called different names according to the type of research it precedes. For instance, a doctoral student preparing for a doctoral dissertation may refer to the research proposal as a dissertation proposal. A master's candidate may prepare a thesis prospectus. Others may simply refer to the proposal as a research plan, although as indicated, the notion of a research plan is frequently used synonymously with research design. In order to avoid semantic problems, research plans may be viewed as integral components of the proposal or prospectus. Research plans constitute the methodological portion of the proposal.

Research proposals vary in length, complexity, and/or sophistication according to the particular standards of the investigator in charge of the research activity. The following format of a research proposal is by no means the only way of outlining a project for social investigation. The various components included (as well as the order in which each is presented) are merely suggested as constituting a possible compilation and arrangement of the bare essentials. Many departures from this scheme are to be expected, especially when we consider the vast array of topics of social interest as well as the diversity of researcher preferences that exists. One way of outlining a research proposal is as follows:

1. Introduction
2. Statement of objectives
3. Review of the literature
4. Theoretical structure and/or conceptual scheme
5. Hypotheses
6. Methodology
7. Statement of theoretical and substantive implications.

Short discussions of each of these components follow. The discussions are general in nature. They are included to indicate the importance and/or significance of each section, and they are designed to be broadly applicable to projects reflecting diverse interests.

Introduction. The introduction of a research proposal should place the problem to be studied in some kind of historical perspective. The researcher should briefly illustrate the historical development of the current problem under investigation. Researchers should also locate their particular interests in the problem fairly precisely. In short, researchers reveal the problem to be studied and what dimension or dimensions of it will be given extensive analysis or treatment. For example, if researchers were to be interested in studying the social and psychological effects of automation in a business setting, they might begin by describing the early origins and applications of automation in various work environments. They could follow up this historical description by discussing present uses of automation in specific settings. At this point, they could reveal their precise interests in learning about the potential social and psychological impacts of automation in contemporary businesses.

Another way of looking at the introduction is as a way of moving from very general to very specific subject matter you intend to study. When we say "Put the problem you study in a historical context," we mean to provide a historical foundation for the problem. For instance,

> Labor turnover among probation departments throughout the United States has increased during the last four decades. From 1950 to 1990, the proportion of probation officers leaving probation work annually to seek alternative employment has increased from 4 percent to over 30 percent. In California by 1990, labor turnover among probation officers had reached 40 percent. According to Jackson (1991:3), the costs of training new probation officers to replace those who quit are prohibitive. This study examines the problem of labor turnover among California probation officers . . .

From here, you specify and introduce what specific aspect of probation officer labor turnover you plan to describe in your thesis.

Statement of Research Objectives. The objectives of research projects detail what researchers wish to accomplish as the result of their investigative activity. What are the specific goals to be achieved? Sometimes this section is broken down into subparts to include *major* and *minor* objectives. There are primary concerns of investigators as well as secondary concerns. In this event, researchers possibly arrange their objectives into a hierarchical fashion, listing them from most important to least important. Some proposals make explicit the distinction between major and minor (primary and secondary) objectives (goals).

There is no limit to the number of research objectives. Decisions about how many objectives will be identified are based on the breadth of the research; the interests of the investigator; and the time, cost, and personpower considerations. Some studies may have a single objective, whereas other projects may have 20 or 30 of them. Although there are no limitations concerning the number of research objectives a project may have, it is possible for investigators to bite off too much of a given problem. There is little wisdom spreading oneself too thin, however. If researchers have too many research objectives, they may encounter great difficulty in trying to tie together a lot of loose ends. Too many research objectives also necessitate a more complex theoretical scheme. Therefore, it is recommended that investigators limit their objectives to a reasonable number. What is "reasonable" again depends upon the time limitations, budgetary considerations, and personpower restrictions under which researchers must often work. It is possible, for example, for a single objective in one study to involve more time and effort to achieve than ten objectives in a related study. Researchers must assess subjectively the objectives of their research in determining whether they have the capability to deal effectively with the problem they have chosen. It is wise to pick objectives that are challenging, but not impossible to achieve.

Fairly precise statements of objectives are functional guidelines for research activity. Using the automation example cited earlier, vague or nebulous objectives might be "to see if the introduction of automation into an employee work setting will bring about attitudinal change" or "to see if the introduction of automation will bring about significant role changes among employees." These statements are considered vague because they fail to specify which attitudes and which employee work roles are involved or possibly affected by automation. Of course, it can be argued that an exploratory study may be loosely constructed so as to identify more specific research targets to be investigated with greater precision at a later date. But it would be more meaningful to state which attitudes of employees are considered most relevant for examination. A more specific statement of an objective might be "to investigate the impact of the introduction of electronic data processing (a form of automation) on employee depersonalization (an attitudinal variable)." This statement clearly indicates that the specific independent variable, *electronic data processing*, may be followed by a change on a specific dependent variable, *depersonalization*. One interest of researchers, therefore, is to examine the relationship between these variables as a means of more accurately depicting some of the potential social and psychological implications of technological change on people in work environments.

Review of the Literature. The literature review is designed to familiarize the investigator with any relevant information pertaining to the topic being studied. Opinions vary concerning the extent to which a literature review should be conducted. Some researchers may be concerned with identifying all available literature on a given subject, whereas others are content to review literature in major professional journals for the most recent ten-year period. In research proposals, it is usually not necessary to discuss all relevant and available literature uncovered by the researcher. A positive feature of a literature review in a proposal is to highlight representative ideas from current articles and books on the subject investigated. For instance, if there are 1,000 articles on a particular topic that reflect varying and opposing points of view, investigators may select 20 or 30 of them that seem to represent the major viewpoints and conflicting opinions and/or findings. Of course, when a dissertation or thesis is involved, the expectation may be that researchers will review a much larger portion of the literature in the final research report, thesis, or dissertation.

The question of how many articles should be included in a research proposal is difficult to answer in quantitative terms. If the research topic is relatively new, it is likely that little or no information exists in the available literature that bears directly on the subject. Researchers may be forced to cite available literature that is only remotely connected to the topic under investigation. For example, in the 1950s, little, if anything, was known about the impact of electronic data processing systems on school structure and administration. However, there were articles in existence that examined the impact of electronic data processing systems in petroleum refineries and airline reservation offices. If researchers had elected to study this automation form and its impact on school systems, they would have included in their literature review only information that was indirectly relevant to this chosen topic. Any pioneering effort (a research project delving into previously unexplored social/psychological/criminal justice/criminology areas) is subject to this significant limitation. On the other hand, if there is an abundance of material on a given topic, it is up to the researcher to determine how many articles will be selected for a representative review. There are no clear-cut standards to dictate how many articles should be reviewed. Again, we return to the matter of how many sources are considered reasonable. Reviewing too many articles may be regarded by some researchers as superfluous activity. Other researchers may consider a particular literature review to be too scanty and inadequate. When researchers themselves feel comfortable with the articles they have reviewed, this subjective criterion will usually suffice.

Footnoting and referencing in literature reviews in proposals and in research reports can be handled quickly and easily by following certain conventional procedures established by such professional associations as the American Psychological Association. Although several footnoting and referencing styles exist, some are much more simple to follow than the others. For instance, "Smith (1993:222–224) indicates that . . ." is considerably less awkward than "James R. Smith, *Problems of the Inner City*, Holt, Rinehart, and Winston, New York, NY, 1993, pps. 222–224, indicates that . . ." Another style of footnoting is "Smith (15) says that . . ." In the first footnoting case ["Smith (1993:222–224)"], a list of references is compiled and placed at the end of the proposal. The entire reference to Smith's work is included there. The second instance ["Smith (15)"] is indicative of a referencing system that numbers the authors alphabetically. "Smith (15)" means that this work is the fifteenth in the list of references included at the end of the proposal. This is not an especially desirable footnoting style, however. What if researchers want to add one or two more references to their list of references? Then they will have to renumber all references and make those renumbering changes throughout the entire proposal. The first footnoting style is preferred because of its simplicity. Multiple articles or writings by a single author in the same year are also handled easily. What if Smith has written three articles from which you have quoted? These can be cited as Smith (1993a), Smith (1993b), and Smith, (1993c).

The literature review should have an effective summary, highlighting the important findings that bear directly upon the problem to be studied. This helps the reader to understand the relationships between the various articles presented. Of course, it is assumed that the researcher has presented the articles reviewed in a coherent fashion and has woven them together meaningfully in the main presentation. A summary following their presentation will be of great assistance and value to readers as well as to the researcher.

In the quest for scientific objectivity, researchers should make every effort to present articles (particularly in controversial areas) that represent a balanced position. Discussing articles favorable to one viewpoint while ignoring those favoring the opposing view reflects researcher bias. This practice should be avoided because it is misleading and contrary to the canons of science and scientific inquiry.

Theoretical Structure and/or Conceptual Scheme.   In a sense, this section is the heart of the research proposal. This is where researchers formulate and develop an explanation for the relationships between variables investigated. How does it come to be so that variables X and Y are associated with one another? Not only are the variables X and Y defined here, but their logical connection is delineated. Also included here are the assumptions, propositions, and definitions of variables researchers use to develop the explanatory framework upon which the entire research project rests. Subsequent research will either support or fail to support the existing theoretical framework presented here.

Hypotheses.   Hypotheses are logically deduced from the theoretical framework. Within the context of the research proposal, hypotheses may be viewed as specific statements of theory in testable form. There is no limit to the number of hypotheses that can be derived from the theoretical scheme and subjected to empirical test. However, it should be noted that usually the number of hypotheses (as well as their nature) coincides closely with the numbers of objectives of the project stated earlier. In other words, by subjecting the various hypotheses to empirical test, some or all of the objectives of the researcher's project are achieved partially or fully.

Methodology.   The methodology section makes explicit the study design and constitutes the "how to do it" phase. This section includes the following:

1. The population to be studied
2. The type of sampling plan to be followed (e.g., simple random sampling, stratified proportionate random sampling, quota sampling)
3. The size of sample to be drawn and the rationale for this sample size in relation to the population size
4. The type of instrumentation and/or data collection procedures (e.g., questionnaires, interviews, participant observation, analysis of secondary sources such as statistical records, letters, autobiographies, and so forth)
5. The statistics to be used (e.g., gamma, lambda, the *t* test, the *F* test for analysis of variance, **multivariate analysis,** path analysis, the Pearson *r*, etc.) and the rationale for selecting these procedures
6. The type of tabular presentation (e.g., graphs, tables, charts, figures, etc.)
7. Some **dummy tables** illustrating how you plan to graphically portray your data to be analyzed

The methodology section is the blueprint for researcher activity and specifies how the investigator intends to test the hypotheses, study the people or research subjects, or describe the social settings. Researchers are at liberty to choose from among a variety of data collection techniques and to study designs as well as alternative approaches to the problem. Because so many options are available to the investigator in order to study the same problem, this has led some persons to label social research an "art" as opposed to a body of scientific strategies that have specific and limited applications.

Statement of Theoretical and Substantive Implications.   Although some researchers seldom give a lot of thought to the relevance of their research activity theoretically and substantively, others are more comfortable investigating topics for which several *raisons d'être* exist. If someone were to ask us the question, "So what?" at the end of our research proposal or project, what kinds of answers could we provide to demonstrate the theoretical and practical utility or relevance and significance of the investigation? Although there are some researchers who pursue knowledge for the sake of knowledge and give little attention to the meaningfulness of their research activity from the standpoint of practical application to problems in the real world, there are many other investigators who sense an obligation to themselves and to others to defend the studies they have undertaken or propose to undertake.

Research can be assessed from several dimensions. Some people react favorably to social research if they can see some immediate and direct benefits, such as reducing crime, divorce rates, and the psychological stresses associated with urban renewal programs. Can the research help people to overcome some of their social adjustment problems? Can the results of research be of value in the solution of ecological crises? A different kind of assessment is made of social research in terms of the time dimension. Will the results of research today be applicable 20 or even 50 years from now even though no practical value of it is presently apparent? The work of Sigmund Freud is a case in point. In his day, people were quick to discard his notions on the significance of dreams and to label the id, ego, superego, and libido as nonsensical. Present-day psychologists and psychiatrists and other social researchers find his work fascinating and insightful for assisting people with various sorts of psychological problems.

Research can also be assessed in terms of its theoretical value. Does the research contribute to (support or help to substantiate) existing theories of social behavior? Or does the research refute existing theoretical schemes and orientations? Couched in the context of a relation to existing social theories, research in given areas can eventually prove to have profound significance for the nature and growth of the academic discipline.

However, it must be acknowledged that some people prefer to study a topic simply for the pleasure and interest of understanding it more fully. They are unconcerned about the opinions of others relating to the theoretical and/or practical (substantive) significance of what they do. There must be tolerance and room for all positions taken and motives reflected in the process of social inquiry.

■ SOURCES FOR REFERENCES

There are many sources for references. The most common are (1) research articles in professional journals, (2) books and monographs, and (3) papers presented at professional conferences.

Research Articles in Professional Journals.   Professional journals contain both research articles and essays about a myriad of criminological subjects. Most university and college libraries have modest collections of sources for students to consult when they are preparing papers. In recent years, *Criminal Justice Abstracts* have been made available on CD-ROM in many libraries. Thus, students can search these CD databases for key words involved in their research topics.

Abstracts of articles are brief synopses of what the articles contain. Most of these abstracts summarize the major article findings or article contents. Students can make a fairly easy determination of which articles they might wish to examine more closely. If the library doesn't have the journal with the article desired, then the article may be acquired often through an interlibrary loan service. There may or may not be a nominal charge for this service.

Often, however, article abstracts will have sufficient information about the study conducted that students can determine what was found as well as its significance. It is not unheard of for someone to write an entire paper based on abstract information. This may sound strange, but a review of many abstracts shows that much rich information is presented. Some sample abstracts from the 1999 *Criminal Justice Abstracts* CD follow.

SAMPLE ARTICLE ABSTRACTS

TI: Police misconduct and malpractice: a critical analysis of citizens' complaints
AU: Lersch-Kim-Michelle
JN: Policing, 21, (1), pp. 80–96.
PY: 1998
AB: A study tests several hypotheses suggested by conflict theory about official complaints lodged against a large police department in the southeastern U.S. from 1992–94. Because a single complaint of misconduct may include allegations against 2 or more officers, the 527 complaints translated into 682 allegations of wrongdoing. Data were drawn from agency personnel files.

In support of the hypotheses, minority citizens and those with less power and fewer resources were more likely to file complaints of misconduct and to allege more serious forms of misconduct than those with greater power and more resources. There appeared to be some relationship between the complainant's race and the substantiation rate of complaints: when the bivariate relationship was examined, race was a significant predictor. Findings are consistent with conflict theory's view that policy brutality and misconduct are used by dominant groups to protect their hold on society's limited resources.
DE: POLICE-ACCOUNTABILITY; POLICE-COMMUNITY-RELATIONS;
POLICE-MISCONDUCT
CL: Police (P)
AN: 74294

TI: "They're making a bad name for the department": exploring the link between organizational commitment and police occupational deviance . . .
AU: Haarr-Robin-N
JN: Policing, 20, (4), pp. 786–812.
PY: 1997
AB: A study examines links between Sun Valley (AZ) Police Department patrol officers' levels of organizational commitment and their attitudes toward, and participation in, a continuum of deviant behaviors. Data were derived from 580 hours of onsite field and participant observation, including patrol unit ride-alongs, and in-depth, unstructured interviews with 48 patrol officers. Patrol officers with low levels of organizational commitment tended to engage in patterns of work avoidance and manipulation, and in employee deviance against the organization, in part to undermine its goals and/or strike back. In contrast, patrol officers with high levels of commitment were likely to engage in employee deviance activities to work toward organizational goal attainment. All patrol officers accepted informal rewards.
DE: POLICE-MISCONDUCT; POLICE-OFFICERS; POLICE-PATROL
CL: Police (P)
AN: 73178

TI: Police decertification: changing patterns among the states, 1985–1995
AU: Puro-Steven; Goldman-Roger; Smith-William-C
JN: Policing, 20, (3), pp. 481–496.
PY: 1997
AB: Decertification is similar to removal of licenses common to most other professions: peace officers whose conduct has been found to be in violation of state statutes or regulations in the U.S. have their certification revoked, preventing them from continuing to serve as law enforcement officers in the state. A study describes the major shifts in state practices that have occurred in decertification between 1985 and 1995. Data sources included state statutes and regulations, and 20 telephone interviews with officials of Peace Officers' Standards and Training Commission (POST) in 15 states.

Over the period examined, 11 states moved into the broad decertification classification. Currently, 30 states are in this classification, among the 39 that have any decertification authority. Three other states moved from no decertification to limited decertification. Additional inquiry is needed to determine if decertification serves as an effective means of controlling police misconduct.
DE: POLICE-ACCOUNTABILITY; POLICE-MISCONDUCT
CL: Police (P)
AN: 73158

TI: Shielded from justice: police brutality and accountability in the United States
AU: Human-Rights-Watch
PY: 1998
PB: New York, NY
PD: 440p., Appendix
AB: A study examines police brutality in 14 American cities: Atlanta; Boston; Chicago; Detroit; Indianapolis; Los Angeles; Minneapolis; New Orleans; New York; Philadelphia; Portland, OR; Providence, RI; San Francisco; and Washington, DC. Interviews and correspondence were carried out with attorneys representing victims alleging ill treatment by police, representatives of police department internal affairs units, police officers, citizen review agency staff, city officials, and others.

Police brutality is one of the most serious, enduring and divisive human rights violations in the U.S. The problem is nationwide and its nature is institutionalized. Police officers engage in unjustified shootings, severe beatings, fatal chokings, and unnecessarily rough physical treatment in cities, while their superiors fail to control them or even to record the full magnitude of the problem. A victim seeking redress faces obstacles at every point in the process. Minority groups have alleged that they are disproportionately targeted by police human rights violations. Severe abuse persists because overwhelming barriers to accountability make it all too likely that officers who commit abuses will escape punishment and continue their conduct.

The costs of pervasive police abuse include police criminality, the corruption of ideals of public service, public mistrust, and the tens of millions of dollars in damages that cities pay every year in response to victims' civil lawsuits. Recommendations are offered for police administration, the use of civil remedies, local criminal prosecution, federal criminal civil rights prosecution, and federal data collection.
DE: MINORITY-GROUPS; POLICE-ACCOUNTABILITY; POLICE-MISCONDUCT;
POLICE-USE-OF-FORCE
CL: Police (P)
AN: 73503

Since I have my own copy of the *Criminal Justice Abstracts* in CD-ROM format, I was able to scan the *Criminal Justice Abstracts* CD and search for "Police Misconduct." Almost 200 article abstracts were generated. I scanned the first several articles and marked four of them to include in this book. Next, I downloaded them to a diskette on my computer and translated them into WordPerfect, a popular software word processing program. An examination of these abstracts reveals the following abbreviations:

TI = Title of work/article/book

AU = Author(s)

JN = Journal (may be publisher if a book), volume and page numbers

PY = Publication year of work

AB = Abstract material

DE = Alternative search terms one might use besides "Police Misconduct"

CL = Article/book classification

AN = Reference number

Thus, *all* relevant information for a citation is presented in this annotation. Notice in the first article by Kim Michelle Lersch that the study is a test of conflict theory involving complaints filed against police officers in a large southeastern police department. There were 527 complaints and 682 allegations of wrongdoing. The findings were that minorities were more likely to file complaints of misconduct against police officers. The study provided support for the conflict theory's view that police brutality and misconduct are used by dominant groups to protect their control of scarce resources.

The second article abstract by Robin Haar is a study of the Sun Valley (Arizona) Police Department. Police officers were studied using participant observation and involved over 580 hours of on-site field experience. Unstructured interviews with 48 police officers revealed that officers with low levels of organizational commitment were more likely to engage in deviant conduct, including misconduct.

The third article by Steven Puro, Roger Goldman, and William C. Smith investigated the decertification process in various states. Telephone interviews were conducted and these researchers found that during the period 1985–1995, major shifts in state decertification practices occurred. Specific statistics were reported showing the results of their investigation. The journal for the Lersch, Haar and the Puro-Goldman-Smith articles is *Policing*. It is likely that a university library would have this journal, since it is popular and well known.

The fourth article by Human Rights Watch focuses upon police brutality in 14 American cities, which are listed. Through interviews and written correspondence, researchers interviewed defense attorneys who represented victims of police misconduct. In this particular article abstract, several general statements were made about the extensiveness of police brutality. Alluded to were several recommendations for using civil remedies and other strategies for combating police brutality. However, if one wanted to learn more about these findings, the article or report itself would have to be inspected. This is where the interlibrary loan service comes in handy if the library doesn't have the particular document. In this case, the study is published in New York by Human Rights Watch. Here, at least, the student might have to write or call this organization directly and order a copy of the publication, if more information is desired. It is unlikely that the average university library would have materials from this organization.

It is not necessary for students to purchase their own copies of *Criminal Justice Abstracts* or the *CJ Abstracts* CD. Most libraries have copies of these documents, either in hard copy (the journals themselves) or on CD-ROM. Accessing this information is most often a free library service.

Books and Monographs. Besides research articles and theoretical pieces published in professional journals and magazines, books may be consulted. Some books are readers, where editors compile numerous articles written by others.

These articles are usually focused around an integrating theme, such as community policing, or probation and parole. Many books are called monographs because they are specialty books or trade publications written for fairly narrow audiences. Someone may write a book about juvenile transfer hearings or the pros and cons of the death penalty. The topics of such books are well defined. It is unlikely that specific courses in criminology and criminal justice might use such specialized books. More often than not, these books might be used as supplemental reading because of their limited scope.

Textbooks are another source of information. However, while textbooks are useful at providing factual information about a broad array of events and topics, they are often dated. It usually takes about one year for a textbook to be published once the author has submitted the final manuscript to the publisher. Much time is spent copy editing the work and proofreading several more refined versions at different publication stages. Thus, source materials may be as much as two or three years old by the time the textbook is in print. This is not the fault of the author. Rather, the pace of publishing causes this dating to occur. Thus, textbooks may not contain up-to-date information that might be found in the latest research articles. It is recommended that the most recent journals should be consulted in preference to textbook sources.

Papers Presented at Professional Conferences. Annually different regional and national organizations hold conferences. These organizations include the Midwestern Criminal Justice Association, the American Sociological Association, the American Society of Criminology, the Academy of Criminal Justice Sciences, the Western Society of Criminology, the Southern Sociological Society, the Southern Criminal Justice Association, the Western and Pacific Criminal Justice Association, the American Correctional Association, and the American Probation and Parole Association. The proceedings of these associations are often published and can be acquired by those attending the conferences. The American Society of Criminology, for instance, publishes abstracts of papers presented. These abstracts are the same as article abstracts published by *Criminal Justice Abstracts*.

Using abstracts from recent criminological and criminal justice conferences is one way of obtaining the most recent, up-to-date information about various subjects, since paper presenters are often in the midst of writing up their research for journal article submissions and other publication outlets. Many researchers scan these conference proceedings and write letters to presenters with requests for copies of their papers if available. It is often the case that these papers presented at professional conferences will eventually be published in research journals one or two years later. Therefore, it is obvious that obtaining the freshest research from presenters gives the student an edge over those who rely on textbooks or even recently published journals.

■ LEGAL RESEARCH IN CRIMINAL JUSTICE

When students examine legal cases from different sources, they may wish to quote from them or cite them in their papers. The material below provides some conventional practices relating to legal citations.

The U.S. Supreme Court cases cited in this section, as well as cases cited from U.S. district courts or circuit courts of appeal and state courts, are cited by the *names* of persons involved in the cases as well as the *volume numbers* and *page numbers* where the cases can be found. A *hypothetical* citation might appear as follows:

Smith v. Jones, 358 U.S. 437, 112 S.Ct. 229 (1993)

Or a citation might appear as

Smith v. Jones, 226 F.Supp. 1 (1992)

or

Smith v. Jones, 442 P.2d 433 (1989)

These citations are important to anyone interested in legal research or learning about what the law says and how it should be interpreted or applied. They specify particular sources or *reporters* where these cases can be found. A *reporter* is a collection of books containing published opinions of different courts. Most of the cases discussed in this book are U.S. Supreme Court cases, while several are from state supreme courts. The first numbers in each citation above specify a *volume number*, while the second number is a *page number* in the volume. In the hypothetical example above, *Smith v. Jones* is found in the 358th volume of the *United States Reports*, on page 437. Also, the same case can be found in volume 112 of the *Supreme Court Reporter* on page 229. Below are several rules or guidelines governing legal citations and information about what is contained in them.

U.S. Supreme Court

All U.S. Supreme Court opinions and decisions are printed in various sources. The *official source* for all U.S. Supreme Court opinions is the *United States Reports*, abbreviated as *U.S.*, and it is published by the U.S. Government Printing Office. The U.S. Supreme Court convenes annually for a *term*, where numerous cases are heard and decided. All U.S. Supreme Court actions are recorded in the *United States Reports*. There is a substantial time lag between the time the U.S. Supreme Court delivers its opinions and when they are published in the *United States Reports*, however. Other sources exist, therefore, that distribute these opinions in a more timely fashion to interested lawyers and researchers.

Unofficial sources also print U.S. Supreme Court opinions in bound volumes on an annual basis. These unofficial sources include West Publishing Company's *Supreme Court Reporter* and the Lawyer's Cooperative *United States Supreme Court Reports, Lawyer's Edition*. The *Supreme Court Reporter* published by West is abbreviated as *S.Ct.*, while the *United States Supreme Court Reports, Lawyer's Edition* is abbreviated as *L.Ed.* Within days following a particular ruling by the U.S. Supreme Court, unofficial versions of the entire text of U.S. Supreme Court opinions are published by West Publishing Company and the Lawyer's Cooperative. For instance, West Publishing Company distributes *ad-*

vance sheets to its subscribers. *Advance sheets are booklets published about once every two or three weeks that contain recent U.S. Supreme Court actions.* During any given U.S. Supreme Court term, as many as 22 to 24 booklets or advance sheets will be sent to subscribers.

Other sources are *United States Law Week*, which is published by the Bureau of National Affairs, Inc., and the *United States Supreme Court Bulletin*, published by Commerce Clearing House, Inc. The *United States Law Week* is abbreviated as *U.S.L.W.* A major strength of the unofficial *United States Law Week* is that the most recent U.S. Supreme Court opinions are made available to interested legal researchers and lawyers within days following particular decisions.

Whenever a U.S. Supreme Court opinion is cited, more than a few scholars use *parallel citations* to indicate where any given case can be found. For instance, a case with its *typical* parallel citations might be *Brewer v. Williams*, 430 U.S. 387, 97 S.Ct. 1232, 51 L.Ed.2d 424 (1977). According to the Harvard Law Review Association in Cambridge, Massachusetts, as well as Kunz, et al. *The Process of Legal Research* (1992), it is proper to rely exclusively upon the *official* reporter, which would be the *United States Reports* in U.S. Supreme Court cases. Thus, we would only need to cite *Brewer v. Williams*, 430 U.S. 387 (1977), and this citation would be sufficient to comply with legal protocol. However, because of the time lag between U.S. Supreme Court opinions and the publication of the *United States Reports*, it is proper to cite the next most recently available *unofficial* source. This would involve a citation from the *Supreme Court Reporter* published by West. Thus, if we didn't know the *United States Reports* citation yet, *but* we knew the *Supreme Court Reporter* citation, we could cite as follows: *Brewer v. Williams*, ____ U.S. ____, 97 S.Ct. 1232 (1977). The blank spaces indicate that we do not know yet which volume or page number *Brewer v. Williams* will be found in the *United States Reports*. Later, when the *United States Reports* is published as the official version of U.S. Supreme Court opinions, we can supply the appropriate page numbers.

There are several hundred volumes of each of these reporters. Obviously, it would be very expensive for any college or university library to acquire each of these compendiums of U.S. Supreme Court opinions. Many libraries subscribe to the *United States Reports*, while other libraries might subscribe to the *Supreme Court Reporter*. Other libraries might subscribe to the *United States Supreme Court Reports, Lawyer's Edition*. Several large law school libraries have all of these volumes and more. However, since many colleges and universities cannot afford to maintain all three versions, and since these are *parallel citations* and are virtually identical opinions, it makes little sense for an average library to have three different compendiums of opinions that say the same thing. Therefore, many libraries will have either one source or another. Scholars sometimes give three standard parallel citations whenever cases are cited. Thus, researchers can look up the same U.S. Supreme Court opinion in any one of these sources, depending upon which version is maintained by their library.

When students read introductory textbooks in criminology or criminal justice, therefore, it should not be considered unusual or confusing to see the *same* case in different books with *different* citations. For example, one criminology book may cite *Brewer v. Williams*, 97 S.Ct. 1232 (1977), while another criminology book may refer to *Brewer v. Williams*, 430 U.S. 387 (1977). Yet another criminology book may use the Lawyer's Cooperative version and cite *Brewer v. Williams*, 51 L.Ed.2d 424 (1977). All of these citations are considered proper. When an author of a textbook provides *all three* parallel citations, it may not be necessary, but it may be helpful for persons more or less restricted to particular sets of U.S. Supreme Court volumes.

When "2d" or "3d" follow a reporter, this doesn't mean that a new edition of the source has been published. Rather, it means that the publishing company has started over with a fresh numbering system. For instance, the *Brewer v. Williams*, 51 L.Ed.2d (1977) means that the case can be found in volume 51 of the *United States Supreme Court Reports, Lawyer's Edition, Second Series*. There are no fixed rules governing when publishing companies will commence new series for their volume renumbering.

There are *no* official sources for reporting the opinions of lower *federal* courts, such as the different circuit courts of appeal or U.S. district courts. However, West Publishing Company publishes the *Federal Reporter*, abbreviated as *F*, or *F.2d*, to indicate where various opinions can be found for the U.S. circuit courts of appeal. Not all of these opinions are published each year. Whatever opinions are published are at the discretion of the publisher, and often decisions to include or not include particular circuit court of appeals opinions is influenced by their constitutional relevance. Another source, also published by West, is the *Federal Supplement*, abbreviated as *F. Supp.* This source publishes selected opinions from U.S. district courts, the U.S. Customs Courts, and the U.S. Court of International Trade.

Separate state supreme court reporters are published. Several publishing companies, including West Publishing Company, publish these state supreme court opinions. A chart provided below shows which outlets publish which state supreme court opinions and which abbreviations are used for such compilations.

Reporter	States Included
Atlantic Reporter (A or A.2d)	Connecticut, Delaware, Maine, Maryland, New Hampshire, New Jersey, Pennsylvania, Rhode Island, Vermont, and District of Columbia
Northeastern Reporter (N.E. or N.E.2d)	Illinois, Indiana, Massachusetts, New York, and Ohio
Northwestern Reporter (N.W. or N.W.2d)	Iowa, Michigan, Minnesota, Nebraska, North Dakota, South Dakota, and Wisconsin
Pacific Reporter (P or P.2d)	Alaska, Arizona, California, Colorado, Hawaii, Idaho, Kansas, Montana, Nevada, New Mexico, Oklahoma, Oregon, Utah, Washington, and Wyoming

Southeastern Reporter (S.E. or *S.E.2d)*	Georgia, North Carolina, South Carolina, Virginia, and West Virginia
Southwestern Reporter (S.W. or *S.W.2d)*	Arkansas, Kentucky, Missouri, Tennessee, Texas, and Indian Territories
Southern Reporter (So. or *So.2d)*	Alabama, Florida, Louisiana, and Mississippi

Individual states publish their supreme court opinions in separate publications. For example, the Alabama Supreme Court has its opinions published in the *Alabama Reports.* The Colorado Supreme Court's opinions are published in the *Colorado Reports.* Other reporting outlets include the *North Dakota Reports, Ohio State Reports, Tennessee Reports, Virginia Reports,* and *Wisconsin Reports.* These and other report sources can be consulted to find specific state supreme court opinions for different years.

Federal and State Statutes. Criminal and civil statutes for the federal system are contained in the *U.S. Code.* Connecticut has *The General Statutes of Connecticut.* Tennessee has the *Tennessee Code Annotated.* Texas has *Vernon's Texas Code Annotated.* Virginia has the *Virginia Reports.* Washington has the *Revised Code of Washington Annotated*, and so on. These statutory compilations are being rewritten annually as new laws are passed and old or existing laws are modified or eliminated.

Answers to Mathematical Problems at the Ends of Chapters

Chapter 12

4. (a) 89.5 and 109.5   (b) 1499.5 and 1599.5   (c) .195 and .295
   (d) .00545 and .00595   (e) 135.5 and 139.5   (f) 199.5 and 249.5
6. (a) 64.7   (b) 139.5   (c) 152.8   (d) 35.9   (e) 99.5   (f) 61.5
   (g) 169.5   (h) 69.5
8. (a) .36%   (b) 15.6%   (c) 97%   (d) 11.58%   (e) 55.5%   (f) .04%
9. 34.5, 44.5, 54.5, 64.5, 74.5, 84.5, 94.5, 104.5, 114.5, 124.5, 134.5, 144.5, 154.5, 164.5, 174.5, 184.5, 194.5

Chapter 14

1. (a) $s^2 = 193.2$ $s = 13.9$ (b) 39.7
2. (a) 522   (b) 524.9   (c) 527
3. Mode = 14, median = 12.5, mean = 12.6
4. Mode = 15, median = 24, mean = 35.8
6. 42.5
7. Mean = 56.4, median = 5
8. Mode = 132, median = 142, mean = 143.8
9. Range = 13.7, $s = 3.9$
10. $s = 13.7$, range = 56
11. $s = 31.3$
12. Range = 58, $s = 17.3$

Chapter 15

1. **(a)** .0735   **(b)** .9901   **(c)** .5000   **(d)** .6554   **(e)** .0233   **(f)** .1587
2. **(a)** .0782   **(b)** .9030   **(c)** .4666   **(d)** .0026
3. **(a)** 4.10   **(b)** 0   **(c)** -1.50 **(d)** -3.00
4. **(a)** 137   **(b)** 242   **(c)** 267   **(d)** 220
5. **(a)** .6255   **(b)** .0146   **(c)** .8389   **(d)** .4880   **(e)** .8665   **(f)** .9871
   (g) .2090   **(h)** .8413
6. **(a)** 35   **(b)** 40   **(c)** 55   **(d)** 15   **(e)** 40   **(f)** 31
7. **(a)** .2843   **(b)** .8475   **(c)** .3413   **(d)** .7726   **(e)** .0003   **(f)** .8790
   (g) .8593   **(h)** .3284
8. **(a)** 1.31   **(b)** 3.00   **(c)** 1.50   **(d)** .34   **(e)** 2.03   **(f)** 2.50
9. **(a)** .1587   **(b)** .9970   **(c)** .9998   **(d)** .8944
10. **(a)** 0   **(b)** 10.67   **(c)** -4.33 **(d)** -1.00 **(e)** -9.33

Chapter 16

4. **(a)** 96.82 to 104.18   **(b)** 96.74 to 103.26   **(c)** 93.43 to 106.57
5. **(a)** 94.12 to 105.88   **(b)** 96.16 to 103.84   **(c)** 95.68 to 104.32
6. **(a)** 326.76 to 333.24   **(b)** 325.92 to 334.08   **(c)** 327.84 too 332.16
8. **(5a)** 1.96   **(5b)** 1.28   **(5c)** 1.44   **(6a)** 1.56   **(6b)** 1.96   **(6c)** 1.04
9. **(a)** 120.55 to 123.45   **(b)** 120.02 to 123.98   **(c)** 121.06 to 122.94
10. ± 2.58 (critical value of Z for .01 level of significance, two-tailed test); observed $Z = 1.67$, not significant; confidence interval = 99%CI = 17.26 to 32.75 (based upon a Z value of 2.58)
11. **(a)** 65   **(b)** 6   **(c)** 71   **(d)** 6.47   **(e)** 196.8   **(f)** 5.07
    (g) 3.09

Glossary

Accidental sampling. Selecting elements for one's sample based upon immediate accessibility and cooperativeness of respondents; for example, questionnaires distributed to students in the classroom are distributed to "accidental samples"; and the roving reporter on the street interviews "accidental sample" elements.

After-only design. Method seeking to compare an experimental group with a control group *after* an experimental variable has been introduced to one group but not the other.

Alpha error. Known as *Type I* error, alpha error (α) is defined as the probability of rejecting H_0 when it is true and shouldn't be rejected; also known as the probability at which the hypothesis is tested; also the level of significance.

Alternative hypothesis. Same as the research hypothesis in relation to a null hypothesis.

Altruistic appeals. Cover-letter appeals to respondents who are requested to complete and return their questionnaires as a favor to others.

Analysis of secondary sources. Data collection strategy that utilizes materials collected by other investigators for purposes other than those of the present investigator; includes studies of public documents, letters, diaries, and private reports.

Analysis of variance. Known as the *F* test, a statistical test designed to determine the significance of difference between *k* sample means; answers the question of whether there is a significant mean difference somewhere among the means; does not indicate where significant differences exist between means.

Anonymity. Assurances given to respondents in one's research that their answers will be confidential and disclosed to no one.

Applied research. Investigations undertaken primarily for practical reasons; policy-relevant form of research.

Arbitrary reference point. Random interval midpoint selected by researchers for determining the mean for grouped data; any interval midpoint may be chosen as the arbitrary reference point, since the grouped data formula for the mean computation is self-correcting, depending upon the interval chosen.

Arbitrary scales. Indices developed and based upon face validity and individual discretion.

Archival analysis. Use of historical records, court documents, in order to discover patterns.

Area sampling; area probability sample. See Multistage sampling.

Association. Preferred term to describe relationships or correlations between two or more variables, regardless of level of measurement of test variables.

Assumption. Similar to empirical generalizations, these are statements that have a high degree of certainty; they require little, if any, confirmation in the real world. Examples of assumptions might be "All societies have laws" or "The greater the deviant conduct, the greater the group pressure on the deviant to conform to group norms."

Asymmetrical. Skewed or nonnormal distribution; applied to association, a correlational measure that yields a different *PRE* interpretation depending on which variable is used as independent and which is used as dependent.

Asymptotic property. Characteristic of unit normal distribution where the ends of the curve extend exactly the same way but in opposite directions, approaching the baseline of the curve but never touching it; ends of the curve extend toward infinity.

Atheoretical evaluations. Descriptive research that is not directly connected to a theoretical scheme; a study of some event simply to know what causes the event; not grounded in any particular theory.

Attitudes. Tendencies to think or act in given ways; intangible dispositions of persons, measured by scales, intended to differentiate persons according to their dispositions and inclinations; inferred dispositions from paper-pencil questionnaires containing scales.

Attributes. Characteristics of people or things.

Autobiographical information. Method of studying persons by paying attention to their own accounts of their lives and social events.

Average deviation. Mean or average amount of fluctuation of all scores around the mean of their distribution.

Axiomatic theory. Use of truisms or axioms in a logical fashion to derive testable statements about events; ordering of propositions and assumptions in ways that yield other statements capable of being tested.

Axioms. Truisms; statements about reality that are largely unquestioned; assumptions.

Bar graphs. Graphic representations of either vertical or horizontal bars that represent frequencies of occurrence of different values.

Basic research. Investigations conducted to test theoretical issues; contributes to the knowledge base of criminal justice or criminology.

Before-after method or **design.** An improvement over the after-only method or design, the before-after method or design consists of obtaining measures on some dependent variable for two groups that are presumed equivalent for experimental purposes, then introducing an experimental variable to one group and withholding it from the other, and then comparing the two groups after the experiment has been completed.

Bell curve; bell-shaped curve. The normal curve produced by the unit normal distribution.

Beta error (β). Known as *Type II error* (β), beta error is the probability of failing to reject H_0 when it is false and ought to be rejected.

Between-group variation. In the F test for analysis of variance, any differences observed between k samples.

Bias. A misrepresentation of reality as the result of inappropriate measures or inaccurate measures; any question encouraging a particular response.

Biased estimator. Statistic that underestimates the population parameter of which it is an estimate.

Bimodal distribution. Score distribution having two modes.

Biographical information. Method of acquiring information about persons by studying accounts written about them by others.

Birth cohort. Aggregate of persons born in the same year and studied at different intervals over time.

Bivariate normal distribution. Assumption of the Pearson product-moment correlation coefficient or Pearson r; two correlated variables are both assumed to be normally distributed.

Bogardus social distance scale. Measurement technique for determining willingness of persons to associate with others who are different ethnically or racially, disclosing varying degrees of closeness among such persons.

Branching technique. The method of asking questions that narrow the focus of the topic; used in situations where sensitive topics such as rape or incest are discussed.

Canned data sets. Readily available databases of information compiled by private and public sources; made available to researchers for diverse purposes.

Case study. A qualitative study where the researcher collects large amounts of information from individual cases; reliance upon interview or observational information.

Case study design. Thorough examination of specific social settings or particular aspects of social settings, including detailed psychological and behavioral descriptions of persons in those settings.

Categorical variable. Any factor measured according to a nominal scale.

Cause-effect relation. See Causal Relation.

Causal relation. In a causal relation, one variable, designated as independent, functions to create changes in another variable, designated as dependent; a relation where one variable follows another variable's occurrence.

Causality. A relationship between two or more variables, where values for one variable are determined or strongly influenced by another variable; study of factors that elicit other factors; process of linking one condition with another, such that one condition elicits changes in another in predicted or anticipated directions.

Cell frequencies. Number of observations in a particular cell of any $r \times c$ table.

Census. The study of an entire population; U.S. Census Bureau collects information periodically about the U.S. population.

Centiles. A measure equivalent to one percent in frequency distributions; a method of dividing a distribution of scores into single percentage points.

Central tendency. Score accumulations around certain points in a distribution of scores; includes mean, mode, and median.

Chi square test, single sample, two samples, *k*-samples. Goodness-of-fit nonparametric procedure for data that is measured according to a nominal scale that has been cross-tabulated into a $1 \times c$ or $r \times 1$ or larger tables; determines whether observed frequencies differ from what would be expected according to chance; weakest nonparametric procedure; available for one-sample, two-sample, and *k*-sample situations.

Classical experimental design. A design used if there are two or more cases, and in one of them observation Z can be made, while in the other it cannot. If factor C occurs when observation Z is made, and does not occur when observation Z is not made, then it can be asserted that there is a causal relationship between C and Z.

Cluster sampling. See Multistage sampling.

Code of conduct. Outline of expected moral and ethical behaviors for members of an organization or profession.

Code of ethics. Prescription for moral behaviors and standards expected of members of an organization or profession.

Coding. Assignment of numbers to information collected by investigator; questionnaires are coded when questions and responses are classified numerically, and numbers are transmitted to software programs designed to facilitate data analysis.

Coding manual or **code book.** A document compiled by researcher to identify meanings of numbers assigned to different variables and variable subclasses.

Coefficient of association. Numerical expression of the degree of relationship or correlation between two or more variables; ranges in magnitude from ± 1.00, respectively meaning either perfect negative or perfect positive association; $0 =$ no association.

Coefficient of reproducibility. Measure used in conjunction with Guttman scaling that determines whether one's responses to individual items may be predicted solely on the basis of knowing one's total test score; .90 means that the scale is reproducible, hence, unidimensional; .80 is a quasi-reproducible scale.

Cohort. Any aggregate of persons studied at different points in time; birth cohorts are persons born in the same year and subsequently studied periodically.

Collapsing tables. Reducing a table size, with a certain number of rows and columns, to a smaller table size with fewer rows and columns; refers to combining certain row and column cells into fewer of them to create a smaller table. The intent of collapsing is to increase the numbers of cell frequencies in remaining cells.

Comparative research. Investigations seeking to contrast persons of different cultures; sometimes called cross-cultural research; generally any comparison research highlighting characteristics and differences between two or more groups.

Computer-Assisted Telephone Interviewing (CATI). A method of contacting respondents by dialing telephone numbers at random; objective is to circumvent problems in contacting respondents with unlisted telephone numbers.

Computer-determined draw. Software program designed to generate random digits; method of generating random samples of elements by using the random-numbers program on a computer.

Concepts. Terms used in language that have direct empirical referents.

Conclusions. Final observations and deductions about collected and analyzed data; final tentative interpretations of the significance about what one has found.

Concurrent validity. Form of test validation where scores of predicted behavior are obtained simultaneously with the exhibited behavior.

Confidence interval. An interval about an observed sample mean that has a specified probability of overlapping the population mean that the sample mean is attempting to estimate.

Confidentiality. The privilege requirement that any information disclosed by participants in a study will not be made public or available to outsiders; provision that information collected will not be used to harm research subjects in any way.

Constant. Any variable that doesn't change in value during the course of a study.

Constructs. Terms used in language that have indirect empirical referents.

Construct validity. Both a logical and a statistical validating method; also known as *factorial validity,* construct validity is useful for measuring traits for which external criteria are not available, such as latent aggressiveness; this type of validity is determined through the application of *factor analysis.*

Contamination of data. Experiences or events that might adversely affect the experimental or control group and thus disrupt the experiment and undermine experimental integrity.

Content analysis. Systematic qualitative and quantitative description of some form of communication.

Content validity. Face validity based upon the logical inclusion of a sampling of items taken from the universe of items that measure the trait in question. The only way content validity can be demonstrated is by examining the test or instrument items and comparing them with the universe of items that could theoretically be included, if known.

Contingency coefficient. See Pearson's *C.*

Contingent conditions. Factors acting as intervening links in the presence of an observed relation between two other variables; any factor or variable that intervenes and modifies the relation between an independent and a dependent variable.

Continuous variables. Any factors that have an infinite number of subclasses.

Contributory conditions. Factors that influence the occurrence and degree of change in other phenomena; not necessarily followed by the caused event. Contributory conditions or variables, acting with other conditions or variables, operate to change dependent variables.

Control. Holding constant one or more factors while others are free to vary; manipulation of variables to elicit predictable effects. Also a reference to the groups or individuals, known as the control group, who are not exposed to experimental variables, whatever they might be.

Control group. Persons not receiving experimental stimulus. For example, if we were to administer a particular drug to persons in one group and withhold the drug from persons in another group, the group receiving the drug would be called the *experimental group,* whereas the group not receiving the drug would be called the *control group.* Ordinarily, the reactions of the experimental group and the control group are observed and compared; differences between the two groups are attributed largely to the effects of the experimental stimulus, or in our example case, the drug.

Control of variables. Manipulating variables so as to determine their experimental impact on other variables; distributing variable subclasses in tables to determine their influence on other variables with which they have been cross-tabulated.

Control variable. Any factor that is held constant in an attempt to further clarify the relation between two other variables.

Convenience sampling. Method of selecting elements because of their availability to the researcher; same as accidental samples. Researchers sometimes study those with whom they work, or they may take advantage of their teaching situation and use large classes of students that are conveniently available.

Convention. Practice of following whatever is customary; applied to criminology and criminal justice, certain actions of professionals are guided by convention, including setting particular significance levels such as .05 or .01 in statistical tests. Convention also applies to tabular formats and certain kinds of data presentation consistent with the customary usage within the academic discipline.

Cornell technique. See Guttman scaling.

Correlation. See association.

Cost-benefit analysis. Comparison of the useful and practical results of an intervention or experimental variable and the costs of these results compared with alternative interventions.

Cramer's *V*. Measure of association for two variables, where each has been measured according to a nominal scale; lacks *PRE* interpretation.

Crime clocks. Circular portrayals of the frequency of occurrence of particular crimes; see Pie charts.

Crime rate. Number of crimes during a given period, such as one year, divided by the population, and then multiplied by 100,000.

Criterion validity. See Predictive validity.

Critical region. Area on sampling distribution of any statistic that is defined by critical values of that statistic; also known as *region of rejection,* since statistical observations that occur on the line of or in critical regions result in rejections of null hypotheses.

Critical values. Tabled statistical values that usually must be equaled or exceeded by observed statistics in order for statistical significance to be indicated.

Cross-sectional study. Survey designed to elicit opinions or attitudes about one or more issues from designated persons at one point in time.

Cross-tabulation. Tabular arrangement where two or more variables and their subclasses are arranged so that "interactions" between variables may be observed.

Cross-tabulations of variables. Tabular representations of data, where two or more variables have been placed in tables with several rows and several columns to determine their interaction and influence upon one another.

Cumulative frequency distributions. Displays of frequencies where the frequencies of intervals containing smaller scores have been added to successive intervals; the last interval contains all scores in the distribution; the curve drawn is an ogive curve.

Cursor. Blinking point on a computer screen to advise users of location of marker for typing reports or preparing documents.

Curvilinearity. Property of an association between variables, where regression line is curved rather than straight.

Data. Collected information.

Data analysis. Evaluation of the significance of collected information by means of statistical assessment or the significance of the contents.

Data cleaning. Close inspection of responses to questionnaire and coding procedures to detect any errors in recording information.

Data collection. Process of acquiring information about research subjects, usually through interviews or questionnaires.

Data collection methods. Any way of obtaining information about events; includes questionnaires, surveys, interviews, observation, and analysis of secondary sources.

Data entry. Process of creating machine-readable data sets from collected data; process of entering values into a statistical software program, such as *SPSS*.

Data set. Collection of variables for a group of research subjects to be studied.

Deception. Deliberately deceiving research subjects about the nature of the experiment, study, or research being conducted and the role played by these subjects in the research.

Deciles. Division of frequency distribution into 10 percentage–point intervals.

Decision rules. Criteria established in advance of conducting hypothesis tests. Rules govern how researchers will evaluate statistical test outcomes; some decision rules include specification of sampling distribution of a statistic, a level of significance at which a hypothesis is tested, and an area on the sampling distribution containing the critical region(s).

Deduction. Process of deriving conclusions logically from several related theoretical statements.

Deductive theory. A theory based on reasoning as explained in the work of the ancient Greek philosopher Aristotle (384–322 B.C.); logical statements are deduced or derived from other statements; typically, assumptions are made and conclusions are drawn that appear to be logically connected with these assumptions; a common example is "All men are mortal. Aristotle is a man. Therefore, Aristotle is mortal." Symbolically, "All A's are B's; C is a B, therefore, C is also an A"; using deduction, we abstract by generalizing.

Definitions. Indicators we consider significant in influencing various events assist us in constructing a logical explanatory framework or theory.

Degree of association. Magnitude of the association or relationship between variables; degree ranges from 0 to either ±1.00.

Degrees of freedom, *df.* Number of values in a set which are free to vary; for tabular arrangements, *df* are determined by (rows − 1) (columns − 1); for samples, $df = N - 1$.

Dense sampling. Selection of elements where approximately 50 percent of the population is obtained; method of obtaining sample is irrelevant, since it is assumed that the overwhelming numbers of such a sample, even obtained accidentally, would be sufficient to warrant some amount of generalizing to and inferences about the population.

Dependent variable. Any factor whose value is determined by other variables.

Description. One of several functions of statistical procedures; to depict sample and population values and characteristics.

Descriptive design. Considerably more structured than casual descriptions of social settings; involves depictions of social patterns that persist over time. The most common design objective in criminology and criminal justice.

Descriptive research. Any investigation that depicts patterns of behavior or elaborates relationships between variables.

Descriptive statistics. Broad class of statistics that depict the central tendency and dispersion or variability of a distribution of scores; includes mean, mode, median, standard deviation, interdecile range, range, and interquartile range.

Deviation score. Difference between a raw score and its mean.

df. See Degrees of freedom.

Diagonal distributions of frequencies. In 2 × 2 tables or larger, distributions of frequencies which are considered desirable, in that cell frequencies accumulate in cells *a* and *d* or *b* and *c*.

Dichotomous variable. Factor that can assume only two values as subclasses; gender is a dichotomous variable, since it yields only two variable subclasses: male and female; in the general case, any variable that can be divided into two subclasses.

Dichotomy. Division of three or more subclasses on any variable, measured according to any level of measurement, into two subclasses only.

Diffusion of treatment. Occurring when control groups learn about and imitate the experimental group, thus contaminating and confounding study results.

Dimension. A specific facet or aspect of a concept.

Directional hypothesis tests. Any statistical verification of a statement where a specific direction of difference has been indicated.

Direction of association. Fluctuation of scores on two variables in one direction or the other, in relation to the other; positive association means that two variables change in value in the same direction, whereas negative or inverse association means that as one variable increases (or decreases) in value, the other variable decreases (or increases) in value.

Directory. Areas on computer disks where files and other types of information are stored.

Direct relationship. Positive correlation between two or more variables; two variables change in the same direction in relation to one another.

Discrete variables. Any factors that have a finite number of subclasses.

Disk drive. Hardware device accepting either 3½″ or 5¼″ disks that "reads" such disks electronically, transmitting information to the computer for processing.

Dispersion or **variability.** Refers to the spread or distribution of scores around the mean of the distribution.

Disproportionate stratified random sampling. Probability sampling plan where one or more variables are controlled; elements obtained are chosen such that these characteristics are not distributed throughout the sample in the same way that they are distributed within the population.

Distribution. Array of collected scores and their arrangement.

Distribution-free statistics. Any statistical test of significance that does not assume normality for its proper application.

Double-barreled questions. Two questions contained in a single statement; cannot be answered with a single response.

Dual-submission policy. Regulation adopted by most professional journals that prohibits authors from submitting their original scholarly articles to more than one journal at a time. In past years, some authors would send their articles to several different journals at once, whereupon two or more journals might subsequently publish the same article; currently this is an unacceptable practice.

Dummy tables. Blank tables that are constructed prior to conducting research; intent of these tables is to suggest the type of data to be collected to answer research questions.

Egoistic appeals. Cover-letter appeals to respondents that are designed to solicit their opinions as a way of increasing response.

Elements. Persons or objects; in social research, one person selected for inclusion in a sample from a larger population.

Empirical. Amenable to the senses; measurable.

Empirical generalizations. Facts; observable regularities of human or social behavior.

Empirical referent. Any object or idea referred to by a single word.

Empiricism. Belief that measurable data can lead to understanding problems and issues.

Environmental factors. Field conditions under which questionnaires are administered or studies are conducted.

Epistemic correlates. Parallel phenomena that indicate the existence of a variable; behaviors that are concomitants of the term describing the behaviors.

Equal-appearing intervals. See Thurstone scaling.

Equality of draw. Provision in probability sampling that states that each element has the same chance of being drawn each time elements are included.

Equivalent groups. Persons in two or more samples that are considered similar in a sufficient number of respects.

Error. Amount of unexplained variation in a variable when using another variable as a predictor of it.

Estimation. Procedure that attempts to determine population values by examining corresponding sample values.

Eta, the correlation ratio, η. Measure of association between two variables, where one variable has been measured according to an interval scale and the other measured according to a nominal scale; has *PRE* interpretation.

Ethics. Normative standards of professional groups or organizations, articulations of what is right and wrong; a morally binding normative code upon members of a group.

Evaluation research. Investigations that attempt to answer practical and applied questions; any investigation geared to test the efficacy of a strategy or intervention in relation to some event, such as delinquency or criminality.

Expected frequencies. In any goodness-of-fit test, the frequencies that are expected according to chance, based upon the distribution of marginal frequencies in any $r \times c$ table.

Expected value. The mean of the sampling distribution of any statistic.

Experiment. Study attempting to approximate laboratory conditions for identifying causal relations between variables.

Experimental designs. A method of experimentation with the objective of implicitly or explicitly including the control of variables. Researchers experiment by observing, under controlled conditions, the effects of one or more variables on others.

Experimental groups. Persons receiving experimental stimulus during experiment.

Experimental mortality. The loss of subjects in an experiment over time.

Experimental research; experimental social research. Any investigation where variables are controlled or manipulated by researchers in order to determine cause-effect relationships between variables; any study conducted where hypotheses are tested; generally refers to controls exerted over different variables to determine their effects on other variables; characterized by high degree of control over extraneous variables.

Experimental stimulus. See Experimental variable.

Experimental variables. Factors manipulated during an experiment; stimulus given experimental group; also known as *treatment variable.*

Explained variation. Amount of variation in a dependent variable which is accounted for by an independent variable.

Explanations. Rationales for why an event occurs; theorizing about the nature of phenomena and their occurrence.

Exploratory design. Characterized by several features, including the assumption that investigators have little or no knowledge about the research problem under study; potentially significant factors may be discovered and may be subsequently assessed and described in greater detail with a more sophisticated type of research design.

Exploratory research. Investigations undertaken when little is known about the phenomena studied; purpose of exploratory research is to discover subject matter that might be studied in greater detail later.

External reliability checks. Any method used to assess the dependability of a measuring instrument through either parallel forms of the same test or test-retest.

External validity. Generalizability of a study to other social situations.

Face-to-face questionnaire administration. Conducting a questionnaire administration directly with respondents rather than by mail.

Face validity. See Content validity.

Factor analysis. A statistical technique designed to determine the basic components of a measure.

Factorial validity. Statistical means of determining the contents of a measuring instrument that purportedly measures two or more separate variables; application of factor analysis to numerous items. Measure is said to possess factorial validity if it "factors" into predictable parts associated with measured variables.

Field experiment. A test of the relation between variables under real conditions in social settings.

Field notes. Written observations of social interactions and events recorded by observers and researchers.

Fishbowl draw. Method of obtaining a sample by drawing numbered pieces of paper or other items from a fishbowl.

Fit. See Goodness of fit.

Fixed-response items. Individual instrument questions with limited choices as alternative answers.

Fixed-response questionnaire. Questionnaires consisting of items (questions or statements) that have a finite list of alternative responses.

Floppy disk. Either a $3\frac{1}{2}''$ or $5\frac{1}{4}''$ disk used for data storage; disks for lap-top computers may be of other sizes. Disks are used in disk drives and may be read electronically by data retrieval systems in computers; data disks of larger sizes are available for specific types of disk drives, such as an Iomega 100 meg disk.

Focused interview. Interviews with respondents who have shared some common experience that has, in turn, been carefully scrutinized by investigators to generate hypotheses about the effects of the experience on participants; the interview context focuses upon the actual effects of the experience as viewed by the participants.

Focus group. Persons brought together for a specific experimental purpose, such as to evaluate their reaction to witnessing an execution.

Follow-up questions. Any query designed to elicit more detailed information after a respondent has answered a certain way to a previous question.

Frame of reference. The way chosen by a researcher for looking at or approaching a problem for scientific study.

Freedom of Information Act (FOIA). Legislation passed to permit private citizens access to government documents collected about them.

Frequency. Number of times an observation occurs.

Frequency distributions. Tallies of occurrences of values according to intervals of a designated size.

Frequency distribution control matching. Group matching method relying upon group characteristics as matching criteria; equating groups according to group properties rather than individual ones.

Frequency polygons. Interconnected points disclosing the distribution of frequencies across several intervals; connected points are at the upper-most points where the number of frequencies in the interval are found, and at each interval midpoint; frequency polygons may be drawn from histograms.

F ratio. MS_{bet} divided by MS_{within}.

F test for analysis of variance (ANOVA). Parametric test for analysis of variance, designed to determine whether two or more sample means differ; answers the general question, Does a difference exist between k sample means?

Gamma (γ). Measure of association for two ordinal-level variables; has *PRE* interpretation.

Generalizability. Degree to which study findings can apply to other social settings or situations.

Goodman and Kruskal's gamma (γ). Popular measure of association for two variables measured according to an ordinal scale; has PRE interpretation.

Goodness of fit. Match between what is observed and what is expected according to chance; applied in chi square test situations; the better the goodness-of-fit, the less significant the differences observed.

Grand mean. Average or arithmetic mean of two or more sample means.

Graphs. Any chart or figure depicting fluctuations of events or occurrences.

Graphic presentation. Any visual or pictorial portrayal of data, either through charts, stick figures, bars, pie charts, maps, or other illustrative data.

Group distribution matching. See Frequency distribution control matching.

Grouped data. Arranging scores into a frequency distribution with interval sizes greater than 1.

Guttman scaling. Method of attitude measurement professing to measuring a single dimension of an attitudinal phenomenon; devised by Louis Guttman.

Guttman's coefficient of predictability, lambda (λ). Measure of association for two variables, where each has been measured according to a nominal scale; has both symmetric and asymmetric *PRE* interpretation.

Halo effect. Assigning higher scores or giving great weight to persons who have scored well or performed well in other test conditions; false credit assigned to persons who are believed to be special in relation to some other characteristic they exhibit; observer bias through prejudging those observed and deciding which ones are better than others.

Hard drive. Hardware computer component capable of storing large amounts of information; amount of information stored on a hard disk is equivalent to the amount of information stored on numerous floppy disks.

Hartley F_{max} test. Homogeneity of variance significance test, associated with one of the underlying assumptions of the F test for analysis of variance; the largest variance divided by the smallest variance.

Hawthorne effect. Effect of being observed, where observed persons who know they are being observed will act differently from the way they would act under conditions when they don't know they are being observed.

Hawthorne experiment. An experiment in the 1920s at the Hawthorne plant of the Western Electric Company, involving bank wiring for telephones; workers were given special attention by observers and behaved differently compared with their behavior when not being observed.

Histograms. Bar graphs constructed for frequency distributions, where height of each bar is determined by number of frequencies in each interval, and bars are centered over each interval midpoint.

Historical method. Use of case histories and archival data to discover social patterns. See also Archival analysis.

H_0. The null hypothesis.

H_1. The research hypothesis.

Homogeneity of variance. Equal variances. See Hartley F_{max} test.

Homoscedasticity. Property of an association between two variables measured according to the interval level of measurement, where the intersecting points form a football-shaped pattern around the regression line.

Human subjects. Any participants in one's research; also called research subjects or study elements.

Human subjects committee. Any university or organizational body designed to oversee the physical and psychological effects of anticipated research projects by faculty or organization members.

Hypotheses. Statements or assertions derived from theory; statements to be tested by scientific inquiry, capable of being refuted. Tests of hypotheses result in support or non-support for the theory from which they were derived.

Hypotheses of association. Any statement indicating a relationship or correlation between variables.

Hypothesis of difference. Any statement specifying a difference between some observed statistic and a hypothesized parameter; any hypothesis seeking to determine the significance of difference between two or more groups on some measured characteristic. Technically, all hypotheses are hypotheses of difference; for example, hypotheses of association specify that an observed coefficient of association will be "different" from zero or "no association."

Hypotheses of point estimation. Any statement proclaiming a parameter to be of some specified value.

Hypothesis sets. Pair of hypotheses, including a research hypothesis and a null hypothesis; conventional presentation of hypotheses in statistical analyses.

Hypothesis testing. Process of determining truthfulness or falsity of any speculative statement, usually derived from a theory; most frequently involves statistical tests.

Icon. Graphic symbols that depict computer functions; used with computer mouses.

Independence of draw. In probability sampling plans, the provision that the draw or selection of one element will not affect the chances of inclusion of remaining elements.

Independent samples. Samples that are mutually exclusive of one another and are not related through any type of matching.

Independent variable. Quantity that determines values, value fluctuations, or subclass distributions on other quantities or variables.

In-depth interviews. Any questioning of respondents designed to uncover detailed information about their behaviors or characteristics.

Index. Type of composite measure that summarizes several specific observations and represents some more general dimension.

Indicator. An observation that is considered a reflection of the variable studied.

Individual matching. Used for experimentation, a method for equating groups by matching persons in groups to be compared according to individual properties.

Inductive logic; induction. Use of specific cases to form generalizations or theories.

Inductive theory. A process whereby a specific event is examined and described, and where generalizations are made to a larger class of similar events; using induction, we generalize by abstracting.

Inference. Process of making generalizations about population parameters by examining their statistical counterparts from a sample of elements.

Inferential statistics. A broad class of statistics intended to provide information about unknown population parameters.

Informant. Someone who is knowledgeable about the social setting studied, and who will provide inside information about what is going on and why.

Informed consent. Agreement given by research subjects that they are aware of what will occur in an experiment, and that they are knowledgeable of the facts and potential harm that may accrue.

Institutional review boards. Organizational screening committees that examine research projects and attempt to discover anything that might be harmful to human subjects; a quality-control board that oversees ethical procedures used in conducting research.

Instrument. Questionnaire or interview guide containing questions or items intended to measure variables.

Intensity continuum. Continuum of attitudinal expression, representing extremes of low to high, with moderate points near the center.

Interdecile range. See 10–90 range.

Internal consistency. Amount of correlation between items on a scale intended to measure a variable.

Internal reliability checks. Any method designed to determine the dependability of a measuring instrument through either item discrimination analysis or the split-half procedure.

Internal validity. The soundness of the actual study conducted; evaluated according to the accuracy of instruments used to measure variables, soundness of theory, adequacy of sample selected, appropriateness of statistics chosen for data analysis; study integrity.

Interpretation. Explanation of an event based on data analysis; the research outcome in which a control variable is discovered to be a mediating factor through which an independent variable has an effect on the dependent variable.

Interquartile range. The distance over which the central 50 percent of the scores in a distribution are spread; measured by the difference between the first and third quartiles.

Interrupted time series. Multiple measures at different points in time before and after an experiment.

Interval estimation. Creating an interval around an observed sample mean, based upon a knowledge of the sample standard deviation and sample size; the interval has a probability of overlapping the population mean.

Interval level of measurement. Scale where distance between values is equal; such information can be averaged arithmetically.

Interval midpoints. The theoretical dividing point in an interval that cuts the interval into two equal parts.

Interval size. Magnitude for including certain scores in a frequency distribution.

Intervals. Fixed numerical groupings for portraying scores.

Intervening variable. A third variable that may affect the relation between two other variables.

Interview. A verbal communication with one or more research subjects for the purpose of acquiring information.

Interview guide. A loosely structured set of open-ended questions that interviewers may use as a general guide for conducting interviews with respondents.

Interview schedule. A questionnaire consisting of a predetermined number of questions and fixed-response replies that interviewers can fill in themselves when they conduct interviews.

Item analysis. See Item discrimination analysis.

Item discrimination analysis. An internal consistency method for improving instrument reliability. The objective is to eliminate items that poorly differentiate between subjects who possess some attitudinal property to varying degrees; eliminating poorly discriminating items creates greater internal consistency.

Item weights. Numerical values assigned alternative responses to items in an attitudinal measure; summated weights enable researchers to determine one's attitudinal position relative to others.

Jaspen's *M*. Measure of association for two variables, where one variable is measured according to an ordinal scale and the other measured according to an interval scale; has *PRE* interpretation.

Judgmental sampling. Handpicked samples from designated populations; believed in some cases to be superior to randomness, especially if those selecting the sample are quite familiar with the population; used in community research.

Kendall's tau (τ). Measure of association for two variables measured according to an ordinal scale; has *PRE* interpretation.

Key informants. Persons who have access to a restricted group or organization; able to provide information to researchers about behaviors of organizational participants or group subjects.

Kilobytes (k). Unit of measurement depicting the amount of space consumed by information stored on floppy or hard disks; high-density $3\frac{1}{2}''$ floppy disks, for instance, may store 1,400k of information; this is equivalent to about twelve textbook chapters.

Kurtosis. Curve peakedness; refers to the flatness or peakedness of curve shapes that depart from the normal, bell-shaped curve model.

***K*-variable hypotheses.** Any statement containing two or more variables or factors.

Labeling theory. Explanation for deviant and criminal conduct that focuses upon social definitions of acts of crime and deviance rather than on the acts themselves. Some of the assumptions underlying labeling theory are that (1) no act is inherently criminal, (2) persons become criminals through social definition of their conduct, (3) all persons at one time or another conform to or deviate from the law, (4) "getting caught" begins the labeling process, (5) persons defined as criminal will, in turn, cultivate criminal self-definitions, and (6) they will eventually seek out and associate with others who are similarly defined and develop a criminal subculture.

Lambda, λ, Guttman's coefficient of predictability. Yields the amount of correlation between two variables where both are measured according to a nominal scale; has both a symmetric and an asymmetric *PRE* interpretation.

Leptokurtic. Any peaked distribution which is not normal; scores tend to accumulate near the center of distribution, producing a very peaked and pointed distribution as opposed to a normal bell-shaped curve.

Leptokurtosis. A nonnormal condition and curve shape, where the curve is extremely peaked or tall near the center of the distribution; characterized by scores "bunching up" near the center of distribution; few scores in the curve tails.

Level of significance. Probability set by researcher in advance of statistical test; amount of probability associated with rejecting H_o when H_o is true and shouldn't be rejected; also known as Type I error or alpha error (α).

Levels of measurement. Four levels of measurement identified by S. S. Stevens, including the nominal, ordinal, interval, and ratio levels; each of these levels of measurement are equated with certain permissible arithmetic procedures; statistical tests and measures require satisfaction of a certain measurement level before they may be applied properly.

Lie detector tests. Polygraphs designed to measure one's heart rate and other physical factors to determine whether one's responses to questions are truthful; not reliable for criminal court use. See also Polygraph.

Lie factors or **lie scales.** Questions or items included in questionnaires that measure respondent truthfulness.

Likert scale. Named after Rensis Likert, this method of summated ratings is based on the idea that variable numbers of items with alternative responses may be weighted to yield ordinal-level attitudinal positions; most popular attitudinal scaling device.

Linear. Having a straight-line relation between two variables when displayed on a scatterplot or scatter diagram.

Linearity. A straight-line association between two variables, where the line refers to the "regression line" or "best-fitting" line that theoretically may be drawn through the intersecting points for values on both variables.

Literature review. Examination of existing sources focusing upon a particular topic of study; a preliminary examination of materials available as resources to bolster one's ideas about and explanations for events.

Longitudinal research or **study.** Any research conducted over time; designed to examine trends or changes; time interval may be measured in months or years.

Mailed questionnaire. Survey distributed through the U.S. Post Office to respondents; considered an inexpensive way of obtaining large amounts of data from large numbers of respondents separated from one another geographically; enhances respondent anonymity.

Matching. Method of equating two or more groups according to individual or group properties shared by persons in each group.

Maturation. Biological or psychological changes occurring within research subjects over time that are not attributable to the experimental variable.

McNemar test for significance of change. Nonparametric, nominal-level test for two-sample situations where persons are used as their own controls in a before-after experiment; determines whether persons change from one condition to another, where the test variable has been dichotomized.

Mean. Arithmetic average, obtained by summing scores and dividing by the number of scores.

Mean of means. See Grand mean.

Measure of association. Any of a class of procedures designed to show the amount of relationship or correlation between two or more variables, regardless of the level of measurement obtained.

Measurement. Assignment of numbers to characteristics and the degree to which they are possessed by individuals or groups.

Median. Theoretical point in a distribution of scores that divides that distribution into two equal parts.

Megabytes (Mb). Unit of measurement depicting the amount of space consumed by information stored on floppy or hard disks; hard drive capacities measured in megabytes; common hard drive sizes are 30Mb, 40Mb, 80Mb, 800Mb; $3\frac{1}{2}''$ high-density floppy disks store approximately 1.4Mb of information.

Mesokurtic. A flat-appearing distribution of scores; widely dispersed scores around some central point.

Mesokurtosis. Nonnormal condition and curve shape which is most like the normal curve; curve bulges near center of distribution, reflecting greater proportions of scores apart from those expected in similar areas on the normal curve.

Meta-analysis. Literally, analysis of analysis; statistical analysis of numerous studies of the same phenomena in order to determine general findings.

Method of agreement. Statement that if the circumstances leading up to a given event have in all cases one factor in common, then this factor may be the cause sought.

Method of concomitant variation. If variation in the intensity of a given factor is followed by a parallel variation in the effect, then this factor is the cause.

Method of difference. If two sets of circumstances differ in only one factor, and the one containing the factor leads to the event and the other does not, we may consider the factor as the cause of the event.

Method of equal-appearing intervals. See Thurstone scaling.

Method of summated ratings. See Likert scaling.

Methodology. Study of research methods.

Mode. For data in ungrouped form, the most popular or most frequently occurring score; for data in grouped form, the interval midpoint of the interval containing the most frequencies. Several modes may be reported, where more than one value occurs most frequently. Limit is conventionally established at three modes; if more than three values occur most frequently in a distribution, there is no mode.

Model. Any logical collection of concepts and statements designed to explain a phenomenon.

Modem. Telephonic device that serves to link computers in various locations with one another. Personal computer users may access library computer systems through modem linkages, which are telephonic devices.

Mouse. Small computer device that has several levers that may be pushed with the fingers; the mouse is moved on a board, which activates a pointer on the computer monitor. Users may use the mouse or the computer keyboard to perform various computer functions.

Multidimensional scales. Any attitudinal measure containing two or more dimensions of an attitudinal phenomenon; Likert scales and Thurstone scales are multidimensional scales.

Multiple correlation (R). Multiple regression coefficient that shows relation between two or more variables simultaneously.

Multiple time-series design. Similar to conventional time-series design except an additional comparison group is included.

Multistage sampling. Also called a cluster or areal sampling, a multistage sampling is composed of successive selections of squares from horizontal and vertical grids of geographical areas. Smaller areas represent square miles or city blocks within which reside those who are designated for inclusion.

Multivariate analysis. Statistical study of simultaneous relationships among several variables.

Mutually exclusive. Occurs when an observation cannot fall into two different categories; for example, a male cannot be included in both "male" and "female" subclasses of the gender variable.

N. Population size; N is often used to apply to samples of elements and for formula terms; a distinction between N and n is made only to illustrate sampling techniques.

n. Sample size; n is commonly used in formulas to represent sample size rather than entire population size.

National Crime Victimization Survey (NCVS). Victim survey conducted annually by U.S. Census Bureau; investigates 60,000 households.

National Youth Survey (NYS). An ongoing longitudinal study of delinquent behavior and alcohol and drug use among the American youth population; uses a fairly typical sample of youth ranging in age from 11 to 17. Self-report questionnaires are administered, where youths disclose whether they have committed any status or criminal offenses and whether they have been apprehended for any of these offenses. The study utilizes this sample of youth over successive time periods as a panel.

Necessary conditions. Those factors that must occur if the phenomena of which they are a cause are to occur.

Negative skewness. Distribution of scores where tail of curve tapers off toward the left; represented by a skewness factor of minus ($-$).

Nominal definition. Dictionary definition of various phenomena, where inherent properties of concepts are described; definition is far-removed from numerical expression. Nominal definitions are useful for theory-building; eventually, nominal definitions are operationalized to yield operational definitions.

Nominal level of measurement. Lowest of four measurement levels described by S. S. Stevens. Nominal-level measurement consists of describing variable subclasses of attributes; numerical quantities assigned nominal-level measurement differentiate subclasses from one to another, without any implication that values serve any other purpose.

Nondirectional hypothesis tests. Any statistical verification of a statement's truthfulness, where the direction of difference has not been specified.

Nonparametric procedures; nonparametric statistical tests. Class of statistical tests and measures considered less restrictive compared with parametric procedures; for the most part, these procedures are designed for variables measured according to nominal or ordinal scales. The assumption of a normal distribution is relaxed; smaller samples may be handled easily; these procedures are less powerful compared with parametric procedures.

Nonparticipant observation. Nonparticipant observation is structured observation of others with or without their knowledge, and without actually participating in the behaviors and activities being observed.

Nonprobability samples; nonprobability sampling plans. Elements for these samples are selected in a way that will not permit generalizations to larger populations in a probability theory context.

Nonresponse. The proportion of the sample that does not return questionnaires sent to them by researchers or who refuse to answer interviewer questions.

Normal curve. Bell-shaped line produced for a normal distribution, based upon a mathematical equation; the normal curve is popular in estimation work and statistical decision making; also known as the *bell curve* or *bell-shaped curve*.

Normal distribution. Any distribution of scores which is approximately bell-shaped in appearance and having the features of the unit normal distribution.

Normality. Condition of distribution of scores, where distribution resembles a normal distribution or bell-shaped curve.

Null hypothesis. Any hypothesis that has been created from a research hypothesis; the purpose of null hypotheses is to permit indirect tests of research hypotheses. Such hypotheses are usually, though not always, statements of no difference.

Nuremberg Code. Set of principles specifying conditions under which human subjects can be used in medical and/or social experimentation.

Obedience research. Questionable investigation of the propensity of research subjects to follow orders from research directors, even though such orders are potentially harmful to experimental subjects.

Objectivity. Detached approach to research from an unbiased perspective; nonjudgmental.

Observational research; observational study. Method of data collection seeking to preserve the natural context within which observed behaviors occur.

Observed frequencies. Any actual distribution of frequencies in any $r \times c$ table.

Observation. Method of data collection that involves the visual inspection of research subjects.

Ogive curve. Line drawn from cumulative frequency distributions.

One-shot case study. Intensive examination of a single element or group or social setting at a single point in time; no provisions are made for follow-ups or subsequent observation or testing; a study of a group at one point in time only.

One-tailed test. Directional hypothesis test, where direction of difference is expected and predicted; refers to statistical test of significance where only one "tail" or extreme region of the sampling distribution is used as the critical region.

Open-ended or **open-end items.** Questions asked in interviews or on questionnaires that require respondents to answer questions at length; written replies are requested.

Open-ended or **open-end questionnaires.** Consisting of questions that require short or lengthy written replies by respondents.

Operational definition. Product of operationalization; numerical indicator of attitudinal phenomenon; being able to point at phenomenon measured while enunciating the term, according to George Lundberg.

Operationalization. Process of converting constructs into concepts; creating numerical expressions of nominal definitions; bringing less tangible phenomena into the empirical world.

Ordinal level of measurement. Scale where scores may be ranked or ordered in relation to one another, but where the distances between scores are unknown.

Oversample. Selecting more elements for a sample than are actually desired, anticipating that some nonresponse will occur; a means of obtaining a desired number of elements taking into account some nonresponse or unusable questionnaires.

Panel, panel study. Designated sample that is studied repeatedly over time, and comparisons are made between "panels" or the responses given by these youths within each time frame.

Parallel forms of the same test. A major reliability check is the use of parallel forms of the same test; researchers use parallel forms of the same test by devising two separate measures of the same phenomenon.

Paradigm. Model or scheme that provides a perspective from which to view reality.

Parameter. A characteristic of the population of elements about which we seek information.

Parametric procedures; parametric statistical tests. Class of statistical tests and measures considered the best for data analyses, provided their stringent assumptions are met. A crucial assumption underlying these tests is a normal distribution for the variable measured; such tests normally require that the variables analyzed be measured according to an interval scale; other rigorous assumptions accompany some of these procedures.

Participant observation. Structured observation of social settings of which the observer is a part. This is a popular form of observation, since researchers may find it convenient to describe the settings wherein they work or the groups in which they have membership.

Path analysis. Form of multivariate analysis in which the causal relations among variables are presented in a graphic format.

Pearson's *C*, coefficient of contingency. Used in conjunction with chi square, an index number that reflects the amount of association between two variables measured according to nominal level of measurement. This coefficient cannot achieve 1.00 without a correction factor being applied; correction factor varies according to table size.

Pearson's *r*. Most popular parametric measure of association for two variables, where each variable has been measured according to interval scaling; also assumes linearity, homoscedasticity, bivariate normal distribution, and randomness; has *PRE* interpretation.

Personal computer (PC). Smaller version of mainframe computer that is used for personal projects, including data processing, report writing, data analyses, statistical compilations.

Persons used as their own controls. Method for creating equated groups for experimental purposes; method uses persons over time, through various experimental periods, where different stimuli are introduced. Individual reactions of persons are charted over time to determine experimental effects.

Phi coefficient, ϕ. Measure of association for two variables where each has been measured according to a nominal scale; has *PRE* interpretation.

Pie charts. Type of graphic presentation, such as crime clocks, shaped like pies, to portray proportions of a whole.

Pilot studies. Pretests that are designated as trial runs of questionnaires before audiences similar to those where the final form of the questionnaire is to be administered. Pilot studies are small-scale implementations of the actual studies researchers are prepared to conduct; they enable investigators to detect faults associated with their research instruments and obtain ideas about how best to carry out the final project.

Placebo; placebo effect. Tendency of control groups to react to believed treatment in a positive manner. Often used in biochemical research, the placebo is the introduction of a bland substance with no known properties to affect human behavior, but the placebo induces changes in behavior anyway, since research subjects believe the substance is mind-altering or affects their behavior in some way. A placebo is a "sugar-coated" pill designed to trigger placebo effect.

Plagiarism. Using someone else's work as your own; taking credit for work done by another.

Platykurtic. Flat-appearing distribution of scores; a nonnormal distribution where scores are dispersed widely around central point.

Platykurtosis. Nonnormal condition and curve shape that is flat-appearing; scores in the distribution are dispersed over a wide area, including larger proportions of scores in curve tails than would otherwise be expected under normal curve conditions.

Point estimate. The predicted value of a parameter.

Point estimate hypothesis; hypothesis of point estimation. A hypothesis that forecasts population values and against which sample values are compared.

Point estimation. Process of guessing the population mean and comparing an observed sample mean with it in a statistical test of significance.

Policy analysis. Study of the causes and consequences of governmental mandates and behaviors.

Polygraph tests. Polygraph tests are designed to measure physical responses while the subject is answering questions; the tests are calculated to discriminate between truthful and untruthful responses to questions; not reliable for criminal court use.

Population. Aggregate of elements about which we seek information; the target number of elements from which we will obtain our sample.

Positive skewness. Distribution of scores with tail of curve tapering off toward the right, indicated with a positive skewness factor (+).

Postcard questionnaires. Abbreviated versions of survey instruments confined to a single postcard, which is mailed to designated respondents.

Posttest. A reexamination of study subjects once an experimental treatment has been administered.

Potentates. Very powerful people or those protected by law from researchers, such as children.

Power of tests. Ability of statistical tests to reject false null hypotheses; power of tests is generally increased by increasing Type I or Alpha error (α), by increasing sample size, or by decreasing the standard error of the mean term.

Pragmatic validity. Either concurrent or predictive validity; a form of validity based upon the successfulness of any particular attitudinal measure as a predictor.

***PRE* measure.** Any correlational procedure capable of providing an account of how much error is explained in either of the two variables correlated; proportional-reduction-in-error; amount of variation in one variable by another variable.

Prediction. Attempts by researchers to forecast social and psychological events with a knowledge of certain variables; specifying patterns of behavior in advance of their occurrence, on the basis of criteria.

Predictive validity. Also known as criterion validity, predictive validity is based upon the measured association between what an instrument predicts behavior will be and the subsequent behavior exhibited by an individual or group.

Pretest. Testing study subjects prior to the introduction of an experimental variable. See also Pilot study

Pretest effects; pretest bias. Possible familiarity of experimental subjects with questionnaire administered to them may skew subsequent test results; possible familiarity with research goals and interests of investigators may elicit untrue responses from subjects; pretest bias may result from repeated testing.

Probability. Likelihood that an event will occur.

Probability distribution. Any statistical distribution, such as the t or F or Z distribution, where probability values can be determined; decisions about sample statistics can be made based on comparisons of observed statistical values compared with tabled values for a particular statistic, such as t or F.

Probability sample. Random sample selected in such a way so that each element has an equal and an independent chance of being included.

Probability sampling; probability sampling plan. Drawing a sample in such a way that each element has an equal and independent chance of being included.

Probability theory. Explanatory context in which scientific observations are made when statistical tests are applied; some uncertainty always exists, which is attributable to studying only samples from populations rather than total populations of elements. Over time, our certainty about events and their explanations increases through replication research and additional study.

Probes; probing. Follow-up questions in an interview or questionnaire.

Problem formulation. Selection, identification, and specification of the research topic to be investigated.

Prompts. Symbols that appear on computer monitors and indicate actions to be taken. Users enter letters or other symbols when prompts are displayed; computer functions according to entered information.

Proportional-reduction-in-error (_PRE_). Amount of variation accounted for in one variable by using another as a predictor of it.

Proportionate stratified random sampling. Method of including elements where one or more variables are controlled, such that the sample element characteristics are distributed proportionately similar to the way those same characteristics are distributed in the population.

Proportion. Quantity obtained by dividing a part of the sum by the sum.

Propositions. Statements about the real world that lack the high degree of certainty associated with assumptions; examples of propositions are "Burnout among probation officers may be mitigated or lessened through job enlargement and giving officers greater input in organizational decision making," or "Two-officer patrol units are less susceptible to misconduct and corruption than one-officer patrol units."

Pure research. Investigations undertaken simply for the sake of knowing.

Purist. Researcher who insists that all assumptions underlying statistical tests be satisfied before applying such tests.

Purposive sampling. See Judgmental samples.

Q-sort. Attitudinal scaling procedure in which respondents sort questions on cards into predetermined categories; a way of determining item intensity.

Qualitative data. Any information collected through interviews or observation; nonnumerical information.

Qualitative research. Investigations that do not rely heavily on statistical analyses; participant observation, historical method, and content analysis are examples of qualitative research.

Quantitative data. Any information where numbers have been assigned to variables and variable subclasses and scores have been calculated.

Quantitative research. Investigations that involve heavy use of statistical procedures; statistical manipulations of data considered primary in an effort to discover patterns of behavior.

Quartiles. Dividing points in frequency distributions according to 25 percent designations.

Quasi-experimental design. Experiments where random assignment has not been used to establish equivalent experimental and control groups; such experiments utilize matching, frequency distribution control matching, or persons used as their own control in before-after experiments.

Questionnaire. A self-administered inventory that seeks descriptive information about people and their opinions about things.

Questionnaire length. Actual number of pages or numbers of items contained on a survey instrument.

Quota sampling. Persons selected to ensure the inclusion of elements with particular characteristics.

Random assignment. Method for equating two or more groups by using randomness to assign persons from a larger group to two or more smaller groups; the basis for true experiments or true experimental designs.

Randomness. The primary control in probability sampling plans; elements are selected so that each has an equal and independent chance of being included; no attempt is made to deliberately include or exclude certain elements.

Random numbers. Digits generated by computer that occur in no particular order and with no consistent frequency; digits are not dependent upon the occurrence of other digits.

Random sample. Persons drawn in accordance with probability sampling principles; sample drawn in such a way so that each element has an equal and an independent chance of being included.

Rand Seven-Factor Index. Measure of an offender's potential for dangerousness and recidivism.

Range. Distance over which 100 percent of the scores in a distribution are spread; for ungrouped data, the distance between the upper limit of the largest score and the lower limit of the smallest score; for grouped data, the distance between the upper limit of the interval containing the largest scores and the lower limit of the interval containing the smallest scores.

Ratio level of measurement. Highest scale of measurement where proportional statements can be made about numerical information; 1 is to 2 as 4 is to 8; an absolute zero point exists for ratio scales.

Ratios. Proportions of elements in relation to a common standard, such as 4 to 1 or 2 to 1.

Raw scores. Uncoded actual scores that persons receive on a questionnaire, test, or scale.

Reactivity. Atypical or artificial behavior produced by respondent's awareness of being studied.

Region of rejection. See Critical region.

Regression. Statistical technique designed to predict scores on a dependent variable from a knowledge of scores on one or more independent variables.

Regression line. Slope of line intersection of dependent and independent variable values that have been cross-tabulated.

Related samples. Two or more different samples that share several common characteristics; they cannot be considered independent samples; persons may act as their own controls in before-after experiments.

Relationship. See Association.

Reliability. Property of a measuring instrument that enables researchers to say that whatever is being measured is being measured consistently; the reliability of a measuring instrument is the ability of that instrument to measure consistently the phenomenon it is designed to measure.

Replication; replication research. Conducting a subsequent study based on the general guidelines of a previous study; an attempt to obtain the same results from a different sample by conducting fresh research at a later point in time; repetition of experiments or studies that utilize the same methodology.

Representativeness. The degree to which sample characteristics are similar to the population characteristics and the population from which the sample was drawn.

Reproducible scales. According to Louis Guttman, Guttman scales that may disclose individual item responses based upon one's total test score, with at least 80 percent accuracy.

Research. Investigations, studies, or any systematic investigative efforts designed to increase our knowledge about events and their occurrence.

Research design. Detailed plans that specify how data should be collected and analyzed.

Research hypotheses. Testable tentative statements directly deduced from theory.

Research problem. Any event in need of an explanation; may be criminal activity, recidivism, correctional officer stress and burnout, employee turnover, or any other phenomenon that needs to be explained.

Research process. All activities that pertain to problem formulation and definition; includes developing a theoretical explanation for why problems exist, collecting information that will verify or refute the explanation of problems, analyzing, presenting, and interpreting this information, and drawing tentative conclusions that will either support or refute the theoretical explanation provided.

Research question. Any query for which no immediate answer is apparent; investigations are guided by queries seeking solutions to research problems.

Respondent. A person who provides data for analysis by answering questions in an interview or by completing a questionnaire.

Response rate. The number of persons participating in a survey divided by the original number selected for the sample.

Response set. Answering all questionnaire items by selecting the first answer, or the same answer, regardless of whether it is descriptive or not descriptive of one's attitudes or characteristics; usually indicative of respondent carelessness in taking seriously the study or answering questions truthfully.

Robustness. Ability of a statistical test to yield reliable results, despite certain assumption violations; an example is the robust *F* test for analysis of variance, which, despite violating the homogeneity of variance assumption, yields results similar to those that would have been obtained if the assumption had been satisfied originally.

Rounding; rounding rule. Limiting the number of places in which a numerical value is expressed; for example, we might limit 1.4444555 to 1.4.

Rows and columns; $r \times c$. Number of subclasses on two variables in a cross-tabulated table, represented by $r \times c$.

Salient Factor Score (SFS 81). Parole prediction scheme used to forecast parole success and potential for recidivism.

Sample. A smaller proportion of elements taken from a larger population of them.

Sample representativeness. See Representativeness.

Sample size. Number of persons in one's sample.

Sampling. Method for obtaining smaller proportion of elements from larger population.

Sampling distribution. Array of all possible values a given statistic can assume for samples of a given size taken from a given population size.

Sampling distribution of a statistic. Distribution of all possible statistical values a given statistic may assume when computed for samples of a specified size drawn from a specified population.

Sampling error. The amount of difference between the characteristics of a sample and the characteristics of the population from which it was drawn; some error is always present when the full population is not available; sampling error usually declines as sample size increases.

Sampling fraction. Designated proportion of sample elements considered ideal in relation to population. Sample size is usually considered to be one-tenth of the population as a conventional sampling fraction; this is not an absolute standard, however.

Sampling frame. The actual list of persons in the population from which the sample is derived.

Sampling without replacement. Method of obtaining elements from a population in which elements once drawn cannot be drawn again.

Sampling with replacement. Method of obtaining elements from a population and replacing them in the population before drawing other elements; the possibility exists that some elements may be drawn two or more times under such a sampling condition; an assumption underlying all tests of statistical inference.

Saturation sampling. Selection method of elements from populations, regardless of the sampling method used, where over 90 percent of the population elements are obtained.

Scale. Index designed to measure a variable and how much each person possesses it; a collection of questions or items focused upon a single variable; for example, such a variable might be police professionalism.

Scalogram analysis. See Guttman scaling.

Science; scientific inquiry. Method of acquiring information about events by relying on empirical observations; pursuing questions about events by adhering to objectivity, ethical neutrality, and limitations to empirical phenomena.

Secondary analysis; secondary source analysis. Any type of analysis of secondary sources or any information originally collected for purposes other than their present scientific one.

Seed money. Small sums allocated for pilot studies or small-scale research projects in order to determine the feasibility of undertaking at a later time a more elaborate research enterprise.

Selection bias. Including elements in a sample who have already been screened according to other criteria; affects generalizability and representativeness.

Self-administered questionnaire. Survey instrument requiring respondents to write their responses or to indicate answers that best represent them; respondents complete their own questionnaires.

Self-reports. A data collection method relying on disclosures by respondents of personal behaviors, including deviant or criminal conduct.

Sellin-Wolfgang Index. Procedure for assigning weights to crime seriousness.

Semantic differential. Consists of a series of bipolar characteristics, such as hot-cold, popular-unpopular, witty-dull, cold-warm, sociable-unsociable; the semantic differential is a useful measure of psychological, social, and physical objects to various respondents.

Serendipity. Unusual, surprising, and unanticipated findings or outcomes.

Set response. Respondent tendency to mark first responses to individual items in a questionnaire with fixed-responses; indicative of carelessness or failure to read items; set responses may be detected by a high rate of inconsistency of responses that purportedly measure the same thing.

Shield laws. Statutes that protect researchers from being compelled to reveal their sources of information in court.

Significance level. The probability at which a hypothesis is tested; Type I error, or alpha (α) error; the probability of rejecting H_0 when H_0 is true and should not be rejected.

Sign test. Nonparametric test for the ordinal level of measurement; determines significance of difference in scores between two related samples.

Simple random samples. The most basic probability sampling plans, where elements are selected from a larger population without controlling for inclusion of specific characteristics; such elements have an equal and an independent chance of being included.

Simulation. Game that attempts to emulate key features of reality.

Single samples. One-sample scenario where researchers obtain no more than one sample from the population for subsequent study; also known as one-shot studies, since only one sample is investigated.

Single-variable hypotheses. Any statement containing one variable only, such as "The mean of group 1 is 50."

Skewness. Condition of a curve when scores "bunch up" in one end or tail of the distribution; measured by "three times the mean minus the median, divided by the standard deviation"; has no precise interpretation. Negative skewness shows scores bunching to the right, while positive skewness shows scores bunching up toward the left; tapering tail of the curve determines whether skewness is positive or negative, apart from the calculation for this value.

Snowball sampling. Type of relational analysis, using a sampling technique where those interviewed disclose friendship relations with others who are subsequently interviewed; process continues until social patterns can be identified or charted.

Social desirability. Propensity of respondents to place themselves in a favorable light when being interviewed or questioned.

Social responsibility. Moral integrity and obligation to uphold code of conduct of one's organization or profession.

Somers' *d*. Measure of association between two variables, where each has been measured according to an ordinal scale; has *PRE* interpretation.

Spearman's rho (r_s). Measure of association for two variables measured according to the interval level of measurement; conventionally applied to two ordinal-level variable situations; has *PRE* interpretation.

Split-half technique; split-half reliability method. Designed to correlate one half of the test items with the other half of them; an internal reliability test.

Sponsored research. Any investigation underwritten by an external agency; funded investigations where the funding source is other than the researcher undertaking the research.

SPSS. Statistical Package for the Social Sciences; a multipurpose software program designed for sophisticated analyses of data; includes numerous tests and procedures for significance and correlation.

Spuriousness. An apparent relation between two variables that is subsequently explained by the presence of a third, unknown, variable; a false relationship that can be explained away by other variables.

Spurious relationship. Any association between two variables which may be explained away by introducing a third, more powerful variable in the original two-variable relation.

Standard deviation. Best measure of variability, the standard deviation identifies distances on either side of the mean of a distribution containing consistent proportions of scores; used for inferential purposes; the square root of the variance; the square root of the sum of the squared deviation scores divided by N.

Standard error. Unit of measurement along the horizontal axis of any sampling distribution.

Standard error of a statistic. Standard deviation of the sampling distribution of some statistic.

Standard error of the difference between two means. Denominator term for parametric t test for differences between two sample means; assumes interval level of measurement associated with measured characteristic or variable.

Standard error of the mean ($s_{\bar{x}}$). Standard deviation of the sampling distribution of sample means.

Standard normal distribution. See Unit normal distribution.

Standard score; standard value. Z scores; scores along the horizontal axis of the unit normal distribution; scores cut off consistent proportions of curve area.

Statistic. Characteristic of a sample of elements; a procedure or measure for analyzing sample characteristics and making a decision about them.

Statistical analysis. Application of significance tests to collected data; determining the significance of one's findings through quantitative methods.

Statistical hypothesis. Symbolic expression of research and null hypotheses.

Statistical inference. See Inference.

Statistical significance. Probability associated with conducting a test of the relation between two variables or the difference between two or more groups on some measured characteristic; arises from the magnitude of observed values, which are in part a function of sample size and standard error.

Statistical significance of association. Significance test applied to correlation coefficients to determine their significant departure from zero (0).

Statistics. Field of study; refers to numerical evidence that has been compiled, such as the "Vital Statistics" compiled by the U.S. Bureau of the Census; a collection of tests and techniques used to describe and make decisions and inferences about collected research data.

Stratification. Grouping of persons into homogenous aggregates before sampling from the population.

Stratified random sampling plans. Any means of drawing elements where control is exercised over the inclusion of persons with specific characteristics (such as year in school or type of prior offense) and where elements are selected in a way that each element has an equal and an independent chance of being included.

Stratified samples. Elements distributed either proportionately or disproportionately according to one or more traits or characteristics.

Stratifying. See Stratification.

Strength of association. Arbitrary interpretation of correlation coefficient in terms of its magnitude; no or low association would be 0 to $\pm$ .25, whereas strong association would be any observed correlation coefficient in excess of $\pm$ .75.

Structured interviews. Consist of a predetermined list of fixed-response questions or items.

Subclass. Any subdivision of a variable.

Subjects. Any person included in an experiment or study.

Subpopulation. Smaller population within a larger population.

Subsamples. Different samples of elements that may be created from a single, larger sample.

Substantive implications. Research results that have practical applications.

Sufficient conditions. Factors that are always followed by the phenomena of which they are a cause.

Survey design. Specifications of procedures for gathering information about a large number of people by collecting information from a smaller proportion of them.

Survey research. Method of gathering information about a large number of people by interviewing a few of them.

Symmetric and asymmetric *PRE* interpretations. Certain measures of association have asymmetric *PRE* interpretation, where it makes a difference whether one variable is used as independent and the other dependent. Most measures of association with *PRE* interpretations have symmetric *PRE* interpretations only; this means that regardless of which variable is used as the independent one, the coefficient yielded is the same in both situations.

Systematic sampling. Technique for including elements where elements are selected according to their location in an ordered list; researchers select every nth person from list. Considered a random sampling plan by some investigators.

Table of random numbers. Method of drawing elements from numbers that have been randomly generated by computer. Digits in this type of table occur in no particular order, and no digit occurs any more frequently than any other digit; the systematic derivation of a sample from a table of random numbers is, by definition, a random sample.

Tabular presentation. Any portrayal of information in a cross-tabulated fashion, with one or more rows and one or more columns.

Target population. Aggregate of persons about which one seeks information.

Telephone interview. Any questioning of respondents by telephone; dialing respondents and asking them questions by telephone instead of face-to-face.

10–90 range or **interdecile range.** Distance over which the central 80 percent of the scores in a distribution are spread.

Testing effect. Pretest effect or bias introduced, resulting from research subjects having been pretested.

Test-retest. External reliability check based upon comparison of the attitudinal measure's results over two separate time periods. If persons receive same or similar scores on same attitudinal measure over two different time periods, without the intervention of an experimental stimulus of any kind, then the measure possesses reliability on the basis of test-retest.

Tests of significance. A broad class of tests designed to reveal statistical differences between observed statistics and predicted parameters; any procedure yielding a probability that significance exists or does not exist between two or more groups according to some measured characteristic.

Tests of significance of difference. Any procedure designed to determine the statistical differentiation between two or more samples according to some measured characteristic.

Theoretical implications. Research results where there may or may not be immediate application; contribution is largely designed to explain a theory and how it enhances our understanding of events.

Theory. Integrated body of propositions, assumptions, and definitions that are related in ways that explain and predict relationships between two or more variables.

Theta, coefficient of differentiation (θ). Measure of association when researcher has one variable measured according to nominal scale and another variable measured according to an ordinal scale; has *PRE* interpretation.

Thurstone scaling. Method of attitudinal scaling, devised by L. L. Thurstone, based upon judges' ratings and averages of item weights. Items are sorted into 7, 9, or 11 categories by judges; choices of responses by respondents are weighted in advance; average of items selected purportedly discloses respondent position on attitudinal intensity continuum.

Time-series design. Measurement of a single variable at successive points in time.

Treatment variables. Known as experimental variables; variables introduced to elicit predictable effects in experiments.

Trend information. Type of longitudinal research where a given characteristic of some population is monitored over time.

Triangulation. Use of two or more data-gathering strategies when investigating the same sample of elements or a common research problem; intent of triangulation is to verify accuracy of reported information disclosed by different data-collection techniques.

True experiment. Procedure in which randomization, pretests and posttests, and experimental and control groups are used.

True range. Actual distance over which 100 percent of all scores in a distribution are dispersed.

Tschuprow's *T*. Measure of association between two variables, where each has been measured according to a nominal scale; lacks *PRE* interpretation.

t **test.** Parametric test for determining difference between a hypothesized population mean and an observed sample mean; parametric test for determining difference between two sample means. The inference is made that if two sample means differ, the population means of which they are estimates also differ. Appropriate for smaller sample size applications.

Tuskegee Syphilis Study. Notorious medical experiment conducted by U.S. Public Health Service at Tuskegee Institute between 1932 and 1970, involving 1,000 black research volunteers who were diagnosed with syphilis. Some volunteers received treatment while others did not receive treatment, in order to study the progressiveness of syphilis; considered unethical research and widely condemned for insensitivity to the human subjects.

Two- and *k*-sample situations. Research scenarios where investigators study two or more samples simultaneously; samples may be related or independent.

Two-variable hypotheses. Any statements containing two factors or variables.

2 × 2 tables. Most common tabular form, where the table is constructed with two rows and two columns.

Two-tailed tests. Hypothesis tests involving two extreme areas of a sampling distribution of some statistic; a nondirectional hypothesis test, where simple differences between values are tested without any expectation of directional differences.

Type I error (α). Probability of rejecting a true null hypothesis; also alpha error (α) and the level of significance at which hypotheses are tested.

Type II error (β). Probability of failing to reject a false null hypothesis.

Typology. Classification of observations in terms of their attributes on two or more variables.

Unbiased estimate. Any statistic having a sampling distribution with a mean equal to the parameter the statistic is designed to estimate.

Unethical conduct. Any behavioral departure from expected and articulated codes of a profession or association that would raise moral issues.

Ungrouped data. Tabular arrangement of scores according to their actual frequency of occurrence.

Unidimensionality. Property of an attitudinal measuring instrument that means the instrument measures only one dimension of the phenomenon. See also Guttman scaling.

Unidimensional scale. In the case of attitude statements, this means that a person with a more favorable attitude score than another person must also be just as favorable or more favorable in his response to every statement in the set than the other person. When responses to a set of attitude statements meet this requirement, the set of statements is said to constitute a unidimensional scale.

Uniform Crime Reports (*UCR*). Annual FBI publication of official statistics of reported crime by law enforcement agencies.

Unit normal distribution; normal distribution; or standard normal distribution. Theoretically derived distribution; bell-shaped curve; characteristics include identical mean, mode, and median; parameters are a $\mu = 0$ and $\sigma = 1$; curve has asymptotic property, where ends of curve extend toward baseline of horizontal axis but never touch it; used in inferential work and statistical decision making.

Universe of items. Abstract and theoretical population of items from which attitudinal items are selected and used for test purposes by researchers; an infinite population of items.

Unobtrusive measures. Ways of studying groups so that they remain unaware of being studied, thus eliminating reactivity.

Unstructured interviews. Loosely constructed interview guides with open-ended questions; most flexible interview tool, where researchers may probe extensively in different directions, depending upon responses given from subjects interviewed.

Upper and **lower limits of intervals.** Theoretical upper-most and lowest points in each interval, showing the actual distance over which the interval is spread.

Validity. The property of a measuring instrument that enables researchers to say that they are measuring whatever it is they say they are measuring.

Values. Standards of acceptability we acquire from our peers or from society in general; cause us to prioritize or to allocate greater importance to some things and less importance to others.

Variable subclasses. Any number of subdivisions on a variable.

Variables. Any phenomena, quantities, factors, or attributes that can assume more than one value or subclass.

Variance, s^2. Square of the standard deviation.

Variation. Amount of dispersion among scores; how much scores differ from one another.

Verification. Confirmation of the accuracy of one's findings.

Weighted mean. Giving greater or lesser weight to larger or smaller sample sizes when computing a grand mean or mean of means; taking into account variations in sample sizes when calculating the overall mean of several means.

Weighting. Multiplying individual sample means by their respective sample sizes, if sample sizes differ; also refers to assigning different values to item responses that can be gradated from high to low (for example, this value system: Strongly Agree = 1, Agree = 2, Strongly Disagree = 6).

Wilcoxon's theta. See Theta, the coefficient of differentiation.

Within-group variation. In F test for analysis of variance, any dispersion of scores among each group.

Working hypotheses. Testable statements derived from theory that are subsequently operationalized.

Z score; Z value. See Standard score, Standard value.

Z test. Identical to the t test in functions; uses the normal distribution for determining significance of observed Z values; appropriate for larger sample size applications.

References

Abbott, Jack Henry (1981). *In the Belly of the Beast*. New York: Random House.

ACJS Today (1998). "Draft #7: Academy of Criminal Justice Sciences Code of Ethics." *ACJS Today* **17:**14–21.

Adams, Reed and Ron Vogel (1986). "Perceptional Foundations of Deterrence: The Case of Prostitution." *American Journal of Criminal Justice* **10:**131–139.

American Correctional Association (1993). *The State of Corrections*. Laurel, MD: American Correctional Association.

Amnesty International (1994). *Conditions for Death Row Prisoners in H-Unit Oklahoma State Penitentiary*. New York: Amnesty International.

Anderson, Patrick R. and L. Thomas Winfree Jr. (1987). *Expert Witnesses: Criminologists in the Courtroom*. Albany, NY: State University of New York Press.

Andrews, D. A. (1990). "Does Correctional Treatment Work: A Clinically Relevant and Psychologically Informed Meta-Analysis." *Criminology* **28:**369–404.

Anson, Richard H. (1983). "Inmate Ethnicity and the Suicide Connection: A Note on Aggregate Trends." *The Prison Journal* **12:**191–200.

Backstrom, Charles H. and Gerald D. Hursh (1963). *Survey Research*. Evanston, IL: Northwestern University Press.

Bahn, Charles and James R. Davis (1991). "Social Psychological Effects of the Status of Probationers." *Federal Probation* **55:**17–25.

Bailey, Kenneth D. (1987). *Methods of Social Research* (3e). New York: Macmillan.

Ball, Richard A. and Robert J. Lilly (1985). "Home Incarceration: An International Alternative to Institutional Incarceration." *International Journal of Comparative and Applied Research* **9:**85–97.

Barker, Tom and David Carter (1990). " 'Fluffing Up the Evidence and Covering Your Ass': Some Conceptual Notes on Police Lying." *Deviant Behavior* **11:**61–73.

Beck, Robert J. (1997). "Communications in a Teen Court: Implications for Probation." *Federal Probation* **61:**40–48.

Becker, Gary (1968). "Crime and Punishment: An Economic Approach." *Journal of Political Economy* **78:**169-217.

Bernstein, Ilene N., William R. Kelly, and Patricia A. Doyle (1977). "Societal Reaction to Deviants: The Case of Criminal Defendants." *American Sociological Review* **42:**743-755.

Bersani, Carl, Huey-Tsyh Chen, and Robert Denton (1988). "Spouse Abusers and Court Mandated Treatment." *Journal of Crime and Justice* **11:**43-60.

Black, James A. and Dean J. Champion (1976). *Methods and Issues of Social Research.* New York: John Wiley.

Blalock, Hubert M. Jr. (1972). *Social Statistics.* New York: McGraw-Hill.

Bonjean, Charles M., Richard J. Hill, and S. Dale McLemore (1967). *Sociological Measurement: An Inventory of Scales and Indices.* San Francisco: Chandler.

Bonta, James, Moira Law, and Karl Hanson (1998). "The Prediction of Criminal and Violent Recidivism Among Mentally Disordered Offenders: A Meta-Analysis." *Psychological Bulletin* **123:**123-142.

Boone, Harry N. Jr. (1994). "Recommended Outcome Measures for Program Evaluation: APPAs Board of Directors Survey Results." *APPA Perspectives* **18:**19-20.

Bowery, Margaret (1997). *Private Prisons in New South Wales.* Sydney, Australia: New South Wales Department of Corrective Services.

Brandt, A. M. (1978). "Racism, Research, and the Tuskegee Syphilis Study." *Hastings Center Report* **7:**15-21.

Brannigan, Augustine, J. C. Levy, and James C. Wilkins (1985). *The Preparation of Witnesses and Pretrial Construction of Testimony.* Calgary, Alberta: Research Unit for Socio-Legal Studies.

Breci, Michael G. (1997). "Female Officers on Patrol: Public Perceptions in the 1990s." *Journal of Crime and Justice* **20:**153-165.

Brooks, Alexander D. (1996). "Megan's Law: Constitutionality and Policy." *Criminal Justice Ethics* **15:**56-66.

Burlington, Bill (1991). "Involuntary Treatment: When Can Mentally Ill Inmates Be Medicated Against Their Will?" *Federal Prisons Journal* **2:**25-29.

Chamlin, Mitchell B. and Steven G. Brandl (1996). "A Quantitative Analysis of Vagrancy Arrests in Milwaukee, 1930-1972." *Journal of Crime and Justice* **19:**23-40.

Champion, Dean J. (1996). *Probation, Parole, and Community Corrections* (2e). Upper Saddle River, NJ: Prentice-Hall.

Champion, Dean J. (1988). "Private Counsels and Public Defenders: A Look at Weak Cases, Prior Records, and Leniency in Plea Bargaining." *Journal of Criminal Justice* **17:**253-263.

Champion, Dean J. (1981). *Basic Statistics for Social Research* (2e). New York: Macmillan.

Champion, Dean J. and Alan M. Sear (1969). "Questionnaire Response Rate: A Methodological Analysis." *Social Forces* **47:**335-339.

Charles, Michael T. (1989). "Research Note: Juveniles on Electronic Monitoring." *Journal of Contemporary Criminal Justice* **5:**165-172.

Cohen, Morris R. and Ernest Nagel (1934). *An Introduction to Logic and the Scientific Method.* New York: Harcourt Brace.

Coleman, James S. (1959). "Relational Analysis: The Study of Social Organizations with Survey Methods." *Human Organization* **17:**28-36.

Coleman, James S., E. Katz, and H. M. Menzel (1957). "Diffusion of Innovation among Physicians." *Sociometry* **20:**253-270.

Colley, Lori, Robert G. Culbertson, and Edward J. Latessa (1986). "Juvenile Probation Officers: A Job Analysis." *Juvenile and Family Court Journal* **38:**1-12.

Conley, J. A. (ed.) (1979). *Theory and Research in Criminal Justice: Current Perspectives.* Cincinnati, OH: Anderson.

Coston, Charisse T. M. and Lee E. Ross (1996). "Criminal Victimization of Prostitutes: Empirical Support for the Lifestyle/Exposure Model." *Journal of Crime and Justice* **19:**53-70.

Crank, John P. et al. (1986). "Cynicism Among Police Chiefs." *Justice Quarterly* **3:**343-352.

Cretney, Antonia and Gwynn Davis (1997). "Prosecuting Domestic Assault: Victims Failing Courts, or Courts Failing Victims?" *Howard Journal* **36:**146-157.

Crouch, Ben M. and James W. Marquart (1990). "Resolving the Paradox of Reform: Litigation, Prisoner Violence, and Perception of Risk." *Justice Quarterly* **7**:104-123.

Dembo, Richard, Kimberly Pacheco, and James Schmeidler (1997). "Drug Use and Delinquent Behavior Among High Risk Youths." Journal of Child and Adolescent Substance Abuse **6**:1-25.

Denzin, Norman K. (1989). *The Research Act: A Theoretical Introduction to Sociological Methodologies* (3e). Upper Saddle River, NJ: Prentice-Hall.

Dicks, Shirley (1991). *Victims of Crime and Punishment: Interviews with Victims, Convicts, Their Families, and Support Groups.* Jefferson, NC: McFarland.

DiRenzo, Gordon J. (ed.) (1966). *Concepts, Theory, and Explanation in the Behavioral Sciences.* New York: Random House.

Dixon, David (1997). "Ethics, Law, and Criminological Research." *Australian and New Zealand Journal of Criminology* **30**:211-216.

Edwards, A. L. (1957). *The Social Desirability Variable in Personality Assessment.* New York: Dryden.

Ehrlich, I. (1975). "The Deterrent Effect of Capital Punishment: A Question of Life and Death." *American Economic Review* **65**:397-417.

Elliott, Delbert S. (1994). "1993 Presidential Address: Serious Violent Offenders: Onset, Developmental Course, and Termination." *Criminology* **32**:1-21.

Elliott, Delbert S., Franklyn W. Dunford, and David Huizinga (1987). "The Identification and Prediction of Career Offenders Utilizing Self-Reported and Official Data." In *Prediction of Criminal Behavior,* John D. Burchard and Sara Burchard (eds.). Newbury Park, CA: Sage.

Elliston, Frederick A. and Jane van Schaick (1984). *Legal Ethics: An Annotated Bibliography and Resource Guide.* Littleton, CO: Fred B. Rothman.

Empey, Lamar T. and Maynard Erickson (1972). *The Provo Experiment: Evaluation of Community Control of Delinquency.* Lexington, MA: Lexington Press.

Esbensen, Finn-Aage (1991). "Ethical Considerations in Criminal Justice Research." *American Journal of Police* **10**:87-104.

Esbensen, Finn-Aage and L. Thomas Winfree (1998). "Race and Gender Differences Between Gang and Nongang Youths: Results from a Multisite Survey." *Justice Quarterly* **15**:505-526.

Fagan, Jeffrey, Martin Forst, and T. Scott Vivona (1987). "Racial Determinants of the Judicial Transfer Decision: Prosecuting Violent Youth in Criminal Court." *Crime and Delinquency* **33**:259-286.

Farkas, Mary Ann (1997). "The Normative Code Among Correctional Officers: An Exploration of Components and Functions." *Journal of Crime and Justice* **20**:25-40.

Faulkner, Paula L. and William R. Faulkner (1997). "Effects of Organizational Change on Inmate Status and the Inmate Code of Conduct." *Journal of Crime and Justice* **20**:25-38.

Feierman, Jay R. (ed.) (1990). *Pedophilia: Biosocial Dimensions.* New York: Springer-Verlag.

Fisher, Bonnie S. et al. (1998). "Crime in the Ivory Tower: The Level and Sources of Student Victimization." *Criminology* **36**:671-710.

Fitzgerald, Jack D. and Steven M. Cox (1987). *Research Methods in Criminal Justice.* Chicago: Nelson-Hall.

Frank, Mark G. et al. (1995). "Individual Perspectives on Police Ethics." *Ethics and Policing* **125**:1-27.

Frazier, Charles E. and Donna M. Bishop (1990). "Obstacles to Reform in Juvenile Corrections: A Case Study." *Journal of Contemporary Criminal Justice* **6**:157-166.

Fyfe, James J., David A. Klinger, and Jeanne Flavin (1997). "Differential Police Treatment of Male-On-Female Spousal Violence." *Criminology* **35**:455-473.

Garofalo, James (1977). *Local Victim Surveys: A Review of the Issues.* Washington, DC: U.S. National Criminal Justice Information and Statistics Service.

Gaskins, Donald "Pee-Wee" and Wilton Earle (1992). *Final Truth: The Autobiography of Mass Murderer/Serial Killer.* Atlanta, GA: ADEPT.

Gendreau, Paul, Claire E. Goggin, and Moira A. Law (1997). "Predicting Prison Misconduct." *Criminal Justice and Behavior* **24**:414-431.

Gendreau, Paul, Tracy Little, and Claire Goggin (1996). "A Meta-Analysis of the Predictors of Adult Offender Recidivism: What Works?" *Criminology* **34**:575-607.

Glaser, Barney and Anselm Strauss (1967). *The Discovery of Grounded Theory: Strategies for Qualitative Research*. Chicago: Aldine.

Glass, Gene V. (1976). "Primary, Secondary and Meta-Analysis." *Educational Researcher* **5**:3-8.

Goldhammer, Gary E. (1994). *Dead End*. Brunswick, ME: Biddle.

Goode, William J. and Paul K. Hatt (1952). *Methods in Social Research*. New York: McGraw-Hill.

Grasmick, Harold G., Robert J. Bursik Jr., and John K. Cochran (1991). "'Render Unto Caesar What Is Caesar's: Religiosity and Taxpayer's Inclinations to Cheat." *Sociological Quarterly* **32**:251-266.

Greenwood, Peter W. and Allan Abrahamse (1982). *Selective Incapacitation*. Santa Monica, CA: Rand Corporation.

Gunderson, D. F. (1987). "Credibility and the Police Uniform." *Journal of Police Science and Administration* **15**:192-195.

Guralnik, David B. (1972). *Webster's New World Dictionary of the American Language*. New York: World.

Guttman, Lous (1944). "A Basis for Scaling Qualitative Data." *American Sociological Review* **9**:139-150.

Hafley, Sandra Riggs and Richard Tewksbury (1996). "Reefer Madness in Bluegrass County: Community Structure and Roles in the Rural Kentucky Marijuana Industry." *Journal of Crime and Justice* **19**:75-94.

Hagan, Michael and Robert P. King (1992). "Recidivism Rates of Youth Completing an Intensive Treatment Program in a Juvenile Correctional Facility." *International Journal of Offender Therapy and Comparative Criminology* **36**:349-358.

Hammett, Theodore M. and Nancy Neveloff Dubler (1990). "Clinical and Epidemiologic Research on HIV Infection and AIDS Among Correctional Inmates: Regulations, Ethics, and Procedures." *Evaluation Review* **14**:482-501.

Hanke, Penelope J. (1996). "Putting School Crime into Perspective: Self-Reported School Victimizations of High School Seniors." *Journal of Criminal Justice* **24**:207-226.

Hashimoto, Henichi et al. (1968). "A Study of the Treatment Effect on Juveniles in Reform and Training Schools." *Bulletin of the Criminological Research Department* **6**:21-23.

Hassine, Victor (1996). *Life Without Parole: Living in Prison Today*. Los Angeles: Roxbury Press.

Helfgott, Jacqueline (1997). "Ex-Offender Needs versus Community Opportunity in Seattle, Washington." *Federal Probation* **61**:12-24.

Henderson, Joel H. and Ronald L. Boostrom (1989). "Criminal Justice Theory: Anarchy Reigns." *Journal of Contemporary Criminal Justice* **5**:29-39.

Hirschi, Travis and Hanan C. Selvin (1967). *Delinquency Research: An Appraisal of Analytic Methods*. New York: Free Press.

Hoffman, Peter B. and James L. Beck (1985). "Recidivism Among Released Federal Prisoners: Salient Factor Score and Five-Year Follow-Up." *Criminal Justice and Behavior* **12**:501-507.

Holmes, Malcolm D. and William A. Taggart (1990). "A Comparative Analysis of Research Methods in Criminology and Criminal Justice Journals." *Justice Quarterly* **7**:421-437.

Humphreys, Laud (1970). *The Tearoom Trade*. Chicago: Aldine.

Hyman, Herbert (1955). *Survey Design and Analysis*. Glencoe, IL: Free Press.

Iannuzzi, Joseph "Joe-Dogs" (1993). *Joe Dogs: The Life and Crimes of a Mobster*. New York: Simon & Schuster.

Johnson, Richard E. (1986). "Family Structure and Delinquency: General Patterns and Gender Differences." *Criminology* **24**:65-84.

Jones, Mark (1996). "Do Boot Camp Graduates Make Better Probationers?" *Journal of Crime and Justice* **19**:1-14.

Josephson, Trevor K. and Wally R. Unruh (1994). "A Q-Sort Assessment of Personality and Implications for Treatment in Child Welfare and Young Offender Settings." *Residential Treatment for Children and Youth* **12**:73-84.

Jurgens, Ralf and Norbert Gilmore (1994). "Divulging of Prison Medical Records: Judicial and Legal Analysis." *Criminology* **27**:127-163.

Kaci, Judy and Shira Tarrant (1988). "Attitudes of Prosecutors and Probation Departments Toward Diversion in Domestic Violence Cases in California." *Journal of Contemporary Criminal Justice* **4**:187-200.

Kakar, Suman (1998). "Delinquency Prevention Through Family and Neighborhood Empowerment." *Studies on Crime and Prevention* **7**:107-125.

Kakar, Suman (1998). "Youth Gangs and Their Families: Effect of Gang Membership on Family's Subjective Well-Being." *Journal of Crime and Justice* **21**:157-172.

Kaplan, Meg S. (1990). "The Impact of Parolee's Perception of Confidentiality of Their Self-Reported Sex Crimes." *Annals of Sex Research* **3**:293-303.

Kelling, George L. et al. (1974). *The Kansas City Preventive Patrol Experiment: A Summary Report and a Technical Report.* Washington, DC: The Police Foundation.

Kenney, Dennis J. (1986). "Crime on the Subways: Measuring the Effectiveness of the Guardian Angels." *Justice Quarterly* **3**:481-496.

Kerlinger, Fred (1965). *Foundations of Behavioral Research.* New York: Holt, Rinehart, and Winston.

Klofas, John and Ralph Weisheit (1987). "Guilty But Mentally Ill: Reform of the Insanity Defense in Illinois." *Justice Quarterly* **4**:39-50.

Knight, Kevin and Matthew L. Hiller (1997). "Community-Based Substance Abuse Treatment: A 1-Year Outcome Evaluation of the Dallas County Judicial Treatment Center." *Federal Probation* **61**:61-68.

Kowalski, Gregory S., Alan J. Shields, and Deborah C. Wilson (1985). "The Female Murderer: Alabama 1929-1971." *American Journal of Criminal Justice* **10**:75-104.

Krisberg, Barry et al. (1987). "The Incarceration of Minority Youth." *Crime and Delinquency* **33**:173-205.

LaPiere, Richard T. (1934). "Attitudes vs. Actions." *Social Forces* **14**:230-237.

Larzelere, Robert E. and Gerald R. Patterson (1990). "Parental Management: Mediator of the Effect of Socioeconomic Status on Early Delinquency." *Criminology* **28**:301-324.

Launay, Gilles (1994). "The Phallometric Assessment of Sex Offenders: Some Professional and Research Issues." *Criminal Behavior and Mental Health* **4**:48-70.

Lemert, Edwin M. (1951). *Social Pathology.* New York: McGraw-Hill.

Levine, Irene (ed.) (1996). "Preventing Violence Among Youth: Introduction." *American Journal of Orthopsychiatry* **66**:320-389.

Likert, Rensis (1932). "A Technique to Measure Attitudes." *Archives of Psychology* **21**, No. 40.

Lucas, Wayne L. (1987). "Staff Perceptions of Volunteers in a Correctional Program." *Journal of Crime and Justice* **10**:63-98.

MacKenzie, Doris Layton and James E. Shaw (1990). "Inmate Adjustment and Change During Shock Incarceration: The Impact of Correctional Boot Camp Programs." *Justice Quarterly* **3**:15-32.

Magnusson, David (1967). *Test Theory.* Reading, MA: Addison-Wesley.

Maguire, Kathleen and Ann L. Pastore (1998). *The Sourcebook of Criminal Justice Statistics.* Albany, NY: The Hindelang Criminal Justice Research Center.

Markey, Vicki K., Sunny Ariessohn, and Margaret Mudd (1997). "Outcome-Based Supervision for Pregnant, Substance-Abusing Offenders." *APPA Perspectives* **21**:21-23.

Marquart, James (1986). "Doing Research in Prison: The Strengths and Weaknesses of Full Participation as a Guard." *Justice Quarterly* **3**:15-32.

Matthews, Timothy, Harry N. Boone, Jr., and Vernon Fogg (1994). "Evaluation of Probation and Parole Programs: The Development of Alternative Outcome Measures." *APPA Perspectives* **18**:10-12.

Maxfield, Michael G. and Terry L. Baumer (1992). "Pretrial Home Detention with Electronic Monitoring: A Nonexperimental Salvage Evaluation." *Evaluation Review* **16**:315-332.

McCamey, William P. and Gayle Tronvig Carper (1998). "Social Skills and Police: An Initial Study." *Journal of Crime and Justice* **21**:95-102.

McCulloch, Sue (1993). "Social Skills and Human Relationships: Training for Sex Offenders." *Australian and New Zealand Journal of Criminology* **26**:47-58.

McIntyre, Thomas J. (1986). "The Freedom of Information Act." *International Criminal Police Review* **39**:58–64.

McShane, Marilyn D. (1987). "Immigration Processing and the Alien Inmate: Constructing a Conflict Perspective." *Journal of Crime and Justice* **10**:171–194.

Meadows, Robert J. and Lawrence C. Trostle (1988). "A Study of Police Misconduct and Litigation: Findings and Implications." *Journal of Contemporary Criminal Justice* **4**:77–92.

Mednick, S. A. and J. Volavka (1980). "Biology and Crime." In *Crime and Justice: An Annual Review of Research,* N. Morris and M. Tonry (eds.). Chicago: University of Chicago Press.

Merton, Robert K. (1957). *Social Theory and Social Structure.* New York: Free Press.

Merton, Robert K., M. Fiske, and Patricia L. Kendall (1956). *The Focused Interview.* New York: Free Press.

Milgram, Stanley (1974). *Obedience to Authority: An Experimental View.* New York: Harper.

Mill, John Stuart (1930). *A System of Logic.* New York: Longmans.

Miller, Delbert C. (1991). *Handbook of Research Design and Social Measurement.* New York: David McKay.

Miller, J. L. and Glenna Simons (1997). "A Case of Everyday Justice: Free Press v. Fair Trial in A Burglary Case." *Journal of Crime and Justice* **20**:1–22.

Minnesota Corrections Department (1972). *A Follow-Up Study of Boys Participating in the Positive Peer Culture Program at the Minnesota State Training School for Boys: An Analysis of 242 Boys Released During 1969.* Minneapolis, MN: Minnesota Corrections Department Research Information and Data Systems Division.

Minor, Kevin (1988). *An Evaluation of An Intervention Program for Juvenile Probationers.* Ann Arbor, MI: University Microfilms International.

Morn, F. T. (1980). *Academic Disciplines and Debates.* Washington, DC: Joint Commission on Criminology and Criminal Justice Education Standards.

National Archive of Criminal Justice Data (1990). *Data Available from the National Archive of Criminal Justice Data.* Ann Arbor, MI: The Inter-University Consortium for Political and Social Research.

National Association of Attorneys General Committee on the Office of Attorney General (1976). *Privacy: Personal Data and the Law.* Raleigh, NC: National Association of Attorneys General.

National Council on Crime and Delinquency (1979). *Information Needs in Juvenile Justice.* Hackensack, NJ: National Council on Crime and Delinquency.

National Institute of Justice (1997). *Policing Research and Evaluation: Fiscal Year 1997.* Washington, DC: U.S. Department of Justice.

Neidig, Peter H., Harold E. Russell, and Albert F. Seng (1992). "Interspousal Aggression in Law Enforcement Families: A Preliminary Investigation." *Police Studies* **15**:30–38.

Norusis, Jarija (1993). *SPSS for Windows: Base System User's Guide.* Chicago: SPSS.

Osgood, Charles (1965). "Cross Cultural Comparability in Attitude Measurment via Multilingual Semantic Differentials." In *Current Studies in Psychology*, I. D. Steiner and M. Fishbein (eds.). New York: Holt, Rinehart, and Winston.

Peatman, John G. (1963). *Introduction to Applied Statistics.* New York: Harper & Row.

Pettus, Ann Burnett (1986). "An Investigation of Jury Decision Making Based on Posttrial Interviews." Ann Arbor, MI: University Microfilms International.

Porterfield, Austin L. (1943). "Delinquency and Its Outcome in Court and College." *American Journal of Sociology* **49**:199–208.

Prenzler, Tim (1994). *Attitudes to Police Gratuities.* Brisbane, Australia: Griffith University.

Quillen, Jim (1991). *Alcatraz from Inside: The Hard Years, 1942–1952.* San Francisco: Golden Gate National Park Association.

Rachal, J. Valley et al. (1975). *A National Study of Adolescent Drinking Behavior, Attitudes, and Correlates.* Research Triangle Park, NC: Research Triangle Institute.

Regoli, Robert M. et al. (1987). "Police Professionalism and Cynicism Reconsidered: An Assessment of Measurement Issues." *Justice Quarterly* **4**:257–286.

Riedel, Marc and Tammy A. Rinehart (1996). "Murder Clearances and Missing Data." *Journal of Crime and Justice* **19**:83–102.

Rose, Arnold M. (1965). *Sociology: The Study of Human Relations.* New York: Alfred A. Knopf.

Rosen, Karen Hanula (1992). "The Process of Coping with Dating Violence: A Qualitative Study." Ann Arbor, MI: University Microfilms International.

Rosenblatt, Jennifer A. and Michael J. Furlong (1997). "Assessing the Reliability and Validity of Student Self-Reports of Campus Violence." *Journal of Youth and Adolescence* **26**:187-202.

Rouse, J. J. (1985). "Relationship Between Police Presence and Crime Deterrence." *Police Journal* **58**:118-131.

Sampson, Robert J. (1986). "Crime in Cities: The Effects of Formal and Informal Social Control." In *Communities and Crime,* Albert J. Reiss, Jr. and Michael Tonry (eds.). Chicago: University of Chicago Press.

Schroeder, Kathleen (1983). "A Recommendation to the FDA Concerning Drug Research on Prisoners." *Southern California Law Review* **56**: 969-1000.

Sellin, Thorsten and Marvin Wolfgang (1966). *The Measurement of Delinquency.* New York: John Wiley.

Selltiz, Claire, S. W. Cook, and L. S. Wrightsman (1976). *Research Methods in Social Relations* (3e). New York: Holt, Rinehart, and Winston.

Selltiz, Claire et al. (1959). *Research Methods in Social Relations.* New York: Holt, Rinehart, and Winston.

Seng, Mangus (1996). "Theft on Campus: An Analysis of Larceny-Theft at an Urban University." *Journal of Crime and Justice* **19**:33-44.

Shah, Saleem A. and Loren Roth (1974). "Biological and Psychophysiological Factors in Criminology." In *Handbook of Criminology*, Daniel Glaser (ed.). Chicago: Rand McNally.

Shockley, Carol (1988). "The Federal Presentence Investigation Report: Postsentence Disclosure Under the Freedom of Information Act." *Administrative Law Review* **40**:79-119.

Short, James F. Jr. and F. Ivan Nye (1958). "Extent of Unrecorded Juvenile Delinquency: Tentative Conclusions." *Journal of Criminal Law and Police Science* **49**:296-302.

Siegel, Judith (1985). "The Measurement of Anger as a Multidimensional Construct." In *Anger and Hostility in Cardiovascular and Behavior Disorders*, M. Chesney and R. Rosenman (eds.). New York: Hemisphere.

Siegel, Sidney M. (1956). *Nonparametric Statistics for the Behavioral Sciences.* New York: McGraw-Hill.

Silverman, Mitchell and Manual Vega (1988). "Reactions of Prisoners to Stress as a Function of Personality and Demographic Variables." *International Journal of Offender Therapy and Comparative Criminology* **34**:187-196.

Simon, Leonore M.J. (1996). "The Effect of the Victim-Offender Relationship on the Sentence Length of Violent Offenders." *Journal of Crime and Justice* **19**:129-148.

Smith, Carolyn A. and Marvin D. Krohn (1991). *Delinquency and Family Life: The Role of Ethnicity.* Hindelang Criminal Justice Research Center.

Smith, R. L. and R. W. Taylor (1985). "A Return to Neighborhood Policing: The Tampa, Florida Experience." *Police Chief* **52**:39-44.

Smodish, Susan D. (1974). "Recent Legislation Prohibiting the Use of Prison Inmates as Subjects in Medical Research." *New England Journal on Prison Law* **1**:220-243.

Smykla, John Ortiz (1987). "The Human Impact of Capital Punishment: Interviews with Families of Persons on Death Row." *Journal of Criminal Justice* **15**:331-347.

Snell, Tracy L. (1998). *Capital Punishment 1997.* Washington, DC: U.S. Department of Justice.

Stephan, James J. (1997). *Census of State and Federal Correctional Facilities, 1995.* Washington, DC: U.S. Department of Justice.

Stevens, S. S. (1951). "Mathematics, Measurement, and Psychophysics." In *Handbook of Experimental Psychology*, S. S. Stevens (ed.). New York: John Wiley.

Sutherland, Edwin H. (1937). *The Professional Thief.* Chicago: University of Chicago Press.

Sykes, Gresham (1958). *The Society of Captives.* Princeton, NJ: Princeton University Press.

Taylor, Janet (1953). "A Personality Scale of Manifest Anxiety." *Journal of Abnormal Social Psychology* **48**:285-290.

Theoharis, Athan (ed.) (1991). *From the Secret Files of J. Edgar Hoover.* Chicago: Ivan R. Dee.

Thompson, Kevin M. (1989). "Gender and Adolescent Drinking Problems: The Effects of Occupational Structure." *Social Problems* **36**:30-47.

Thompson, Wendy M., James M. Dabbs, and Robert L. Frady (1990). "Changes in Saliva Testosterone Levels During a 90-Day Shock Incarceration Program." *Criminal Justice and Behavior* **17**:246-252.

Thurstone, L. L. and E. J. Chave (1929). *The Measurement of Attitudes*. Chicago: University of Chicago Press.

Todd, W. G. (1975). "Non-Therapeutic Prison Research: An Analysis of Potential Legal Remedies." *Albany Law Review* **39**:799-825.

Torres, Sam (1997). "The Substance-Abusing Offender and the Initial Interview." *Federal Probation* **61**:11-17.

Tripodi, Tom and Joseph P. DeSario (1993). *Crusade: Undercover Against the Mafia & KGB*. Washington, DC: Brassey's.

VanderZanden, James W. (1984). *Social Psychology*. New York: Random House.

Vito, Gennaro F. and Thomas J. Keil (1998). "Elements of Support for Capital Punishment: An Examination of Changing Attitudes." *Journal of Crime and Justice* **21**:17-38.

Vohryzek-Bolden, Miki (1997). "Ethical Dilemmas Confronting Criminological Researchers." *Journal of Crime and Justice* **20**:121-138.

Walker, Anne Graffam (1986). "Content, Transcripts, and Appellate Readers." *Justice Quarterly* **3**:409-427.

Walters, Stephen (1988). "Correctional Officers' Perceptions of Powerlessness." *Journal of Crime and Justice* **11**:47-59.

Wang, Zheng (1996). "Is the Pattern of Asian Gang Affiliation Different? A Multiple Regression Analysis." *Journal of Crime and Justice* **19**:113-128.

Wansell, Geoffrey (1996). *An Evil Love: The Life of Frederick West*. London, UK: Headline.

Ward, Tony et al. (1995). "A Descriptive Model of the Offense Chain for Child Molesters." *Journal of Interpersonal Violence* **10**:452-472.

Wardlaw, Grant R. (1979). "Aversion Therapy: Technical, Ethical and Safety Issues." *Australian and New Zealand Journal of Criminology* **12**:43-54.

Webb, Vincent J., Charles M. Katz, and Nanette Graham (1997). "Citizen Ratings of the Importance of Selected Police Duties." *Journal of Crime and Justice* **20**:37-54.

Websdale, Neil and Byron Johnson (1997). "The Policing of Domestic Violence in Rural and Urban Areas: The Voices of Battered Women in Kentucky." *Policing and Society* **6**:297-317.

Weeks, Robin and Cathy Spatz Widom (1998). "Self-Reports of Early Childhood Victimization Among Incarcerated Adult Male Felons." *Journal of Interpersonal Violence* **13**:346-356.

Weiss, Alexander and Steven M. Chermak (1998). "The News Value of African-American Victims: An Examination of the Media's Presentation of Homicide." *Journal of Crime and Justice* **21**:71-89.

Wells, L. Edward (1991). "The Utility of Meta-Analysis in Criminal Justice Research." Paper presented at the Academy of Criminal Justice Sciences, Nashville, TN (March).

Whitbeck, Les B., Danny R. Hoyt, and Kevin A. Ackley (1997). "Families of Homeless and Runaway Adolescents: A Comparison of Parent/Caretaker and Adolescent Perspectives on Parenting, Family Violence and Adolescent Conduct." *Child Abuse and Neglect* **21**:517-518.

Wicharaya, Tamasak (1995). *Simple Theory, Hard Reality: The Impact of Sentencing Reforms on Courts, Prisons, and Crime*. Albany, NY: State University of New York Press.

Williams, Kirk R. and Richard Hawkins (1992). "Wife Assault, Costs of Arrest, and the Deterrence Process." *Journal of Research in Crime and Delinquency* **29**:292-310.

Willis, C. L. (1983). "Criminal Justice Theory: A Case of Trained Incapacity?" *Journal of Criminal Justice* **11**:447-458.

Wilson, Deborah G. and Gennaro F. Vito (1990). "Persistent Felony Offenders in Kentucky: A Comparison of Incarcerated Felons." *Journal of Contemporary Criminal Justice* **6**:237-253.

Winer, Ben J. (1962). *Statistical Principles in Experimental Design*. New York: McGraw-Hill.

Wiseman, Jacqueline P. (1970). *Stations of the Lost: The Treatment of Skid Row Alcoholics*. Englewood Cliffs, NJ: Prentice-Hall.

Wolfgang, Marvin (1983). "Delinquency in Two Birth Cohorts." In *Perspective Studies of Crime and Delinquency,* Katherine Teilmann Van Dusen and Sarnoff A. Mednick (eds.). Chicago: University of Chicago Press.

Wolfgang, Marvin, Robert M. Figlio, and Thorsten Sellin (1972). *Delinquency in a Birth Cohort.* Chicago: University of Chicago Press.

Wright, Richard A. and Colette Soma (1996). "The Most-Cited Scholars in Criminology Textbooks, 1963-1968, 1976-1980, and 1989-1993." *Journal of Crime and Justice* **19**:45-60.

Yokoyama, Minoru (1994). "Treatment of Prisoners Under Rehabilitation Model in Japan." *Kokugakuin Journal of Law and Politics* **32**:1-24.

Zimbardo, Philip G. (1972). "Pathology of Imprisonment." *Society* **9**:4-6.

■ CASES CITED

Furman v. Georgia, 408 U.S. 238 (1972)

Gregg v. Georgia, 428 U.S. 13 (1976)

Skinner v. Oklahoma, 115 P.2d 123 (1942)

Tennessee v. Garner, 105 S.Ct. 1694 (1985)

Brewer v. Williams, 430 U.S. 387 (1977)

Name Index

C

Carper, Gayle Tronvig, 191
Carter, David, 130
Chamlin, Mitchell B., 305-306
Champion, Dean J., 28, 46, 59, 206, 237, 270-274, 584, 605
Charles, Michael T., 145-146, 197
Chave, E.J., 350-355
Chen, Huey-Tsyh, 201
Chermak, Steven M., 136
Clemmer, Donald, 137
Cochran, John K., 132
Cohen, Morris R., 323
Coleman, James S., 199-201
Colley, Lori, 216, 218-219
Comte, August, 18
Conley, J.A., 67
Cook, S.W., 36
Coston, Charisse T.M., 178-179
Cox, Steven M., 50
Crank, John P., 201, 340
Crouch, Ben M., 184
Culbertson, Robert G., 216, 218-219

D

Dabbs, James M., 333, 336
Davis, James R., 260
Dembo, Richard, 244
Denton, Robert, 201
Denzin, Norman K., 48
DeSario, Joseph P., 306
Dicks, Shirley, 131
Dingwall, R., 67
DiRenzo, Gordon J., 323
Dixon, David, 132
Doyle, Patricia A., 40
Dubler, Nancy Neveloff, 132
Dunford, Franklyn W., 243
Durkheim, Emile, 18, 49-50, 65-66

E

Earle, Wilton, 306
Edwards, A.L., 354, 356
Ehrlich, I., 73
Elliott, Delbert C., 242-243
Elliston, Frederick A., 103
Empey, Lamar T., 10
Erickson, Maynard, 10
Esbensen, Finn-Aage, 130, 142, 144

F

Fagan, Jeffrey, 203
Farkas, Mary Ann, 136, 263-266

Faulkner, Paula, 139, 266
Faulkner, William, 139, 266
Feierman, Jay R., 306
Figlio, Robert M., 8-9
Fisher, Bonnie S., 263
Fishman, Joseph, 137
Fiske, M., 259
Fitzgerald, Jack D., 50
Flavin, Jeanne, 74
Fogg, Vernon, 32
Forst, Martin, 203
Frady, Robert L., 333, 336
Frank, Mark G., 103
Frazier, Charles E., 146
Furlong, Michael J., 244
Fyfe, James J., 74

G

Garofalo, James, 130
Gaskins, Donald "Pee Wee," 306
Gendreau, Paul, 316-319
Gilmore, Norbert, 132
Glaser, Barney, 46
Glass, Gene V., 316
Goggin, Claire E., 316
Goldhammer, Gary E., 131
Goode, William J., 154, 156
Graham, Nanette, 267
Grasmick, Harold G., 132
Greenwood, Peter W., 363-365
Gunderson, D.F., 52, 56, 58
Guralnik, David B. 36
Guttman, Louis, 355-361

H

Hafley, Sandra, 25-26, 200, 248
Hagan, Frank E., 50
Hagan, Michael, 29
Hammett, Theodore M., 132
Hanke, Penelope J., 244
Hanson, Karl, 316
Hashimoto, Henichi, 362
Hassine, Victor, 306
Hatt, Paul K., 154, 156
Hawkins, Richard, 131
Helfgott, Jacqueline, 179
Henderson, Joel H., 67
Hill, Richard J., 233
Hiller, Matthew L., 159
Hirschi, Travis, 59, 61
Hoffman, Peter B., 363
Holmes, Malcolm D., 311-312
Hoover, J. Edgar, 307
Hoyt, Danny R., 243
Huizinga, David, 243
Humphries, Laud, 112-113, 298

Hursh, Gerald D., 142
Hyman, Herbert, 59, 142

I

Iannuzzi, Joseph "Joe-Dogs," 306

J

Johnson, Byron, 74
Johnson, Richard E., 44-45, 56
Johnston, Mildred E., 75
Jones, Mark, 6-8, 10, 20
Josephson, Trevor K., 362
Jurgens, Ralf, 132

K

Kaci, Judy, 343-344
Kakar, Suman, 158-159, 243
Kalmuss, Debra, 75
Kaplan, Meg S., 245
Katz, Charles, 267
Katz, E., 199
Keil, Thomas J., 136
Kelling, George L., 157-158
Kelly, William R., 40
Kendall, Patricia L., 259
Kenney, Dennis J., 195
Kerlinger, Fred, 331
King, Robert P., 29
Klinger, David A., 74
Klofas, John, 313-314
Knight, Kevin, 159
Kowalski, Gregory S., 140
Krisberg, Barry, 144
Krohn, Marvin D., 243

L

LaPiere, Richard, 367-368
Larzelere, Robert E., 177
Latessa, Edward J., 216, 218-219
Launay, Gilles, 118-119
Law, Moira, 316
Lemert, Edwin M., 40
Levine, Irene, 244
Levy, J.C., 103
Lewis, P., 67
Likert, Rensis, 338-350
Lilly, Robert J., 24
Little, Tracy, 316
Lombrosco, Cesare, 18
Long, Nigel, 139
Lucas, Wayne L., 198

M

MacKenzie, Doris Layton, 193, 567-568, 572-573
Magnusson, David, 381
Maguire, Kathleen, 452
Markey, Vicki K., 26-27
Marquart, James, 4, 184, 296-298
Matthews, Timothy, 32
Maxfield, Michael G., 30
McCamey, William P., 191
McCulloch, Sue, 28-29
McIntyre, Thomas J., 307
McLemore, S. Dale, 233
McShane, Marilyn D., 186
Meadows, Robert J., 178
Mednick, S.A., 41
Menzel, H.M., 199
Merton, Robert K., 37, 259
Milgram, Stanley, 113-114
Mill, John Stuart, 56-58
Miller, Delbert C., 233
Miller, J.L., 285, 314-315
Minnesota Corrections Department, 30
Minor, Kevin, 132
Morn, F.T., 67
Mudd, Margaret, 26-27

N

Nagel, Ernest, 323
National Archive of Criminal Justice Data, 315
National Association of Attorneys General Committee on the Office of Attorney General, 307
National Council on Crime and Delinquency, 362
National Institute of Justice, 127-128
Neidig, Peter H., 245
Nye, Ivan, 240

O

Osgood, Charles, 361

P

Pacheco, Kimberly, 244
Pastore, Ann L., 452
Patterson, Gerald R., 177
Peatman, John G., 334
Pettus, Ann Burnett, 47
Porterfield, Austin L., 240
Prenzler, Tim, 103

Subject Index

Computer-Assisted Telephone Interviewing (CATI), 268
Computer-determined draw, 183-184
Computers in criminal justice research, 631-646
Computer software packages, 632-634
Concepts, 36, 332
    defined, 332
Conceptualization of problem for study, 3-4
Conceptual schemes, 656-657
Conclusions, research, 36, 91-92
Concomitants, 332
Concurrent validity, 381-382
    criticisms, 382-383
    defined, 382
Confidence intervals, 555-564
Confidentiality, 116-117, 129-130
    anonymity, 117
    informed consent, 129-130
    governmental safeguards, 116-117
Confidential records and information, 115-116
Constructs, 332-334
    defined, 332
Construct validity, 383-387
    criticisms, 386-387
    defined, 383
Content analysis, 311-315
    advantages and disadvantages, 315
    defined, 311
Content validity, 378-381
    criticisms, 380-381
    defined, 378
Contingency questions, 234-235
Contingent conditions, 59
Continuous variables, 54
Contributory conditions, 59
Control groups, 142, 149
Convenience sampling, 194-195
    advantages and disadvantages, 194-195
    defined, 194
Cornell Technique 355-361
Correlations, 592-606
Cost-benefit analyses, 165-168
    criticisms, 168
    defined, 165-166
    examples, 166-168
Coston, Charisse T.M., personal profile, 299
Countables, 334
Cramer's *V*, 597
Crime Bill of 1994, 10
Crime rate, 8, 424-425
    computation, 424

Criminal Justice Abstracts, 20, 82-83, 243-244, 319, 333, 361, 658-662
    illustrated, 658-662
Criminal justice and science, 17-18
Criminology, 311-313
Criterion validity, 381
Critical essays, 650-651
Critical regions, 543-549
Critical values, 567
Cross-tabulations of variables, 445-454
Cultural date of test and validity, 399
Cultural factors on questionnaires, 247-248
Cumulative frequency distributions, 437-438
Curvilinearity, 594, 604

D

Dalley, Lanette, personal profile, 402-403
Das, Dilip, personal profile, 209-210
Data analysis and interpretation, 11-12
Data cleaning, 420-423
    defined, 420
Data collection and analysis, 5
Data collection methods, 89-90
Data editor for SPSS, 635-636
Data presentation, 423-454
Data verification, 420-423
Deception and lying to respondents, 115
Deciles, 438-441
Decision-making functions, 28
Decision rules, 533-550
    levels of significance, 541
    regions of rejection, 543-549
    sampling distributions of statistics, 534-540
    Type I and Type II errors, 541-542
Deductive theory, 43-45
Definitions, 37-41
Deng, Xiaogang, personal profile, 422-423
Dense sampling, 200-202
    advantages and disadvantages, 201-202
    defined, 201
Department of Health and Human Services, 129
Dependent variables, 51-54
    defined, 53-54
    examples, 53
Description and inference, 487-488
Description and interviewing, 269-270
Descriptive designs and objectives, 139-140
    defined, 139
Descriptive functions, 26-27

F

Face-to-face interviews and validity, 400
Face-to-face questionnaire administration,
   8-9, 229-230
   comparison with mailed questionnaires,
     230
Face validity, 378-381
Factor analysis, 383
Factorial validity, 385-386
Farkas, Mary Ann, personal profile,
   264-265
Federal Bureau of Investigation (FBI), 315
Feld, Barry C., personal profile, 460-461
Field notes, 298-299
Final report, 6
Fishbowl draw, 181-182
   defined, 181
   example, 182
Fixed-response questionnaires, 220-227,
   399-400
   advantages and disadvantages,
     226-227
   compared with open-ended items,
     225-226
   defined, 220
   validity, 399-400
Focused interviews, 257-263
   defined, 259
Focus group, 264
Follow-up questions, 255
Frames of reference, 36, 75-78
   theory, 76-78
   values, 75-78
Fraudulent research, 111
Freedom of Information Act (FOIA),
   307-310
Frequency distributions, 430-443
   characteristics, 435-437
   constructing, 430-434
   defined, 430
   grouped data applications, 431
   interval midpoints, 436-437
   ungrouped data applications, 431
   upper and lower limits of intervals,
     436-437
Frequency polygons, 441-443
F ratio, 581
F test for analysis of variance (ANOVA),
   577-584
   assumptions, advantages, and
     disadvantages, 584
   between- and within-group variation,
     579-583
   degrees of freedom, 580-582
Furman v. Georgia (1972), 160, 164

G

Gaining access to organizations, 284-285,
   307
Gang Reduction and Sports Program
   (GRASP), 158-159
Gang Resistance Education and Training
   (G.R.E.A.T.), 143-144
Gender of respondents and validity, 401
Generalizability, 173-174
"Get-tough" movement, 161
Goodman and Kruskal's gamma, 601-603
   strengths and weaknesses, 602-603
Goodness of fit, 584-585
   tests, 584-591
Grand mean, 503-504
Graphic presentation, 426-443
   bar graphs, 429-430
   cumulative frequency distributions,
     437-438
   frequency distributions, 430-443
   functions, 426-428
   pie charts, 428-429
   types, 428-443
Granting permission to study subordinates,
   119
Gregg v. Georgia (1976), 160, 164
Grounded theory, 46-48
Grouped data, 431-438, 497
   creating intervals, 431-438
"Guilty But Mentally Ill" (GBMI), 313-314
Guttman scales, 355-361
   advantages and disadvantages, 360-361
   defined, 355-356
Guttman's coefficient of predictability,
   lambda, 599-601
   strengths and weaknesses, 600-601

H

Halo effect and validity, 406-407
"Hands-on" research, 85
Harris, Diana K., personal profile, 241
Hawthorne effect, 302
Hawthorne experiments, 301-302
Henley, Stacy L., personal profile, 64-65
Henriques, Zelma Weston, personal profile,
   326
Histograms, 441-443
Historical method, 305-306
Homoscedasticity, 605
Human subjects, 129
   rights, 129
Hypotheses, 63-68, 325-329, 458-481, 657
   defined, 325-327

Hypotheses (*cont.*)
dissertations, 657
examples, 66
interpreting results, 478–481
k-variable, 474–475
null, 463–466
operationalizing variables, 330–332
origins, 469–470
point estimates, 473–474
refinements, 470–473
research, 462–463
single-variable, 473–474
statistical, 466–469
testing, 475–478
theory, 458–462
two-variable, 473–474
Hypothesis testing, 325–329, 475–478
data collection procedures as a
consideration, 481
defined, 475
factors affecting, 480–481
measurement considerations, 481
participant observation as a
consideration, 481
sampling considerations, 480–481
statistical considerations, 481
theoretical considerations, 480

I

Ideal and real sampling considerations, 210
Illegal behavior and ethics, 132–133
Illumination experiments, 302
Impact of observed on observer, 303–304
Impact of observer on observed, 301–303
Independence of draw, 179–182
Independent samples, 203–204
defined, 203
Independent variables, 51–52
defined, 51
In-depth interviews, 263–267
defined, 263
Index offenses, 86–87
Individual matching, 150
Induction, 45
Inductive logic, 45–46
Inductive theory, 45–46
Inference, 487–488, 554–564
Inferential statistics, 554–564
Informants, 307
Informed consent, 121, 129–130
respecting confidentiality, 129–130
Instructional clarity and validity, 400
Instrument contents and validity, 399–400
Interdecile range, 506–507

Internal consistency, 389
Internal reliability checks, 395
split-half method, 389–390
Internal validity, 410
Interpretation and conclusions, 5–6
Interpreting hypothesis test results,
478–481
Interquartile range, 506–507
Interuniversity Consortium for Political and
Social Research, 315
Interval level of measurement, 334–336
defined, 336
Interval characteristics, 431–437
Interval estimation, 558–564
compared with point estimation,
563–564
Intervals, 431–437
lower and upper limits, 435–437
midpoints, 435–437
size, 432–436
Interval size, 432–436
Intervening variables, 60
Interview construction, 274–283
Interview guide, 257
Interviews, 8, 252–290
advantages and disadvantages,
289–290
arranging, 284–285
characteristics, 253–254
compared with questionnaires, 255
conducting, 283–289
construction, 274–283
dangers, 288–289
defined, 252
description, 269–270
dressing appropriately, 286–287
exploration, 270–274
functions, 269–274
gaining access to organizations, 283–284
in-depth interviews, 263–267
lie detectors, 288
personality factors, 285–286
polygraph tests, 288
probing, 287
structured, 257–263
telephone interviews, 267–269
training and orientation of interviewers,
285
types, 255–269
unstructured, 256–257
videotaping and tape-recording,
287–288
Item discrimination analysis, 390–395
defined, 390
strengths and weaknesses, 394–395
Item weights, 341–342

Interview schedule, 257
Investigations from a distance, 85–86

J

Jaspen's *M*, 605
Jensen, Eric L., personal profile, 308–309
Jones, Mark, personal profile, 180–181
Journal of Criminal Justice, 311–313
Judgmental sampling, 196–198
  advantages and disadvantages, 197–198
  defined, 196
Justice Quarterly, 311–313
Juvenile justice and delinquency
    prevention, 146
Juveniles, studies of, 119–120
  confidentiality, 119–120
  potentates, 210–211

K

Kakar, Suman, personal profile, 495–496
Kansas City Preventive Patrol Experiments,
    157–158
Kendall's tau, 601
Key words, 238–239
Klein, Lloyd, personal profile, 366–367
Knox, George W., personal profile, 93
Knox County (Tennessee) Sheriff's
    Department, 407
k-sample situations, 203
Kurtosis, 530–533
  leptokurtic, 532
  mesokurtic, 532–533
  platykurtic, 532
k-variable hypotheses, 474–475

L

Labeling theory, 40–41
Law Enforcement Assistance
    Administration, 18
Legal citations, 664–667
Length of test and validity, 399
Leptokurtic distributions, 532–533
Level of measurement–statistical choices
    relation, 370–372
Levels of measurement, 334–338, 493
  interval level, 336
  nominal level, 334–335
  ordinal level, 335–336
  ratio level, 336–338
  statistical applications, 337–338, 493

Levels of significance, 541
Lie detectors in interviews, 288
Lie factors, 226–227, 246–247
Likert-type scales, 338–350
  advantages and disadvantages, 349–350
  compared with Thurstone scales,
      354–355
  "don't know" or "undecided" responses,
      347–350
  forms of response, 343–345
  item weights, 341–342
  meaning of raw scores, 345–347
  numbers of items, 343
Linear, linearity, 593
Literature reviews, 80–85
  sources, 81–85
Long Beach (California) Police Department
    (LBPD), 247
Longitudinal research, 8–9
Los Angeles Police Department (LAPD), 178

M

Mailed questionnaires, 8, 228–229
  compared with face-to-face
      questionnaire administration, 230
Mail-order papers, 110
Master's theses, 651–658
Matching, 150
Maturity level of respondents and validity,
    401
Mean, 501–504
  compared with mode and median,
      504–505
Mean of means, 504–505
Mean squares, 581–582
Measurement issues, 365–372
  attitude-action relation, 365–369
  level of measurement–statistical choices
      relation, 370–372
  response sets, 370
  social desirability, 369–370
Measurement of criminal justice variables,
    323–373
  defined, 323–324
  functions, 324
  statistical applications, 324–325
Measures of association, 592–606
Measures of dispersion or variability,
    505–512
  average deviation, 507–508
  defined, 505
  range, 505–506
  standard deviation, 508–512
  variance, 508–512

Mechanical factors and validity, 400
Median, 499–501
    compared with mean and mode,
        504–505
Memory or recall of respondents and
        validity, 401
Mesokurtic distributions, 532–533
Meta-analysis, 316–320
    advantages and disadvantages, 319–320
    defined, 316
Method of agreement, 56
Method of concomitant variation, 56
Method of difference, 56
Method of summated ratings, 338–350
Midwestern Criminal Justice Association, 129
Miller, J. Mitchell, personal profile, 489
Minnesota Multiphasic Personality
    Inventory (MMPI), 247, 368
    built-in lie factor, 247
Mode, 498–499
    compared with mean and median,
        504–505
Monitoring the Future Survey, 240–241
Multiple regression, 604
Multiple time-series designs, 165
    criticisms, 165
Multidimensional Anger Inventory, 344–345
Multidimensional scales, 356
Multiple correlation, 368
Multistage sampling, 189–192
    advantages and disadvantages, 192
    defined, 189
Mutually exclusive samples, 203–204

N

National Center for Juvenile Justice, 316
*National Criminal Justice Reference
    Service Document Data Base*, 83
*National Crime Victimization Survey
    (NCVS)*, 86–88, 175, 242–243, 263,
    493
    criticisms, 87–88
    defined, 87
    examples of questions, 276–282
National Judicial Reporting Program, 316
National Prisoner Statistics, 73
National Research Act, 129
National Rifle Association, 129
National Youth Survey (NYS), 144, 242,
    254
Necessary conditions, 59
Nominal definitions, 330–332
    defined, 330
Nominal level of measurement, 334–335

Nondirectional hypothesis tests, 468–469
Nonparametric tests of significance,
    584–591
    advantages and disadvantages, 566
    defined, 565
Nonparticipant observation, 298–299
Nonprobability sampling plans, 192–202
    accidental sampling, 194–195
    defined, 193
    dense sampling, 200–202
    purposive or judgmental sampling,
        196–198
    quota sampling, 198–199
    saturation sampling, 200–202
    snowball sampling, 199–200
    systematic sampling, 195–196
Nonresponse, 94, 206–207, 236–238,
    249–250
    defined, 206
    strategies for dealing with, 207
Normal curve, 493, 518–520
    characteristics, 519–520
    defined, 518
"Not Guilty by Reason of Insanity" (NGRI),
    313–314
Null hypotheses, 463–466
    defined, 463
    examples, 463–465
Nuremberg Code, 120–121
    defined, 121
    informed consent, 121

O

Obedience research, 113–114
Objectivity in scientific research, 22–24
Observation, 295–320
    advantages and disadvantages, 299–301
    defined, 295
    nonparticipant, 298–299
    participant, 296–298
    purposes, 295–296
    types, 296–299
    unobtrusive, 298–299
Observed frequencies, 585
Official records, 315–316
Ogive curves, 443–444
One-shot case studies, 202
One-tailed tests, 468–469
Open-ended items, 224–228
    advantages and disadvantages, 227–228
    compared with fixed-response items,
        225–226
Open-ended questionnaires, 224, 399–400
    validity, 399–400

Operational definitions, 330–332
    defined, 330
Operationalization, 330
Operationalizing variables, 330–332
Ordinal level of measurement, 335–336
    defined, 335
Oregon Youth Study, (OYS), 177
Organized reserve, 407
Oversampling, 207

P

Parallel forms of the same test, 397–398
    advantages and criticisms, 397–398
    defined, 397
Parameters, 172, 486
Parametric tests of significance, 564–584
    advantages and disadvantages, 566
    defined, 565
Participant observation, 296–298
Path analysis, 368
Pearson r, 603–605
    strengths and weaknesses, 604–605
Pearson's C, 598–599
    strengths and weaknesses, 599
Permission required to study subjects, 94
Personal documents, 306–310
Personal factors and validity, 400–401
Phi coefficient, 597
Pie charts, 428–429
    defined, 428
Pilot studies, 233
Placebo, 408
Placebo effect, 408
Plagiarism, 109
    by professors, 110
Platykurtic distributions, 532–533
Point estimate hypotheses, 473–474
Point estimates, 473
Point estimation, 555–558
    compared with interval estimation,
        563–564
Police Professionalism Scale, 340–343, 407
Polygraph tests and interviews, 288
Population change measures, 425
Population parameters, 486
Populations, 172
Position papers, 650–651
Postcard questionnaires, 232
Posttests, 153
Potentates, 119, 210–211
Power of statistical tests, 542
Pragmatic validity, 381–383
    concurrent, 382–383
    predictive, 381

PRE, proportional reduction in error,
    595–597
Prediction, 12, 41–43
Predictive validity, 381
Presentation of findings, 90–91
Pretest bias, 404
Pretest effects and validity, 403–404
    bias, 404
Pretests, 153
Prison Community, The, 137–138
Prisoners, 131–132, 210–211
Probability distribution, 539
Probability sampling, 176
Probability sampling plans, 177–192
    area (I) sampling, 189–192
    cluster sampling, 189–192
    defined, 177
    disproportionate stratified random
        sampling, 186–187
    equality of draw, 181
    fishbowl draw, 181–182
    independence of draw, 181–182
    multistage sampling, 189–192
    proportionate stratified random
        sampling, 187–189
    randomness, 179–181
    simple random sampling, 182–185
    stratified random sampling, 185–187
Probability theory, 20–22
Probes, 255
Probing and interviewing, 287
Problem formulation, 88–89
Proportional reduction in error (PRE),
    595–597
Proportionate stratified random sampling,
    187–189
    advantages and disadvantages, 188–189
    defined, 187
Propositions, 36–41
    defined, 37
Pure research, 9–10
    defined, 9
Purist view, 208–210
Purposive or judgmental sampling, 196–198
    advantages and disadvantages, 197–198
    defined, 196

Q

Q-sort, 361–362
Qualitative research, 11–12, 135–136
    defined, 135
Quantitative research, 11–12, 135–136
    defined, 136
Quartiles, 438–441

Statistics (*cont.*)
    inference, 487
    measurement, 324-325
    tests of significance, 488-490
Stimulus-response experiments, 118-119
Stratification, 185
Stratified random sampling, 185-189
    disproportionate stratified random
        sampling, 186-187
    proportionate stratified random
        sampling, 187-189
Stratifying, 185
Strength of association, 592-594
Structured interviews, 257-263
Studies, 78-80
    choosing topics, 78-80
Subpopulations, 187-188
Subsamples, 186
Substantive implications, 6, 657-658
Sufficient conditions, 59
Sums of squares, 581-582
Survey research, 142
Surveys, 142-144
    advantages and disadvantages, 145
    compared with case studies, 147-149
    defined, 142
Systematic sampling, 195-196
    advantages and disadvantages, 196
    defined, 195

T

Tabular presentation, 444-454
    cross-tabulations of variables, 445-452
    defined, 444
    rows and columns, 444
Tampa (Florida) Police Department, 156
Target population, 187
Taylor Manifest Anxiety Scale, 331-332
Tearoom Trade, 112-113
Telephone interviews, 267-269
    criticisms, 269
    defined, 267
10-90 range, 506-507
Term papers, 648-649
Testing effect, 404
Testing or pretest effects and validity,
    403-404
Test-retest, 395-397
    advantages and criticisms, 396-397
    defined, 395
Tests of significance, 488-493, 564-591
Tetrachoric r, 597
Theoretical implications, 6, 657-658
Theory, 36-43

axiomatic, 48-50
complementary of research, 63
deductive, 43-45
defined, 36
frames of reference, 76-78
grounded, 46-48
hypotheses, 63-67
inductive, 45-46
types, 43-50
value of, 67-68
verification, 325-329
Theses, 651-658
Thurstone scales, 350-355
    advantages and disadvantages, 354-355
    compared with Likert scales, 354-355
    defined, 350
Time-series designs, 160-164
    criticisms, 165
    defined, 160
Treatment variables, 149
Trend information, 452-454
Triangulation, 215
True experiments, 158-159
True range, 505-506
Tschuprow's T, 597
t test for single sample, 567-570
    assumptions, advantages, and
        disadvantages, 571-572
t test for two samples, 572-577
    assumptions, advantages, and
        disadvantages, 575-577
Tuskegee Syphilis Study, 112
2×2 tables, 445-446
Two-sample situations, 203
Two-tailed tests, 468-469
Two-variable hypotheses, 473-474
Type I and Type II errors, 541-542

U

Unbiased estimates, 538
"Undecided" responses, 347-349
Unethical conduct, 102
Ungrouped data, 431, 497
Unidimensional scales, 356
Uniform Crime Reporting Program, 86-87
Uniform Crime Reports (UCR), 73, 86, 175,
    241-243, 315, 493
    criticisms, 87-88
Unit normal distribution, 518-520
University guidelines for human subjects,
    124-126
    human subjects committees, 126
    institutional review boards, 126
Unobtrusive observation, 298-299